W9-CLH-900

For Steffi and Steve,

with love,

Lenni

The Marriage Contract

The Marriage Contract

Spouses, Lovers, and the Law

Lenore J. Weitzman

 THE FREE PRESS
A Division of Macmillan Publishing Co., Inc.
NEW YORK

Collier Macmillan Publishers
LONDON

Copyright © 1981 by Lenore J. Weitzman

All rights reserved. No part of this book may be reproduced or
transmitted in any form or by any means, electronic or mechanical,
including photocopying, recording, or by any information storage
and retrieval system, without permission in writing from the
Publisher.

The Free Press
A Division of Macmillan Publishing Co., Inc.
866 Third Avenue, New York, N. Y. 10022

Collier Macmillan Canada, Ltd.

Library of Congress Catalog Card Number: 80–69645

Printed in the United States of America

printing number

1 2 3 4 5 6 7 8 9 10

Library of Congress Cataloging in Publication Data

Weitzman, Lenore J.
  The marriage contract.

  Includes index.
  1. Antenuptial contracts—United States. 2. Un-
married couples—Legal status, laws, etc.—United
States. 3. Husband and wife—United States. I. Title.
KF529.W43   347.7301'6   80-69645
ISBN 0-02-934630-4   347.30616   AACR2

This book is sold with the understanding that the author and publisher are not engaged in
rendering legal advice. If legal advice or other expert assistance is required, the services of a
competent professional person should be sought. Cases reported herein may be modified
or reversed on appeal. Articles and suggested clauses in the model contracts have not been
edited for legal accuracy and may not be applicable in all jurisdictions.

—L.J.W.

To my mother and father
for all they gave to us
and to each other

Contents

Acknowledgments

This book has been written and rewritten so many times over the past ten years that I am indebted to a large number of people who have helped me in this struggle.

It began in 1969 when I was a Russell Sage Postdoctoral Fellow at Yale Law School. A tutorial with Joseph Goldstein started me on this journey, and I am still grateful for his never ending challenges to my assumptions. I also wish to thank Richard Schwartz, Ann Freedman, and Stanton Wheeler for the stimulating questions they raised at that time.

In 1974, a much abbreviated first version of this book was published in the *California Law Review* as "The Legal Regulation of Marriage: Tradition and Change—A Proposal for Contracts Within and in Lieu of Legal Marriage." In writing that article I benefited greatly from the thoughtful and detailed comments of Herma Hill Kay and William J. Goode. Conversations with Brigitte Bodenheimer, Kathryn Gehrels, Caleb Foote, Mary Dunlap, Joan Graff, and Beth Summers were also most helpful. I owe a particular debt to my two assistants, Sheila Cronan and Mary Jean Hamilton, not only for their legal research but for their patience and perseverence in finding impossible cites to answer the Law Review editors' endless queries.

In rethinking and rewriting this book over the past six years several groups of colleagues have been especially helpful. First, the sociologists and lawyers at the Center for the Study of Law and Society at the University of California at Berkeley who provided stimulation, support, and fellowship during my years at the Center—Sheldon Messinger, Caleb Foote, Phillip Selznick, Phillipe Nonet, and, most significant, the Chair of the Center, Jerome Skolnick, to whom I owe a special intellectual and personal debt.

Second, law professors Carol Bruch and Marjorie Schultz have discussed, probed, debated, and dissected most of the major issues in this book with me. Their patience with my legal queries, and their constant encouragement have been tremendously helpful. Professor Bruch also provided detailed comments on the entire manuscript. Her keen eye, unerring judgment, and constant quest for precision have saved me from many errors of legal form and judgment.

Third, my close friends and colleagues Arlene Skolnick and Lillian Rubin. Our ongoing discussions on the family and sex roles, men and women, work and life, have been a fountain of intellectual and personal delight.

Fourth, I want to thank the members of the Faculty Women's Research Forum. Although they have not contributed directly to this book, they have contributed a great deal to my life and to my thinking over the past five years: Victoria Bonnel, Cynthia Brantley, Clair (Vickery) Brown, Patricia Brown, Carol Bruch, Nancy Chodorow, Ruth Dixon, Susan Ervin-Tripp, Eleanor Glass, Judith Gruber, Barbara Heyns, Gertrude Jaeger, Suad Joseph, Gail Lapidus, Flo Livson, Jean Love, Dale Marshall, Karen Oppenheim Mason, Marcia Millman, Karen Paige, Ruth Rosen, Lillian Rubin, Marjorie Shultz, Arlene Skolnick, Judith Stacey, Ann Swidler, Laura Tyson, Frances Flanagan Vanloo, Norma Wikler, Abby Wolfson, and Barbara Zoloth.

I am especially grateful to my parents, Charles Colman Weitzman and Ethel Goldberg Weitzman, for their constant love and encouragement, and to my brother Irving Joel Weitzman.

I also want to express my debt to three women who have been vital role models for me: Betty Friedan, Rose K. Goldsen, and Sheila Tobias.

The mechanics of getting this book done have been horrendous and I am grateful to a number of people who have helped to make this task easier. The creative pencil of my editor, Carol Norton, miraculously transformed run-on sentences, sociological jargon and legal obfuscation into clear English prose. Superb research assistants have helped me in hundreds of ways: Joseph Barberri, Laura Bean, Peggy Bernardy, Joyce Bird, Carol Dixon, Susan Feller, David Lineweber, Steven Lokeitz, Neil McGinn, Lyndon Stambler, Kyra Subbotin, and Holly J. Wunder. Several typists have worked on the manuscript, and each has been patient beyond belief with the countless revisions: Millie Becerra, Roberta Carlston, Ann Gordon, Bette Haberl, Lois Strand, Pamela Trainor, and Natalie Tripp.

I am especially indebted to the couples who allowed me to use their contracts in Chapter 12. Because each of these couples was assured anonymity I cannot thank them by name. But I do want to mention my special gratitude to those who took the time to write and to talk to me about their experiences in "living" with the contract.

I also want to thank those who have provided me with research support over these years: The Center for the Study of Law and Society at the University of California at Berkeley; the National Institute of Mental Health (grant MH27617); the National Science Foundation (grant GI-39218); The Ford Foundation Fellowship Program for Faculty Research; the Hoover Institution, the Boys Town Center, and the Center for Research on Women at Stanford University; the German Marshall Fund of the United States; Nuffield College and the Centre for Socio-Legal Studies at Wolfson College at Oxford University.

Finally, I want to express my profound debt to Professor William J. Goode. He has been a constant source of inspiration and encouragement. I am grateful for his endless wisdom in reading each successive draft of this manuscript, and for his endless patience. I am also grateful for his insistence on high standards of scholarship, although there were many times when I wished I could have ignored them. There is no doubt that his influence has made this a far better book.

Introduction

The idea of a contract within marriage will strike many as incongruous, for marriage is typically thought of as the most intimate and private social relationship, while a contract is typically regarded as the prototype of rational business transactions. And yet, upon closer examination, it will become clear that there is an implicit contract that governs every marriage—an unwritten contract that is imposed by law.

Clearly, this "marriage contract" is unlike most contracts: its provisions are unwritten, its penalties are unspecified, and the terms of the contract are typically unknown to the contracting parties. Nor are prospective spouses allowed any options about these terms.* In fact, one wonders how many men and women entering marriage today would freely agree to the provisions of the marriage contract if they had the chance to consider the rights and obligations to which they were committing themselves. No state, how-

*This point is further elaborated by Morris Ploscowe, Henry H. Foster, and Doris Jonas Freed in *Family Law Cases and Materials* (Boston, Mass.: Little, Brown & Co., 1972), p. 11. As they note, "the parties are not free to prescribe any terms they choose . . . even the intervention of an act of God is no excuse for nonperformance."

ever, asks prospective spouses if they are willing to assume the duties, rights, and obligations their marriage contract specifies. It is simply assumed that everyone who gets married will abide by the state-imposed unwritten contract known as legal marriage.

This book describes and analyzes this unwritten marriage contract and explores its far-reaching effects on the social, psychological, and economic structure of marriage. In addition, it shows how the legal stucture of marriage influences not only the behavior of husbands and wives, but also the nature and meaning of alternatives to legal marriage such as cohabitation.

The Unwritten Contract

Most people who enter marriage in the United States have no direct experience with a formal marriage contract of any kind.* Historically, since marriage was an alliance of families, a written contract provided a vehicle for family control over marriage and property arrangements. In modern Western societies, however, free courtship has become the rule, and written contracts before marriage

*Most Jews who marry sign a ketuba, or contract, but the agreement is typically regarded as a symbolic document rather than a financial contract. Nevertheless, in one recent case cited by Sokolov, one party to a ketuba persuaded the court that the agreement, even if not enforceable *per se*, should at least be respected as evidence of an enforceable implied contract. In *Wener* v. *Wener*, Mrs. Wener sought child-support payments for a child who had lived with the couple for thirteen months without ever having been formally adopted. At the time of their marriage the couple had signed a ketuba which provided, among other things, that the husband assumed all obligations "as are prescribed by our religious statutes." One of these religious laws imposes a duty on the head of a household to provide for the support of any child who is taken in as a member of the household. The trial court found that Mr. Wener was obligated to support the child on two grounds: first, his promise as expressed in the ketuba, and second, his agreement to adopt the child, which, in itself, had created an obligation to support. The appellate court affirmed this decision on the second ground only.

Wener v. *Wener*, 59 Misc. 2d 957, 301 N.Y.S. 2d 237 (Sup. Ct. 1969), aff'd, 35 App. Div. 2d 50, 312 N.Y.S. 2d 815 (2d Dep't 1970) as described in Margaret Sokolov, "Marriage Contracts for Support and Services: Constitutionality Begins at Home," *New York University Law Review* 49 (December 1974):1195. Other commentators have suggested that the court should have enforced the ketuba as an ordinary contract. See, for example, Note "Enforceability of Religious Law in Secular Courts—It's Kosher, But Is It Constitutional?" *Michigan Law Review* 71 (1978):1643-44.

have disappeared except in rare cases involving a great deal of property. It is unusual for prospective spouses to think of signing a contract because, after all, mutual trust is essential in marriage, and two people who trust each other should not need to sign contracts.

But even those spouses who oppose a formal marriage contract have unknowingly entered one just the same. It is only when they begin to disagree about their respective obligations or to make arrangements for their responsibilities after divorce that they discover, usually upon consulting their respective lawyers, to what extent their freedom to decide their own fate is restricted by the terms of the state-dictated marriage contract that is codified in family law. (This unwritten contract, known as legal marriage, is described in Part I of this book.)

There is the further irony that many of these same couples will discover that the unwritten contract that governs their relationship is based on outmoded assumptions about the family, assumptions often contradicted by the reality of their own experience but nevertheless applied to them by law. (The sociological assumptions embodied in legal marriage are examined in Part II of this book.)

Still more ironically, if spouses decide to reject the law's traditional definitions of proper roles for husband and wife, and attempt to write their own contract based on what they believe each should owe the other, they too will find that provisions that seem just and fair to them are invalid and unenforceable in a court of law. That is, they are *not* free to write a contract to structure their marriage as they choose. (The restrictions on contracts between husbands and wives, and suggested remedies for change, are discussed in Chapter 13.)

Finally, if a couple decides to forgo legal marriage and still live together, the state may nevertheless apply certain legal assumptions about marriage to their relationship. (The legal consequences of living together without marriage are discussed in Chapters 14 and 15.)

Clearly, the unwritten and relatively unknown legal marriage contract has a profound and pervasive influence on the status of marriage and the social relations between spouses. It is partly to illuminate this set of relationships and to demonstrate how the implicit legal assumptions affect people's lives that I have written this volume.

Sociologists who study the family have typically focused on the norms and values that govern family life while ignoring its underlying legal and economic structure.* On some level it offends us to think that our most intimate personal relationships are determined by or even influenced by laws and legal constraints. Nevertheless the law does impose a contract on everyone who enters legal marriage,† and this contract is enforceable in court. Legal marriage establishes the rights and responsibilities of husbands and wives and provides sanctions for those who do not comply.

The major aim of this book is to analyze the implicit marriage contract and the common-law tradition from which it developed. This analysis goes beyond the lawyer's task of explaining "what the law says" to an exploration of "what the law really means" for the men and women who enter legal marriage. The goal of this analysis, then, is to explore the impact of the law on the social, psychological and economic structure of marriage, to show how the legal structure of marriage shapes the everyday lives of men and women in intimate relationships, as husbands and wives, as lovers and cohabitors, through their joining together and breaking up, in parenthood and widowhood, with its arrangements for their lives and its arrangements for their deaths.

Thus my aim is *not* to provide the most comprehensive up-to-date portrait of the law today, although I have made every possible effort to state the law accurately as of January 1980, but rather to explore the broader sociological implications of our family law: to examine its underlying assumptions, and to illuminate the social consequences of its perspective. Sociologists of law have always assumed that the reality of the law is to be found not in legal tomes alone but in the social definitions of ordinary people. While the actions of citizens may sometimes render null various provisions of the law, the force of the law can also change people's behavior. Ordi-

---

*The thrust of sociological analysis, as exemplified by Emile Durkheim, has been to uncover the important role of norms, values, and informal organization in what has otherwise been assumed to be a formal, rational structure. Durkheim, for example, focused our attention on the noncontractual elements in the contract; that is, the extent to which implicit social understandings control the scope of the contract. These norms and values restrict what a contract may state or do: "Everything in the contract is not contractual . . . [w]herever a contract exists, it is submitted to regulation which is the work of society and not that of individuals." Emile Durkheim, *The Division of Labor in Society*, translated by George Simpson (Chicago: Free Press, 1960) p. 1135.

†The term "contract" is used in a very broad sense here and includes what Weber referred to as status contracts as well as purposive contracts. See Max Rheinstein, ed., *Max Weber on Law in Economy and Society* (Cambridge, Mass.: Harvard University Press, 1954), p. 105.

nary people sometimes discover with chagrin or rage that the law has its own power, which can override their definitions—and can compel them to act in specific ways. A special case of this discovery is the experience of spouses or ex-spouses within the institution of marriage.

From Status to Contract?

While this book shows the inadequacies of the marriage contract, it nevertheless argues for contracts within marriage—and for contracts as alternatives to marriage—that are devised and executed by the parties themselves. To understand the nature of the legal contract in marriage, we must first examine the blending of the two seemingly polar extremes in social relations—status and contract—in the institution of marriage.

Maines's famous "law of progress" envisioned the movement of progressive societies from status to contract.[1] In the nineteenth century, contract was perceived as the mechanism for freeing individuals from the vestiges of antiquated status-based institutions: "The law of contracts embodied values of freedom, equality, self-government and legal competence."[2]

But marriage has not moved from status to contract. It has not changed from a relationship based on status—in which rights and obligations flow from one's position—to a contractual relationship in which rights and obligations are freely negotiated by the parties. Rather, marriage has moved from a status to a status-contract. That is, while the individuals who enter marriage have the same freedom of choice that governs entry into other contractual relations, once they make the decision to enter, the contract analogy fails, because the terms and conditions of the relationship are dictated by the state. The result is that marital partners have lost the traditional privileges of status and, at the same time, have been deprived of the freedom that the contract provides.*

*Both Mary Ann Glendon and Walter Weyrauch, two leading scholars argue, however, that the legal status of marriage is becoming less distinct and that recent changes in the laws of cohabitation have brought the "withering away of marriage" as a highly regulated state-controlled institution. See, generally, Mary Ann Glendon, "Marriage and the State: The Withering Away of Marriage," *Virginia Law Review*, 62, no. 4 (May 1976): 663–720; idem, *State, Law and Family* (New York: North-Holland, 1977); and Walter Otto Weyrauch "Metamorphoses of Marriage," *Family Law Quarterly*, 13, no. 4 (Winter 1980): 415–440.

In the past the state has been able to justify the unusual restrictions of the marriage contract by claiming that they were necessary to preserve the traditional family.[3] However, our society has undergone profound transformations in the past century, and the structure of marriage and families has also changed. Yet the traditional contract continues to impose unnecessary and inappropriate sex-based obligations on both husbands and wives. While new societal and individual needs require more flexibility and options in family forms, the rigid obligations imposed by traditional legal marriage appear increasingly anachronistic. Clearly, the purported state interest in preserving the traditional family may no longer be appropriate or important enough to override the equally important individual and societal needs.

There are three basic objections to the traditional marriage contract imposed by law. The first is that it creates an unconstitutional invasion of marital privacy. The second is that it discriminates on the basis of gender by assigning one set of rights and obligations to husbands and another to wives. Third, the law denies the diversity and heterogeneity in our pluralistic society by imposing a single family form on everyone—irrespective of the parties' age, race, class, values, needs, life-style, previous marital experience, obligations to children, etc.

Recent constitutional interpretations have begun to challenge the state's complete control over marriage, as well as the traditional legal conception of marriage. In *Griswold* v. *Connecticut*[4] and *Loving* v. *Virginia*,[5] the U.S. Supreme Court recognized that "traditional state control of the marital status has [had] to give way to current notions of individual liberty and the right to privacy."[6] Thus, "no longer may it be assumed that states have autonomy over rules and law governing marital status."[7]

The *Loving* decision refers to marriage as "a basic civil right of man [sic]."[8] If this is so, then marriage should be treated as are all other basic civil rights, and any attempts to restrict or infringe on this civil right should require careful scrutiny. Clearly the time has come for the courts to reevaluate the state-imposed restrictions in the traditional marriage contract in light of our expanding constitutional right to "marital privacy" and the growing recognition of marriage as a basic civil right.

The second objection to the traditional marriage contract is that it unconstitutionally uses sex as a basis for assigning the rights and responsibilities of marital partners. It therefore comes under increasing attack as the legal instrument for the subjugation of women. Traditional marriage was clearly a hierarchical and patriarchal institution. Under common law the wife lost her independent legal identity, which was merged with that of her husband. The husband was head of the family and, in return for his duty to support her, he gained the right to manage her property and income, to claim her household and sexual services, and to custody of their children.[9]

Although the more "onerous aspects of patriarchal authority over married women" have gradually been removed,[10] vestiges of the traditional system remain firmly entrenched in modern family law. The movement to a truly egalitarian structure for legal marriage has been slow.

The third objection to traditional legal marriage is that it rigidly imposes a single family form that denies the diversity characteristic of families in a pluralistic society. The traditional model assumes that all people marry when they are young and that they stay married to the same person for the rest of their lives. Not only does this model ignore the social reality of marriage, divorce, cohabitation, and remarriage throughout the life cycle, but it is based on the assumption that the state can decide what form marriage should have regardless of its citizens' needs and desires. A single legal structure for all marriages is at odds with our highly valued tradition of protecting diversity in individual beliefs and values.

The contract model proposed in the second half of this book would overcome these objections. It would facilitate the freedom of married and unmarried couples to order their personal relationships as they wish and to devise a structure appropriate for their individual needs and values. Contracts are also suitable instruments for establishing egalitarian relationships, as indicated by the case study of contracts discussed in the Appendix. Finally, contracts can be used to legitimate and structure relationships between people who are barred from legal marriage, such as homosexual couples, and between people, such as unwed cohabitants, who reject the sex-based structure and/or other rigidities in legal marriage but who nevertheless want to join together in a legal partnership.

An Overview of the Book

Part I provides a comprehensive analysis of traditional legal marriage and its social and psychological consequences. It begins with an examination of the traditional law and the terms of the unwritten marriage contract. The traditional marriage contract created a hierarchical family structure and defined the basic rights and obligations of husbands and wives on the basis of gender. It recognized the husband as head of the family and made him responsible for family support. The wife was responsible for the home and was obligated to provide domestic services and child care. Each of the four chapters in Part I focuses on one of these time-honored provisions of the traditional law and examines its social, psychological, and legal effects on husbands and wives. Each chapter also discusses recent developments in the law, along with prospects for future change.

Part II contrasts the law's assumptions about the nature of marriage with social reality. The present marriage laws are based on the assumption that all marriages are first marriages of young, white, middle-class, monogamous couples who bear children, divide the labor in the family along sex lines, and remain together for a lifetime. This model ignores the current evidence concerning divorce, marriage in middle age and throughout the life cycle, childless marriages, more egalitarian family patterns, diverse family forms among ethnic minorities and the poor, and alternative family forms among homosexuals, communards, and others who live together without marriage. Furthermore, the law unnecessarily restricts those who do not conform to the traditional legal assumptions.

Each of the chapters in this part, Chapters 5 through 9, focuses on one of the social assumptions in the traditional law: lifelong commitment; first marriage; separate roles for husbands and wives; the white, middle-class family; and the monogamous heterosexual norm. Each reviews sociological data (for example, the divorce and remarriage rates) which challenge the accuracy and appropriateness of the legal assumptions.

The three chapters in *Part III* present the case for intimate contracts. Chapter 10 discusses the legal, social, and psychological advantages of a contract and attempts to answer the objections of those who fear that contracts will undermine trust and destroy romance. Chapter 11 presents a detailed list of possible provisions and suggests a number of questions that contract writers may wish to address. These issues are further explored in Chapter 12, which presents the case histories and intimate contracts of ten couples, five legally married and five cohabiting couples.

Finally, *Part IV* examines the legal consequences of alternatives to traditional legal marriage. While its primary focus is on contractual alternatives, it also examines the legal consequences of living together without a contract. After reviewing recent developments in this rapidly changing area of the law, it argues that most people would be better off with a contract (rather than getting married or living together without a contract).

Chapter 13 focuses on contracts between husbands and wives. Although the courts have traditionally refused to enforce most contracts between married persons, in the last decade a number of courts have begun to recognize the legitimate interests of husbands and wives who wish to arrange their relationship by contract. Chapters 14 and 15 explore the legal consequences of the major alternative to marriage: unwed cohabitation. Chapter 14 examines the legal consequences of living together without a contract. It reviews the sociological data on the growing incidence of unwed cohabitation and describes the laws that negatively affect cohabiting couples—both during an ongoing relationship and at the point of dissolution. Chapter 15 then explores the ways and extent to which a contract improves the legal situation of unwed cohabitants. After reviewing the law's traditional refusal to recognize the validity of contracts between an unmarried man and woman, the chapter focuses on recent developments in the law spurred by the 1975 California Supreme Court decision in *Marvin* v. *Marvin*. The cases that follow *Marvin* have drastically improved the prospects for a man and woman who wish to order their relationship by contract—whether in writing or by oral agreement. The chapter ends with an exploration of the evolving case law and prospects for the future enforcement of intimate contracts such as those proposed in this book.

The *Appendix* describes an empirical study of 60 contracts, relying heavily on quotations from contracts written by three types of couples: married partners, unwed cohabitants, and couples entering a trial relationship. The aim of this study was to compare relationships established by contract with those established by traditional family law, and to analyze the extent to which these contracts support more egalitarian family patterns.

PART I

The Legal Tradition: Terms of the Traditional Marriage Contract

Blackstone, the renowned English legal scholar, described marriage under the common law of England as the merger of husband and wife into a single legal identity:

> By marriage, the husband and wife are one person in law. . . . [T]he very being or legal existence of the woman is suspended during the marriage, or at least is incorporated and consolidated into that of the husband, under whose wing, protection, and cover she performs everything; and is therefore called . . . a *femme-covert*; and her condition during her marriage is called her *coverture*.[1]

As U.S. Supreme Court Justice Black observed, "this rule has worked out in reality to mean that though the husband and wife are one, the one is the husband."[2]

Under this doctrine of coverture, a married woman lost control of her real property as well as ownership of her chattels. She could not make a contract in her own name, either with her husband or with third parties, and she could not sue or be sued in her own name.[3] If she worked, her husband was entitled to her wages, and if she and her husband were to separate, her husband invariably gained custody of the children.[4] Upon marriage a woman's husband

1

not only gained complete control over his wife's income and property, he also controlled her person: "She was bound to accept his sexual advances, whether friendly or forcible" and was always subject to his physical restraint.[5]

The husband's power and authority over his wife was so pervasive, and the concept of the unity of husband and wife as a single person so complete, that a married woman was even absolved of full criminal responsibility for her own conduct: criminal acts committed by a woman in her husband's presence were assumed to be done under the husband's command, and he was therefore held responsible.[6] Because it was assumed that the husband and wife had a single legal identity, contracts between them were precluded during the course of their marriage.[7]

Some of these barriers, most notably those restricting a married woman's rights to property, were removed with the passage of the Married Woman's Property Acts, first enacted in Mississippi in 1839, and soon adopted in some form by all American jurisdictions.[8] As Professor Kanowitz notes:

> [T]hese laws generally granted married women the right to contract, to sue and be sued without joining their husbands, to manage and control the property they brought with them to the marriage, to engage in gainful employment without their husbands' permission, and to retain the earnings derived from their employment.[9]

Yet although these acts removed the more egregious property restrictions,[10] many of the economic, social and legal disabilities imposed on married women remained unchanged. It is only in recent years, more than a century later, that these basic obligations of marital partners under the English common law have begun to change.

In essence, the traditional marriage contract embodies four provisions:

1. The husband is head of the household.
2. The husband is responsible for support.
3. The wife is responsible for domestic services.
4. The wife is responsible for child care, the husband for child support.

Each of these provisions is rooted in common law, and each, to one degree or another, remains alive today. While recent developments in the law—and in society—have brought increasing challenges to the traditional legal "contract," what is most surprising is the extent to which present statutory and case law continue to uphold the traditional obligations of husbands and wives.

In the following four chapters we examine each of these time-honored provisions—and the challenges and changes they face. Each chapter begins with a statement of the traditional law and its effects on husbands and wives. Then recent developments in the law are discussed along with prospects for future changes.

The relative stagnation in the traditional law of marriage stands in sharp contrast to the major reforms that have taken place in the laws governing divorce. In the past decade most states in the United States have adopted some form of no-fault divorce law,* laws which clearly establish the individual's right to decide when and why a marriage should be dissolved.[11] In light of this new freedom granted to couples upon divorce, it seems especially ironic that most states do not grant couples the same freedom to structure their marriage. The terms of the legal marriage contract remain, for the most part, fixed by law.

Although the divorce law changes have been heralded as the beginning of a new era in family law, no true modernization can be effected until the legal restrictions of marriage are modified. Hopefully when the new era fully arrives, family law will reflect many of the suggestions for change proposed in the following pages.

---

*First passed in California in 1969. By 1980 only two states, Illinois and South Dakota, had not adopted some no-fault option for divorce.

CHAPTER 1

The Husband Is Head of the Family

The common-law tradition of coverture is still apparent in legal marriage, for the law continues to assume that marriage creates a unified legal identity of husband and wife. Although the merger of identities is not as complete today as it was under the common law, and although the married woman's legal and social identity is not as completely subordinated as it was under the common law, it is nevertheless evident that the law and the legal assumptions surrounding marriage still largely require that a married woman assume her husband's legal and social identity.[1] The husband is still considered the head of the family, and both his wife and his children are typically expected to assume *his* name, *his* domicile, and *his* social and economic status. The law continues to structure their legal identities as an adjunct to his.

Consider, for example the following case decided in California in May 1980. Patricia Herdman and Jason Schiffman separated in June 1977 after a 6 month marriage.* Patricia was pregnant when

---

*These facts are summarized from *In re Marriage of Schiffman* 102 Cal. App. 3d 714; 162 Cal. Rptr. 620 (1980).

they separated, and in November 1977 she gave birth to a baby girl whom she named Aita Marrie Herdman. At the divorce trial Jason Schiffman argued that he, as the child's father, had a legally "protectible interest" in having his child bear his name. Patricia objected, arguing that the common law rule was outmoded, and that she had a right to have her child, who had never lived with the father, bear *her* name. The trial court agreed with Schiffman and ordered the mother to change the child's surname to Schiffman. Patricia Herdman was outraged and appealed the ruling, asserting that she had been deprived of her equal right to have her child bear her name. The Court of Appeal, however, upheld the decision, citing the common law rule that "the father of the child born in lawful wedlock has a 'protectible interest' or a 'primary right' in having his child bear his surname." The absence of such a rule, the appeal court contended, would lead to "unnecessary mischief."*

In this chapter we examine the ways in which traditional marriage law merged the identities of husband and wife and thereby established the husband as the head of the family. This hierarchical relationship has been maintained by sex differentials in the age at which boys and girls can marry, by laws and customs dictating that a married woman assume her husband's name, by statutes requiring a married woman to take her husband's legal domicile as her own, and by rules establishing the husband's right to his wife's services and affection. In each of these areas, as we will note, the traditions surrounding marriage have denied wives equal rights and privileges under the law.[2]

While examining the traditional law, we will also note the changes that are now taking place. Recent cases and statutory reforms point toward a partnership concept of marriage and to a growing recognition that wives and husbands should be treated equally.

To note the trend toward the partnership model of marriage is not, however, to assert that it is already a reality. In fact, what is most surprising is the extent to which the traditional coverture-inspired model of marriage persists despite major social and economic changes in the position of women in our society.

---

*After this book went to press the California Supreme Court reversed this opinion and held that "the sole consideration when parents contest a child's surname should be the child's best interest." *In re Marriage of Schiffman*, 28 Cal. 3d 640; 169 Cal. Rptr. 918, 62 P. 2d 579 (1980).

Age of Marriage

The first way in which the common law fostered the hierarchical structure of marriage was by establishing different age-of-marriage requirements for the two sexes. The traditional rule was that girls could marry at 18 (or 16 with parental consent) and boys at 21 (or 18 with parental consent). It was assumed that boys had to prepare to earn a living; they therefore needed to defer marriage in order to pursue their education and training.[3] In contrast, it was assumed that girls required no special education or training for their life's work—as they were expected to be housewives and mothers.[4]

As of 1977, 23 states in the United States still had unequal marriage ages for men and women.[5] An additional number set different age requirements with parental consent.[6]

Although it is impossible to separate the effects of legal regulations from the influences of social custom, age differences at marriage had two major effects. First, on a structural level, the husband was usually older than his prospective wife, and the disparity in their ages helped to assure his authority as head of the household. It was "natural" for the younger, less educated and less well trained wife to assume her husband's identity upon marriage, just as it was "natural" for her to assume a subordinate role and status within the family. Both the age discrepancy and the different marital obligations that the law assigned to husband and wife fostered a hierarchical relationship between the two that supported the patriarchal structure of traditional marriage.

Second, on a psychological level, these laws suggested to young women that marriage was their proper life choice. As Professor Leo Kanowitz has argued, age differences for marriage have the psychological effect of telling both sexes that only men have to postpone marriage to acquire career training. He observed:

> [The law assumes] that the married state is the only proper goal of womanhood. [T]he male, and only the male, while not to be denied the benefits of marriage, should also be encouraged to engage in bigger, better and more useful pursuits.
>
> Recognizing that early marriage impedes preparation for meaningful extra-family activities, society has decreed that males should not be permitted this digression from life's important business at too

early an age. Since women's participation in meaningful activities outside the home was until recently socially inconceivable, no great harm was seen in permitting females to follow their biological inclination and to marry earlier than males.[7]

Kanowitz correctly perceived that early marriage for a woman often leads to her premature removal from educational and occupational opportunities. Although we have come a long way from the 1800s when education for women was widely believed to be unnecessary (and even harmful), the net effect of allowing women to marry earlier remains: even today women who marry early are likely to interrupt their education, drop out of school, and simply lower their educational and occupational aspirations. Further, as Kanowitz noted, early marriage increases the likelihood of early pregnancy, which further alters a woman's life course and thus perpetuates different roles for the two sexes.[8] Thus these laws reinforce social pressures that already exist: they encourage a woman to choose marriage over a career when she perceives a conflict between the two, and they reinforce the structural differences in the positions of the two sexes.

According to Professor Homer Clark, by 1980 many of the states that had age differences in marital eligibility had changed their laws because of the change in voting age brought about by the 26th Amendment, the reduction in the age of majority from 21 to 18, and the 1974 U.S. Supreme Court decision in *Stanton.* * *Stanton* invalidated a Utah law that required parents to support their daughters until they were 18, but to support their sons to age 21. This law was based on the assumption that only sons had to acquire further education and training for their life's work.[9] When the Supreme Court overturned the Utah law it expressly rejected the law's traditional assumptions about the necessity of different educational requirements for the two sexes:

> No longer is the female destined solely for the home and the rearing of the family, and only the male for the marketplace and the world of ideas. . . . If a specified age of minority is required for the boy in order to assure him parental support while he attains his education and training, so, too, it is for the girl. To distinguish between the two on educational grounds is to be self-serving: if the female is not to be sup-

---

*Professor Homer Clark, of the University of Colorado School of Law, concludes that by 1980 there was a substantial consensus among the states that the marriage age should be 18 for both sexes. Personal conversation, October 1980.

ported so long as the male, she hardly can be expected to attend school as long as he does, and bringing her education to an end earlier coincides with the role-typing society has long imposed.[10]

Although the Stanton opinion dealt only with the issue of child support, it clearly implies that state laws that maintain sex differences in the age of marital eligibility will be held unconstitutional.*

A Married Woman's Name

The married woman's loss of an independent identity is most clearly symbolized by the loss of her name: upon marriage she typically assumes her husband's surname. In the past, married women who tried to retain their birth-given surnames have had difficulty registering to vote, obtaining a driver's license, securing credit, running for office, and obtaining a passport.[11] Married women have been unable to recover for injuries suffered in automobile accidents if their cars were registered in their maiden names,[12] and to become naturalized citizens using their maiden names.[13] And, until 1975, Michigan forced a woman with minor children to retain her husband's name after divorce.[14]

However, throughout most of history the law did not compel married women to take their husbands' names. Their subordinate status was so accepted that no such laws were deemed necessary:

> As long as most women quietly accepted wifehood and the feminine sphere, their names were not an issue. In fact there were no laws on the subject, other than common law, which allowed persons to take any names they chose.[15]

Not until the nineteenth century, when women began to assert their autonomy, did they begin to lose their common law right to their own name. Confusion about names grew, and when the controversy reached the courts, judges began to "build precedents out of hot air and patriarchal sentiment."[16] By the 1930s it became "accepted law" that women lost their maiden names at marriage.

*As of October 1980, Professor Homer Clark counts 42 states and D.C. that set the eligible age for the marriage at 18, for both men and women. Some states still have unequal age requirements, e.g., Ark. Stat. Ann. Sec. 55–102 (Supp. 1977) and Del. Code Ann. tit. 13, Sec. 123 (1975), but it seems likely that such statutes would be held unconstitutional if challenged. Personal conversation, October 1980.

Restrictions During Marriage

The types of name restrictions married women face are illustrated by voter registration laws.[17] In the majority of states in the United States, when a woman marries, her birth-name voting registration is cancelled and she is required to register with the Board of Elections under her married name. In other states women registering to vote must specify a prefix "Miss" or "Mrs.," and those with the "Mrs." prefix must use the same surname as their husbands.

Driver's license regulations are similar. As recently as 1972, in *Forbush* v. *Wallace*, the U.S. Supreme Court upheld an Alabama law requiring a married woman to use her husband's surname on her driver's license.[18] The decision was premised on the Alabama common law requirement that "upon marriage the wife, by operation of law, takes the husband's surname." Because Alabama's motor vehicle regulations require that a driver obtain a license in "one's legal name," a married woman must use her husband's surname on her driver's license even if she is not known by that name in her other everyday transactions. The rationale for the Alabama regulation was that it served the state's "administrative convenience"; however, it would seem that "administrative convenience" would be better served if women *retained* their birth names throughout life, thereby obviating the need to change existing records.

Although many women want to assume their husband's surname when they marry, "a coerced change of name," as Professor Herma Hill Kay has noted, "is resented by the woman who wishes to retain her birth name in order to establish a continuity of identity throughout her life."[19] When Mary Smith becomes Mrs. John Jones, her former name (and social identity) are completely obliterated: she becomes an extension of John Jones—an appendage to his social identity. A woman in public or professional life may incur a serious loss of recognition if she alters her name upon marriage, particularly if she marries more than once.

The problem of a married woman's professional identity is illustrated by the 1976 case of *Whitlow* v. *Hodges*.[20] Whitlow, a college instructor, had used her birth name throughout her marriage and acquired a professional reputation under that name. When she accepted a post at the University of Kentucky School of Journalism and moved with her husband to Kentucky, she applied for a driver's license in her professional name. Her application was denied because Kentucky common law requires that a married woman receive a driver's license in her husband's surname, regardless of what name she may use for other purposes. Whitlow argued that the requirement was irrational in her case because her personal and professional identification was well established in her birth name. Further, she contended, she had not used her husband's name for any purpose. The U.S. District Court nevertheless dismissed her complaint and the Court of Appeals affirmed the decision. *

There has been considerable controversy over both the origin and the legality of the rule that requires a woman to adopt her husband's name upon marriage. Is it custom or law? Research indicates that it was historically a matter of custom in England[21] as well as in most states in the United States.[22] In the past decade courts in Arkansas, California, Connecticut, Florida, Indiana, Maryland, New Jersey, New York, Ohio, Tennessee, and Wisconsin[23] have affirmed that their state laws *do not require* a woman to assume her husband's name, relying on the common law rule that a person may adopt and use any name he or she wishes as long as the change is not made for fraudulent purposes.[24] Similar rulings have been issued by the attorney generals of Pennsylvania, Michigan, and Massachusetts.[25]

Although the recent trend in state courts has been toward upholding the married woman's right to retain her birth name upon marriage and her right to reassume her birth name during marriage (if she did not do so when she first married), the decisions are by no means uniform. For example, in a 1974 lower court opinion in New Jersey, *In re Lawrence*, a married woman who had assumed her husband's name after marriage was denied the right to resume her birth name.[26] The woman asserted that her request was justified because she was about to enter a career in law. (Her petition also noted that her husband did not object to the change.) The court nevertheless denied the petition; it asserted that the couple's use of different names "would cause great confusion in the community in which they live and could well have a traumatic effect upon any children they might have."[27]

This holding was later reversed on appeal (as an abuse of discretion),[28] but a similar ruling in another state was not. In the 1975

*The U.S. Supreme Court denied certiorari (refused to hear the case) and thereby let stand the ruling of the Court of Appeals.

case of *In re Mohlman*,[29] a North Carolina court denied the name-change petitions of several married women who had adopted their husbands' surnames and wished to resume the use of their birth names. The court said the North Carolina name-change statute required a showing of "good and sufficient" reasons for the change, and the petitioners' assertion of personal and professional reasons did not meet this requirement.

Restrictions After Divorce

Most states have some divorce-decree provision allowing a divorced woman to resume the use of a birth-given or prior surname.[30] However, this right may be denied to women in certain situations or may be left to the judge's discretion. Trial court judges have refused to restore the birth names of women who are at fault in the divorce action, who are recipients of alimony, or who have minor children.[31] Some statutes also allow an order to *prohibit* a woman's use of her former husband's surname upon divorce, regardless of her wishes.[32]

The most common name restriction after divorce affects the woman who retains custody of her minor children. For example, in the 1974 California case *In re Marriage of Banks*,[33] a superior court judge refused to allow a divorced woman to resume her birth name on the grounds that her three minor children would be harmfully affected if her surname was not the same as theirs. When pressed by Mrs. Banks' attorney, the judge stated:

> I consider the sanity of the children and a lack of frustration over a different name is of considerably greater importance at this point than a resumption of her maiden name. I don't see what is to be gained by resuming her maiden name. . . . I would advise Mrs. Banks that a rose by any other name is a rose just the same. It doesn't make any difference what your name is. And my concern at this stage of the game is with these children. That's my major concern.[34]

Similarly, a 1975 New Jersey trial court denied the petition of three women (all obtaining uncontested divorces, all having custody of minor children) to have their former surnames restored in *Egner* v. *Egner*.[35]

The trend in recent appellate court decisions, however, is to *uphold* the woman's right to resume her birth name. Both *Banks* and *Egner* were reversed at the appellate level, and the New Jersey appellate court made it clear that the right to choose one's own name cannot be limited by "court-created exceptions based on conjectures about the effects of such name changes on others."[36] Further, in response to the lower court's argument that a change of name would be harmful to the children, the higher court indicated it did not "perceive any significant problem affecting minor children's welfare,"[37] and pointed out that many children are raised by remarried mothers who have taken the surname of their new husband.

Thus, while the law in this area is changing, a married woman who prefers not to assume her husband's surname would still be well advised to take appropriate legal action[38] if she does not want to contend with unwritten law, administrative regulations, and social pressures that continue to reinforce this coverture-inspired custom.[39]

A Child's Name

Official policy and long-standing custom have traditionally dictated that children shall assume the surname of their fathers. This rule, according to Brown et al., ensures that a child's surname reflects both the child's "legitimacy" status and the married father's dominance over his family's identity.[40] The traditional view has been that the father, as head of the family, has a right to have his children bear his name and his identity—and to have his children carry on his family line.

Today more and more married women are choosing not only to retain their birth names after marriage, but also to have their children's names reflect their own identities. Some couples use hyphenated names for themselves and their children; others assign surnames to their children according to the sex of the child, each having the surname of his or her same sex parent.* However, these couples still confront considerable official resistance from state health departments and vital statistics bureaus.

Parental interests in children's names are most likely to conflict after a divorce. Here again, the common law rule has been that the father has a protected "property right" to have his progeny bear his name.[41] Most courts continue to abide by this rule. Even those

*See, for example, pages 435–436 on names in the Appendix.

courts that readily grant a divorcee's request to resume her maiden name are reluctant to grant her request to change the names of minor children in her custody. The father is almost always successful in blocking her request, especially if he has continued to support the children. Even if the child is born after the parents have separated and has never lived with the father, as in the 1980 Schiffman case cited in the beginning of this chapter,* the father can still assert his right to have his child bear his name. Similarly, a natural father's opposition to his children assuming the surname of the mother's second husband is invariably respected by the courts.

The issues involved in changing the name of a minor child are complex. While it is difficult to know what standards or presumptions will be best for the child, it seems more reasonable to base the decision on the child's best interests than on an arbitrary sex-based rule favoring the father. While some courts have begun to utilize sex-neutral rules such as "the best interest of the child," they have typically construed the rule to imply that it is in the child's best interest to retain the father's surname.

Such decisions reflect the strength of the presumption that the father has a "right" to have his children bear his name. They also point to the need for more explicit standards to guide the courts. Brown, et al. have suggested that courts consider such factors as "which parent has custody, the presence of other children in the family with another surname, the social difficulty the children may encounter in the use of a particular name, and the value of retaining a tie to the noncustodial parent."[42]

A Married Woman's Domicile

Another example of the married woman's loss of independent legal identity is provided by her traditional assumption of her husband's domicile upon marriage.[43] Under common law the husband had the right to decide where the family would live: he was head of the household and had the authority to choose the marital abode. His wife was obliged to follow him wherever he went and to live under whatever circumstances he chose. "The husband may choose any reasonable place or mode of living and the wife must conform thereto."[44]

*In re Marriage of Schiffman, 102 Cal. App. 3d 714; 162 Cal. Rptr. 620 (1980) discussed on pages 5–6.

This basic rule is still the law in many states.[45] It means that when a woman marries she "loses her domicile and acquires that of her husband no matter where she resides, or what she believes or intends."[46] Domicile rules often serve to exclude wives from independent eligibility for the range of benefits offered by both state and national governments. For example, a woman who is, and always has been, a state resident, and is therefore eligible for free tuition at the state university, may suddenly be charged out-of-state tuition if she marries a man whose legal domicile is in another state.[47] Further, she may lose her right to vote in local and state elections or to run for office in her home state.

The location of a person's domicile affects a broad range of legal rights and duties, including not only the place where he or she may vote, run for public office, or receive free or lowered tuition, but also where he or she may serve on juries, be liable for taxes, sue for divorce, receive welfare assistance, register a car, and have an estate administered. Although the privilege of choosing one's own legal domicile is accorded to all other adults, the married woman may find herself with no choice in the matter and thereby severely disadvantaged. For example, if a married woman owns personal property in the state in which she is residing, her property may be taxed at the higher rate of the state of her husband's domicile.[48] As of 1975 only ten states allowed a married woman to establish her own domicile for purposes of taxation.[49]

In many states married women are prevented from retaining their own domiciles for purposes of voting, running for office, having their estates probated, and serving on juries.[50] As of 1977 only five states in the nation—Arkansas, Colorado, Maine, Maryland, and Oregon—had laws declaring that the domicile of a person shall not be abridged or denied on the basis of sex, and that a married person may establish his or her own domicile on the same basis as all other adults.[51] A married woman can establish her own domicile for voting in only fifteen states, for election to public office in only six other states, and for probate and jury service in only five other states.[52]

Thus, in many cases the law fails to recognize a wife's equal interest in the location of the marital domicile and thereby denies her equal protection of the law. As Professor Kanowitz has observed, the practical effect of the domicile rule is to "deprive wives of certain governmental benefits they would otherwise have."[53] For example, a wife is typically disqualified from receiving unemployment benefits when she moves to assume her husband's new domicile.[54]

The domicile rule may cause a more severe hardship at the time of divorce. In most states that retain the option of fault-based grounds for divorce, a woman who refuses to accept her husband's choice of domicile is considered to have deserted him. A woman found guilty of deserting her husband would be "at fault" in a divorce action and could be deprived of property and her right to alimony. For example, in the 1974 New York case of *Cavallo* v. *Cavallo*,[55] the court found a wife's refusal to move to a location that her husband selected to be constructive desertion. Similarly, in a 1974 Pennsylvania case the court found an 88-year-old wife guilty of desertion for leaving her 92-year-old husband's chosen domicile (with his unmarried daughter), and for refusing to live with him unless he would live where she wanted to live. The woman's behavior, the court asserted, "flies in the face of everything sacred which decrees that the husband must choose the domicile and the wife must conform thereto."[56]

The traditional legal rule that forced a wife to take her husband's domicile was derived from the common law doctrine of coverture—and the accompanying notion of a single identity and unity of husband and wife.[57] More recently, the domicile rule has been justified by the assumption that the husband must be able to choose the family's domicile in order to maintain his job (so that he can support the family). This in turn assures that the husband alone is responsible for family support. As the court reasoned in *Carlson* v. *Carlson*:[58]

> The general rule by the great weight of authority is that the wife *must* adopt the residence of the husband and that she cannot without just cause maintain a separate domicile. There are sound reasons for this rule. *The law imposes upon the husband the burden and obligation of support, maintenance and care of the family and almost of necessity he must have the right of choice of the situs of the home.* There can be no decision by majority rule as to whether the family home shall be maintained. . . . The *violation of this principle tends to sacrifice the family unity, the entity upon which our civilization is built. [O]ne domicile for the family home is still an essential in our way of life.*[59]

This rationale is outmoded in three respects. First, it is no longer realistic to assume that the location of the homestead is determined solely by the husband's work: the needs and wishes of wives and children also play a role in residential decisions. Second, it is no longer realistic to assume that husbands are solely responsible for family support. In the growing number of two-career families the career needs of both spouses must increasingly be considered. Third, a single-family residence may not be appropriate when spouses work in different cities or states. Some two-career couples live in separate domiciles for substantial periods of time.

Let us briefly examine further these challenges to the domicile rule.

First, consider the assumption that the husband's work determines the family domicile. It is clear that even when the husband assumes the role of primary breadwinner, his career and the financial advantages of a move for him are often weighed against the potential costs to other members of the family. Wives and children have become increasingly aware of the social and psychological costs of relocation[60] and many are loath to endure those costs for the sake of a man's occupational mobility. Berkwitt reports that more wives of business executives are unwilling to give up their established interests and identities to follow their husbands to new locations, and, as a result, more husbands are refusing to relocate.[61] Similarly, Lake asserts that many corporations have had to alter their policies on transfers in response to family-oriented concerns among their executives.[62]

Further, it is likely that in the future the social and professional needs of wives will play an increasingly significant role in the decision of whether or not to change the family domicile. Thus the domicile law will become even less appropriate than it is today. Dr. Seidenberg has aptly summed up the absurdity of the traditional legal and social assumptions on domicile:

> It is indeed ironic that the *housewife* whose life centers around the *home* should, under the law as well as iron-clad custom, have *no right to domicile*.[63]

Consider now the second assumption underlying the domicile rule: that all families are single-career families in which the husband is solely responsible for family support. This assumption ignores the growing number of dual-career couples whose residential choice may involve compromising the needs of two careers.[64] By 1977 two-earner families represented over 47 percent of the total number of husband-wife families in the United States.[65]

In one study of two-career families Professor Lynda Holmstrom found that when the family established a single-family domicile, the wife's career significantly influenced the family's decision in 12 out of 15 cases.[66] Typically, when the couple decided to move they negotiated simultaneously for two positions that took into account the occupational needs of both the husband and the wife. A similar trend is observable in Britain, where Rapoport and Rapoport[67] and Fogarty[68] found that mobility among highly educated men and women is determined by the career situations of both husband and wife, not by the husband's alone.[69]

This is not meant to imply that these decisions are truly egalitarian. As Holmstrom notes, although many husbands "were restricted in the sense that they went out of their way to live in places where their wives could also obtain employment, it was still the wives who typically made the greater career sacrifices when deciding where to live . . . it was the women who accommodated to their husbands' careers more than vice versa."[70] Similarly, in a sample of 107 dual-career couples with Ph.D.'s in psychology, Wallston, Foster and Berger found that although about 80 percent of the couples ascribed to egalitarian norms in their search for professional jobs, in the face of institutional constraints, about 60 percent of the sample reported a decision in which the woman followed the man.*

When faced with difficulties in finding two jobs near each other some couples decide to alternate the priorities given to each person's career or to each forgo their first-choice location for a compromise location where both can find acceptable jobs.[71]

The domicile rule's third assumption, that a family will have only one residence, is challenged by other two-career couples who decide to establish separate domiciles for significant periods of time.† Some of these couples are forced to live apart for reasons of

---

*Barbara Strudler Wallston, Martha A. Foster and Michael Berger "I Will Follow Him: Myth, Reality or Forced Choice—Job Seeking Experiences of Dual Career Couples" in Jeff Bryson and Rebecca Bryson (eds.), *Dual Career Couples* (New York: Human Sciences Press, 1978). Wallston, Foster and Berger note that many couples felt frustrated by the institutional constraints that hampered their attempts to follow an egalitarian job-seeking strategy and they recommend policy changes and programs to educate employers. See also page 432 of the Appendix for a discussion of the variety of domicile arrangements made by two-career couples.

†Other couples may marry after establishing domiciles that each spouse wishes to retain. For example, in 1976, when U.S. Representative Andrew Jacobs, an Indiana Democrat, married U.S. Representative Martha Keys, a Kansas Democrat, they retained their separate domiciles. Both were re-elected from their respective districts after the marriage.

health, education, parenting, or military service; many more choose to do so to maximize career opportunities.[72]

In 1976, sociologist Naomi Gerstel studied "The Feasibility of Commuter Marriage" in a sample of 94 couples.[73] Her sample was limited to dual-career families whose primary motivation for commuting was to maximize both partners' opportunities, personal satisfaction, and involvement in work. In 32 percent of the families the woman did all the traveling between homes, in 52 percent the man did all the traveling, and the spouses alternated in 16 percent of the cases. Gerstel concluded that commuting was most feasible at two points in the family's life cycle: before the children were born and/or after the children were grown and had left the home. *But* family life and commuting proved extremely difficult if it occurred very early in the marriage, or just after the children were born, or in retirement. Further, she noted that commuting was most successful when it was defined as a temporary situation, whether or not the couple had specific plans for reuniting.[74]

Nevertheless, legal assumptions continue to ignore the possibility that many "normal" married couples may live apart for substantial periods of time.* As a result, the law continues to impose unwarranted burdens of taxation, insurance, and employment-linked restrictions on dual-career marriages.

Before ending this section it is important that we note two exceptions to the established domicile law that may portend a brighter trend. The first is a 1974 New York case, *Weintraub* v. *Weintraub*.[75] The wife, a New York police officer for 13 years, did not want to give up her job, or its prospect of excellent retirement benefits after 20 years of service, to move with her husband to Alabama. When she sued for support after her husband moved, her husband contended she had abandoned him because she had not moved with him. In a clear break with tradition, the New York court ruled that the husband's right to choose the family domicile was not absolute. Instead the court recognized the wife's legitimate interest in retaining financial independence and a sense of self-worth, and held that these interests justified her refusal to move to Alabama. The court ordered the husband to continue to provide

---

*A notable exception is provided by the pending Wisconsin legislation on property law reform sponsored by Representative Mary Lou Munts et al. Recognizing that a happily married couple may not always live together, it allows spouses who maintain two bonafide principal residences, one of which is within and one without the state, to designate the law of the jurisdiction of their choice which shall govern their property rights. A.B. 370 Section 766.20 (1981).

some support for her and their children while she remained in New York.

In a second case, *Blair* v. *Blair*,[76] a Maryland court tried to carve out a broader exception to the domicile rule by allowing the wife to initiate the move. In this case the wife was the family bread-winner, the sole supporter of her student husband. The court ruled that she was not guilty of desertion when she did not take her husband's domicile at college but instead returned to their previous home in the state where she had been employed.

Consortium

A final indication of the married woman's submerged identity under common law is provided by the laws governing suits for loss of consortium. Consortium is the right of a spouse to the other's services, companionship, affection, and sexual relations. As Clark states, consortium includes:

> ... the husband's rights to his wife's services, society, companionship, assistance and sexual relations. [C]onsortium could be summed up as referring to the variety of intangible relationships prevailing between spouses living together in a going marriage.[77]

At common law, only the husband could sue for loss of consortium when a third party negligently injured his wife.[78] The husband's right was founded, at least in part, on the notion that a married woman was the property of her husband and owed him household as well as sexual services.[79] The wife, on the other hand, had no cause of action for the loss of her husband's consortium "because a married woman was unable to bring suit in her own name, because she had no right to her husband's services, and because, upon marriage, her identity became part of a legal unity represented by the husband."[80]

The persistence of these differential standards was long an enigma even to legal scholars. As the Supreme Court of Alabama observed in 1974 (in a decision extending to wives the right to sue for loss of consortium):

> At common law a wife had no independent legal status of her own. In legal contemplation she existed largely as a non person. On this basis a wife was denied a cause of action for the loss of her husband's consortium. Despite change in a wife's status through the years, . . . the

common law doctrine that a wife could not sue for the loss of her husband's consortium was continued in the decisions of this country. Realizing that the old common law basis for the rule had become unrealistic in the more modern social fabric, new reasons were assigned for its continuance. *In this manner the old doctrine denying a wife's action for loss of her husband's consortium was retained as a vestigial appendage in the body jurisprudence.*[81]

The law on suits for loss of consortium has changed considerably in recent years. As of 1977, 38 states and the District of Columbia recognized a married woman's interest in her husband's consortium, although in most of these (30) recognition was extended by judicial decision rather than by affirmative legislation.[82] Of the remaining twelve states, six did not allow married women to sue for loss of their husbands' consortium, and six had abolished such suits for both sexes.[83] The courts invalidating the traditional rules have recognized that sex-based differences in the legal rights accorded to husbands and wives are in violation of the equal protection clause of the Fourteenth Amendment. These same courts may well soon recognize similar violations in the other sex-based obligations of the traditional marriage contract.

In summary, it is important to note the circular and reinforcing nature of the social and legal stereotypes embodied in the traditional marriage contract. Once the husband is defined as the legal head of the family, it follows that decisions about the family name, the family domicile, and family finances are properly *his* decisions. It is not that the legal system or the social system has marshaled resources to treat the wife as a person of secondary importance. Rather, questions about the wife's role, or the wife's power, or the wife's separate identity simply do not arise when the family is treated as a single unit.

The coverture-based assumption of family unity implies that a wife has no need for her own name, her own domicile, her own credit, her own status, or her own identity. It assumes that she derives great benefits from the identity and protection of her husband and that these benefits are essential to the family unit. Thus, a series of legal assumptions gives rise to a host of social customs and administrative regulations that combine to enhance the husband's strictly legal rights as head of the household and, as a result, further diminish those of his wife.

Women today are increasingly challenging these assumptions.* They are asserting that they derive neither benefit nor protection from the coverture-inspired conception of marital roles. In addition, they are calling into question the law's assumption that the identities of husband and wife should merge upon marriage and, more emphatically, the assumption that any merger necessitates subordination of the wife.

While the focus in this chapter has been on the disadvantages the first provision of the marriage contract imposes on married women, it is clear that the traditional contract also imposes inappropriate and unnecessary burdens on married men. Some of these burdens are discussed in the next chapter.

*Changing attitudes (and behavior) of both men and women are discussed more fully in Chapter 7.

CHAPTER 2

The Husband's Responsibility for Support

The Legal Tradition

In the traditional state-imposed marriage contract the financial responsibility for the family was delegated to the husband; he was obligated to provide their support, and privileged to control the family's property. Presumably, the husband exchanged his financial support of the family for his wife's services as a housewife and mother. Although recent changes in the laws governing property, and the U.S. Supreme Court's disapproval of gender-based alimony statutes in *Orr v. Orr*, discussed below*, suggest the beginnings of a trend toward a more sex-neutral family law, the legacy of the tradi-

---

*Orr v. *Orr*, 440 U.S. 268 (1979). In *Orr* the Supreme Court invalidated an Alabama law that imposed alimony obligations on husbands, but not on wives. Since only 10 states limited alimony to wives prior to Orr (most states had sex-neutral statutes but nevertheless awarded postdivorce support almost exclusively to women) the decision created more of a symbolic revolution with its declaration that gender-based support obligations are illegal. As a practical matter, however, the responsibility for postdivorce support is likely to remain with men in light of the different needs, experiences and capacities of the two spouses after divorce. *Orr* is discussed on page 44 in the section on support after divorce.

23

tional system still remains. Professor Homer Clark summarizes this traditional system of spousal obligations as follows:

> [T]he courts say that the husband has a duty to support his wife, that she has a duty to render services in the home, and that these duties are reciprocal. . . .
>
> The husband is to provide the family with food, clothing, shelter and as many of the amenities of life as he can manage, either (in earlier days) by the management of his estates or (more recently) by working for wages or salary. The wife is to be mistress of the household, maintaining the home with the resources furnished by the husband, and caring for the children.[1]

The traditional rules thus dictated a strict division of labor within the family, with the husband responsible for the economic sphere and the wife responsible for the internal sphere of the home. It was a reciprocal but sex-based assignment of marital obligations.

Although one might suppose this statement of spousal obligations merely represents an old fashioned ideal, it is important to recognize that these definitions are still entrenched in modern family law in a variety of spheres. As recently as 1974 Professor Herma Hill Kay concluded that "Even a superficial examination of the law of spousal and family support during marriage discloses that virtually every state, including those with community property systems, places the primary obligation of family support upon the husband . . . he is to provide necessities for both his wife and his children."[2] At that time two-thirds of the states *never* held a wife responsible for the support of her husband, and the others held her responsible only if her husband had become incapacitated or a public charge.[3]

The husband's obligation for family support was regarded as his major marital responsibility. As a 1973 Pennsylvania court stated, "*The husband has an absolute moral and legal obligation to support his wife.* . . . This obligation does not arise out of debt or contract; *it is an incident of the marital status imposed by the law*."[4] Similarly, a 1973 New York decision proclaimed:

> [B]oth at common law and presently by statute . . . the primary obligation of a husband or father [is] to support his wife and children. Presumably, interwoven in the latter obligation is the recognition that *natural order*, taught both by history and reason, *designates the male as the provider* in the usual marriage relation. That duty [is] different in recognizable degree than the other mutual duties of marriage. . . .[5]

And again, in 1975, in response to a direct challenge in *State* v. *Barton*[6] the husband's responsibility for family support was reaffirmed. In that case the State of Louisiana charged Douglas Barton with criminal neglect for failing to support his wife. Barton contended that Louisiana law discriminated against him on the basis of sex because it allowed criminal nonsupport charges to be brought against husbands, but not against wives. However, the Supreme Court of Louisiana found the statute reasonable and fair:

> Despite the increasing activities of women in the marketplace of commerce, it presently remains a fact of life that, between two spouses, the husband is invariably the means of support for the couple. Thus, the classification drawn by the statute, i.e., that only husbands are liable for criminal nonsupport, constitutes a reasonable legislative classification.[7]

While it is clear that such explicit sex-based differences would not be upheld after the Supreme Court's decision in *Orr*, discussed below,* the legacy of this approach remains, and there is little doubt that most courts continue to view the husband as the family's primary breadwinner, the wife as secondary. Similarly, his responsibility for child support stems from a legal tradition† in which a wife was asked to contribute only if her husband was unwilling or unable to do so.[8] For example, in a 1974 Alabama divorce case the father, who was seeking child custody, requested child support from his ex-wife. The trial court awarded custody to the father but refused to order the mother to contribute to the child's support. On appeal, the higher court affirmed this decision, reasserting that the primary support obligation rested with the father.[9]

Similarly, in 1974, in *Dill* v. *Dill*, the Georgia Supreme Court unanimously upheld as constitutional a Georgia statute that placed the primary obligation of child support after divorce upon the father, holding the mother responsible only if the father was dead, missing (and unlocatable), or incapable of support. The different treatment of male and female parents was affirmed by the Georgia high court[10] as both appropriate and reasonable.‡

Orr v. *Orr*, which involves support after divorce, is discussed on page 44.

†This discussion refers to his *legal responsibility*. Actual practice is discussed in Chapter 4: "The Responsibility for Children."

‡However, in 1974 in Pennsylvania *Conway* v. *Dana*, 456 Pa. 536, 318 A.2d 324 (1974), a court held that different support obligations based solely on the sex of a parent violated the state's equal rights amendment. Nevertheless, the language of this decision, which directs lower courts to consider the capacity and

In light of the courts' traditional view of the husband's total responsibility for family financial support, spouses were not allowed to make private contracts to alter or limit the husband's obligation.[11] As San Francisco Judge Isabella Grant summarized the law: "[A] prospective husband may not be absolved from his duty to support his wife nor can this duty be qualified or limited. The husband's duty . . . is an obligation imposed by law and cannot be contracted away."[12] Even in cases in which a man married a wealthy woman on the condition that he would not be obligated to support her, the courts nevertheless affirmed the unalterability of his obligation and held him liable for his wife's support.[13]

Legal Consequences: Financial Control and Property

One major effect of placing the primary support obligation on men has been to reinforce the husband's position as head of the household and, more specifically, his financial authority in the family. While the husband's obligation for support does not alone bestow upon him the mixed blessing of financial authority and financial responsibility, much of his legal power over the family's finances stems directly from this duty. The link between support and the control of family property and income may be traced directly back to the common law. Historically, upon marriage, the husband acquired ownership and control of all of his wife's property and possessions, as well as the duty to provide for her welfare. He was thus given both the lifelong resources and the lifelong responsibility for her financial well-being. As Clark explains:

> Upon her marriage the wife's personal property and possessions became the property of her husband, and on his death passed to his personal representatives. The same was true of personal property which she acquired during marriage. Even her paraphernalia, clothing, and jewelry belonged to him, but this sort of property did come back to her on her husband's death. . . . The rules were different with respect to the married woman's real property, but no more favorable to her interests. The use of her estates of inheritance in land belonged to her husband during the marriage, and for that time he was entitled to the

---

ability of both parents, still suggests that the primary responsibility lies with the father: "When we consider the order to be assessed against the father, we must not only consider his property, income, and earning capacity, but also what, if any, contribution the mother is in a position to provide."

rents and profits of the land. If the marriage produced a child born alive, the husband became a tenant by the courtesy, as a result of which he was entitled to the rents and profits of his wife's land during his life. The estate of inheritance remained the wife's property, but the husband could convey his interest and the wife could not convey hers without his consent, nor could any conveyance be made between husband and wife. On his death the property passed to the wife or her heirs.[14]

Of course, the theory behind these regulations was that since the husband had the responsibility and duty to support his wife, she had no need or use for her "own" property. Later, when married women began to earn money, their husbands were also entitled to their wages, just as they were entitled to the wages earned by their children's labor.[15]

Although the law today has come a long way from these absolute prohibitions, it nevertheless retains many traditional presumptions that preserve the husband's position as master of the family treasury. One extreme example is provided by "free dealer" statutes. These statutes require a woman to obtain her husband's permission before she can open a business. Five states still have free dealer or "sole trader" statutes, which typically compel a married woman to set forth in a petition her character, habits, education, and mental capacity for business, and to explain why she should be exempted from the disabilities of other married women and allowed to open a business of her own.[16] She is usually required to serve her husband with a copy of the petition or to otherwise obtain his signed consent.* Similarly, a husband's permission, or signature, may be required before his wife can trade in commodities.†

*Professor Marjorie Fine Knowles reports that the last state statute to prevent a married woman from conveying her separate property without her husband's consent was invalidated in Alabama in 1977. Knowles, "The Legal Status of Women in Alabama: A Crazy Quilt," *Alabama Law Review* 29 (1978): 439.

†A 1972 story in *The Wall Street Journal* reported: "Several Wall Street firms have long-standing policies aimed at discouraging women from trading in the volatile commodity market. The brokers apparently believe women are too emotional to keep pace with the frequent changes in the commodities market." "Woman Wins Round in Her Bias Action Against Walston & Co.," *The Wall Street Journal*, February 8, 1972, p. 38, cols. 4–5. (This story concerned the complaint of a female attorney and orange grove owner who was restricted from trading in juice concentrate commodities futures because she would not sign a "Women's Commodity Account Agreement" that released the firm from liability for any losses that might be incurred.)

The penumbra of financial powers that flow from the husband's assumed position as master of the family treasury now embraces newly emerging areas such as pensions, insurance, Social Security, and dependency allowances, as well as the more traditional areas of income and real property. On the national level, administrative regulations regarding unemployment insurance, Social Security benefits, federal survivors and disability insurance, home mortgage loans, and public assistance similarly reinforce the assumption that the husband is the financial head of the household.[17] These regulations are directly related to the husband's support obligation and the financial authority over the family coffers that it brings. As John Kenneth Galbraith observes:

> With the receipt of the income, in the usual case, goes the *basic* authority over its use. This usually lies with the male. . . . The place where the family lives, . . . the level and style of expenditure. . . . More important, in a society which sets store by pecuniary achievement, a natural authority resides with the person who earns the money. This entitles him to be called the *head* of the family.[18]

The husband's legal control over family finances is most significant with respect to property. While it is impossible to detail the variety of marital property schemes in the 50 states, several basic principles can be outlined to suggest the extent of the husband's rights.

Separate v. Community Property Systems

Marital property law takes two basic forms. Most states in the United States (42 states and the District of Columbia) have a "separate" or "common law" property system. The remaining minority of eight states (Arizona, California, Idaho, Louisiana, Nevada, New Mexico, Texas, and Washington) have a "community" property system.

In the separate property jurisdictions, a spouse retains all the property he or she brought into the marriage, and all the property he or she earns or inherits during the course of the marriage. The other spouse has no legal right or interest in his or her partner's income or separate property. Since each is the sole owner of his or her earnings, each has also the sole right to contract with regard to those earnings, to obtain credit based on them, and to manage and control them. Thus, in a separate property system a wife who is a full-time homemaker has no right to her husband's income—or to any of the property he acquires; they are his alone. Her sole economic right is to be supported by her husband.

In the eight community property states, each spouse retains separately all the property he or she had before marriage, and any property inherited during marriage. Once married, however, the earnings of each party, together with all other uninherited property acquired during the marriage, become "community property." Each spouse has one-half interest in this community property—and thus in any property or income the other spouse earns during the marriage. In some states the earnings produced by separate property are also community property.

The community property system assumes that both spouses are equally responsible for the economic assets of a marriage, whether acquired through earnings or household maintenance, and that both are therefore the equal owners of all those assets. Thus, in theory, the married woman who is a fulltime housewife is much better off in a community property state, where she is entitled to half of her husband's postmarriage earnings, than in a separate property state. While the community property system is typically advantageous to employed wives as well, it is useful to examine the effects of the two systems during marriage, in the event of divorce, and after death.[19]

Property Rights During Marriage

In the course of her marriage a full-time housewife in a separate property state can obtain money or property by her husband's support, or gift, or by using his credit. But she has absolutely no legal right to any of her husband's income or property.* The disadvantage this rule places on housewives is illustrated by a 1966 Wiscon-

---

*Some exceptions to this blanket rule have recently evolved in the 14 common law states that have adopted Equal Rights Amendments to their state constitutions. In Pennsylvania for example, the state ERA expanded the wife's right to joint ownership of household property. Previously, all household property was presumed to belong to the husband unless the wife could prove she had contributed monetarily to the purchase of the goods. A similar situation existed in New Mexico before its ERA; the husband's rights to the income and assets of the marriage were exclusive. "A married woman could not even advertise the family washing machine for sale without her husband's consent." *Women Today* X (December 12, 1980):218.

sin case* in which the money a housewife saved for her sons' college education was awarded to her husband:

> Margaret and Harold Rasmussen, like most people married in the forties, chose a traditional relationship: Harold brought home the paycheck, while Margaret remained in the home to care for their sons, Eric and Ky. Each week, Harold turned his paycheck over to Margaret; she did the family's bookkeeping, paid the bills, and rationed out the money for household and personal expenses.
>
> The Rasmussens didn't have much money. For most of their married life, they lived with Mrs. Rasmussen's mother, not even able to afford a home of their own. But Margaret believed that her boys should go to college, and she managed to save a little here and there for their education. She economized in all the little ways in which a housewife can economize. Occasionally, her mother made a donation to the college funds. Slowly but surely, two savings accounts grew.
>
> When Margaret Rasmussen died in 1963, she left her teenage sons two savings accounts: $2,000 in trust for Ky and another $3,000 in trust for Eric.
>
> Harold Rasmussen remarried and moved out of his mother-in-law's house. $5,000 seemed like a lot of money to him. He wanted it, and he went to court to get it. "I earned that money," he argued, "and I never gave it away. I merely entrusted it to Margaret to pay the bills. The surplus belongs to me." The court agreed—despite the fact that there would have been no surplus without Margaret's careful economizing, despite the fact that Margaret's mother had contributed some of the funds. "The general rule in separate property states," said the court, ". . . is that the excess left after paying the joint expenses of . . . the family remains the property of the husband. . . ." The boys' college money went to Harold and his new wife. Margaret's long years of scrimping and saving were an exercise in futility.[20]

If the Rasmussens had lived in a community property state, half of Harold's earnings would be Margaret's—both during the marriage and as part of her estate.

Until recently, married housewives, even in community property states, were practically disadvantaged by a rule that allowed husbands to manage and control community property during marriage. Although wives theoretically *owned* half of their husband's income, since the law gave the husband the power *to manage and*

---

*This case summary was prepared by Norma Briggs, Executive Secretary of the Wisconsin Governor's Commission on the Status of Women for their publication *Real Women Real Lives: Marriage, Divorce and Widowhood* (1978).

control the community property during the marriage, the husband alone could decide how the money was spent.

In the 1970s, however, all of the eight community property states extended the wife's right to control the community property during marriage.[21] Louisiana was the last community property state to recognize the husband as the "head and master" of the community property, and the inequities of the old rule are poignantly illustrated by a 1978 case in which a wife lost the home she bought (with her own wages) because her husband had exclusive control of her property:[22]

Married at 18, Selma Martin worked double shifts as a nurse to support her husband through four years of college. Her salary paid for all household expenses and she saved enough to buy a small home. Her husband was unemployed for most of the year after he graduated from college, and Selma continued to support the family. When her husband proposed that they mortgage the house to borrow $5,000, Selma objected. But under the Louisiana "head and master" rule her husband had the full power to mortgage the home she bought—and to control all of their community property—without even asking her. So he ignored Selma's objection, and without her signature or consent, he mortgaged the home to take out a loan. When he failed to repay the loan the credit company sought to foreclose the mortgage and take their home. Selma Martin objected and challenged the constitutionality of the head and master rule. It was unfair, she said, for her husband to have the power to mortgage the home without her knowledge or permission. And it was unfair that he should control every cent she earned and every item she bought. But the Louisiana Supreme Court denied her appeal, and the U.S. Supreme Court refused to hear the case,[23] thus leaving her creditors to foreclose the mortgage and letting the head and master rule stand.*

Today, in contrast, both spouses have access to the community property in all eight community property states, and the consent of both is typically required for the pledge or sale of important community assets.

In general, then, *housewives* in community property states are better off than those in common law systems. In addition, since

*This case may still have an impact as it potentially affects rules that give the husband the authority to manage joint property in common law states. (See, for example, the male management scheme of tenancy by the entirety in Massachusetts.) Interview with Phyllis Segal, Legal Director of NOW Legal Defense and Education Fund, January 1979.

most employed wives currently earn less than their husbands, they too are likely to benefit from community property rules. However, it is important to note that both housewives and employed wives in community property states are expected to share most, if not all, of the husband's debts along with his earnings.

The relative advantages for housewives under the community property system are also evident with regard to consumer credit. Although the 1974 Equal Credit Opportunity Act (ECOA) prohibits discrimination "on the basis of sex or marital status with respect to any aspect of a credit transaction,"[24] the creditor *may* take into consideration the marital property laws of the state in which a woman lives when deciding whether to extend her credit.

If a married woman in a separate property state is a full-time housewife (as are 52 percent of all U.S. wives)[25] she can apply for credit in her husband's name if her husband signs an agreement promising to be liable for her debts. This means, of course, that she is using her husband's credit, not her own, and she thus acquires no independent credit rating or credit history.

If a married woman in a separate property state is employed (as are 48 percent of all U.S. wives) she may still be disadvantaged if she does not apply for credit in her husband's name.[26] Since credit in her own name will be based solely on her own earnings, and since she is likely to earn less than her husband, it is probable that less credit will be available to her than if their incomes are pooled (and he thereby becomes liable for her debts). Thus, whether she is employed or not, a wife in a separate property state is likely to acquire credit through her husband.

In seven community property states a wife can obtain credit on exactly the same terms as her husband, whether or not she is employed, with or without his consent or signature, and the credit thus obtained will be hers alone. (Texas is an exception because both spouses manage their own earnings.) The community property system is therefore generally advantageous to both housewives and employed wives.

Property Rights After Divorce

In most separate property jurisdictions, each spouse is legally entitled to keep his or her separate property after divorce. It is easy to see how this rule, although couched in sex-neutral terms, typically has an adverse impact on women. The woman who has devoted her married years to caring for home, husband, and children is not likely to have any separate property of her own at the time of divorce.[27]

Clearly, the separate property regulations discussed above make it difficult for a wife to acquire and retain her own property during marriage. Even if she has been employed she is less likely to have accumulated property than her husband; and if she has been a housewife during most of the marriage, she probably has not accumulated any property at all. Although she may have helped her husband to earn money and acquire property, if he holds the title to the property, he is the sole legal owner of that property upon divorce. Thus, by allowing each spouse to retain his or her property, the system effectively ignores the housewife's contribution to the wages and property her husband acquires. Consider the inequities in the following 1974 Illinois case in which the court held that the property accumulated during 22 years of marriage belonged solely to the husband:

John and Norma Norris were married in 1950. They lived on a farm in Illinois that John had inherited before they were married. At first, Norma was a housewife, caring for their children, performing the usual household tasks, gardening, preserving large quantities of food, and cooking five or six daily meals for the hired hands who worked on the farm. Later on, when the children were in school, Norma took on an outside job. She continued to do the traditional tasks, and in addition contributed part of her income for family expenses.

After 22 years of marriage, John divorced Norma. The court awarded her no alimony. Her share of their marital property consisted of only her own clothing and personal effects, a few household items which she owned prior to the marriage, and an automobile which she had purchased in her own name with her own funds. The house and furnishings, the farm with its machinery and livestock, the savings—all went to John.

Norma appealed the decision. "Surely, after 22 years of hard work, I am entitled to at least a portion of the assets I helped to accumulate," she thought. But the legal system saw things differently. The appellate court upheld the lower court's division of the property.

A spouse seeking part of the other spouse's property, explained the court, must show that she or he made valuable contributions to the property's worth. The court defined a valuable contribution as "money or services other than those normally performed in the marriage relation"; Norma's years of cooking, cleaning, and child rearing did not meet the court's definition of "valuable."

But the money Norma contributed for family expenses from her outside employment was "valuable"; would she not be entitled to some recompense for this financial contribution? No, said the court; she did not keep clear records of what property was acquired through her own effort, and consequently all property was properly awarded to her husband.

In other words, the court told Norma, her 22 years of hard work and unselfish consideration of her family—during most of which she held down an outside job as well as a full-time job at home—entitled her to nothing when the marriage ended. The labor and money she contributed to what she assumed was a joint enterprise enriched her husband, but was totally lost to herself. In middle age, Norma was forced to start over economically.[28]

In a community property state, Norma Norris would have been treated as the legal owner of one-half of the property acquired in the course of her marriage, instead of being cut off without any share of her home and farm.*

"As a practical matter," Professor Barbara Ann Kulzer observes, "the propertyless state of most wives [in separate property states] requires that some provision be made for them on divorce. Most commonly, this is alimony. But alimony does not alter prevailing concepts of property as individually owned by the husband who acquired it . . . and a court historically could not or would not require the property-owning spouse to surrender his own assets."[29]

If alimony is not awarded (it rarely is, as we shall see below) the housewife who "has not been employed and who has not inherited money with which to acquire her own property, is at the sufferance of her husband with respect to what, if anything, she will own."[30] While the traditional fault-based system of divorce may give her a bargaining lever if her husband wants to leave the marriage, and while she might also appeal to her husband's sense of moral respon-

---

*Today, Norma might also fare better in Illinois. The new Illinois divorce law gives the court the power to divide marital property (all property acquired by either spouse subsequent to the marriage) in "just proportions" taking into account "all relevant factors". Among the ten factors mentioned is the contributions of a spouse as a homemaker. (Ill. Ann. Stat. Ch. 40 Sec. 503 (c)(1).

The Illinois law, however, has a glaring deficiency according to Bartke and Zurvalec. It attempts to resolve the division of property at dissolution without changing the respective property interests of the spouses during the existence of the marriage. Since married persons continue to own separate property, and can dispose of it during marriage in whatever way they choose, a propertied spouse could transfer his (or her) property before dissolution and leave the nonpropriated partner with the right to a share of an empty chest. Richard W. Bartke and Lori A. Zurvalec, "The Low, Middle and High Road to Marital Property Law Reform in Common Law Jurisdictions," *Community Property Journal*, Summer 1980: 217.

sibility, guilt, or good-will, she actually has, in short, "no property rights."[31]

The manifest unfairness and harsh results of these separate property rules have led some common law states to adopt laws allowing the judge to make an "equitable division of property" upon divorce. But equitable court rulings depend on individual judges' perceptions of what is equitable, and in common law states judges start with the assumption that "separate" property belongs to one party. As a result, equitable division rules make the wife's prospects for property ownership wholly contingent on a judge's concept of equity—instead of on a codified legal recognition of her entitlement to share in assets acquired during her marriage.

The wife in a community property state is likely to fare much better at the time of divorce. Two of the community property states require that the property be equally divided upon divorce; the other six allow the courts to make an "equitable" division. However, the starting point for an "equitable" division in a community property state is a 50–50 division because of the basic presumption of equal ownership.

As Professor Ann Bingaman observes, in a separate property system the basic premise is that property is owned by the person who earned it during the marriage, but in a community property system the basic premise is just the opposite: property acquired during marriage is owned by both spouses regardless of who earned it: "With such premises as the starting points for the 'equitable' property division by courts, it seems inevitable that the wife in a community property state will receive a larger share of the property accumulated by either of the spouses during marriage than will the wife in a separate property jurisdiction."[32]

Although most wives will undoubtedly fare much better after divorce in a community property state, there is one problem that even community property states have not dealt with adequately. It involves the recognition of the intangible assets of the marriage and, consequently, their division upon divorce. In most marriages in which there is a single wage earner the couple does not invest in and acquire physical property alone. They typically invest their time, energy and resources in the "human capital" of the breadwinning spouse by using family resources to finance his education, to help him succeed in work, to cultivate contacts and clients for him, and to develop a life-style that supports and gives priority to his career. The results of these investments are what I call "career assets." These career assets typically include a number of items of value such as the value of an education or training; job experience; seniority at a particular company or in an industry; the ability to earn a specific salary; insurance coverage for accidents, illness, hospitalization, disability and unemployment; the goodwill value of a professional practice or business; and the right to pensions, retirement benefits, and Social Security. If the property accumulated during marriage is to be divided upon divorce, I would argue that the law should recognize career assets as major assets of the marriage. In fact, since most couples have little physical property to divide at divorce (other than their home, cars and furnishings) it is likely that the value of these career assets will be equal to or greater than the value of their physical property.

Recent years have brought increased awareness of the importance of these career assets and there is now a discernable trend in both community and common law property states toward recognizing some of them as part of the marital property. Many states now consider a pension a marital asset to be divided upon divorce, and a few, such as California, New Jersey, Washington and Oregon, recognize the good will value of a professional practice as well.* These new types of marital property are discussed further in Chapter 3.† They will undoubtedly play an increasingly important role in divorce settlements in the future.

Property Rights After Death

If a wife predeceases her husband in a separate property jurisdiction, her estate may include only that property she personally accumulated in life. For the wife who was unemployed, this may mean that virtually nothing is left to her intended heirs.

Although it is often assumed that husbands and wives will have identical interests in distributing their estates, and that it "doesn't

*Fred Kennedy and Bruce Thomas, "Putting a Value on Education and Professional Goodwill" *Family Advocate*, Vol. 2, Summer 1979, p. 40. Kennedy and Thomas conclude their review of recent cases in this newly emerging area with the following comment: "It seems manifestly unjust for the spouse of a surgeon making $300,000 a year to receive half of the couple's assets while the specialist receives his half *along with* a degree, a license, and a specialty certificate."

†See pages 89 to 97 discussing the community's interest in a professional education, the good will value of a professional practice and pension and retirement benefits.

really matter" which party has the estate because each would designate the other spouse and their children as beneficiaries, this clearly is not so. Previously married spouses may have children from a former marriage and the interests of their children may conflict with those of the second spouse and/or the children from the second marriage. A 1957 Wisconsin case is illustrative:

> Laura and William Budney were married in 1921. William supported the family through his work as a manual laborer; Laura was the homemaker. Each week, William turned his earnings over to Laura, who paid the bills, purchased household supplies, and saved a little when she could.
>
> Laura didn't trust banks. She squirreled the savings away in odd places around the house—the proverbial cookie jar, her dresser, her sewing cabinet, and numerous other places. When she died in 1955, Leone, her daughter from a previous marriage, and William found more than $7,000 tucked away in small bills.
>
> Laura had not made a will. Under the law some of the money—if it *was* her money—would go to her daughter. But her husband wanted it all. He argued, "All that money came from my paycheck. I never gave it to her to keep. Anything left over belongs to me alone."
>
> The court agreed with William. Since Laura had not worked in paid employment during the 33 years of her marriage, clearly the money was not hers. Not one cent of Laura's frugal saving could be passed on to her daughter.[33]

In community property states, in contrast, a woman is free to dispose of her half of community property as she sees fit. If she dies without a will, her heirs are nevertheless entitled to their inheritance.

What happens when a woman outlives her husband? How do the two systems provide for widows?

If a woman outlives her husband in a separate property state she is likely to benefit from one of the common law doctrines of "dower" or "widow's election." Dower gives the wife the right to a life estate of one-third to one-half of all real property owned by the husband during his life. A life estate gives the wife only a beneficial use of the property during the remainder of her life; it does not grant her legal title, and therefore she cannot bequeath it or otherwise dispose of it. A widow's election gives the wife a one-third to one-half legal ownership of all property owned by the husband at the time of his death. Subject to these restrictions, the husband is otherwise free to bequeath his separate property as he wishes. Only a few common law states—Georgia, North Dakota, and South Dakota—allow a husband to completely disinherit his wife (and vice versa).

Although dower and the widow's election were designed to mitigate the essential unfairness of the separate property system, there are four difficulties with these remedies. First, they are based on the faulty assumption that all marriages last for the lifetime of the spouses. If a marriage ends in divorce or dissolution, or if the wife dies before her husband, the unemployed wife in a separate property state is left without a guaranteed share of the property accumulated during the marriage.

A second problem with these remedies is that many states allow the widow only a third—rather than half—of the property her husband acquired during marriage. As Kulzer asserts, the schemes that allow the widow a third of the estate are "flawed by their premise that the property being distributed . . . is a share of [the husband's property]. They fail to recognize the ownership of marital property as vested in both spouses."[34]

A third difficulty involves the "widow's tax." Since the separate property system treats the family ranch or farm as the husband's separate property, when he dies his widow is typically required to pay inheritance tax on any property she inherits. As a result, farm widows may be forced to sell the family farm in order to pay federal estate taxes. While the 1978 tax reforms allow a widow to exclude the first $250,000 of an estate's value from federal inheritance tax, to do so she must prove that she "materially participated" in acquiring the property. To meet this standard a widow typically has to demonstrate a financial contribution, through a salary for example, rather than a lifetime of work. This is an especially difficult standard for full-time farm wives.

Even if the widow meets this test, she may nevertheless be forced to sell her property in order to pay the tax because of the rapid increase in the appraised value of many family farms. Charging that the "widow's tax strikes at the very heart of the American agricultural system" Senator Nancy Kassebaum (R–Kan.) proposed that the first $600,000 of an estate be exempt from federal tax, and that inheritance taxes be eliminated for surviving spouses. *

*San Francisco Chronicle, February 5, 1981, p. 12, cols. 1–3. The latter is already the rule in California (a community property state), which as of 1981 abolished the state inheritance tax on property left to a spouse.

A fourth problem with dower and the widow's election is that they do not protect the wife whose husband chooses to dispose of some or all of his separate property while he is alive. Because the husband has complete legal control of his separate property during his lifetime, he can legally sell it or give it away before he dies. For example, in *In re Weger*[35] a Wisconsin widow assumed that she had been the co-owner of a recently sold family motel business. It was only when her husband died (after 25 years of marriage) that she discovered he had put the proceeds from the motel sale into a joint account with his son from a previous marriage. Inasmuch as Mrs. Weger had used her separate property (from an auto accident settlement) as the down payment for the motel, and then managed the business with her husband, she argued that half of the $252,000 for the sale belonged to her:

> I bought the land the motel stands on. I signed the loans for the money to build it. I helped operate it, day in and day out. I signed the land contract, and my name is on the mortgage. That money is half mine.[36]

But the court denied her claim. Since her husband held the title to the property in his name alone, it was his separate property, and the proceeds put into the joint tenancy account with Mr. Weger's son became, upon her husband's death, the sole property of the joint tenant son.

If Mrs. Weger had been living in a community property state, the motel and the profits from its sale would have been at least half hers. Her husband could have given *his* half to his son, but as a widow in a community property state she would retain her ownership of half of the community property. Both widows and widowers in community property states are entitled to half of the assets accumulated during marriage. The disposition of the other half, owned by the decedent, can be fully controlled by the decedent in a will or by other arrangements made during his or her lifetime.

Although it may seem that we have moved far afield from the law of support, that law provides the basis for the common law property rules discussed above. For as the reader will recall, the common law rule that gave the husband the right to his earnings (and the property acquired with them) arose from the assumption that the husband had to manage the family funds to fulfill his obligation to support his wife.

The Law of Support During Marriage and After Divorce

Ironically, although the husband's obligation to support his wife has been vigorously proclaimed in the written law, the courts have rarely been forceful in exacting this obligation. Because the situation is somewhat different during an ongoing marriage and after divorce, we will deal with each period separately.

Support During Marriage

If a husband and wife are living together, the courts have traditionally refused to enforce the husband's responsibility for family support because they do not want to "interfere" with the marital relationship. In the leading case in this area, *McGuire* v. *McGuire*,[37] the wife complained that for the past three years her husband had provided her with neither money nor clothing. She further alleged that although he was a man of substantial means (he owned assets worth more than $100,000), he had refused to purchase furniture and other household necessities beyond groceries (for which he paid by check). The court refused to enforce the wife's right to support, however, because the parties were still living together and it did not want to intervene in the internal affairs of the marriage. In the language of the court:

> The living standards of a family are a matter of concern to the household, and not for the courts to determine, even though [this] husband's attitude toward his wife, according to his wealth and circumstances, leaves little to be said in his behalf. As long as the home is maintained and the parties are living as husband and wife it may be said that the husband is legally supporting his wife and the purpose of the marriage relation is being carried out. Public policy requires such a holding.[38]

As *McGuire* indicates, wives whose husbands fail to provide adequate support have typically been told by the courts that the level of support remains a matter of the husband's discretion. As head of household he has the "right" to set the family's standard of living, and the law gives him "almost unbounded discretion as to expenditures and style of living."[39] His obligation to support is "an obligation that is defined and controlled solely by him."[40]

As another example, in *Commonwealth* v. *George*[41] a wife asked the court to order her husband to give her a fixed sum of money each month "to take care of items of food and clothing for herself and the children and [to have] spending money for herself and the children" so that she didn't have to go to her husband to "ask for fifty cents." The woman complained that

> the bills were not paid promptly . . . that he differed with her as to the necessities of dental expenditures . . . that she had to use $500 given to her as a gift by her mother to pay off certain charges [for] one of the children.[42]

The court denied her request, reiterating that "the arm of the court is not empowered to reach into the home and to determine the manner in which the earnings of the husband shall be expended."[43]

It seems clear, as Blanche Crozier observed, that what is called the wife's "right to support" is little more than "the privilege of living with the husband" on his terms:

> So long as the spouses are living together, the wife's right of support is not a right to any definite thing or to any definite amount even in proportion to the husband's means. . . . To be sure, it is said that he should support her in accordance with his means, but that is no more than an ideal, with which he may or may not comply.[44]

If a wife cannot get the court's assistance in obtaining support during her marriage, it becomes meaningless to speak of a husband's legal obligation to support his wife. The U.S. Citizens Advisory Council on the Status of Women aptly describes the present situation: "A married woman living with her husband can, in practice, get only what he chooses to give her."[45] Thus the law's promise of support is a hollow guarantee, one that affords a married woman no more protection than her husband will willingly grant. As long as a woman is living with her husband, she can take no direct legal action to enforce his duty to support her. She cannot compel him to give her an allowance, either for herself or for the household. Nor can she legally claim a share of his earnings or the property he acquires.

The rationale for the courts' refusal to enforce support is that they cannot afford to become involved in day-to-day disagreements between husbands and wives. With respect to minor disputes, this position has merit. However, family support is hardly a minor matter: the duty to support is purported to be one of the essential obligations of legal marriage. Further, by their refusal to become "involved" the courts indirectly encourage marital dissolution, for the only way a woman can obtain an order for support is to become separated or divorced from her husband.

Krauskopf and Thomas suggest another reason for judges' reluctance to recognize a wife's complaint against her husband: the courts in general do not wish to undermine the husband's authority. Instead they seem to believe "that keeping the wife barefoot will indeed keep her home."[46]

This observation finds support in numerous cases. For example, in *Garlock* v. *Garlock* a New York court refused to uphold an agreement between the spouses in which the husband promised to give his wife a fixed level of support, because to do so would interfere with a "desired flexibility" in family economic affairs.[47] But since the wife in this case had "no remedy available to enforce payments, desired flexibility meant that the court thought it was desirable for the husband to have the arbitrary power to decide how he would support the family."[48]

Although the courts have also staunchly contended that any interference on their part serves to disrupt marital harmony, it seems evident that the harmony in these marriages has already been disrupted (or else the matter would hardly have come to the court's attention), and a just resolution of the issue would do more to restore balance and tranquility.

Remedies During Marriage

There are four legal options available to the wife whose husband fails to provide adequate support; however, none of them is very effective. One option is to pledge her husband's credit for "necessaries" such as food, clothing, shelter, and medicine.[49] Her husband is then obligated to pay the supplier. Under the common law this obligation was entirely sex-based: the wife could legally obligate her husband for both her own and the children's needs, but the husband could not so obligate his wife.[50]

Although the creditor who supplies a wife with necessaries has the right to collect the bills from the husband, the merchant is typically reluctant to take the risk of extending credit to her—and to incur the potential burden of collection. In addition, the term "necessaries"[51] leaves unclear precisely what articles are covered.* Finally, the rule that a wife who has wrongfully left her husband cannot legally pledge his credit creates another situation in which the merchant may have difficulty collecting on his bill.[52] Thus the law of necessaries does not provide a wife a reliable means of securing support. In addition, the "right" to the money belongs to the creditor, not to the wife.

Two other ways in which support obligations may be enforced, in theory, are the "poor laws" or family responsibility statutes in force in 33 states, and the criminal nonsupport statutes in force in nearly all states.[53] The aim of these laws is to keep women and children off the public dole, but neither has proved a realistic means of enforcing a wife's common law right to support. Ironically, most criminal nonsupport statutes do not apply unless nonsupport is accompanied by desertion, and therefore they do not help the woman who is still living with her husband. As Krauskopf and Thomas note, "the law does not allow the husband to desert his wife and starve her, but he may stay at home and starve her."[54]

The only other legal means of relief open to the nonsupported wife is to sue for legal separation or divorce. Then various civil remedies become available to her. If she wishes to continue living with her husband and/or to remain married, however, her pleas for legal assistance from the courts will usually fall on deaf ears.

Support After Divorce

A husband's responsibility to support his former wife theoretically continues after divorce. However, it is almost as difficult for a woman to enforce this obligation after divorce as it is during an ongoing marriage.

Traditionally the English ecclesiastical courts granted divorce only *a mensa et thoro* ("from bed and board"): the husband and wife were authorized to live apart but their marital obligations remained. The husband's obligations to support his wife continued

---

*The merchant's risk is minimized in extending credit for wealthy families. For example, in one New York case, whalemeat and caviar were held to be "necessaries." *Bloomingdale Bros., Inc.* v. *Benjamin*, 200 Misc. 1108, 1110, 112 N.Y.S. 2d 33, 35 (N.Y. City Ct. 1955). And a Pennsylvania court held a husband liable for a mink coat because he had stated, "To be successful, you have to look successful." *Gimbel Bros., Inc.* v. *Pinto*, 118 Pa. Super 73, 145 A. 2d 865 (1959).

until their marriage was dissolved by death, as did his rights over her income and property.[55]

At that time alimony (from the Latin "to nourish") was an unquestioned necessity for the financially dependent wife. Since her husband gained control over all her property and income when they married, and since he retained that control if they separated, he remained responsible for her economic support. Employment opportunities for the separated wife were virtually nonexistent, and alimony typically provided her sole resource for financial survival.[56]

Today, virtually all states continue to have statutory provisions for alimony (or spousal support or maintenance) following a divorce.[57] This is, however, one area in which recent years have brought about a dramatic symbolic change in the law. In 1979, the U.S. Supreme Court ruled, in *Orr* v. *Orr*, that wife-only alimony statutes were based on sexual stereotypes and were invalid.[58] William Orr had been ordered to pay his ex-wife $1,240 monthly alimony by an Alabama court. When charged with contempt of court for being in arrears in his payments, he argued that Alabama's statutes were unconstitutional because they authorized courts to place an obligation of alimony on husbands but never on wives. A majority of justices of the Supreme Court agreed. Justice Brennan, writing for the court, concluded that

> Where, as here, the State's compensatory and ameliorative purposes are as well served by a gender-neutral classification as one that gender-classifies, and therefore carries with it the baggage of sexual stereotypes, the State cannot be permitted to classify on the basis of sex.[59]

Not suprisingly, the decision extended the already common practice of stating the postdivorce support obligation in sex-neutral terms (by calling it "spousal support" or "maintenance") and of making postdivorce support available to both partners. In fact, prior to *Orr*, only ten states limited alimony to wives.[60] These states, as Foster and Freed observed, were overprotective of the wife's right to support because they failed to give her any right to property held in her husband's name.[61] Today postdivorce support must be equally available to both spouses but, as a practical matter, alimony (by whatever name) serves primarily to enforce the husband's support obligation after divorce.

When one examines the actual pattern of alimony awards it becomes evident that *Orr* is unlikely to have much impact. This is because alimony itself does not play a large role in the financial arrangements of former spouses. The fact is that alimony is awarded in only a small minority of all divorces. Research from the California Divorce Law Research Project indicates that in 1977 alimony was awarded in approximately 17 percent of California divorce cases.[62] Further, it seems this percentage is not unusual. The limited data available from other states indicate similarly low percentages. Only 14 percent of divorced wives in a 1975 national poll commissioned by the National Commission on the Observance of International Women's Year said they had been awarded alimony.[63] Similarly, only 16 percent of the divorced women interviewed by the U.S. Census Bureau in April 1979 reported having been awarded alimony.*

What is perhaps more surprising is that these figures do not reflect a new trend but rather a well-established pattern: available data indicate that alimony has always been awarded in a minority of all divorces. Even if we examine data from fifty to seventy-five years ago, the pattern is clear. For example, national data from the U.S. Census reveal that from 1887 to 1906, 9.3 percent of divorces included provisions for permanent alimony. In 1916 the percentage was 15.4; and in 1922 alimony was awarded in only 14.7 percent of the nationwide sample of decrees.[64] It seems, then, that the promise of alimony has always been a myth, hardly more enforceable in reality than the "right to support" in an ongoing marriage.

While it is often asserted that the no-fault divorce laws (and the women's liberation movement) of the past decade have been responsible for a drastic reduction in alimony awards, our California data indicate minimal changes between 1968 and 1977. In 1968, two years before California's no-fault divorce law was instituted, 19 percent of the divorced women in Los Angeles and San Francisco counties were awarded alimony.[65] In 1977, as we have noted, the percentage was 17 percent. This small difference can be accounted for by the decline in awards to women after short marriages. In 1968, 14 percent of the women married between one and five years were awarded alimony. By 1977, with no-fault divorce and a new norm of self-sufficiency for young women, the comparable proportion dropped to five percent.[66]

*This figure was calculated from Table 3, page 8 of the U.S. Bureau of the Census "Child Support and Alimony: 1978" *Current Population Reports* series p. 23, no. 106 (1980). It differs from the frequently reported 14 percent figure which includes separated as well as divorced women.

While a no-fault divorce established a clear norm of self-sufficiency for younger women who were capable of supporting themselves after divorce, the law was also designed, in theory, to protect those women who could not support themselves. In particular, three groups of women with compelling financial need were singled out for support: those with full-time responsibility for young children, those who require transitional support to become self-supporting, and those who are incapable of becoming or too old to become self-supporting. The third category recognized that a housewife's *earning capacity was typically impaired* during a long marriage in which she devoted herself to her home and children. Homemakers with "earning disabilities" as a result of long marriages were therefore assured, in theory, the right to continued support.

But contrary to these explicit goals, our California data indicate that the law failed to provide support for these women. In fact, the first group, mothers of young children, experienced the sharpest decline in alimony awards under the new law, more than any other group of women. (Only 12 percent of the mothers of preschool children were awarded any alimony in 1977.) While women in longer marriages are significantly more likely to be awarded support, still, only 46 percent of the women married 15 years or more were awarded any alimony in 1977.* (The much larger proportion of divorces that occur after short marriages explains their relatively greater weight in the overall statistics cited above.) Thus despite the law's persistent rhetoric about "the obligation of support" it is disheartening to find that *only half* of the women married for a goodly number of years are ever awarded alimony.

Four additional factors conspire to further diminish the real amount of alimony that divorced women receive. First, tax regulations encourage a man to label his "child support" as "alimony."[67] Thus, the true number of alimony awards may be even less than the above statistics suggest. Second, the amount of money typically awarded as alimony is too meager to be considered a bona fide means of support. For example, in 1977 California divorce decrees

---

*These awards are, of course, strongly influenced by the husband's income as well as by the duration of marriage. Among California women married 18 or more years to men earning over $30,000 a year, the proportion of alimony awards rose to 62 percent. Nevertheless, when one considers the amount of alimony these women are awarded, we find that they have, on the average, less than half of the postdivorce income of their former husbands. These statistics are covered further in Lenore J. Weitzman and Ruth B. Dixon, "The Alimony Myth: Does No-Fault Divorce Make a Difference?" *Family Law Quarterly* 14, no. 3 (Fall 1980):141–85.

the median alimony award was $210 per month.[68] That kind of award may help defray welfare costs, but it can hardly provide any economic protection for a dependent spouse.

Of course, the amount of alimony is influenced by both the duration of the marriage and the husband's income, and longer-married wives of higher-income husbands do receive more monthly alimony. However, even the wives of fairly well-to-do men are *relatively deprived* when the wife's postdivorce standard of living is compared with that of her former husband. For example, in families with predivorce incomes of $20,000 to $29,000 a year, women married 18 or more years were awarded, on the average, $350 a month ($4,200 a year) in *combined* alimony and child support. When we compare their postdivorce incomes (from any source) with that of their former husbands, we find that in the first year after the divorce, these long-married wives had postdivorce incomes that were 24 percent of the previous family incomes, while their former husbands had incomes that were 87 percent of the previous family income.*

Overall, the consistent pattern across all income groups is that whatever the family's standard of living before divorce, wives (and children) have much *lower* standards of living than husbands after divorce. Men are more likely to retain a standard of living that is roughly comparable to the predivorce family standard, while women (and children) are reduced to relative poverty with post-divorce incomes of never more than a half (and often as low as a quarter) of the family's former standard of living. The contrast between the two is even greater when one realizes that the divorced woman is likely to have minor children in her household and her income is likely to be shared with them—thus leaving the husband with an even larger share of the family's total resources.

These data probably *underestimate*, if anything, the relative position of former spouses because our calculations assume that the

---

*Along the same lines, in families with incomes of $30,000 to $39,000 in the year before the divorce, women married more than 18 years had postdivorce incomes of 46 percent of the previous family income, while their husband's postdivorce income was 83 percent. Finally, in families with predivorce incomes of $40,000 or more, the wife's postdivorce income was 26 percent of the former family income, while her husband's was 68 percent. Overall, in all income groups, the postdivorce incomes of men averages at least *twice* the dollar income of the women who helped them to build their earning capacities. While some of this disparity may be attributed to the different earning capacities of men and women, it must also be recognized that judges play a major role in creating the disparity because they establish the meager support awards for divorced women.

alimony and child support ordered by the court is actually paid. Thus, to calculate the postdivorce income figures reported above, the amount of alimony and child support the court ordered was added to the wife's postdivorce income from other sources (such as employment or welfare) and subtracted from the husband's postdivorce income. In fact, however, many men do not pay alimony or child support, or do not comply fully with the court order. We found that within six months of the divorce decree one out of every six men was already in arrears on alimony payments owing, on the average, over $1,000 each.[69] In addition, by the end of the year, 48 percent of the divorced women reported that they had many problems collecting court-ordered alimony, while 43 percent reported "a lot of difficulty" in collecting their child support awards. And, unfortunately, the rate of noncompliance is likely to increase over time. As a result, the figures reported above probably overestimate the wife's postdivorce income, underestimate the husband's, and minimize the actual discrepancy between the two.

The third factor that diminishes the real amount of alimony that divorced women receive is, as we have just noted, the high rate of noncompliance with court orders. Thus many of the women who are "awarded" support never actually receive it. In California we found that only 52 percent of the wives awarded alimony reported that they collected it regularly in the *first year* after the divorce. On a national scale, a 1975 survey undertaken by the National Commission on the Observance of International Women's Year showed that only 46 percent of the divorced wives who were awarded alimony actually collected it regularly.[70] Another 21 percent *never* received it and the rest received it rarely (21 percent) or sometimes (8 percent).

The time, effort, and money required to secure compliance (to locate a nonsupporting husband, to find and pay an attorney, to pursue the matter in court, and to collect the award) are enough to dissuade many women from even trying.[71] As a result, most separated and divorced women must either work outside the home or accept welfare, for even those few who are awarded enough support to meet their needs have less than a 50 percent chance of collecting it.

The fourth and final factor that diminishes these alimony awards is inflation. Even an award that is adequate at the time it is made may rapidly become inadequate in a period of high inflation. For example, if we assume a 12 percent rate of inflation, we find that an award of $500 per month in 1980 is worth only $284 of purchasing power five years later. Since less than ten percent of the 1977 California awards for alimony and child support included cost of living increases, the burden of having the award modified (with all the costs and difficulties of returning to court) falls, once again, on the wife. Most likely the original order will stand only to be gradually eaten away by inflation with each passing year.

In sum, despite the myth of generous alimony awards and "alimony drones," for four out of five divorced women in the United States alimony is just that—a myth. And the woman who relies on the law's promise to ensure her husband's support is likely to find herself in financial despair.

Social and Economic Effects on the Husband

The legal rule that the husband shall be responsible for family support may be analyzed with respect to its effects on male and female roles within the family. In the following pages we will argue that the husband's unilateral support obligation imposes unrealistic and burdensome roles on both husband and wife. We begin by examining the economic burden of this role and then consider its social and psychological consequences.[72]

Economic Consequences

The responsibility for family support exerts an unnecessary pressure on a man to be his family's breadwinner. Men who feel the constant pressure to work overtime, to moonlight after work, or to hold down two full-time jobs are often responding to more than economic necessity. They are responding to a legal and cultural norm that makes the total economic well-being of the family exclusively *their* responsibility.

In order to evaluate fully the consequences of the husband's economic responsibility, one must first note its obvious benefits: the sole provider is accorded both status and respect. As psychologist Robert Brannon observes, "Even if his job is dull and routine, he leaves the home, labors, and returns with a paycheck. . . . This bastion of status within the family is traditionally available to virtually every male. It is a haven in which one basic demand of the male role can be satisfied."[73] Without his paycheck he feels less "like a man," less entitled to the respect and privileges that are ascribed to him as head of the household.

However, there are "costs" to maintaining this status. The first is an economic cost. When a husband's masculinity is threatened by the idea of a working wife, he may force or persuade her to stay at home and thereby deprive his family of the economic advantages of a two-income family. His paramount concern is to keep his wife "in her place, which is in the home, so that her second-class status can assure him of his first place."[74]

Sociologist Lillian Rubin observes that a working wife is especially threatening to a working-class man: "Historically it's been a source of status in working-class communities for a woman to be able to say, 'I don't *have* to work.' Many men and women feel keenly that it's his job to support the family, hers to stay home and take care of it. *For her to take a job outside the house would be, for such a family, tantamount to a public acknowledgement of his failure.*"[75]*

Professor Mirra Komarovsky aptly describes the paradoxes of this situation in her book *Blue Collar Marriage*. In Komarovsky's sample, it was the less educated, poorer white working-class husbands who most strongly insisted that their wives not work.[76] And yet, as Komarovsky observed, these very men were the ones for whom an extra income could make the difference between a bearable standard of living and an unbearable one. As one woman in Howell's study of lower-middle-class white families complained:

> He wouldn't let me work. . . . He wants to be the one who supports the family, who makes all the money, and he'd rather us live in goddam filth and the kids go without any clothes on their backs and we not eat, before I go out and work. He wants to be the big worker, but hell, look what he's doing.[77]

And sociologist Rubin concludes, "In a society where people in all classes are trapped in frenetic striving to acquire goods, where a man's sense of worth and his definition of manhood rest heavily on his ability to provide these goods, it is difficult for him to acknowl-

*These status concerns were clearly articulated by one of Rubin's working-class men: "I'd like to feel like I wear the pants in the family. Once my decision is made, it should be made, and that's it. She should just carry it out. But it doesn't work that way around here. Because she's working and making money, she thinks she can argue back whenever she feels like it." *Worlds of Pain* (New York: Basic Books, 1977), p. 177.

edge that the family really does need his wife's income to live as they both would like."[78]

Another consequence of allocating the sole responsibility for support to the husband is that it encourages men to remain in dead-end jobs instead of accepting the challenges that lead to better long-range prospects. The sole provider is unfortunately likely to sacrifice long-term economic (and social) gains for a secure paycheck, and to remain locked in a meaningless job because it provides "food for the table."[79]

It is important to underscore the fact that it is not just blue-collar workers, but all men, at all occupational levels, who become trapped because of their breadwinning responsibilities. For example, psychologist Robert Brannon writes of an executive who was earning over $50,000 a year in an assignment he actually enjoyed and was good at. *His* problem was an impending promotion:

> Having proven his competence at this level of the company hierarchy, he was expected to move on to the next level. It meant more money but a substantially different kind of work, which he was fairly sure he wouldn't like as well, and he'd have to commute a lot farther. It made sense to stay where he was . . . but he couldn't. . . . He couldn't resist the temptation to move upward and make more money.[80] (He got his promotion, and, as predicted, hated his new assignment.)

Social and Psychological Consequences

The law's assumption that the husband is solely responsible for the family's economic well-being may also take its toll on men physically—in their higher rates of stress and illness due to strenuous work, in their higher rates of suicide and heart attack, and in their younger ages at death.[81] And there are psychological costs too. As Myron Brenton has noted, the American male treads dangerous ground when he "puts all his psychic eggs into one basket" and depends on his breadwinning role to validate his sense of himself as a man.[82] For when a person's identity is tied to a single role, the pressures and tensions of that role increase, as do the chances of failure.

One consequence of focusing all one's psychic energy on the breadwinning role is that it increases the devastating effects of anything that can be interpreted as a failure—a layoff, the denial of a promotion, a job reassignment, getting a smaller raise than one's associates, or not being selected as foreman. The tragedy of this standard is that it is so pervasive and all-encompassing *that any man can fail at any time.** Even those in well-paid, prestigious careers cannot altogether escape feelings of failure: there will always be someone else who makes more money, or advances more rapidly, or attains a higher position, or gets more recognition.

The man who measures his self-worth solely in terms of his work is also in a precarious position in a society undergoing rapid economic and occupational changes. And furthermore, a total investment in work makes him especially vulnerable upon retirement. He is likely to have more difficulty adjusting to retirement than the man with multi-dimensional interests. Myron Brenton sums up these perils and offers a word of advice:

> Many people invest too much of their psyches in work. A wide variety of circumstances—limited native capacity, skills that become obsolescent, impersonal socio-economic forces, capricious judgments by superiors—make the prediction and control of occupational success very hazardous. Accordingly, a prudent man would do well to develop other sources of ego-gratification.[83]

But the psychological costs do not end in the arena of succeeding and spending. The totally work-oriented man frequently forgoes both the pleasures and the validation available from other roles in the family and community. Such a man limits his ability to feel satisfied with his accomplishments at home, or in sports, or in leisure activities—and to enjoy his relationships with his wife, friends, neighbors, and children.[84]

No less a luminary than Olof Palme, former Prime Minister of Sweden, has noted that when men are looked upon exclusively as family supporters their relationships with their children are impaired.[85] This observation is echoed on a more personal level by Warren Farrell, reporting the frustrations of a truck driver who found himself working overtime so often he hardly knew his children (but still, "it would be an insult to have the old lady to go work").[86]

Perhaps the most poignant picture emerges from Elliot Liebow's research on black lower-class streetcorner men. Many of these men deliberately distanced themselves from their wives and

---

*In fact, Joseph Pleck argues that "no man can live up to the ideals he has been socialized to hold for himself about his performance relative to other men." Joseph Pleck, "My Sex Role—and Ours," in Deborah S. David and Robert Brannon, eds., *The Forty-Nine Percent Majority* (Reading, Mass.: Addison-Wesley Publishing Co., 1976), p. 263.

children, some left home altogether—all because they felt they could not be husbands and fathers if they failed as breadwinners:

> The streetcorner man who lives with his wife and children is under legal and social constraints to provide for them, to be a husband to his wife and a father to his children. The chances are, however, that he is failing to provide for them, and failure in this primary function contaminates his performance as father in other respects as well. The more demonstrative and accepting he is of his children, the greater is his public and private commitment to the duties and responsibilities of fatherhood; and the greater his commitment, *the greater and sharper his failure as the provider and head of the family.* To soften this failure, and to lessen the damage to his public and self-esteem, he pushes the children away from him, saying, in effect, "I'm not even trying to be your father, so now I can't be blamed for failing to accomplish what I'm not trying to do." [Once the father is] separated from his children, there is no longer the social obligation to be their chief support.[87]

Thus when they most needed the emotional support that families provide, these men felt they had to limit these relationships if they weren't earning enough money.

So long as society and the law continue to view the less than optimal provider as a failure, an incompetent, and something less than a man, so long will that man and his family adopt a similar view, thus reinforcing a vicious cycle. By assigning the total responsibility for family support to the husband the law not only imposes an unfair burden on men, it also undermines the more realistic and less burdensome alternative of having both spouses contribute to and share the responsibility for family support according to their individual talents and abilities.

Social and Economic Effects on the Wife

The legal rule that makes the husband responsible for family support has negative effects on the wife as well, economically, socially, and psychologically.

Economic Consequences

When the law assumes that husbands must be held responsible for the financial support of the family, it makes the parallel assumption that wives must be economically dependent, as Professor Kay observed:

> [T]he support laws embody the legal view that a married woman is an economically nonproductive person dependent upon others for the necessities of life. [T]he married woman continues to be treated as a legal dependent, like the children and insane persons with whom the law formerly classified her.[88]

Here as elsewhere the law's assumption is in the nature of a self-fulfilling prophecy. When wives are assumed to be economically dependent, their financial authority is restricted and they are precluded from developing and exercising the financial skills they need. Thus the law can "create" as well as perpetuate financial dependency.

This is not to imply that women's dependency or "trained incapacity" in financial matters has its basis solely in legal regulations.[89] As we have noted, social and legal stereotypes are complexly interrelated and mutually reinforcing. However, legal regulations arising out of social stereotypes frequently add new barriers in the way of women's financial independence and thus serve further to reinforce the stereotypes.

One example of this process can be seen in the practices surrounding testamentary trusts. A testamentary trust allows a man in a separate property state to leave up to half of his taxable estate to his wife, free of estate taxation, through a device called the marital deduction.[90] Although available to both spouses, testamentary trusts are typically established by men, because men control the family property (and because they commonly expect to die before their wives). According to attorney Susan Plover, the typical testamentary trust is based on the assumption that a widow is incapable of wisely managing her husband's estate; consequently the trust is structured so that she will have no control over its assets. Consider the patronizing attitudes expressed by one legal expert in this field:

> It has been my experience that *a woman unaccustomed to the use and management of money* will shortly adjust her life with inescapable tragic consequences based on certain illusions which she will certainly harbor. In due course she will unconsciously make an election between *absurd niggardliness* or *ridiculous extravagance*. She will be her own worst enemy as she functions under one or the other equally untenable illusion of poverty or wealth. . . . [W]e can create an atmosphere for our beloved widow . . . through the use of a proper

trust, preferably with an institutional trustee, designed and drawn with her happiness, comfort, and peace of mind foremost in our thoughts.[91]

Plover quotes another expert who cautions against "leaving money to widows because of their inability to refuse relatives with hard luck stories, . . . and their tendency to bury the money in a little tin box."[92]

Since the trust is established by the husband, the widow cannot choose the person who will administer it and her preferences in its management and investment may be ignored. In fact, unless she can prove the administrator's gross incompetence, her wishes are considered irrelevant. She is therefore effectively deprived of any control over her own money. Although most men with comparable amounts of money (trusts occurring almost exclusively among the wealthy) manage their finances with the help of lawyers, accountants, bankers, and stockbrokers, they choose their own advisers. The trust, on the other hand, is structured on the assumption that the widow will be taken advantage of if she is allowed any choice.

When women's rights to make financial decisions are restricted by the assumption that they are financially incompetent and gullible, their inexperience and dependency in financial matters are perpetuated. The result is a vicious cycle that steadily enhances the husbands' financial skills and just as inexorably reduces the skills of their wives. Indeed, if married women were not less financially competent than their husbands initially, the imposition of financial restrictions would certainly serve to make them so, for it is far more difficult for a married woman to develop financial competence when she is deterred from gaining the very experience she needs.

The first economic effect of the law that assumes women's financial dependency is, then, to place women in a position that makes it difficult for them to develop the personality attributes, educational background, and practical experience they need to become financially competent and independent.

The second economic effect is a devaluation of the wife's actual contribution to family support. Almost half of the married women in the United States are employed and making a basic contribution to the family treasury. In Chapter 7 we will discuss the growing labor force participation of married women and the extent to which their wages contribute to basic family support. Here it is sufficient to underscore the challenge that these data present to the law's assumption that the husband is—and should be—his family's sole breadwinner.

The third economic consequence of the law's assignment of family support to the husband is to ignore the financial value of the unpaid services the wife provides. "The law fails to recognize that the wife's prodigious contributions to the household are valuable to society" because it labels her services in the home as nonproductive and without economic value.[93] The value of the housewife's services is discussed further in Chapter 3.

Social and Psychological Consequences

Just as the law fosters a sociopsychological framework that encourages husbands to define themselves as breadwinners, it fosters a sociopsychological framework that encourages wives to define themselves as dependents, for legal marriage supposedly brings the guarantee of lifelong support by the husband.

More specifically, the law provides two directives for young women: the first is to marry well; the second is to aid and support her husband's career.

With respect to the first message, not only has the aim of marrying well been the culturally approved pattern, but the law itself was organized to protect the woman's prospects for marriage. Traditionally, if a man and woman were engaged and the man broke the engagement, she could sue him for breach of promise. Thus the law provided the woman with legal recourse if her eligibility for marriage was impaired.

Breach of promise suits originated as tort actions that recognized injuries to the woman's feelings, pride, and reputation.[94] It was assumed that once she had been rejected, her value on the marriage market would be lower and her chances of marrying well would be substantially impaired. Later breach of promise suits were also founded in contract. An engagement was considered a contract to marry, and if the contract was broken, damages were allowed for "loss of the bargain."[95] If the engaged woman had also been seduced, she was entitled to aggravated damages.* Thus the

*The father of a woman who was seduced also had the right to sue the seducer. The seducer then had the choice of agreeing to a "shotgun wedding," which would serve to preserve her (and her father's and male kin's) honor, or to face the charges. Such drastic measures were deemed appropriate since "it was assumed that [seduced] women were practically unmarketable and that a woman's

law allowed a jilted woman to recover damages because it recognized the extent to which her future would be impaired by her diminished marital prospects.

Breach of promise suits are currently recognized in the majority of states in the United States.[96] Only 22 states have abolished such actions,* although a few others have limited the recovery of punitive, vindictive, and aggravated damages.[97]

While the continued validity of breach of promise actions may be surprising to some readers, breach or fraud in entering marriage is still considered a serious offence—even in a "modern" relationship in which a couple has lived together before marriage. For example, in the 1968 New York case of *Calloway* v. *Munzer*, a woman who had lived with her fiance before they married discovered she had been deceived into entering a void marriage. She was awarded damages for her injuries: public ridicule, shame, humiliation, and other mental anguish.[98]

The second directive implicit in the support law is that a young woman must do everything she can to aid and support her husband's career. Although there are no legal remedies comparable to the breach of promise suits to enforce this message, it is nevertheless clear that by emphasizing the husband's responsibility for support, the law is telling the wife that her economic well-being will always be tied to her husband's success. It therefore seems reasonable for a young woman to forgo her own education and training to further her husband's career, for *her* talents and earning potential are irrelevant so long as *his* talents and earning potential provide the key to her future happiness. Thus both the middle-class college graduate who forgoes graduate school to put her husband through medical school, and the high school graduate who forgoes college to build a family, are doing what the law encourages them to do.

However, the woman who follows the mandate of the traditional marriage contract may experience much the same sense of depri-

---

first opportunity [for marriage] probably was her last." Herma Hill Kay, "The ERA and Family Law: The Last Frontier for Change" keynote address to the National Conference on Women and the Law, 1977, Madison, Wisconsin, p. 6, and Ploscowe, Foster and Freed, *Family Law: Cases and Materials*, 2nd ed. (Boston: Little, Brown & Co., 1972), p. 133.

*Alabama, California, Colorado, Connecticut, Delaware, Florida, Indiana, Maine, Maryland, Massachusetts, Michigan, Montana, Nevada, New Hampshire, New Jersey, New York, Pennsylvania, Vermont, Virginia, West Virginia, Wisconsin, and Wyoming. Personal Conversation with Professor Homer Clark, October 1980. Clark notes that a Washington court recently refused to abolish the action by judicial decision. *Stanard* v. *Bolin*, 88 Wash. 2d 614, 565, P. 2d 94 (1977).

vation and resentment as the man who totally embraces the narrow legal role of breadwinner. This woman is likely to find that her "trained incapacity" and dependency are handicaps, and to feel she has missed both the personal enrichment and the financial benefits of having a career or avocation of her own. As one woman explained:

> I, too, had stayed home and raised children. I, too, had felt resentment as I served my husband's breakfast day after day, year after year, like some kind of downstairs maid, as he read the paper and eagerly went out into the world. . . . He was achieving, developing, thriving. . . . I was losing my identity. I was a satellite orbiting around my mate. My life was defined by him, by his job, his salary, his everything. . . .
>
> Most painful of all was the idea that I felt thwarted and suffocated by the human being who was closest to me. Pain, anger, and resentment eventually led to deep depression. . . .[99]

Along with these feelings of personal dependency and inadequacy come regrets about relinquished career opportunities and the financial dependency that results from a lifetime as a full-time housewife. For the woman who has sacrificed educational and vocational opportunities for her marriage typically finds herself without the skills and experience she needs to re-enter the job market and command a good salary in the event of divorce or her husband's death. She may fear she has lost her potential for new development, or that others who assume that she has will be reluctant to "risk" hiring her. Thus from the wife's perspective, the first effect of the law that obligates the husband for family support is that it fosters her social and psychological dependence.

A second effect is to encourage a false sense of security in the wife. Although it is clear that many women fully rely on the law's promise that their husbands will support them, it is equally clear that the law's guarantees are illusory: most married women cannot enforce their husband's obligation to support them during marriage, and few are awarded, upon divorce, the support the law promised them. Unfortunately, however, most women do not discover that until it is too late for them to change their lives—and too late for them to develop the skills and experience they need in order to be financially responsible for themselves. The tragedy here, as with the dependency the law encourages, is that women often discover the importance of foregone options only when they are past the point where they can easily choose a different course. As Betty Friedan has aptly described the woman's disillusionment with the traditional marriage contract, "If there is anything that makes a feminist, it is growing up and believing that love and *marriage will take care of everything*, and then one day waking up at 30, 40, 50, and facing the world alone and facing the responsibility [alone]."[100]

CHAPTER 3

The Wife's Domestic Responsibility

The Legal Tradition

In legal marriage a husband provides financial support in exchange for his wife's services as companion, housewife, and mother. A wife has a duty "to be his helpmate, to love and care for him in such a role, to afford him her society and her person, to protect and care for him in sickness, and to labor faithfully to advance his interests."[1] Likewise, she must perform "her household and domestic duties . . . without compensation, for a husband is entitled to the benefit of his wife's industry and economy."[2]

The husband's right to the services of his wife has been most clearly articulated in two types of actions: suits for loss of consortium, and suits for alienation of affection. As we noted in Chapter 1, if a third party negligently injures the wife, her husband may sue for his loss of her consortium. In addition to housework and child care, her consortium includes her love, affection, companionship, society, and sexual services.[3]

A husband also has a right to sue for alienation of affection if another man interferes with his marital relationship by seducing his wife. Three types of actionable interference are enumerated by Professor Prosser: enticement or harboring of the wife, committing adultery with the wife (which constitutes the tort of "criminal conversation"), and alienating the wife's affections or adversely influencing her mental attitude toward her husband.[4] For example, in a 1972 Texas case, the husband alleged that:

> . . . the defendant visited a lounge owned by [the husband] and his wife, where his wife worked as a bartender; that the defendant intentionally set out to seduce and have sexual intercourse with his wife; and that he finally accomplished his purpose during the early morning hours of February 27, 1971, when he took plaintiff's wife to a lakehouse and kept her there until approximately 6:30 a.m.
>
> Plaintiff further alleged that as a result of the defendant's intentional and wrongful acts, he was deprived of the services, affections, and consortium of his wife, Mary Ann McMillan; that a trespass was committed by the defendant upon the plaintiff's rights to the affection, love, consortium, and exclusive sexual relationship with his wife; that the defendant alienated the affections of the said Mary Ann McMillan; and that defendant's conduct was the controlling cause of the separation between him and his wife and his loss of consortium. His prayer was for actual as well as punitive damages.[5]

Both the lower court and the Texas appellate court upheld the husband's right to his wife's affection and sustained his claim for damages for his "mental anguish and other injuries."

Similarly, a 1968 Ohio jury awarded a husband $30,000 for the "conversion" of his wife by the Radio Church of God, which resulted in her leaving him.[6] Although that verdict was reversed on appeal, two more recent awards for alienation of affection were not: a North Carolina court awarded a husband $70,000 in compensatory and punitive damages in 1974, and the Oregon Supreme Court upheld a $10,000 award to the husband of a wayward wife in the same year.[7] Most recently, a 1979 Rhode Island court awarded a husband $80,000 after finding his best friend guilty of seducing his wife, thereby violating "the husband's exclusive right to physical intercourse with his wife."[8] The jury upheld the husband's request for damages for the loss of his wife's company and services as the mother of their two sons, for the mental pain and anguish he suffered, and for punitive damages.

As of 1973, only 12 states had enacted statutes to abolish the torts of alienation of affections, criminal conversation, and breach of promise to marry.[9] While these suits are not common, their continued legality indicates that the law considers the wife's marital obligations a serious matter. In fact, the married woman's domestic obligations have occupied such a central position in the formulation of family law that much of the case law that ostensibly deals with other issues can be seen as merely a vehicle for ensuring that women are not sidetracked from these all-important duties.

This perspective is clearly evident in U.S. Supreme Court decisions dealing with women's roles over the past century: with remarkable consistency these decisions elevate women's domestic obligations above all else. The pattern began in 1873 with *Bradwell* v. *Illinois*, in which the Supreme Court upheld an Illinois state court decision that denied a married woman the right to practice law because women's destiny was "to be wives and mothers."* Justice Bradley's concurring opinion states:

> Man is, or should be woman's protector and defender. The natural and proper timidity and delicacy which belongs to the female sex evidently unfits it for many of the occupations of civil life. The constitution of the family organization, which is founded in the divine ordinance, as well as in the nature of things, indicates the domestic sphere as that which properly belongs to the domain and functions of womanhood. The *paramount destiny and mission of women are to fulfill the noble and benign offices of wife and mother. This is the law of the Creator.*[10]

Later Supreme Court justifications for women's domestic roles were to become more sophisticated, relying less on the "law of the Creator" and more on "sociological truth." In *Muller* v. *Oregon*, which tested an Oregon law limiting work hours for women to ten a day, a brief prepared by Louis Brandeis introduced a vast amount of sociological data to support women's differential treatment because of their social roles as wives and mothers.[11] The Court's ruling, in Brandeis's favor, was based on these sociological "givens":

> That woman's physical structure and the performance of maternal functions place her at a disadvantage in the struggle for subsistence is obvious. This is especially true when the burdens of motherhood are upon her. [A]s healthy mothers are essential to vigorous offspring, the

*In 1853, almost 20 years before this question was raised in court, Elizabeth Cady Stanton wrote to Susan B. Anthony: "I feel, as never before, that this whole question of women's rights turns on the pivot of the marriage relation, and, mark my word, sooner or later, it will be the topic for discussion." Alice Rossi, *The Feminist Papers: From Adams to De Beauvoir* (New York: Columbia University Press, 1973), p. 392.

physical well-being of women becomes an object of public interest and care in order to preserve the strength and vigor of the race.

The two sexes differ in structure [and] in the functions to be performed by each. . . .[12]

Muller established a precedent for many later decisions that upheld special legislation for women if it supported their roles as wives and mothers. Although minimum hour laws were considered a benefit to women at the time of the *Muller* decision, the courts often used the same reasoning to women's detriment, most notably in a wealth of decisions upholding the exclusion of women from various work situations. For example, courts have upheld laws that exempt women from specific occupations such as bartending, from civic duties such as jury service, from certain work assignments such as those requiring heavy lifting and overtime, and from employment immediately before and after childbirth.[13] The range and recency of many of these exclusions indicate the extent to which courts have consistently endorsed the notion that women's domestic responsbility should be a primary determinant of their legal status. For example, in the 1961 decision in *Hoyt* v. *Florida*, the U.S. Supreme Court upheld a Florida law exempting all women from jury service because of their domestic responsibilities, declaring that "woman is still regarded as the center of home and family life."[14]*

The latest Supreme Court decisions, based on equal protection rules, have invalidated many of these sex-based exemptions.† In addition, a growing constitutional challenge to all sex-based distinctions has been evident in the efforts to secure state and federal Equal Rights Amendments.

But although the pattern of judicial decisions is changing, the Supreme Court clearly is not yet willing, on its own, to rule *all* sex-based classifications unconstitutional.[15] For example, in 1974 in

*Similarly, in 1966 the Supreme Court of Mississippi concluded: "[T]he legislature has the right to exclude women so they may continue their service as mothers, wives, and homemakers, and also to protect them (in some areas they are still upon a pedestal) from the filthy, obscene, and noxious atmosphere that so often pervades a courtroom during a jury trial." *State* v. *Hall*, 187 So. 2d 861, 863 (Miss.), appeal dismissed 385 U.S. 98, 87 S. Ct. 331 (1960). *Hall* and *Hoyt* were overruled in 1975 by *Taylor* v. *Louisiana*, 419 U.S. 522.

†It was not until 1979 that the Supreme Court invalidated laws that gave women, but not men, the option of being exempted from jury service. However, this time the Court's opinion relied not on equal protection principles but on the Sixth Amendment right of a defendant to a trial by a jury selected from a cross section of the community. It did not discuss equal protection for women jurors. *Duren* v. *Missouri*, 99 S. Ct. 664 (1979).

Kahn v. *Shevin*,[16] the Supreme Court upheld a Florida law allowing widows a tax exemption not allowed to widowers; and in 1976 the Court upheld the exclusion of pregnancy-related disabilities—and thus the exclusion of specific classes of women—from a company disability benefits plan in *Geduldig* v. *Aiello*.[17] Thus in the absence of state and federal Equal Rights Amendments, the courts may continue to allow some sex-based differences that reinforce traditional marital and family responsibilities—and thus undermine the partnership model of marriage.

Let us now examine the effects of placing the responsibility for domestic service on the wife. We shall focus first on the legal consequences of this state-imposed obligation, then on its economic, social, and psychological effects.

Legal Consequences

The rule that obligates a wife to perform domestic services for her husband has three major legal consequences. First, it deprives her of the legal right to her own labor; inasmuch as her husband is "entitled to" and "owns" the products of her labor, it is he, not she, who can sue others whose actions result in the loss of her services.

Second, the wife's role in building the family wealth and property is ignored and, with it, her right to share in the ownership of the fruits of her labor. Third, the wife is not entitled to compensation for her work in the home because the law does not allow her to be paid for services "legally owed" to her husband.

Let us briefly examine each of these legal consequences.

The Husband's "Right" to His Wife's Labor

When a woman marries, her spouse acquires the right to her wifely services and to all the benefits derived from them. He is legally entitled to her industry and economy, and he "owns" the results of all her labor in the home. Thus, the wife who, in the hope of putting aside a little money for herself, engages in paid activities at home, such as typing, editing, dressmaking, or babysitting, may discover that her earnings actually belong to her husband.[18] In addition, if a third party negligently injures her (in an automobile collision, for instance), it is her husband who has a legal claim against the wrongdoer: for her husband is entitled to recover the value of the household services she is unable to perform.[19]

In criticizing the legal rule that a wife's services belong to her husband, Blanche Crozier argued that the economic relationship between husband and wife "is the economic relationship between an owner and his property, rather than that between two free persons."* As Crozier observed: "In no other department of life has anyone had such ownership of the time and labor of another person since the abolition of slavery."[20]

If the slavery analogy seems extreme, consider this observation, in another context, by Gunnar Myrdal:

> When a legal status had to be found for the imported Negro servants in the seventeenth century, the nearest and most natural analogy was the status of women and children. The ninth commandment—linking together women, servants, mules and other property—could be invoked, as well as a great number of other passages of Holy Scriptures.[21]

Inasmuch as the legal status of both women and children has changed considerably since the seventeenth century, it is all the more remarkable that there has been "no change in the basic requirement arising from the marital relation that the wife's total services in the home belong to the husband without compensation."[22] In fact, law Professors Sylvia Law and Nadene Taub argue that the analogy to involuntary servitude is still, in many respects, singularly appropriate. Whereas the decision to marry is voluntary today, once women enter marriage they "are compelled, by law, to perform housework without pay [and] the obligation cannot be altered."[23] Along the same lines is economist John Kenneth Galbraith's observation that while servants were available only to a minority of the pre-industrial population, today "the servant-wife is available, democratically, to almost the entire present male population."[24]

The woman's obligation to serve remains one of the essential duties of marriage, and within the present law it cannot be altered or

*As John Stuart Mill declared, "Marriage is the only actual bondage known to our law. There remain no legal slaves, except the mistress of every house." J. S. Mill, "The Subjection of Women," in *Essays on Sex Equality* by J. S. Mill and Harriet T. Mill, Alice Rossi, ed. (Chicago: University of Chicago Press, 1970), p. 217.

varied. Yet any law that regards the labor of one human being as the property of another clearly runs counter to the fundamental values of freedom cherished in our country.[25]

The Wife's Contribution to Family Income and Property

A second effect of the wife's legal obligation to provide services for her husband is that the value of her services is ignored and she is therefore denied the right to the fruits of her labor. Indeed, in the forty-two common law states, in return for her legally required services she is entitled to no material compensation whatever—neither money, nor goods, nor services, nor a share in the assets she helped to accumulate. As one critic has observed, "She may be the best housekeeper and the most considerate and compassionate mother and wife, but she is not entitled to an allowance, to a claim on the husband's earnings, to wages, or to a share in any of the property that she has indirectly helped the husband to earn."[26] Even if she devotes herself *exclusively* to advancing her husband's work—by typing his papers, entertaining his clients, preparing his office payroll, organizing his business trips, working as his lab assistant, or whatever—she has no claim to a share of his income. Finally, if she goes so far as to sacrifice her own education or career to help her husband get ahead in his—no matter how much effort, how much time, how much psychological support, or how much skill she provides—her contribution gains her no legal interest in the results.

Beyond question this glaring inequity does not accord with the intentions and expectations of most spouses. Most married couples today hope to have a relationship based on principles of sharing. As Professor Susan Westerberg Prager persuasively argues, the wife who toils and sacrifices to advance her husband's career (whether by rendering sustained services and support or by subordinating her own career opportunities to his) does so precisely because she assumes the relationship will be stable and enduring and that she will thereby share in its future profits and successes.[27] Empirical evidence of the pervasiveness of this assumption is presented in the Appendix to this book, which reports the findings of a recent study of intimate contracts written by couples living together under a variety of arrangements. The overwhelming majority of the couples in that study, whether married or not, elected *to share* all income and property acquired by either party during their relationship—that is, to treat it all as community property.*

In fact, most couples who marry believe they *are* entering a partnership, a union to share everything for better or worse. Both expect to work to advance their common interest, whether in the home or in the labor force, and both expect to share the benefits (and burdens) of their common endeavor. Furthermore, the law in every state claims to recognize marriage as a partnership. But the law's provisions belie the claim: in practice, the wife's contribution is largely negated in the 42 common law property states, and marital assets acquired as a result of the joint efforts of husband and wife are typically treated as the property of the husband alone.

The potentially harsh and unreasonable effects of this legal situation are well illustrated by the 1973 Wisconsin case of *Skaar* v. *Department of Revenue*.[28] Ellen Skaar, a farm wife, worked for 20 years alongside her husband on the family farm. Despite the fact that both spouses testified that they had an agreement to share the farm's revenues, the court ruled that since her husband was "entitled to his wife's services," all the farm profits were considered his alone. The facts of the case are dramatically summarized by the Wisconsin Commission on the Status of Women:

> The farm couple, Eugene and Ellen Skaar, were married in 1942. After Eugene returned from military service in 1945, they began farming. They purchased their land as joint tenants, and worked it together. Ellen did a substantial amount of the farm labor—probably more than Eugene did, since he was active in community affairs and his official duties often took him away from the farm. Twice a day Ellen helped to milk and feed their cows; she took care of chickens; baled hay; planted, harvested, and stripped the tobacco crop; and drove the tractor. Her farm work usually took her about 12 hours per day.
>
> All the Skaars' financial dealings were handled through one joint checking account, and all income—primarily the milk check, which was made out to both Eugene and Ellen—was deposited in it. Eugene and Ellen had an oral agreement that they would work together, make farm decisions together, and manage the farm jointly. For many years, they proceeded with this arrangement, always abiding loyally by their agreement.
>
> In the late 1960s, the Wisconsin Department of Revenue audited the Skaars' tax returns. It challenged their assertion that they were

*See the review of property allocation in Appendix pages 426–8 and 454–6.

partners in a joint enterprise and that half their income belonged to Ellen. (More tax was due, of course, if the income was all Eugene's.) The [Wisconsin] supreme court agreed with the Revenue Department that there was no partnership and that all the income had been earned by Eugene. The court's decision was based on the fact that the Skaars had not entered into a written partnership agreement and had not (on their accountant's advice) filed business partnership tax returns. Additionally, their financial records (which Ellen kept, along with her other farm duties) did not reflect any division of profits resulting from the farm operations.

The Judge said: "Joint tenancy in land or the sharing of gross returns from the land do not of themselves constitute a partnership. *The husband is entitled to the services of his wife performed for him in the conduct of his business* and the profits thereof derived are therefore not her separate property. . . ." So, despite the Skaars' understanding and intentions, under Wisconsin tax law the result of their joint efforts belonged to Eugene alone. Ellen earned nothing for herself in the more than 20 years she worked 12 hours daily on their farm.[29]

The Skaars were not atypical in their expectations. Probably most farm couples regard the family farm as "theirs," not his. But in common law states the law considers it his, and in those states the farm wife acquires no legal right to "her husband's" farm.

Along the same lines, a husband-and-wife decorating company, in which the wife worked full time in the store as a sales manager and interior decorator while the husband hung wallpaper and laid carpet, was held to belong to the husband alone.[30] The husband in this case, like Mr. Skaar in the previous case, was required to pay back taxes on "his income."

The law's failure to recognize a housewife's contribution to a marriage becomes most evident at the time of divorce. In many states the housewife's role in building family wealth and property is ignored upon dissolution, to the great shock of many a hitherto unsuspecting woman.

The unjust result in the 1974 Canadian case of *Murdoch* v. *Murdoch* is illustrative.[31] When the Murdochs married in 1943, she owned two horses; he owned 25 to 30 horses and eight head of cattle. They hired themselves out as a team of ranch hands for several years, saved their money, and invested in a dude ranch. Thereafter, over the years, they worked side by side and accumulated more valuable property. Mrs. Murdoch not only performed the usual household chores but participated fully in outdoor ranch work: "haying, raking, swathing, mowing, driving trucks and tractors and teams, quieting horses, taking cattle back and forth to the reserve, dehorning, vaccinating, branding, anything that was to be done."

Mr. Murdoch presently began spending five months each year away from the ranch as an employee of the national Forestry Service. During his absences, the wife managed the property alone. In addition, she contributed financially to their joint ventures. She purchased household furnishings and appliances, and the couple used money that she earned for down payments on various pieces of property.

In 1968, Mr. Murdoch wanted to sell a piece of property and asked his wife to sign a paper releasing her dower rights to it. When she refused, he beat her so badly she had to be hospitalized. Subsequently they separated, after 25 years of marriage, with Mr. Murdoch remaining in possession of the property.

Mrs. Murdoch went to court, asking for a legal separation, ownership of their ranch home and the land surrounding it, and a one-half undivided interest in the land, cattle, cattle brand, and other assets. The court granted the separation but ordered only that she be paid maintenance of $200 a month. All the land, cattle, and other assets—including the family home—went to Mr. Murdoch. The judge justified the order in this way:

> The land was held in the name of Mr. Murdoch at all times. The cattle and equipment were also held in his name; income tax returns were filed in his name; no declaration of partnership was ever filed . . . ; and I, therefore, do not form the conclusion that the [Murdochs] were partners, or that a relationship existed that would give [Mrs. Murdoch] the right to claim as a joint owner in equity in any of the farm assets.[32]

Irene Murdoch had thus devoted 25 years of her life to making her husband a wealthy man and was rewarded with a severe beating and the promise of $200 a month. *

Similarly, when a Missouri farm wife tried to prevent her husband from disposing of their personal property, livestock, and canned goods (which she had grown as well as canned), she was told by the court that she had no rights to "his" property.[33] The common law courts have consistently presumed that all household

*It is important to note that the public outrage which greeted the Murdoch decision was instrumental in bringing about a reform of Canadian property laws.

goods for which no documentary title exists are the property of the husband.[34]

Even the wife who works in the paid labor force and earns her own money may find her contribution unrecognized in law. The "shocking unfairness" of the "obsolete and archaic" marital property laws[35] of many traditional states* is illustrated by the New York case of *Wirth* v. *Wirth*,[36] which attorneys Henry Foster and Doris Jonas Freed summarize as follows:

> [B]oth husband and wife were employed and for 22 years of their marriage their earnings were pooled. She also raised two children. In 1956 it was agreed between them that the husband would start a "crash" savings program and that family expenses would be met out of her income and his would be used for investments. According to the wife, the husband said that the program was "for our latter days" and "for the two of us." All of the investments were taken in the husband's name and none were held by joint ownership. Upon divorce it was held that she had no interest whatsoever in the assets they had accumulated as a nest egg for both of them, and that although she might be entitled to alimony (after some forty years of marriage), he got to keep all of the investments.[37]

The well publicized facts of the Wirth case, due in large part to the dedicated efforts of Foster and Freed, helped to mobilize support for property law reform in New York, which was finally enacted in 1980. Other separate property states, however, continue to rely on title and thereby to disregard the wife's contribution to family property.† In these states a woman who has made extensive contributions to her husband's business, property, or income may nevertheless find that her contribution is flatly ignored: upon dissolution

---

*Writing in 1974, Foster and Freed counted 15 common-law jurisdictions that did not subject separate property to equitable distribution upon divorce. However, even in the other 29 common-law jurisdictions the wife was not guaranteed half of the property because separate property was typically distributed as "justice and equity require." Henry Foster Jr. and Doris Jonas Freed, "Marital Property Reform in New York: Partnership of Co-Equals?" *Family Law Quarterly* 8 (1974): 170.

†According to Professor Foster, by 1980 there were possibly only five common-law jurisdictions that barred equitable or equal distribution of marital property upon divorce. With the subsequent addition of New York, there are now at least 37 states which provide for equitable distribution of property upon divorce. Henry Foster Jr., "Equitable Distribution" *New York Law Journal*, July 24, 1980, p. 1, col. 2. However, as we noted above, women in these 37 common law jurisdictions are not *guaranteed* half—or even a third—of what may still be regarded as "the husband's separate property" as it is divided according to judges' concepts of "justice and equity." See pages 32–36.

the partnership is treated as a one-man business, and she is cheated out of a fair share for her half of the enterprise.

No wonder that one of the top five recommendations adopted by the 1980 White House Conferences on the Family was for the law to recognize the financial worth of the homemaker. Along the same lines was a 1974 recommendation of the Citizens' Advisory Council on the Status of Women, urging a careful evaluation of the economic effects of divorce laws to ensure recognition of the home-maker's contribution to the marital property. *

The law could achieve this end in one of two ways: one approach, adopted by the community property states, is to treat all income and property accumulated during marriage as the product of the two partners and to guarantee the homemaking partner *a half share* of those products. The second approach would be to calculate the monetary value of the homemaker's contribution and provide for (or at least allow) her to be *paid* for her work and to receive job-related benefits. We have seen how the present law fails in the first instance by negating the wife's right to an equal share in the income and property accumulated during marriage. We now turn to an examination of the law's position with respect to the second.

The Prohibition on Wages for Domestic Services

The assignment of domestic services to the wife effectively precludes her from receiving any monetary compensation for a major share of her life's work. Because the courts have always considered a wife's domestic services to be owed to her husband, they have traditionally refused to enforce contracts in which a husband agrees to pay his wife for her work on the grounds that such a contract is void for lack of consideration: a person cannot receive special compensation for performing a job he or she is legally obligated to perform.[38] Housekeeping, entertaining, child care have all been deemed "wifely tasks";[39] so have such "extras" as participation in the husband's business or doing heavy farm labor. For all these services the courts have voided husbandly promises to pay wives for their work.

For example, in *Youngberg* v. *Holstrom*[40] and in *Frame* v. *Frame*[41] wives worked extensively on their husbands' farms. In

*Specifically they have urged that states adopting no-fault divorce laws change their laws on the division of property, alimony, child support, and enforcement so that the law explicitly recognizes the contribution of the homemaker. See *Rieger* v. *Christensen*, 529 P 2d, 1362 (Colo. App. 1974) and The California Civil Code, § 4801 (a)(1) which adopt this view.

Youngberg the wife raised poultry and hogs and cared for a large garden. In *Frame* the wife kept accounts, cooked for hired hands, collected rents, helped supervise field work, and marketed produce. Neither wife was able to recover for her services.

Similarly, in the 1975 North Carolina case of *Taylor* v. *Taylor*, the court denied compensation to a wife who worked without pay in her husband's business during 40 years of marriage.[42] The court in this case held that a wife has neither the right to recover for work she has done, nor the entitlement to compensation for increasing the value of her husband's business. (Paradoxically, the law recognizes that a husband's efforts may increase the value of his wife's farm or business, and entitles him to compensation for his work. *His* efforts are not considered part of his normal duty as a spouse.)[43]

The courts have applied the same principles to invalidate a husband's pledge to pay his wife a wage for special nursing services. For example, in *Brooks* v. *Brooks*, the court not only refused to uphold a husband's agreement to pay his wife a monthly sum for nursing services, it also ruled that the wife was obligated to *reimburse* her husband for any amounts he had already paid her.[44] If two unmarried parties had made an agreement whereby one agreed to pay the other for nursing, their contract would, of course, be valid. However, if those parties subsequently married, their agreement would automatically terminate, since one of the terms of the marriage contract is that the wife's services will be performed without compensation.[45]

In summary, then, the law places an insurmountable barrier in front of the married woman who seeks to gain some financial recompense for her services. The inevitable result is that hundreds of thousands of women who work without pay (in 1974, 78 percent of all unpaid family workers were women) on "their husband's" farm, or house, or business have no assets whatever to call their own if they happen to live in any of the 42 separate property states.[46] The State of Wisconsin affords a case in point. In that heavily agricultural state, in 1978 one-third of all the women had *no* personal income and another one-third earned less than $2,000—simply because most Wisconsin wives received no monetary compensation for the services they performed.[47]*

*No wonder that Wisconsin is leading the movement toward property law reform in the common law states. It is likely to be the first common law state to enact a system of marital partnership property. 1981 Wisconsin Assembly Bill 370. (Assembly Substitute Amendment 4, passed by the Ass. Judiciary Committee on Feb. 19, 1980.)

It is axiomatic that the only way most of us can acquire income and property is through our own labor. When the law treats a woman's labor as her "wifely duty" and denies her compensation for it, she is deprived of her major (and often her only) means of financial gain. Moreover, as Professor Herma Hill Kay concludes, when a wife's labor is "seen as a service she owes her husband rather than a job deserving the dignity of economic return," the value of the work she does is greatly underestimated.[48]

The compensation workers receive in most jobs takes various forms: apart from wages, they receive an array of fringe benefits, including health insurance, paid vacation, seniority rights, pensions, and so on. The housewife, however, receives neither salary nor fringe benefits for her labor. Theoretically, of course, she is entitled to support from her husband in exchange for her home services; but as we know (see Chapter 2), the courts will not compel him to support her and in 42 states she has no legal right to share his salary or property. In a society that rewards its citizens with money and typically measures individual worth by the salary one commands, the law's refusal to accord the wife an economic reward for her services suggests that those services are considered to be without value. The message is not lost on the populace. As one middle-aged woman notes:

> Because I haven't been paid for the work I've done for the past quarter century—raising a family, managing a home—what I've done doesn't count. So much so that, now that my kids are grown, they have the gall to say to me: "Why don't you get a job, Mother? Why don't you *do* something?" After all these years of slaving for them, they seem convinced I'm some kind of parasite.[49]

"Real work" seems to be defined as labor that has an acknowledged monetary value.[50] If it is not paid, it is not "work."

The Citizen's Advisory Council on the Status of Women has concluded that while "there has been much rhetoric about the value of homemaking and child rearing, . . . there has not been enough actual recognition or action to give homemaking status, dignity, and security. . . . It is very important to change the law to recognize explicitly the contribution of the homemaker."[51] How can the law best recognize the homemaker's contribution? Should housewives be paid for their work? Or should they be guaranteed lifelong support? Or should all full-time homemakers be given a share of the income and property accumulated during marriage? These questions are addressed in the final section of this chapter. However, before turning to remedies, we will assess the economic and social consequences of the present legal rule.

Social and Economic Consequences

The law that obligates a wife to provide domestic services has several important economic effects. First, it restricts the wife's opportunities for paid employment. Second, it deters her from developing her own earning power. Third, it prevents her from making provision for such contingencies as illness, divorce, or old age. All these limitations also reinforce the wife's economic dependence on her husband and thereby increase his burden for family support.

Restricted Opportunities for Paid Employment

To the extent that a wife devotes herself to the homemaker's responsibilities mandated by law, she necessarily forgoes opportunities for paid employment. As Law and Taub explain:

> The duty to serve in the home inequitably limits the married woman's opportunities for work outside the home. This is not entirely a matter of symbolic effect. . . . It may also have concrete legal effects in limiting work opportunities for married women.[52]

One concrete effect, as these writers note, is that employers can use women's domestic responsibilities as a basis for discriminating against them in a variety of ways.

If a married woman works in the paid labor force instead of in the home, she earns a salary for her labor and has the option of spending it to acquire assets of her own. Without a salary, as we have seen, she has no such power in most states of the United States. The time spent in unpaid housework thereby deprives her of the use of her time for paid employment and the monetary resources it brings.

Impaired Earning Capacity

To the extent that a wife spends her time in homemaking and child rearing and husband care, she inevitably relinquishes opportunities to develop her own earning capacity. Since earning power increases with education, job training, seniority, and practical employment experience, the wife loses time and opportunities each day she spends as a housewife. As Krauskopf notes:

> Day by day and year by year in the homemaker role, the woman falls farther behind in earning power. When her full economic worth is eaten up by marital duties, she has neither property nor earning ability. And yet the common law system accords her no rights for that sacrifice. The wage-earning husband may retain all his earnings in excess of what he chooses to use for family support, and, in addition, he gains pension and Social Security rights and that all-important growth in earning power.[53]

Often a wife helps her husband increase his earning potential by sacrificing her own. Ironically, his gain is likely to increase her sacrifice; for the more the disparity in their earning power grows, the more she must give up to "protect her investment" in her husband. All the while, her chances for building an independent earning potential steadily diminish.*

Vulnerability in Old Age, Divorce, Illness, and Disability

One of the major consequences of a wife's restricted employment is that she is likely to have limited provision for costly contingencies. As Professor Kay has observed, when the housewife is not compensated for her work, she is not entitled to contribute to Social Security and has no pension or retirement plan of her own.[54] Most steady employees are directly covered by medical insurance, disability insurance, workmen's compensation, unemployment insurance, life insurance, Social Security, and pension or retirement plans, and the coverage changes to meet shifting economic realities. The housewife typically is able to benefit from these protections only indirectly—as a dependent of her husband—and then only selectively and in a manner subject to a battery of restrictions. If her marriage should end in divorce, of course, most (if not all) of her indirect benefits will be withdrawn.

*As of 1980 the California Civil Code § 4801 (a)(1) requires that courts awarding alimony must consider "The earning capacity . . . of each spouse, taking into account *the extent to which the supported spouse's present and future earning capacity is impaired by periods of unemployment that were incurred during the marriage* to permit the supported spouse to devote time to *domestic duties.*" (emphasis added)

For example, the housewife who has been entitled to health and hospital insurance by virtue of her husband's employment typically finds, upon divorce, that she is suddenly without coverage. Some companies may allow her to purchase a conversion policy which provides much *less* protection for much *more* money, but often she does not even have this option. A woman of 45 or 50, especially one with a history of illness or a disability is likely to have considerable difficulty obtaining any coverage at all—and is typically left without adequate protection at the very point at which she needs it the most. The divorced housewife is also likely to be totally cut out of her husband's retirement and pension benefits.* In addition, if she has been married less than 10 years she loses her right to Social Security benefits as a spouse. While she retains this right if married more than 10 years, her entitlement is only one-third of a couple's benefits—an amount so low that it is likely to thrust her into poverty. †

*In 1980 Representative Patricia Schroeder introduced legislation to remedy this situation in federal government retirement plans for employees of the foreign service, civil service and the military. Her proposals seek to accomplish two goals. First, to make survivors' benefits mandatory unless the spouses agree in writing to waive the survivors' annuity (in order to maximize the joint income from their lifetime annuity). Second, to entitle divorced spouses to a pro-rata share of the retirement and survivors' annuities based upon the years of marriage during covered employment. *The Spokeswoman*, October 1980, p. 2 and January 1980, p. 17.

Schroeder's Amendment to the Foreign Service Act of 1980 was passed, and became effective February 15, 1981. Anyone married to a Foreign Service officer for a decade or more is now "presumptively entitled" to a pro-rata share of the officer's retirement and survivor's benefits, subject to court review. In addition, an employee may not elect against providing survivor benefits without the consent of his spouse or former spouse.

The 1980 Congress also amended the Civil Service retirement system to make clear that Civil Service pensions are subject to division by a divorce court. Representative Schroeder has reintroduced legislation to provide more secure pension benefits for divorced Civil Service and military spouses.

†Before 1978 a divorced wife who had been married for less than twenty years was not entitled to any of the benefits that would ordinarily have come to her when her husband retired or died. Although the divorced housewife who has been married for more than ten years is now entitled to Social Security benefits as a spouse, her entitlement is clearly inadequate. As Representative Geraldine Ferraro (D–NY), a member of the Congressional Task Force on Women and Social Security noted, "Since a divorcee is only entitled to one-third of the couple's benefits, many divorced women who rely entirely on their Social Security benefits for their income find that they are thrust into poverty because of the inadequacy of benefits paid to divorced spouses." "Women under Social Security," *The Spokeswoman* December 1979, p. 7. In addition, a divorcee cannot collect social security until her ex-husband decides to retire, and many men are delaying retirement to keep up with an inflationary economy.

The housewife who is widowed may also find herself in a precarious situation as a result of her financial dependence on her husband during marriage. One possibility is that she will be left totally without survivors' benefits because most survivors' benefits are optional for the employee. Many widows do not discover that their husbands have not elected survivors' benefits until after he has died. As pension plans allow the worker alone to decide whether to opt for survivors' benefits, without a spouse's knowledge or consent, and since most plans give the worker an actuarial incentive *not* to elect survivors' benefits (because the workers' retirement pay and lifetime annuity are typically reduced to pay for the cost of a survivors' annuity), many widows find themselves cut off from the one form of insurance "protection" that they assumed they could always count on. *

Even if her husband has elected a survivors' option a widow may find herself in similar straights if her husband dies before he is eligible for retirement or if he dies before his pension has vested. In fact, if her husband has changed jobs and been unable to transfer his pension, or if he dies at an early age, all of his retirement contributions may be lost. Thus when the dependent housewife loses her husband she may also lose her sole source of income. In addition, if he dies before *her* 60th birthday she is not eligible for Social Security benefits. As a result many widows face the prospect of no immediate income until they reach age 60. The years between 55 and 60, or between 45 and 60, can be years of dire hardship and despair for the housewife who has never worked outside the home. And, after a lifetime without a paid job, her earning capacity has typically been impaired to the point where she is simply not equipped to support herself.

It is important to note that the increased vulnerability in divorce and widowhood is not limited to the full-time housewife. Many women who work in the labor force before they marry, or before their children are born, or after their children are in school, as well as those who maintain continuous part-time jobs throughout marriage, are often excluded from full employee benefits because they have not worked for enough years, or enough hours, or

---

*A homemaker can now establish an Individual Retirement Account with her husband—*if* her husband is eligible for an IRA (many are not). In 1979 U.S. Representative Paul Trible (R–Va.) introduced *The Homemaker Retirement Act* to permit homemakers to set up their own retirement accounts instead of requiring joint accounts with their husbands. *Women Today*, July 11, 1979, p. 73.

in the right position or industry to qualify. Some may be penalized by company policies that limit fringe benefits to full-time employees, others by restrictions on accumulating retirement benefits in discontinuous periods of employment, and still others may not work long enough for their pensions to vest. When a housewife makes her home and her family her *primary responsibility*, even if she maintains a part-time job and/or has held full-time jobs at various points in the marriage, she is, typically, simply unable to accumulate and maintain the benefits that accrue to continuous employees. As a result, her *primary status* remains that of her husband's dependent and she too is excessively vulnerable in the event of divorce, illness, old age, and widowhood.

Finally, even a housewife who does receive pension and insurance benefits as her husband's surviving dependent, may nevertheless face years of widowhood on a decreasing income as inflation eats away at her fixed-payment pension benefits.

It is no wonder that older women are the fastest growing poverty segment in the United States: in 1979 forty percent of all older women lived in poverty and seven out of every ten Social Security recipients who were eligible for welfare were women. *

Thus, once again, the law has the economic effect of pathetically—and dangerously—increasing the wife's vulnerability in illness, disability and old age, and of thereby also increasing her dependence on her husband. A woman's consequent dread of future contingencies and her fear that she will be unable to cope with them is well expressed by Howe:

> What if I become ill or incapacitated? . . . What if the source of family income is lost? . . . What if my home breaks up by desertion or divorce? . . . What if I want more control over the financial management of my life? . . . What if the homemaking job gets too much for me to handle? . . . What if I need to refresh myself and grow? . . . How will I live if my husband dies? All those what if's, . . . it can all look hunky-dory until suddenly he gets laid off or sick or wants out and then you realize how dependent you've been all these years on his good fortune . . . or his good will. [55]

The issue, as U.S. Representative Patricia Schroeder (D–Co.) concluded in her 1980 testimony before the President's Commission on Pension Policy, is

---

*Geraldine Ferraro "Women under Social Security," *The Spokeswoman* December 1979, p. 7.

If we value the role of mother and homemaker, we must attach an economic value to it, so that she will be economically protected in old age. Personally, I would like to see a society where women have the option to drop out of the paid labor force to raise children or take care of elderly parents, without being penalized for it. . . .

Who should bear the cost of childbearing and childrearing in our society—women themselves, or employers, or society? The way we answer that question will have long term ramifications for both older women and their retirement security and younger women in terms of their options to leave the work force to have children and to raise them.*

Reinforced Dependency of Wives

By now it is obvious how the legal rule that obligates a wife's domestic services to her husband reinforces her economic dependence on him. So long as a woman spends all her energy and time in the home, where the law assumes she should be, her economic dependence on her husband is assured.[56] But her dependence extends beyond the economic sphere. The rule has social and psychological implications as well. One without economic resources has difficulty achieving either personal or social autonomy. As English feminists Edmond and Fleming assert, when a woman has to rely on her husband for money she is constrained to subordinate her own needs to his:

> We are saying that we women need money of our own—if we weren't forced to depend on men for money, we wouldn't have to put their needs before ours, to service them sexually, physically, emotionally. We could begin to find out what *our* needs are.[57]

Without doubt, the most profound effect of the law's refusal to recognize the housewife as a productive person is that it affects the way women think and feel about themselves. They come to think of themselves as dependent, powerless, unimportant and nonproductive beings—to regard themselves as "*only* housewives." In so doing they deprecate their productive work and their productive capacities. This not only lowers their feelings of low self-worth, it fosters an even more emotionally destructive psychological dependence on

---

*The Spokeswoman, January 1980, p. 17. In 1980 Congress passed Representative Schroeder's "Displaced Diplomats Bill" providing for retirement and survivors' annuities for divorced spouses of foreign service personnel. *The Spokeswoman*, October 1980, p. 2.

their husbands. As Lillian Rubin describes it, they make their own needs and desires—their very selves—ancillary to those of their husbands'.[58]

Reinforced Male Roles

The legal stress on wives as homemakers serves to strengthen and reinforce the male role of family breadwinner, and often with burdensome results. In fact, men with dependent wives are most likely to feel the full pressures of the male support obligation. Edmond and Fleming contend that a woman utterly dependent on a man's wages for her own survival necessarily imposes a discipline on him to hold on to a regular job and at all costs to keep the paychecks coming in.[59] A husband not *strictured* by such pressures, they assert, has greater control over his work because he is in a far stronger position to press his on-the-job demands and risk trying out alternative jobs.

Defining domestic responsibilities as "women's obligations" also encourages employers to make excessive occupational demands on men. Employers who assume that men have no family responsibilities are more likely to expect them to be totally available for work. As Law and Taub note,

> The law, employers, and society generally now assume that men have no duties in relationship to the care of their children or the maintenance of the home environment. Indeed, the general assumption reinforced by legal expectations is that there will be someone else, i.e., the wife, to handle all of that.[60]

If the law were to recognize that men and women *both* have obligations and responsibilities to their families and their homes, men undoubtedly would be better protected against excessive occupational demands.

The Nature and Value of a Housewife's Work

In order to decide how the law could best compensate the housewife's work, we must first analyze the work she performs. We begin this section with an analysis of the nature of the wife's productive services. Next we examine various approaches to evaluating these services. The final section of this chapter then deals with appropriate means of compensation.

The Nature of the Wife's Productive Services

The housewife usually provides three types of productive services: home care, home administration, and people care (inputs to human capital). The first category, which embraces what is typically called housework, may be broken down into various discrete chores: cleaning, cooking, shopping, doing laundry, paying bills, etc. Because it is relatively easy to enumerate these tasks and to calculate their market value, several analysts have tried to calculate the value of the housewife's work by focusing exclusively on this category and ignoring the other two components of the wife's work.

The second type of service the housewife provides—home administration—includes all of her responsibilities in managing the home: planning meals and eating schedules, organizing car pools and lessons and social activities for the children, administering the household budget, arranging for home maintenance (cleaning, repairs, etc.), planning family vacations and leisure activities, and acting as the family purchasing agent and comparison shopper.

Although some upper-middle-class women may manage to escape doing housework, as Professor Nona Glazer correctly observes, it is difficult if not impossible for married women to escape the responsibilities of household management: "Regardless of their social class position, women are responsible for the functioning of the household even if only (among the rich) to supervise others to whom the more mundane responsibilities have been delegated."[61]

The third category of women's domestic work—people care—is also performed by all wives regardless of socioeconomic status. Translated into economic terms by Wellesley economist Carolyn Shaw Bell, women's work in caring for husbands and children involves the production and maintenance of "human capital." As she explains: "human beings yield a return over time by working productively. [By] keeping human beings fed and warm and clothed and clean and even happy, women keep them productive and efficient."[62]

In other words, people care (or husband care or child care) involves attending to the psychological needs of other family members: loving, nurturing, supporting, stimulating, and soothing.

Although this component of women's work is probably the most difficult to measure in terms of both input and results, providing emotional and psychological support is the very essence of "being a mother" and "being a wife." As two feminists explain it, it consists of nothing less than the "production of people" who have the inner strength to deal with the world outside:

> We produce and reproduce in other people and ourselves the ability to work and go on working, we produce labour power. All other production would grind to a halt tomorrow if women weren't producing these workers.[63]

The Value of the Housewife's Contribution

There are two basic strategies for valuing the housewife's services and her contribution to the marriage. The first approach has been used by economists, the second is embodied in family law. To further complicate the situation, within each of these two general perspectives there is a bifurcation of opinion. For example, as we have noted, within family law one standard is used by community property states, while those with the separate property system employ a substantially different model. Let us first examine the two *economic* methods for valuing the housewife's contribution: the market value approach, and the opportunity cost approach. Then we will turn to the methods used in family law.

The market value approach attempts to assess the wife's value or contribution to the family by calculating what it would cost the family to replace her. This calculation involves listing the tasks the housewife does, finding their current wage rate in the marketplace, and adding the results to arrive at a total cost of the work.[64] This approach is typically used in wrongful death actions by courts called upon to estimate the economic cost of replacing a wife's services. Using the market cost approach, a Metropolitan Life Insurance Company study in 1976 estimated: "Based on her work as cook, nurse, housekeeper, chauffeur and more, the stay-at-home wife is worth more than $13,000 a year. If anything happened to the wife, it would cost the husband close to that amount to take over all of those jobs."[65] Similarly, economists for the Chase Manhattan Bank analyzed the amount of time an "average" housewife spent on various tasks, estimated the hourly cost of hiring a person in the free labor market to do each of these tasks, and calculated that it would have cost \$13,391 to purchase the services performed by this "average" housewife in 1970.[66]

These wage-rate calculations are inaccurate in three respects.* First, wages for domestic work are chronically depressed in the free market because married women are obligated to do the work without pay.[67] Second, housework is only one component of the housewife's role. The estimates cited above ignore the more difficult (and, in the marketplace, more highly paid) aspects of the wife's role—what we have referred to as home administration and the maintenance of human capital. These estimates might be more accurate if they calculated the costs of psychiatric and management services instead of concentrating primarily on the lower paying domestic work. Two more recent estimates appear to be more sensitive to these deficiencies. In 1979 a *Parents* magazine article concluded that a young mother with two preschool aged children, if paid for all her work, would receive a check for \$699 a week, or a yearly income of \$35,000, and in 1980 a Chicago divorce lawyer calculated that with an average work week of 90.6 hours in various service roles, the cash value of the houswife was over \$40,000 a year.[68]

A third problem with the market approach is that its wage estimates are based on salaries for those who work normal daytime hours on a routine schedule. Inasmuch as the housewife works on a 24-hour "demand" schedule, more appropriate calculations would be based on wages for night work, overtime work, and on-call services—all of which are recompensed at premium rates.

The opportunity cost approach to estimating the economic value of housework calculates the salary the housewife forgoes to work at home. This assumes that the cost of a woman's work in the home is equal to the salary she could earn in the paid labor force. As economist Richard Posner explains:

> The value of a housewife's services, and hence the cost to the family if those services are eliminated, is the price that her time would have commanded in an alternative use. Suppose she had been trained as a lawyer and could have earned \$15,000 working for a law firm but chose instead to be a housewife. Suppose further that the various functions she performed as a housewife could have been hired in the market for \$8,000. Since she chose to stay at home, presumably her

*I am indebted to economist Clair Vickery Brown for guidance in analyzing the deficiencies of these models.

services in the home were considered by the family to be worth at least $15,000; if not, the family could have increased its real income by having her work as a lawyer and by hiring others to perform her household functions. The decision that she remain at home may have been quite rational, for her skills as a housewife, particularly in child care, may have exceeded what could be obtained in the market at the same price. Therefore, the [value of her services in the home is] at least $15,000.[69]

Calculated in this way, the wages of working wives vary sharply and are especially influenced by age and education. In 1964, the average opportunity cost for a 30-year-old woman to remain a housewife was calculated at $2,556, if she had less than 12 years of education. If she had a college degree, the opportunity cost was $5,892. A 50-year-old wife with a college degree forfeited some $7,186, and so on.[70] Of course, the wife who was already established in law, medicine, real estate, finance or corporate management, would have a much greater opportunity cost. Posner notes that although the courts have not typically used the opportunity cost approach in determining damages in wrongful death or disabled housewives cases, "they have approximated it by allowing testimony on the quality of the housewife's household services. This is an oblique method of avoiding the pitfall of valuing such services at the cost of domestic servants."[71]

The opportunity cost approach offers some clear advantages over a simplistic market valuation of the wife's domestic services because it recognizes that different women have different values to their families. This perspective moves at least some of the financial estimates away from "averages" and the depressed market for domestic labor. Clearly a family that elects to have a woman who could earn $40,000 a year as an attorney stay home instead to raise her children, places a very high value on the unique upbringing she can provide for her children. Her potential wages provide a more accurate estimate of the cost that her family is paying for *her services* at home than the cost of hiring domestic help.

Nevertheless, both of these economic approaches share a major flaw: they both deal with potential, rather than actual, earnings. This conceptual device leads to both theoretical and practical problems in court proceedings. On a theoretical level, it invites contradictory testimony from competing experts (usually economists) concerning the needs of the local labor market, current salary levels, the skills and merits of a particular woman, etc. On a practical level, the courts are asked to rule on the disposition of income and other assets which the family never had. If the expert's testimony is used to calculate what an insurance company ought to pay in a wrongful death action, hypothetical figures may be useful. But when the matter at issue is a settlement in a divorce case, the fact that a wife never earned the money in question can have a major effect on the amount of money and/or property her husband can reasonably be expected to pay. In addition, in a divorce case one would have to calculate and deduct from her award the value of the wife's room and board, her own gains from raising her children, etc.

To say the least, those kinds of economic calculations do little to foster the notion that marriage is a partnership, and that is probably one reason why family law has adopted a very different approach. Both of the *legal* approaches to the housewife's contribution begin instead with the premise that the law cannot go beyond the actual financial circumstances of the marriage.

The first legal approach, what we call *the exchange model*, is adopted by the separate property states and is set forth in the basic provisions of the marriage contract: the wife's services are exchanged for the husband's support. In theory, family law provides for the housewife by guaranteeing her lifelong support. In this model the "value" of her services is whatever her husband chooses to pay her, with certain safeguards to ensure her support in the event of divorce (by means of alimony) or the husband's death (through dower rights). While the legal approach may at first seem to avoid the question of what the wife's services are worth, the law does in fact answer that question: it values her services according to her husband's standard of living—the home he provides, the food on the table, the clothes she wears, the travel and entertainment he pays for, the money she has to spend, and the gifts he buys for her. This formula, which closely accords with the reality of family life, characterizes the working rules of the common law states.

The major difference between this position and the rules adopted by the community property states is that the latter assume that the marriage contract includes an additional provision—that the husband and wife *share* virtually everything acquired in the course of their marriage. This approach, which we refer to as *the partnership model*, also values the wife's contribution in practical terms: it calculates the wife's contribution as equal to *one-half* of whatever the marital partnership has produced.

The partnership model assumes that the wife is responsible for one-half of the family's earnings and assets even if they are derived from the husband's salary. It also assumes that the marital partnership is akin to *an economic partnership* in which two individuals agree to pool their assets and abilities and to share the fruits of their common venture. In some marriages the couple may decide to divide their partnership responsibilities in the traditional manner, with the husband responsible for financial support, the wife for homemaking and child care. Others may choose to share both responsibilities in a more egalitarian manner with both husband and wife working in the home and the paid labor force. But whatever the division of labor, *both partners are assumed to be contributing to the joint enterprise and both are entitled to share fully in its accomplishments.* The partnership theory is based on the premise that the very essence of the marital bond is the partners' mutual commitment to share everything—for better or for worse.

As we have noted above, one of the advantages of this partnership policy is that it recognizes the value of the wife's contribution to the assets acquired during the marriage. As Levy notes, it is widely recognized that "the wife who spends almost all of her married life in homemaking and child rearing contributes significantly to the family's economic welfare *by making it possible for the husband to earn income and amass property during the marriage.*[72] The partnership theory assumes that whatever her precise role, the housewife's services enable her husband to earn money, increase his earning power, and acquire property—and that as his partner she is entitled to an equal share of these assets.

Another advantage of the partnership model over the exchange model is that the former more closely approximates the expectations of most people who enter marriage; thus, it embodies societal ideals of what a marital union should be. Certainly the court decisions in most of the cases reviewed in the first part of this chapter (in which farm wives and business wives in separate property states were denied the right to share in the ownership of the property they helped to build) not only violate most married couples' conceptions of fairness, but they are also contrary to the everyday assumptions about togetherness and sharing with which most couples enter marriage.

A third advantage of the partnership model is that it provides a realistic measure of the wife's contribution because it takes into account what the family actually accomplishes as a result of her efforts. This perspective avoids the patently inaccurate calculations of the simple market value approach, as well as the need for the more complex and intricate valuation that takes into account the wife's on-call managerial and psychiatric services. The partnership model also is preferable to the opportunity cost approach, because when the wife, in fact, is not employed in the paid labor force, her *real* contribution to the family can be most accurately assessed in terms of what the family gains thanks to her support and services.

Compensating the Housewife

One practical approach to the question of how the housewife can be compensated for her services in the home is the one adopted by the 42 common law states; that is, one can assume that the husband's support constitutes the housewife's reward. This model is more or less compatible with the National Organization for Women (NOW) proposal that housework be paid.[73] A husband and wife can, in theory, agree on a "fair wage" as his means of support. Although, as Jessie Bernard has aptly put it, "the very thought of paying women for their housekeeping services is a horrifying anathema (since) women are still expected to do things because of love and/or duty,"[74] there are some clear-cut advantages to this proposal.

An assured monthly income would provide the full-time housewife with disposable income of her own, as well as unequivocal recognition and reward for her work. It would also help to lessen her dependency on her husband. The NOW proposal urges that housework be treated as a bona fide occupation complete *with* the normal *fringe benefits* of employment—health insurance, old age and disability coverage, Social Security, and a retirement and/or pension plan.[75] The job package could even include unemployment insurance as a partial cushion against divorce.

There are many ways to calculate an appropriate "wage" for the housewife. The market value approach (in its more sophisticated form) and the opportunity cost approach provide two possibilities. Another formula would forthrightly allocate one-half of the husband's salary to the housewife. This approach, known as the earnings-sharing or earnings-splitting scheme, could have widespread applications beyond the single-wage-earner family. Once the principle of splitting income between an employed husband and a full-time housewife is established, it could be continued when the wife takes a part-time job or returns to full-time work—or when her husband takes a work sabbatical, or a year off to go to school, or paternity leave to care for a newborn child.

On a societal level it would certainly be helpful if the fringe benefits of employment that are controlled by the U.S. Government (such as Social Security, unemployment compensation, and disability insurance) were also available to the housewife*—or were allocated to the married couple as a unit,† instead of to the individual wage earner. For example, one of the most promising proposals for reforming the Social Security system would establish an earnings-sharing plan for married couples.‡ Under this plan the total income of a married couple (whether from a single wage earner or from two wage earners) would first be combined. Then one half of the total would be assigned to the wife, one half to the husband. An individual wage record would be maintained for each spouse separately, and future benefits would be based on this record. In the event of divorce, both spouses would retain their individual records and credits. The earnings-sharing plan could be adopted to private employee benefits as well as to those controlled by the government.

A second, and not incompatible, approach to compensating the housewife, would be to adopt the community property or partnership model, and recognize the wife's right to half of all the income, property, and other assets acquired during the marriage. This could be most easily accomplished if the common law states adopted a system of community property—applicable both during marriage and after divorce. A California-type system that gave both partners an equal right to manage and control the community property would also allow the wife access to family income and property on a day-to-day basis.§

*The December 1980 final report of President Carter's Advisory Committee on Women recommended a feasibility study by the government on the inclusion of homemakers in unemployment compensation, disability insurance, and Social Security. It also recommended the formation of other policies that recognize marriage as an economic partnership. *The Spokeswoman* 11, no. 1 (Jan. 1981):8.

†The terms "housewife" and "married couple" are used interchangeably with "homemaker" and "household unit" here and are not intended to suggest that these benefits should be awarded on the basis of marital status. Evidence of dependency, or a shared household and/or a pooling arrangement might be preferable criteria for these benefits.

‡See, generally, the 1979 reports of the HEW and Congressional Task Forces on Women and Social Security summarized in "Recommended Changes in Social Security—Greater Equality for Working Women," *Marriage and Divorce Today*, August 18, 1980, p. 2.

§This has been proposed in the new Wisconsin legislation that seeks to create a system of marital partnership property in what has traditionally been a separate property state.

However, even the community property states have not yet worked out the specific means to effect an infallibly equitable division of marital assets in the event of divorce. Although they adhere to the partnership principles that presume both spouses to be entitled to an *equal share* of the assets of the marriage, even these states fail to carry out the spirit of the law because they typically limit the definition of community assets to tangible items (such as a house, a car, or a going business). As we noted in Chapter 2, this definition excludes the extremely valuable career assets which should be recognized (and divided) as community property.*

Dividing Career Assets

A more equitable system would recognize that literally every uninherited asset acquired during a marriage is community property. As we noted in Chapter 2, an education, job experience and an ability to earn a living, what we have called "career assets," are assets that are typically acquired in the course of a marriage by one or both partners, and these assets have a monetary value as surely as income and real property do.

It is evident that many families, especially single-income families, devote most of their resources (of time and money) to building the husband's career. The wife may have left school "to put him through school," or postponed her education to help him get established, or quit her job to move with him, or used her skills to directly aid and advance his career. In fact in *most* single-income families the single career might well be conceptualized as a "two-person career," the product of a cooperative effort by the partners. †

Once it is recognized that the family's major asset or wealth may exist in the form of career assets, it follows that both partners have a right to share in the fruits of that career. Just as income earned by one spouse is recognized to be the product of joint efforts and therefore an asset belonging to both spouses, a career that is de-

---

*Because these assets are not recognized as community property the husband typically leaves with *all* of them upon divorce, as noted on pages 35–36.

†The term "two-person career" originates with Hanna Papanek, who defines the "two-person-single-career" as a "(s)pecial combination of roles whereby wives are inducted by institutions employing their husbands into a pattern of vicarious achievement." According to Papanek, this pattern serves as a social control mechanism that derails the occupational aspirations of highly educated women into a subsidiary role determined by her husband's career. Papanek shows how the husband's career suffers if the wife does not cooperate, and vice versa. See Papanek, "Men, Women and Work: Reflections on the Two-Person Career," *American Journal of Sociology* 78 (January 1973): 852.

veloped in the course of a marriage is certain to be the product of joint efforts and should be similarly recognized as a community asset.

The issue is no less pressing in two-earner families, for even though both spouses may have worked during the marriage, it is likely that they, as a marital unit, chose to give priority to one person's career and that they both expected to share in the benefits of that decision.

In order to establish the value of a career, courts could draw on traditional economic methods for calculating the value of having an education or on the job training; the value of having a secure job (especially in a high-unemployment economy), work experience, and seniority rights; a professional license, or union membership, or certification in a trade; job-related benefits such as health, accident, and life insurance; goodwill in a business or profession; a pension or retirement program; and the value of Social Security coverage. (This list is meant to be suggestive, not comprehensive.) Precedents for such calculations have already been developed in many other areas of the law—for example, in workmen's compensation cases, disability cases, personal injury suits, wrongful death actions, and suits for loss of consortium.

Three newly emerging areas of family law suggest promising analogies for the task of defining and apportioning the career assets accumulated during marriage. The first deals with a professional education, the second with the good will value of a professional practice, and the third with pensions and insurance benefits. Let us briefly examine some of the developments in each of these areas.

A Professional Education

A number of efforts have been made recently to establish the community's interest in an education, especially in a professional education. The issue typically arises when one spouse, usually the woman, has supported her mate through school "in the hope of improving future community earnings" which she expects to share.[76] If the marriage is dissolved upon graduation, the erstwhile student walks away with a valuable education acquired at community expense. Since a college or professional degree and a license to practice are assets of substantial economic worth, and since community earnings have been drained to pay for the educational expenses, a sound argument can be made for establishing the community's interest in the education. As attorney Thomas Schaeffer argues:

> An education is a valuable asset. Its worth should not be allowed to "walk away" from the marital community that has contributed to its acquisition. . . . When an education, acquired at the expense of the community's funds and labors, is held to be an intangible possession of the student spouse upon dissolution, unjust enrichment and unusual hardship result.[77]

Schaeffer suggests two approaches to evaluating a professional education. One approach involves ascertaining the cost value of the education (which is calculated by adding its purchase price plus its indirect costs). For example, in a 1978 Iowa case the wife supported her husband through law school, contributing approximately $18,000 to his education. When the marriage dissolved, after the husband's graduation from law school, the family had acquired few other assets. The wife claimed an interest in her husband's law degree and the court awarded her $18,000.* Similarly, in a 1980 New Jersey case, a woman who worked to put her husband through medical school was awarded 20 percent of her ex-husband's medical degree, which the court valued at $306,000.†

A second approach to evaluating a professional education involves ascertaining its capacity to produce future income. Once such a value is established, the total sum can be divided, or a percentage awarded to each spouse over time.

A third approach to effect fairness for a couple that has invested solely in one person's education would be to award the second spouse an equivalent educational opportunity. Though this remedy may be limited to younger and less well educated spouses, it would provide equity through reimbursement in-kind. For example, in a 1975 New York case, *Morgan* v. *Morgan*,[78] a wife who put her husband through college and law school sued for reimbursement in-kind so that she could attend medical school. She had dropped out of school to work as an executive secretary in order to support the

---

In re Marriage of Horstmann, 263 N.W. 2d 885 (Iowa, 1978): Although the court awarded the wife an amount roughly equal to her contribution to her husband's education, its justification for the award was the increased value of the husband's earning capacity. This rationale seems to uphold the property value of the license to practice rather than the education per se.

†In this case New Jersey Superior Court Judge Conrad Krafte ruled that the wife was entitled to "some of the value of the medical degree." *American Bar Association Journal* 67 (Jan. 1981), p. 36.

family and pay for her husband's education. Her husband, a Wall Street attorney at the time of the divorce, was now in a position to do the same for her. The lower court granted her request, but the decision was reversed on appeal. Nevertheless, the lower court's opinion sparked considerable interest and undoubtedly will inspire other similar suits.

While claims for a marital interest in a professional degree would seem to stand a better chance of success in community property states where the community's interest in other intangible products of the marital partnership is already recognized, one of the first states to recognize the marital interest in a professional degree was the common law state of Kentucky. In 1979 the Kentucky Court of Appeals ruled that the value of a dentist's license was to be included in the marital property divisible upon divorce.[79]

Professional Goodwill

A second developing area of law establishes the community's interest in the "goodwill value of a professional practice." In the community property states of California and Washington the courts have long recognized the extent to which the professional practice of a lawyer, doctor or dentist can be an asset built through the joint efforts of both partners.[80] In recent cases the financial worth of this goodwill value has been factored into the division of community property upon divorce. Two common law states, New Jersey and Oregon, have also concluded that professional goodwill must be considered marital property in a dissolution action.[81] Unfortunately no court that has recognized goodwill value has yet recognized the existence of a similar type of community asset in a nonprofessional career, such as the value of a union membership, or a painter's or electrician's license, but the principles for that recognition have been established.

Thus far the courts have utilized two different definitions of goodwill:[82] one considers goodwill the advantage a person or enterprise has because of the reputation or position it has established in a business or professional community. The narrower definition, typically used by accountants and economists, considers goodwill the *excess* earnings produced by a person or business over what is considered normal in the field or profession. With these competing definitions and the absence of an established method for calculating goodwill value, the major task for attorneys who claim that goodwill is a divisible marital asset remains that of establishing its value.

Life Insurance and Pensions

The third and the most extensive recognition accorded to intangible assets of marriage concerns life insurance policies and pensions. In both cases the courts have treated the right to future benefits, even though those rights are not guaranteed, as property rights nonetheless. Most insurance policies that are divided at divorce have a cash surrender value. Similarly, many pensions have already vested at the time of the divorce (that is, they are already guaranteed to the wage earner, whether or not the time for retirement has yet arrived). But what is more significant is that the courts have also recognized the community's interest in life insurance policies with no current cash value and in nonvested pensions.[83] The rationale, in both cases, is that these assets have been acquired with community funds (and community efforts) and are therefore part of the marital property.

With respect to insurance, in 1979 the average American family had a $32,400 investment in life insurance.[84] Since insurance policies are typically acquired and maintained with community funds, their inclusion as marital assets would seem obvious. While the cash value of most policies can be ascertained and divided upon divorce, Douglas Anne Munson suggests the usefulness of working out a divorce agreement that provides for the insurance policy (on, let us say the breadwinner's life) to be maintained so that the proceeds can be used as security to assure the ex-spouse's or children's continuous receipt of support.[85] This can be done by designating the ex-spouse or a trust for the children as the irrevocable beneficiary of the policy.*

Along similar lines, pensions are increasingly being recognized as marital assets to be divided upon divorce. For many long-married couples the husband's pension is the most valuable asset acquired during the marriage. In a recent Montana case, for example, the pension of an Air Force colonel who retired after 20 years of active duty was valued as $442,307.

*Munson outlines the necessary procedures to insure this result. Douglas Anne Munson "Putting a Value on Insurance Policies" *Family Advocate* Vol. 2, No. 1 (Summer 1979): 10–13.

The division of pensions has been approached in two ways. In some cases what we call the buy-out method is used: the cash value of the pension at the present time is calculated (by using basic actuarial principles*) and included in the total property to be divided upon divorce. Invariably the pension is awarded to the worker while the spouse is given an offsetting asset (such as a house or stocks and bonds) of *equal* value.

The second approach to dividing a pension, what we call the future-share method, ignores the present value of the pension and focuses instead on the *percentage* that the community owns. Each spouse is then awarded a percentage of the future pension when (and if) it is paid. For example, the Foreign Service Act of 1980 now entitles the divorced wives of Foreign Service officers to a share of their ex-husband's retirement and survivor benefits. The wife's share is pro-rated according to the number of years of the marriage.

To illustrate the future-share method, let us say that a certain California worker's pension permits retirement after 20 years of employment. This worker was employed for ten years prior to his marriage, and has remained employed with the same firm for ten years as a married man. The community thus has a one-half interest in the pension. Since community property is divided equally upon divorce, each spouse is entitled to one-half of the community's share, or one-fourth of the total. In this case then, three-quarters of the vested pension would belong to the husband (his single half plus a quarter from his share of the community) and one-quarter to the wife.

While the divorce court can order a pension to be divided in specific proportions in the future, when it is actually paid, other legal precautions are often necessary to insure that each spouse is awarded his or her appropriate share.† In addition, since the worker is often given the option of deciding the date of retirement and whether or not to elect survivors' benefits,‡ both of which will have a large effect on the amount of monthly payments, these and other items have to be specified at the time of divorce.

*See, generally, Murray Projector "Putting a Value on a Pension Plan" *Family Advocate* Vol. 2, No. 1 (Summer 1979): 37, 41.

†It is important to have a knowledgeable and experienced attorney work out these arrangements.

‡Under the Foreign Service Act of 1980 an employee may not elect against providing a survivor benefit, without the consent of his spouse or former spouse.

When the divorcing couple is young or middle-aged they typically prefer the first (buy-out) method of dealing with the pension to effect a "clean break" in their financial relationship. In addition, there are obviously many more risks involved in the future-share procedure. However, the latter may be useful for families that have no offsetting assets and no means of securing a loan or bond to effect a buyout.

Two recent cases have challenged the right of state courts to divide federal pensions (in contrast to private or state pensions) upon divorce.* While the California Supreme Court and the highest courts of several other states have held that federal pensions are part of the community property, state courts in Texas and Alaska have held that federal law requires federal pension benefits to be paid exclusively to the federal employee, and not to a former spouse. The 1981 U.S. Supreme Court adopted the latter view and upheld the appeal of an Army physician who challenged a California court's division of his military pension upon divorce.†

There is no question, however, about the divorce court's jurisdiction in dividing private and state pensions acquired during marriage according to state law. Divorce court judges in California are currently calculating the community interest in life insurance policies and nonvested pensions, if they have been acquired partially or wholly during marriage, and awarding each spouse a proportionate share of that interest upon divorce.

The courts in the future might use a similar approach to estimate the extent of the community's interest in one partner's career. While the task would be considerably more complicated than the

*In 1979 a male railroad employee appealed a California court decision that awarded his wife a share of his retirement benefits upon divorce in *Hisquierdo* v. *Hisquierdo* 439 U.S. 572 (1979). The U.S. Supreme Court ruled that the husband's pension was covered by the Railroad Retirement Act which forbade the assignment or attachment of the annuity and that this federal law preempted the state's community property law. A similar appeal from a California court's award of a military pension was upheld by the U.S. Supreme Court in June 1981 in *McCarty* v. *McCarty*, Case No. 80–5 discussed below.

†In *McCarty* v. *McCarty* the California court awarded half of the doctor's military pension to his wife when they divorced as they had been married for his entire term of military service. The physician claimed that military pensions were established solely for the benefit of military personnel and that they were covered by the federal law specifying that military pension payments are not assignable. The 1981 U.S. Supreme Court agreed and ruled that state courts may not divide military pensions as part of the community property upon divorce. Case No. 80–5.

exercise cited above, that factor should not deter the courts from recognizing the need for a fair division of *all* the assets of a marital partnership.*

Thus far we have focused this discussion of career assets on the single-income family in which the wife is not employed outside the family enterprise, whatever that enterprise. But what about dual-career families? Should they be treated differently? Professor Susan Prager argues persuasively that they should not—for inevitably both spouses' careers will be products of the marriage. As Prager observes,

> By and large it is not practicable for each spouse in the two-earner marriage to make employment decisions on a completely individualized basis, for each decision affects both spouses in very different ways.
>
> Some couples may attempt to make employment choices that will maximize opportunities for both of them. . . .
>
> In some marriages one spouse's career will be subordinated temporarily, perhaps because of the need for education or the presence of children. Educations may be obtained in serial fashion, in order to maximize economic potential, with each spouse supporting the other while he or she is in school. . . .
>
> Other couples may conclude that it is desirable to structure their choices to give permanent priority to the advancement of one of them rather than to equalize opportunities. . . .
>
> Still others may see the two-earner marriage as an opportunity to reduce the importance of work. Having two shared incomes may make it economically possible for both to work less or to hold less demanding jobs. This may seem desirable for numerous personal reasons, including considerations of health or the attraction of more leisure time. . . .[86]

A scheme that provides for all marital assets, including the career assets of both spouses, to be divided equally would establish an equitable arrangement for sharing the benefits and sacrifices of a dual-career marriage. The California courts have already adopted the approach in dealing with the pensions of the two spouses at divorce. There would be little difficulty extending the scheme to other career assets and it is a system that is eminently applicable to the evolving patterns of modern families.

*Once courts recognize careers as marital assets they should have no more difficulty in valuing two careers than they now have in valuing and dividing a family's two pensions.

The community property approach to compensating house-wives is more likely to appeal to couples in longer marriages while the wage-benefit approach may seem more appropriate to others, and, as we have noted, the two are not mutually exclusive. Here as elsewhere, we strongly advocate giving couples the option to choose among alternatives. To allow them that choice, the present restrictions on pay for housewives, and on contracts between husbands and wives, must be abolished. From the societal perspective, however, community property principles are strongly recommended for all states because they would most effectively bring the law into line with the ideals of most couples entering marriage,* and would most truly reflect the partnership ideals that family law theoretically seeks to encourage.

*Note the overwhelming preference for community property and sharing principles among both married and cohabiting couples reported in the Appendix on page 427.

CHAPTER 4

The Responsibility for Children

The Legal Tradition

Procreation has always been considered one of the essential purposes of marriage, if not its prime justification. As the U.S. Supreme Court stated in *Skinner* v. *Oklahoma*, "Marriage and procreation are fundamental to the very existence and survival of the race."[1] "Marital intercourse, so that children may be born, is an obligation of the marriage contract, and . . . the foundation upon which must rest the perpetuation of society and civilization."[2] As the Massachusetts Supreme Judicial Court noted in *Reynolds* v. *Reynolds*,[3] ". . . one of the leading and most important objects of the institution of marriage under our laws is the procreation of children. . . ."[4] And as recently as 1967 the Supreme Court of Mississippi declared "Marriage is [the] legal . . . union of two persons . . . for the purpose of establishing a family."[5] In 1972 the Ohio Supreme Court echoed the same utilitarian view: "Marriage is a device intended to perpetuate family groups. . . ."[6]

The law's assumption that procreation and the rearing of children are primary in marriage has been so widely shared in the larger society that it has rarely been challenged directly, and hence has rarely been dealt with *explicitly* in judicial opinions. However, it is implicitly endorsed in many areas of law in one way or another: annulments are granted on the basis of procreative failure and fraud; premarital and extramarital sexual relationships are prohibited to ensure that procreation occurs only within marriage; and same-sex unions are banned because they cannot produce children. The law's encouragement of procreation is also reflected in the priority the law gives to women's maternal roles; the structure of incentives it embodies in tax laws; the numerous obstacles it places in the way of contraception, voluntary sterilization, and abortion; and the series of government programs it has created to reward citizens for having children.

The procreation assumption has deep historical roots. According to Professor David Daube, the concept of a duty to procreate goes back to a time well before the dawn of the Judeo-Christian era when Nomadic tribes faced the ever-present danger of being outnumbered and overrun by their enemies.[7] At such a time obligatory procreation served the ends of cultural survival through sheer numbers. The Romans attempted to further similar political aims by legislation: "[The law] penalized men between twenty-five and sixty, and women between twenty and fifty, if unmarried or married but childless."[8] Religions in the West (and elsewhere) translated this ancient imperative into divine law.

In this context it is not surprising to find that one of the major concerns of family law has been the establishment of rules and procedures to ensure that children are born, cared for, and supported within a legal marriage. The traditional marriage contract assigned the responsibility for the child's care and nurturance to the mother and obligated the father to provide the child's support. This division of parental duties paralleled those enumerated in the first three chapters, with husbands charged with breadwinning, and wives with care and nurturance.

And yet even a brief investigation into legal history discloses that our current assumptions about appropriate male and female parental roles are by no means grounded in immutable natural law. For example, in the past it was assumed that fathers should have the major responsibility for their children. "The English tradition was that the father was the natural guardian of the children and controlled their education and religious training."[9] He had the primary right to his children's services and, in return, he was liable for their support and maintenance. Child care was perceived primarily as child training, and fathers were presumed to have superior skills and knowledge (especially where boys were concerned) for this vocationally oriented relationship.

It is therefore not surprising to find that if the parents separated, the English law gave custody of a legitimate child to the father, not the mother.[10] As Blackstone stated the common law rule, the father had a "natural right" to the custody of his children; the mother had no power over them; she was entitled only to their reverence and respect.[11] For example, in one widely cited English case in 1804, *King* v. *De Manneville*, a nursing mother took her infant and fled home to escape her French husband's physical cruelty and abuse. A British magistrate, Lord Ellenborough, ordered the infant returned to his father, because the father was "entitled by law to custody of his child."[12] In view of the well-known English reluctance to accord privileges to the French, the only way to understand such an order is to recognize that in that day children were seen as property, pure and simple, and like all other types of property and chattel they had to be returned to their legal owner if they were "stolen" from him.

"The common law preference for the father was secure," Foster and Freed note, "as long as feudalism flourished, but it disintegrated with the advent of the industrial revolution."[13] As fathers moved off the farm into wage labor in factories and offices, women's maternal instincts were "discovered," and mothers became increasingly associated with child care. Thus, it was only when women assumed the *de facto* full-time responsibility for child rearing that legislators and judges came to view the mother as the person "naturally" responsible for children.

Today, however, labor force composition is changing again, and women are no longer likely to be full-time housewives and mothers. Indeed, the most rapid increase in female labor force participation has been among women with young children. By 1975, 37 percent of the mothers of preschool children were in the labor force, as were 52 percent of the married women with children between the ages of 6 and 17.[14] With the dramatic drop in full-time motherhood, even among mothers of very young children,* the

*These statistics are discussed in greater detail in Chapter 7.

law's assumption that women can and should bear the full-time responsibility for child care is growing increasingly inappropriate. Nevertheless, this assumption remains entrenched in family law.

The clearest reflection of the law's continuing assumption that women's primary responsibility lies in child care is to be found in child custody decisions. Twentieth century case law has established the presumption that prefers mothers as the custodians of their children after divorce, particularly if the children are of "tender years."[15] This maternal presumption was established almost entirely through judicial decisions rather than by statutes. For while most statutes have put the wife on an equal footing with the husband, and have instructed the courts to award custody in the best interest of the child, judges typically have held that *it is in the child's best interest not to be separated from the mother*—unless she has been shown to be unfit.[16]

"The child's best interest" has thus evolved into a judicially constructed presumption that the love and nurturance of a fit mother is always in the child's (and society's) best interest. The result has been a consistent pattern of decisions that both justify and further reinforce the maternal presumption. In fact, as one 1942 decision states, the preference for the mother is "not open to question, and indeed *it is universally recognized that the mother is the natural custodian of her young. This view proceeds on the well known fact that there is no satisfactory substitute for a mother's love.*"[17]

Over the past fifty years the assumption that the mother is the natural and proper custodian of the children has been so widely accepted that it has rarely been questioned, and even more rarely challenged. As Alan Roth asserts, many of the rationales offered by the courts for the maternal preference have the ring of divine-right doctrine.[18] One Idaho court, for example, concluded that the preference for the mother "needs no argument to support it because it arises out of the very nature and instincts of motherhood; Nature has ordained it."[19] Similarly, a Florida court declared: "Nature has prepared a mother to bear and rear her young and to perform many services for them and to give them many attentions for which the father is not equipped."[20] A 1958 New Jersey Court found "an inexorable natural force" dictating maternal custody awards[21]; and a Maryland decision found:

> The so-called preference for the mother as the custodian particularly of younger children is simply a recognition by the law, as well as by

the commonality of man, of *the universal verity that the maternal tie is so primordial that it should not lightly be severed or attenuated.*[22]

More recent justifications for the mother presumption seem to have shifted from the "ordination of Nature" to what a 1975 Utah court referred to as the "wisdom inherent in traditional patterns of thought."[23] Similarly, a 1973 appellate court found:

> In Pennsylvania, supported by the wisdom of the ages, it has long been the rule that in the absence of compelling reasons to the contrary, a mother has the right to custody of her children over any other person, particularly so, where the children are of tender years. . . . In fact, *that the best interests of children of tender years will be best served under a mother's guidance and control is one of the strongest presumptions in the law. . . .*[24]

The wisdom of maternal presumption has also been supported by child psychologists emphasizing the unique relationship between an infant and its mother. Social scientists have asserted that women have "an inherent nurturing ability that predisposes them to be more interested in and able to care for children; that they are biologically and psychologically destined to rear the children; and that the well-being and optimal development of children requires mothers in a way that does not require fathers."[25]

More recently the social science evidence adduced to support the maternal presumption has been challenged, but the presumption itself has been considered wise because it avoids "the social costs" of contested cases.[26] In fact, it is interesting to note that both those who favor the presumption and those who oppose it agree that it serves the purpose of expediency: it spares the court the time and effort required for thorough investigation. For example, Professor Robert Levy candidly states that one advantage of the rule is to "relieve the judge of extensive fact-finding and decision-making responsibility."[27]

In light of the courts' widespread reliance on the mother presumption, it is surprising to learn that as of 1975, only three states had an implicit maternal preference in their statutes for divorce actions.[28] Most statutes are sex-neutral: they provide for custody to be awarded in "the best interest of the child."[29] But this standard leaves the judge with an enormous amount of discretion, and judges can easily maintain an explicit maternal presumption by equating the child's best interest with maternal care.[30] For example, the statutory language of the Uniform Marriage and Divorce Act clearly provides for custody to be awarded according to the sex-neutral criterion of the "best interest of the child." But the comments appended to explain the custody section of the Act include a passage that suggest a mother presumption:

> Although none of the familiar presumptions developed by the case law are mentioned here, the language of the section is consistent with preserving such rules of thumb. *The preference for the mother as custodian of young children* when all things are equal, for example, *is simply a shorthand method of expressing the best interest of children* —and this section enjoins judges to decide custody cases according to that general standard.[31]

Thus, even though the majority of the commissioners who drafted the Act did not formally endorse the mother preference, it found its way into the commentary as an "example" of a desirable rule of thumb.

Our California research suggests that most judges believe that mother custody is, in fact, in the best interest of the children. Eighty-one percent of the Los Angeles family court judges interviewed in 1975 thought that they and their colleagues still held a presumption in favor of the mother for custody of preschool children.[32] Similarly, a 1976 Illinois report indicates that judges hearing divorce cases held an "underlying assumption that the mother would assume custody and the father would assume support obligations."[33]

Even in the last decade, when many sex-based laws have been challenged, and when the passage of state Equal Rights Amendments would seem to require the elimination of the maternal preference, the case law in many states has continued to uphold it. For example, in 1974 the Utah Supreme Court "brushed aside" a father's equal protection challenge to a maternal preference custody statute stating that "the contention might have some merit to it in a proper case *if the father was equally [as] gifted in lactation as the mother*."[34] Along the same lines a 1978 Oklahoma court decided that gender-based preferences did not constitute illegal sex discrimination because "the old notion that a child of tender years needs a mother more than a father" was still sound:

> We believe that consideration of the cultural, psychological and emotional characteristics that are gender-related make this custodial preference one of "those instances where the sex-centered generalization actually [coincides with] fact. . . . [T]his statute is not concerned en-

tirely with the "rights" of parents to their children. In addition to, and far beyond, their rights, the paramount purpose of the statute is to serve the welfare and best interest of children.[35]

As of 1978, according to attorneys Henry Foster and Doris Jonas Freed, the tender years doctrine remained "gospel" (unless clearly in conflict with a child's best interest) in 14 states, and in at least 12 other states there was still a preference for a fit mother, other things being equal.[36] Even among the 17 states with Equal Rights Amendments the maternal presumption was "alive and well" in eight states, although it supposedly had been discarded in the other nine.

The empirical pattern of child custody awards clearly reflects the strength of the maternal presumption. Since the turn of the century mothers have been awarded custody of their children in the overwhelming majority of divorce decrees,* and the pattern has remained relatively stable over the years. After reviewing the minimal empirical data available from nine states between 1875 and 1949, Jacobson found that mothers typically received custody of their children in all states and in every decade.[37] Goode reports that women received custody of their children in 95 percent of the divorce cases he examined in Michigan in 1948,[38] and a 1960 Maine

---

*For about 25 years after the close of World War II there was a steady increase in the proportion of divorces in which children were involved. In 1948, 42 percent of the divorcing couples had children, whereas by 1966 the percentage had increased to 62 percent. During those years the number of children per divorcing couple also increased from .85 in 1953 to 1.34 children per divorce in 1968. Jessie Bernard, "No News, But New Ideas," in P. Bohannan, ed., *Divorce and After: An Analysis of the Emotional and Social Problems of Divorce* (Garden City, N.Y.: Doubleday, 1970), p. 6.

More recently, however, the percentage of divorcing couples with children has declined. Data from the California Divorce Law Research Project indicate that the percentage of Los Angeles divorcing couples with minor children declined from 62 percent in 1968 to approximately 50 percent in 1977. The mean number of minor children per divorce also has dropped, from 1.28 in 1968, to .98 in 1972, to .87 in 1977. Lenore J. Weitzman, *No-Fault Divorce in California*, unpublished manuscript, California Divorce Law Research Project, Center for the Study of Law and Society, University of California at Berkeley, 1980.

But despite the percentage decrease of divorces involving children and the declining average number of minor children involved in each divorce, a nationwide *rising divorce rate* has caused a steady rise in the *absolute numbers* of children involved in divorce. A high of 1,123,000 children were involved in a divorce in 1975; since then the number has remained virtually unchanged, and currently more than one million minor children are involved in divorces each year in the United States. U.S. Bureau of the Census, "Divorce, Child Custody and Child Support," *Current Population Reports*, series P–23, no. 84 (1979):1.

study showed mother custody in 87 percent of the cases.[39] On a nationwide basis, it has been estimated that mothers received custody in 90 percent of the divorces in 1968.[40]

The pattern of custody awards in California provides an illuminating example of the persistence of the maternal preference despite conscious legislative attempts to institutionalize a sex-neutral standard. Until 1973, the statutory law in California contained an explicit maternal preference regarding custody awards of young children. In 1973 that directive was removed and custody was thereafter to be awarded "according to the best interest of the child." Nevertheless, mothers were awarded custody in the overwhelming majority of divorces granted under both laws. A random sample of 1968 California divorce decrees disclosed that mothers were awarded sole physical custody of their children in 88 percent of the cases, fathers in 9 percent, and in the remaining 3 percent the children were either divided between the two parents, or awarded jointly to them or to third parties.[41] In 1977, *four years* after the new sex-neutral standard was instituted, the distribution of custody awards remained virtually unchanged: mothers continued to receive physical (and legal) custody of their children in nearly 90 percent of all cases.

It would be clearly erroneous, however, to attribute the overwhelming predominance of maternal custody awards to judicial attitudes alone. In most cases the divorcing couple decides (or takes it for granted) that their children will be better off living with the mother, and in other cases their attorneys may assume or suggest that the wife should have custody.* Custody decisions are obviously influenced by many factors, including prevailing social norms and assumptions about the mother as the primary caretaker. Nevertheless, courts and laws have an impact on custody decisions because they establish the normative framework within which custody decisions are made. Judges thus set the boundaries that restrict the cus-

---

*In 1977–1978 interviews with 228 recently divorced California men and women, 96% of the mothers reported that they wanted custody of their children after divorce compared to 57% of the fathers. However, the father's interest in custody fluctuated considerably depending on how the question was asked, and only 13% of the fathers "wanted" custody enough to pursue the matter in the legal process, either formally or informally. These data are discussed further later in this chapter on page 112 and in more detail in Lenore J. Weitzman and Ruth B. Dixon,"Child Custody Awards: Legal Standards and Empirical Patterns for Child Custody, Support and Visitation After Divorce," *University of California at Davis Law Review* Vol. 12, No. 2 (Summer 1979).

tody options that divorcing couples (and their attorneys) perceive to be available. It is to these effects of the legal system—and their consequences—that we now turn.

Legal Consequences of the Maternal Preference

The law's preference for the mother as the child's caretaker and for the father as the child's source of financial support has important legal and social effects. Here we will examine the legal consequences of the maternal presumption. The social effects are examined in the following section; the final section focuses on the law governing child support.

The major legal consequence of the preference for the mother as the child's caretaker has been to use women's parental responsibilities as a justification for excluding them from full work and citizenship roles. A second effect has been to deprive the father of an equal chance to become the custodial parent after divorce. And a third effect has been the court's tendency to neglect the child's interests and needs.

Since this discussion focuses on the negative effects of the maternal presumption it is important to emphasize that the presumption —and maternal custody—has had many positive effects as well. It is only because the literature of the last century has so universally assumed that *all* the effects of the mother preference were positive (and beneficial to women) that it is necessary to discuss the less well recognized burdens that accompany this "privilege."

The Exclusion of Women from Nonmaternal Roles

As we note above, the law has typically assumed that a woman's responsibility for child care takes precedence over everything else; hence it is not surprising that this responsibility has been used as a justification for treating everything else women do as secondary. Furthermore, the courts have tended to treat *all* women as wives and mothers, whether they were married or not and whether or not they had children—from the 1872 *Bradwell* decisions that barred married women from the practice of law because their "paramount destiny" was as wives and mothers,[42] through the 1909 *Muller* decision that upheld "protective" labor laws for women (to safeguard their ability to produce future generations of "vigorous off-spring");[43] to the 1961 *Hoyt* decision that allowed Florida to exclude women from jury service so they could remain at the center of home and family life.[44] However, as we saw in Chapter 3, many of the legal regulations that were designed to give women "privileged" treatment have served, in practice, to deny them equal participation as citizens and as workers.

This pattern is perhaps most clearly evident in the rules and regulations surrounding pregnancy. Pregnant women and new mothers seeking to maintain employment continuity have been forced to take unpaid leave from jobs for fixed periods of time before and after the birth of a child,* and have been systematically denied normal employee rights and benefits such as health insurance, job security, seniority, sick leave, and disability coverage. In fact, as recently as 1977 the U.S. Supreme Court upheld an employer's right to exclude pregnancy-related disabilities from a company health insurance program.[45]† As Babcock et al. conclude, treating pregnancy as unique allows employers to relegate mothers to the position of second-class employees, and thereby reinforces the primacy of their child-care responsibilities at home.[46]

While the law that assigns child care to women has frequently been justified as "natural," it is important to distinguish the capacity to bear children, which nature has given to women, from the responsibility for rearing them, which is a socially (and legally) assigned role. The second does not necessarily follow from the first. The law has long behaved as if it did, however. Today, a woman's role in childbearing remains central to the legal view of her proper role and place,[47] making "this unique physical characteristic perhaps the most fertile ground for stereotype and misunderstanding and the last, most stubborn and intractable bastion of discrimination."[48]

*Elizabeth Duncan Koontz, former director of the Women's Bureau observes that: "Such policies are left over from the days, extending into this century—when pregnant women were forced to remain at home—when pregnancy was viewed as obscene. This feeling is still widespread, frequently disguised as concern for the protection of women's interest." Elizabeth Koontz, "Childbirth and Child-rearing Leave: Job Related Benefits," *New York University Law Forum* 17, p. 480.

†In 1978, however, in the closing hours of the 95th Congress, U.S. lawmakers negated this decision by passing the pregnancy disability bill as an amendment to Title VII of the 1964 Civil Rights Act. This law now forbids discrimination on the basis of "pregnancy, childbirth, or related medical conditions." See *The Spokeswoman*, vol. 9, no. 6 (December 15, 1978), p. 3.

The Father's Interest in Custody

In many respects the maternal preference doctrine has been convenient for men. As Wisconsin Supreme Court Justice Heffernan aptly recognizes, "child rearing and child care, by and large, have worked out very nicely for the males. A substantial portion of parental responsibility has thus been transferred with good conscience to the female, because by it she is rewarded and 'ennobled'."[49]

On the other hand, it is easy to see how the hard-to-overcome maternal presumption may at times work against fathers and even threaten their right to equal protection of the law.[50] As Lila Tritico notes, "if the rationale behind a preference to the mother is based upon the idea that the mother, because she is a woman, is better suited for rearing children, this denies the father's interest in his children and places a great burden upon him to assert this interest by rebutting the presumption."[51]

In other words, from the father's perspective there are two negative legal effects of the presumption: an abridgement of his constitutional rights to due process and equal protection of the law, and an unwholesome pressure to defend his interests through the use of evidence likely to have a detrimental effect on the continuing relationship between the two parents, as well as on the child.

A 1973 New York case first recognized the constitutional issue. In *Watts* v. *Watts*, the father contended that the judicial preference for maternal custody denied him equal protection of the law.[52] Judge Sybil Hart Cooper of the New York Family Court agreed, and ruled that arbitrary gender-based presumptions about which spouse is better suited to care for young children were impermissible. *Watts* is the strongest constitutional assault on maternal preference to date.[53] It is especially noteworthy because the New York presumption was established by judicial interpretation of a sex-neutral statute (i.e. the best interest of the child). It therefore suggests that common law as well as statutory preferences for the mother are open to constitutional challenge.

The second legal consequence of the traditional rule is to encourage fathers to rely on moral accusations to bolster their contentions that they would be superior custodial parents. Since a father's custodial qualifications are not usually considered under a mother-presumption standard until he can prove the mother unfit, he bears the double burden of showing not only that he can provide a desirable environment for his child, but also that an award to the mother will be detrimental to the child's welfare.[54] To do this he must typically document her immoral conduct, her mental instability, or her cruelty to the child. For example, the *Family Law Reporter* offers the following advice to lawyers representing fathers in contested custody cases:

> Perhaps the quickest route for a divorcing father to take when he wants custody of his young offspring is to show that his wife is personally and emotionally unstable. What with the traumas inherent in any divorce, such a showing is often easy to make. And when there is a flavor of sexual indiscretion about the instability, this is often enough to overcome the "tender years presumption" that still holds sway in many states and prefers the mother over the father when young children are involved in a custody battle.[55]

Such standards of maternal unfitness may in fact have little bearing on the wife's real effectiveness as a mother, and can easily serve to increase antagonisms between the two adults who will, after the contest and shouting, both continue to be the child's parents.

Fathers who want to obtain a *change* of custody (that is, after the children have been awarded to the mother) are urged to follow much the same evidentiary formula.[56] For example, in 1980 the U.S. Supreme Court upheld an Illinois state court ruling (by refusing to rehear the case) that awarded custody of three children to the father because the mother was living with a man to whom she was not married. The Illinois Court held that the mother's behavior had demonstrated a "disregard for existing standards of conduct" and could be harmful to the children.* Along the same lines in *Brim* v. *Brim*,[57] a father persuaded a 1975 court to take his children away from their mother and grant him custody instead because the mother was living with a man she had no intention of marrying. In another 1975 case, *Carper* v. *Rokus*, custody was changed to the father because the man the mother remarried was seven years younger and the court considered the mother's choice of a younger husband a clear indication of abnormality (because "normal women" do not marry men seven years younger).[58] In this case, the natural father was living with his parents, who agreed to care for the children when he was at work. These rulings suggest that fathers

*Jarrett v. *Jarrett*, No. 79-1735, decided October 20, 1980. Illinois is one of the states in which unmarried cohabitation is still a crime. The states which make cohabitation and fornication criminal acts are listed in Chapter 14, pages 367–8.

stand a good chance of gaining custody if they can show that the mother's life-style deviates from the traditional "moral" model.*

One may certainly question the wisdom of basing custody decisions on standards that may have little to do with the effective care of children. In fact, these evidentiary rules tend, if anything, to discourage fathers who are sincerely interested in their child's welfare, and to encourage those who want to use custody as a vehicle for harassing or punishing their ex-wives.† Ironically, it is the father who "plays dirty" (by monitoring his ex-wife's behavior to expose "immoral" acts that will prove her unfit) who is most likely to win custody.

In contrast the system discourages the fathers who, by dint of their preference for a reasoned challenge, are more likely to be just and loving custodial parents. In fact, the sincerely caring father may abandon his efforts to obtain custody rather than subject his child to the effects of a hostile and protracted court battle based on moral accusations. Meanwhile, the father who cares less about the effects of a custody battle on his children and who is willing to resort to moral blackmail—in short, the father who is probably least fit to be a "good" custodian—is encouraged to pursue his claim.

While this discussion has focused on the legal effects of the maternal preference, it is important to underscore the social and emotional deprivation that many fathers feel when they are compelled to live apart from their children after divorce. Many fathers perceive the legal standards for custody (and visitation) as obstacles to their enjoyment of a full parental relationship with their children.

Clearly, forcing the father to prove the mother unfit has detrimental results for everyone involved. It greatly heightens the adver-

---

*In a few recent cases judges have ignored these old moral standards. For instance, in *Marriage of Moore* (531 P.2d 995, Colo. App., 1975), an apellate court reversed a lower court that had granted a father's motion for change of custody. The mother was living with a man and the lower court deemed her conduct immoral, even though a welfare report had recommended her as the preferable custodian. In returning custody to the mother, the appellate judge found absolutely no evidence that the mother's relationship with the man was in any way detrimental to her children.

†The extent to which custody contests are used by vindictive spouses to embarrass or harass an ex-spouse or to gain an advantage in a property settlement is discussed in Lenore J. Weitzman, *No-Fault Divorce in California*, unpublished manuscript, Center for the Study of Law and Society, University of California, Berkeley, 1980.

sary nature of the divorce process and contributes to what Margaret Mead considered one of the major shortcomings of our system of divorce —its failure to provide "some kind of viable relationship between parents who are no longer married to each other, so that there may be continuing relationships between the child and both his parents, and so the child's identity is not shattered by divorce."[59] The labeling of one parent as unfit or bad not only distorts the reality of most relationships, it may also create serious conflicts for the child (and may be traumatic for at least one of the adults as well).[60]

The legal context in which child custody is awarded can easily lead one to assume that the low rate of father custody awards is a result of legal bias against men who seek custody. A second explanation for the low rate of father custody awards is that most men have little interest in obtaining custody to begin with: both they and their wives prefer to have the children live with their mothers after divorce. There appears to be some merit in each of these views.

Undoubtedly, maternal preference encourages bitterness and resignation in the father who feels that he has little chance of receiving either custody or due process in his claim. This is the assertion of Equal Rights for Fathers, an organization formed to monitor and ensure the enforcement of laws that theoretically give men an equal right to child custody.[61] They contend that there is a "quiet conspiracy" among judges, probation departments, conciliation courts, and even the fathers' attorneys to dissuade divorced men from gaining custody of their children. *

This conspiracy theory has some basis in fact. Professor Levy, for one, has frankly advocated writing a mother preference into the Uniform Marriage and Divorce Act precisely to discourage fathers from entering custody battles because of the "social cost" of contested cases and the trauma they seem to produce.[62]

However, the legal bias explanation presupposes that when fathers do ask for custody their success rate is low. Our California

---

*As of March 1980 there were approximately 175 fathers' rights and divorce reform organizations in the U.S. Bob Hirschfeld, publisher of *Single Dad's Lifestyle*, surveyed the 175 organizations and found that "they provide local lawyer referrals, assistance in pro-se filings, support groups/rap sessions, legislative lobbying, courtroom observers, picketing/demonstrations, publicity/consciousness raising, activities for custodial or noncustodial children, and sympathetic listening to problems of newly divorced dads. Seventy-two percent of the organizations publish a newsletter. None have daycare facilities for smaller kids." *Marriage and Divorce Today*, Vol. 5, No. 33 (March 31, 1980): 2.

data indicate that, on the contrary, when fathers ask for custody their chances of obtaining it are very good indeed: in 1977, fully 63 percent of the divorced fathers who requested sole physical custody of their children were awarded it.[63] Further analysis of these cases reveals that the mother had often agreed to the arrangement either explicitly or implicitly. However, even in the subsample of cases in which there was no parental agreement—and custody was *fully contested* in court, *the judge awarded custody to the father in one out of three cases.*

This success rate for fathers suggests that most men do not have custody because they do not want it. Further support for this view comes from our interviews with recently divorced California men. Among those with children under 18, 40 percent indicate they have never thought of having custody of their children and if given the option would simply reject it. Both they and their wives assume that children belong with their mothers. Another 20 percent of the divorced men report having had positive thoughts about having their children with them after divorce, but when they are "being practical," they say they are not really willing to assume custody.

The remaining 40 percent of the men say they have seriously considered seeking custody at some point in the divorce process. Some of them were later dissuaded by their wives, others by their lawyers, and still others by their own realization of the practical and financial difficulties they might encounter. Many of these men talk of inevitable conflicts between their work commitments and their children's needs. Others focus on their lack of homemaking and child-care skills, still others on their need for time and their new social lives. Finally, the financial cost of housing, food, clothing and other child-related expenses seem formidable to many. It is also likely that at least some of the men who profess to be considering custody are doing so primarily to threaten their ex-wives or to gain some advantage in economic bargaining. Eventually, our figures indicate, only 13 fathers in 100, one out of every eight divorced fathers decides he wants custody enough to pursue the matter through the legal process, either formally or informally.

These data suggest that the major reason for the low rate of father custody awards is that the vast majority of divorcing fathers simply do not want custody of their children after divorce. This finding does not, however, negate the importance of the maternal presumption barrier for the fathers who do.

Detrimental Effects on the Child

When custody battles focus on the parents—and in particular on the mother's "fitness"—factors crucial to the child's well-being are often overshadowed. Professors Goldstein, Freud, and Solnit argue that the law should make the child's needs paramount both in initial custody decisions and in decisions about change of custody.[64] They contend that these needs are best served when the child maintains a continuous relationship with a single adult—the "psychological parent."*

The contrast between this position and the automatic mother presumption is highlighted in the 1972 case of *Estes* v. *Estes*.[65] In *Estes* a mother originally awarded custody after a divorce, temporarily ceded it to her ex-husband for economic reasons. After the children had lived with the father for three years, the mother sought to regain custody. The trial court found that the father had provided "excellent care" and a sound environment for the children and that they had blossomed in his charge. The mother presented no evidence to show that the children needed to be removed from the father's custody or that they would fare better with her. Nevertheless, the court again awarded custody to the mother reasoning that unless a mother is proven unfit it is in the children's best interest to live with her. However, Justice Barham's dissenting opinion in this case clearly states the argument against the court's reliance on the traditional maternal preference:

> Neither the trial court nor the majority has given one single reason why the ultimate best welfare of these children will be served by removing them from an ideal home situation where they lived happily and securely over three years. Both have simply decided that because the mother is a *woman*, some superior right rides with her. . . .
>
> In this day and time there is less and less reason for granting preference to the mother. The physiological basis which once existed for the very young infants has almost disappeared. For infants not nursing there is no physiological basis. The social basis for favoring the

---

*Goldstein, Freud, and Solnit argue that it is best for the child to have a single, permanent custodial parent who has power to make unilateral decisions concerning all aspects of the child's well-being, including visitation arrangements and the extent of the child's relationship with the other parent. (They also propose elimination of the court's continuing jurisdiction over visitation and custody.) If this proposition were widely adopted, it is possible that most divorced fathers would have even less contact with their children than they do now.

mother which once existed because the mother was the homemaker and child tender while the father was the breadwinner has almost totally disappeared. . . .

There was absolutely no showing that the children *needed* to be removed. Moreover, there was no showing that removal would be *beneficial* to the children. The trial court stated not one advantage which would obtain in the mother's custody. There was no basis for changing the custody of these children.[66]

A few courts are now beginning to focus more sharply on the child's needs, and on the parents' relationship to the child, instead of upholding the mother presumption and traditional moral standards of fitness. For example, in 1975, a New York court[67] allowed a mother to retain custody of her children even though she was living with a man whom she did not intend to marry. The court decided that the mother's living situation did not interfere with the quality of her care for the children. Whereas a traditional court would probably have evaluated this woman's behavior in terms of moral fitness and on that basis judged her an "unfit mother," a court that is focused on the children could view the same behavior as irrelevant to the more important issue of the quality of the parent–child relationship.

The new emphasis on the parent–child relationship is not confined to mother–child interaction. Courts looking to the child's needs have used the same standard to compare the parents. For example, in 1973, in *Moezie* v. *Moezie*[68] a Washington, D.C., court awarded custody of three children to the father because of his superior nurturing abilities. The *Moezie* court recognized that both parents were "fit" and could provide a good home for the children; the decision was based wholly on the court's assessment of the superior quality of the father–child relationship. *Moezie* set an important precedent in using a sex-neutral standard that emphasized the child's needs.

If more courts were willing to accept the possibility of paternal nurturance and to base their custody decisions on the quality of the relationship between the parents and the child, all parties would gain. Not only would the child benefit from being placed with the more effective caretaker, but both parents would benefit as well— for these standards would signal an end to the outmoded moral criteria for judging a mother's fitness that, as we shall see below, has often been as much of a burden for the mother as it has been for the father.

Social and Psychological Effects of the Maternal Preference

The maternal preference has three important social and psychological consequences. First, it creates pressures for custodial mothers to conform to the traditional (and narrow) legal ideal of a "good" or "fit" mother. Second, it serves to reinforce the mother's traditional role as housewife and mother, and thus her dependency on her ex-husband. Finally, it may cause the woman who does not want custody to feel guilty and deviant, and thus impede her efforts to break out of the traditional female role after divorce.

While the law's assumption about appropriate maternal roles may appear reasonable to the ideal-typical divorced mother who wants to devote herself totally to raising her children (and has the financial resources to do so), the reality of most divorced mothers' lives is far from this ideal. Most of them have to work, and most of them cannot devote themselves entirely to their children. They face a multitude of competing demands as employees, homemakers, and all-around social beings. In this context, the mother who spends a lot of time and energy on her career (or on simply holding onto her job) and the mother who begins dating or living with a new man may (accurately) perceive that the legal system could question their "fitness" and take away their children.

Most of the contested custody cases cited above make it evident how the custodial mother who does not conform to traditional standards of morality might indeed be successfully challenged by her ex-husband. The concern of the employed mother is no less justified: one of the instances in which courts appear most willing to change custody from mother to father is that in which the mother works and the father promises to care for the children personally or to provide another female relative (such as his mother or his new wife) to care for them.

Such was the case in one 1974 Colorado action,[69] in which a father was able to gain custody after he remarried and his new wife agreed to stay home and care for the child while the natural mother worked. Similarly, in a 1976 Iowa case, a father was granted custody when the child's grandmother (the father's mother), who had cared for the child during the marriage, assured the court that she would continue her care under her son's custody[70] whereas the wife would have placed the child in a day-care center while she worked.

A divorcing mother who is openly committed to a job or career may be threatened with a custody battle for that reason. For example, in a 1977 Virginia divorce case the father was awarded custody of his two daughters, aged two and four, because, even though *both* parents worked full time, the court thought "the mother was less willing than the father to place her obligations to the children ahead of her job and her involvement with a male co-worker."[71]

Reacting to the implicit double standard used for "working mothers" vs. "working fathers," a team of feminist attorneys, headed by Kristin Booth Glen and aided by an *amicus curiae* brief from the National Organization for Women appealed a similar decision in New York. The case* involved a remarried father who attempted to regain custody from his now single former wife. The father, a high school graduate, was employed as a butcher. His second wife was a full-time housewife. The mother, who was originally awarded custody, went back to school after the divorce and obtained a college degree. She financed her education through grants, scholarships, and part-time work including part-time teaching in a Head Start program in which her son was enrolled. She planned a career in teaching.

The lower court transferred custody to the father even though it found that the mother was *not* unfit. It reasoned, however, that the mother's work was inconsistent with the child's best interest and that the father's second wife could be a *full-time* mother for the child. On appeal from this decision Glen and NOW argued four major points. First, that the court had "created a blatant inequity by taking custody away from the mother just because she was a working mother." As they asserted:

> How are Ms. R.'s interests in teaching, and her prospective status as a teacher—with its long vacations and shorter working hours outside the home—inconsistent with the best interest of her son John? By the same standard, how does Mr. R.'s work as a meat butcher make him better equipped to be the custodial parent?
>
> The court's rejection of Ms. R. as the custodial parent because of her lifestyle, her aspirations for a college degree, and the fact of her employment embodies all of *the invidiousness of a double standard; it is fine for the father to earn his living, at any pursuit, but it apparent-*

---

*The case, which was not identified by name, is discussed fully in "Feminist Arguments for a Working Mother's Custody," *Women's Rights Law Reporter*, Vol. 1, No. 6 (Winter 1974): 23–25. The following discussion and excerpts are summarized from this article.

ly is not permissible for the mother to seek a career to become self-supporting.

Second, when it treated the father's second wife and the mother as if the two were interchangeable, the court ignored the rule of law that prefers the *natural parent* over the stranger. The natural mother may be compared to the natural father, but not to a stranger. Third, in addition to her parental right, the attorneys pointed to the mother's well established social and emotional relationship with her son, and the importance of that continuity for the child.

Fourth, the feminist attorneys argued that the court was trying to replace the natural mother because she did not conform to the court's stereotyped image of a mother as a full-time stay-at-home housewife:

> It is clear that the court's attempt to substitute the father's second wife in the place and stead of the natural mother, springs not from the child's needs, but from the court's equation of "motherhood" with those domestic activities in which the second wife, a stay-at-home housewife, engages. The court's employment of this invidious stereotype is an arbitrary and capricious violation of Ms. R.'s fundamental liberty to live as she, and not the state, feels is best for herself and her son.

These arguments proved successful and the attorneys won a reversal of the Family Court's revocation of custody.

This case also illustrates a second result of the law's assumption that the mother will be the custodial parent, that of reinforcing her traditional roles as a housewife and a mother—and as a perennial dependent. Sole custodianship clearly intensifies the traditional mother role, causing many custodial mothers to feel like "200-percent mothers" because no other adult shares the responsibility of parenthood. Hetherington, Cox, and Cox found that "divorced mothers [have] significantly less contact with adults than do other parents, and often [feel] . . . locked into a child's world."[72] Thus, when the mediating influence of another parent is withdrawn, the mother's relationship with her children often becomes more intense and more isolated. This may put an enormous (and unrealistic) strain on the mother–child relationship to provide the kinds of support both would otherwise seek and receive from peers. Nevertheless, the courts clearly encourage the custodial mother to stay home with the children and spend all her time as homemaker and caretaker. This encouragement serves, in turn, to further isolate her and confine her to the world of children.

Margaret Mead asserted that placing the total responsibility for child care on the mother is a form of anti-feminism:

> [The] insistence that the child and mother or mother surrogate must never be separated; that all separation even for a few days is ultimately damaging and that if long enough it does irreversible damage . . . is a mere and subtle form of anti-feminism by which men—under the guise of exalting the importance of maternity—are tying women more tightly to their children than has been thought necessary since the invention of bottle feeding and baby carriages.[73]

When women are expected to be full-time mothers it is difficult for them either to earn money or to improve their earning potential, with the consequences that they continue to be financially dependent on their husbands, or ex-husbands, or on welfare when they are unable to collect adequate support.

The court's interest in ensuring the children a stay-at-home mother may have detrimental effects on the mother's psychological well-being, as well as on the psychological well-being of her children. Hetherington, Cox, and Cox found that divorced women who worked were less likely to feel bound to a child's world than nonworking women, even though both sets of mothers had custody.[74] Their research suggests that custodial mothers may be better off psychologically (and may, therefore, be better mothers to their children) if they have some work (or other) commitments.

It is easy to see the double bind that many divorced women feel when pressed to be both financially independent and full-time mothers. On the one hand, the courts may imply that a woman who devotes less than full time to her children will be deemed an unfit mother. On the other, she faces pressure to become financially independent so that she will not have to rely on her ex-husband or welfare for her children's and her own financial support. If she takes a job (especially if it is a full-time job of the kind that will provide the money she will need for full support) she runs the risk of "neglecting" her children and having them taken away. And if she takes to heart the court's interest in a full-time child guardian, and remains at home to devote herself exclusively to child care and homemaking, she thereby isolates herself socially and remains financially dependent on her former husband or on welfare funds. Thus, the legal system seems to put custodial mothers in the position of having to choose between losing their children and losing their major opportunities to build a new economic and social life.

A third effect of the maternal presumption is that the mother who considers giving up her children, even temporarily, to build a new life, is made to feel guilty, deviant, and unwomanly. Thus, in yet another way the custody presumption can subtly but effectively operate to foreclose a mother's options. Because it is assumed that all mothers want custody of their children, women feel strong pressures to assume that role regardless of its consequences. Further, with custody awarded to the mother so routinely, the woman who is brave enough to admit she does not want custody is viewed with distinct suspicion by the legal system as well as by society:

> The court that deprives the mother of custody displays her to the world as morally unfit. To avoid this stigma, the mother often chooses to fight the father for the children even if she does not really want their custody.[75]

A Market Opinion Research poll of over 1500 U.S. women commissioned in 1975 for International Women's Year revealed that few women support the automatic mother presumption in custody. As the report states:

> Where minor children are involved in a divorce, 37 percent of women say that both parents should be considered equally for custody and 45 percent say that custody placement should depend upon the circumstances. Only 17 percent are automatically saying that custody of minor children should be given to the woman.[76]

Nevertheless many women may be coerced into assuming custody because of the strength of the prevailing social and legal assumptions. In one rare 1975 case in which a mother admitted she did not want custody, the court admonished her for being selfish. In denying her request to grant her husband custody of their six children, the judge chastised her for seeking "to develop her own talents and abilities as a person" (by enlisting "in the U.S. Army in a program which will offer her opportunities and education which were previously denied her") instead of considering the well-being and protection of her children.[77] (The children were already living with the father but he opposed his wife's joining the Army.)

In recent years there has been increased interest in joint custody as a way of relieving some of the disadvantages of the present system for both mothers and fathers. Joint custody gives both parents concurrent legal responsibility for the child while allowing for alternating physical custody. Ideally it could mitigate the deprivation that many fathers currently feel as well as the intense all inclusive pressures on full-time custodial mothers. Preliminary research indicates that joint custody can work extremely well when the parties live in the same residential area and are truly committed to shared postdivorce parenting, but it is clearly not a solution for parents who cannot get along or one that is viable when one parent is determined to have sole custody.*

Having examined the social and psychological consequences of the present system of awarding child custody, let us now turn to the economic consequences and examine the system of awarding child support.

The Responsibility for Child Support

The traditional law assigned the father the major responsibility for child support both during marriage and after divorce. The practical and legal effects of this obligation in an ongoing marriage were discussed in Chapter 2. Here we will focus on the financial responsibility for children after divorce. Although the primary duty of support still rests with the father, the custodial mother, as we shall see, comes to bear the greater—indeed, frequently the total—burden of child support after divorce.

The Law on the Books: The Father's Responsibility

As a continuation of the husband's common-law obligation for support, all states imposed the primary responsibility for child support after divorce on the father. Although statutes with gender-based language (i.e. those that name the father or husband as solely responsible) are likely to be invalidated under the reasoning in *Orr*, the principle of obligating the spouse with greater financial resources to pay for the children will remain, and thus most states will continue to place the major responsibility for postdivorce child

*See, generally, H. Jay Folberg and Marva Graham "Joint Custody of Children following Divorce," *University of California at Davis Law Review*, Vol. 12, No. 2 (Summer 1979) for the legal aspects of joint custody and Alice Abarbanel's unpublished Ph.D. dissertation "Joint Custody Families: A Case Study Approach" Calif. School of Professional Psychology, 1977, for a sociological study of parents with joint custody.

support on the father. Today most divorced fathers are in fact ordered to pay child support. The amount of money ordered is, in theory, established by the child's needs and the father's resources. As Clark summarizes the law:

> Within the limits of the husband's means, the child is entitled to an adequate provision for his needs, one which reflects the income level and scale of living of the family before the divorce. The child . . . should not be limited to the bare necessities of life unless the husband is unable to provide more than that.[78]

Judges are accorded a great deal of discretion in setting "an appropriate award" for child support; most, however, implicitly or explicitly, rely on a formula so that child support awards tend to be quite standardized within any given court's jurisdiction. Many counties publish "child support schedules" which "suggest" appropriate amounts for "temporary orders" in "average" cases. This qualified language seeks to preserve both judicial discretion and the flexibility to deviate from the schedule. But in practice, deviations are rare, and a heavy burden of proof is placed on the custodial parent to justify any more generous allotment. Michigan Law Professor David Chambers found that actual awards show virtually no variation from the amount suggested in the support schedule.[79] In fact, the schedule seems to put a ceiling on potential awards—an unfortunate result because the amount of support suggested is typically quite low.

There are two types of child support schedules. One type uses a flat percentage or a sliding percentage of the noncustodial parent's net income to calculate the award. For example, a set of 1977 Seattle, Washington guidelines specified the following percentages: 24 percent of the father's net income for 1 child, 35 percent for 2 children, 42 percent for 3 children, 48 percent for 4 children; and the percentages continue to increase in an Illinois schedule which allows 50 percent for 5 children, and 55 percent for 6 or more children.[80]

The second type of support schedule establishes a fixed amount of support for each level of husband's income. For example, consider the 1979 guidelines for Superior Courts in the San Francisco Bay Area, reprinted below, which combine support for the wife and children in one schedule.

The first three columns of this schedule assume a full-time custodial wife. But if the wife is employed, the suggested amount is

1979 Guidelines for Support Orders*: San Francisco Bay Area Superior Courts

Husband's Net Monthly Income	Wife and One Child (1)	Wife and Two Children (2)	Wife and Three Children (3)	Child Support Only† (per child)
$ 400.00	$ 100.00	$ 100.00	$ 100.00	$ 50.00–$ 75.00
500.00	200.00	200.00	200.00	75.00– 100.00
600.00	300.00	300.00	300.00	75.00– 100.00
700.00	350.00	375.00	400.00	75.00– 100.00
800.00	400.00	425.00	450.00	100.00– 125.00
900.00	450.00	475.00	500.00	100.00– 125.00
1000.00	500.00	550.00	600.00	100.00– 150.00
1200.00	600.00	650.00	700.00	100.00– 150.00
1400.00	700.00	800.00	850.00	125.00– 175.00
1600.00	800.00	900.00	950.00	125.00– 175.00
1800.00	900.00	1000.00	1050.00	150.00– 250.00
2000.00	1000.00	1100.00	1150.00	150.00– 250.00
Above 2000.00	40 percent plus $150 to 200			Court's discretion

*Special provisions for handicapped wife or children not specified. If wife's income is less than 60 percent of husband's income, then one half of her net earnings (after child care expenses are deducted) should be deducted from these figures to determine support award.
†When wife's income reaches 60 percent of husband's income, use this column alone. (The total is not to exceed the amount in the previous column.)

reduced by one half of her net earnings (after deductions for child care expenses) until her net income reaches 60 percent of her former husband's. At that point she is not eligible for any support for herself: the final column is used to set child support. The percentage of the husband's income awarded for support in this schedule varies considerably with his income level. Men with take-home pay of $400 a month are required to pay $100—or 25 percent of their net income—irrespective of family size. On the other hand, men with a monthly net income of between $900 and $1400 are ordered to pay 50 percent of their net income for a wife and one child—and sometimes, where more children are involved, as much as 60 percent. Once the husband's net income reaches $2,000 a month the percentage again declines.

Even though this is a relatively typical schedule, many of its recommended awards clearly would constitute inadequate support for the children—or for the wife and children. No family of two, three, or four could live in 1979 on $100 to $300 a month, and few families could make it on $400 to $600 a month. Further, it is easy to see how a mother might feel the balance is unjust when the father, a single person, is given 40 to 75 percent of the income while she and the children, two or three or four people, are expected to share the remaining 24 to 60 percent. Nevertheless, most judges are reluctant to award more than one-half of a man's net income because they do not want "to remove a man's incentive to earn."[81] Thus for all the law's ideology about the mother as full-time custodial parent, economic reality must sooner or later dictate that she will work outside the home to help support the children.

The Law in Action: The Mother's Burden

It is empirically doubtful whether fathers have ever actually assumed the major burden of child support after divorce. As Congresswoman Martha Griffiths reported to the U.S. House of Representatives in 1974:

> All states require parents to support their children, and all states provide civil and criminal remedies for nonsupport. However, the law on the books is not the law in action. Upon divorce, separation, . . . courts do not automatically order child-support payments to be made. Even when a support order is issued, chances are that payments will not be sufficient to furnish half of the child's support.[82]

A combination of factors guarantees the accuracy of Griffith's conclusion that child support payments are not sufficient to furnish half of the child's support. First there is the low level of court-ordered child support awards, and that is typically compounded by a high incidence of noncompliance. If we add up the wife's expenses for the child's food, clothing, housing, entertainment, babysitting and other child-care services, and her own opportunity costs (in terms of foregone employment and career advancement) it becomes evident that the custodial mother typically shoulders the lion's share of the cost of raising children after divorce.

California data offer evidence in support of these assertions.[83] While child support was awarded in 80 to 85 percent of all cases involving children, the median Los Angeles award in 1972 was $75 per child and $121 per family. These data suggest that *mothers were carrying more than half the responsibility for child support at the time of the divorce,* for the average child support award in 1972 provided less than one half of the direct cost of raising children in a low-income family. Indeed, when compared to the estimated cost of raising two children to age 18 made by a large national Consumer Expenditure Survey in 1960–61, the median amount of total child support ordered in our 1972 sample was only one half that required nationwide for low-income families in 1960–61.[84]

The low median level for support awards is due in part to the large number of low-income families in the divorcing population. According to Los Angeles County Superior Court guidelines for temporary support orders, a "provider" spouse would not ordinarily be expected to pay more than half of his net monthly income to a nonemployed custodial spouse, regardless of the number of children. Thus, the ex-wife and two children of a man who takes home $1,000 per month could expect an award of no more than $500, while the husband would retain at least that much for himself. At lower income levels, of course, the possible amount of support diminishes proportionately: a man bringing home $600 per month would be expected to pay not more than $300 per month for a dependent spouse and one, two, or three or more children. (The figure of $600 is not unrealistic: the reported median net monthly income of Los Angeles husbands receiving final decrees of divorce in 1972 was $587.) At that level and below, a nonemployed custodial mother would almost certainly require state assistance.

In 1972 divorced fathers in the Los Angeles area were ordered to pay an average of 25 percent of their net incomes in child support. This percentage, varying with the husband's income level and the number of children, in fact tended to be lowest at the lowest income levels, a reflection of the fact that, far from assessing the allowable 50 percent, most judges were granting only token awards (of $15 or $20 per month) to dependents at those levels. The percentage increased in the middle income range (up to the full 50 percent for a wife and several children), and decreased at levels over $2,000 a month.

A second California sample, drawn in 1977, revealed little change in these patterns. Although the median child support award per child had risen to $100 per month by 1977, and the median total award from $141 to $150, these amounts clearly had not kept up with the interim cost of living (calculated at an increase of 8 percent per year).[85] Nor were they equal to even half of the actual cost of raising a child, even in a low-income family. *

Although these figures indicate that the child support awards are less than half the cost of raising a child in a low-income family, as sociologist Karen Seal notes, the burden on the single mother is actually greater because childrearing costs are based on two-parent families: "The calculations assume that one parent works while the other is available to care for the child. In one-parent families where the mother is forced to return to work, the cost of child care alone may exceed the child support award."[86]

Two other factors serve, in practice, to further diminish the noncustodian's share of the childrearing costs, and thus to further increase the burden that the custodian must bear alone: inflation and noncompliance. Let us briefly look at the effects of each of these.

The Effects of Inflation

In October 1980 *Parents* magazine issued a shocking estimate of what it would cost to raise a new born baby to age 18—$254,000—and that did not include the cost of college.[87] Thomas Tilling criticized the low estimates projected by the U.S. government (at $65,000) and the Population Reference Service (at $85,000 including 4 years of college) for failing to take account of the effects of inflation. Using the $65,000 figure issued by the government as a starting point and adding a mere 10 percent inflation each year raises the cost from $65,000 to $175,000. Another 10 percent was added to make up for gross underestimates† bringing the total to $193,000. The final $61,000 figure is earnings lost to the mother from the child's birth to enrollment in kindergarten based on a $10,000-a-year salary, plus inflation, for five years.

These projections make the court orders for child support reported above almost laughable—as less than ten percent of the

*Monetary cost estimates do not take into account the mother's time expenditures which, if added, would demonstrate that the custodial parent assumes an even greater share of the total cost of rearing the children. See, e.g., Clair Vickery's innovative analysis of time and monetary resources in "The Time-Poor: A New Look at Poverty," *Journal of Human Resources* 12 (1977): 423.

†The magazine found some of the federal figures ludicrous and wondered whether the government's estimators had children of their own. One figure cited was the government's estimated $22 a week to feed a teen-age boy. *Parents*, October 1980.

child support awards in our California study were tied to potential increases in the husband's income or to the cost of living. In an inflationary economy the real value of these awards—which were inadequate to begin with—will diminish to almost nothing in a matter of years. Consider attorney Philip Eden's example of how inflation flaunts the court's order:

> A support order of $500 was awarded a decade ago for three children aged one, three, and five. What has happened since then?
>
> > The growth of the children in the last decade increased the amount needed to maintain the original living standard to $633.
> >
> > The purchasing power of the original amount has been eroded by inflation down to $275.
> >
> > The proportion of the noncustodial spouse's income used for support of the children has dropped from one-third down to one-sixth.
>
> While the original award represented a certain standard of living for these children, their growth and inflation have combined to reduce the buying power of that same $500. For each dollar now needed to purchase that original standard of living, they have only 43 cents.[88]

The Noncompliance Problem

Whether or not support awards are adequate or equitable, the fact of the matter is that most fathers do not support their children as ordered.[89] As Congresswoman Griffiths has aptly stated, the debate about the fairness of the amount of support ordered is largely "academic, since relatively few appear to be paid."[90] In fact, noncompliance with support orders is the rule rather than the exception.

The first complete study of compliance with child support orders was conducted in the 1960s by Professor Kenneth Eckhardt in Wisconsin.[91] Eckhardt examined a jurisdiction in which all child-support payments had to be made through the courts, so that he could compile complete and reliable data on rates of compliance. Eckhardt's findings, summarized in the table below, indicate that even in the first year after the court order was made, 62 percent of the fathers failed to comply fully with the order. In fact, 42 percent did not make a *single* child support payment. By the tenth year 79 percent of the fathers were in total noncompliance and contributing nothing whatever to their child's support.

Similarly, in an Indiana sample of child-support payments that were made directly to the court, Steininger found arrearages in 89

The Probability of a Divorced Woman Collecting Any Child Support Money (by Years Since the Court Order)*

Years Since Court Order	Number of Open Cases	Full Compliance	Partial Compliance	No Compliance
One	163	38%	20%	42%
Two	163	28	20	52
Three	161	26	14	60
Four	161	22	11	67
Five	160	19	14	67
Six	158	17	12	71
Seven	157	17	12	71
Eight	155	17	8	75
Nine	155	17	8	75
Ten	149	13	8	79

*Based on data from Eckhardt, "Deviance, Visibility, and Legal Action: The Duty to Support," *Social Problems* 15 (1968):473–74.

percent of the cases. He also reported that *no payments* were ever made in 47 percent of the cases.[92]

Data from a 1975 market poll conducted for the U.S. Commission on International Women's Year indicated that only 44 percent of the divorced mothers were awarded child support, and of those only 47 percent were able to collect it regularly.[93] Another 29 percent collected it sometimes or "rarely," and the remaining 21 percent reported they were never able to collect any of the child support ordered by the court. Along the same lines, a 1979 U.S. Census Bureau report indicated that about a quarter of the divorced, separated, remarried, and never-married custodial mothers in a national sample actually received child support.*

The critical importance of the child support for these families is highlighted by the fact that it often makes the difference between poverty and nonpoverty. As the census report states, "in many instances, women near the poverty line who received child support would have fallen below the poverty level if those payments were eliminated. In fact, when child support income is excluded from

*A poorly constructed question in the Census survey did not permit a "yes" response with respect to both child support and alimony. Thus women who indicated they were receiving both kinds of contributions are not included in the data reported above. About 60 percent of the women who received child support received less than $1,500 a year. Child support payments constituted *less than 10 percent* of the total household income for approximately half of the women who received support. U.S. Bureau of Census, "Divorce, Child Custody, and Child Support," *Current Population Reports*, series P-23, no. 84 (June 1979), p. 3.

their total income, the poverty rate for mothers who received it rises from 12 percent to 19 percent."[94] Overall about a third of the women (32 percent) who did not receive child support fell below the poverty line, compared to 12 percent of the women who received support.

Child support is also a major determinant of whether or not a woman has to apply for public assistance. In the census sample 38 percent of women without child support from the father of their children received public assistance income, compared to only 13 percent of women with child support income.[95]

Because neither of these national surveys controlled for the length of time elapsed from the original award, it is impossible to compare these data directly with Eckhardt's.[96] However, even using the most conservative figures from these studies we can ascertain *three consistent findings*. First, fewer than half of the fathers comply more or less regularly with court orders to pay child support.[97] Thus, despite the law and despite the court orders, it can hardly be said with assurance that divorced fathers will assume the responsibility for child support. Second, it is evident that a majority of fathers who comply do so irregularly and are often in arrears (perhaps as many as 89 percent, if we accept Steininger's figures).[98] While some contribution is certainly preferable to total noncompliance, irregular and infrequent child support can nevertheless cause serious hardship for the dependent mother and children. As Blank and Rone note:

> The economic problem is not always one of total default. The husband/father/obligor who is chronically late in his payments, who pays regularly but not always the full amount of the award, or who pays erratically and permits large blocks of arrears to accumulate causes a tremendous hardship.[99]

Third, all the research indicates that a very sizable minority of fathers—a hefty 47 percent—never make a single court-ordered payment.[100] How is this possible? How can so many men successfully evade the law? How do the authorities responsible for enforcement answer this question?

The Ability to Pay

There is a general belief that the noncomplying father simply does not have the means to support two families. He is portrayed as a man engaged in a desperate economic struggle to support a former family as well as a new family. Or if the ex-wife and her children are receiving welfare assistance, the assumption is that the father has disappeared and is unlocatable. Government agencies are purportedly fighting a gallant battle to locate these vanished men and make them face their financial responsibilities, but are constantly thwarted by a lack of cooperation from deserted spouses.

Evidence from other sources, however, paints a different picture. First, it is clear that many noncomplying fathers have the financial capacity to support their children. For example, one 1971 study, conducted by Winston and Forsher for the Rand Corporation, found that many truly affluent fathers, including a number of physicians and lawyers, had evaded child-support obligations until their families were forced onto welfare.[101] The study concluded that much middle-class poverty is attributable to nonsupport by fathers who clearly have the financial ability to comply with court orders. Furthermore, as they note, the amount of support ordered was by no means exorbitant:

> The amount of child support awarded was not unreasonably large. For those nonsupporting fathers who were already under court order to contribute to their children's support, the typical payment ordered was $50 a month. In 33 percent of the nonwelfare cases, the order called for $50 or less.[102]

Congresswoman Griffiths concluded, after congressional hearings on the subject, that there appears to be little relationship between compliance and ability to pay:

> We found no clear or consistent relationship between compliance with support orders and absent parents' income. Eighty-one percent of the parents earning less than $6000 were not substantially complying with their support orders or agreements—but neither were 66 percent of those earning between $6000 and $12,000 or 70 percent of those earning $12,000 or more.[103]

One indepth study of a small sample conducted by Judith Cassetty revealed that the overwhelming majority of absent men (86 percent) "were better off than their former wives and children, and even for many of the officially poor mothers in the sample, enough money was available to raise them above the poverty level without causing the fathers either to fall below the poverty line or to reduce their income below that of their families."[104]

Cassetty found only a tiny minority of the absent fathers who were truly unable to contribute anything toward the support of their children, while most could contribute much more than the authorities believed possible. She concluded that "there appears to be an enormous untapped source of funds that could be used to improve the economic status of children in female-headed households."[105]

By now it is obvious that the "ability to pay" depends to a large extent on enforcement procedures. Although a man may claim that he can't pay because he doesn't have the money, having spent it on something else, as E. Uhr observed, "if the IRS were to collect taxes only from those people who had money left over after meeting other obligations, few taxes would be paid."[106]

The Lack of Enforcement

The obvious conclusion from the research cited above is that it is not the financial incapacity of the fathers, but rather the lack of enforcement machinery that leads to widespread noncompliance with child support orders. As the congressional response indicates:

> [I]nvestigators . . . point to the difficulty of proving the income of the self-employed, the ease with which unwilling fathers can conceal their assets, the statutory barrier to collecting from military personnel and federal employees, and the low priority given child-support investigations by the understaffed district attorneys' offices.[107]

One excuse officials give for not enforcing child support orders is that the nonsupporting fathers have disappeared. However, Winston and Forsher found that only a minority of them are unlocatable. Most, in fact, are still living in the same city as the ex-wife.[108] Similarly, Jones, Gordon, and Sawhill, citing a 1973 New York City AFDC (Aid to Families with Dependent Children) study, noted that only one out of every four nonsupporting fathers could not be located[109]; yet procedures were initiated to secure compliance in only one out of every seven cases.

The problem, then, is not the fathers' lack of finances or their physical absence, but rather the absence of an effective enforcement machinery. The expensive and time-consuming burden of enforcing the court order typically falls on the mother. It is she who must hire an attorney, and attorneys are often unwilling to take these cases because they assume they will have trouble collecting their fees. Blank and Rone, writing in 1975, found that the attorney's fee for an enforcement action can run to several thousands of dollars.[110] Further, the judge who hears the case is likely to be unsympathetic. As Blank and Rone observe:

> Even when a woman knows the whereabouts of her former spouse and can afford the high cost of enforcement services, overcrowded courts and the low priority given enforcement actions may delay relief for months or even years. Once a woman finally has her day in court, she will find judges reluctant to use the full panoply of remedies available in order to assure her continued support and thus to relieve her of the necessity of investing repeatedly in legal actions. . . . Viewed in its worst light the attitude of many male judges is that alimony and child support awards are punitive, that women should be primarily responsible for the children, and that if women want to be equal to men, they should get a job and support themselves.[111]

Recent years have brought increased awareness of the magnitude of the problem, and new legislation aimed at rectification has been passed on both the state and national levels. On the national level, Public law 93–647 has provided the first major federal effort to aid child support enforcement. Effective in 1978, it established a federal parent locator service to assist states in locating absent (nonsupporting) parents.[112] Child support enforcement bureaus in each state are also given access to Social Security records and may obtain aid from the Internal Revenue Service's collection service in certain cases.

New federal legislation has also increased access to the wages of federal employees to satisfy child support orders. Before 1975 the wages or pensions of federal employees (including military personnel) were not subject to garnishment for alimony or child support. Since then they are, although 1978 federal legislation exempts 40 percent of federal wage and retirement income from garnishment (50 percent if the employee is supporting a second family). These exceptions, however, may be decreased by 5 percent if there are substantial arrearages.

In the past, enforcement remedies on the state and local level have typically been utilized after a parent is in noncompliance. However, prospective enforcement efforts may be more effective. For example, a court could require child support payments to be made directly to the court so that they could be monitored from the beginning. Alternatively a court could order a wage assignment, i.e. a routine payroll deduction, at the time of the initial child support order.

Recent California legislation has moved in this direction. It gives the judge the option of ordering a wage assignment or of requiring the posting of security (such as a bond) when a child support order is first made.[113] In addition, it is now mandatory for a judge to order a wage assignment if the total amount of arrearage reaches the equivalent of two months of court-ordered support. Further, children in California are preferred creditors (which means that child support must be paid before other creditors) and one can put a lien against a house to secure money for existing child support arrearages when a house is sold. Finally, as of 1980, reasonable attorneys' fees are to be awarded in any action to enforce an existing order for child support.[114]

The most persuasive argument in favor of both prospective and vigorous enforcement procedures was made by Michigan law Professor David Chambers after seven years of extensive empirical research on the effects of different methods of child-support enforcement.[115] Chambers set out to examine the effects of prison sentences on compliance patterns in 28 counties in Michigan. He used over 17 data sets based on 13,000 case files along with interviews with fathers, ex-wives, court personnel, judges and jail keepers. After a rigorous analysis of these data Professor Chambers concluded that no-nonsense methods of enforcement, including incarceration, resulted in much higher rates of compliance:

> The sad finding of our study has been that, in the absence of sanctions, so many fathers fail to pay. . . . swift and certain punishment can reduce the incidence (of noncompliance) so long as potential offenders perceive a clear link between their own behavior and a system that leads to punishment.[116]

The Michigan counties with the highest rates of compliance had two characteristics: a self-starting system of collecting child support and a high jailing rate.[117] In a self-starting system child support payments are made directly to the court so that court personnel can keep a careful watch on compliance. As soon as a father is delinquent, action is initiated by the Friend of the Court, a publicly supported collection system which pursues nonsupporting fathers whether or not their ex-wives are on welfare. The Friend of the Court does not wait for a complaint from the mother to begin enforcement efforts. It takes the initiative itself with reminders, prodding letters, and warnings. If these fail it follows up with mandatory wage assignments, judicial reprimands, probation—and, eventually, jail.

As noted above, the probability of jail for delinquent fathers is the second essential component of an effective deterrent system. Michigan, which jails one out of seven divorced fathers under court orders to pay child support, collects more child support per case than any other state in the country.[118] (Professor Chambers argues however, that the sequence of steps before jail, especially the mandatory wage assignments and the work of the Friend of the Court, are equally responsible for Michigan's success.)

In one analysis Professor Chambers matched subgroups of fathers by factors that influence compliance rates (such as the father's occupation) and compared fathers in a high-jailing self-starting county (Genessee) with an identical subgroup in a low-jailing non-self-starting county (Washtenaw). Men in Genessee had uniformly higher compliance rates (20–25 percentage points more) across all subgroups.[119] These results clearly point to the conclusion that aggressiveness makes the difference: in fact, Professor Chambers asserts that the uniformity of the findings suggest that "there are few men so unable to pay that the threat of jail does not produce substantial additional payments and, conversely, that there are few men so self-motivated to pay that they will pay as well as they are able without threat."[120]

On a policy level Professor Chambers recommends the establishment of a nationwide system of direct child-support deductions from wages. This would require a federal system whereby child support would be deducted from wages along with income taxes from the first moment of the court order.[121] Sadly, without this type of comprehensive system, it seems likely that the major burden for postdivorce child support will remain with the custodial mother.

In summary, we have seen that the practical effect of making the mother the custodian of the children is to endow her with primary responsibility for their support. For when her former husband fails, for any reason, to help to support his children, she, as their custodian, is left to bear the responsibility alone.

Yet the law does not recognize a woman's right to compensation for her child care, either during marriage or after divorce. Not only is she expected to perform these services without pay, but the law typically fails to recognize the options she foregoes and the opportunities she misses when she is compelled to put these responsibilities above all else. Even the Uniform Marriage and Divorce Act, which represents the enlightened vanguard view in family law, makes no provision for a custodial parent to be compensated for time and labor expended in taking care of children. One can certainly ask why, if our society truly values children, we cannot find a better way to support and reward the people we charge with the responsibility for their care.

Legal Assumptions Versus Social Reality

The major thesis of the five chapters in Part II is that the basic assumptions of legal marriage are anachronistic and inappropriate: they do not accord with social reality, and they infringe on the strongly valued and politically protected heterogeneity and diversity of our society. Each chapter in Part II examines one assumption of legal marriage and the extent to which it is challenged by current sociological data. Each also discusses how the law might be changed to more accurately reflect contemporary social reality.

To assert that legal norms should conform to social reality is not to suggest that the legal system ought to respond to superficial fluctuations in social patterns. The changes that form the basis for the present challenge are manifestations of complex, long-developing societal alterations. In particular, the increasing industrialization and urbanization of our society in the past century have compelled profound changes in the nature and functions of the family.

When this country was founded, the family was the basic social and economic unit of an agrarian society. Ogburn's classic statement of the seven functions of that family included production, prestige and status conferral, education, protection, religion, recreation, and affection-procreation.[1] Of these, the economic function was foremost: the family was often a self-sufficient economic unit that produced most of what it consumed. Farm families were less mobile residentially; they typically stayed in one community and had an opportunity to establish reputations: the family thus conferred prestige and status on its members. The family was also the primary center of education, not only for the infant or preschool child, but for the vocational instruction of its youth. Girls were taught domestic skills by their mothers; boys were taught their fathers' vocations. Higher education, if any, was most often provided by a tutor who lived with the family, or through a son's professional apprenticeship with a lawyer, doctor, or clergyman. The protective role of the family included not only the physical protection of family members but the assurance of care for the sick and elderly. Both religious and recreational activities centered around the home. Finally, the family provided affection and companionship for the spouses, and a stable environment for the procreation and rearing of children.

Over the past century, largely as a result of sweeping technological change, the functions of the family have changed. As work moved from the farm to the factory, store, and office, the major economic tasks of the family have shifted from production to consumption. Education, especially vocational training, has gradually been transferred to the school (although parents still assume the major task of preschool socialization and informal education throughout the school years), and recreation has similarly moved outside the home. Religion, diminished in importance, now centers around the church or synagogue. Protection has been increasingly transferred to state agencies, and responsibility for the handicapped and aged has similarly been slowly shifting to institutions outside the home. Family status is no longer the central prestige-conferring mechanism in an age of mobility and urban anonymity.

Today's family remains, however, the basic unit for the procreation and rearing of young children, and it is still the center of affectional and emotional life. Indeed, its role as the major source of psychological and emotional support for its members has, if anything, greatly increased. Today "the conjugal family serves as an oasis for the replenishment of the person, providing the individual with stable, diffuse and largely unquestioning support."[2]

Goode's analysis of the evolving functions of the family in industrialized societies points to the "fit" between the affectively based conjugal unit and the achievement-oriented society.[3] He notes that the conjugal family is uniquely suited to provide the psychological and emotional support individuals need to make their way in an industrial system that endlessly and impersonally demands individual achievement. In such a system the emotional support of family members provides crucial redress for the tension, stress and bureaucratic impersonality characteristic of work and day-to-day life in industrial society.

Thus one challenge to the legal assumption of a strict division of labor within the family—with the husband as breadwinner and the wife as homemaker—is that it ill serves our modern society's requirement of sharing, companionship, and emotional solace in the marital bond. The partnership model of marriage seems far better suited to the needs of families today.

A second challenge to the legal imposition of sex-based marital obligations is that it denies individual autonomy. It instead enforces a rigidity and specificity that undermines the diversity of families in a heterogeneous society such as ours. Thus, even if it could be demonstrated that a majority of American families conformed to the assumptions and norms underlying legal marriage, there would still be compelling reasons for restraining the state from enforcing a rigid relational structure upon the minority who choose otherwise. The very concept of a single structure for all intimate relationships is in its nature tyrannical: it implies that the state can decide what form marriage should take regardless of the parties' ages, life circumstances, and individual wishes.

This interference in private lives cannot be justified on grounds of state interest, for, as we shall argue, the preservation of outmoded social forms is inevitably, over the long run, antithetical to state interests. Further, even if the state could assert a short-run interest in preserving the traditional form of marriage, that interest would not be important enough to supersede individual rights to privacy and freedom. As long as there are critical differences in the needs and values of a diverse citizenry, the state's imposition of a single norm on all simply cannot be justified.

The following five chapters document many of the changes in contemporary marital patterns and highlight the great diversity of our pluralistic society.

The present marriage laws are based on the assumption that all marriages are first marriages of young, white, middle-class, monogamous couples who bear children, divide the labor in the family along sex lines, and remain in a lifelong marriage. However, this model ignores the current evidence of divorce, of marriage in middle age and throughout the life cycle, of childless marriages, of more egalitarian family patterns, of the different family forms among the poor and ethnic minorities, and of alternative family forms among homosexuals, communards, and others who live together without marriage.

In view of the ethnic, racial, religious, social, and normative differences in our society, and the great variety of family forms that they give rise to, it hardly seems necessary to argue that we need a more flexible legal structure. The current institutionalization of a single set of norms for all marriages infringes on the beliefs and practices of millions of citizens, and it violates this nation's tradition of protecting the diversity of individual beliefs and values.

CHAPTER 5

The Lifelong Commitment

The Traditional Legal Contract

The law conceives of marriage as a permanent lifelong union. This conception is based on the Christian doctrine of marriage as a holy union of man and woman ordained by God, and therefore meant to last for the life of the parties: "We take each other to love and to cherish, in sickness and health, for better, for worse, until death do us part."[1]

The dominance of the religious influence in civil laws pertinent to marriage* is a result of the Church's long-standing jurisdiction over matrimonial causes in England.[2] The Church once had full authority to enforce its view of marriage as a sacrament that could not be dissolved by mere mortals: "Those whom God hath joined to-

---

*The philosophy of marriage under Jewish law is quite different from the traditional philosophy of marriage according to Christian teachings. As Shiloh notes, although Jewish marriage is celebrated in a religious ceremony it "remains, in essence, a business transaction, a contract between two parties of equal legal capacity, creating mutual rights and duties that terminate" upon the occurrence of various conditions. For example, according to Jewish law [a] woman is entitled to say to her husband, "I don't expect any maintenance from you and I do not want to work for you." (The Talmud, Baba Kamma, 8b.) The Christian marriage, in contrast, is more than a mere contract; it is based on the idea of the sacramental fusion of flesh and blood, symbolizing the union of Christ and the Church. Shiloh, Marriage and Divorce in Israel, *Israel Law Review* 5 (1970):479, 492-93. Cited in Margaret Sokolov, "Marriage Contracts for Support and Services: Constitutionality Begins at Home," *New York University Law Review* 49 (December 1974): 1195.

gether let no man put asunder."[3] Although this absolutist stance has gradually been modified in the English Church as well as in the law, an examination of its historical evolution discloses that in many ways the legal conception of marriage is still anchored in the religious ideal of a lifelong bond between husband and wife.[4]

Before the seventeenth century the indissoluble union of a marriage could be ended only by the death of one of the parties. In the late seventeenth century, rare exceptions were made and divorce was permitted by special act of Parliament. As Rheinstein observed, however, a parliamentary divorce was so "cumbersome and expensive that it was available only to the most affluent."[5] As only a few parliamentary divorces were granted each year, "under the general law of the land, marriage remained indissoluble."[6]*

"Divorce, in the modern sense of a judicial decree dissolving a valid marriage and allowing one or both partners to remarry during the life of the other, did not exist in England until 1857."[7] In that year the ecclesiastical courts transferred their exclusive jurisdiction over marriage and divorce to the civil court system, and divorces were authorized for adultery. But the underlying premise of divorce law remained the same: marriage was still regarded as a sacrosanct and essentially permanent union which the Church—and then the state—had to protect and preserve. And it was still assumed that the holy bond of matrimony would best be protected by restricting access to divorce. As Clark observes:

> [Officialdom believed] that marital happiness is best secured by making marriage indissoluble except for very few causes. When the parties know that they are bound together for life, the argument runs, they will resolve their differences and disagreements and make an effort to get along with each other. If they are able to separate legally upon less serious grounds, they will make no such effort, and immorality will result.[8]

The religious justification for indissoluble marriage soon led to a more secular argument—indissoluble marriage was necessary to maintain a stable society:

> Even if monogamous marriage, and the family grounded upon it, were not divinely established institutions, their continued maintenance would be required as the basis of society, and their integrity was considered to be endangered by the possibility of easy divorce. An

---

*The Church also permitted divorce *a mensa et thoro* (literally, divorce "from bed and board"), which allowed the parties to live apart; however, this legal separation did not sever the marital bond.

occasional individual might suffer under the yoke of an unhappy marriage; [but] it would still be better to ignore such suffering, to maintain the stability of the institution.[9]

Divorce laws in the United States were heavily influenced by the English tradition. They too were based on the idea that the strength of the family would be preserved by keeping people married—and making divorce difficult.

It is interesting to note that even in the mid-nineteenth century, liberals and feminists were arguing that the law's assumption of "indissoluble unions" was obsolete and oppressive. Elizabeth Cady Stanton advocated the acceptability of divorce as a protection for women mistreated by "tyrannical, profligate or abusive husbands," and argued against the naive legal assumption of lifelong bliss. Referring to the number of suicides among wives, she asked: "Do you believe . . . that all these wretched matches are made in heaven? that all these sad, miserable people are bound together by God?"[10]

Although the United States today records one of the highest divorce rates in the world, a divorce is still treated as a deviation from the legal norm. This view is most evident in the contrasting provisions that most state laws have for widowed and divorced spouses. In almost every state a divorced woman loses the rights and economic benefits she is entitled to, while a widow retains them.[11] As New York attorney Doris L. Sassower testified, "What are the wife's legal rights in the property her efforts helped the husband acquire? . . . [T]he shocking answer is that [if they divorce] she has none. Gone also are her rights to inherit from his estate, her right to elect against his will, employment benefits of health and survivors' insurance, as well as retirement benefits which might have been hers were she upon his death his widow rather than his ex-wife."[12]

While one might assume that the high divorce rate would provide an impetus for equalizing the provisions for divorced and widowed persons of similar status, recent decisions indicate that, if anything, the distinction has become more rigid. In 1976, in *Mathews* v. *de Castro*,[13] the U.S. Supreme Court made it clear that it did not consider a divorced woman with dependent children, a woman who had been married for more than 20 years, entitled to the same benefits as a similarly situated wife.* Thus the law seems to have

Mathews dealt with disparities in the Social Security Act. The Supreme Court ruling referred to the purpose of the Social Security Act as that of providing basic protection to workers and their families, and clearly indicated that it did not consider divorced spouses with dependent children, even if married twenty years, a family for the purposes of the Act.

partial vision: it protects the widowed because a marriage that endures until death accords with the legal view of what marriage ought to be. Meanwhile, it remains coldly oblivious to the real needs of those who endure the increasingly common experience of divorce.

Not only do most states fail to anticipate the needs of divorced spouses, they typically go even further and prohibit the spouses themselves from anticipating divorce and making adequate provisions for it. In most states, contracts in contemplation of divorce are considered contrary to public policy; and if they are made, they are usually declared void by the courts. *

There is clearly a punitive element in the courts' attitude toward divorce. They seem to be saying that even if people do get divorced, they shouldn't. And if people insist on violating the legal norm of a lifelong marriage they cannot expect the same degree of protection from the state.

Social Reality: The Impact of a High Divorce Rate

The Growing Rate of Divorce

Sociological and demographic data indicate a continuing increase in the number of divorces in the United States each year, and a rapidly diminishing probability that any marriage will last until the death of one of the parties. Today we have the highest divorce rate in U.S. history and there is every indication that the rate will continue at this high level.

Over the past century there have been four major shifts in the divorce rate:[14] first, a slow, gradual increase between 1860 and 1940 to a divorce rate of 2.0 per 1,000 total population; second, after World War II, a divorce boom (with the rate reaching 4.3 in 1946); third, a drop and leveling off in the early fifties; and fourth, a phenomenal rise in recent years. In the twelve years between 1963 and 1975 the divorce rate increased a dramatic 100 percent.

With each successive year since 1974, the divorce rate has surpassed all previous records for this country. † In terms of absolute

---

*But see Chapter 13 for a discussion of new developments in the law.

†A more precise "divorce rate" (recently employed by the U.S. Census) is the rate per 1,000 married women aged 15 years and older. The changes in that rate parallel the changes discussed above: from 9.4 in 1940, to a postwar high of 17.9

numbers, for the first time in the history of the United States, there were more than one million divorces in a twelve-month period in 1974. By 1979 the number reached 1,170,000, and the divorce rate reached an all-time high of 5.3.[15]

Demographer Kingsley Davis concludes that the most significant change in the pattern of marital termination over the past century has been the shift from death to divorce as a common way of ending a marriage. Great numbers of marriages that will be ended voluntarily, by divorce, in 1980 would have been ended by death in 1880.[16] Davis contends:

> The stability of the combined rate of marital dissolution is . . . a function of the long-run downward trend in dissolutions by death and a long-run compensatory upward trend in dissolutions by divorce. The compensatoriness of the trends may be in part motivational. *As the probability of escaping a bad marriage by death approaches zero, the willingness to consider divorce must surely rise.* . . . There is nothing to stop the legal divorce trend from rising until it displaces death as the chief cause of dissolution. . . .[17]

According to a recent U.S. census report, more women in the United States today (aged 14–75) have had their first marriage end in divorce than in widowhood.[18]

Clearly there is an increasing probability that any single marriage will end in divorce instead of in death. At current rates of divorce, Glick and Norton of the U.S. Bureau of the Census predict that 40 percent of all current marriages will end in divorce.[19]* But this prediction is probably a conservative estimate of the chances of divorce for those entering marriage today. The reason is twofold. First, the Census Bureau bases its estimates on the experience of those who have gotten divorced in the past, as they provide the only data we have. However, in a period of rapid change, the experiences of the last one or two generations are considerably different

---

in 1946, to a leveling off at the prewar level in the 1950s and a dramatic increase from the early 1960s (around 9.4) to the present (22.0 in 1978). U.S. Bureau of the Census, "Divorce, Child Custody and Child Support," *Current Population Reports*, series P-23, no. 84 (1979), p. 7, Table 1.

*Using an alternative method of predicting the probability of divorce for those currently entering marriage, Preston, using 1973 data, estimated that 44 percent of all marriages would end in divorce. Since the probability of divorce has continued to increase since 1973, today's estimate with Preston's method would be somewhat higher. Samuel H. Preston, "Estimating the Proportion of American Marriages that End in Divorce," *Sociological Methods and Research* 3, no. 4 (May 1975):435–60.

from those of the current generation. Because the divorce rate has been increasing rapidly in recent years, any estimate based on past generations is likely to be overly conservative.

The marriages of the younger generation already reflect a vastly different rate of divorce. In fact, among the younger cohorts, it is much more likely that a first marriage will end in divorce. Thus, according to the Bureau of the Census, it is expected that 38 percent of the first marriages of all women born between 1945 and 1949 will end in divorce, compared with 13 percent of the first marriages of women born from 1900 to 1904.[20] The same trend holds true for second marriages: 44 percent of the second marriages of the younger cohort of women may end in divorce, compared to 5 percent of the older cohort.[21]

A second conservative bias is built into Census Bureau divorce projections in that they are typically based on the divorce experiences of persons up to the age of 54. While the rate of divorce does decline with the age, it is no longer accurate to assume that a person has "completed" his or her marriage-divorce-remarriage life history by age 54. In fact, the number of divorces among persons of middle age and older, and among persons who have been married for many years, appears to be increasing.[22] Although only 4 percent of all divorces filed 30 years ago involved marriages of more than 15 years duration, the current figure is 25 percent, and about 16 percent of those involve couples married 25 years or more.[23] And we have reason to predict that the middle-aged divorce rate will continue to rise.* Sociologists James Bossard and Eleanor Boll found that marital unhappiness (among couples currently married and living together) is greatest in the late forties and early fifties for women, and in the fifties for men.[24] Similarly, Campbell, Converse, and Rogers report that marital satisfaction generally declines with the length of the marriage.[25]† As divorce becomes more common more of these

*One source of this increase is the growing number of people who divorce after a second marriage (discussed further in Chapter 6). In 1975, 18 percent of the redivorcing men were 35–39, 28 percent were 40–49, and 28 percent were 50–75. In total, 74 percent were over 35. U.S. Bureau of the Census, "Number, Timing and Duration of Marriages and Divorces: 1975," p. 7, Table H.

†They report that after the low point at the twentieth year of marriage, marriage satisfaction sweeps upward again into very old age, perhaps because by then many of the unhappy couples have gotten divorced and "dropped out" of the relevant population. Angus Campbell, Philip E. Converse, and Willard L. Rogers, *The Quality of American Life: Perceptions, Evaluations, and Satisfactions* (New York: Russell Sage, 1976), p. 325.

middle-aged people who are dissatisfied with marriage will divorce.

Children Affected by Divorce

Dr. Paul Glick, the Senior Demographer of the Population Division of the U.S. Census Bureau, predicted that, at current rates, the proportion of children under 18 whose parents had ever obtained a divorce would reach 32 percent by 1990. That is, by 1990 close to one-third of U.S. children are expected to experience a parent's divorce before they reach the age of 18.[26]

Surprisingly, even this estimate seems quite low if we look at the pattern over the last two decades. In 1960 less than 1 percent (0.7) of the children under 18 were involved in a divorce each year. The proportion rose to 1.2 percent in 1970 and 1.7 percent in 1976. Using this 1.7 percent, Dr. Glick calculates that over 18 years 18 times 1.7 percent, or 30.6 percent of the children will have been through a parental divorce. Adjusting for the fact that some of these children will go through a divorce more than once reduces the 1976 figure to 28 percent. Thus Dr. Glick estimates that the proportion will increase a very modest amount between 1976 and 1990, from 28 percent to 32 percent. If, however, the divorce rate continues to rise, we may well find that about half of the children under 18 experience a parental divorce by 1990.

Dr. Glick does project that by 1990 half of the children will spend some time during their childhood living in a single-parent household (a definition which includes separated and widowed parents as well as divorced parents). This represents a dramatic increase from 1960, when only 27 percent of the children under 18 did not grow up in a home with their two natural parents.[27]

The New Trends

Since the high incidence of divorce poses such a fundamental challenge to the legal assumption that marriage is—and should be—a lifelong union, it is useful to examine the societal trends which suggest that *a relatively high divorce rate should now be considered a predictable feature of American society.* At least four trends are contributing to and supporting a high divorce rate. First, the social stigma attached to divorce is declining and divorce is increasingly seen as a normal event. Second, increased alternatives to a present marriage are available today, either through remarriage or in remaining single. Third, women's increased labor force participation and independent earnings mean that they have more options, especially economic options, for a viable existence outside their present marriage. And fourth, the rising standard of expectations for marital happiness makes it difficult for both men and women to justify remaining in an unsatisfactory marriage.

The Declining Stigma of Divorce

The decline in the strength of the social stigma traditionally attached to divorce is one of the most striking changes in the social climate surrounding divorce. The growing acceptance of divorce as normal is contrasted by Professor William J. Goode with the climate at the turn of the century, when people who had been divorced were excluded from many social circles and almost everyone who divorced was considered to have lost respectability to some extent.[28]

In 1977–78 interviews with recently divorced Californians we found that only 26 percent of the men and 31 percent of the women reported that they felt there was any stigma attached to divorce.[29] In addition, only a fifth of the men and a third of the women reported feeling that someone thought less of them because they were divorced. On the other hand, a third of both sexes reported receiving more favorable treatment or having someone perceive them as more interesting, sophisticated or desirable because they were divorced.

Since these interviews were conducted in California, the state where "creative divorce" and "the happy divorce movement" were first invented, one may suspect that they are atypical. However reports from states as diverse as Georgia, Michigan and New York echo the same themes: divorce is being redefined as a period of personal growth, and divorced people are more likely to be seen as interesting, coping people who are taking control of their own lives.[30] These non-traditional attitudes are, of course, more prevalent in certain segments of the population. For example, Professors Prudence Brown and Roger Manela found that among 253 divorced women in Michigan, those with more nontraditional sex-role attitudes were *more likely* to define divorce as a time of well-being and personal growth.[31] They were also more likely to have higher self-esteem and a greater sense of personal effectiveness after divorce.

One powerful influence on the changing image of divorce is the media. As Dr. Sheila Kessler, Director of the National Institute of Divorce Counselling noted, in the past the media reflected a national blind spot whereby "after divorce one either became a swinging single going to all kinds of gala affairs or one was a party to the great American tragedy."[32] Today, however, there is a more balanced approach emphasizing the real complexity of the emotions involved—including new learning and joy as well as loneliness and deprivation. This much more realistic assessment of divorce has been aided, no doubt, by the phenomenal growth in the sheer number of people who have been divorced who do not fit the old stereotype, as well as by the new approaches to divorce adopted by marriage and family counselors.

Increased Life-Style Alternatives

A second trend, resulting in part from the increased acceptability of divorce, is toward an increased number and variety of alternatives to marriage. This trend is enhanced by the large number of currently divorced people who serve as models for those who are still married: when disgruntled married people come into contact with happily divorced people, they themselves are encouraged to consider divorce an acceptable alternative.

Sociologist Jessie Bernard has emphasized the importance of successful models in explaining the increase in divorce among middle-aged women. She observes that "so many women used to be frightened by divorce, but now they see their friends leaving home and surviving. Women are finding out that living alone and being free can be great."[33] Similarly, Spence and Lonner, in studying middle-aged women, found successful divorce models an important factor in encouraging an unhappy woman to contemplate a divorce.[34]

The social alternatives available to divorced people today include not only the possibility of remarriage (which is discussed in some detail in the next chapter) but also the increasingly popular option of remaining single. Recent years have brought a dramatic increase in the number of single adults—and a concurrent increase in the respectability of being single. More people are currently remaining in their after-divorce single status for longer periods of time, and a growing percentage of never-married young adults have chosen to maintain their single life-style. From 1960 to 1976 the percentage of persons never married increased (from 20 percent to 34 percent) in every age group and for both sexes.[35] There are now over 43 million single adults whose very presence attests to the possibility of creating an acceptable single life-style after divorce.[36]

Economic Options for Women

A third factor in the high divorce rate lies in women's new economic options. As Carter and Glick have shown, in the nineteenth-century United States marriage was essential to economic security. A divorced woman had few economic options:

> Women who contemplated divorce in 1890 were unlikely to obtain a comfortable livelihood. If they sought employment, their limited education and training made the outlook, other than for unskilled or semiskilled work, anything but bright; if they returned with their children to the home of their parents, they might be placing a heavy responsibility on persons who were approaching retirement age. Remarriage following divorce was made difficult by the widespread disapproval of divorced persons. Thus the unhappy wives of 1890 were often constrained to tolerate conditions that wives of the 1960s would find intolerable. So, also, the unhappy husbands of 1890 were reluctant to seek divorce because of strong community disapproval of such action. And if the husband was a farmer, as so many were, the wife was an indispensable member of the production team; this fact was a strong economic motivation for avoiding a legal ending of the marriage.[37]

Today both men and women can find economically feasible alternatives to their present marriage, but it is for women that the changes have been most striking. Women's increased labor force participation means that more women have paychecks of their own —and that gives them a new measure of independence. They are more likely to be able to support themselves when the need arises, or at least to feel that their present marriage is not their only option for economic survival. As sociologist Jessie Bernard has observed, the increased labor force participation of middle-aged women today vastly expands their options, and, equally important, it enhances their awareness of alternatives to their present marriage:

> With their children grown up more women are moving into the labor force and have more options available to them. More and more women are saying, "What's the point of hanging on to a bad marriage?"[38]

The empirical data on the impact of women's employment on divorce are mixed because of the vast number of other variables involved. (The amount of income a woman earns, the steadiness of her job, her occupational status, and her prospects for advancement will obviously affect her perception of her alternatives to her present marriage.) However, if a woman's work can ensure her an adequate life-style and standard of living outside her present marriage, her labor force participation is more likely to have an "independence effect"—that is, to make her more independent of her marriage. Several studies have reported evidence of this effect among women who are employed outside the home, especially among those working in highly paid jobs. For example, Sawhill reports that women with higher salaries in 1968 were more likely to have separated or divorced by 1972.[39]

Offsetting the independence effect is the positive impact that a wife's salary can have on the family's standard of living. As Hofferth and Moore have noted, "a wife's working can raise the couple's joint standard of living—and perhaps improve their quality of life—thereby increasing the pleasures of remaining in the marriage."[40] When two spouses are working at highly paid jobs the life-style they can enjoy together often far exceeds what either one could have alone. Thus a wife's employment (and salary) may increase the likelihood of marital stability by providing both spouses with the added benefits that her income brings. In fact, a 1980 national survey indicates that, overall, wives' employment does not seem to affect marital adjustment and companionship from either the husband's or the wife's point of view.[41] If the wife is unhappy in her marriage, however, she is much more likely to divorce if she can envision viable economic alternatives outside marriage.

Along these lines, employment outside the home also expands a woman's access to noneconomic opportunities that may similarly work to increase her self-reliance. As Paul Glick of the Bureau of the Census observes, "Women who enter the marketplace gain greater confidence, expand their social circles independent of their husbands' friends, taste independence and are less easy to satisfy— and are more likely to divorce later."[42]

It is interesting to note that women's labor force participation also affects husbands' perceptions of the economic and social viability of divorce. If a husband is unhappy in his marriage, his wife's employment may make divorce more feasible for him. In fact, one could explain the upsurge in middle-age divorce from the man's point of view: liberalized divorce laws and employed wives have given husbands new opportunities to leave marriage without having to bear a heavy financial burden.

Glick and Norton also point to the impact of the declining birth rate on women's option to divorce.[43] Many married couples today, especially among the younger groups, have few or no children; thus a woman's return to single life is likely to be far less complicated now than it was when large families were the rule. In 1976, 43 percent of the divorcing couples were childless, and those who did have children had, on the average, only one or two.[44]

Rising Standards for Happiness in Marriage

A fourth societal trend is the rising expectation for happiness in marriage, which makes it more difficult for both men and women to justify remaining in an unsatisfactory marriage. Increased dissatisfaction with marriage may be attributed at least in part to the new romanticization of marriage, as Carter and Glick suggest:

> Much has been written about the over-romantic attitude of young people toward marriage, abetted by popular literature and songs with much to say about the blissful state that comes with the perfect marriage. These attitudes deserve at least some of the credit for the frequent development of disillusionment and increasing divorce.[45]

Each of these factors has been closely associated with the rise in the divorce rate over the past century, and each will probably continue to stimulate further rises in the future. But whether or not the divorce rate continues to increase, the assumption of lifelong marriages already runs contrary to the facts of the modern era.

Implications for the Legal System

The sociological data point to the need for a legal system which recognizes the possibility that individuals may wish to contract for marriage on a less-than-lifetime basis. In any case, the legal regulation of marriage should reflect the present realities. In 1975 the average first marriage that ended in divorce had lasted less than seven years, down from nearly eight years the decade before.[46] Second marriages that ended in divorce were even shorter lived: about

5.3 years. In fact, by 1975 thirty percent of the divorces involved persons married three years or less.[47]

A society with this high rate of marital dissolution should, at a minimum, have legal provisions for marriage contracts, term marriages, and limited-purpose marriages for persons wishing such alternatives. But most important, the legal provisions for divorce should be restructured to provide some real protection for the men, women and children who experience divorce. Although many states have revised their divorce laws in the last decade with an eye toward eliminating the more egregious aspects of the fault system, only a few states have undertaken the serious steps necessary to reformulate their divorce laws in light of the changing social patterns and timing of both marriage and divorce. Fewer still have recognized the need to increase a couple's options in structuring their own marriage—and their own divorce.[48]

In Part I of this book we discussed many of the changes that are necessary to bring modern divorce law into line with present social reality. Two types of reforms are worthy of special emphasis: one concerning property, the other support. First, there is a need for divorce laws to recognize the partnership nature of marriage in general, and the wife's contribution to the assets acquired during marriage in particular. As a practical matter this necessitates laws that provide for the division of *all* marital property upon divorce, including the intangible assets of the marriage such as the career assets discussed in Chapter 3. Social Security accounts, pensions, retirement benefits, professional education and goodwill, and insurance coverage should all be recognized as products of the marital partnership and divided as marital property upon divorce.

Second, there is a need for divorce law reforms to provide better *economic* protection for the women and children who are the casualties of the current laissez-faire system of divorce. We have to recognize that divorced spouses and their children need the kind of economic protection that has been traditionally reserved for widows and their children. For children this means the institution of adequate child support schedules and the establishment of a viable system of enforcement. This could include a system of automatic wage assignments from the inception of the child support order, and, when necessary, the realistic application of more forceful sanctions, such as jail. For the younger women, especially those who have been housewives and/or have subordinated their own careers for their husbands and families during the marriage, this means the adoption of support rules that enable her to get education and retraining to develop a satisfactory earning capacity for the future. For older women, especially those whose earning capacities have been impaired while they were housewives in marriages of long duration, this means the adoption of support rules that equalize the net income available to both spouses after divorce. Clearly one of greatest inequities in the current law is the almost punitive treatment of divorced wives after long-duration marriages. They, like widows, deserve survivors' benefits.

Finally, for the custodial parent (or parents), whether male or female, special social and economic supports are needed. Consider, for example, the economic consequences of divorce for the custodian of young children in Norway as reported by a Norwegian social scientist who was herself recently divorced:

> Everyone knows that *divorced parents need more money* and more social support because of the additional pressures involved in raising children as a single parent . . . So, as soon as I got divorced *my income went up*: both the local and national government increased my mother's allowance, my tax rate dropped drastically as I was now taxed at the lower rate of a single head of household, and my former husband contributed a significant sum for child support. . . . It also helped to have the possibility of 24-hour day care and a husband who was willing to take some of the responsibility for parenting during the week.

Even this brief illustration suggests the advantages of a legal (and social) system that takes seriously its responsibility to provide protection and support for divorced parents—and their children.

In conclusion, it is clear that the legal assumptions of the traditional marriage contract must give way to a new social reality. No longer can marriage be viewed as a lifelong union and divorce as a deviant phenomenon. Robert Schoen and Verne Nelson have estimated that the average woman now can expect to spend 6.5 years of her life as a divorced person.[49] Clearly, the legal system must recognize the legitimate legal concerns of these average citizens, just as it has always recognized the concerns of those who remain married until death.

CHAPTER 6

First Marriage, No Remarriage

The Traditional Legal Contract

The assumption that marriage will last a lifetime is closely linked to the assumption that all marriages are first marriages of the young. The ideal scenario is that two people marry when they are young and set out to travel the road of life together. They soon have children and struggle to provide a good home for them. They share the hard work in the early years hoping to reap the benefits in later years. Their joint efforts begin to bear fruit in middle age, and by the time they reach retirement they are assured security and comfort through whatever golden years remain.

The assumption that every marriage is a first marriage is evident when one considers the scope of the obligations in the traditional marital contract. While the law obligates the husband to support his wife and children, it does not specify how this responsibility should be balanced against the needs of a former spouse or the children of a former marriage. Nor is there any consideration of a wife's similar responsibility to divide or balance her obligations to children from a former marriage.

The same assumption is reflected in the treatment of property acquired during marriage: here again, traditional law omits any provision for balancing the competing interests of first and second families. This omission can be most troublesome when a former spouse dies, for while most state laws contain some automatic provision for a surviving *spouse* to inherit a specified share of a deceased mate's estate, they accord no such recognition to a surviving *former spouse*, even if she or he has played a greater role in building the estate than the current spouse has. Also, except by antenuptial or postnuptial agreement or by disinheritance in a will, it is impossible to prevent a spouse of short duration from inheriting a fixed share of one's estate. For these reasons attorneys have often advised antenuptial contracts for previously married persons.[1] They are necessary because the traditional marriage contract completely ignores so many real needs by assuming that all marriages are first marriages.

Even a superficial review of the types of persons to whom attorneys routinely recommend a special contract before marriage[2] gives a clue to the number of relationships traditional legal marriage fails to consider: divorced men and women with property they wish to control; widows and widowers who have inherited a former spouse's estate; persons with children from a former marriage and persons marrying someone with children from a former marriage; persons with grandchildren and persons marrying someone with grandchildren; and persons eligible for pensions or other widow's benefits as a result of a former marriage.[*] But antenuptial contracts do not adequately offset the legal system's failure to take into account the problems routinely faced by people entering second marriages. In the following pages we shall see that second (and third) marriages now account for close to one-third of all marriages. Surely the legal conception of marriage must be expanded to include this significant proportion of the marrying population.

*In order to determine exactly what group of people most often used antenuptial contracts, Charles W. Gamble tabulated all antenuptial contract cases in volume 16 of the *Seventh Decennial Digest* (covering 1956–1966). He found that 80 percent of the men and 70 percent of the women had been previously married; 90 percent of these men and 94 percent of the women had children from their former marriages. Among the women whose ages were reported, the average age was 49 years with 81 percent over 40. Charles W. Gamble, "The Antenuptial Contract," *University of Miami Law Review* 26 (1972):732.

Social Reality: The Increase in
Second (and Subsequent) Marriages

Both the number and proportion of second (and subsequent) marriages has increased substantially in recent years. Although the vast majority of all marriages are still first marriages, as early as 1960 nearly one out of every five men who married had been married before.[3] By 1975 more than a quarter of the men entering marriage—29 percent—were entering a second marriage.[4]

This growing remarriage rate can be linked directly to the rising divorce rate. Sociologist William J. Goode found a high divorce rate accompanied by a high remarriage rate in all societies,[5] and this has clearly been the recent trend in the United States. The process works in two ways. First, high divorce rates create a large pool of unattached men and women who are available as potential remarriage partners. Second, the presence of a large number of divorced men and women in the population provides potential (and real) alternatives to currently married persons, and may thereby stimulate more divorce—and more eventual remarriage. In other words, the high divorce rate and high remarriage rate together represent the ever-present possibility of changing spouses throughout the life cycle.

Most of the recent rise in the incidence of second marriages is a result of remarriage after divorce rather than after the death of a spouse. For example, in 1975, 24 percent of all marriages were remarriages after divorce, while only 5 percent followed widowhood.[6]

Divorced persons are generally more likely to remarry than are widowed persons, even when age is held constant. For example, a 1975 census study showed that half of the people in the early fifties age group whose first marriages had ended in widowhood had remarried, compared to about four-fifths of those whose first marriages had ended in divorce.[7] Part of the difference between these two groups may be related to the fact that many people divorce in order to remarry, while few people enter widowhood with that intent.[8]

Two aspects of the current remarriage rate have particularly important implications for the legal system because they both indicate that the number of people entering second and subsequent marriages is likely to increase in the future. The first is the high percentage of divorced people who eventually remarry; the second is the relationship between age at divorce and at remarriage.

Overall, a strikingly high proportion of divorced people remarry—over 80 percent, or four out of every five divorced persons.[9] The probability of remarriage after divorce is highest for men: four out of five divorced men and three out of four divorced women eventually remarry. With the number of divorces currently at more than one million a year, there is a high probability that in the future an ever increasing number of persons will continue to be frustrated by the "first marriage" assumptions built into the legal structure of marriage.

With respect to age, as might be expected, the younger the age at divorce the more probable it is that the parties will remarry. Thus, a 1975 survey conducted by the U.S. Bureau of the Census revealed that 76 percent of the women divorced before they were 30 had remarried, 56 percent of those divorced while in their thirties had done so, and 32 percent of those divorced in their forties had remarried. Of those divorced between the ages of 50 and 75, only 12 percent had remarried.[10] Probably some of those not remarried by the survey date will eventually do so (especially if their marriages ended a short time before the survey).

Because age at divorce is related to probability of remarriage, it is important to note that although people are marrying later, the average age at divorce is declining[11] (because those marriages that end in divorce are lasting fewer years). Today, first marriages that end in divorce last an average of seven years, and the median age at divorce is 27 for women and 29 for men.[12] Most of those who remarry do so a short time after their divorce. Among people who divorce in their 20's the average time is less than four years between marriages.[13] One-half of all remarriages occur within three years of the divorce; two-thirds occur within five years. With this short time-span between marriages the median age at remarriage is 29 for women and 33 for men.

These current trends—toward briefer marriages, younger ages at divorce, and younger ages at remarriage—portend a continued increase in the number of remarriages.* But while there seems to be

*There is also a growing number of remarriages after a second divorce. Because the incidence of redivorce is also increasing, these people are also much younger. Half of all redivorces have occurred by age 41 for men and 38 for women. Paul C. Glick and Arthur Norton, "Marrying, Divorcing and Living Together in the U.S. Today," *Population Bulletin* 32, no. 5 (1977):6, 36.

little room for doubt that the *number* of people entering second and third marriages will continue to grow, the *rate* of remarriage after divorce may continue to fluctuate, as it has over the past few decades.[14]

It is difficult to ascertain the absolute number of persons marrying now who have been married previously because of certain limits in census data. We do know that in 1978, 22 percent of the intact marriages between persons 45 to 54 years old involved at least one partner who had been married before.[15] However, this is a conservative estimate of the total percentage, for two reasons. First, the data on which it is based are weighted towards persons in an older, and therefore more conservative, generation; as we have already noted, men and women in successive generations are divorcing and remarrying at younger ages and in greater numbers. Second, because these data are drawn from a sample of currently married people, they exclude people who have been through a second or third marriage but are now separated, divorced, or widowed. We know that 23 percent of currently divorced persons have been married more than once, as have 20 percent of the currently separated persons.[16]

When the data are adjusted for these factors, we can realistically estimate that about one-third of all marriages will soon involve a previously married spouse. In fact, as we have noted above, that figure is already close to attainment, with 29 percent of the men who married in 1975 entering a second or subsequent marriage. Furstenberg suggests that in the next 15–20 years, 25 percent of women in mid-life will have had a second marriage.[17]

Children Affected by Remarriage

In 1980 there were about 25 million stepparents in the United States.[18] Estimates of the number of children currently living in remarriage or "reconstituted" families varies from 13 to 20 percent of all American children under the age of 18.[19]

If one includes children who have lived with stepparents in the past, and those who will live with a stepparent in the future, it is likely that one out of four children in the U.S. will live in a stepparent family before they reach 18. In addition, many of the children who live in single-parent families will spend some time living with or vacationing with stepparent families formed by noncustodial parents. As we noted in Chapter 5, about a third of all children will experience a divorce before they are 18 and many of these children will also have the experience of living in a reconstituted family.

Implications for the Legal System

Two consequences of this divorce–remarriage phenomenon must particularly concern sociologists and legal scholars. One is that persons entering a second marriage have *different concerns* from those beginning their first marriage; and their concerns need to be recognized by the legal system. Most persons entering a second marriage bring with them some responsibilities and obligations from their first marriage. They are likely to be older than persons entering first marriages, to possess more property, and to be more concerned with how that property will be distributed after their death. In addition, persons entering a second marriage are likely to have children (and in some cases, grandchildren), and they are likely to want to structure their new relationships so that they can remain social, economic, and psychological parents to those children.

A second highly significant consequence of the divorce–remarriage phenomenon is the growing pattern of *serial monogamy*, or serial family formation, in which people go through the formative phase of establishing a new family with a new spouse more than once. Full recognition of the increasing importance of serial monogamy could well transform our legal and social expectations of a "normal" family life cycle, and might even alter profoundly the role of marriage within our society. These two consequences are further explored below.

Social and Legal Concerns of Reconstituted Families

In a classic analysis of remarriage sociologist Andrew Cherlin argued, in 1978, that remarriage was an "incomplete institution."[20] While most family behavior is "habitualized"—that is, in most everyday situations parents and children know what is expected of them—there are no clear social norms for behavior in reconstituted families. Cherlin argued that this lack of social norms creates additional pressures on these families, which helps to explain the higher rate of divorce among second marriages. He notes that

. . . families of remarriages after divorce that include children from previous marriages must solve problems unknown to other types of families. For many of these problems, such as proper kinship terms, authority to discipline stepchildren, and legal relationships, no institutionalized solutions have emerged. As a result, there is more opportunity for disagreements and divisions among family members and more strain in many remarriages after divorce.[21]

Remarriage families are structurally more complicated in three respects. First, there is the problem of sheer numbers. Because the new kin in a remarriage after divorce do not replace the kin from the previous marriage, children often have two sets of fathers and mothers, four sets of grandparents and an assortment of half brothers and sisters along with their birth siblings.

Jessie Bernard's classic study of remarriage emphasizes the competition and conflict between former and present family units and the impact this may have on the various sets of spouses and children.[22] The basic problem, as Leslie Aldridge Westoff put it, is that "a second marriage resembles a Cecil B. DeMille production with a cast of thousands: most remarrying people . . . are involved not only with each other but with children and parents and parents-in-law and new children and ex-wives and ex-husbands."[23] It is not surprising that an English study of reconstituted families concluded that the couples' major desire was for all these people to leave them alone so that they could get on with the work of their "own" (self-contained) family.[24]

In addition to an expanded network of relatives, and the expanded obligations that follow, there is a need for an expanded vocabulary of kinship: how does one refer to multiple moms and dads and brothers and sisters each with new spouses and former spouses who are all "members of the family."

The second structural complexity is ecological: the family is often "expanded in space over more than one household."[25] The wife's children, who may normally live in the new household may frequently leave to visit (or live with) their father, while the husband's children, who may normally live with his ex-wife, may join the household. This extension over three households is often further complicated by vacations at yet another "summer house" or winter ski cabin.

The third complication stems from conflicting obligations and norms for roles in the new family, what Liz Einstein calls "Catch-

22 roles."[26] While children may want a stepparent to act like a "real" father or mother in some ways, at the same time they may also want them to know their place. Spouses also have conflicting expectations. For example a stepfather may be expected to help rear and support his new wife's children but not to discipline them.

In 1980 Goetting reported little consensus among remarried men and women about norms for appropriate behavior.[27] Goetting asked a sample of 90 remarried men and 90 remarried women what they considered appropriate behavior in a variety of situations involving interaction between current and former spouses. Although it was generally agreed that former and current spouses ought to say hello to one another if they meet by chance, and that a former spouse should be called about a health emergency, on the whole, there was little consensus on what was the proper thing to do in most of the situations the researchers posed. For example, there was no agreement as to whether an ex-spouse should be invited into the new spouse's home while waiting to pick up his or her children. Since this is a common event in the lives of most of the respondents, it reflects the lack of norms for even the most routine tasks of stepfamily interaction.

Dr. William Nicols, 1980 President of the American Association of Marriage and Family Therapy called the remarriage family the major clinical problem of the 1980's. As he observed, "taking the characteristics of the nuclear family and placing them on another totally different sociological/cultural entity—the remarriage family —just will not work."[28]

The same can be said of the attempts to impose the legal structure of marriage—a structure designed for a first-marriage nuclear family—on second and third marriages. It is evident that the legal responsibilities of remarried parents to each other and to their various sets of children must be defined differently than those of spouses in a lifelong partnership. In addition, the law must apportion and reallocate traditional family obligations among two or three families.

If, for example, both husband and wife remarry, they not only have to reallocate their support responsibilities for their common children, but each may now have responsibilities for the new spouse's children from a former marriage, as well as for children of the current union. The extent to which our society has lagged behind in dealing with such emotional and legal complexities is re-

flected in the dearth of terms available to define the emerging relationships. Westoff asks: "How, for instance, does a new husband
designate his relationship to his current wife's ex-husband's new
wife?"[29] Similarly, what term does a child who is living with his
mother use to describe his relationship with his father's new wife?
Not surprisingly, the legal (and social) rights and duties of the child
and the woman toward each other are unclear.[30] As anthropologist
Paul Bohannan put it, the relationships of these quasi-kin "approach chaos, with each set of families having to work out its own
destiny without any realistic guidelines."[31]

Consider the following situation as an example of the typical legal (and social) issues that may arise with remarriage. A remarried man is legally obligated to support his two children from a former marriage and the young child he has fathered with his new
wife. At the same time, his wife's two children from her former
marriage are currently living with him, and by virtue of their presence in the household (at the dinner table, etc.) he finds himself
supporting them as well. While he is not legally obligated to support his wife's children if he has not legally adopted them—and let
us suppose that neither he nor the children's natural father wants
that adoption to take place—in practical terms, he inevitably contributes to their support because they are members of his new
household. The situation is further complicated by the fact that his
new wife's ex-husband has also remarried and started a new family,
and has not been paying her court-ordered child support. Our man
feels the law should either relieve him of his financial obligation to
support his own two children by his ex-wife (who are now living in
another man's household) or force his present wife's ex-husband to
pay his support obligations. He is disconcerted to learn that there
are no legal guidelines to allocate and apportion support responsibilities among several families.

On the other hand, consider how the present system may provide a windfall for a second spouse while unjustly depriving the
first. At age 58, a corporate vice president falls in love with his secretary and decides to divorce his wife of 34 years. (The two children
of this marriage already have families of their own.) Aside from a
substantial home the major assets of this marriage are in the husband's career, in generous company benefits (including full medical, hospital and life insurance and an excellent retirement program) and executive perks (a luxurious car, a large expense account,

investment options and extensive travel at company expense). His secretary, who is 28 at the time of the marriage, has two young children whom the executive agrees to adopt. If, let us say, the executive has a heart attack the following year and dies suddenly, in most states, a third to a half of his estate would go to his new wife, with the remainder divided among the four children (two from his last marriage and his new wife's two children). His first wife will receive nothing—neither survivors' insurance nor a survivors' pension nor a share of the estate—and both she and his natural children are likely to feel that they have been treated unjustly. A legal rule that would allow some weighted apportionment between the two wives would seem more just.

Given such situations, it is not surprising that Schwartz found that the typical family seeking help from a family service agency has changed from the intact first-marriage family to one of the new kinds of extended family—either that headed by a divorced spouse or that involving new mates—and their respective sets of children. An increasing number of remarried parents are having trouble defining their relative obligations to "his, her, and their children."[32]

One would think the large number of children involved in these new family networks would alone provide sufficient justification for a new legal analysis. In the past two decades the number of children involved in divorce has more than tripled: in 1954 there were 341,000 children under the age of 18 in divorcing families, by 1975 the number had increased to 1,123,000.[33] As we noted in Chapter 5, close to one-third of the children in the United States are likely to experience a parents' divorce before they reach the age of 18.

Margaret Mead insisted that in coming to grips with the growing phenomenon of divorce (and remarriage) we must define kinship in new terms so that children in changing family relationships can have the security of knowing that certain important people will have lifelong responsibility for them.* Thus, a permanent term for co-grandparents is needed to reflect a permanent relationship; and a term for "my child's father who is no longer my husband" is needed to reflect the reality and legitimacy of that continuing rela-

---

*Mead also suggested that current laws about incest fail to provide adequate security and protection for children in households of remarriage. Margaret Mead, "Anomalies in American Postdivorce Relationships," in Paul Bohannan, ed., *Divorce and After: An Analysis of the Emotional and Social Problems of Divorce* (New York: Doubleday, 1970), pp. 97–112. See also Brenda Maddox, *The Half-Parent: Living with Other People's Children* (New York: M. Evans & Co., 1975).

tionship between two adults no longer married to each other. It is clear, however, that the need Mead seeks to satisfy cannot be met by terminology alone. The legal system must respond as well by trying to articulate principles and assign responsibilities and rights fairly to members of these new kinship and quasi-kinship networks.

Men and women about to enter a second marriage will find it useful to discuss and specify their obligations to prospective and existing children as well as to current and former spouses. When there are children from a former marriage, they may want to make explicit arrangements for visitation, support, adoption, inheritance, and custody.

Support and property obligations to former spouses will also be of concern to those entering a second marriage. In addition to monthly support obligations, questions will arise as to who shall be the beneficiaries of life and accident insurance, medical coverage, retirement benefits and pension rights, and shared investments in careers, real estate, business, and other property. Some may want to specify how income and property will be apportioned between first and second spouses; others will want to ensure the inheritance rights of each spouse as well as those of the various offspring. For example, it may be important to have a second wife agree to the first wife's retention of her rights to health coverage, pension benefits, and life insurance, and to her new husband's pledge to continue to support his children through college. The second wife often feels that her new husband's income has been committed in advance by a divorce court, leaving little flexibility for his second family. At a minimum, the nature and extent of the husband's financial obligations should be made known and agreed to in advance.

Remarriage After 60

At the other end of the life cycle, those who remarry after the childbearing years and after their children have left home also have distinct concerns which the legal system tends to ignore. The United States has one of the highest rates of marriage in the world for men and women over 60.[34] In 1970 alone, 60,000 people aged 65 or older got married.[35] The rate of marriage in this age group has remained fairly stable, but the proportion of the U.S. population over 65 is increasing,[36] and thus the *number* of such marriages is expected to rise. In 1975 the marriage rate (per 1,000 unmarried) for those over

65 was 2.4 for women and 16.8 for men.[37]* Recent statistics show that if a man of 65 marries a woman his age or younger, they can look forward to at least ten years of life together.[38]

Persons retired or about to retire may be especially interested in specifying a property settlement in the event of dissolution or death. They are less likely to have day-to-day concerns about the support of their children, who are likely to be financially independent by the time their parents are 65. Nor are they likely to have more children; thus they need not consider the obligations incident to child-rearing. Former spouses may also be less relevant to partners who may themselves be widows and widowers. (In 1974, two-thirds of these brides were widows.[39]) However, elderly persons may well want to retain their separate property and to ensure that the bulk of their estates will go to their blood kin, which is to say the children and grandchildren of their first marriage.[40] As Foster points out, "In all probability, each spouse's assets antedated their relationship, and there is no economic reason to force upon either spouse an interest in the property of the other merely because they are married."[41] Finally, elderly couples may want to specify or limit their financial obligations to each other with respect to support, medical costs, health and accident insurance, and retirement and pension benefits.

Today's system of laws, however, not only frustrates elderly persons' efforts to choose the economics of marriage best suited to their circumstances; it discourages them from entering into marriage. Sociologist Arlie Hochschild reported in 1974 that many older people were then living together in lieu of marriage to avoid losing pension or Social Security benefits based on former spouses' earnings.[42] Until recently, Social Security provisions provided a disincentive to remarriage in that widow's benefits were terminated upon remarriage; now, if a widow and widower marry, both may retain their separate Social Security benefits. However, many private pension plans still terminate a widow's benefits if she remarries, and they therefore provide a strong economic disincentive to remarriage for widows. Despite these obstacles, however, increas-

*This sex-based difference is due to two factors: the greater number of men who marry considerably younger spouses, and the larger absolute number of women over 65 compared to men. In 1974 there were more than 12.8 million women over 65 in the U.S. population compared to 9.0 million men, a difference of 3.9 million. By 1985 it is expected that women over 65 will outnumber men by 5.3 million. "Profiles of Elders in the United States," *Statistical Bulletin* (Metropolitan Life) 15 (April 1975):8.

ing numbers of older persons are entering new legal marriages each year.

In response to current attempts to redefine age roles, it seems reasonable to expect more remarriage among persons over 65 in the future. As gerontologist Bernice Neugarten notes, Americans between 55 and 75—those she calls the "young-old"—are vastly altering our stereotypes of old age. In contrast to the familiar poor, sick, isolated, passive and incompetent stereotype of the elderly, the young-old are well educated, politically active, in good health, and have a great amount of leisure time.[43]

In support of Neugarten's vision are Masters and Johnson's findings that sexual response and performance for men may extend beyond the age of eighty, and for women "there is no time limit drawn by the advancing years."[44] Female age roles, in particular, have been undergoing redefinition in a break with the traditional measure of a woman's worth in terms of her physical beauty—a standard that excludes all but the young.[45] With these trends in mind, it is reasonable to expect that the number and variety of social, sexual, and legal relationships among elderly persons will increase in the future. Unfortunately, it also seems likely that these relationships will be increasingly restrained and thwarted by the traditional legal model.

The Implications of Serial Monogamy

As noted above, another trend in American society is the movement toward serial monogamy, or serial family formation. There are two demographic bases for this trend. The first, of course, is the increase in divorce and remarriage, which we have already reviewed. Demographers Schoen and Nelson have found that as a result of the growing pattern of marriage, divorce, and remarriage, the average U.S. male already participates in 1.67 marriages in his lifetime.[46]

One characteristic of the new pattern is the formation of new families throughout the life cycle. This inevitably leads to a greater diversity in the functions and purposes of marriage. Some of the new units want to raise children, others do not. Some focus on shared leisure activities, others on work or a career. Some of the new families will last for 20 to 40 years, others for but two or three. And while some will seek to build a total life together, others quite frankly will want limited-sphere relationships in which the spouses will decide in advance to share only a stage or period in life, such as going through graduate school, working in a foreign country, raising small children, traveling in middle age, participating in a campaign or a political cause, or weathering the empty-nest period or the time before and after retirement.

The second demographic basis for the pattern of serial monogamy is the continuing increase in life expectancy—and, therefore, in the years available to spend in family life. With increased longevity, the couple in an enduring marriage today can reasonably anticipate many years of life alone together. For example, the expected duration of marriage contracted in the years 1900–1902 between a man of 23 and a woman of 21 was 31.3 years. In 1969–1971, by contrast, the expected duration was 42.5 years, an increase of more than ten years.[47] Thanks to a significant reduction in mortality in the United States since the turn of the century, the chances that the principals in today's typical first marriage will both survive the next fifty years are more than twice as great as they were in 1900–1902.[48]

In addition to increased longevity, one must consider the current trends toward fewer children and closer child spacing and the consequent decrease in the number of years the average family spends in childrearing. These trends leave the average parents with many more years alone together after the children have left home. The proportion of children born to women over 30 years old has decreased, owing to a decrease in the median age at which women bear their children.[49] Today the average woman completes her childbearing by the time she is 26, and she is in her middle-forties when the last child attains majority.[50] With children more commonly moving out of the family home at that point, the number of years the parents will spend alone together further increases. The result is a very different family pattern from that of fifty years ago, when minor children commonly lived at home with parents who were in their fifties and sixties. Even if we take the marriage of the last child as the point at which major parental responsibilities end, we find that women today tend to be about fifty years old when their last child is married, which leaves them with the prospect of ten to twenty-five years of marriage in the "empty nest."[51]

The departure of children creates an increased stress on each spouse to fulfill the other's needs. And as Jessie Bernard observes, "This post-parental stage of marriage is a brand-new phenomenon in human history. People did not live long enough in the past to reach it. One spouse or the other had died long before the youngest child had left home or was married."[52] Lawrence Kubie points out that today divorce "is accomplishing some of the reshuffling of marriages which only a few years ago occurred through death."[53] In fact, Kubie asserts that it is our increased longevity that "has now exposed the fact that the human race never has been mature enough for enduring marriages, a fact which used to be obscured by early death."[54]

Bernard suggests that with increased longevity it may be wholly unreasonable to expect both exclusivity and permanence in marriage. Either serial monogamy or institutionalization of extramarital relations may be necessary to cope with the expanded time burden placed on marriage. As Bernard explains, in our modern world with its evolving realities, some major adjustments seem to be taking place:

> If we insist on permanence, exclusivity is harder to enforce; if we insist on exclusivity, permanence may be endangered. The trend . . . seems to be in the direction of exclusivity at the expense of permanence in the younger years but permanence at the expense of exclusivity in the later years.[55]

Marital sabbaticals have been suggested as one means of providing variety in very long-term marriages.

As our expectations for marriage increase and change, and as social and psychological pressures on the two-person bond multiply, the social influences toward serial monogamy are becoming as powerful as the demographic ones. Each of these changes presents a challenge to the traditional marriage contract. Clearly, a more flexible legal model is needed in a society with increasing serial family formation throughout the life cycle.

CHAPTER 7

Separate Roles for Husband and Wife

The separate roles that legal marriage presents for husbands and wives have been extensively documented in Part I of this book. The marriage contract assigns the husband the primary responsibility for the family's economic support, and designates him head of the household. The wife's duties are to care for her husband, her home, and her children.

This assumed division of labor is challenged by recent economic and sociological data. The economic data on married women's labor force participation and earnings challenge the law's assumption that the husband should—and does—singlehandedly bear the responsibility for family support. The sociological challenge is posed by data showing increasingly varied and egalitarian role patterns within the family. Each of these challenges is explored in more detail below.

Economic Reality: Shared Responsibility for Family Support

Three types of economic data challenge the law's continued assignment of the responsibility for family support to the husband. The first is the increase in the number and percentage of married women in the labor force. The second is the increase in the number and percentage of mothers, especially mothers of young children, who work outside the home. The third is the increasing importance of women's wages in meeting the day-to-day living expenses of the family.

Labor Force Participation of Married Women

Women have always worked. But in the past most women were engaged in domestic employment or agricultural work, and in both types of work their jobs were obtained through, and supervised by, their male kinsmen—their fathers, uncles, and husbands.[1] The major change in that picture has taken place in the last century, with women's greatly increased participation in the nonagricultural, nonfamilial, industrialized labor force[2] and their ability "to obtain jobs and promotions without the help or permission of their men."[3]

In 1890 less than 5 percent of all U.S. married women worked outside the home for wages and salaries.[4] By 1940 this figure had increased to 17 percent. The most dramatic increases, however, have occurred in the past few decades, since World War II. In 1947 one out of five married women (20 percent) was employed in the paid labor force. The proportion rose to one in four (25 percent) by 1950, roughly one in three (32 percent) by 1960, and to one out of two by 1980. Today a married woman is as likely to be employed outside the home as she is to be a full-time housewife.

Economist Ralph Smith points to the sharp, sustained increase in employment of *married women* as the most profound change in women's labor force participation.[5] Married women accounted for the greatest part of the increase in women's labor force participation in the 1970's. (The rise for single, divorced, and widowed women has been less pronounced because a substantial percentage of unmarried women have always worked.)

There are several explanations for the change. Smith contends that the increase in real wages offered by employment has outstripped the rewards of working at home. In his words, "more women have shifted part of their work activity to the marketplace because the 'opportunity cost' of staying home all day has become too great."[6]

Sociologist Valerie Oppenheimer characterizes the great postwar rise in female labor force participation as "in good part, a *response* to increased job opportunities" at a time when labor shortages caused employers to abandon their prejudices against employing older married women.[7] Economist Francine Blau draws upon Oppenheimer's thesis to suggest that many more married women would be working today if they were afforded sufficient opportunities to do so.[8]

The average woman worker in 1920 was a single woman in her late twenties employed as a factory worker or clerk until she got married;[9] the average woman worker today more closely resembles the profile of the average American woman. She is married, in her thirties, and might be found in a great variety of occupations.[10]* In terms of age, racial composition, educational attainment, marital and family status, and most other characteristics, the female labor force is like the total female population. For example, in 1974, the median age of working women was thirty-six, only five years younger than the median for the entire female population. Thus, "it is rapidly becoming more difficult to consider working women an unrepresentative or atypical group."[11]†

Projecting current trends, economist Ralph Smith forecasts that by 1990, 67 percent of all married women—two out of every three—will be in the labor force.[12] Without doubt, family law's assumption that all married women are full-time housewives is increasingly anachronistic.

---

*However, the growing numbers of working women who have been absorbed into the labor force does not indicate that there has been an across-the-board expansion of employment opportunities. Rather, there has been an expansion of traditionally female jobs (particularly in the clerical and service categories), of new occupations that have been rapidly defined as female, and an occasional shift in the sex composition of some occupations from male to female. Francine D. Blau, "The Data on Women Workers, Past, Present, and Future," in Ann H. Stromberg and Shirley Harkess, eds., *Women Working: Theories and Facts in Perspective* (Palo Alto, Calif.: Mayfield, 1978), p. 44.

Thus, despite the increased proportion of women in traditionally male fields (from 2.4 to 4.7 percent in law, and from 7 to 9 percent in medicine), women are still concentrated in a relatively small number of occupations. In 1970, 97.6 percent of secretaries and 94.2 percent of typists were women. By 1985 it is expected that 98.6 percent of the secretaries and 93.2 percent of the typists will still be women. Women's Bureau, *Women Workers*, pp. 91–93. "So for every woman who goes on to direct films, perform brain surgery, run a university or win a seat on the stock exchange, many more will be sitting behind typewriters." Georgia Dullea, "Vast Changes in Society Traced To the Rise of Working Women," *New York Times*, November 29, 1977, p. 28.

†In fact, the "typical" picture of a wife who stays home to care for children will be true for only 25% of the married women under 55 by 1990. *Marriage and Divorce Today* 5, no. 12 (Nov. 5, 1979):1.

Mothers in the Labor Force

A second major change in the labor force participation of married women has been the increase in the number of employed mothers. Between 1940 and 1978 the labor force participation rate of mothers with children under age 18 showed a phenomenal 500 percent increase—from 9 percent to 50 percent.[13] In fact, by 1978, more than half (58 percent) of all American mothers of school-age children were in the labor force.[14]

Perhaps more surprising is the number of employed mothers with preschool children, that is, children under six years. In 1950 only one out of ten (12 percent) wives (in intact marriages) with children under six were in the labor force; by 1960 the proportion had risen to one out of five (19 percent), and by 1970 it was close to one out of three (30 percent).[15] In 1978 the proportion was rapidly approaching one out of two (it was 42 percent)—and Smith predicts it will exceed fifty-five percent by 1990.[16]

In other words, it is rapidly becoming as common for married mothers with preschool children to work in the labor force as it is for them to remain at home to care for their children.* In addition, even women with children under three years of age are entering the labor force in large numbers. By 1975, 33 percent of all mothers with children under three were employed—twice the 1960 rate.[17]

Thus, the law's traditional assumption of a household mother whose exclusive attention is devoted to her children is clearly inappropriate today.

The Economic Contribution of Working Women

Most of the married women in today's labor force are contributing basic financial support to their families. Three-quarters of those

*In a recent study of working women with small children Gordon and Kammeyer found that economic need was the most important determinant of their working status. Henry A. Gordon and Kenneth C. W. Kammeyer, "The Gainful Employment of Women with Small Children," *Journal of Marriage and the Family* 42, No. 2 (1980):327–36.

In addition, it is likely that more women in this group might work outside the home if child care were available. When nonworking women were asked why they did not work, in a 1980 national survey, a significant number mentioned either the high cost or unavailability of child care.

American Research Corporation, *American Families, 1980*, Poll conducted by the Gallup Organization for the American Research Corporation (Newport Beach, Calif.: 1980), p. 128.

who work are working full time, and contrary to the myth that married women work for pin money or extras, the facts show that the wages of these workers are of vital importance to their families.[18] In an era of double-digit inflation, when an ordinary car costs $10,000 and a modest house goes for $100,000, most families desperately need two incomes just to pay their bills.*

Among families in which the wife worked full time year round in 1978, she contributed a median 38 percent of the total family income.[19] Not surprisingly, families with working wives typically have higher incomes than those with full-time housewives. Some have surmised that a high family income accords a woman the status and the freedom from domestic worries to work outside her home. But, Smith cautions:

> Casual examination can lead to the correct, but misleading conclusion that wives who work are in higher-income families than are wives who do not. Their families are in higher-income brackets precisely *because* they work.[20]

The importance of a wife's contribution to total family income is most obvious, of course, where it raises a family above the poverty level. For example, in 1976, only 2 percent of husband–wife families with employed wives had incomes below $5,000, in contrast to 6 percent of the families with nonemployed wives.[21] At this level, many of the working wives earned more than their husbands: their contribution was clearly essential to family survival.[22] In minority families the wife's employment was particularly significant. In the black family, for example, the wife employed full time contributed some 39 percent of the family income and raised the mean family income to over $12,000.[23]

This is not to suggest that the wife's income makes a significant difference only at the lowest income levels. Wives' incomes are equally crucial to families above the poverty line. For example, in 1978 Rawlings reported that close to 70 percent of the married women whose husbands earned from seven to ten thousand dollars a year were in the labor force.[24] Obviously few families feel they

---

*In a 1980 national survey half of the working women said they worked mostly for the money. Another quarter said they worked for money and satisfaction, while only a quarter claimed personal satisfaction alone as the primary cause of their employment. American Research Corporation, *American Families, 1980*, Poll conducted by the Gallup Organization for the American Research Corporation (Newport Beach, Calif.: 1980), p. 126.

can make ends meet on a single salary of less than $10,000; a second paycheck helps to pay for basic necessities.

While these middle-income husbands rely on their wives' paychecks for what they consider necessities, upper-income men, who would seem to be more self sufficient, nevertheless come to depend on their wives' incomes for "basic expenses" in much the same way. For example, sociologist Cynthia Epstein reports that the young women attorneys she studied, who were earning $35,000 to $50,000 a year in 1978, perceived considerable support for their careers from their husbands, partially because these men had grown accustomed to the life-style they enjoyed with a combined family income of $50,000 to $100,000 a year.[25]

The consistent pattern across all income groups, as economist Clair Vickery observed, is that family expenditure patterns quickly adjust to the expectation of two paychecks.[26] Within a relatively short period of time the family "needs" the wife's paycheck for rent and groceries (or the car payments, or mortgage, or the children's dental bills) as much as it "needs" the husband's.

One indication of the extent to which American families have come to rely on the wife's income is the phenomenal increase in life insurance policies written on women workers. New England Mutual Life reported that individual women policy holders doubled between 1970 and 1979.[27]

Although husbands generally have higher salaries than their wives, overall one out of three working married women in 1978 earned about as much as or more than her husband.[28] The relative size of a wife's contribution to the family income obviously depends, in part, on her work schedule. For example, when the wife worked full time the year round in 1974 she contributed a median 38 percent of the family income; when she worked 27 to 49 weeks she contributed 29 percent; and when she worked either part time or full time for less than half a year she contributed 12 percent.[29]

The wife's relative contribution to the family income is also affected by wage discrepancies between men and women. In 1979, the median income of full-time, year-round, working women was only 59 percent of that of men who worked full time the year round.[30] The gap between men's and women's wages has not been narrowing: in 1970 also women earned 59 percent of what men earned.[31] Part of this discrepancy is due to men's greater average work-life experience, since women's careers are typically interrupted. But at least equally important is women's continued concentration in relatively low-wage occupations and industries.[32]

Even after adjustment for factors such as education, work experience, and occupation, the pay differential beween men and women remains. For example, in 1974, women professional and technical workers earned 66 percent of what men in the same occupational group earned; women sales workers, 41 percent.[33] As economist Francine Blau has noted, a growing body of research supports the view that discrimination accounts for a significant share of the male–female pay differential:

> After controlling for education, experience, and other factors that might tend to cause productivity differences between men and women, the proportion of the sex differential attributable to pure discrimination has been estimated at between 29 and 43 percent of male earnings.[34]

Discrimination notwithstanding, fully half of all U.S. married women are in the labor force today, and they are clearly contributing to family support. Today neither marital nor parental roles preclude women from active participation in the labor force, nor do they prevent them from sharing the family-support burden. Thus economic reality strongly contradicts the economic assumptions of traditional legal marriage.

In addition, public opinion has begun to reject the old model. For the first time in U.S. history, less than half of the population supports the traditional family model as the "preferred" family form. Results of a 1980 Roper Poll for Virginia Slims indicate that a diminishing minority (42 percent) of women and men support the traditional concept of marriage with the husband assuming the responsibility for providing for the family, and the wife running the house and taking care of the children.* A majority of women in 1980 (52 percent) perceived marriage as a responsibility to be equally shared by both partners, with both husband and wife earning salaries and sharing family and household responsibilities. And nearly half of the American men (49 percent) agreed with this interpretation.

---

*National NOW Times, June 1980, p. 15. These beliefs receive even stronger endorsements from younger women and those with college educations. A sizeable majority of younger women (66 percent) and a roughly similar number of college-educated women support this interpretation of the marital relationship.

Sociological Trends: Toward More Egalitarian Patterns

Sociological trends are similarly challenging traditional family law assumptions about the husband's role as head of the family, and the strict division of family tasks between husband and wife.

Although the ideal of male authority was more widely accepted in the past than it is today, it is questionable whether men as a group actually ever exerted anything close to the absolute power attributed to them. A close analysis of the relationships between the sexes indicates that while women in the past may have deferred to men in public, they often had great covert power and, in some spheres, considerable control over men.[35]* Nevertheless, the formal system of authority gave men the legal right to make decisions for the family, and it is likely that many men (and women) believed this arrangement proper and just.

What has changed is the legitimacy of male power. A major shift in family ideology has taken place: we have moved from the belief that the male *should* be head of the family to the belief that egalitarian arrangements are best. Further, as a 1977 nationwide survey conducted by *The New York Times* and CBS News disclosed, "Americans today are more likely to believe that marriages in which partners share the tasks of breadwinner and homemaker are a more 'satisfying way of life' than the traditional marriage in which the husband is exclusively a provider and the wife exclusively a homemaker and mother."[36]

The likelihood of increasingly liberal views toward marriage and sex roles in the future is evidenced by the wide disparities in the views of the young and the old in the *New York Times*–CBS poll sample. While 48 percent of the general population preferred

*In addition, men and women have often exercised different kinds of authority. As Goode explains: "[Those] who have observed first- or second-generation immigrant families from Italian, Greek, or Eastern European Jewish backgrounds are likely to have noticed that though the rhetoric of male dominance is common, the middle-aged or elder matriarch is to be found in many homes. The woman seems to be the center of initiative and decision. However, the male head of the family seems to be conceding this authority, reserving the right to take it back when he wishes. If he wants to oppose her will, he can do so successfully. That is, a distinction should perhaps be made between day-to-day initiative and direction, and negative authority—the right to prevent others from doing what they want." William J. Goode, *The Family* (Englewood Cliffs, N.J.: Prentice-Hall, 1964), p. 75.

shared roles, and while 43 percent preferred traditional roles, among respondents aged 18 to 29, only 27 percent preferred traditional marriage, in contrast to 59 percent of those over 45.[37]

Thus, while it would clearly be inaccurate to say that all of us currently have, or desire to have, egalitarian family forms, we certainly seem to be moving in that direction. Further, three major societal forces suggest that trend will continue.

The first is the changing expectation of what marriage should accomplish, with heavy emphasis on the emotional and psychological needs of the spouses—tenderness, sexual fulfillment, intimacy, companionship, emotional support, security, and ego enhancement. Even as the traditional economic functions of the family have declined, the emotional interdependence of family members has increased, and these emotional and psychological needs would appear to be better met in more egalitarian relationships.

The second thrust in the direction of egalitarian family patterns is coming from women's increasing dissatisfaction with the traditional roles of housewife and mother, and their resulting demands for more independence, greater participation and compensation in the labor force, and more sharing of domestic chores by husbands and children. Jessie Bernard has forcefully described the great emotional strain that marriage puts on women: "traditional marriage makes women sick—both physically and mentally."[38] As Bernard explains, every marriage is really two marriages: the husband's marriage and the wife's marriage, the one beneficial and the other destructive. For the average husband, marriage enhances mental health, happiness, career success, income, and life expectancy. Married women, on the other hand, are more depressed, have more nervous breakdowns and more feelings of inadequacy, and are generally less healthy, both mentally and physically, than single women. Dr. Bernard writes that women are "driven mad, not by men but by the anachronistic way in which marriage is structured today—or rather, the life-style which accompanies marriage today and which demands that all wives be housewives."[39]

Of course, women have recently been expressing their dissatisfaction with the roles they have been "assigned" and are increasingly demanding changes in their marriages.[40] Their very disaffection should provide a powerful force in the restructuring of relations between the sexes in marriage.

Third, the changing occupational and ideological position of women in the larger society creates strong pressures for change in their status in the family—and thus for change in the nature of the family. The increased labor force participation of women and their changing patterns of employment have already provided considerable impetus for such change, and it is likely that as more married women enter full-time work, for more pay and at higher occupational levels, their roles, power, and authority within the family will continue to change.

As economist Ralph Smith states it, the movement of larger numbers of married women into the paid labor market has created a revolution in the sense that it is bringing about a fundamental change in social and economic conditions:

> The division of labor between the sexes in which men work outside the home for pay while women engage in unpaid housework is breaking down. And, as more women work outside the home . . . female–male relationships in every aspect of society are being questioned and are changing. The movement of women into the labor force is part of this larger social revolution, both as a cause and as an effect. The economic power provided by paid employment enhances the bargaining power of an individual in the marketplace, the political arena, and the home.[41]

What is more, apart from the occupational impetus, the ideology of equality has played, and will continue to play, a major independent role in propelling "the revolution." As sociologist William J. Goode notes:

> I believe that the crucial crystallizing variable—i.e., the necessary but not sufficient cause of the betterment of the Western woman's position—was ideological: the gradual, logical, philosophical extension to women of originally Protestant notions about the rights and responsibilities of the individual undermined the traditional idea of "woman's proper place."[42]

We shall now examine a number of spheres within the family that give evidence of a trend toward more egalitarian family forms. Before doing so, however, one caveat is in order. In some of these areas the *ideology* has changed but not the behavior; in others behavior has changed under pressure from outside forces, but before the participants were able to incorporate it into their vision of "how things ought to be done." Because social change is a complex and uneven process, it is difficult to document any unilateral and all-pervasive trend. Nevertheless, we believe that significant developments can already be observed in the following areas.

Family Decisions (and Power)

It seems reasonable to expect that as more wives work in the paid labor force, as the wife's contribution to the total family budget assumes greater relative importance, and as norms of equality between the sexes become more widely accepted, wives will have more to say in family decisions. This appears to be the case in the findings from Moore and Sawhill's investigation of wives' bargaining power,[43] and in Bahr's study of women's power in family decisions concerning finance.[44] Decisions on family expenditures, savings, and the general "struggle for financial security" are now more likely than ever before to be made jointly, or at least to be apportioned on a less sex-stereotyped basis.

Another recent shift in the management of family finances has been the increase in the percentage of wives with checking and savings accounts of their own. A 1980 Roper Poll revealed that the number of married women with checking and savings accounts in their own names nearly doubled between 1972 and 1980.* Although the majority of married couples still maintain joint accounts for checking, savings, consumer loans and home mortgages, when compared to eight years ago, married women today also have more credit cards and bank loans in their own names.†

Similarly, selecting the family domicile and deciding when and where to move have increasingly become democratic decisions, with the needs and interests of the wife and children assuming greater importance than in the past. Although both of these trends represent a decline in the traditional authority of the husband, they may be attended by a decline in the domestic authority of the wife as the husband assumes a greater role in household tasks and decisions.

It would seem reasonable to predict that women's power in the family would increase directly with their labor force participation. While this is generally true,‡ several factors still work against wom-

---

*National NOW Times, June 1980:15. As might be expected, single women are more than twice as likely to have checking and savings accounts in their own names as married women. However when these single women marry, some will retain their separate accounts and this will eventually influence the pattern among married women.

†Nevertheless, the percentages are still appallingly low. In 1980 only 19 percent of the married women had credit cards in their own names.

‡In one study of this relationship Brown concluded that changes in household tasks that were defined as exclusively for the wife occurred simultaneously with

en's attainment of equal status within the family. The wife in most two-paycheck families is still likely to work in a lower status job than her husband and to earn less money, even in families in which both adults are professionals.[45] This means that the relative status of their roles is not yet seriously challenged by the wife's work or the wife's income.

An interesting example of the continuing truth of the saying that "money talks" is provided by sociologist Constantina Safilios-Rothschild. Rothschild discovered that although working-class women may find jobs of greater occupational prestige than their husbands (wives of blue-collar workers often have white-collar jobs), their work is not disruptive to the marriage, apparently because their husbands still generally earn more money and thus consider their own work more important.[46]

As this example suggests, the effect of the wife's work also differs by social class. In general, sociologists have found a strong egalitarian ethic in middle-class families, with more sex-stereotyping and a sharper division of family decision making along sex lines in working-class families. However, sociologist William Goode has noted an apparent paradox in the correlation between social class and male authority: toward the lower strata, the husband is likely to claim authority simply because he is a male, but he actually has to concede considerable authority to his wife; toward the upper strata, men are less likely to assert the values of patriarchal authority, but are more likely to wield actual power. As Goode explains:

> On a commonsense basis, it can be seen that upper strata men have more resources by which to have their way. Their wives are less likely to work, and even if they do work, they contribute a smaller percentage of the total family income than would be true in the lower social strata. . . . Thus the husband's position in role bargaining is stronger.[47]

In line with Goode's observation, after a 1975 review of the literature, Bahr concluded that lower-class wives gain more power through employment than do middle-class wives.[48]

It is important to note that while most employed wives today may earn less money and enjoy less status than their husbands, this

---

increased female labor force participation while the shift to joint decision making followed *after* the labor force increase. Bruce W. Brown, "Wife-Employment and the Emergence of Egalitarian Marital Role Prescriptions: 1900–1974," *Journal of Comparative Family Studies* 9, no. 1 (1978):5–17.

pattern may be less pronounced in the future. As Rothschild observes, the diffusion of women's liberation ideology has largely freed wives of the compulsion to keep their status lines lower than those of their husbands, and many are now exhibiting a greater interest in work, higher achievement aspirations, and an increased determination to enter male-dominated, high-prestige, high-pay occupations such as medicine and law.[49] As wage and promotion discrimination against women decreases, married women's occupational roles are expected to more closely approximate the male range of occupational roles, and more women will have income, prestige, and power that they themselves have achieved. Rothschild further predicts that more women will have higher job status than their husbands because they will feel free to marry "men to whom they are attracted because of appearance, personality, or other status-irrelevant skills and characteristics (such as being good lovers)" instead of choosing husbands for their occupational or financial prospects.[50]

But whatever the relative occupational status and income of the two spouses, one critical aspect of their relationship will never be the same again—the husband's centrality. As sociologist William Goode observes, "men have come to expect that women will always assume that whatever a man is doing is more important than whatever it is that a woman is doing herself . . . and husbands resent this loss of centrality in the lives of their wives more than they fear the competition from women at work."[51] Author Caroline Bird seconds this observation:

> Husbands don't always realize how unconsciously they assume that they will be the center of attention. A breadwinner expects the meals to be served when he is ready to eat them. He expects that she will listen when he wants to talk and shush the children when he wants to sleep. When she has a job of her own she may not be able to adjust to his timetable. Even worse, he may discover that she has something else she really would rather do. . . . As wives develop interests and friends of their own, husbands lose the power to keep them at home. They are startled and ashamed to admit a sense of loss when they find that the phone rings for her—and that the conversation is so interesting that she leaves their dinner to cool, or to be served and eaten by others. They are used to being scolded by their wives for leaving the dinner for an important phone call for themselves, but the reverse is inconceivable. And its occurrence can be traumatic.[52]

Household Responsibilities

The emergence of more egalitarian housework patterns should also follow from the increased labor force participation of married women. In this sphere, however, the change, though visible, has so far been less than impressive. "In general, husbands of working wives do engage in slightly more child care and housework than do husbands of women who are not earning income, although it does not appear that the rapid movement of women into the labor force has been matched by a very significant increase in husbands' willingness to help around the house."[53]

Time-use studies generally indicate that the major burden of housework still falls on women. Women employed full time (thirty hours or more per week) spend an average of 4.8 hours per day on household work, while their husbands spend an average of 1.6 hours per day.[54]

Thus, in most cases, a woman's labor force participation has not meant a decline in household tasks but rather a double work load, with the factory or office job merely added to household responsibilities. On the average, American working women still work from .8 to 3.5 more hours per day in housekeeping and child care activities than their husbands do.[55] The marriage in which husband and wife share housework equally is decidedly the exception.

This pattern apparently holds true world wide. There are no countries in which employed women are known to spend less than an hour and a half on housework each day, even when they spend more hours at work than their husbands.[56] A 1968 study of 1,300 husband–wife families in Syracuse, New York, further showed that children spend even less time on household chores: 1.1 hours compared to 1.5 hours a day for husbands and 4.8 for wives—and that these time allocations are *not* significantly affected by the employment status of the wife.[57]

What is perhaps more surprising is that the average married American woman who works full time (40 hours a week) in paid employment, now spends more total time working (in the market and at home) than did a rural woman in 1926! In 1926 the average rural woman spent 52 hours a week on housework and 10 on farmwork, totaling 62 hours of work a week. A 1965–66 national sample of employed women revealed that the average respondent spent 26 hours a week on household tasks, which, when added to 40 hours of paid employment, totals 66 hours.[58]

In the decade between 1965 and 1975 the amount of time spent on housework by all women in the U.S. population decreased by 2.5 hours per week. However, as John Robinson notes, the difference was not attributable to better technology or to greater participation from husbands, but to be a reordering of preferences and a greater tolerance for the results of less housework.[59]

As might be expected, the husband's participation in household tasks is influenced by a number of factors, including the family's class status and the income and prestige of the wife's job.

With respect to social class, as we have already noted, the working-class wife typically gains power from her outside work and her husband takes on more household responsibilities. Middle-class men are more likely to resist, whether their wives work or not. The key variable seems to be the discrepancy between the wife's and husband's status. Professional and middle-class men who are far better educated and earn far more than their wives are also far more successful in resisting their wives' pressures to share household tasks. Conversely, in one survey of 1,212 couples in the Philadelphia area about the division of household tasks, Ericksen, Yancey and Ericksen found that couples in which the husband did not have a high income, the wife was highly educated, and there were no children under 12 were all more likely to have shared work roles.[60] These results are interpreted to support the hypothesis that marital power is strongly related to household division of labor. To the degree that the wife's status relative to her husband's is higher, the household tasks are more likely to be evenly divided.

Another factor that influences how tasks are divided is the amount of time husbands and wives spend doing things together. In the lower-class families, husbands and wives tend to engage in complementary but independent activities, and each spouse spends considerable time with same-sex friends.[61] It is harder to get lower-class men to participate in women's chores that are sex-segregated. In middle-class and professional families, on the other hand, there is more emphasis on the husband–wife bond and couples spend more time together. In this respect they may share some household tasks that are done together, such as shopping and cooking, just as they more often share leisure and recreational activities. In addition, middle-class wives are more successful in getting their husbands to accept responsibility for tasks that the men consider enjoyable or "interesting" such as gourmet cooking or backpacking trips with older children.

A third factor that influences household responsibilities is the wife's occupational status. Women with prestigious, financially remunerative jobs often have little time for traditional domestic chores. They are likely also to be married to high-status, high-income men, and both spouses in this situation are likely to favor hiring others to take over some of the household tasks rather than redistributing the tasks between them. Thus both men and women in these families do fewer routine household tasks. Nevertheless, the wives still bear the major burden of administering the household, supervising the help, and organizing meals. What has changed in these families, and in many middle-class families as well, is the ideology—the norms about appropriate behavior for husbands and wives.* Husbands of professional women are much more likely to be supportive of their wives' careers and to believe that they themselves should share more household responsibilities.† This is especially true of younger men who do, in fact, share much more of the actual work with their wives.

Clearly we are in a state of transition. While the new norms of sharing household responsibilities are becoming widely accepted throughout the population, men have been much slower to change their actual behavior. In some homes this means that women are still doing all the work, in others they are delegating some of it to others—including their children, and in still others the standards have changed—the beds are changed less frequently, the house or apartment isn't as clean or as neat as it used to be, and the family

*One indication of this is men's new stake in asserting that they are doing more. In fact, the extent of the husband's participation in household tasks that is reported depends, in large part on who you ask. Both husbands and wives tend to underestimate their spouse's contribution and overestimate their own. Spouses show the least agreement about the wife's contribution to tasks usually considered to be "male," and the husband's contribution to child care tasks. In general, however, there is more disagreement about husbands' contributions to household tasks than there is about the wives' contributions. Sarah Fenstermaker Berk and Anthony Shih, "Contributions to Household Labor: Comparing Wives' and Husbands' Reports," in *Women and Household Labor*, Sarah Fenstermaker Berk, ed., (Beverly Hills, Ca.: Sage Publications, 1980).

†Nevertheless, in a study of English professional families with children Edgell found that there was still high traditional role segregation in carrying out domestic tasks. Stephan Edgell, *Middle Class Couples: A Study of Domination and Inequality in Marriage*, George Allen and Unwin, London: 1980.

eats out more often. However, in many homes the division of labor is changing so that each partner has his or her weekly tasks (of laundry or shopping) and his or her nights to prepare dinner—along the lines suggested in the contracts in the Appendix to this book.* In fact, the care and planning that are obviously reflected in the schemes for dividing household tasks in the contracts indicate that this is clearly an area in which there are already blueprints for major changes in the near future.

Parenthood

Accompanying the general trend among married couples to subscribe to (if not yet to adhere to) a norm of egalitarian family patterns, is a growing acceptance of a more equal sharing of parenting. Psychologist Arlene Skolnick sees parenthood as "coming to be defined more and more as a joint enterprise of both the husband and the wife . . . not only because the women are insisting that men share some of the load, but because many young professional men themselves no longer accept as their fate the compulsive male careerism that dominated the 1950s."[62] They too are considering alternative roles and rediscovering some of the joys of fatherhood.

However, males' willingness to assume primary parenting roles should not be exaggerated. As Komarovsky reports of her 1973 interviews with male college seniors at an Ivy League university, "Many respondents expressed their willingness to help with child care and household duties. Similarly, many hoped to spend more time with their own children than their fathers had spent with them. But such domestic participation was defined as assistance to the wife, who was to carry the major responsibility."[63] Among Komarovsky's respondents 24 percent intended to marry a woman who would be satisfied to remain at home as a housewife and mother. Another 16 percent were willing to "allow" their wives to work, but qualified their statements with impossible conditions. Another 48 percent expected their wives to interrupt their work during the early years of childbearing and childrearing. Only 7 percent indicated a willingness to change their own marital roles.

As we have seen, sex-typed parenting roles are at the very core of the traditional legal assumptions about marriage and the as-

*See pages 433 to 434 in the Appendix.

sumed natural division of labor between husbands and wives. Law Professor Herma Hill Kay has noted:

> The social attitude that a mother's place is in the home is further reflected in the myriad confusing, inconsistent, and totally inadequate regulations dealing with childbearing and childrearing leaves of absence. The lack of job security for the childrearing parent during the early months of an infant's life, together with the virtual absence of good child care centers and the still meager tax support for child care expenses make it imperative in most families that one parent stay home during the child's infancy.[64]

Some progress has been made outside the courts toward official acceptance of parenting roles being shared by men. For example, the New York City Board of Education now allows male employees to take child care leaves, formerly granted only to women. This policy change followed a suit brought by a teacher-father charging the Board with discriminatory practices for refusing to allow him an unpaid leave to participate in caring for his children.[65] Some private corporations, such as Prudential Insurance, have also begun to publicize "paternity leave" programs which offer male employees the same childbirth leaves as female employees. The New York Telephone Company, which offers men six months of unpaid paternity leave, reported that 51 men within the Bell system had taken advantage of the policy in 1979.[66]

In addition, while most men are still reluctant to assume the role of the child's primary caretaker, there is a clear and discernable increase in the number of men who are willing to *share* parenting. The development of fathers' rights organizations discussed in Chapter 4, the new social science interest in the father's role in child development, and the increased participation of fathers in cooperative day care centers, all attest to men's increased interest in their paternal roles.[67] In addition, the number of fathers who share or have custody of their children after divorce continues to grow. These men have already made their roles as fathers a much more central part of their lives and their new attitudes are likely to persist through remarriage and the formation of new families—and new family patterns.

In the past, social scientists have asserted that a homebound mother was essential to the proper development of the child,[68] and that clearly differentiated parental sex role models were necessary to ensure a child's normal sex role development.[69] Freud's identification theory was once widely championed by social scientists, and the American sociologist Talcott Parsons urged the importance of strong distinctions between the roles of mother and father in teaching the child proper sex role behavior.[70]

More recently, however, social scientists have begun to question this theory. Philip Slater, for one, has argued that adult role models who exhibit stereotyped sex role differentiation may impede, rather than facilitate, a child's sex role identification.[71] Children more naturally identify with less differentiated and less stereotyped parental role models, Slater contends, and it is easier for them to internalize parental values when nurturance, the assertedly feminine role, and discipline, the allegedly masculine role, come from the same person. Thus children can learn a wider range of traits and develop their more "natural" talents if they are not pushed into predetermined sex role boxes.

Two other areas of much concern among social scientists in the past—fears about the "maternal deprivation suffered by latch-key children" and alarm about the "harmful effects" of working mothers on their children—have all but completely evaporated. After an extensive review of the pertinent literature, psychologist Lois Hoffman concluded that mothers who are satisfied with their employment status do a better job of mothering than the full-time mothers who stay home out of "a duty" to the child.[72] In addition, it now appears that working mothers may provide more positive role models and more effective parents for growing children of both sexes. For example, Reis found that working mothers communicate more effectively with their children than do nonworking mothers.[73] They also exchange more information with their children and their children (aged 7–10) are more likely to help adults when asked. Her findings confirm working mothers' emphasis on the quality of time spent with children.

In general, "maternal employment is associated with less traditional sex role concepts and a higher evaluation of female competence."[74] Daughters of working mothers, in particular, compare positively with daughters of nonworking mothers, particularly with respect to independence and achievement-related variables. For example, in two studies with children of various ages Gold and Andres found that children's sex role concepts were broader and they received better adjustment ratings from their teachers if their mothers were employed.[75]

In fact, sociologist Alice Rossi has suggested that an exclusive devotion to motherhood can have a negative effect on children:

> If a woman's adult efforts are concentrated exclusively on her children, she is likely more to stifle than broaden her children's perspective and preparation for adult life. . . . In myriad ways the mother binds the child to her, dampening his initiative, resenting his growing independence in adolescence, creating a subtle dependence which makes it difficult for the child to achieve full adult stature. . . .[76]

In addition to its potentially negative effect on children, a preoccupation with motherhood may be harmful to the mother herself. Sociologist Pauline Bart found extreme "empty-nest" depression among middle-aged women who had been overly involved with their children.[77] In addition, although employed mothers worry as much about their child care role, they are more likely than nonemployed mothers to enjoy the activities and relationships they share with their children, and to have more positive feelings about themselves.[78] They therefore project an image of greater ability and confidence.

The problem for most women today is no longer whether to combine work with motherhood, but *how* to combine motherhood and work. And the same is increasingly true for fathers. In fact, in one study of dual-career families the *greatest* concern in every family was that of child care.[79] This is one area in which solutions may lie in more egalitarian arrangements within the family, as well as in increased institutional supports (i.e. more child care facilities and more work flexibility for parents). And, until that happens, some couples may be forced to delay parenthood until they can afford to purchase more help themselves, while others may feel pressured to forgo it entirely.*

Nevertheless, even without the institutional changes that are necessary, it is likely that the future will bring a continued modification of the traditional parenting roles in the direction of more

*See, especially, Marilyn Fabe and Norma Wikler, *Up Against The Clock*, (New York: Random House, 1979). In 1980 sociologists Sara Yogev and Andrea Vierra of Northwestern University reported that many more young women faculty have decided to remain childless because they are not confident that they can successfully combine motherhood and a career. Yogev and Vierra report that younger professional women observe that the "superwomen" who are trying to "have it all"—i.e. combine career with motherhood, are enduring such relentless pressure that younger colleagues do not dare to think about having children. "Childlessness Among Professional Women: A Trend?" *Marriage and Divorce Today* (September 15, 1980):4.

egalitarian family patterns. This prospect is enhanced by the inter-play of the new awareness of social science prescriptions, the femin-ist challenge to early sex role stereotyping and the traditional mother role, increased male dissatisfaction with the occupational burdens of the male role and increased interest in fatherhood, and the economic changes discussed above.

Sexuality

A decisive trend toward more egalitarian patterns is visible in the realm of sexuality. In the traditional definition of marital sexuality the wife was the private sexual property of her husband and it was her duty to "afford him . . . her person."[80] As wives were assumed to be completely available to their husbands, a wife could not charge her husband with rape; for by definition, a sexual act be-tween husband and wife did not constitute rape—not even if she re-fused to participate and he assaulted her to force her compliance.[81]

By contrast, the revolution in sexual attitudes of recent years has focused a great deal of attention on the wife's participation and sat-isfaction in sexual relations, and consequently on more mutual and egalitarian sexual relationships. Married women's enjoyment of sex became respectable sometime in the 1950s, though husbands were still seen as the initiators and orchestrators of marital sex.[82] In the late 1960s, however, with the publication of Masters and Johnson's research demonstrating the range of female sexual response, both men and women began to redefine female sexuality and women's sexual needs.[83]

The sexual liberation of women has been one of the primary goals of the women's liberation movement. This goal is reflected in the movement's determination to eliminate the "double standard"; to develop women's potential for multiple orgasms; to sanction non-traditional behavior, such as masturbation, bisexuality, and lesbi-anism; and to establish women's control over their reproductive functions.[84] As one feminist explains:

> As women, we want our own sexuality under our own control. We no longer will allow our sexual behavior, capacities, rights, and relation-ships to be defined or limited for us by men, either individuals or so-cial institutions, for experience has shown that men will define us for their own purposes and pleasures, denying us significant parts of our sexual birthright. Our emphasis is on self-determination. Significant-ly, this implies not only the absence of male domination over female

sexuality but the freedom of individual women to differ from whatever norms or averages may be discovered or postulated.[85]

Attitudes toward female sex have been shifting steadily from negative and repressive to positive and permissive, and it is predicted that the present liberalizing trends will continue.[86] Women in less traditional marriages (as well as those with more education) already report a higher satisfaction with their marital sexual relations than did women in the past.[87]

Some new research also suggests that both sexual satisfaction and companionship are better in more egalitarian relationships. In a 1979 study of two-paycheck couples, author Caroline Bird found that having a job had a positive effect on the sexual response of women: they often feel freer, more uninhibited and more confident.[88] Bird argues that "anything that improves a woman's self-worth makes her sexually more responsive, and nothing improves her self-worth more than success at earning money."[89] Bird cites a study of the Harvard class of 1952 after their 25th reunion. Of the wives earning less than $15,000 a year in their own right, 42 percent reported that they were less interested in sex than they were when they were younger. Among wives earning more money however, 74 percent said they were more interested.[90]

Along the same lines, an admittedly nonrandom sample of the 1980 readers of *Redbook* magazine indicated that women who were more assertive had better sex lives.[91] In addition, more egalitarian couples, those who were able to share their views and arrive at mutually agreeable decisions, reported much higher levels of sexual satisfaction.

In conclusion, the changes we have discussed in this chapter only hint at the profound changes in the internal structure of marriage taking place in our society today. A vast array of sociological data suggests that these trends are nothing less than revolutionary. Clearly, the time has come to bring the law into line with social reality.

CHAPTER 8

The White Middle-Class Bias

The Legal Tradition: The Dual System of Family Law

Recent years have brought a new awareness of the class, racial, and ethnic biases embedded in traditional family law. This awareness was spearheaded by Jacobus tenBroek's monumental work documenting the existence of a dual system of family law: one law for the poor and one law for the rest of society.[1] TenBroek asserted that the legal system differentiates families on the basis of income and discriminates against the principal victims of poverty: racial and ethnic minorities, the economically and socially underprivileged, and the children of broken homes.[2]*

*It should be noted that women in general, and female-headed families in particular, are vastly overrepresented among the poor. Two-thirds of the 15 million people classified as poor are women, as are 70 percent of the aged poor. Female-headed families, which increased from 10 percent of the total number of families in 1950, to 14 percent in 1970, are much more likely to fall below the poverty line: in fact, one-third of all female-headed families are living in poverty (in contrast to five percent of the male headed families). Diane Pearce, "The Feminization of Poverty: Women, Work, and Welfare," pp. 28–35, *The Urban And Social Change Review* 11, nos. 1 and 2 (1978) and *The Spokeswoman* 10, no. 1 (January 1980):5.

According to tenBroek, the family law cases of the rich are heard in civil courts that deal with issues of property and support, while those of the poor are heard in nonjudicial agencies or criminal courts concerned with issues of nonsupport and noncompliance. In the first forum, the rights of the parties are protected; in the second, the state's costs and burdens take precedence over individual rights. As tenBroek concludes, for the poor the law is heavily political and harshly penal, whereas for the middle class it is nonpolitical and civil.[3]

De Jure and de Facto Bias

Family law embodies two kinds of white, middle-class bias. The first, which Carlin, Howard, and Messinger refer to as *de jure* denial of equal protection,[4] is seen in the separate and unequal systems of law and procedures designed to deal with the problems of the poor and certain racial minorities. As a result, many blacks and lower-class whites are systematically denied the protections and benefits the law provides for the rest of society.[5]

TenBroek found *de jure* bias both in the substantive law and in judicial forums. With regard to the substantive law, he found that the rules in the two systems differ fundamentally with respect to the disposition of property, the support responsibilities of husbands and wives, and the creation and termination of the marital relationship.[6] These differences are reflected in the enforcement of child support obligations. Although middle- and upper-class men have a greater ability to pay child support, enforcement proceedings are more frequently brought against poor men.[7] The reason is that the state has no direct stake in the support that middle-class husbands are ordered to pay, whereas it is concerned with the cost of welfare, and therefore has a stake in recovering the public expenditures it has paid to the children and ex-wives of poor men.[8] Foster and Freed point to the devastating effects of this policy on the poor:

> [T]he wholesale defiance of court orders by embittered men may be accounted for, at least in part, by the failure of courts to be realistic and to appreciate that an automatic imposition of the support duty is not in accord with current values and in many cases is highly penal. In the case of the more prosperous, the husband's duty to support or pay alimony may be an unpleasant but tolerable burden, but where a poor or low income husband is involved, even a minimal order may constitute a great hardship or impossible burden. Of necessity, he may

become a fugitive. Moreover, if he remarries or establishes a new family, further complications inevitably arise, making his primary obligation to the first family unrealistic. *In short, both support and alimony law occasion hardship to poor and lower income husbands and in application often force the man into defiance of the law or prevent him from living in dignity.*[9]

With respect to the judicial forum, tenBroek contrasts the respectful treatment of middle-class families in the civil courts with the humiliation of lower-class families in nonjudicial forums and criminal courts. He then likens the dual system of family law to racially separate and unequal schools—"in the feelings of inferiority it generates and the effect it has on the hearts and minds of its victims."[10] The experiences of poor families with the harsh administration of family law in "the foreign land of the New York Family Court" have been dramatically described by Professor Monrad Paulsen:

Each morning a hundred stories of poverty are suggested by the faces and the personal effects of those who wait to appear before the judges. . . . The court's waiting rooms resemble those at hospital clinics. Negro and Puerto Rican families predominate, and many regard the trappings of justice with bitterness and suspicion.[11]

As the Honorable Florence Kelly, Administrative Judge of the New York Family Court, put it: "No one is at home in this court. A poor family journeys into a foreign land."[12]

The second type of bias in the law, what Carlin, Howard, and Messinger refer to as *de facto* bias, relates to ostensibly neutral laws that have differential effects on the poor. Even when the law on the books is unbiased, in practice it may affect the rich and the poor unequally because the correlates of poverty make equality impossible.[13] As they explain, *de facto* bias

. . . is pervasive because so many correlates of poverty such as indigency, ignorance or insecurity can serve as barriers to justice. In essence it is bias by default. It represents a failure of the law to take into account the differential capacity of rich and poor to realize the protections and benefits which the law provides.[14]

As E. Ehrlich suggests, neutral laws may have the effect of accentuating de facto inequality because "the more the rich and the poor are dealt with according to the same legal propositions, the more the advantage of the rich is increased."[15] In the following pages we will examine the *de facto* bias in the law with respect to marriage, divorce, and children.

Common Law Unions

De facto bias is evident in the law's traditional assumption of universal legal marriage and universal legal divorce. The poor are in fact more likely than the rest of society to form common law unions and to terminate these unions with a "common law divorce." On one level, the problem is purely financial. As Foster and Freed observe, for some of the poor, legal marriage and divorce may have priced themselves out of the market; the financial obligations incurred as an incident to marriage and divorce sometimes make both legal statuses luxuries which the poor cannot afford.[16]

On another level, however, the legal problems poor families face are a result of the way the courts are structured. Couples who are not legally married are often sent off to criminal court to have their disputes adjudicated, while the same problems, if they occur in the context of a legal marriage, are handled in the more understanding atmosphere of the "family court."

While it has typically been assumed that the family court, "whose purpose is the preservation of marriage," should not concern itself with "crimes between persons who are living in a meritricious relationship," at least one judge has criticized this position and advanced some telling reasons why the families of the poor, whatever their legal relationship to one another, belong in family court:

> There are countless households where man and woman reside with their offspring in a domestic relationship on a permanent basis without being legally married. Such households . . . [have] behavior problems, support problems, mental and emotional problems. They concern the health, welfare and safety of children. They result in filiation proceedings, support proceedings and juvenile proceedings. In short, from a social point of view, this is a situation where the unique and flexible procedures and services available in the Family Court may possibly find a remedy.[17]

Common-Law Divorce

A second assumption in traditional family law is that marriages are ended solely by legal divorce. However, many marital (and nonmarital) unions are ended by what Foster calls "common-law divorce"—desertion.[18] When legal divorce is perceived as neither affordable nor accessible, the poor are likely to resort to "the poor man's divorce":

> [We] see a substantial number of people at the lower end of the economic scale for whom divorce action is a luxury beyond their financial means. They are no less prone to family breakdown than members of other economic classes but because they cannot afford the legal procedure of divorce, they must resort to the poor man's divorce, that is, separation or desertion. The real problem develops when, like people with conventional divorces, they decide to remarry and want to make the second marriage work.[19]

Historically, the cost of lawyers and court fees, the bewildering jargon of "complaints" and "cross-complaints," the time-consuming and seemingly complex legal process, and the popular association of courts with crime, have served to dissuade the poor from seeking legal divorce. At the point of breakup it often seems much easier simply to separate—or for the man to desert—than to go through the hassles and traumas of a legal divorce. Thus common-law divorce has always been most prevalent among poverty subcultures.[20]

Regional variations in divorce law provide a prime illustration of de facto bias in supposedly neutral laws. In theory, a state with highly restrictive divorce laws makes divorce equally difficult for all classes. However, in practice, O'Gorman found, poorer citizens are more likely to be prevented from getting a divorce because, unlike the middle and upper classes, they cannot afford to travel to a state with more lenient laws to obtain a "migratory divorce."[21]

In 1971 the U.S. Supreme Court attempted to remedy this situation—or at least to remove the financial barriers to legal divorce for the poor. In *Boddie* v. *Connecticut*[22] two welfare recipients seeking a divorce challenged a Connecticut statute requiring them to pay $45 in filing fees and $15 for service of process. The Supreme Court, recognizing the importance of giving all citizens access to marriage and divorce, and recognizing the state's monopoly power to govern marriage and divorce, ruled that the state could not deny indigents access to its divorce courts solely on the basis of their inability to pay court fees and costs.

Even with court fees paid, however, the poor often cannot pay for competent legal advice. After a comprehensive review of the character of legal services for the poor, Carlin, Howard, and Messinger found that the poor are the least likely stratum of society to use lawyers,[23] that when they do go to lawyers they generally have access to the least able and responsible members of the bar,[24] and that the assistance they receive is generally quite limited.[25]

In the 1960s Legal Aid services were established for the express purpose of extending to indigents full access to the law. However, these agencies, consistently understaffed and underfunded, have proved unable to meet the vast need for their services.[26] High case-loads frequently lead to mass processing of cases and thus to routinized, perfunctory service. Divorce cases tend to be given the lowest priority and are often rejected as unnecessary or unimportant.[27] According to Carlin and Howard, the Legal Aid attorney is apt to view divorce as a luxury that should be granted only if a client is deemed morally deserving, or if it is absolutely necessary "to protect either the wife or the children from immediate or threatened physical harm, or moral jeopardy."[28] One attorney explained why he rejected a divorce case:

> She can wait. Her husband [who deserted the family eight months before] isn't around to bug her, and there's no emergency. Her landlord hasn't turned off the heat or the water, and she hasn't been evicted. So what's the rush? She can get her divorce in six months or a year—or whenever I have time. If I took every divorce case that came in here I'd never have time to do the important work.[29]

Child Neglect Proceedings and Coercive Welfare

It is with respect to children that the middle-class bias in family law is likely to cause the most severe hardship for poor families. Throughout the United States, juvenile courts may assert authority over "neglected" children, and poor families are much more likely to be judged "neglectful" and to have their children taken away from them than are middle-class families.[30] The reasons for this may have more to do with middle-class definitions of proper care than with true neglect. As Paulsen explains:

> A statute which defines a neglected child as one who is without proper care because his parent or guardian "neglects or refuses to provide," may sometimes be applied to a youngster with parents who are paupers, not parents who refuse to share what they have. *What one regards as proper care may, indeed, be a matter of dispute reflecting class and cultural differences. Standards of child rearing adequate in*

one cultural setting may seem appalling in another. Neglect defined as raising a child in an environment which is "injurious or dangerous" may create a hazard for parents without means. Unhappily, the environment of the poor is often injurious and dangerous.[31]

Parents whose children are supported by Aid to Families with Dependent Children (AFDC) may be especially vulnerable to charges of neglect. As Professor tenBroek observed, welfare caseworkers on home visits are likely to raise questions about the parents' morality, extramarital relations, drinking, and other personal predilections, and about "the suitability of the home for the rearing of the children."[32] The potential harassment of the poor through this kind of surveillance is illustrated by a case summary provided by Kay and Philips:

> The household was composed of an eighteen-year-old mother and her three children, who ranged in age from two and a half years to eight months. Only the oldest child was supported by AFDC. The mother's husband, father of the two younger children, was absent on duty in the military service. The welfare caseworker, making an unannounced house visit, had found the mother absent from the home and the two older children alone in the house. Upon entering the house accompanied by a neighbor, the caseworker found the house "filthy," one child naked, and mouldy food in the refrigerator. She called the police and insisted that the children be taken into protective custody. The children were taken to the county reception center for dependent children, where they remained from Wednesday until Monday, when the detention hearing was held and they were released to the mother pending the juvenile court hearing. At this hearing, held a month later, the mother and father both appeared. The welfare worker testified that the house was "messy but not dirty" and that she had waited for about twenty or thirty minutes before removing the children. The mother's explanation of her absence was that she had been trying to find a babysitter to take care of the older children while she took the baby to see a doctor. She stated that she had never left the children alone before. The father defended his wife, pointing out that she had had a hard time trying to manage for eleven months while he had been in military service. He seemed bitter towards the worker's actions, and asked the court why, if the "welfare lady" really wanted to help his family, she hadn't offered to babysit for his wife instead of "calling the cops and bringing us to court?" Upon being told by the judge about the worker's responsibilities under the AFDC program, he stated that they had "gone off" welfare in order to avoid the home visits. He asked whether the court couldn't rely on him to take care of

the family. . . . The court, however, accepted the Probation Department's recommendation that there be some supervision for the children. Accordingly, he made them dependent children of the court and placed them in the family home with provision for a further hearing in ten months.[33]

As Foster and Freed note, there is a clear danger that the decision of what is or is not neglect may be determined by the social worker's or judge's middle-class values—and middle-class prejudices.[34] While there are no national data on the number of AFDC children who are labeled "neglected," a Minneapolis–St. Paul study suggests that AFDC families are far more likely to be referred to protective service agencies than are educated, economically independent families.[35]

The "neglected" children of minority parents are likely to suffer a double burden: not only are they removed from their natural home but they are disadvantaged with respect to placement. There is a general dearth of placement facilities for neglected children—especially those of black or Puerto Rican background—and they tend to be kept in temporary shelters for long periods of time. For example, in Judge Justine Polier's 1963 study of the New York Family Court, 14.5 percent of the blacks were in "temporary" shelters for over a year while not one white child was there that long.[36]

The belief that the poor are less able to care for their children, and the popular outrage at soaring welfare costs, have also led to legislative attempts to require sterilization for welfare recipients. While none of these proposals have been enacted, coercion has sometimes been effected under the guise of "voluntary" sterilization. Such was the case under an HEW program, as the Supreme Court decision in *Rolf* v. *Weinberger* indicates:

Although Congress has been insistent that all family planning programs function on a purely voluntary basis, there is *uncontroverted evidence* in the record that minors and other incompetents have been sterilized with federal funds and that an indefinite number of poor people *have been improperly coerced into accepting a sterilization operation* under the threat that various federally supported welfare benefits would be withdrawn unless they submitted to irreversible sterilization. Patients receiving Medicaid assistance at childbirth are evidently the most frequent targets of this pressure, as the experiences of plaintiffs Waters and Walker illustrate. Mrs. Waters was actually refused medical assistance by her attending physician unless she submitted to a tubal ligation after the birth. Other examples were documented.[37]

Racial and Ethnic Variants

Thus far we have treated the poor and ethnic and racial minorities together because they all deviate from the white middle-class legal norm. At this point, however, it is important to note the extent to which family patterns and norms vary among various ethnic and racial groups. The conjugal family model that is assumed by the law is typical of white Protestant families; but Jews, Italians, and Latinos are more likely to live in extended families, and the single-parent family is more common among blacks.[38]

The precise nature and range of these family patterns is clearly beyond the scope of this book. However, in the following pages we will briefly examine one family type, the lower-class black family, as an example of the extent to which the traditional legal model is inappropriate.

The Lower-Class Black Family in Perspective

Before we begin, it is important to emphasize that the following discussion is limited to lower-class black families. The lower-class black family to which we refer is characterized by urban residence, a female-headed household, three-generation residence pattern, presence of illegitimate children, nonlegal termination of marriage, and child care by an extended kin network. This constellation describes only a small minority of all black families. As Professor Andrew Billingsley has observed, only half of all black families are in the lower class, only a third have incomes below the poverty line, only a quarter are headed by women, only a tenth have illegitimate children, and an even smaller proportion combine these conditions and are supported by public welfare.[39] It is this distinct minority of black families that we refer to when we examine the ways in which these poor families deviate from the assumptions of the traditional legal model.

Marriage and Divorce

The lower-class black family has frequently been characterized as a matriarchal (mother-headed) extended family with emphasis on blood ties rather than the conjugal (husband–wife) relationship.[40] One's parents and other members of one's birth family—or what anthropologists call the extended family—constitute one's closest kin. These ties are often considered more important and more enduring than the tie between husband and wife. As Aschenbrenner's study of black families in Chicago reveals:

> [O]ther relationships, such as father–son, mother–daughter, or brother–sister, may be more important in terms of social and economic support than that of husband and wife [and consequently] the marital tie does not enjoy the central and absolute status it generally holds among middle-class whites, who create a socially and economically independent family unit.[41]

Among lower-class blacks premarital sex, coupled with a high value placed on parenthood, often results in a high incidence of premarital pregnancy.[42] According to Stack, the woman's early age at first pregnancy and a mutual lack of monetary resources frequently prevent young couples from marrying and establishing a separate domicile before the birth of their first child.[43] As a result, many young women are unmarried and living in their parents' homes when their first child is born. Thereafter, these women quickly and accurately assess the relative stability afforded them by AFDC as opposed to the extreme economic vulnerability of their male partners and, at least temporarily, commonly forgo legal marriage.[44] The young unmarried mothers then continue to reside with their own mothers after their children are born. In this setting the grandmother is likely to play a substantial role in raising the children.

Although the relatively large number of female-headed households in poor black communities has been widely documented,[45] some scholars have cautioned against exaggerating the extent to which men are absent.* Nevertheless, it is clear that few lower-class black households have a permanent male provider. Carol Stack attributes this to two primary factors. First she cites the lack of permanent, well-paying jobs for men:

> [T]he most important single factor which affects interpersonal relationships between men and women . . . is unemployment, and the im-

---

*TenHouten, for instance, tells us that "substitute father laws and welfare requirements often make financial aid contingent on there being no father in the home. This, of course, creates a strong economic incentive to *conceal the presence of the husband*, and also contributes to husbands' motivation to leave the family unit" (italics added). Warren D. TenHouten, "The Black Family: Myth and Reality," *Psychiatry* 33, no. 2 (1970):145–55.

possibility for men to secure jobs. Losing a job, or being unemployed month after month, debilitates one's self-importance and independence, and for men, necessitates that they sacrifice their role in the economic support of their families. . . .[46]

Second, women come to realize that welfare benefits and ties within kin networks provide them and their children with more security than they can reasonably expect from men. Since a woman may be immediately cut off the welfare rolls if she gets married, she is often reluctant to give up the (limited) financial security of AFDC and her kin network for the risks of marriage.

In fact, marriage and long-term relationships are often difficult to sustain. Low-income black families experience a high rate of divorce and desertion. In 1975, 26.6 percent of the black population aged 25 to 54 were divorced or separated, compared with 8.4 percent of the white population in the same age group.[47] Lee Rainwater, like Stack, attributes the high rate of dissolution to the males' economic difficulties. He noted that unemployed husbands find it hard to maintain either their relationships with their wives or their status when they are not bringing money into the house.[48] In addition, strong kin networks often serve to weaken marital ties by asserting the primacy of kin responsibilities over marriage obligations. As Rainwater observes, the once-married black woman may "see little to recommend it in the future."[49] Overall, it is the mother's kinship network, with its elastic household boundaries and lifelong bonds, that provides, as Stack concludes, the most "resilient response to the social-economic conditions of poverty."[50]

A Challenge to the Provisions of the Traditional Marriage Contract

Black lower-class family patterns challenge every one of the provisions of the traditional marriage contract.

First, the legal marriage designation of the husband as head of household is clearly inappropriate in a three-generation matrilineal household. As both Aschenbrenner and Stack describe the pattern of domestic authority, such a household is most frequently headed by the grandmother. Both adult males and adult females are encouraged to return to their own mothers' homes with their children. In fact, Aschenbrenner reports that the grandmother may encourage her children to remain unmarried in order to maintain her authority and control over the household, particularly with respect to the distribution of monetary resources.[51] Similarly, Stack notes that when women have most of the domestic authority there are clear limitations on the power of a husband or male friend within the women's kin network.[52]

Second, the financial patterns among black lower-class families challenge the provision of the traditional marriage contract that holds the husband responsible for family support. Because the lower-class black husband's earnings can rarely ensure the necessities of life, the family unit is typically dependent on welfare, or on the mother's wages or her kin network for family support.[53] Since women can often earn as much outside the home as their husbands, and because motherhood makes them uniquely eligible for state aid, the main burden of family support and child support usually rests with them. For example, in Liebow's well known study of black "street-corner men," fathers provided financial support irregularly, if at all, and then only on demand or request.[54]

Third, the stay-at-home housewife so taken for granted in the legal model is an ideal that poor black families cannot afford. Since economic circumstances typically require that a lower-class black woman work in the labor force, she is likely to carry the double burden of providing both economic support and domestic services for her family. Francine Blau has shown that minority women have for the past century been likely to carry this double burden.[55] As early as 1890, when only 4 percent of all married women in this country were in the labor force, two groups of married women commonly worked outside the home: black women, the majority of whom still lived in the South, and immigrant women in the textile towns of New England. Blau reports that in 1890 one of every four black married women was gainfully employed, many doing the same kinds of jobs they had done in slavery.[56]

In recent years, with the labor force participation rate for white women rapidly increasing, the gap between black and white women's employment rates has diminished. However, black women over age 24 still are much more likely than their white contemporaries to be employed, and a larger proportion of them work full time the year round.[57]

Fourth, in a way that is perhaps unique, the black lower-class family also challenges the traditional marriage contract's assignment of responsibility for child care to the mother. Since many of the women in the lower-class black community work outside the home, "the responsibility for providing food, care, clothing, and shelter for children tends to be spread over several households."[58] As we have seen, the care of children is typically delegated to the grandmother and the extended kin network rather than to the mother—or to the parents. Indeed, Aschenbrenner reports, "Black Americans may not accept the terms and decrees of a legal system designed for a conjugal family system, in which parents take all responsibility and have sole rights over their children."[59] As she notes, these requirements inappropriately rule out the influence of extended families in which grandparents, aunts or uncles, and older siblings share responsibility for children. *

The traditional legal model assumes that when parents separate, they divorce; and that when they divorce, a court somewhere will award custody of the children.[60] As we have seen, this assumption also does not hold true for black parents afflicted by poverty. In their world, community norms about custody become *de facto* law. The law in most states holds that the child's natural parents have permanent rights to the child's custody, even if they have temporarily left the child with relatives or foster parents. But while children in the black community are acknowledged to be in the ultimate care of their natural mothers in the great majority of cases,[61] a mother who does not fulfill her obligations to her child may lose her claim to parenthood, and the child's caretaker (most often the maternal grandmother) may well acquire "parental rights."

Finally, traditional legal marriage is inappropriate in the lower-class black community in its assumptions about child support. As we have noted, fathers there cannot typically assume the responsibility for either spousal or child support, either during marriage or after divorce. Instead, the mother supports the children from her own wages or with the aid of the state and her kin network.

One hopeful note surfaces in this pattern of legal assumptions that undermine and restrict the social customs and patterns in black lower-class families. In 1977, in *Moore* v. *East Cleveland*,[62] the U.S Supreme Court upheld a grandmother's challenge to a housing ordinance that denied her right to live in an extended family. The East Cleveland ordinance prohibited individuals who were not in the same family from sharing a common dwelling, defining a "family" as parents and their children. Mrs. Moore was convicted of vio-

---

*Stack observed the exchange of children and short-term fosterage among the mother's female friends as well in the lower-class black community she studied. Carol B. Stack, *All Our Kin: Strategies for Survival in a Black Community* (New York: Harper Colophon Books, 1974).

lating the housing ordinance because her two grandsons living in her home were first cousins, not brothers, and therefore not of the same "family" according to the terms of the ordinance. However, the Supreme Court ruled that the ordinance unlawfully interfered with family living arrangements and family privacy.

In his concurring opinion Justice William Brennan discussed the class and racial bias embodied in the ordinance. He explicitly noted the extent to which American family law is a law for white suburbanites, and thus may discriminate against lower-class blacks. Brennan said that since the "nuclear family" is predominantly a phenomenon of white suburbia, "the line drawn by this ordinance displays a depressing insensitivity toward the economic and emotional needs of a very large part of our society."[63]

In this chapter we have seen many ways in which traditional legal assumptions about family patterns may be less than appropriate for ethnic and racial minorities and the poor. At a minimum, the traditional family law imposes inappropriate burdens and responsibilities on persons in these groups; it also often goes so far as to punish them for failing to live up to middle-class norms.

The contract model, discussed in detail in Parts III and IV of this book, provides an alternative legal structure that can encompass the class, racial, and ethnic diversities among families in our society. It would allow families to structure their relationships in accord with their own norms and values. Some of these family groups may want a marriage contract that extends support obligations beyond the conjugal family unit to include grandparents, aunts, uncles, and cousins as providers or recipients. Others might find it appropriate to apportion financial, domestic, and child care responsibilities along generational rather than sex-linked lines. In imposing the white middle-class family concept on all families, the traditional legal marriage has ignored and excluded the special concerns and needs of those who deviate from this limited "ideal."

CHAPTER 9

One Man, One Woman— No Exceptions

The law has institutionalized the Judeo-Christian ideal of monogamous, heterosexual marriage through statutory and case law prohibitions against polygamy, bigamy, adultery, and homosexual unions. This chapter focuses on three distinct components of the traditional law. The first is the assumption that marriage is a union of two single individuals, exemplified by prohibitions against polygamy and bigamy. The second is the assumption of sexual fidelity to one spouse, exemplified by prohibitions against adultery. The third is the assumption of a heterosexual union, exemplified by the denial of marriage licenses to homosexual couples.

Prohibitions Against Bigamy and Polygamy

The assumption that marriage is a union of two individuals is evident in the statutory prohibition, in all the states, against bigamy (marriage to more than one wife or husband), and in judicial decisions dealing with polygamous or multiple marriages. State legislatures have traditionally imposed criminal penalties for bigamy and polygamy and the courts have consistently upheld their right to do so.[1]

As recently as 1946, a fundamentalist Mormon was convicted of violating the Mann Act when he transported a woman across a state line for a plural marriage ceremony and subsequent cohabitation.[2] The U.S. Supreme Court affirmed the invocation of the Mann Act, which specifically prohibits transporting individuals across state lines for the purpose of prostitution, because "the establishment of polygamous households is a notorious example of promiscuity."

Historically, the only systematic challenge to prohibitions against polygamy has been posed by the Mormon Church.[3] Beginning in 1878, the U.S. Supreme Court consistently upheld the prosecution and criminal conviction of Mormons found to be involved in plural marriages. For example, in *Reynolds v.the United States*,[4] a Mormon prosecuted for entering into a plural marriage (and thereby violating the law against polygamy) asserted that his marriage was ordained by his religion and therefore protected under the First Amendment guarantee of freedom of religion. The Supreme Court, however, upheld his conviction, stating: "There has never been a time in any State of the Union when polygamy has not been an offense against society, cognizable by the civil courts and punishable with more or less severity."[5]

While no sociologist would seriously claim that the polygamy prohibition is at odds with the accepted norms of our society, there are two situations in which this prohibition severely disadvantages innocent people and violates equally accepted norms of fairness. The first situation involves a bigamous union resulting from sequential marriages in which one party has not obtained a legal divorce from a former spouse. The second involves persons living in extended families, communes, and other family-like units of two or more adults.

Sequential Bigamy

As we have seen, serial monogamy, the movement from a first monogamous union to a second, is becoming more common in our society. Although serial monogamy usually entails a divorce from the first spouse, many marriages are dissolved by desertion and separation with neither partner securing a legal divorce. If these persons marry a second time, they and their new spouses—and especially the children of the second marriage—may run afoul of the legal prohibition against bigamy. As Foote, Levy, and Sanders observe, the law makes no distinction between these "sequential unions" and "concurrent" bigamy:

> American bigamy statutes draw no distinction between what we might term "concurrent" and "sequential" bigamy. The first is probably extremely rare, and most of our legal problems concern situations where the challenged second marriage is sequential to an earlier family already terminated in fact.[6]

The problem is most common among poor families who, as we noted in Chapter 8, often forgo divorce and dissolve their marriages informally, owing to strained finances and a lack of legal assistance. The prevalence of *de facto* unions among adults who have not divorced their former spouses is suggested by the following plea from a California social worker:

> Forty-three per cent of AFDC [Aid to Families with Dependent Children] children were born to parents who were not [legally] married to each other [although] the parents treated each other and their children in all respects as would a legally married couple. . . . We believe that some form of legal aid should be readily available to families where divorce is indicated . . . particularly to stabilize an existing second home and family for children.[7]

Because bigamy is illegal, when the courts are confronted with bigamy cases they have traditionally ruled that only one marriage is valid.[8] However, if the marriages are sequential, *both* may have been "socially real marriages" and in such situations justice would seem to be best served by legal recognition of their social validity.

For example, let us say a man lives with one wife for three years. He then remarries and lives with a second wife for five years, without ever divorcing the first. If this man then dies without a will, the court would probably award his entire estate to his first (and only *legal*) wife. However, one might easily argue that the second woman has an equal, if not greater, interest in his estate and that a more equitable solution would be to divide the estate between the wives, thereby recognizing the just claims of both. If the law were to recognize the social validity of both families in such cases, the courts could fairly apportion such benefits as insurance, pensions, Social Security, and unemployment compensation among various deserving former wives and their children without the constraints imposed by the requirement that they be "legitimate" heirs.

One unusual decision in California took a major step in this direction. In 1975, *In re Atherley*,[9] both the decedent's legal wife and the woman with whom he had been cohabiting for more than 25 years prior to his death sought to be designated his "surviving spouse." Mr. Atherley had formed the second union without obtaining a legal divorce from his first wife. After fifteen years of cohabitation he secured a Mexican divorce (that later turned out to be invalid) and married the woman with whom he was living. They lived together for an additional ten years until he died. The Atherley court ruled that the first wife was the surviving "spouse," but it nevertheless found that the second "wife" also had an interest in the estate and awarded her a share of the property.

While the *Atherley* decision sets a precedent in recognizing *de facto* bigamy, two factors may limit its application. First, it is clear that Mr. Atherley attempted to establish a legal marriage with the second woman, thus making her a putative spouse (a woman who mistakenly believed that she was married), a status that has traditionally been accorded legal protection. Second, since Mr. Atherley was dead, the court was faced only with dividing his estate—a task that appears relatively straightforward when compared to apportioning nondivisible rights and privileges when all of the adults (and children) are still alive.

The claims of dual spouses—and the two families—are equally pressing after divorce or separation when all the parties are alive. For example, in one 1975 California case, Jane Scherr, the cohabiting partner of Max Scherr, owner of the Berkeley Barb newspaper, sought to recover half of the assets of the newspaper she helped to build during the 12 years that they lived together.[10] Jane and Max had two children together and were known and treated as husband and wife. Max Scherr, however, contended that since he had never divorced his legal wife, Jane had no claim to "his" assets. Jane Scherr's attorney, Fay Stender, persuasively argued that since Jane and Max and their children were a family—in their own eyes and in the eyes of the community in which they lived—their family status, rather than the inappropriate law of bigamy, should govern their legal relationship. Stender contended that justice and fairness called for legal recognition of their family relationship, and that this need not exclude Max's legal wife. In other words, she asked the court to recognize the reality of sequential family formation and to apportion rights between the two families. The trial court judge, however, held that the law recognized only one marriage,* and since Max was still legally married to his first wife, Jane had no claim to the "community" she had helped to build. The legal prohibition against bigamy denied Jane the status (and claims) of a legal wife.

Thus the Scherr case argues for the important but difficult task of recognizing sequentially bigamous relationships for the purpose of fairly allocating family assets and benefits.

"Group Marriage" and Communes

Today a growing number of people are cohabiting in communes and other family-like units of more than two adults.[11] Such alternatives to traditional legal marriage have been urged by some to "obviate the need for paternalistic state regulation" of family relationships,[12] and by others to extend family feelings of warmth, closeness, and acceptance in an alternative community.[13]

Although these groups may function in a manner similar to an extended family, the members typically are not related by blood or conjugal ties. While a detailed description of these relationships is beyond the scope of this book, it is important to note that many actually define themselves as families. Sociologist Jessie Bernard, uses the term "group marriage" to describe the groups of three or more members "who commit themselves to one another and consider all to be married to one another."[14] They are not a cooperative household because the bonds that unite them are genuinely intimate and affectionate.

Communes and group marriages have typically been excluded from many of the benefits and legal protections accorded to families: they cannot file joint income tax returns; receive family benefits under Social Security, disability, and health insurance programs; or avail themselves of the property and tax benefits of inheritance laws.

Apart from these economic restraints, parents living in communes are especially vulnerable to the risk of losing custody of their children. Although there are no laws mandating this result, few judges consider communes desirable environments for children,

---

*The *Scherr* case was decided before the California Supreme Court's decision in the *Marvin* case, which is discussed in Chapter 15, and did not claim an implicit or explicit contractual agreement.

and may therefore consider allegations that such a living arrangement is "unhealthy" as sufficient to deny or change custody, or to order a child removed from a commune.* In addition, the court may require a noncustodial parent who lives in a commune to visit his or her child outside the commune.[15]

Communards face other legal problems that, according to attorney Lee Goldstein, arise from "discretionary harassment" by local officials: selective enforcement of building and zoning codes, police searches, and enforcement of seldom invoked sex laws.[16] In addition, if a commune seeks to buy property as a family, it is likely to encounter difficulties obtaining financing.[17]

On occasion legislators have gone so far as to change existing laws so that persons in communes can be "legally" deprived of benefits they otherwise would be entitled to receive. For example, the U.S. Congress, in response to studies indicating that "hippie" communes were substantially dependent on federal aid programs, changed its definition of "household" in such a way as to make most communards ineligible to receive food stamps. Under the revised rules a household was defined as "a group of *related individuals* (including legally adopted children and legally assigned foster children) or nonrelated individuals over age sixty," living as one economic unit, sharing common cooking facilities, and purchasing food in common.[18] The new regulations were invalidated by a federal court because they denied equal protection to those in communal living arrangements and bore no relevant relationship to the government program's intent of alleviating hunger. The U.S. Supreme Court later affirmed this decision.[19]

Morality laws also have been used to harass communal groups. Indeed, Goldstein claims that "virtually by definition, morality laws are aimed at the oppression of nonconforming minorities"[20] because they are always selectively enforced. The language of such laws tends to be vague, and in small communities neighborhood complaints often lead to convictions with little "proof" demanded. For example, "disorderly conduct" encompasses many activities not normally considered crimes. Similarly, "lewd and lascivious behav-

---

*Attorneys Massey and Warner advise communal parents who face custody battles to emphasize the financial benefits of the living arrangements. Further, they assert that the more the parent–child situation emulates the traditional family, the more likely it is to be viewed as acceptable by the judge. Carmen Massey and Ralph Warner, *Sex, Living Together and the Law* (Berkeley, Calif.: Nolo Press, 1974), p. 177.

ior" and behavior "offensive to public morals" can cover a multitude of circumstances, depending on whether the witnesses consider the behavior offensive. In many communities, a group of unwed men and women living together could be considered an offense to public morals. In addition, communal residences are vulnerable to raids on charges that they are "bawdy" or "disorderly houses." As attorney Goldstein cautions:

> A disorderly house [is] defined as a house "in which people resort to the disturbance of the neighborhood or activities injurious to public morals, health, convenience, or safety." Even if the state's laws do not prohibit a disorderly house, they can get you at common law as a public nuisance. If what is done inside is illegal or immoral, the house may be legally disorderly even though the public peace and quiet are in no way disturbed.[21]

All of these charges, if proven to the court's satisfaction, are punishable offenses.

The legal weapons most commonly used against communards are zoning laws. Zoning laws typically prohibit more than two unrelated adults from living together as a family in single-family residence zones.[22] In *Palo Alto Tenants Union* v. *Morgan* (1970)[23] and *Village of Belle Terre* v. *Boraas*[24] two communities successfully ousted communal groups from "single-family residential neighborhoods." In both cases the ousted groups contended that the zoning restrictions violated their constitutional rights to privacy and freedom of association, and the Palo Alto group specifically asserted they were living together as a family, "treating themselves and treated by others as a family unit."[25] But while the courts acknowledged the value of protection for the traditional family relationship, they were unwilling to attach the same status to the voluntary family. As the court in the Palo Alto case reasoned:

> The communal living groups represented by plaintiffs share few [characteristics of a family]. They are voluntary, with fluctuating memberships who have no legal obligations of support or cohabitation. They are in no way subject to the State's vast body of domestic relations law. They do not have the biological links which characterize most families. Emotional ties between commune members may exist, but this is true of members of many groups. Plaintiffs are unquestionably sincere in seeking to devise and test new life-styles, but the communes they have formed are legally indistinguishable from such traditional living groups as religious communities and residence clubs.

The right to form such groups may be constitutionally protected, but the right to insist that these groups live under the same roof, in any part of the city they choose, is not.[26]

In *Belle Terre* Justice Douglas, writing the majority opinion for the U.S. Supreme Court, justified the community's zoning ordinance as a reasonable environmental measure:

> A quiet place where yards are wide, people few, and motor vehicles restricted are legitimate guidelines in a land-use project addressed to family needs . . . zones where family values, youth values, and the blessings of quiet seclusion and clean air make the area a sanctuary for people.[27]

So far, for all the Court's expressed concern about *environment*, decisions in such cases appear, in fact, to be based exclusively and consistently on the existence or absence of legal or blood ties among the inhabitants of a home. For example, an Illinois "family" of 18 people—a widow, her 12 children, the husbands of 3 of the children, and 2 grandchildren—was held not to violate a single-family zoning law.[28] Similarly, in the 1977 case of *Moore* v. *East Cleveland*,[29] the Supreme Court held that a black extended family could not be excluded from a single-family zone but made it clear that this ruling could not be extended to unrelated persons living together in a single home.

In a series of cases following *Belle Terre*, the courts have consistently upheld ordinances that restrict the living arrangements of unrelated persons. Two married couples and two other unrelated individuals were forced to vacate their residence in Colorado,[30] and a priest and seven male members of a religious society were denied a single-family residence permit in Missouri.[31] The justification for these kinds of decisions was most clearly articulated in a New Hampshire case:

> The State has no particular interest in keeping together a certain group of unrelated persons. The State has a clear interest, however, in preserving the integrity of the biological or legal family. The promotion of this legitimate government purpose justifies the exclusion of a blood related family from the density requirements of the ordinance which applies to an unrelated household.[32]

The only exceptions to this general trend have occurred in New York and New Jersey, where courts have been subjecting zoning regulations to more careful scrutiny. For example, despite single-family zoning, a New York court permitted a group home for ten foster children because they emulated the traditional family.[33] The court said the city could restrict the area to *stable* families, but could not limit the definition of the family to exclude a household that was a family in every sense even though it lacked biological ties. A later New York case adopted this reasoning, as did a New Jersey court, to allow a group home for handicapped preschoolers in a single-family zone.[34]

The restrictions on voluntary families are now affecting more segments of society than many people realize. For example, communal arrangements are on the increase among the elderly,[35]* for whom the financial advantages of the communal household may be especially important. Because many elderly people live on fixed incomes, they may increasingly need to pool and share resources. In one case, *Marino v. Mayor and Council of Norwood*,[36] an unmarried and unrelated elderly man and woman living together in one apartment of a two-family dwelling were accused of a zoning violation. In this case, however, the court found in favor of the couple:

> This court will not conclude that persons who have economic or other personal reasons for living together as a bona fide single housekeeping unit and who have no other orientation, commit a zoning violation, with possible penal consequences, just because they are not related.[37]

Although this ruling antedated *Belle Terre*, both it and the food stamp ruling noted above suggest that one avenue of defense against restrictive definitions of "family" may be that they discriminate on the basis of income.[38]

Sexual Monogamy

The legal ideal is that marriage entails a monogamous sexual relationship between a wife and a husband. Adultery (sexual relations by a married person outside of his or her marriage) has been treated in Western societies as a serious moral and legal transgression at least since the time of the Romans. It is perhaps the oldest cause for

---

*In view of the shortage of older men, some gerontologists and social analysts have suggested legalizing polygamy among the elderly to provide them the economic and social advantages of extended family relationships. Rustum Roy and Della Roy, "Is Monogamy Outdated?" in *Renovating Marriage: Toward New Sexual Life-Styles*, R. Libby and R. Whitehurst, eds. (Danville, Calif.: Consensus, 1973), p. 71.

divorce in our culture and traditionally has been regarded as the most heinous of marital sins—when it is perpetrated by a wife.[39] Historically, here as elsewhere, wives have distinctly been victims of a double standard. "Under some ancient laws a wife who committed adultery might be burned alive, devoured by dogs, stoned to death, or killed by her father or husband," while an adulterous husband received either no punishment at all or a reprimand and a small fine.[40] The justification for the harsher treatment of the wife was that her transgression could bring "strangers" to the blood, whereas the husband's philanderings posed no similar threat.

According to Ploscowe, Foster, and Freed, the double standard was incorporated into Roman law, Anglo-Saxon law, and ecclesiastical law.[41] "Although adultery was an ecclesiastical offense rather than a crime at common law, the American colonies made it a crime and treated it severely, the death penalty was imposed in Massachusetts Bay Colony and the scarlet letter brand in Connecticut."[42] Today, adultery is still a crime in all but five states but is rarely prosecuted as such.[43]

In the past century adultery has provided an important ground for divorce actions under the fault-based laws in effect in most states. Originally, men were permitted to divorce adulterous wives, but wives were barred from asserting similar charges against their husbands. In England, it was not until 1923 "that a woman could maintain a divorce action against her husband for mere adultery."[44] Now, however, the law no longer accords official recognition to the double standard. Marital fidelity is regarded as a mutual obligation, and both husbands and wives can obtain a divorce if their spouses transgress. Nevertheless, the old religious ethic still permeates family law and provides the basis for many judicial decisions. A mother's adultery still weighs against her in a custody contest (although it alone cannot bar her from custody); a wife's adultery deprives her of alimony in most states, regardless of her need; and a divorced wife's illicit sexual activity may cause her alimony to be revoked.[45]

While the monogamous ideal embedded in law probably reflected moral ideals, it is not clear that it ever reflected social reality and it certainly does not do so today. The data on extramarital sex tend increasingly "to support the notion that we pay lip service to the monogamous ideal but in fact maintain a significant variety of other forms of sex life."[46]

In the 1950s Kinsey reported that by the time they reached the age of forty, 50 percent of his male subjects and 26 percent of the females had engaged in extramarital sexual relations.[47] Today, marriage experts commonly estimate that 60 percent of all married men, and 35 to 40 percent of married women have engaged in extramarital sexual relations at some time during their married lives.[48] Because the incidence of extramarital intercourse is most widespread among the younger generation (it is now three times more common among white women 18 to 24 than it was a generation ago), it would seem reasonable to predict further increases in the overall incidence of extramarital sex in the years to come.* However, after completing a comprehensive national survey in 1974, Morton Hunt cautions against too-hasty conclusions: "While most Americans—especially the young—now feel far freer than formerly to be sensation-oriented at times, for the great majority of them sex remains intimately allied to their deepest emotions and is inextricably interwoven with their conceptions of loyalty, love and marriage."[49]

Nevertheless, even a "happy marriage" no longer seems to preclude the possibility of an extramarital relationship. Cuber and Harroff found that a large number of "happily married" upper-middle-class Americans were also engaged in extramarital affairs.[50] The researchers concluded that "there is a growing tolerance of the idea that some men and women need or want enduring sexual as well as platonic relationships with more than one person concurrently."[51]

As the incidence of extramarital sex appears to be increasing, so does its acceptance. For some spouses "the infidelity is condoned by the partner . . . as a kind of basic human right which the loved one ought to be permitted to have—and which the other perhaps wants also for himself."[52] Both Hunt and the Cuber-Harroff research team concluded that extramarital relations are not necessarily destructive to marriage: both one-time flings and more long-term affairs were found to coexist with stable marriages for some couples.

Recent national data confirm the trend to more permissive attitudes toward extramarital relations.[53] In a 1973 national sample of the U.S. population Hunt found that "Mate swapping, virtually

---

*Hunt's national 1974 survey indicated there had been no overall increase in extramarital experience among men, and only a limited increase among women in the generation since Kinsey's work in the 1950s. Nevertheless, the increase among women and those under 24 was significant because they were the two groups most likely to affect a future increase in the amount and acceptance of extramarital sex. See Morton Hunt, *Sexual Behavior in the 1970's* (New York: Dell, 1974).

unmentionable until recently and violative of our most deeply entrenched ideas about sex and marriage, is still wrong in the eyes of the majority—but, surprisingly, not an overwhelming one: only 62 percent of men and 75 percent of women agreed that it was wrong, while a sizable minority—nearly a third of the men and a fifth of the women—felt that it was not."[54]

The increased acceptance of extramarital sex does not, however, indicate that most spouses accept their mates' infidelity. Nor does it mean there are no difficulties in maintaining extramarital relationships; clearly there are.[55] But more couples are choosing to deal with these difficulties instead of paying lip service to the monogamous ideal.* Some of the recent social science literature distinguishes between extramarital sex, which has the "old pejorative meaning of adultery and unfaithfulness," and comarital sex, which "exists alongside of and in addition to a marriage relationship . . . [but] is not competitive with the marital relationship."[56] In addition, there is a growing body of literature that challenges the traditional concept that monogamy is the most satisfying form of relationship. Of course, the double standard has long been used to rationalize male prerogatives to engage in extramarital sex, as Dr. Robert Seidenberg observes:

> The well-known double standard has been rationalized and vindicated in the fiction that the male of the species is basically polygamous, and therefore his transgressions are a part of his basic nature; whereas the woman's is a moral fault. This is another instance where power can write its own favorable rules supported by an ongoing mythology.[57]

What is new is the recent re-examination of our assumptions about female sexuality and its relationship to the monogamous ideal. Professor Pepper Schwartz argues that, in the past, socialization, peer groups, limited access to information, and the structure of the family made a woman feel that love and sex must go together and one man, her husband, should be able to satisfy her.[58] Now, however, with women beginning to discover the extent and degree

---

*Some data suggest a slightly different pattern: while many individuals of both sexes say that extramarital sex is permissible "in general" and for them "personally," they are still reluctant to grant the same freedom to their own wife or husband or nonmarital spouse.

of their own sex drives,* Schwartz predicts that women will generally desire more sexual activity than one monogamous, long-term
relationship can provide, and this will lead to an upsurge of nonmonogamous marriages and relationships outside of marriage.† As
she notes:

> We already know that marriages . . . can tolerate non-marital sex and
> still maintain their continuity. Traditionally, only men have been al-
> lowed the liberty of relating sexually to persons outside the marriage
> and they often have rationalized their actions by saying that they "can
> handle it" while their wives would become "too emotionally in-
> volved." Under a more egalitarian model, we know that non-marital
> sex can exist when adequate rules, ideology, and trust have been es-
> tablished to protect the original couple.[59]

While a complete examination of this position is beyond the
scope of this discussion, it is clear that the traditional assumption of
monogamy, and the importance of monogamy in marriage, is subject to a growing number of theoretical and empirical challenges in
our society.

Heterosexual Unions

The third component of the Judeo-Christian ideal embodied in law
is that of a heterosexual union, a marriage between two individuals
of opposite sex.

Our current social and legal prohibitions against homosexuality
in general, and homosexual marriage in particular, originate in
English common law. This law continued the ecclesiastical tra-

---

*Recent evidence also indicates that women are becoming more likely to as-
sert their desire for satisfaction in sexual relationships. A 1980 (nonrandom) survey of reader's sexual attitudes (conducted by *Redbook* magazine) indicated that
communication between partners and assertiveness in women was positively related to sexual satisfaction. Philip and Lorna Sarrel "The Redbook Report on Sexual Relationships" *Redbook* (October 1980): 73–80.

†Schwartz points to the following "myths" about female sexuality: (1) that
women need a committed (love) relationship for sexual satisfactions, (2) that female sexual satisfaction is best produced in a monogamous marriage, (3) that two
people can satisfy all of each other's sexual needs, and (4) that if the female has a
sexual relationship outside the marital dyad the dyad will be destroyed. See Pepper Schwartz, "Female Sexuality and Monogamy," in *Renovating Marriage:
Toward New Sexual Lifestyles*, Roger W. Libby and Robert N. Whitehurst, eds.
(Danville, Calif.: Consensus, 1973).

dition, which was, in turn, based on Judeo-Christian prohibitions against homosexuality.[60] Whereas homosexual behavior was generally tolerated in the Greco-Roman world, the Christian church adopted the Hebrew prohibition of homosexual conduct for either sex as part of its wider prohibition of any sexual act that did not lead to procreation.

American law, besides adopting the church's condemnation of homosexuality, also adopted its view of the purpose of marriage: "The end of marriage is procreation of children and the propagation of the species."[61] While it is clear that homosexual marriage would not be welcomed by a legal institution that endorses these views, legislation that explicitly excludes or forbids homosexual marriages is rare because it has been so widely assumed that marriage is *ipso facto* a heterosexual union. For example, although the Uniform Marriage and Divorce Act refers to "a marriage between a man and a woman" and its Comment section adds that "in accordance with established usage, marriage is required to be between a man and a woman," the Act does not include same-sex marriages in its list of prohibited marriages.[62] The legal assumption that marriage can occur only between heterosexuals has been so taken for granted that no other possibility was considered until very recently.

Today, however, there are increasing numbers of homosexual couples who want to formalize their relationships. The issue of homosexual marriage was first raised in the courts in 1972, in *Baker* v. *Nelson*,[63] a case in which a male homosexual couple applied for, and were denied, a marriage license in Minnesota. In challenging the state's restrictions on homosexual marriages, they argued that the right to marry is a fundamental right of all persons. Further, they contended that restricting marriages to heterosexual couples was an irrational and invidious means of discrimination. The court disagreed, and affirmed the traditional position that marriage "is the state of union between two persons of the opposite sex."[64] A Kentucky court has followed *Baker* by sustaining the denial of a marriage license to two women.[65]

The denial of a marriage license may impose burdens on a couple beyond the loss of formal legitimacy for their relationship. Legally married persons receive certain economic advantages in filing income tax returns; in obtaining Social Security, disability, unemployment, and pension benefits; in securing mortgages, homes, apartments, and insurance; in receiving loans and credit; and in obtaining family rates and coverage for health insurance, home insurance, and auto insurance. Couples who cannot be legally married are also denied the right to inherit from each other if one party dies without leaving a will, and to recover damages for the wrongful death of the other party. They may also be discriminated against in adopting or obtaining custody of children.

Although this book has stressed the many restrictions imposed by legal marriage, a state-sanctioned union clearly has some social and psychological benefits. But while the freedom to weigh and choose between the restrictions and benefits of legal marriage is accorded to all heterosexual couples, the same freedom is denied to all couples of the same sex. Those who have suggested that homosexual couples be allowed the same choice have pointed to the legitimating effect of legal marriage—as well as to its social and financial advantages:

> For some, marriage means a religious sacrament and commitment. For others it may also take on a legal significance in terms of community property, the filing of joint income tax returns and inheritance rights. Recognition of a Lesbian union might . . . serve to validate the couples who wished to take on the legal responsibility of adopting homeless, unwanted children. It would also simplify insurance problems, making the couple eligible for family policies, for family rates on airlines travel and, for that matter, for "couple" entry to entertainment functions, too.[66]

Another author claims that the formal status of marriage enhances the "stability, respectability, and emotional depth of the relationship between two individuals."[67]

No court, however, has yet recognized the right of homosexuals to obtain marriage licenses, and although homosexuals have been married in religious ceremonies, no state recognizes such marriages as legal.[68] In a recent New York case, a court held that a marriage between two men, one of whom presented himself as a woman, was invalid because "the law makes no provision for a 'marriage' between persons of the same sex."[69] In 1973, Maryland enacted a law that specifically states, "Only a marriage between a man and a woman is valid in this State,"[70] and in 1974 a Florida legislative committee concluded that "the Biblical description of homosexuality as an 'abomination' has well stood the test of time."[71]

Given these attitudes, it does not seem likely that the courts will recognize homosexual unions in the near future. The *Baker* court's dismissal of the petitioners' contentions adamantly affirmed that "the institution of marriage as a union of man and woman is as old as the book of Genesis."[72]

The prohibition of homosexual marriage has been challenged, unsuccessfully, on several constitutional grounds: as a violation of the First Amendment right to freedom of association, as an invasion of privacy as protected by the Fourth, Ninth, and Fourteenth Amendments, and as a denial of due process and equal protection as guaranteed by the Fifth and Fourteenth Amendments.[73] Some champions of the cause believe the prohibition of homosexual marriages would have to fall if the federal Equal Rights Amendment were ratified; but Birch Bayh, ERA's chief sponsor in the Senate, has stated that the Amendment would *not* prohibit states from banning same-sex marriages as long as both males and females are equally denied the right to marry a person of their own sex.[74]

Recent cases suggest that Senator Bayh's interpretation is likely to prevail. In 1974 Washington State's prohibition against same-sex marriage was upheld under that state's Equal Rights Amendment.[75] More recently, the same interpretation of a state ERA was expressed by the attorney general of Colorado, who concluded that under both statutory and case law a county clerk does not have to issue a marriage license to a same-sex couple. Further, he asserted, if such a license is issued it is not valid, nor is an ensuing marriage between such a couple.[76]

Although the courts remain reluctant to legitimate homosexual marriages, they are beginning to be somewhat more willing to allow homosexual parents to retain custody of their children. A number of lesbians have been involved in marriages or other heterosexual relationships that have produced children: Hunter and Polikoff estimate there are now well over 1.5 million lesbian mothers in this country.[77] Similarly, many homosexual males have been married, and remain fathers to the children of those marriages. The problems lesbian mothers and homosexual fathers face in trying to maintain their parental rights constitute a relatively new public issue, since gay parents have only recently begun to live openly in homosexual relationships while trying to retain their parental rights.

Our knowledge of how homosexual parents have actually fared in child custody cases is quite limited, for two reasons. First, custody cases involving homosexuals rarely go to trial since attorneys and clients usually fear that the court will not grant custody to an acknowledged homosexual.* This fear is well grounded. For example, in 1973, in *Bennett* v. *Clemens*,[78] the Georgia Supreme Court upheld a decision that transferred custody of a child from her lesbian mother to the paternal grandparents, even though the father of the child testified he wanted his former wife to retain custody. As a result of this case and others, Hunter and Polikoff have suggested that a lesbian mother's best strategy "is to reach private settlement with the father without judicial intervention."[79]

A second reason for our lack of information is that only a few of the cases that go to trial are officially reported because many family courts seal the case records in order "to protect juveniles" with homosexual parents. For example, in the 1974 case of *O'Harra* v. *O'Harra*,[80] the trial court awarded the father custody of three sons after considering many factors, including the mother's lesbianism, but did not issue a detailed opinion explaining the basis for its decision. The appellate court ruled that "[b]ecause there is a potential for harm to persons involved, we conclude that no useful purpose would be served in publishing a detailed opinion."[81]

A custody dispute involving homosexual parents typically arises in connection with a divorce action, and can take the form of a custody contest at the time of divorce, a request for change of custody after divorce, or an attempt to limit or deny visitation at either time. Because mothers are typically awarded custody upon divorce, most contested custody cases involve a father's claim that a lesbian mother is unfit to raise the children. Thus, the contest is typically between the two natural parents. However, a minority but growing number of cases are being brought by third parties, usually grandparents challenging a lesbian mother's right to custody.

In "ordinary" custody battles between a parent and a non-parent, the natural parent is assumed to have the right to custody unless he or she can be proved unfit. However, as the Georgia decision in *Bennett*, cited above, illustrates, the mother who is a known lesbian may be presumed unfit by dint of that fact alone, and thus deprived of her preference as the natural parent with no further proof

---

*While judges may choose to ignore expert testimony that a parent's homosexuality does not adversely harm the child, it is significant to note that the American Psychological Association adopted the following resolution in 1976: "The sex, gender identity, or sexual orientation of natural or prospective adoptive or foster parents should not be the *sole or primary variable* considered in child custody or placement cases." *Sexual Law Reporter* 2, no. 6 (November/December 1976): 69. It is too early to determine the effects of this resolution on custody rulings.

required.[82] In a well-publicized 1967 California case, *Nadler* v. *Superior Court*, a trial court ruled that a lesbian mother was unfit to have custody "as a matter of law."[83] However, in a landmark decision, the appellate court reversed the ruling and rebuffed the lower court: "[W]e are saying that the trial court failed in its duty to exercise the very discretion with which it is vested by holding as a matter of law that petitioner was an unfit mother on the basis that she is a homosexual."[84] The case was then sent back to the trial court for a "reconsideration of all the evidence with regard to the mother's fitness," but the trial court still found (on different grounds, of course) that it was in "the best interests of the child" to award custody to the father. "The best interests of the child" standard has routinely been interpreted to mean a heterosexual environment.[85]

The result is that the burden of proof is often shifted to the lesbian mother to prove that she is fit—in contrast to the more typical pattern of assuming the mother is fit until she is proved otherwise.[86] She typically must overcome the court's negative assumption by showing her life-style is *not* detrimental to the child.*

Since *Nadler*, several trial courts have awarded custody to women involved in lesbian relationships but have conditioned the award on the lovers not living together. For example, in the widely publicized 1972 case of *Mitchell* v. *Mitchell*, the first case in which an admitted lesbian won a child custody contest,[87] the mother was awarded custody of her children on the condition that she discontinue living with her lover and associate with her only when the children were at school or with their father.

Similarly, in the consolidated cases of *Shuster* v. *Shuster*[88] and *Isaacson* v. *Isaacson*,[89] two women involved in a lesbian relationship were granted divorces from their respective husbands and were awarded custody of their six children. The judge found their living together "not in the best interests of the children" and required them to live "separate and apart"; however, he *did not* require that they stop seeing each other in their children's presence. (The wom-

---

*As Martin and Lyon accurately observe, despite favorable psychiatric testimony regarding the "fitness" of a lesbian as a parent, judges are still inclined to award custody to the father in such cases: "These decisions are not based upon the qualifications of the mother, but rather on the assumption that her children will more than likely become homosexuals. Yet, of the thousands of lesbian women we have met over the years, all were products of a heterosexual union, all were raised in a heterosexual environment, and all were taught a totally heterosexual value system." Del Martin and Phyllis Lyon, "Lesbian Mothers," *Ms.*, October 1973, p. 79.

en moved into apartments across the hall from each other in the same building.[90])

In the *Schuster–Isaacson* cases, both fathers remarried and reinstituted custody proceedings, charging that the mothers had made a movie about their relationship and "flaunted" their life-style, and that the ensuing publicity had created changed conditions that were detrimental to the children. Although the judge was troubled by the publicity, he was convinced by psychiatric testimony that the children were not harmed. Not only did he deny the fathers' motion for custody change, but he removed the prior cohabitation restriction.[91]

In *People* v. *Brown*,[92] acknowledged lesbian mothers were allowed both to retain custody of their children and to live together. Originally, when the two women refused to live apart in order to retain custody, their children were placed in foster homes. On appeal, the judge found "little, if any, material or admissible evidence to support the finding that the appellants' homosexual relationship rendered their home unfit for their children."[93]

Homosexual fathers frequently find their rights to visitation challenged because it is feared the children will be "exposed to improper conditions and undesirable influences."[94] In one 1974 case, a custodial mother sought to limit a homosexual father's visitation, especially for overnight periods. The father argued that such a restriction, based on homosexuality, is prohibited in the U.S. Constitution. The court agreed with the constitutional argument but held that because this father participated in gay rights activities and took his children with him, there was a "possibility of inflicting severe mental anguish and detriment on three innocent children."[95] The judge therefore ordered that during visitation the father could not be with his lover, could not sleep with anyone but a lawful spouse, and could not take the children to his home or to any homosexually related activities.

A similar theme echoes in the 1976 case *In re Jane B.*,[96] in which a divorced father regained custody of his daughter when his former wife became involved in a lesbian relationship. The judge ruled that although her lesbianism per se did not serve to make the mother unfit, "the home environment with her [the mother's] homosexual partner in residence is not a proper atmosphere in which to bring up this child or in the best interest of this child."[97] As this case indicates, custody depositions are never final: any award may be challenged if there is a "change in circumstances." Thus, homosexual parents who have custody of children are always under the threat of further litigation. Moreover, it is clear that many, if not most, courts continue to view the homosexuality of a parent as conclusive indication of unfitness for custody—whether they openly admit it or couch it in terms of the "best interests of the child."

The cumulative effect of the restrictions embodied in traditional legal marriage is to enforce the notion that one man and one woman will find happiness if they commit themselves to each other for life. The expected commitment obviously goes beyond sexual and social monogamy: it implies a spiritual yoke under which each will seek full happiness only with and through the other. This model envisions an intertwining of lives that many today consider oppressive. The prospective result is a form of tyranny that rules out individual choice in the degree of commitment and involvement. Not all people want the same intensity in their personal relationships; some may want intensity in some relationships at some times, but not necessarily in a marriage relationship at all times. Although we know that some individuals all through history have considered traditional marriage unnecessarily confining,[98] the rapidly expanding number of individuals who are now experimenting with new forms of marriage, living together without marriage, and other innovations in personal and family relationships indicates that the limitations of the present legal model are particularly inappropriate for today's world. It is difficult to imagine a single model for personal relationships fitting the lifelong needs of all individuals in a society as diverse as ours.

PART III

The Alternative: Marital and Nonmarital Contracts

In a society highly conscious of individual rights and accustomed to depending on contracts to order many different types of relationships, it is reasonable for people in close personal relationships to consider writing a contract that fits their individual needs and life-styles. Such a contract would allow a man and a woman to decide in advance on the duration and terms of their relationship, as well as the conditions for its dissolution. They could specify their respective rights and obligations for the financial aspects of the marriage (support, living expenses, property, debts and so forth), as well as for their more personal relations (such as responsibility for birth control, household tasks, and child care). Furthermore, they could make some decisions before entering the relationship (such as their intentions with regard to surname, procreation, or adoption), while reserving others (such as domicile changes) for later. They could also specify the process for making later decisions, and for resolving disagreements that might arise. Any and all such provisions could be included in a contract within or in lieu of legal marriage.

Contracts in lieu of marriage would also allow for legal relationships not contemplated under the present structure of state-regulated marriage. For example, some families might want to extend support obligations beyond the conjugal family unit, to include grandparents, aunts, uncles, and cousins, and to apportion domestic and child care responsibilities along generational rather than sex-linked lines. Contracts in lieu of marriage can also be used in situations where legal marriage is impossible—for communes, homosexual couples, group marriages, and other family-like units of more than two adults—and in situations where legal marriage is inappropriate—among unwed cohabitants who reject the sex-based obligations of family law but want nevertheless to join together in a legal union. Intimate contracts provide an alternative model for homosexual and heterosexual couples wishing to legitimate and regularize a nontraditional relationship. Although many of the above-mentioned marital and family forms do not seem to create any "societal problems" the courts have been slow to grant them recognition that contracts provide.

The three chapters in this section of the book present the rationale for intimate contracts—along with the practical details for devising one. Chapter 10 argues the case for intimate contracts. It describes the individual and societal advantages of contracts within and in lieu of marriage. It also examines the social and psychological effects of contracts and attempts to answer the objections of those who fear that contracts will undermine trust and destroy romance. Given the diverse needs and desires of persons who might enter intimate contracts, the variety of possible provisions in such contracts is virtually infinite. Chapter 11 presents a detailed list of possible provisions, and suggests a number of questions that contract writers may wish to address. These issues are further discussed in Chapter 12 which presents the case histories and intimate contracts of ten couples, five within legal marriage, and five in lieu of marriage.

CHAPTER 10

The Case for Intimate Contracts

In this chapter the tone of the book changes into one of advocacy as we present the case for intimate contracts. The first half of the chapter discusses the advantages of a contract for the individual couple (legally, socially and psychologically) and for the larger society. The second half examines the effects of instituting the contractual model and attempts to answer those who have argued against it. *

From the perspective of a couple about to enter a relationship, a contract offers four major legal advantages, which are discussed in the first section of this chapter. First, in contrast to the outdated framework of traditional legal marriage, a contract allows couples to formulate an agreement that conforms to contemporary social reality. Second, it permits an escape from the sex-based legacy of legal marriage and aids couples who wish to establish an egalitarian relationship. Third, it affords couples the freedom and privacy to

*I am especially indebted to Berkeley Law Professors Melvin Eisenberg and Marjorie Shultz for the opportunity to debate these issues in their classes on contract law, and for their personal assistance in numerous discussions over the years.

It is important to note, however, that the views expressed below are mine alone.

order their personal relationships as they wish. Finally, it allows those who have not married (such as unwed cohabitants) and those who are barred from legal marriage (such as same-sex couples and groups of more than two individuals) to formalize their relationship.

In the discussion that follows, the contracting parties may be referred to as "a couple" or "a man and a woman" for linguistic convenience; however, it is important to bear in mind that the model is equally applicable to same-sex couples and to groups.

In addition to its legal advantages, the contractual model provides social and psychological benefits. Contracts facilitate open and honest communication, and help prospective partners to clarify their expectations. Once this is done, the contract creates a normative guide for future behavior. In addition, a contract can help a couple to identify and resolve potential conflicts in advance, and can provide a useful system for dealing with other conflicts that arise in an ongoing marriage. Finally, contracts increase predictability and security. Each of these advantages is discussed in the second section of this chapter.

The third section focuses on the societal advantages of intimate contracts. Clearly, a less uniform and less rigid legal system is needed in a pluralistic society as diverse and heterogeneous as ours. It would seem that the state's interest in promoting family stability would be much better served by a system that supported the divergent needs and circumstances with which people enter into marriage and other intimate relationships. Increased judicial recognition of contracts would also provide a route to reforming and updating our antiquated system of family law.

The fourth section of this chapter examines the psychological effects of contracts on intimate relationships. In so doing, it attempts to answer the assertion that contracts substitute a negative attitude and "the morals of the marketplace" for romance and cooperation, and thereby undermine the trust and love that are essential for an effective intimate relationship.

Finally, the social policy implications of intimate contracts are examined in the fifth section. Here we ask whether contracts adequately protect the individual parties from their own imprudence and from the inevitable changes in their circumstances over the course of a long-term relationship. This section also addresses the concerns that contracts deter people from marriage and undermine "the institution of marriage" and/or that they will increase the work load of the already overburdened judicial system.

Legal Advantages of Intimate Contracts

This section discusses four legal advantages of establishing an intimate relationship by contract, instead of by marriage, from the perspective of the individual parties.

Escape from the Outmoded Legal Tradition

One major advantage of a personal contract is that it affords those who want to legitimate their relationship an alternative to the outmoded scheme imposed by traditional legal marriage. In Part II we surveyed the myriad ways in which the traditional law imposes a socially anachronistic model that fails to meet the changing needs of couples in contemporary society. A personal contract provides an avenue of escape from this legal straitjacket and a means of structuring relationships in accord with a couple's individual situation and needs. For example, instead of the legal assignment of the major responsibility for family support to the husband, a contract could recognize the support commitments of both parties. It could also structure other commitments to take into account the time and work pressures in a dual-career family. Similarly, in contrast to the law's delegation of home and child care responsibilities to the wife, a contract might structure the sharing of these responsibilities. It might also help a young couple plan for the possibility of a divorce, and guide previously married couples in the allocation of responsibilities to former spouses and the children of former marriages.

Under the present legal system, most couples face a choice "between two evils: either to accept the strictures and disabilities arising out of legal marriage, or to run the legal gauntlet that attends an irregular union."[1] A contract, however, not only allows them to avoid that choice, it provides a positive alternative—the option of creating a personally-tailored structure to facilitate their goals and desires. A contract gives their requirements and aspirations legitimacy and aids those couples who want to renounce the outmoded assumptions of legal marriage.

Promotion of an Egalitarian Relationship

A contract promotes egalitarian relationships in two ways. First, a contract allows a couple to reject the patriarchal system of rights and obligations imposed by the legal institution of marriage. Second, the contracting process is, by its very nature, an egalitarian enterprise.

Part I of this book discusses the systematic ways in which the law imposes a hierarchical (and patriarchal) structure on intimate relationships by designating the husband as head of the family and by granting him rights and privileges denied the wife. Couples intent upon creating a partnership of equals have, for over a century, turned to contracts for redress. For example, as early as 1855 Lucy Stone and Henry Blackwell explicitly rejected the superior status that the law bestowed upon the husband by writing their own contract:

> While we acknowledge our mutual affection by publicly assuming the relationship of husband and wife, we deem it a duty to declare that this act on our part implies no sanction of, nor promise of voluntary obedience to, such of the present laws of marriage as refuse to recognize the wife as an independent, rational being, while they confer upon the husband an injurious and unnatural superiority.[2]

Modern-day feminists have similarly embraced the marriage contract as a means of establishing an egalitarian relationship in defiance of the law's sex-based inequalities.[3] For example, a 1973 contract featured in *Ms.* magazine begins with a similar rejection of the law's view of the rights and obligations of husbands and wives:

> Harriet and Harvey desire to enter a marriage relationship, duly solemnized under the laws of the State of Washington, the rights and obligations of which relationship differ from the traditional rights and obligations of married persons in the State of Washington which would prevail in the absence of this CONTRACT. The parties have together drafted this MARRIAGE CONTRACT in order to define a marriage relationship sought by the parties which preserves and promotes their individual identities as a man and a woman contracting to live together for mutual benefit and growth.[4]

Thus, marriage contracts provide married couples who believe in the principles of equal partnership and self-determination with a legitimate means of modifying the sex-based marital rights and obligations imposed by law.

A second way in which a contract promotes an egalitarian relationship is inherent in the structure of the contracting process. A contract is based on the premise of equality, for it requires the voluntary consent of two independent parties. Each must have a say in the drafting of provisions and each must freely consent to be bound by them. Neither party can unilaterally impose a provision on the other; the second party's acquiescence is always necessary. In fact, as we will note further in Chapter 13, a contract cannot be legally enforced if one party has used fraud or duress to obtain the other's agreement. The only permissible foundation for a valid contract is the willing consent of each party.

Privacy and Freedom in Ordering Personal Relationships

Even if the rights and duties imposed by the law were sexually neutral, and even if they conformed more closely to the norms of contemporary society, they still could not encompass the great diversity of individual arrangements that people might construct if they were allowed to structure their own relationships. Contracts would still be necessary to permit individuals to arrange satisfying relationships according to their own needs and desires.

The belief that individuals should have the freedom and privacy to arrange their personal affairs as they wish (as long as they do not endanger others) is fundamental to the philosophy of those who advocate intimate contracts. Indeed the disagreements between advocates and opponents of intimate contracts tend to hinge on the advocates' stress on personal freedom and marital privacy in contrast to societal concerns. As Rausmussen aptly observes, opponents of intimate contracts regard marriage primarily as a public institution, while proponents view it as a private relationship.[5] Those who view it as a public institution stress the ways in which uniformity promotes social stability. Those who see it as a private relationship counter that social stability (and social welfare) are better served by permitting individually satisfying contractual agreements. "Recent judicial and legislative support for individual freedom, privacy, and equality of rights under the law," seem to have buttressed the latter position and the legal support for individual contracts.[6]

*Legitimation and Structuring of Cohabiting, Homosexual,
and Other Nontraditional Relationships*

The legal status of homosexual couples and persons in relationships of more than two individuals (discussed in Chapter 9), and of those heterosexual couples who live together without marriage (discussed in Chapter 14), is similar in that all may suffer a series of legal disabilities as a result of their nonconforming life-styles. As no state has yet seen fit to accord them the same privileges as those who conform to the traditional legal norms, the only way they can legitimate their relationships and establish their rights and obligations is through a contract.

In the absence of a contract, couples who have no legal relationship are likely to be severely disadvantaged by the denial of a variety of benefits, both public and private, that are automatically accorded to married persons. While some of these benefits of marriage are status benefits in that they are accorded only to those who have the status of a spouse (e.g. the widow's right to a forced share of her husband's estate), in many cases the same results may be achieved through private contract.* For example, cohabitors may contract to make mutual wills so that they can inherit from each other, or contract to share in jointly acquired property held in one partner's name, or contract to designate each other as the beneficiary of a life insurance policy. In addition, because a contract formalizes a relationship by specifying each person's rights and obligations, it serves a legitimizing function—and provides the attendant social and psychological advantages that accompany the legitimation of a relationship that one regards as of primary importance.

Social and Psychological Benefits of Intimate Contracts

Clarification of Expectations

The contracting process itself helps the parties articulate and clarify their goals and expectations. It stimulates straightforward, open communication, as each partner reveals his or her needs, hopes,

*This is not to deny that some matters are beyond contractual control today. As Law Professor Marjorie Shultz cautions, "One cannot substitute contractually ordered actions for all of the status outcomes that automatically arise from the status of marriage." For example, there is no way for unmarried partners to contract to acquire spousal privileges in regard to court testimony.

goals, and plans. Couples about to enter a new relationship are likely to benefit from this planning and drafting process because it provides a natural forum for revealing and discussing both parties' expectations for their life together.

In fact, the benefits of facing major life questions in the drafting process might alone justify the contract as a means of facilitating family communication. Once open communication has been established as a norm, a couple is more likely to share feelings and concerns as situations and attitudes change.

Creation of a Normative Blueprint for Behavior

A contract enables the parties to establish a clear normative standard for behavior. This serves two important functions. First, when important agreements are written down in "black and white" they can constantly be read and referred to by the parties.[7] Many of the marital disagreements that result from simple oversight or thoughtlessness can be resolved without rancor by simple reference to the contract, which stands as a constant reminder of all that was mutually agreed upon.

In addition, the contract serves as a written statement of the goals of the relationship. To this end, its existence provides the parties with a good deal of guidance and security, for they know what to expect of the partner and what the partner expects of them. A clearly spelled-out standard of conduct and prescription of duties and obligations constitutes a more or less specific description of what the relationship should be or must be if it is to continue.

Obviously the existence of a contract alone cannot ensure its fulfillment, nor can it guarantee a happy and stable relationship. However, one who agrees in writing to perform certain duties is likely to be willing in fact to perform those duties, just as one who publicly expresses an attitude is likely to behave in a manner consistent with that attitude.[8]

This brings up the second advantage of specifying behavioral expectations: they make it easier to act in accordance with one's

---

Similarly many government benefits, such as social security benefits for surviving spouses, are status benefits in that they are designated as *spousal* benefits by law, and cannot be transferred to a person who is not a legal spouse. (Personal Conversation, October 13, 1980.) While one might argue that individuals ought to be allowed to designate their beneficiaries, in much the same manner that they can designate the beneficiary of a private insurance policy, the public policy issues raised by this argument are beyond the scope of this book.

ideals. We know that many couples who give lip service to the ideal of an egalitarian relationship nevertheless find it difficult to translate their ideals into concrete arrangements (such as household task assignments, years to be supported in school, hours with the children, dollars of discretionary income). Those who do specify these practical matters have a concrete guideline for transforming ideals into day-to-day actions. The specification gives couples a concrete standard against which to monitor and measure their own behavior and thereby keep themselves on track. This is especially important to couples in a legal marriage where it is easier to slip into traditional roles and routines without realizing it. For example, a mother accustomed to being her child's primary parent may find it hard to resist her mate's pleas for "help" with the child care duties he has agreed to perform.

Advance Identification of Potential Problems

The contracting process helps couples to identify potential conflicts before they enter a relationship. There is no doubt that marriage (and any other intimate relationship) provides fertile ground for the development of disagreement and conflict.[9] Open and honest communication in contract discussions can play an important role not only in alleviating conflict, but in helping parties to identify and deal with areas of potential trouble in advance. Attorney Karl Fleischmann asserts that all couples about to marry can benefit from a prenuptial discussion of the values and goals that each will bring to the marriage and the difficulties they foresee or have already encountered in reconciling divergent ideas. He then proposes the resolution of these differences by written agreement.[10] By way of example, he notes that men are particularly prone to view earning money as their primary goal, even when this satisfaction is achieved at the family's expense. An exploration of the values of economic vs. personal goals can bring potential philosophical differences into the open and may help to resolve them before they become a source of conflict.

Fleischmann further advocates the involvement of a professional (that is, an attorney, marriage counselor, or therapist) in these discussions, even though the contractors do not feel they need help. Fleischmann argues that a professional adviser may unmask a problem in the process of drafting what appears to be a straightforward contract, just as the lawyer asked to draw up a simple will may uncover a complex tax consideration.[11] He added, however, that an absence of professional assistance, whether by choice or by circumstance, should not deter couples from drawing their own marriage contracts.

Couples who write their own contracts can gain an important degree of control over their relationships, as can those who draw up their own wills. Nevertheless, Fleischmann cautions, "lay instruments" in both cases entail the risk that the writers' intentions may be frustrated by the writers' lack of legal knowledge and requirements.[12]

Resolution of Conflict in an Ongoing Relationship

Before a marriage reaches the stage where it is in serious trouble there are usually periods of rising (but unresolved) conflict. If a contract has established a mechanism for resolving differences at an early stage, many disputes can be resolved before they grow to proportions that seriously threaten the relationship.

One pioneering effort in this direction has been undertaken by the Conciliation Court of Los Angeles County under the direction of Meyer Elkin.[13] The Conciliation Court was originally established to try to "save troubled marriages" by reconciling couples who had filed for divorce. Now, however, any couple may receive counseling to resolve disagreements before they lead to dissolution proceedings. In addition, parents of children under 18 who have filed for a dissolution or legal separation receive special encouragement to use the counseling services.[14]

Significantly, the major tool used in these counseling sessions is a "Marriage Agreement." This agreement, or contract, is negotiated by the parties with the assistance of the marital counseling staff of the court and covers "practically every facet of married life."[15] All counseling is short-term, from one to six sessions, and is geared to resolving immediate problems. According to James Crenshaw, negotiating the contract helps the couple communicate and "redefine their respective roles and responsibilities in the marriage."[16] When the parties are satisfied with the terms, the document is signed by each partner and the Conciliation Court judge; it then has the status of a court order and is technically enforceable through contempt citations. However, the court has rarely exercised this enforcement power, preferring to rely on the psychological and emotional force of the agreement.[17]

During the first thirteen years of its existence the Conciliation Court counseled more than fifteen thousand families.[18] The effectiveness of the marriage agreement is, according to the court's report, indicated by the fact that 75 percent of those couples who negotiated an agreement were still living together one year after reconciliation.[19]

Contracts have also been used successfully in the therapeutic realm. Many therapists believe that marriage and other intimate relationships are, in large part, contractual relationships; that is, they are based on a set of expectations and understandings between two parties. And while these understandings are rarely articulated, and even more rarely reduced to writing, they nevertheless form the structure of the parties' relationship.[20]

The therapeutic model aims at making each party aware of the contractual basis of the relationship. This insight enables each party to make his or her expectations explicit, which in turn helps the other partner meet those expectations. The therapists argue that the success of any marriage depends in large part on the extent to which the partners are aware of, and attempt to fulfill, each other's contractual expectations. As psychiatrist Clifford Sager and his colleagues explain:

> We use the term marriage contract to refer to the individual's expressed and unexpressed, conscious and unconscious, concepts of his obligations within the marital relationship and to the benefits he expects to derive from marriage in general, and his spouse in particular. But what must be emphasized, above all, is the reciprocal aspect of the contract: what each partner expects to give, and what he expects to receive from his spouse in exchange, is crucial to this concept. Contracts deal with every conceivable aspect of family life: relationships with friends, achievements, power, sex, leisure time, money, children, etc. *The degree to which a marriage can satisfy each partner's contractual expectations in these areas is an important determinant of the quality of that marriage.*[21]

A major complication arises when each spouse is aware of most of his or her own needs and wishes—of the terms of his or her own "contract"—but neither is equally aware of the other's expectations; in this case important expectations on both sides go unfulfilled. "The disappointed partner may react with rage and depression and may provoke marital discord just as though a real agreement had been broken."[22] This response is particularly likely to occur when one partner feels strongly that he or she has fulfilled his or her obligations, but the other has not.

Sager and his colleagues try to elucidate and clarify the spouses' implicit contract terms so they can be dealt with in therapy.[23] When each person's implicit expectations are made explicit the couple is able to negotiate a mutual agreement on the terms of their contract. In addition, once the contract is made explicit the parties have a legitimate forum for expressing concern about unmet expectations.

Another group of therapists and marriage counselors have used the contract negotiation process to resolve a wider range of family problems. For example, Scoresby et al. have developed a procedure for formulating a family action plan (somewhat similar to the contracts used in transactional analysis) to deal with family crises and continuing problems.[24] This type of contract is arrived at through discussion and negotiation between spouses (or among all members of the family, if children are involved), and has been implemented by families on their own with only a minimum of guidance.

Increased Security, Predictability, and Commitment

Many people enter marriage with little or no awareness of the obligations and limitations to which they are committing themselves. A contract ensures that the people entering a relationship know "exactly what they are getting into."[25] This knowledge provides the parties with the security that stems from predictability: the assurance that one's own performance of certain responsibilities will be complemented by the partner's performance of another set of responsibilities. In addition, common sense dictates that parties to a contract will be more committed to rights and responsibilities freely chosen than to obligations that the state has imposed on all husbands and wives. It also follows that the parties will be more likely to comply with the obligations of a freely negotiated contract than with a court order that seeks to enforce duties they may consider unwarranted or unfair.[26] Thus one important result of the contract is a mutually reinforcing sense of security and commitment.

Societal Advantages of Intimate Contracts

Accommodation of Diversity

In our pluralistic society people approach marriage and intimate relationships from widely divergent circumstances, with widely varying needs. While the legal system of marriage imposes a uniform structure on all couples, a contract is a flexible instrument that can be tailored to the needs and circumstances of individual parties.[27]

The very diversity that characterizes intimate relationships in a pluralistic society admittedly makes it difficult, if not impossible, to structure laws that are sexually neutral and universally fair. Indeed, after examining the various marital property systems of Europe, Professor Max Rheinstein concluded that none would be ideally suited to a society as diverse as the United States. Instead, he suggested that individually tailored marital contracts might provide the only realistic and just means to achieve an equitable marital property system.[28]

Legal recognition of individual marriage contracts would establish the basis for a more "elastic" definition of marital property in particular,* and of modern marriage in general. It would permit legal marriage to encompass the diversity of individual relationships which actually comprise contemporary marriage.[29]

Reform of Antiquated Law

Throughout this book we point to the many outmoded assumptions and provisions of legal marriage. Reform has been incredibly slow in coming and the statutes still attempt to enforce a family pattern that conflicts with both contemporary norms and social reality. The law's lag with respect to marriage stands in sharp contrast to its modernization in other areas. As Sokolov notes, for example, while business law has been steadily modified to reflect actual commercial practice, marriage law in every state still preserves "an old and inherently unequal system."[30]

Even if the state does not want to institute a wholesale reform of family law, it could still effect some modernization by according recognition to contractual alternatives—so that individuals who reject the sex-stereotyped roles and assumptions of legal marriage could structure a marital relationship that better reflects their situation and values.

Furtherance of Family Stability

One of the most telling arguments in support of contracts is that they tend to further the state's goal of supporting stability in mar-

---

*Both married spouses and unwed cohabitants already have considerable freedom to contract about property as discussed in Chapters 13 (on contracts between married spouses), 14 and 15 (on unwed cohabitants).

riage and other family relationships. On a common sense level it would seem obvious that if people are allowed to write their own formula for the kinds of relationships they think will make them happy, they are more likely to create relationships that "work" for them and are therefore satisfying and enduring.

A growing body of social science data suggests that, in general, people are most committed to obligations that they themselves elect. This principle ought to affect intimate relationships as well as any other human dealings. Further, both parties to an intimate contract are likely to find their partner's commitment to the terms of the contract a spur to their own commitment.

The Psychological Effects of a Contract on an Intimate Relationship

It is commonly alleged that contracts have "negative psychological effects" on intimate emotional relationships. For example, it is assumed that the contracting process erodes the spirit of romance, love, trust, and cooperation that normally binds couples together, and instead fosters the cold, self-serving "morals of the marketplace." Another objection holds that the process and the product (that is, the contract) create anxiety and insecurity and thereby undermine the parties' commitment to the relationship. This section addresses each of these issues in turn.

Do Contract Negotiations Undermine the Emotional Basis of a Relationship?

The most common negative reaction to proposals for individualized marriage contracts is the assertion that marriage by its very nature makes bargained-for contracts inappropriate. Betrothal is, after all, an emotional commitment that should not be hedged by conditions: the parties involved should be prepared to give themselves totally, and to accept whatever life brings. This argument may appeal to the romantic, but it probably exaggerates the negative impact of the negotiation process, even upon the more romantic-minded. As we have noted, negotiations in the marital context are not likely to be either hostile or adversarial. Instead, they provide an ideal forum for partners to learn each other's goals and plans in a nonthreatening, optimistic setting. Even if some couples prefer to marry in a romantic haze, their honeymoon will end eventually and yield to the necessity of making day-to-day arrangements. At that point some allocation of responsibilities is inevitable, whether as a result of discussion or by de facto decision, and the parties may then discover that each had assumed the other would undertake most of the major family or household responsibilities. While some couples will prefer to take that risk, if our society wishes to prevent unhappy and unstable marriages (and even the romantic could not argue with that goal), it has an interest in encouraging couples to lay out their respective responsibilities prior to the marriage.

A plausible argument can be made for the position that, far from spoiling romance, a marriage contract is an essential prerequisite to preserving it, since romance has a way of evaporating when misunderstandings about roles and responsibilities arise. A contract that assures each partner a fair share of the work and the benefits of the relationship can go far to forestall such misunderstandings.[31]

A final refutation of the assertion that a contract subverts the emotional dimension of a relationship is provided by the success of relationships between contracting partners in other areas. It is the rare business contract that is based solely on rational and economic considerations. Most business contracts and, in particular, most professional partnership contracts (which are more closely akin to intimate contracts) are sustained by friendships, personal preferences, and emotional ties. Many are also cemented by kinship, school, neighborhood, and other network ties. Finally, the need for mutual cooperation and support through some 40 to 60 hours each week builds its own colleagueship and personal commitment. Thus both marriage partnerships and business partnerships combine emotional and practical elements, although certainly in different proportions. Neither is likely to flourish without some attention to both elements.

Do Contracts Foster Negative Attitudes?

Wells and others have asserted that contracts create a negative outlook by focusing on what can go wrong in a relationship.[32] These critics assert, for example, that since most contracts include provisions for divorce (or dissolution) they force couples to "anticipate, perhaps even expect, the worst outcome rather than stability and success."[33] They may thereby create a self-fulfilling prophecy. In addition, some marriage and family experts contend that it is important for couples entering a new relationship to have an optimistic perspective and to assume that the relationship will be permanent—and that these attitudes are "greatly diluted when potential spouses force themselves to deal with whatever might happen if their marriage does not work."[34]

Although these charges may be valid in some measure, the positive advantages of open and honest communication facilitated by precontract negotiations would seem to more than offset the temporary jolt that comes from anticipating a grim possibility. In addition, the ever increasing probability of divorce suggests that contingency planning is more appropriate than blindly assuming everything will work out, for we know that everything will not work out for close to one-half of the couples forming new relationships today.

In contrast to the begin-in-bliss/end-in-enmity syndrome, the contract that provides realistically for the possibility of termination can guide a more orderly transition between marriage and divorce than is presently possible in most states, and may thereby avert much of the emotional trauma and economic hardship that result from an unanticipated and untimely dissolution.

Do Contracts Destroy Trust?
Why Men Say Yes and Women Say No

In the process of discussing this proposal for contracts within and in lieu of marriage I quickly discovered that men are more likely than women to assert that marriage contracts destroy trust. While women find comfort and security in the proposed clear-cut delineation of rights and obligations, men tend to argue that a specification of each person's responsibilities takes the romance and trust out of a relationship. The explanation for this difference may lie in the traditional power difference between the two sexes. Women, who have traditionally had less power, may feel their rights are best protected if they are formalized; men, in contrast, may feel less need for such protection. Indeed, men may (correctly) perceive that they will lose some of their discretionary power if their responsibilities are spelled out and they can be held accountable.

Thus the answer to the question of whether contracts undermine trust must be found, in part, in the structure of the parties' relationship. The larger the power differential in any enterprise, the more likely it is that the subordinate party—the serf or the tenant or the consumer—will prefer a clear statement of each party's rights and responsibilities, while the more powerful party will prefer to rely on "trust." However, when the existing relationship between the two parties is not characterized by a clear power differentiation, a contractual delineation of responsibilities seems more reasonable (and less threatening) to both parties.

It is important to note however that a contract can be a double-edged sword. While allowing individuals to make their own bargains may increase the opportunities for equalization, it may also increase the opportunities for exploitation. Because private ordering often reflects and reinforces power differences that already exist, there is always the risk that men, who typically have more power, will use that power to impose a contract that is even more unfavorable than traditional legal marriage. *

The assertion that equalization is more likely than exploitation rests on the assumption that even though men have more power they nevertheless share an egalitarian ideology and will not think it "fair" or "just" to try to impose an exploitative contract on the women they love. For example, as is noted in Chapter 7, most men in the United States, especially men under 35 who are more likely to be entering intimate relationships, now believe that it is fair to share the housework when both partners are employed outside the home. Having to "put it in writing" is likely to push them to *implement* their ideological position—not to change it. †

In essence the argument rests on the assumption that when there is a discrepancy between ideology and behavior, a system of monitoring is more likely to move behavior into conformity with the ideology. While it is at least possible that the opposite may occur—and that men, when pressed, will change their ideology—the claim that one should rely on *trust* seems to suggest that the egalitarian ideology is fairly secure.

---

*This was stressed by Marjorie Shultz, personal conversation, October 1980.

Below we discuss the closely related traditional concern for the "weak-minded woman in love" who, it is feared, will too readily agree to an unfavorable contract imposed by an all powerful male.

†This is not to naively assume that it will always work in this direction. As Professor Shultz points out, in the economic sector liberals have tried to put a limit on private ordering to protect the weaker parties (e.g. consumers and tenants). Nevertheless, it seems appropriate to assume that the type of overreaching that is profitable in the market sector would be neither profitable nor possible in an intimate contract. This is because parties to an intimate contract are much more likely to begin with norms of fairness and a genuine concern for the welfare of the other party.

Nevertheless, men and women are likely to have different levels of commitment to an egalitarian relationship. While men and women are perhaps equally likely to say they want to structure their relationships along egalitarian lines, some men may not be as fully committed to this ideal as their female partners, or may consider it more burdensome to implement. Such men would be less ready to undertake daily household and child care tasks, and more likely to resent them. In addition, they would be more likely to consider a partner's wish to codify responsibilities indicative of a "lack of trust." Thus, on some level, their very reluctance to assume these responsibilities might well contribute to the partner's lack of trust— for it would suggest that things may not be so egalitarian if left to trust alone.

Do Contract Negotiations Impose
"the Morals of the Marketplace"?

It has been argued that approaching marriage as a bargained-for relationship undermines the cooperative goals of marriage. While preliminary bargaining is a typical (in fact, judicially required) feature of negotiation for enforceable contracts in the business world, it is alleged to be inappropriate in the family context, where the parties should put collective concerns ahead of individual interests. As one court stated, bargaining intrudes the "morals of the marketplace" into an intimate relationship:

> Marriage is the most sacred of the confidential relationships. The undertakings and obligations of the parties are usually secured by the solemn vows of the ceremony. In mutual respect and affection is found the lasting strength of the status. One espoused may enter into the relationship with simple trustfulness relying upon the faithfulness and common decency of the other. *The morals of the marketplace do not determine the rights of the parties or govern their conduct.* The rights of the wife are not to be prejudiced because she failed to detect that which it was her husband's duty to disclose.[35]

One answer to this argument is that it is based on an erroneous view of business dealings. As we have noted, business contracts, especially those which deal with long-term relationships (such as partnerships, employment, leasing, franchising, and servicing agreements),[36] are now guided by a set of principles far removed from the *caveat emptor* morality of laissez-faire economics.[37] The current Uniform Commercial Code suggests a growing judicial activism to ensure that the parties to business contracts have acted in good faith and their contract is not unconscionable.[38] Since the courts will no longer countenance a complete disregard of one party's welfare in business contracts, one would certainly not expect them to enforce such conditions in intimate contracts.*

Thus the first response to the assertion that contracts introduce business morality into personal relationships is that the dichotomy between business morality and personal morality is no longer clear-cut. In fact, the developing standards for business contracts suggest the increasing appropriateness of the contractual model for marriage. As Sokolov has argued, the resemblances between sound businesses and sound marriages may well increase in the future, as businesses learn to live with each other and husbands and wives learn to bargain for their fair share of the privileges and fruits of their union.[39]

A second answer to the "morals of the marketplace" assertion forthrightly challenges the assumption that negotiations undermine cooperation and intimacy. Instead it can be argued that the reciprocity built into the contract provides the best possible basis for cooperation: both parties are assured of help in attaining their own ends if they cooperate in supporting their partner's ends, and each knows that the other is committed to cooperate in achieving mutually advantageous and agreed-upon ends.

Finally, it is important to emphasize that the bargaining process need not be adversarial. Rather, it is likely that the process will disclose many shared desires and goals, and the awareness of these mutual aspirations can only increase the parties' confidence in their relationship and enhance their feelings of intimacy.

Do Contracts Create Impoverished Consent?

A recurring argument against marriage contracts is that they create cold obligations—that is, the parties carry out their family responsibilities because they have a contractual duty to do so, not because feelings of love and affection for their partner or children inspire

---

*Instead, one might more reasonably expect judicial review of intimate contracts to follow the standards set for antenuptial contracts. For example, a court could require complete disclosure of financial assets, or "fair and reasonable" provisions for a dependent partner, or more simply that one party not take unfair advantage of the other. These standards are discussed in more detail in Chapter 13.

them to do so. Thus, the argument runs, an obligation is fulfilled because it is a duty, not because the person wants to do it. Therefore, contracts make for aloof and mechanical relationships.

One objection to this argument is that it is based on a simplistic assumption about human motivation. Most human behaviors cannot be attributed with certainty to any single motivation. For example, does a housewife cook dinner because she loves her family, or because she feels obligated to do it, or because she enjoys cooking? Does a man go to work each morning because he cherishes his wife and family, or because he feels obligated to attain power and financial success, or because he likes his job? If it is difficult to categorize the motivation of any single person engaged in any solitary behavior, it is impossible to define the motives that impel the interactions of millions of husband–wife combinations. The complexity of human motivation undermines the notion that marriage contracts transform voluntary tasks into involuntary obligations.

A second response to the allegation of impoverished consent is that since contracting parties choose the responsibilities they will undertake, contractual obligations are much less likely to be performed unwillingly than are the sex-stereotyped obligations imposed by the state in traditional legal marriage.

Do Contracts Foster Insecurity and Instability?

It has been argued that contracts designed to terminate at a specified time are conducive to instability and insecurity. While a relationship that is defined as nonpermanent may in fact engender few long-range commitments and thus make some persons feel insecure, others may gain security from knowing that they can get out of a relationship that fails to meet their needs without the legal hassles and emotional trauma typically associated with divorce. In addition, it seems inappropriate to insist that all relationships be structured as lifelong unions in cases where one or both parties frankly have other intentions.

Nor does a fixed-duration contract necessarily indicate a short-term relationship (the contract is quite likely to be renewed or renegotiated), any more than a legal marriage necessarily indicates a lifelong union. It is doubtful that either a marriage license or a contract will alone determine whether or not a couple stays together. However, a contract can make a difference in the terms and conditions of a dissolution, and in its economic and psychological impact.

In any event, today's changing society clearly belies the virtue of permanent union as an end in itself: permanence is desirable only when it is a product of a mutually satisfying relationship. Contracts are conducive to permanence when permanence is in the best interest of the parties. However, since it is difficult to predict (or ensure) the survival of any relationship at its inception, some degree of uncertainty may be functional in that it may encourage couples to anticipate dissolution and thereby to avoid some of the difficulties that result from assuming that one does not have to consider the possibility of divorce.

Social Policy Issues

Critics of personal contracts have focused on three types of social policy issues. First, with respect to the parties, there is a concern that contracts will not adequately protect each party from his or her own imprudence or from the overreaching demands of the other party. In addition, there is a concern that unanticipated changes in circumstances may have an unequal and unfair impact on the parties.

Second, with respect to the institution of marriage, there is a concern that contracts will deter people from entering into marriage, foster disputes and litigation between family members, and encourage divorce. Third, with respect to the legal process, there is a concern that contracts will "thrust an unmanageable task into the lap of the judiciary"[40] because it lacks the forum, personnel, and standards to hear personal contract disputes.

Each of these issues is discussed briefly below. Some of these issues—such as the protection of the parties and the problem of changed circumstances—are also discussed in Chapter 13, where we examine appropriate standards for judicial review of contracts.

Concern for the Weak-minded "Woman in Love"

Remarkably enough, one of the most commonly articulated fears concerning marital contracts is that a woman in love will not be emotionally able to protect her rights in contract negotiations. As Ruth Ihne points out, there is a fear that the woman in love may too readily accept unfavorable terms, the full impact of which she may not realize until years later, "when winter comes and the fires glow lower."[41] In fact, Gamble asserts that the courts' traditional approach to reviewing premarriage contracts begins with the assumption that the "mystical relationship anesthetizes the senses of the female partner."[42] Gamble cites as an example an early Ohio decision concerning an antenuptial property settlement, which posed the following rhetorical question:

> What person [is] so exposed to imposition as a woman, contracting, personally, with her intended husband, just on the eve of marriage, at a time when all providential considerations are likely to be merged into a confiding attachment or suppressed from an honorable instinct and sentiment of delicacy. . . ?[43]

As summarized by Ihne, a woman's sex role socialization is assumed to render her incapable of negotiating an agreement in her own best interest:

> A woman in love is unable to deal rationally with the object of her love. . . . [T]he overwhelming majority of them [are likely to] defer to their husbands or prospective husbands, at least in matters of lesser importance, rather than attempt a compromise. The desire to please which is a product of the wife's female role socialization, is accentuated by her infatuation, producing an inequality of bargaining power under which no fair and equitable arrangement could be concluded. The subtle psychological training which each woman undergoes from infancy would virtually guarantee the creation of an unfair agreement, even under circumstances from which neither judge nor jury could justifiably infer duress or undue influence.[44]

A less patronizing version of this position argues that since women have been conditioned to desire marriage more than men, and since they are unaccustomed to asserting their rights in relationships with men, they are likely to accept "grossly unfair bargains in order to get married."[45] In fact, some courts (and commentators) have concluded that husbands are so apt to dominate the marriage relationship that any interspousal agreement must be "presumed to have been entered under duress" and therefore all such agreements should be declared void.[46]

Although one could dismiss these assertions as sexist stereotypes and argue that the law should no longer be based on traditional notions of female weakness and dependency, this response avoids the central issue. The truth is that women in our present society are less assertive and they are less likely to negotiate a favorable bargain with a prospective spouse (or heterosexual cohabitant). However, the woman is surely better off knowing that at the beginning of the relationship instead of blindly trusting the goodwill of her intended partner. In fact, too many women have entered marriage with the romantic illusion that they will be taken care of for the rest of their lives. But if the terms of an unfair agreement are made known to a woman in advance, she might decide not to enter the relationship. In addition, the explicit agreement would be visible to third parties—her family and friends—and they would be likely to try to exert the pressure necessary both to make her insist on, and to make him grant, more favorable terms.

Alternatively, if intimate contracts were judged by family law standards of fairness*, the more egregiously unfair agreements probably would be overturned. Of course, the law cannot protect everyone from making an unwise agreement. In part, the freedom to contract must include the freedom to make a mistake. But even the woman who has entered into a less than optimal contract is likely to be better off knowing that she will not be protected, than one who is surprised to find herself in the inferior position that results from traditional legal marriage.

The Problem of Changed Circumstances

Perhaps the most trenchant criticism of contracts within or in lieu of marriage is that they fail to make allowance for unforeseen changes of circumstances. This criticism highlights the not unfounded fear that by formalizing their commitment and reducing their relationship to a legal instrument, the parties will restrict their ability to adapt creatively to inevitable changes in their individual and collective lives. As Clark explains:

> The real reason for invalidating [antenuptial] contracts seems to be that although the provisions may be fair at the time they are made, they may not be later, when the separation or divorce occurs. The wife may thus be left with entirely inadequate support or the husband with an excessively heavy liability to his wife.[47]

Even previously married persons may not be able to anticipate by contract all the problems that can arise during the course of a marriage, as Ihne indicates:

> One spouse may suffer a disabling injury which would require the rendering of additional services or the application of additional re-

*In Chapter 13 we discuss the different standards of review that are typically used in family law versus contract law. See pages 353–356.

sources by the other spouse; or one spouse may experience such economic success that enforcing the contract's original terms would penalize a spouse who has been an important contributor to that success. Both popular and official attitudes toward marriage will change over time. This in itself may consitute a changed circumstance under which enforcement of an agreement may prove unjust.[48]

There are four levels of response to the changed circumstances objection. First, it is important to realize that the problem of dealing fairly with changed circumstances and unanticipated events is inherent in all long-term relationships, and is, therefore, no less (and no more) of a problem in a legal marriage. Neither a legal marriage nor a legal contract can provide absolute guarantees in the face of unforeseen events.

A second response is that some types of change can be anticipated and provided for—and others can be accommodated by provisions for periodic or extraordinary renegotiation. For example, some of the duties set forth in long-term contracts may eventually invoke resentment (such as commitment to a specific career goal or the promise of lifelong support). In such cases, there is nothing to prevent the parties from rescinding and renegotiating the contract—or from rescinding one offending provision. Provisions for periodic renegotiations, or for renegotiations at the option of either party (perhaps on the condition that the party wishing to renegotiate must bear the burden of justification) can be helpful in this regard. Contracting parties should be aware of the problem of changed circumstances and give their agreements enough flexibility to allow for needed adjustments.

A third response points to recent developments in family law and contract law with respect to standards of review. In family law at present a substantial change in circumstances constitutes grounds for modification of court-ordered support in most states; the same principle could easily be applied to the enforcement of marital contracts.

Contract law has also developed a reasonable set of principles for assessing nonperformance in light of changed circumstances. Nonwillful breaches are excused where performance is rendered impossible by unalterable circumstances; where the purpose of the venture has been "frustrated"; and where the subject matter no longer exists.[49] More recently, the Uniform Commercial Code, a model code of commercial law that has been adopted (with minor variations) by 49 states, has extended the criteria for excusing nonperformance to include "impracticability."[50] In Chapter 13 we argue that contract law standards are generally more equitable than the value-laden standards traditionally used in family courts.

A final response to the problem of changed circumstances acknowledges that the contractual model cannot remedy all the problems individuals face in intimate relationships. Contractual relationships in the business world are in many fundamental ways much like family relationships in that they often depend on mutual goodwill, cooperation, and even affection in coping with the inevitable problems that arise in an ongoing enterprise. It is assumed that each party to the contract will continue to show regard for the other, as well as a continuing interest in the relationship, and that, in order to promote their combined welfare, both will strive to resolve problems that arise. The same principles of goodwill, cooperation, affection, and mutual regard as well as a stake in the joint enterprise should also allow parties to intimate contracts to cope effectively with new and unanticipated situations.

Contracts as a Deterrent to Intimate Relationships

It has been argued that the frank and open discussion required to formulate a contract may deter the parties from entering the relationship. Certainly this is a real possibility if the contracting process uncovers a multitude of differences.[51]

However, it would seem that those most likely to be deterred are those about to make a mistake. For example, the man who discovers unexpectedly that his "sweet little homebody" has plans for a career of her own, and the woman who discovers that her gallant swain wouldn't think of "helping" with the housework, may decide to wait awhile and reconsider the marriage. If so, it can hardly be argued that their discoveries should have been forestalled until their union was a *fait accompli*. Along these lines, Sheresky and Mannes have argued that if the process of negotiating a premarriage contract convinces some couples that they should not marry at all, it has probably made a positive contribution to their lives.[52]

Similarly, from the societal perspective, the state's interest lies in encouraging stable unions. Thus, if a couple is deterred from marrying by a candid discussion of aims and expectations, society is the beneficiary. In fact, an extremely strong argument could be made in favor of contracts if they served no other purpose than weeding out and deterring potentially unstable unions.

Contracts as a Cause of Disputes and Litigation

It has been suggested that people who contract about the conduct of their marriage only widen the range of topics for potential marital disputes. It is also asserted that these burgeoned disputes lead the parties to litigate issues they otherwise would have settled between themselves. Contracts are therefore said to foster, rather than prevent, marital conflict, and to increase the overall amount of litigation.

While these assertions may sound plausible, it is equally plausible to assert that contracts serve to minimize disputes and discourage litigation. If the contracting process helps couples to anticipate and resolve potential disagreements before they enter the relationship, it can eliminate many sources of friction and enable a couple to live together with a minimum of strife. Both the social-psychological and therapeutic literature seem to support this position: discussion and conflict resolution at time 1 typically serves to mitigate and decrease conflict at time 2.

It is also important to note that not all disputes are unhealthy—either for society or for the individuals involved. We know that conflict often engenders creative change. To that end, however, it may be extremely useful for a couple to make provision for outside help in resolving issues that are particularly trying or emotionally disruptive. As Sokolov notes, in the marital context, the method of settling disputes, and the assurance that they will in fact be settled, may be psychologically more important than the relative merits of the disputed issues.[53]

Similarly, from a societal standpoint, it would seem that the provision of a forum for the fair resolution of disputes ought properly to be a function of a responsive legal system. Just as a disagreement about the terms of a commercial contract does not indicate that contracts encourage disputes (much less that commercial contracts should be eliminated), so the existence of conflicts about personal contracts should not suggest that the contractual model is at fault. As Sokolov notes:

> Although there are many disputes over business and labor contracts, these disputes are the price society pays in order to strike a balance between a buyer and seller or an employer and his employees. For better or worse, society has not yet found any fairer means than a contract, bargained out or at least assented to by the parties, to protect the

rights and define the responsibilities of the parties to an economic exchange. . . . [T]he fact that commercial contracts are sometimes the focus of legal disputes does not lead judges to discourage the use of contracts in business. . . . Nor should the possibility of disputes lead judges to discourage the making of marriage contracts.[54]

The Threat to the Institution of Marriage

It is feared that an agreement about the terms of a divorce settlement prior to marriage will facilitate dissolution of the union and will therefore be conducive to divorce—which of course runs counter to the state's interest in preserving the institution of marriage. This argument implies two assumptions: that an undissolved marriage is necessarily a stable marriage, and that marital instability can be controlled (or prevented) by making divorce difficult. However, there is little factual basis for either assumption.[55] We know that many irreconcilable relationships continue to the detriment of both parties: the contract merely helps to define the tolerable limits of dissatisfaction. And making divorce harder to obtain does not eliminate it: it only makes it more troublesome and more painful (and may encourage common-law divorce among those who cannot afford legal dissolution).

The Problem of the Forum

One objection to intimate contracts is that they lack an established forum for adjudication. This, however, can hardly be viewed as an insurmountable barrier, for existing civil or family courts could hear these cases. In fact, family courts in many states are already handling issues of paternity and support for unmarried cohabitants, and the existence of a written agreement would probably facilitate their work.[56]

Furthermore, legislative and judicial attention to the appropriate handling of marriage contracts might well eventuate in a more comprehensive review of the present system of resolving family disputes in light of changing social norms. This in turn might lead to the design of new "family courts" with professional counselors and arbitrators able to provide both married and unmarried couples with a more appropriate forum for the resolution of family disputes.

Another kind of forum is open to contractors who elect to turn to an arbitrator, a marriage counselor, or a previously agreed upon panel of family and friends in case of dispute. Arbitration and counseling provide many advantages over the more formal and legalistic atmosphere of a court—especially for disputes between persons hoping to continue their relationship. While court proceedings tend to be public and adversarial, hearings before an arbitrator are typically held in private with an eye to the overall welfare of the union.[57]

Litigation and the Court Work Load

As we have seen, some opponents of marriage contracts contend that they will result in a proliferation of domestic litigation. An offshoot of this contention is that contracts thus serve to overburden an already burdened court. This fear seems unwarranted for three reasons. First, it is likely that most contractual disputes, like most marital disputes, will reach the courts only after the relationship has broken down. Thus it is not likely that the courts will be called upon to resolve any more cases than it now handles in divorce. Second, if contracts affect court calendars at all, they are likely to lighten them because most issues that are now litigated in divorce cases[58] will already have been resolved by contract.* Third, since it is likely that many contractors will elect to arbitrate their disputes, some of the kinds of cases now heard in divorce court may circumvent the courts entirely.

Nevertheless, even if the fear of increased litigation proved to be realistic, it would hardly justify depriving parties to intimate contracts access to the courts when we freely grant all other contractual litigants the right to have their disputes resolved in court.

*While some couples may contract for the specific and limited purpose of fixing the extent of their obligations to each other in the event of a divorce (as is sometimes the case with previously married people who feel that they were treated unfairly in a prior divorce) it is more likely that most contracts will cover a broader range of issues, such as those suggested in Chapters 11 and 12. In either case, however, there may be a question as to the determinativeness of the contract. If the dissolution is handled as the dissolution of a partnership in civil court, the contract should prevail. If, however, the case is heard in a family court which hears divorce cases there is a risk that the court may decide to override some provisions of the contract—such as those that deal with children—on public policy grounds. The different standards that are typically used in contract law versus family law are discussed in Chapters 13 and 15.

In summary then, it is difficult to sustain the assertion that contracts will encourage disputes and/or create a greater adjudicative burden for society. When weighed against all the positive advantages of intimate contracts—for individuals and for the social order —it would seem that society has only to gain by encouraging couples to order their intimate relationships by private contract.

CHAPTER 11

Topics and Provisions for Intimate Contracts

This chapter presents and discusses 25 topics for individuals to consider in drafting a contract. These topics are by no means exhaustive and certainly are not offered as a list of imperatives to be included in all contracts. Most are introduced as questions in the hope that they will stimulate contracting parties to define the areas and concerns most relevant and important in their particular situation. Different people will wish to order their lives in different ways; individually written contractual agreements would make it easier for them to do so.

Because we have repeatedly stressed the adaptability of the contract model for a wide variety of personal arrangements, in the following sections we have tried to use sex-neutral and number-neutral terms for the contracting parties. They are typically referred to as the partners, the parties, the contractors, the contracting parties or simply as "they." In some sections, however, in the interests of readability and linguistic convenience we refer to the parties as "the couple" or as "two partners" or as "he and she." Thus it is important to bear in mind, once again, that this guide is intended to be applicable to contracts between homosexuals and those among more than two persons, as well as to those between heterosexual dyads.

The reader may find it helpful to read this chapter together with the Appendix, which reports the results of a study of how couples have handled similar matters of concern in actual contracts. Concurrent reference to Chapter 12, which presents excerpts from eight sample contracts, may also be useful.

1. General Purpose of the Contract

The objectives of the partners will influence the kinds of provisions they include and their level of specificity. It is therefore essential for the contracting parties to articulate the purpose of their agreement and what they hope it will accomplish. The following questions may be helpful in attaining this goal.

What is the purpose of this agreement?

1. Is it meant to be a statement of ideals, or a normative guide to the parties' relationship, or a practical blueprint for day-to-day living?
2. Is it primarily a property agreement that defines the parties' respective rights to ownership of current and future property? Or is it a guideline for the parties' interpersonal relations? Or is it both?

Is this agreement intended as a *substitute* for traditional legal marriage, or is it meant to redefine the legal obligations *within* a legal marriage?

1. Are there any obligations of traditional legal marriage that the parties want to renounce or to affirm?
2. What rights and obligations are the parties seeking to establish by this contract?
3. Do the parties wish to include a general statement of purpose (similar to that included in marriage vows) in place of, or in addition to, more specific stipulations?

Are there any particular obligations, situations, or events that have motivated this contract? Are the partners seeking to avoid, or affirm, or change existing obligations?

1. Does one partner want to clarify his or her obligations to a former spouse or to a parent? Or to ensure that an inheritance [or house or pension] will remain separate property?
2. Or to avoid having to support the other in the event of a dissolution?
3. Or to assure his or her children of unchanged allegiance and support?
4. Or to affirm a commitment to create an egalitarian relationship?

2. Legalities

While some partners may write a contract solely as a personal statement of philosophy and intent, and do not care about whether it is legally binding, most will want to construct a legally enforceable instrument. The legality of contracts within marriage and contracts between cohabitants are discussed in detail in Chapters 13, 14, and 15; parties who want their contract legally enforceable would be wise to consider the caveats discussed in those chapters. In addition, they should plan to include a severability provision in their contract (such a provision is included in contract VII in Chapter 12) to ensure that one unenforceable provision will not render the entire agreement void. Here, then, are some questions to be examined:

Is this agreement to be legally binding, in whole or in part?
Will each provision of this contract be treated as severable?
Will the agreement be signed before witnesses or notarized?
What is the consideration* for this contract? Mutual promises?
  Marriage? The exchange of property?

3. The Parties

In reviewing contracts between married or about-to-be-married couples the courts have traditionally required a full disclosure of each party's financial circumstances. As the contracts proposed

---

*Consideration refers to the price, or reason, or benefit, or material cause that induces a party to enter into a contract. It must be something which is of value in the eyes of the law.

here go far beyond the traditional financially based antenuptial contract, it is recommended that the parties also disclose their *social* circumstances. Even contracts that are not written with an eye to legal enforcement are strengthened by an open statement of each party's personal history, education, family background, occupational plans, financial circumstances, and present health.

Age and background

1. How old is each party?
2. Where is each party living?

Educational background

1. How much education does each have?
2. Are the parties now continuing, or do they plan to continue, their educations? When? Where? To what end?

Marital history and children

1. Has either been married before? What type of relationship does he or she have or want to maintain with the ex-spouse?
2. Does either have children? What type of relationship does he or she want to maintain with them?

Family background

1. Are their parents living? Where?
2. What are their parents' occupational and socioeconomic status?
3. What type of social (and financial) relationship does each party have/expect to maintain with his or her parents in the near future? In the distant future?

Occupational circumstances

1. Is each party currently employed? Full time or part time? Where? In what position?
2. How long has each held his or her present job?
3. What are their future occupational and career plans?
4. Does either plan to change occupation, discontinue employment, etc.?

Financial disclosure

1. What are each party's current assets (savings, real property [home, income property, unimproved land, etc.], business or partnership, stocks and bonds, and other major assets)?
2. What is each party's current income? (Current salary? Other regular income?)
3. What are each party's debts and financial obligations?
4. What are their future financial prospects? Is either planning to support or currently supporting a child or an aged parent? Does either expect to receive a large inheritance? Is either involved in high-risk financial ventures?

Health status of the parties

1. Has either had any serious illness in the past? Is it likely to recur?
2. How is each party's current health?
3. Does each have health, accident, and life insurance?

Personal history

Is there anything negative about either person's past that the other person should know about? (A serious personal illness or history of family illness? A felony or other criminal conviction? A bankruptcy or other serious financial problem?)

Secrecy of this disclosure

1. Do the parties wish to restrict the disclosure of any of the information revealed in this part of the contract?
2. Will there be liquidated damages (i.e., monetary payments specified in advance) for disclosure to a third party?

4. Aims and Expectations

This section sets forth the parties' aims and goals for the relationship. It should help each party to clarify his or her expectations for the relationship and to make these known to the other party. Although many of the provisions discussed below would not be legally binding, in interpreting contracts the courts have often looked to such provisions to determine the intentions of the parties and their "states of mind" in entering the contract.

What are the parties' collective goals for the relationship?

1. What do the parties expect to gain (and/or lose) in the relationship (emotionally or otherwise)?
2. What are the parties' goals as a family unit? Does this include or exclude the possibility of children?
3. What type of life-style do they want?
4. What are the parties' financial goals?

What are the parties' individual goals in the relationship?

1. In what ways does each expect to grow, change, and develop?
2. To what extent is each seeking autonomy, a separate identity, privacy?
3. What are the lifelong goals of each? To what extent is this relationship central to (or peripheral to) those goals?

What are the parties' priorities?

1. Have the parties agreed on priorities among their respective goals? Between family and career goals? Between the conflicting demands of two careers? Between leisure and work? Between saving and spending?
2. How will future conflicts be resolved? (See also sections 23 and 24.)

What are the parties' plans for life "phasing"?

1. Do the partners have an overall plan for the phasing of family, career, childbearing, or other events?
2. Do they have any contingency plans?

5. Duration

For those who envision a lifelong union, the question of duration may seem irrelevant. Their agreements should include a statement to that effect. Others, however, may want to fix or limit the duration of their relationship, even though they may later decide to renew their contract. Finally, some couples may contract for a specified period or event.

Do the parties intend this to be a lifelong contract?

Is there a time limit or specific term for this contract?

Is the duration of the contract linked to the achievement of a specific goal (e.g., finishing law school, raising children through college)? Or to the continuation of a social-emotional state (e.g., as long as the parties are in love with each other)?

Will there be a trial period before the contract takes effect?

Will the contract be renewed after a particular event? Or a specified number of years? Or periodically every X years? (See also section 24.)

6. Work and Careers

Although the subject of work and careers may arise in the discussion of many sections of the contract, it seems useful to draw these diverse issues together in a separate section to help clarify the role that work and careers will play.

While it was traditionally assumed that only the husband would work to support the family, many couples today assume that both parties will work and both will have full-time careers. This new orientation raises a series of questions about timing and priorities. Although this section only begins to examine these important questions, it should help the parties clarify their expectations and plans, and that clarification may be of great assistance in future periods of changing expectations and unclear norms. (For example, couples who articulate an egalitarian ideology with respect to the two careers may use the contract to help keep themselves on track.)

Those who choose to follow the traditional model will also find it useful to affirm their choice of that model in writing, for in an era of changing expectations it is especially important that judges (and others) who may be called upon to arbitrate disputes or to enforce the contract be fully aware of a couple's conscious choice of a traditional family style. Another function of the contract for couples who want to follow the traditional male-wage-earner model is that it allows them to redefine the traditional property rights and privileges given to the wage earner.

(It may be useful to read the section entitled "Support and Work Arrangements" in the Appendix for a fuller discussion of the issues raised below and in section 7 on income and expenses.)

What are the parties' career plans?

1. What are the short-range and long-term career goals of each party? What position and salary does each expect to have in two years? Five years? Thirty years? etc.
2. If not currently employed, how will each party choose a job?
   a. Will each make an independent decision? Or will one be obligated to consult with the other or obtain the other's agreement before new employment is accepted?
   b. To what extent will salary considerations enter into choice of employment?

What is the couple's orientation toward work and earned income? (Will there be a single wage earner? Or will both be working for a salary? Or will this vary?)

If a single-wage-earner family:

1. Will the income be treated as the result of the parties' joint efforts and be divided between them? If not, how will the nonearning partner's contribution to the relationship be recognized? How will the nonearning partner be provided with money of her or his own, and a share in the assets and property acquired during the relationship?
2. Will there be provisions to ensure continued support and medical care for a nonincome-earning partner (payment of Social Security tax, health insurance premiums, private pension plans)?

If a two-career family, how will the partners resolve potential conflicts between their careers?

1. Do the parties plan to maximize one person's career? Or will both careers be equally important?
2. Will one spouse's career ever take priority over the other's?
3. Will priorities change over time? (For example, will one party be allowed to finish/obtain an advanced degree but

then be obligated to give the other an equal number of years of career priority?)
4. If a geographical move becomes necessary to the furtherance of one of their careers, will they both move? Or only one? Or will neither move? Or will they rotate this option?

Is either partner expected to aid and support the other's career?

1. In what ways?
2. Is either partner expected to participate in social activities related to the other's work? To what extent?

Do the partners plan to rotate periods of work and household maintenance and/or free time, with one partner acting as "breadwinner" during certain years while the other cares for the home or children or pursues other (nonearning) interests, with a role reversal in the following years?

Will work that produces (more) income be considered more valuable than household or lower paid work, or equally valuable? How will this evaluation be manifested in the relationship?

7. Income and Expenses

This section is closely linked to section 6 because many of its decisions will rest on whether there will be one wage earner or two.

Two cautionary notes are in order here. First, the multiple options may initially seem confusing because there are so many possible ways to handle both income and expenses. However, once the single-income vs. two-income family decision is made, the major question facing each couple will be whether to handle expenses jointly or individually.

The second note of caution concerns discretionary expenses. After comparing income and expenses many couples may find they have no income left for discretionary purchases and therefore conclude that the rest of the questions are irrelevant. However, it is important that they, too, discuss these questions and make decisions about how they would ideally arrange their financial affairs. These "principled" decisions will have important practical implications in the future, when the couple's income increases.

What is each party's current yearly income?

1. What is each party's monthly or annual salary?
2. What other income does each party have (stocks, interest, dividends, capital gains, royalties, rents, etc.)?

What is the sum of each party's anticipated living expenses? (A beginning list might include rent or mortgage payments, utilities, food, telephone, appliances, automobile, household furniture and decorations, medical and dental bills, clothing and personal items, entertainment, leisure activities, vacations, gifts, insurance, taxes, educational expenses, books, sports equipment, charitable contributions, and support of ex-spouse's children or parents.)

How will the parties treat income and expenses?

1. Will all income be pooled (and treated as the result of the parties' joint efforts), and all expenses met jointly?
2. Or will all income be retained by the earner/owner with each person's expenses met by him/her and joint expenses met with equal or proportional contributions?
3. Or will each earner retain his or her income, with expenses being met by equal or proportional contributions from each party?

If all income is pooled and treated as joint income:

1. Will one person be responsible for managing the expenses and be the family bookkeeper and check writer? Or will each have some responsibility for specific expenses and bills?
2. Will the parties set up a joint checking account and pay all bills from that account? Or will each have an account and pay some bills from that account? (Even if income is pooled it may be advisable to have each person sign some checks for tax purposes and to enable each to maintain an independent credit/checking history.)
3. How much personal/discretionary money will each person be allowed? What items will be paid for with joint funds, what with these personal funds?
4. Will the parties have joint credit cards and accounts? Or does each want to establish his or her own credit record by maintaining separate accounts?

If *income is not pooled* and only one party has income (e.g., if there is a single wage earner):

1. Will half (or a fixed share) of his or her earnings automatically be transferred to the other party?
2. If not, will the other party receive any monetary compensation for work in taking care of the household and/or children?
3. How will family expenses be paid?

If *income is not completely pooled* and both parties have income:

1. How will disparities in income be treated? Will the parties try to equalize income or compensate for the disparity in the division of expenses? Or do the parties believe that the person who has the greater income shall have more disposable income?
2. How will expenses be met?
   a. Will each person pay his or her own expenses and contribute to joint expenses?
   b. Or will all expenses be considered joint expenses and met by contributions from each partner?
3. How will each partner's share of the joint expenses be calculated?
   a. Will each pay an equal *amount* of money?
   b. Or an equal *percentage* of his or her income?
   c. Or a *graduated percentage* of his or her income (a higher percentage of each additional dollar earned)?
   d. Will adjustments be made for contributions-in-kind, such as housework or child care?

How will savings be handled?

1. Will each party be permitted a fixed or portional share of income for personal savings?
2. Will the parties save jointly? (What amount or proportion of income will be set aside for savings and/or investments?)

Will there be changes in the financial responsibility for specific items, for specific categories of expenditure, or for different years or stages of life?

How will periods of lessened or suspended income (layoffs, disabilities, education, vacations) be handled?

1. Will the above provisions regarding income, support, and expenses be altered in the event of layoff, illness, or disability?
2. How will the parties ensure support and medical care for a nonearning partner or for a partner who has to stop working?

8. Property Currently Owned

Traditional antenuptial agreements deal almost exclusively with money and property. While the contracts proposed in this book deal with many other subjects as well, it is clear that financial decisions remain a central concern for most contracting couples (and may be every bit as emotionally charged as decisions about love or sex).

This section deals with property that each party currently owns; the next section deals with property acquired during the relationship. The couple's basic decision with regard to any property concerns whether it shall be separate property or community property. (Here again, the discussion of property in the Appendix may be helpful.)*

What property does each party have at the time of contracting?

1. What assets does each person own?
2. What is the present value of those assets?
3. Is there any property that either party expects to receive through gift or inheritance in the future?

How will the property now owned by each party be treated?

1. Will each person retain his or her current assets as separate property?
2. Or will the partners pool their current assets and own them in common as "community property"?†

---

*See especially the concluding comments on separate versus community property on pages 454–456.

†The basic principles of the separate (common-law) and community property systems are discussed in Chapter 2 on pages 28–39.

How will income from and maintenance of separate property be treated?

1. Will the income from separate property (and/or its increased value) be considered separate or community property?*
2. If "community funds" are used to maintain the separate property, will the community acquire a share in it?

9. Property Acquired During the Relationship

Before addressing questions concerning property acquired during the relationship, the parties should discuss and agree upon their definition of "marital property." In law, the term "property" has traditionally referred exclusively to tangible assets (land, homes, cars, jewels, etc.). However, a more appropriate definition of marital property suggested in this book would include certain intangible assets acquired in the course of a relationship, such as education, professional career, job experience, seniority, and pension rights. In many families these assets accumulate as a result of the joint efforts of the parties, and some courts have already recognized that fact when dividing marital assets upon divorce. For example, pension rights earned during a marriage are considered community property in California and are divided equally on dissolution. Although these issues are of greatest practical importance upon divorce or the death of one partner, it is important for contracting couples to consider them here and decide how these assets will be treated during their union as well.

How are the parties defining property?

Will any or all of the property acquired after the contract is signed be held as the separate property of the acquiring party?

1. If so, what will be held as separate property? (Typically, gifts, inheritances, clothing, jewelry, and other personal items remain separate property.)

*Even the community property states differ on how they treat income from separate property. In some states the income from separate assets remains separate property, while in others, the increments to separate property become community property.

2. How will separate property income be treated?
3. If community funds are used to maintain separate property, will the community acquire a share in it?

How will gifts *to the couple* (for example, wedding gifts) be treated?

Will any or all of the property acquired during the the relationship be owned by both parties as "community property"? If so, what will be held as community property?

If (some) property will be treated as community property, how will it be managed and controlled?

1. Will each person be responsible for some of the community assets? Or will one person serve as the community's financial manager? Or will any management be delegated to a third party?
2. Will living possessions (such as pets and plants) be treated any differently?
3. Will the written consent of both parties be required for any purchases (over a specified dollar value)?
4. Will the written consent of both parties be necessary for the sale of community assets?
5. Will the written consent of both parties be necessary to encumber community assets?
6. Are there other safeguards the parties wish to include to avoid dissipation of community funds by one party?

10. Debts

This section begins with questions designed to draw out the parties' feelings about incurring and financing debts, because social habits and emotions often play an important but unconscious role in debt decisions. Once these feelings are articulated and clarified, the parties can more easily move on to practical decisions.

What is each party's feelings about debts? Is he or she:

1. Comfortable living with a large debt as long as he or she can make monthly payments?

2. Comfortable with only limited debts?
3. Willing to use credit freely? For major necessities? For luxuries? Or for unexpected opportunities?
4. Unwilling to have any debts, afraid of debts, etc.?

If disparities arise in answers to questions 1–4 above, what sort of debt policy will the parties adopt?

1. Will they assume (any) joint liability for (any) future debts? (For what debts? Will there be a dollar limit? What about a home mortgage?)
2. Who will be responsible for the management of debt payments?

Does either party presently have any debts or financial obligations?

1. To whom and for what items are debts owed?
2. How much is owed?
3. How is it being, or will it be, repaid?

Does either party presently have any responsibility to support a third party? (For example, a former spouse? Aged parents? Children?)

1. Are these court-ordered or voluntary obligations?
2. How much money is involved, and how is it being paid?

Will either party assume any financial responsibility for the prior financial obligations of the other?

Does either party expect to assume a major financial obligation in the (near) future? (For what? How much money will be owed? How will this affect the debt policy articulated above?)

11. Domicile and Living Arrangements

The choice of a legal domicile is an important contract concern. It is one of the husband's prerogatives in the traditional marriage contract and it entails a series of civic rights and obligations (see Chapter 1).

Where do the parties plan to establish their residence and legal domicile?

1. Will the parties live together? Apart? Both?
2. Who will determine the legal domicile?
3. Where will the legal domicile be located?
4. If the parties will not live together, where will each reside?

Where do the parties plan to live?

1. Do they have a preference for the city or the country?
2. Do they have a preference for a specific geographic area?
3. Do they want to live alone (as a nuclear family)? Or in an extended family or commune?

Do the parties have plans to buy a house?

1. Will title be held as "joint tenants" or as "tenants in common"?*
2. Does either own a house or condominium?
   a. If so, how will the existing mortgage(s) be paid?
   b. How will other expenses on the property be paid?
   c. Will the title(s) be changed?

Are there plans for moving? How and when will decisions about moves be made? If a career opportunity should arise for one partner in another city, how will the decision of whether to move be made?

1. Will either partner be able to exercise a veto power over moves? Or will the decision be rotated to allow one partner to choose the first residence (to maximize his or her educational or career opportunities) and the other partner to choose the second (after a specified number of years or when he or she has a promising career opportunity)?
2. If the parties' occupational needs diverge, are they willing to live apart for periods of time?

*Joint tenants each own half (50 percent) of the property and if one partner dies the other automatically becomes the full owner of the entire property. In contrast, tenants in common may each dispose of his or her share of the property in a will (or, if one dies intestate, his or her estate acquires the share). In addition, tenants in common may own a property equally (each owning 50 percent) or unequally (with, let us say, one party owning 60 percent, the other 40 percent).

Are there provisions for, or restrictions on, additional people visiting or joining the household unit?

1. Is there a policy on guests?
2. Who may visit? For how long?

12. Responsibility for Household Tasks

Much of the debate over so-called marriage contracts has focused on apportionment of household tasks. As Fleishmann notes, "This is an area thoroughly explored by the Women's Liberation contracts and it is far from trivial. Life together is the summation of the activities of individual days; if onerous household tasks are a part of those days the parties must come to a conscious decision on who shall perform them and why."[1]

It is easy to see how a detailed and clear-cut division of household tasks can increase household harmony. A mutually agreed upon schedule (to ensure that one person does not end up doing more than his or her share) reduces conflicts about household chores, facilitates their completion, and serves as a blueprint to help couples who subscribe to egalitarian ideals translate their ideals into practice.

How will responsibility for household tasks be allocated?

1. Will tasks be shared and/or divided, or will one person be responsible?
2. Will some tasks (such as cleaning one's study) be defined as one partner's sole concern?

If one party is assigned primary responsibility for household tasks, is an explicit trade-off or compensation involved (e.g., financial support, or sharing of one's career)?

If tasks will be shared or divided, how will this be accomplished?

1. Will each person have a fixed set of tasks?
2. Or will task assignments be rotated every week or month?
3. Or will some tasks be fixed and others rotated?
4. Are there provisions for changing or phasing of responsibilities (alternating by month, season, year, stage of life)?

Will there be a work schedule?

1. What tasks will be included in it? A beginning list might include cooking, cleaning, shopping, gardening, laundry, taking care of the car, straightening up the house, appliance maintenance, writing checks, planning shopping and dinners for the week, various child care tasks (covered in section 18 below), and administering the work schedule.
2. Will the schedule be set forth in this contract? Or attached as a revisable amendment?

Will either party have the option of paying the other or a third party for household work? Or for specific tasks?

Is there a time period in which the parties must perform tasks (or be considered in noncompliance)?

Will the parties stipulate to the amount of liquidated damages that will be assessed for failure to perform assigned tasks?

13. Surname

As we noted in Chapter 1, the legal tradition has been that the wife adopts her husband's surname upon marriage. Because many view the married woman's automatic loss of her birth name as a symbol of her loss of an independent identity upon marriage, her right to choose (and retain) her own surname may be seen as a critical element in an egalitarian relationship. Similarly, because the courts have always regarded as "sacred" the father's right to have his children bear his name, a contract that affirms a woman's equal right to decide the surname of her children constitutes a significant renunciation of the traditional discrimination borne by married women.

What will be the surname of each partner?

1. Will each retain his or her current surname?
2. Or will one partner adopt the other's surname as his or her own?
3. Or will the partners adopt a hyphenated or new surname as their common surname?

What surname will the children (if any) bear? Will this vary by child, or will all children share a common surname?

Will the child's surname remain fixed in the event of a divorce?

1. If not, will the custodial parent be given the right to authorize a change? Or will a change require a joint decision?
2. Will a minor child be given a choice? At what age?

14. Sexual Relations

Many partners consider agreement on sexual matters essential to their relationship. Although the subject of sexual relations has previously been regarded as the most private of all marital concerns, people are now much more willing to openly discuss their sexual relationships. For example, it may be useful for the parties to establish a norm about sexual fidelity or infidelity. "To pay lip service to the notion of monogamy while harboring the willingness, if not the intention to conduct extramarital affairs, sets the groundwork for future problems."[2]

While some partners may feel that a candid discussion of sexual norms is sufficient to their needs, others will want to state those norms in their written contract. If they want their contract to be legally enforceable they should be cautioned, however, that an agreement about sexual practices poses potential legal difficulties. Most courts will not enforce contracts for sexual services and, in the past, many courts have invalidated entire contracts because they included (or implied) a provision for sexual services. (See Chapter 14 for a further discussion of the traditional and current legal reasoning.) Partners who want to include an agreement about sexual relations should be cognizant of the current state of the law and include a severability provision in their contract.

What kind of sexual relationship do the parties want? (See also section 15 below).

Will the relationship be monogamous?

If the relationship *is* monogamous:

1. How will a violation be handled?

2. Will a violation trigger dissolution? Or will liquidated damages be assessed? Or will the response depend on the circumstances?
3. Will there be any rules about disclosure?

If the relationship is *not* monogamous:

1. Are there any guidelines or ground rules for outside affairs?
2. Are there rules or norms about disclosure?

15. Personal Behavior and Ways of Relating

Some couples see the process of clarifying and defining norms for the intimate aspects of their personal relationship as an end in itself and the sole function of their contract. (See, for example, the third contract in Chapter 12.) Others view behavioral norms as a means of accomplishing the larger goals of the contract. Still others, cognizant of the fact that these provisions are not likely to be legally enforceable, may consider them irrelevant or inappropriate for a formal contract. However, a clarifying discussion about personal behavior may be useful even for those couples who choose to omit the topic from their formal contract.

Do the parties want to make any declarations about their emotional commitments? Or about their feelings for one another?

Do the parties want to stipulate ways of relating to each other?

Do the parties want to make any agreements about the way they treat each other in public? In private?

Do the parties want to affirm (or pledge to change) habits such as drinking, smoking, gambling, drug use, dieting, exercise, playing music in the house, etc.?

Do the parties want to affirm (or agree to change) any mode of behavior toward each other (such as teasing, put-downs, sarcasm, jealousy, anger, dependence, nurturance)?

Do the parties want to set aside certain hours or days to spend together (or agree to do specific things to make the relationship special)?

Do the parties want to set aside certain hours, or days, or places for each to be alone?

1. Will each person have a room or other physical space as a "private area"?
2. Does either party want to ensure his or her freedom to engage in specific activities alone? To take a separate vacation or trip?

How will decisions be made about the frequency and type of joint entertainment, leisure activities, activities with friends, and vacations? (Will any norms or decisions be a part of this agreement?)

Are there provisions for the illness or incapacity of one party? For example, are there provisions for:

1. Financial arrangements to be made (e.g., health insurance) in anticipation of such an event?
2. Responsibilities or tasks from which the incapacitated (or the healthy) party is (temporarily) excused?
3. Responsibilities of the healthy partner to the incapacitated one, either emotional or financial?
4. Time limits (if any) on the above? (E.g., if one party is permanently disabled, will these provisions be renegotiated after a specified period of time?)

16. Relations with Family, Friends, and Others

Mother-in-law jokes have always tapped a reservoir of sympathy, for it is not unusual for in-laws to become a source of conflict for new (and not so new) relationships. Ex-spouses, friends of both sexes, and stepchildren similarly constitute a "natural" source of competition for time, energy, interest, money, and emotional resources. Although a frank discussion and clarification of these relationships and obligations may not eliminate all the problems, it will allow both partners to know what to expect, and once each understands the scope (and limits) of the other's expectations, both will be in a better position either to adjust to them or to negotiate acceptable alternatives.

This is an area in which compromise can be especially effective. As Fleischmann suggests, the wife who is attached to her mother and the husband who cannot abide her ought to be able to reach agreement on some reasonable number of joint social contacts, supplemented by occasions when the wife sees her mother alone.[3]

What is the nature and extent of permissible social relations with others?

1. Will each continue to have separate friends of the same sex? Of the opposite sex?
2. Are there any limits to or understandings about these relationships?

Does either party have any existing or potential future commitments to parents, siblings, or other relatives (such as an expectation to house parents after their retirement or in case of incapacity)?

1. What are they?
2. Does the partner understand the impact that these obligations will have on their relationship?
3. Is the partner expected to participate? In what ways? How often?
4. Are the commitments to be limited or restricted in any way? Will the partner participate in a decision to change them?

Does either partner have any existing or future *financial* obligations to parents or other relatives (for support, in medical crises, etc.)?

1. What are they?
2. Does the partner understand how this will affect joint funds?
3. Are the obligations to be limited or restricted in any way? Will the partner participate in a decision to increase or decrease them?

Does either partner have financial or social commitments to a former spouse (for support, visiting, housing, child care, debts, etc.)?

1. What are they? Are they limited or restricted in any way?
2. Is the other partner expected to participate? In what ways? How often?
3. Does the other partner understand the impact these obligations will have on the relationship? On their joint funds?
4. Will time be set aside for a continued relationship between the previously married spouse and his or her previous spouse?

Does either partner have financial or social obligations to children or stepchildren?

1. What are they?
2. Will the children of a former marriage be part of the new household?
3. If not, how often will they visit?
4. What will be the obligations (if any) of each partner to the other partner's children?

What are each partner's social and/or community and/or work-related social commitments?

1. Is the other partner expected to participate in or to support these activities?
2. If so, is an exchange or tradeoff involved?

How do the parties plan to spend holidays or other "family" occasions?

17. The Decision to Have (or Not to Have) Children

The decision to bear and raise children is one of the most important decisions intimate partners face, because children cannot fail to have a profound effect on their lives. Although the law (and most married couples) have traditionally assumed that children are an essential part of marriage, many conflicting pressures and competing social norms now surround the issue of childbearing.[4] Many potential parents continue to feel that raising a child is in itself one of the most gratifying and rewarding of human experiences. Others, even those in second and third marriages, believe that the only way to "legitimate" their union is by having a child. In contrast, some couples may not want children to intrude on or interfere with their relationship or life-style. Others, particularly young career-oriented women, may fear that having children will damage their occupational mobility. And still others endorse the new antinatalist view that large families are a selfish indulgence in the light of current world population crises.

The vigor with which each of these conflicting norms is urged by various advocates suggests the importance of really "thinking out" the decision to bear children to be certain that one or both partners are not responding to someone else's "script."

Do the parties already have children?

1. What are their names, ages, sexes, etc.?
2. Are they from this or a previous relationship?

Do the parties intend to have or adopt children?

1. When? How many?
2. Do the parties wish to periodically review this decision or to postpone it to a specific date or event?
3. If the parties decide to have (or not to have) children and one party changes his or her mind, how will this be handled?

How will having children affect the parties' life-style?

1. Is one parent expected to stop working or to work only part time in order to stay home with the children? For how long? How will he or she be compensated?
2. Will the parents alternate work and childrearing roles if they have children? Or will both partners continue to work full time and use day care, babysitters, etc.?
3. Will having children alter other aspects of their life-style, such as where they live, with whom they associate, the types of extramarital relationships they have?
4. If unmarried, will the parties get married or renegotiate the contract if they have a child?

Are there plans for birth control?

1. Is one person responsible for birth control? Or will responsibility be shared or rotated? How? When?
2. Are there contingency plans if birth control fails?
3. Will there be an abortion if birth control fails? Will this be at the woman's discretion?

Will the man have a vasectomy or will the woman have a tubal ligation after they have the number of children they have planned?

Are there plans for maternity arrangements? For a hospital or home birth? How will income and expenses be adjusted before, during, and after childbirth?

If either partner has a child in the future with someone outside the contract relationship, how will this be handled?

18. Plans for Raising Children

It is important to note that issues that involve the rights of third parties, (particularly minor children) and issues that implicate constitutionally protected rights (such as religion) are qualitatively different from most of the other issues discussed in this chapter. Thus far, most of the issues discussed in this chapter raise enforcement issues only in so far as they challenge the State's definition of the nature of marriage (as discussed further in Chapter 14). But provisions that involve children's rights may be subjected to scrutiny of a wholly different order (as discussed further in Chapter 15). However, even though provisions about children stand the risk of a more difficult legal challenge, they are nevertheless of great importance and couples are strongly encouraged to include childrearing plans in their contracts.

Although this section is relatively straightforward, it is necessary to underscore the fact that however parents allocate and divide the responsibility for child care, their children may not "cooperate" and crises may not "wait" to be handled by the appropriate person at the appropriate time. Nevertheless, these situations are likely to be handled more easily when parental responsibilities are defined in advance.

How will the responsibilities for childrearing be allocated?

1. Will one person be the primary caretaker?
2. Or will the responsibility be shared or divided?
3. Or will the responsibility vary by day, month, or year?

If one party has the primary responsibility for childrearing:

1. Will the other party be expected to do anything?
2. Will the primary parent have any "time off" for leisure activity or to be alone?
3. Will the primary parent receive any compensation, money, credit, or benefits for his or her child care work?

If the responsibility for childrearing is to be divided or shared:

1. Who will be responsible for what tasks, activities? (A list for a preschool child might begin with morning dressing, breakfast, day care or school drop off or morning activities, lessons or play groups, lunch, afternoon naps, dressing, play, doctor's appointments, afternoon pickup, help with school work or projects, dinner, after-dinner play, bath, getting ready for bed, bedtime stories, etc.)
2. Are there provisions for rotating these responsibilities by the time of day, or by the day of the week, or by month or year?
3. Are there provisions for changing these arrangements for a second child?

What is each partner's philosophy of childrearing?

1. Are the partners permissive? Strict?
2. Do they believe in physical punishment? Or rewards only?
3. How will differences and conflicts about childrearing be reconciled?

Who is responsible for child discipline? Or will each supervise and discipline specific activities?

Will any childrearing be undertaken by other individuals (e.g., grandparents or hired help)? At what age (of child)?

Will one partner have the financial responsibility for children's support? Or will it be apportioned? Will this change over time?

How will decisions about the children's education be made?

1. Will day care be used? At what age?
2. Will children attend public or private schools?

How much autonomy, responsibility, and freedom will the children be given to make their own decisions, and how will limits be established?

What stipulations need to be included regarding children's inheritance? Is this affected by any existing children (from previous marriages)?

Do the parties want to make provisions now for the children's care and support in the event of a divorce? Or will these be amended to the contract after the children are born?

19. Religion

The courts have had considerable experience in trying to resolve religious conflicts between parents—especially with regard to their children's religious education and/or church or synagogue attendance. Here again, future conflicts may be avoided or mitigated by discussion of the following issues in advance.

What are the religious commitments of each party?

1. If they differ, does each agree to respect the other's beliefs?
2. Or is there an agreement that one will convert to the other's faith?

What role will religion play in the relationship?

Is there an agreement about church or synagogue attendance?

How will religious practices and responsibilities be allocated in the home?

In what faith will the children (if any) be raised? What religious education and training will children receive?

20. Health and Medical Care

One of the primary purposes of a contract is to help people plan for unanticipated events that could cause severe hardships—and to help them take reasonable precautions to avoid those hardships. It is often difficult for healthy people to take seriously the possibility that they may one day suffer a severe illness or injury. Nevertheless, careful thought about these possibilities now may lessen the negative impact of a serious illness or disability in the future.

What medical, dental, hospital, and disability insurance does each party have? If one party has no coverage:

1. Can the uninsured party be covered as a dependent on the partner's policy? (If not, will the family now obtain independent coverage for that partner?)
2. If one party remains uninsured, how will his or her medical and dental bills be paid?

What life insurance do the parties have or plan to obtain?

Do the parties want to commit themselves to any physical fitness regime, special diet, or schedule of yearly checkups, etc.?

21. Inheritance and Wills

Wills are especially important to couples who are not legally married because in that case neither partner has an automatic legal claim to the other's estate. In the absence of an explicit will, an unwed but cohabiting partner might be barred not only from obtaining a promised inheritance but also from obtaining his or her share of jointly acquired assets. (The traditional law in this regard is discussed further in Chapter 14.) Thus, even though the death of either partner may seem a remote possibility to persons entering an intimate relationship, all contractors should be able to specify some agreement concerning the making of wills.

Although the courts have traditionally upheld holographic wills (that is, wills written in the disposing party's handwriting), even if they have not been witnessed, if a will deals with complex financial matters or contains unusual provisions (for example, if a spouse is completely omitted or if everything is left to a nonrelative), then it would be prudent to have it reviewed by an attorney and signed before witnesses.

Does either party currently have a will? How will it be modified to provide for the partner? For any children of this relationship?

If both partners do not have current wills, is there an agreement to draft them?

1. Do they plan to make mutual wills?

2. If not, what will each leave to the other partner?
3. Does either party plan to establish a trust for the other partner?

What inheritance provisions will be made for children of this or former relationships?

22. Liquidated Damages

Specification of damages that will be assessed for a breach of contract affords several advantages. First, it puts the parties on notice as to what they can expect if they fail to comply with specific provisions of their contract. Second, it serves to avoid post hoc disputes about the extent of damage (or harm) that the noncomplying partner has caused. Third, it can assist the partners in resolving disputes informally and may help them avoid a legal battle in court. Finally, if the parties must go to court, it documents the parties' intentions for the judge. The last point is especially important if the judge happens not to agree with the parties' intent because, lacking a statement, the judge may independently assess the damages much higher (or lower) than the parties intended.

This section deals with monetary damages because the courts have traditionally refused to enforce "specific performance" provisions (that is, provisions for specific behaviors) in interpersonal contracts. (Their reasoning is discussed further in Chapter 14.) Monetary damages are not only easier to exact legally, they are also easier to handle socially: it is much easier to make someone pay a $25 fine for not cooking dinner than to compel the same person to cook dinner. Partners who are less concerned about legal enforcement may want to consider specifying certain nonmonetary damages as well.

Do the parties want to specify damages for the breach of any part of this contract?

1. For what type of breach will damages be assessed?
2. How and by whom will the breach be assessed?
3. What fines or penalties will be assessed?
4. Will the fine be assessed for each day of a continuing breach (e.g., $100 a day for noncompliance), or will a single fine be established for each type of breach?

How will damages be paid? From separate or from community funds? Do the parties want to post a bond to cover these expenses?

23. Resolving Disagreements

One of the major advantages of a contract is its potential for resolving disputes and reducing family conflict. If couples have established ground rules and procedures in advance, they are more likely to utilize them than if they have to decide how to proceed in the middle of a dispute. In addition, they are likely to take conciliatory action (such as consulting a marriage counselor) at an early stage in a continuing conflict, and to settle their differences more smoothly. Some of the advantages to be gained by using extralegal procedures (such as conciliation and arbitration) to resolve disagreements are discussed in Chapters 10 and 14.

Are there ground rules for arguments (such as no arguing when angry, or no physical violence)?

What are the procedures for resolving continuing conflicts?

1. Do the parties agree to set aside time to discuss them?
2. Or to seek professional assistance in resolving them?
3. Or to consult a conciliator or personal friend? Do the parties want to specify a person (or panel of persons) to act as conciliator?

If one party wants to seek professional assistance, will the other party agree to go along? For how long?

If disputes cannot be resolved by agreement (or with professional help), will the parties submit to arbitration?

1. Will there be an outside arbitrator? Who? How will the arbitrator be chosen?
2. Will the contract be binding on such arbitration?

24. Changing, Amending, and Renewing the Contract

Since the contract is meant to be a "living document," it is likely that over time some of its provisions will have to be revoked or altered to adjust to the changing needs and circumstances of the parties. However, because the future situation and requirements cannot be foreseen, the parties will not be able to anticipate the substantive nature of the contractual changes they may seek. This section therefore focuses entirely on the procedure they will follow to alter the contract.

Establishing a fair and responsive procedure for renegotiation is a difficult undertaking. On one hand, the procedure should facilitate changes which both parties feel are necessary to meet new life situations. (If, for example, an unplanned child is born, it would be reasonable to amend the contract to include provisions for the care and support of the child.) On the other hand, the procedure should not encourage frequent or capricious changes. It is important that both parties regard the contract as a fixed and definite agreement that cannot be easily altered. Thus, it may be wise to stipulate to a presumption in favor of the existing contract and to lay the burden of proof on the party who wants to change it.

Will there be a fixed date for reviewing the contract? Or will it be renewed after some event (such as completion of school, or the birth of a child)?

Will there be scheduled periodic reviews of the entire contract or of specific sections? How often? Annually? Every five years? Will there be a ceremony on the occasion of these renewals?

If reviews are not established in advance, how will requests for renegotiation be handled?

1. How much notice will be required?
2. Must the other party respond to every request? Or will there be a limit to the number of requests or to the raising of specific subjects in any one- (or two- or five-) year period?
3. Will certain financial provisions, such as a tradeoff or an agreement to hold property as joint tenants, be set aside as unalterable?

Will certain events (a childbirth, a severe illness, a bankruptcy, a financial windfall) automatically trigger renegotiation of specified provisions?

What will be the procedure for renegotiation?

1. Who will arbitrate in the event of a disagreement?
2. What burden or standard of proof will have to be met by the party who initiates the change?

Do the parties want to state a presumption in favor of the existing contract (with the burden of proof put on the party who wants the change)?

25. Dissolution

Although the provisions for dissolution discussed in this section may seem excessively detailed and specific to persons establishing a first relationship, previously married persons are likely to find solace and security in a precise delineation of their obligations in the event of a future dissolution. In fact, those who have been through an antagonistic and costly divorce may consider the clarification and specification of a postdissolution regime to be an essential prerequisite to forming a new relationship.

To those couples disinclined to make plans for dissolution on the grounds that the subject is too "negative" or the possibility too remote, we once again urge the merits of anticipating the possibility of an unpleasant event in order to avoid its more devastating effects. In addition, the current rising divorce rate suggests that dissolution is not as unlikely as some couples suppose: it seems that in all too many cases neither good intentions nor well-laid plans suffice to prevent it.

Another objection to anticipating dissolution has to do with the parties' inability to anticipate the future. But whereas provisions drafted at the time of the initial contract cannot fully anticipate the parties' circumstances at the point of dissolution, they can provide a set of equitable principles or guidelines for that time. In addition, broad principles that are established at the beginning of a relationship, when each partner has noble intentions and wants to be fair, may serve the relationship better than a more detailed settlement negotiated in acrimony.

Most of the antenuptial contracts that have come before the courts so far were written by previously married couples who wanted to specify their property rights upon divorce (or death);

therefore, a considerable body of law has developed for dealing with these contracts. (This law is discussed further in Chapter 14.)

When (and why) will the relationship be dissolved?

1. Will it terminate on a specific date? Or after a specific event?
2. Will grounds or justifications be required? Or can it be dissolved at the desire of either party? Or will it require the "consent" of both parties? (As this provision would be contrary to some no-fault laws, partners who include it would be wise to specify liquidated damages for a nonconsenting dissolution.)
3. If only one partner wants the dissolution, will the unwilling partner be given any additional incentives or compensation (such as fees, property, the option of remaining in the joint residence, or the promise of conciliation efforts)?

What are the procedures for dissolution?

1. How much notice will be required?
2. Will conciliation efforts be required? How many sessions? For how long?
3. Will a trial separation be required as part of the conciliation effort? For how long? If so, what will be the financial and residential arrangements during this period?
4. How long after failure of conciliation and/or trial separation will dissolution occur?

What will be considered community property for the purpose of division of assets upon dissolution (that is, will it include pensions, education, life insurance benefits, careers, etc., as well as real property)? For example, if one partner's homemaking services contribute to the other partner's career (and earning power), then the earning partner's career might be considered community property and the nonearning partner may be deemed to have a vested interest in it.

How will property and assets be divided upon dissolution?

1. Is there an agreement to divide the assets equally? Or according to some formula?

2. Will specific assets be linked to other decisions (such as a presumption that the house will be awarded to the parent who has custody of the children)?

Will the following items be taken into consideration in the property division?

1. Reimbursement for educational support?
2. Creation of a partnership interest in the earning partner's career?
3. Compensation for the loss of earning potential during the relationship?
4. Preservation of an ongoing business or professional practice? (The operating partner might be allowed to retain a business or practice intact while reimbursing the other partner for his or her share of its value by securing a bank loan or a note.)
5. Preservation of the family home for minor children? If minor children are living in the home at time of dissolution, the parties may agree to award its title to the children's custodian (as a form of compensation for their care) without penalty in the division of the rest of the property.

How will debts be divided?

1. Will they go with the asset for which the debt was incurred (for example, the car loan with the car)?
2. Or will they go to the prime beneficiary of the loan (for example, a student loan might become the sole obligation of the one who received the education)?
3. Or will they be divided equally?

Will there be a termination fee?

1. Will it be paid by the party who wants to end the relationship?
2. Or will it be paid only in the event that one party is severely hurt or handicapped by the dissolution, regardless of who requested it?
3. Or will it be paid only if one party breaches the contract and causes the dissolution?
4. Is the sum specified, or will it be linked to the timing or cause of the dissolution?

Will one party be obligated by agreement to support the other after dissolution?

1. If so, will the amount of support be set now, or will there be a formula for calculating the amount? (If amounts are set in current dollars, this clause should specify that they will be adjusted for changes in the cost of living.)

2. If postdivorce support is uncertain, what will the decision depend on? (Factors might include each party's age, labor force experience, current salary, job prospects, the length of their relationship, whether one party has contributed to the other's education or career, whether one party's career or financial position is greatly disadvantaged as a result of the relationship, whether one party seeks education or retraining, whether one party will care for minor children.)

3. If support will be tendered, how long will it continue? Will the number of years be fixed? Or linked to the duration of the relationship? Or linked to the completion of a trade-off agreement? Or will support continue until the parties approach equity in their earnings? Or until the supported partner enters a new relationship?

4. Under what conditions can the amount and/or duration be renegotiated (for example, unemployment of the now-earning partner)?

How will custody of children be determined?

1. Have the parties agreed on any presumptions or guidelines for the custodial decision?
2. Will the children be given a role in the decision? At what age?

How will child support be determined?

1. Will one party be solely responsible for child support? Or will support be a fixed or proportional share of each party's income?
2. How will the needed amount of child support be determined?
3. Will the custodial parent's time be included as part of the cost of raising the child, and will that parent be given a credit against his or her assessed share of support?

4. How long will child support last? Until the child is 18? Or graduates from college? Or from graduate school?

How will disagreements about the dissolution provisions be handled?

1. Will they be submitted to binding arbitration?
2. Under what conditions will the parties go to court?

CHAPTER 12

Case Studies: Ten Contracts Within and in Lieu of Marriage

This chapter presents excerpts from ten contracts. They are not hypothetical examples: their terms were formulated by real people in real relationships.* The first five were written by couples who were about to be or who were already legally married. The second five are contracts in lieu of marriage, written by couples who either rejected legal marriage or were barred from it.

Because the motives for drawing up contracts will differ from couple to couple, the orientation, content, and provisions of these individual contracts differ greatly. Some focus on finances and property, others on home and child care, others on equality of career opportunity, and others on interpersonal relations. In addition to these differences in purpose, some contractors consider their contract a private agreement to which they are ethically and morally

---

*Some minor deletions and changes have been made to protect the identity of the parties.

While each of these contracts is original, in the sense that it was drafted by or for each individual couple, it is apparent that two couples used some provisions from a contract published in Ms. Magazine, and one couple (Contract 8) used portions and modifications of Dr. Paschal and Janette Baute's Equalog Contract I™, which is reprinted here in modified form with their permission.

291

bound, while others want their contract to be enforceable in a court of law (and still others want both). While questions of enforceability are reserved for the last section of this book, it will be evident to the reader that some of the contracts presented below were written with an eye to legal considerations while others were not.

Even couples with similar needs may opt for radically different solutions. For example, some couples seeking to establish an egalitarian relationship may believe that this will be possible only if they merge all their holdings and income as community property. Others, striving for an equal partnership, may believe it necessary first to have a strong and independent financial base—and to establish a separate property system whereby each controls his or her own money and resources before they are merged to meet common expenses and investments.*

The contract excerpts presented in this chapter were chosen for their range and variety. None covers all contingencies, and none is intended to serve as an ideal model for the topics it covers. Each one addresses a particular issue or set of issues in a unique way.

The first of the five contracts within marriage is a simple statement of principles for a marriage. Since Beth, a second-year student in a masters of business administration program, and Larry, a doctor beginning a surgical residency, feel they cannot yet make concrete plans for the future, they have written a contract that sets forth only the basic principles that will govern their forthcoming marriage.

The second "marriage contract" describes a relatively traditional marriage. In Contract 2, David, a medical student, has persuaded Nancy, an aspiring dancer, to give up her potential career in return for the promise of a comfortable life-style and status as a doctor's wife. Nancy agrees to support David through medical school and his internship. After that she will be a full-time wife and mother. Their contract assures her of a vested interest in David's career, a generous standard of living, and a guarantee of financial compensation in the event of dissolution. This contract is unlike traditional marriage only in that the wife is guaranteed compensation for her contribution to the marital partnership.

The third contract focuses on equality of educational and occupational opportunities for a young dual-career professional couple. Although Susan, who plans to be an attorney, and Peter, who plans

*These two perspectives are further discussed in the Appendix on pages 453–456.

to be a child psychologist, want to share their future lives, both are deeply committed to their work and feel their careers need not be sacrificed for their personal relationship. Their contract, which was drafted with the assistance of Susan's family attorney, allows both of them to pursue active professional careers.

Contract 4 involves the renegotiation of an existing marriage. Barbara and Robert have been married for 20 years and have two teenage children. After 16 years of marriage Barbara returned to school, and soon after graduation she found a job. Her attempts to renegotiate her household responsibilities in light of her new work load were less than successful. Robert was jealous of her new activities and had an affair to get her to pay more attention to him. After filing for divorce they decided to see a marriage counselor for the children's sake—and in the counseling process realized that they wanted to stay together and to attempt to reconstruct their marriage. Their contract is an attempt to make explicit the terms and conditions of their new relationship.

The final marriage contract (Contract 5) involves two previously married and previously divorced partners: Betty, a hair stylist, and Joe, a municipal bus driver. Their contract deals with two primary concerns. First, since Betty feels that she got the short end of her first marriage (and her divorce settlement), this contract tries to ensure that she "gets something" for her extra work in the home. Second, since both Betty and Joe have children and both are concerned about the financial impact of another divorce, this contract tries to protect their (limited) assets and to provide some financial security for their children in the event of dissolution.

The next five contracts were intended as contracts in lieu of marriage. The first (Contract 6) was written by a homosexual couple seeking to formalize an alternative life-style. Chris, a sailboat enthusiast, and Robin, a painter, have two major aims: they want to rotate work and support responsibilities so that each is supported for six months out of each year while he pursues his special interest. Their second aim is to protect their jointly acquired property from members of their respective families who might try to challenge their wills.

The next contract in lieu of marriage (Contract 7), written by two well-to-do, middle-aged attorneys, is surprisingly nonlegalistic. It is a gentle and humane document that covers a wide range of topics. Its provisions for children and for enforcement (through arbitration) are especially noteworthy.

Contract 8 is the least legalistic contract in this chapter. Written by a California couple who have been living together and are about to have a child, it focuses almost exclusively on ways of relating between the couple and with others.

In striking contrast is Contract 9, which looks almost like an employment contract. Neither Tom, a widower, nor Linda, a divorcee, wants to remarry, but each wants the companionship and family ambience the other can provide. Tom agrees to pay Linda for her housework and child care and to provide her with other job-related benefits that housewives rarely receive: time off, Social Security coverage, medical and hospital insurance, guaranteed raises, and a pension.

The final document (Contract 10) was written to avoid the consequences implicit in the *Marvin* decision, which established the possibility of property rights resulting from a cohabiting relationship. Written by two middle-aged professors at an Ivy League university, Contract 10 sets apart and describes the separate properties of each of the parties and clarifies their intention that neither party shall acquire an interest in the separate property of the other as a consequence of their relationship.

Contract 1: An Agreement on Principles Between Prospective Spouses

Beth, a second-year student at the Stanford Graduate School of Business, and Larry, a first-year surgery resident at Stanford University Hospital, met at the beginning of the fall semester at Stanford University. They decided to marry in December before either of them had a clear idea of their job prospects or plans for the following year. While they felt that many of their life decisions would of necessity remain in a state of flux, they wanted to write a statement of principles to guide their future relationship. Their one-paragraph contract sets forth two general guidelines.

An Agreement on Principles for Our Forthcoming Marriage

This contract establishes two principles for our forthcoming marriage.

1. First, we agree to make our marriage an equal partnership. All career and personal decisions will be made to balance and equalize each party's benefits and burdens.

2. Second, we agree to treat all of our assets and income as community property. We pledge to share equally all of our assets without regard to which party earned or acquired them, and to be jointly responsible for all expenses and debts.

3. Since we do not know where we will live next year, we want to make certain that this agreement, rather than the laws defining the rights and obligations of married spouses in the state(s) where we reside, will govern our relationship.

Contract 2: A Traditional Marriage Between a Medical Doctor and a Housewife, with Full Partnership Rights for the Wife

David is a first-year medical student who may have to drop out of medical school for lack of financial support. Nancy, an aspiring professional dancer, has recently received an offer of a two-year fellowship for a special training program in Paris. Although David and Nancy have known each other only three months, they are madly in love. David wants Nancy to give up Paris and her dancing to marry him and stay in New York. In return he promises her a comfortable life as a doctor's wife. He asks that she get a job to support him through his medical schooling and internship. In return he assures her of generous support once he enters practice as a physician. Nancy decides that she could be happy as the wife of a successful doctor, and she agrees to accept David's proposal on the condition that they have an explicit agreement guaranteeing her a share in David's future career and making adequate provision for her in the event of dissolution.

Aims and Expectations

Each party wants to state their goals and future expectations at the time this contract is signed.

1. Nancy has always wanted to be a professional dancer. She has good reason to believe she is talented because she was recently awarded a special fellowship for two years of study and training in Paris. Nancy realizes that if she gives up her fellowship it will be very difficult—if not impossible—for her to recapture the professional opportunities and the years of youthful training she will have lost.

2. Nancy agrees to give up her career aspirations and to support David through medical school and his internship. In return for her contribution to David's education and training, she expects financial security, the assurance that she will enjoy the usual benefits of being a doctor's wife (i.e., a beautiful home and summer home, expensive clothing, vacations in Europe, child care and private schools for her children, and a full-time housekeeper), and a future interest in David's career.

3. David understands that Nancy's efforts will make it possible for him to obtain his medical education in a fairly comfortable fashion. Her support will ensure that he will not have to drop out of school to earn money and that he will not have to spend any time on part-time jobs or housework. He will be able to devote all his time to his studies. In return, he wants to guarantee Nancy a share in his future career.

4. Nancy realizes that she will have to work hard and make do with very little money while she supports David. Further, she understands that David's studies will be time-consuming, and that he will be a less than ideal companion. However, she is willing to sacrifice these short-run benefits for David's guarantee of a better tomorrow.

5. David realizes that Nancy is making a great sacrifice for the relationship, and for him personally. He views Nancy's continuing efforts on behalf of their partnership to be of the same worth as his. He wants her to devote her talents to nurturing him and their children and to creating the type of elegant and beautiful home that only Nancy's presence could create. He considers these activities to be worth as much as his income-producing activities as a physician.

6. Nancy knows that her life plans will be drastically altered in the event of a divorce, and that she can never recapture the professional opportunities she is giving up now, for she will later be too old to become a great dancer. Thus she wants to be sure that her partnership interest in David's career will be protected even if their marriage dissolves. Further, she expects to be compensated for her psychological, educational, and financial loss if the marriage dissolves.

7. David has offered Nancy much more than this agreement provides because he feels he cannot live without her. He willingly agrees to compensate her if they divorce, although he cannot believe it will ever happen.

Statement of Interest

1. The parties consider this a contract for a lifetime partnership.

2. The parties consider themselves equal partners in this contract and in their relationship.

3. The parties recognize that although Nancy's contribution to the partnership will be less tangible financially, her financial support during school, her home and child care afterwards, and her continuing emotional and psychological nurturance are of equal worth to the partnership.

4. The parties agree to share equally all income, property, and other gains that may accrue to either partner. They consider any gains that accrue to the income-earning partner to be the result of their joint efforts — and thereby to belong to both parties equally.

Property

1. All income, assets, and property of the parties, however acquired, shall be jointly owned as community property.

2. Nancy will manage and control the community property and will take care of all other household business matters.

Support

1. Nancy will work as a secretary in order to support David until he has finished medical school and an internship.

2. After David finishes his internship, he will support the family by taking a (paying) residency or by beginning to practice medicine.

3. To guarantee her support, David will carry $200,000 of life insurance with Nancy as the beneficiary.

4. Nancy will not work outside the home after David's career has commenced.

Domicile

The location of the family domicile will be decided by David; the main consideration in making such a decision will be the best interest of David's career.

Name

Both parties will use David's surname.

Housekeeping Responsibilities

Nancy will be responsible for the administration of the household, eventually with the assistance of a full-time housekeeper.

Other Responsibilities

1. Nancy agrees to further David's career by maintaining appropriate social relationships with other doctors and their wives.

2. Nancy agrees to participate actively in church and country club activities, to serve on medical auxiliary and hospital benefit committees, and to socialize with David's colleagues and other physicians.

3. Nancy promises to give a dinner party or to otherwise aid David's professional advancement by entertaining at least twice a week.

4. David agrees to accompany Nancy to the ballet at least once a month.

5. David also agrees to schedule at least two two-week vacations with her each year, at least one of them in Europe.

Children

1. Children will be postponed until David's education is completed.

2. If Nancy should become pregnant prior to that time, she will have an abortion.

3. Nancy will have full responsibility for the care of the children; financial responsibility will be fully met from the income from David's practice.

Termination

1. This partnership may be dissolved by either party, at will, upon six months notice to the other party.

2. If this partnership is terminated by either party prior to the completion of David's education, Nancy's obligation to support him will cease. Moreover, once David's career has begun, he will have the obligation of supporting Nancy at the rate of $50,000 a year (in 1979 dollars with built-in cost-of-living and inflation adjustments) for as many years as she supported him. If necessary, David will secure a loan to repay Nancy for her support. If Nancy prefers a lump-sum settlement equal to the value of this support, David will arrange a loan to provide it. Both parties agree to treat Nancy's original support of David as a loan of the value specified above. David's obligation to repay this loan has the standing of any other legal debt.

3. Once David finishes his residency, Nancy will acquire a one-quarter vested interest in his future earnings. If the partnership is termi-

nated after that date, Nancy will be entitled to one-fourth of his net yearly income, to be paid quarterly, for as long as he continues to practice medicine. David will purchase insurance or a bond to guarantee this payment. It is agreed that this payment is not alimony, and that it shall be continued unmodified regardless of her earning capacity or remarriage. The parties consider this Nancy's reimbursement for investing in and helping to launch David's career. It is agreed that her efforts will have been crucial to any future success that he has, and that her vested interest in his career is the consideration for that support.

4. David agrees to pay Nancy the fixed sum of $50,000 if their marriage terminates within 15 years, as liquidated damages for the pain and suffering she will experience from the change in her expectations and life plans.

5. David also agrees [in the event of termination of the marriage] to pay for Nancy's medical expenses or to provide her with adequate insurance at the rate of one year of coverage for every year of marriage. It is explicitly agreed that psychiatric and dental bills be included in the above.

6. Community property will be divided equally upon termination.

7. If there are children, Nancy will have custody of the children. David will have full responsibility for their support, as well as the responsibility for compensating Nancy for her services in caring for them (at the then current rate for private nurses). Suitable visiting arrangements will be made.

Death

1. Both parties agree to make wills stipulating the other partner the sole legatee.

2. If the marriage is terminated this obligation will cease, but David's support obligations for Nancy and the children will continue and will be stipulated in his will.

Contract 3: An Antenuptial Contract for a Young Dual-Career Professional Couple

Susan and Peter are currently seniors in college. Susan is an aspiring attorney; Peter plans to become a child psychologist. Both are dedicated to their future careers as well as to each other. After discussing and reaching agreement about their future plans, they asked an attorney to help them draft a contract to formalize their agreement. Although they planned to marry, they wanted to be sure their relationship would not be governed by the traditional laws of their state. They wanted a contract that would reflect their equal status as husband and wife and, at the same time, maximize their career opportunities as well as their personal relationship.

Recital of Intention

Susan Wher and Peter Weiss, hereinafter referred to as Susan and Peter, desire to enter into a marriage relationship duly solemnized under the laws of the State of Florida, the rights and obligations of which differ from the traditional rights and obligations of married persons in the State of Florida which would prevail in the absence of this contract. These customary and traditional rights and obligations, the parties feel, impose inequalities and unequal burdens upon married persons.

The parties have together drafted this contract in order to define a marriage relationship sought by the parties that preserves and promotes their individual identities as human beings. Susan and Peter are of sound mind and body and have a clear understanding of the terms of this contract and of the binding nature of the agreements contained herein. They freely and in good faith choose to enter into this marriage contract and fully intend it to be legally binding upon themselves.

Now, therefore, in consideration of their affection and esteem for each other, and in consideration of the mutual promises herein expressed, the sufficiency of which is hereby acknowledged, Susan and Peter agree as follows:

Recital of Facts

1. Susan was born in 1958 and is 20 years old. Her father, a physician, and her mother, a high school teacher, are alive and healthy. They own an appliance repair store and live in Miami, Florida. Susan plans to graduate from the University of Miami in June, 1978 and to enroll in its law school in September, 1978.

2. Peter was born in 1958 and is 20 years old. His parents are divorced. His father, David Weiss, is remarried and resides in Hollywood, Florida. He manages a retail clothing store. His mother, Ruth Weiss, resides in Miami Beach, Florida. She is currently employed as a secretary-receptionist in a doctor's office in Miami Beach.

3. Both parties to this agreement have made to each other, and in the future will make to each other, a full and complete disclosure of the nature, extent and probable value of all their property, estate, and expectancies, amended to this agreement in Appendices A and B.

Names

Susan and Peter affirm their individuality and equality in this relationship. The parties reject the concept of ownership implied in the adoption by the woman of the man's name. Therefore, both parties will retain their own surnames. Female children will be given Susan's surname, and male children will be given Peter's surname.

Identity

The parties are individuals with their own identities, families, interests, histories, and careers. They do not view themselves as an inseparable couple who do not exist apart from each other.

Educational and Living Expenses

1. The parties agree to take turns going to school, so that the non-student partner can support the other until he or she receives a degree. They, therefore, agree to the following eight-year financial arrangement that shall be severed and binding irrespective of the status of the rest of the contract.

2. The parties recognize that their joint income will be maximized by allowing Susan to attend school first. Peter, therefore, agrees to be solely responsible for Susan's educational expenses and support for three full years. Susan agrees to assume the same responsibilities for Peter's education and support for the following five years.

3. If the partnership is dissolved at any time during these first eight years, each shall have the following financial obligation to the other:

   a. If dissolution occurs during the first three years, Peter will be obligated to pay Susan's remaining tuition (up to three full years' tuition in law school) and pay her $6,000 a year (in 1978 real dollars) for living expenses.

   b. Thereafter, Susan will be obligated to pay Peter's remaining tuition (up to five full years of tuition in graduate school) and pay him $6,000 a year (in 1978 real dollars) for living expenses.

c. All living expenses will be paid at the rate of $500 a month. All of the dollar amounts specified are in 1978 real dollars and are to be tied to the cost-of-living index for yearly adjustments.

Domicile

1. The parties agree that the choice of marital domicile shall be mutual. Peter hereby waives any legal right he may have to determine the legal domicile of the parties.

2. The parties agree to maintain a joint domicile for the first eight years of the relationship. The location of the domicile will be determined by the student partner to maximize his or her educational opportunities.

3. After eight years, domicile decisions will be made jointly, with no presumption that the career of either is of greater importance in making the decision.

4. If we cannot agree on a mutually acceptable domicile, the first decision will be Susan's—for a period of four years. Peter will then have the right to choose the location for the following four years. We will continue to rotate the domicile decision on a four-year basis.

5. We realize that career opportunities may not coincide with this prearranged schedule. We therefore agree to exchange the right of decision for a given period or to make other equitable agreements that would then be incorporated into this contract.

6. Each party will always retain the option of establishing a temporary separate residence, at his or her own expense, to utilize a special career opportunity.

Property

1. For the next eight years (until 19___) all income and property, excluding gifts and inheritance, shall be considered community property. The income-earning partner shall have sole responsibility for its management and control.

2. An inventory will be taken of all community property on June 30, 19___. In the event of a divorce, this property will be divided equally.

3. From June 30, 19___ on, all property acquired by either party, of whatsoever nature and wheresoever located, whether real, personal, or mixed, including but not limited to any earnings, salaries, commissions, or income resulting from his or her personal services, skills, and efforts

shall be and remain his or her sole and separate property, except as herein otherwise provided.

4. Each party's separate property will be subject to his or her control and management, to use and dispose of as he or she sees fit.

5. Any and all income resulting from either party's separate property shall also be his or her separate property.

6. Neither party will have any present or future rights to a share in the separate property of the other.

7. Any joint purchase of over $1,000 will be covered by a separate agreement concerning its ownership.

8. Each party will maintain a separate bank account and financial records.

Household Expenses

(This part of the agreement shall go into effect eight years hence.)

1. Household expenses will consist of rent, utilities, food, and housekeeping expenses.

2. Susan and Peter will each contribute 75 percent of their net income to household expenses. Their contributions will be made in monthly installments of equal amounts and be placed in a joint checking account.

3. Responsibility for the joint account and for paying the above expenses will be rotated at three-month intervals so that each party will be responsible six months each year.

4. Each partner will be responsible for his or her own expenses for food and entertainment outside of the household. Each will maintain a separate car and a separate phone and will take care of these expenses separately.

5. If money in the joint account is not exhausted by household expenses, it may be used for joint leisure activities.

6. Both parties recognize that Susan's income is likely to be higher than Peter's in the future, and that 25 percent of her income will allow her more money for separate expenses. The parties therefore agree that if the income of one party exceeds the income of the second party, clause 2 above will be automatically revised to read: The higher income party will contribute that proportion of his or her net income (i.e., take-home pay) to household expenses so that his or her remaining income does not exceed the remaining income of the lower income party by more than 20 percent.

Care and Use of the Household

1. Susan and Peter recognize the need for allocation of time and labor for household tasks. The parties reject the tradition that the responsibility for housework and domestic services rests solely with the woman in the family. They hereby agree to share the work and responsibility of maintaining their home.

2. All necessary tasks will be divided into two categories. On even-numbered months (e.g., February, April, June, etc.) Susan will be responsible for category 1 and Peter for category 2; and vice versa on odd-numbered months.

3. Each party will do her or his own cooking and cleanup afterwards for breakfast and lunch, as well as keeping her or his own study clean.

4. Cooking dinner and cleanup will be considered part of the housework, to be rotated as specified above.

5. In the event that one party neglects to perform any task, the other party may perform it and charge the nonperforming partner $25 per hour for his or her labor, or agree to be repaid in kind.

Childbearing

1. While the parties have decided to have two children at some time in the future, birth control will be practiced until a decision to have a child has been reached.

2. Responsibility for birth control will be shared equally. Susan will have this responsibility for the first six months of the year, Peter for the second six months.

3. Since the parties believe that a woman should have control over her own body, the decision of whether or not to terminate an accidental pregnancy shall be Susan's alone. If Susan decides to have an abortion, the party who had responsibility for birth control the month that conception occurred will bear the cost of the abortion. This cost will include medical expenses not covered by insurance and any other expenses or loss of pay incurred by Susan.

4. However, if Susan decides to have the child and Peter does not agree, Susan will bear full financial and social responsibility for the child. In that event, Susan also agrees to compensate Peter should he be required to support the child.

5. If the parties agree to have a child and Susan changes her mind after conception has occurred, she will pay for the abortion. If Peter changes his mind after conception has occurred and Susan agrees to an abortion, he will pay for it. If she does not agree, Peter will share the social and financial responsibility for the child, just as if he had not changed his mind.

Childrearing

1. The parties reject the concept that the primary responsibility for raising children rests with the woman. They believe such a restriction would deprive them of experiences and opportunities as individuals and as parents and would be detrimental to the growth and development of their children. Therefore, the parties agree that childrearing shall be a mutual privilege and responsibility. In allocating childrearing time and duties the parties shall take into account the demands of their respective careers, their needs as individuals to establish, maintain, and cultivate social and business contacts outside the marriage, their individual skills and desires, and the best interests of their children.

2. Once a planned child is born the parties will assume equal financial responsibility for the child. Child-related costs will be born by the joint fund. If this is not sufficient, each party will be assessed an additional 5 or 10 percent of his or her income as necessary for childrearing expenses. Costs will be assessed by the primary parent (see clause 5 below).

3. If it is necessary for Susan to take time off from work in connection with her pregnancy or with the birth of a child, Peter will pay her one-half of his current salary to compensate her for the loss. If either party has to take time off from work to care for the child, the other party will repay that party with one-half of the working partner's earnings for that period.

4. All child care, medical, and educational expenses will be shared equally.

5. Since Peter expects to become a psychologist, he will become the primary parent for the first child. If necessary he will take a paternity leave after the birth in order to care for the child, and will have primary responsibility for the child until arrangements can be made for a full-time nurse or day care. Susan will compensate him at the rate of

one-half of her salary. Responsibility for caring for the child on evenings and weekends will be divided equally.

6. Primary responsibility for the second child (as defined above) will be Susan's.

Evaluation and Amendment

1. Susan and Peter recognize the importance of change in their relationship and intend that this contract be a living document and a focus for periodic evaluations of their partnership.

2. The parties agree that either party may initiate a review of any provisions of the articles in this contract for amendment with the exception of the section entitled "Educational and Living Expenses." The parties agree to honor such requests for review.

3. The parties further agree that in the case of unresolved conflict between them over any provisions of this contract, they will seek mediation, professional or otherwise, by a third party.

Dissolution

1. If there are children, both parties agree to submit to at least six months of conciliation sessions prior to termination.

2. If a decision to dissolve the partnership is made, both parties agree to submit to binding arbitration if they are unable to reach a mutual decision regarding the issues of child custody and/or child support.

3. A list of mutually agreeable arbitrators is attached to this agreement.

4. The following principles should govern this arbitration:

   a. While both agree that custody should be determined according to the best interests of the child, a presumption exists in favor of Peter, since he will have had superior training and experience with children.
   b. Each party should assume half of the financial burden of caring for the child.

5. If there are no children, this household agreement can be terminated by either party for any reason with a 60-day written notice. Upon separation, each party will retain his or her separate property, and any jointly owned property will be divided equally.

6. Neither party will have any financial or other responsibility toward the other after separation and division of property with the exception of the provisions in the section entitled "Educational and Living Expenses."

Recordation

This antenuptial agreement, or a memorandum thereof, may be recorded in the Official Records of Dade County by either of us.

Saving Clause

If any portion of this antenuptial agreement be unenforceable under the laws of Florida, it is the intention of the parties that the remaining portions thereof shall remain in full force and effect.

Now, therefore, Susan Wher and Peter Weiss make the following declarations:

1. They are responsible adults.
2. They freely adopt the spirit and material terms of this contract.
3. This marriage contract entered into in conjunction with a marriage license of the State of Florida, County of Dade, hereby manifests their intent to define the rights and obligations of the marriage relationship as distinct from those rights and obligations defined by the laws of the State of Florida and affirms their right to do so.
4. They intend to be legally bound by this marriage contract and uphold its articles before any court of Law in the Land.

Contract 4: A Contract Between an Already Married Husband and Wife

Barbara and Robert Sloan, husband and wife, are both 42 years old. They have been married for 21 years and have two children: Steven, age 20, and Susan, age 18. For the first 16 years of this marriage Barbara was a full-time housewife and mother. Four years ago she returned to school. After completing her college degree she obtained a job as a keypunch operator for a computer company. Robert Sloan is a life insurance agent employed by a large company, a job he has held for the past 22 years. When Barbara returned to school she continued to manage the household while carrying a full college course load. Although Robert and the children tried "to help," she still bore the major burden and her resentment grew.

At the same time, Robert began to resent Barbara's outside activities and started seeing another woman. He now realizes that his involvement with the other woman was aimed at making his wife jealous and getting her to pay more attention to him. He also hoped to prevent her new interests from usurping the central place he had always held in her life. After filing for divorce, the couple decided to see a marriage counselor for the children's sake, and in the course of counseling they realized they really wanted to stay together and try to reconstruct their marriage.

Their contract, the result of months of discussion, was written to affirm their new understanding of their relationship. Although their children are not parties to this contract, they participated in the discussions, and both of them have agreed to support and honor the spirit of this contract.

The excerpts presented below focus on their interpersonal relationship.

Living in Partnership

Barbara and Robert desire to continue their marriage and to make it a full and equal partnership. The parties share a commitment to the process of negotiations and compromise that will continue to strengthen their equality in the partnership. Decisions will be made with respect for individual needs and equality. The parties hope to maintain such mutual decision-making so that the daily decisions affecting their lives will not become a struggle between the parties for power, authority, and dominance.

Therefore, the parties agree that such a process, while sometimes time-consuming and fatiguing, is a good investment in the future of their relationship and their continued love and esteem for each other.

Names

The parties do not ascribe to the concept of ownership implied by the woman's adoption of the man's name. However, since Barbara has used Robert's name for the past 21 years and is known to all her friends at work by this name, it would not be practical for her to resume her birth name at this time. Therefore, the parties agree to retain and use the family name of Sloan.

Careers

Barbara and Robert value the importance and integrity of their respective careers and acknowledge the demands that their jobs place on them as individuals and on their partnership. Although commitment to their work will sometimes place stress on the relationship, they believe that their experiences at work contribute to individual self-fulfillment and thereby strengthen the partnership.

Relationships with Others, Jealousy, and Trust

1. The parties acknowledge their desire to retain a monogamous sexual relationship. They, therefore, agree to be sexually faithful to each other.

2. Barbara freely acknowledges her jealousy and insecurity when Robert is involved with persons of the opposite sex. Robert acknowledges that he would be equally upset if Barbara became involved with someone else.

3. Therefore, the parties agree to discuss plans for activities that involve persons of the opposite sex when the other party is not involved, and when such activities are not directly a part of one's work.

4. They also agree to allow each other the power to veto such activities for a six-month period. Thus, if Robert's activities cause Barbara undue anxiety (even if they are innocent and/or helpful to his work), he will change his plans. The parties feel that they are currently in a financial position to forgo some of Robert's extra commissions if, in order to obtain them, he has to engage in social activities that make Barbara uncomfortable. At the same time, Barbara will try to become a more trusting person. However, since she has been deeply hurt by Robert's affair, this trust will have to be built over a period of time.

5. Realizing that trust is built by practical plans as well as by good intentions, the parties also agree to set aside one evening during each week and one evening each weekend to spend alone together. In addition, they will spend one evening each week at some social activity as a couple. The choice of what to do will be made on a weekly rotation basis, with one partner determining the weekday evening and the other the weekend and social activity each week. A calendar will be posted

two months in advance. Both parties will enter their plans on the large calendar in the kitchen.

Care and Use of the Home

1. The partners reject the concept that the responsibility for housework rests with the woman while the duties of home maintenance and repair rest with the man. They also reject the notion that children should be taken care of instead of sharing home maintenance tasks.

2. Therefore, the parties agree that all household tasks, including cooking and meal management, laundry, cleaning, gardening, car repair, shopping, etc., will be shared by *all* members of the household. The household work schedule now in effect (which assigns household tasks to us, our daughter Susan and our son Steven—until he goes to college in the fall) will be attached as a modifiable amendment to this agreement.

3. Because Robert has higher standards of cleanliness and home neatness than Barbara (and Susan and Steven), and because in the past conflicts have arisen over the condition of the home, the parties agree to continue their current practice of assigning one person the task of inspecting household work for cleanliness and neatness. Once a month, when Robert is inspector, we will conform to his standards. We will conform to the standards set by the three other inspectors on their weeks.

4. Each party has a room in the house for a study and/or bedroom and all matters regarding the care and activities within that room shall be the party's private concern.

Financial Arrangements

1. Barbara and Robert intend that their accumulation of assets and liabilities, wages, salaries, and other incomes during their 21 years of marriage represent an economic partnership of two equal partners. This shall be reflected in the ownership of property, and in the control of their income.

2. The parties therefore agree that these articles of their marriage contract shall replace the property laws of the state whereby Robert alone would be the sole owner of most of their property except the house, which is in joint tenancy.

3. To accomplish these aims all current (and future) property, wages, salaries, and other income, tangible and intangible assets (with

the exception of inheritances), and liabilities will be transferred to and held in joint tenancy with the right of survivorship.

4. The parties agree that all debts and loans against the joint assets will be mutually agreed upon, and co-signed by both parties.

5. The parties agree to designate each other full beneficiary of any benefits which they now own or may acquire during this marriage in insurance, retirement funds, or other co-signed benefits, with the exception of the following clause.

6. The parties have established trust funds for the college education of each of their children, Steven and Susan. These funds should be sufficient to cover tuition, books and basic room and board for four years. The student will be expected to cover other expenses through part-time or summer work. The children are also the beneficiaries of life insurance policies of $100,000 on Robert's life and $100,000 on Barbara's life.

7. The parties agree that in case of divorce the original sum of any inheritance will become the sole property of the inheritor. Any further profits or losses realized from an inheritance will be considered to be owned jointly and will be equally divided between the two parties.

8. Further, the parties agree that all other properties jointly owned and managed by the partnership will be equally divided in case of divorce.

Renewal and Resolving Conflicts

1. We agree to an annual review of the provisions of the contract, including the work schedule appendix, on or about the anniversary date of the execution of the contract.

2. We agree that if we have unresolved conflicts over any provisions of the contract, we will seek assistance from R. S., a licensed social worker and marriage counsellor, who has helped us to understand each other's point of view and to work things out in the past.

Contract 5: A Marriage Contract Between Two Middle-Aged Divorced Persons

Betty and Joe have each been married and divorced before, and each wants to avoid what he or she regards as the financial mistakes of the previous relationship.

Betty, a 34-year-old hair stylist at a neighborhood beauty parlor, has a six-year-old daughter, Lilly. Her ex-husband, who was ordered to pay her $200 a month in child support, remarried last year. He now has a son with his new wife, and continues to find excuses for not being able to pay Betty each month. Betty is furious (especially since she agreed to forgo alimony in exchange for his promise to help support Lilly), but she cannot afford to hire a lawyer or to take time off from her work to go to court to force him to pay. She feels she got the short end of the marriage and the divorce settlement, and she is determined never again to be dependent on a man. Betty has $6,000 in savings (which she got as her share from the sale of their house) and wants to be sure that "nobody can get their hands on that money."

Joe, a 37-year-old municipal bus driver, has two children from his previous marriage: Susie is 8, Tom is 11. Both children live with his former wife, and Joe pays her $300 a month child support. Joe wants and expects Betty to do most of the household chores (which he considers women's work). Betty does not mind doing the work, but she wants to feel it is appreciated and she wants to have something to show for it. They agree that Betty will earn and acquire a 12 percent interest in the house for each year of housework she performs until she owns a full one-half (50 percent) interest.

Betty and Joe are committed to a long-term relationship. However, they want to work out a plan to equalize what each puts into the relationship—financially and otherwise—so that neither is unduly vulnerable if the relationship is terminated. Since both have been divorced before, they are particularly concerned about providing for their own financial security and for the financial security of their children in the event of dissolution. They have devised a unique scheme for a reserve fund, which is essentially a type of self-insurance to help the parties in the event of death or divorce.

Financial Disclosure

1. Betty, a hair stylist, earns approximately $6,000 a year in take-home pay, or $500 a month. Because some of her monthly income comes from tips, she can count on only $400 a month. By court order, Betty should receive another $200 a month from her ex-husband to help pay for Lilly's support, but such payments as she has actually received average about $50 a month.

2. Joe, a municipal bus driver, earns $1,100 net (after taxes and other deductions) a month, but after child-support payments to his ex-wife of $300 per month he is left with take-home wages of about $800. His mortgage payments are $329 a month.

3. Betty has $6,000 invested in a savings account at American Savings, and a 1973 automobile worth about $2,000.

4. Joe has a vested pension from the city, a 1978 automobile, and $2,000 in savings. In 1974 he purchased a home for $53,000. He paid $13,000 down and took out a 30-year mortgage. The value of the house has increased to $106,000 so he has close to $70,000 equity in the house.

Financial Agreement

1. Each partner will retain whatever property he or she currently holds as his or her separate property (with exceptions as provided below).

2. All future income and acquisitions, from whatever source, including gifts or bequests, will be held as separate property.

3. Each partner is expected to pay for clothing, gifts, and other personal expenses from his or her separate property.

4. Each month each partner will retain $200 from his or her salary and contribute the remaining salary to a joint checking account. The money in this account will become community property. All checks written from this account will require both signatures.

5. The parties agree to use $225 per month from the joint account to pay Joe's former wife for the support of his two children. Joe will contribute the remaining $75 from his separate property.

6. Each month $150 will be transferred from the joint account to a reserve fund to be used primarily for the support of Betty's daughter in the event of divorce or the death of one party. The partners agree to appoint their friend Robert Trent trustee of the reserve fund. His duties shall be limited to ensuring (1) that the fund is kept in a high-interest account at a savings bank, and (2) that neither party draws on the account until the other party dies or a formal separation agreement is signed by both parties.

7. All other expenses (including food, laundry, car and furniture payments, entertainment, leisure activities, and travel) will be paid out of the joint checking account. Any surplus funds in the joint account at the end of each month will be transferred to the reserve fund.

8. Any advances made to either partner from the separate property of the other or from the community accounts will be considered loans to be repaid at the current treasury note rate of interest.

9. Each partner agrees to support and care for the other in the event of illness, disability, or unemployment while this agreement is in effect. Inasmuch as Joe's job provides comprehensive medical insurance, he will arrange medical coverage for both partners, and for Betty's daughter.

10. Each month $329 will be drawn from the joint account to pay for the mortgage on Joe's house. Because this money will be taken from community funds, and because Betty will be contributing more household services than Joe, Betty will acquire a share of the equity in the house according to the following schedule:

    a. Each month Betty will acquire a 1 percent interest in the house until she owns 50 percent.

    b. After six months, when she will own a 6 percent interest, the deed to the house will be changed to reflect Betty's part ownership.

    c. Thereafter Betty's ownership shall accumulate at the rate of 1 percent per month and shall be recorded at six-month intervals.

    d. Thus she will own 12 percent of the house at the end of one year, 24 percent at the end of two years, 36 percent at the end of three years, 48 percent at the end of four years and 50 percent at the end of the second month of the fifth year.

Housekeeping Responsibilities

Betty will have the responsibility for running and maintaining the household. She will do the grocery shopping, cooking, cleaning, laundry, etc. Joe agrees to wash the dishes two nights a week, to mow the lawn, and to repair broken or damaged items to the best of his ability.

Children

1. Both parties agree that Joe's children may live with them (or vacation with them) for up to two months and 10 weekends a year, and that the expenses thus incurred will be community expenses.

2. Further, the parties agree to be jointly responsible for the support of Betty's daughter so long as this agreement is in effect. During

that time her support will be provided by community funds. It is also agreed that community funds will be used to pay for her education if necessary.

3. Although Betty will have the major responsibility for taking care of Lilly, Joe agrees to participate in the following ways: he will be responsible for every other trip to the doctor and dentist, for taking care of her from 9 A.M. to 2 P.M. on Saturdays (to enable Betty to catch up on housework) and from 9 A.M. to 1 P.M. on Sundays so Betty can have the morning off. He also agrees to attend teacher conferences and open school week.

Termination

1. Upon separation, each party will retain her or his separate property.
2. All community property will be divided equally.
3. The house:

   a. If Joe wishes to retain the house as his residence, Betty will be obligated to allow him three months to secure a second mortgage or loan to buy out her share.
   b. The parties shall jointly select a real estate broker to set a fair market price for the house.
   c. If Joe does not wish to retain the house as his residence he shall give Betty the option of buying his share according to the above terms.

4. Neither party will have any responsibility to support the other after separation.
5. Upon termination the reserve fund will be divided as follows: 70 percent to Betty for Lilly's support, 30 percent to Joe. This should allow each party sufficient funds for the transitional period after divorce.

Special Provisions for Use and Division of Reserve Fund

1. *Educational trusts for children.* If the partnership is still in effect when Joe's son Tom graduates from high school, one-third of the reserve fund will be put into trust for their three children (Tom, Susie, and Lilly) to be used for their college education. The educational funds will be divided as follows: 40 percent to Tom, 30 percent to Susie, and 30 percent to Lilly. These differences are intended to reflect the fact that the accounts for Susie and Lilly will earn additional interest before

they are used. Each child will have the option of withdrawing the money at age 25 if he or she does not attend college.

2. *Division of the reserve fund.* When Joe reaches age 60, monthly contributions to the fund will cease and half of the remaining reserve fund may be withdrawn and divided equally between the parties for each to use as separate property. When Betty reaches age 60, half of the then remaining funds may be withdrawn and divided equally between the parties, as above. Similar withdrawals and divisions may be made when Joe reaches age 65, and when Betty reaches age 65. When Joe reaches age 70 all remaining funds may be withdrawn and divided.

Contract 6: An Alternative Life-Style Contract for a Homosexual Couple

Chris and Robin, a homosexual couple, have decided to enter into a household agreement after living together for several years. Chris is a sailboat enthusiast; Robin is a painter who has sold very few paintings. Both have worked on and off at various jobs such as waiting on tables, dishwashing, and doing clerical work. They have decided that in order for Chris to have time for sailing and Robin for painting, they will take turns supporting each other to afford each an opportunity to pursue his primary interest on a full-time basis. This is possible even though neither is able to make much money, inasmuch as both partners are content to lead frugal lives. Neither wants to father children.

Support

1. Chris and Robin each agree to take turns working six months a year to support the household. Robin will work from March to September so that Chris can have the summer for sailing. Chris will work from September to March. Each agrees to work at irregular jobs in order to earn enough money to cover their combined living expenses.

2. All household expenses and the personal expenses of both parties will be assumed by the party who is employed at the time.

3. In the event that Robin becomes financially successful as a painter and earns enough to support them both throughout the year at the equivalent of double their current annual income of $6,000 a year,

then Robin agrees to assume the responsibility for all living expenses. At that point Chris agrees to devote the equivalent of six months a year to managing Robin's work by talking to galleries, arranging exhibits, etc. However, if Robin becomes successful enough to hire a half- or full-time agent he will do so unless Chris decides he wants to continue in that capacity.

Property

1. Both partners will retain separately whatever property they presently hold.

2. Any property or income from property (including salary) which either acquires during the term of this agreement will become community property.

3. All community property will be jointly managed and controlled with the exception of Chris's sailboat and Robin's paintings, which will be managed and controlled by Chris and Robin, respectively. However, community funds will be used for supplies for both of these activities.

4. Income from the sale of Robin's paintings will be jointly managed and controlled.

5. All community funds will be kept in joint savings and checking accounts.

Housekeeping Responsibilities

Both parties will be responsible for their own cleanup and laundry. Cooking and other household chores will be assumed by the partner who is not employed at the time.

Medical and Health

Inasmuch as a serious accident or illness could jeopardize this agreement (and the parties' work plans), the parties agree to purchase medical, hospital, and disability insurance for each party. Even though such coverage will be costly and difficult to maintain in their current position, the parties view this insurance as of the utmost importance.

The parties also agree to name each other as beneficiary of any current or future insurance they may acquire.

Wills and Inheritance

Each party agrees to write a will leaving all his property to the other in the event that death should occur while this agreement is in effect.

Legal Relationship

The parties realize that in case of the death of either one of them the other might have difficulty establishing ownership of a jointly acquired asset and/or his share of the community property. They are also aware of, and concerned about, the possibility that their wills might be contested. For example, if Chris inherits a share of his father's estate and devises it to Robin , it is likely that in the event of Chris's death his sister would contest his will. Similarly, if Robin's paintings become valuable and he leaves his estate to Chris, his parents might contest his will. Since neither partner's family knows of the parties' relationship, and since they wish to maintain their privacy, the parties agree to take the following steps to try to ensure the enforcement of their property contract:

1. To write and sign this agreement before witnesses.
2. To hire an attorney to draft mutual wills and to have each party discuss the contents of his will (and sign it) before separate witnesses.
3. To record the title to Robin's paintings in both names whenever possible.
4. To hold all major assets as joint tenants with right of survivorship.
5. To keep all community funds in a joint bank account with right of survivorship.

Termination

1. If one party wants to end this relationship, both parties agree first to participate in three conciliation sessions with a mutually acceptable third party. If after conclusion of the three sessions one or both parties still desire termination, it will then take place after 60 days notice.

2. Upon separation, both parties will retain their separate property and all joint property will be divided equally.

3. No financial or other responsibilities will continue between the parties after separation and division of their community property.

Contract 7: A Contract in Lieu of Marriage Between Two Lawyers

Heather Johnson and William Rogers III are both practicing attorneys in Boston. Both are "established," professionally and financially. Heather is 38; William is 54. William's ex-wife, a magazine editor, and his two sons, a 30-year-old lawyer and a 28-year-old professor, are financially independent. The following contract was written before Heather and William began living together. It is entitled a "Contract Relating to the Terms and Conditions of Our Life Together."

Names

1. We both intend to continue to use the names we were given at birth.
2. We will each contribute equally to the naming of our children.
3. If we have only one child and it is a girl, she shall have Rogers as a last name and Johnson as a middle name. If it is a boy, he shall have Johnson as a last name and Rogers as a middle name.
4. If we have a second child, it shall be given the last and middle names not given to the first child.
5. If we have more than two children, we will agree on names prior to birth.

Domicile

1. Our joint and individual domiciles will be in Boston, Massachusetts, for the next four years.
2. Either of us is free to establish a separate, temporary residence within reasonable driving distance for a period of up to one year.
3. If we disagree as to domicile and we choose to live together in the place that one of us desires, after one year the person being accommodated will then accommodate the desires of the other for a similar period.

Commitment to Ourselves

1. Absent truly extraordinary circumstances, we agree to spend at least one evening a week enjoying each other — alone together. An evening begins at 7 P.M.

2. Absent truly extraordinary circumstances, we agree to spend at least three weekend days a month together enjoying each other.

Sex

1. We recognize the central importance of sex in human relationships and commit ourselves to putting time and creative energy into realizing our sexual potential.

2. We do not intend that our love and commitment to each other shall exclude other relationships in work, friendship, or sex.

3. We do intend that our relationship with each other shall be a primary one and that each other's feelings and needs should be a major consideration in our other actions.

4. We will tell each other when we have sex with other people, and we will make an effort to communicate honestly about all other important relationships in our lives.

Finances, Support and Income

1. We agree that so long as we continue to live together, we shall be mutually responsible for the support of each other.

2. We shall, from time to time, determine the amount and nature of our common expenses. We shall each contribute to our common fund an equal pro rata share of our earned income, prorated on the basis of the amount earned individually.

3. Each of us will have individual control over the income we earn individually, in excess of that contributed to the fund for common expenses. To the extent that we are able to provide it, each of us shall have $1,000 a month in personal spending money.

4. If one of us continues to work at a job that is less than satisfactory in order to meet a large portion of common expenses, that person should notify the other of his or her dissatisfaction. After one year, or another agreed upon period, the other person is obligated to earnestly seek work to meet a large portion of our common expenses. The complaining party (who has worked in a job that is well paid but otherwise unsatisfying) will then have the right to spend a similar period working

without concern for earning income to meet a large portion of common expenses.

5. After determining our common expenses, we shall distribute 20 percent of our remaining disposable income to socially useful causes.

6. Our current common expenses are approximately $80,000 a year (in 1978 dollars).

Children

1. We agree to attempt to have a child.

2. We will attempt to have additional children only after mutual agreement.

3. Any additional child will be subject to the same contractual provisions as our first child.

Child Raising

1. We will both have equal rights and responsibilities in relation to the raising of our child. To the degree that biology dictates a particular contribution in child raising, that contribution will be considered in determining the equality of our rights and responsibilities.

2. In deciding to bring a child into our lives, we commit ourselves to making the space to know and enjoy that person.

3. We will set definite limits for our child, limits that respect freedom and individuality to the greatest extent possible.

4. We hope that we can teach our child to know the joys of caring deeply for others as well as taking seriously the quality of his or her own life. We hope that our child will come to understand the world and act in a useful and just manner in it. We hope that our child will grow to experience and give love freely. We hope that our child will have a terrific sense of humor about it all.

5. Consistent with our other principles, we will be flexible about child raising and try to accommodate each other's outside needs and interests.

Child Support

1. To the extent that money can buy health and safety, we will place the highest priority on spending money to ensure the health and safety of our child.

2. To the extent that our child is able to enjoy the standard of living that we ourselves enjoy, we should share that standard of living with our child.

3. We believe that, in general, more democratically accessible experiences are likely to be of deeper educational value than less democratically accessible experiences. Specifically, we believe that public school education is educationally preferable, unless it poses a threat to our child's physical or emotional security. Within these principles, we would place the highest priority on providing our child with sound educational experiences.

4. While we are living together, money for child support should come out of our common fund.

5. If living apart, we will continue to provide child support on an equal, pro rata basis. Child support will be accorded high priority in our mutual and individual expenses.

Child Custody

1. In the event that we decide to separate or to have separate domiciles but continue to live in the same city or within commuting distance, one of us shall have custody of all children during school weeks, one weekend a month, and for one month during the summer. The other shall have custody during the rest of the time.

2. In the event that we decide to separate and live more than commuting distance apart, one of us will have custody during the school year and the other will have custody during the summer and most of Christmas vacation, if feasible.

3. We will try, if at all possible, to reach decisions on child custody by mutual agreement. The best interest of the child will be the major factor in the decision. The child's best interests will be judged by all the relevant factors, including: our wishes as the child's parents; the wishes of the child; the relationship of the child to each of us, to any siblings, and to any other person who may significantly affect the child's best interests; the child's adjustment to home, school, and community; the physical and mental health of everyone involved.

4. If we cannot agree on custody, we will determine by random lot which parent gets custody at what time.

Purchase of Homes

1. We are already in the process of purchasing a townhouse for our joint domicile in Boston as equal tenants in common, with each of

us owning a 50 percent share. Each of us will contribute 50 percent of the down payment and settlement costs. For tax purposes William will pay the loan fee and a larger percentage of the monthly mortgage payments because he is in a higher tax bracket and this will result in greater joint savings. However, this will in no way affect our equal ownership. Heather will assume the cost of the telephone, utilities, and housekeeper to effect a proportionately equal contribution to our joint expenses.

2. We plan to purchase a second house on Cape Cod by mutual consent, as equal tenants in common.

Conditions of Separation

1. We agree to stay together, absent intense pain, for four years or until our child is three years old, whichever is earlier.

2. After that time, we can separate at any time that we freely and mutually agree to do so.

3. In the event that one of us wants to separate and the other does not, we agree to:

a. Give explicit notice of the desire to separate.
b. Work to mend our relationship for a period of six months after such notice.
c. Make time for each other during that period, and seek professional assistance if either of us believes it would be useful.

4. We recognize that the process of growth is the process of change. We respect each other's freedom and separate character. We hope that we will always freely choose to grow together, but we recognize that we may not. We agree always to try to treat each other gently, politely, and with consideration. We agree that, even if we separate, we will do it in a loving way.

5. Our common property will be divided upon separation. We will each leave with the possessions we brought with us into the relationship, plus any gifts given to us individually. Property purchased with common funds, or given to both of us, will be apportioned equally.

6. The equity in both houses will be divided equally. However, if one of us wishes to remain in our residence he or she shall have the option of purchasing the other party's share. If both of us wish to remain we will draw lots to decide which of us will have the option. The other party will have first option on our summer house.

Amendments

1. Any provision in this contract may be amended by mutual agreement.

2. We agree to review this contract at least once a year at the time of our anniversary.

3. We recognize that either or both of us may enter into contracts with other important people in our lives, whenever we mutually agree. At such times, we will review this contract and amend it as appropriate.

Enforcement

1. This contract is entered into with the firmest intention that we will be mutually and legally bound by the specific provisions of each contract.

2. In our professional judgment, we have entered into a judicially enforceable contractual relationship.

3. Each article and each provision should be treated as severable.

4. It is our firm intention not to seek judicial enforcement of any of the terms of this contract, or judicial resolution of disputes concerning any of the subjects covered by these agreements, but rather to be bound by the decisions of our arbitrators, as specified in clauses 5–7 below.

5. Our arbitrators shall be Barbara Cohn, John Low, and Judy Stevens. In the event that one of these arbitrators shall be unable or unwilling to continue to serve in this capacity, the other two arbitrators shall select a third person after consultation with us.

6. Either of us may submit to the arbitrators any question which we cannot resolve by mutual agreement involving the meaning or enforcement of any term of this contract.

7. While we continue to be a couple, the arbitrators may provide us with advice and aid in conciliation of disputes. After separation or breakdown, we shall be bound by any decision of the majority of our arbitrators with regard to the terms and conditions of this contract.

Contract 8: A Relationship Contract for a Couple About to Have a Child Together

Mona and Alex have been living together for three years in Mendecino, California, a rural artisan community on the northern California coast. They have no intention of marrying because they regard marriage as a bourgeois and bureaucratic institution. However, they are about to have a child together and want to declare and celebrate their love and commitment to each other.

Their contract* reflects their moral and emotional commitment and focuses on behavioral norms and ways of relating. Property and financial matters, clearly of secondary importance in the minds of this couple, are left somewhat vague.

Statement of Intent

1. We are writing this contract at this time because we have chosen to have a child together and want to declare our commitment to each other and to that child.

2. This contract is an affirmation of our continuing love for each other. We want to make our relationship more open, stronger, and more enduring still.

3. We expect to continue to grow together and individually in this relationship and will work to create an environment in which both types of growth will flourish.

4. We want the companionship, the mutual nurturing, and the responsibility that come with a primary relationship; we also desire our autonomy as separate and complete persons, needing individual space, time, and freedom.

5. We declare ourselves to be of legal age, free and independent persons, in full control of our lives, with no obligations that prevent our entering fully into this agreement.

Relating to Each Other

1. We agree that our relationship will be primary: we will invest our time and energy in each other and in the relationship.

2. We agree to treat each other with esteem and affection through ongoing companionship and sharing.

3. We each agree to be responsible for our own feelings, needs, and attitudes, acknowledging that while each does influence the other, neither is responsible for keeping the other happy.

4. We agree to give support, comfort, and nurturance when the other needs and asks for such, though never fostering an unhealthy dependency.

*Large parts of this contract have been adopted from the Equalog Contract I™ developed by Paschal and Janette Baute, 6200 Winchester Road, Lexington, Kentucky 40511, © 1977, and are reprinted with their permission.

5. We agree that we shall not expect the other to guess our feelings, wants, or intentions, and therefore we shall ask directly for everything we want from the other; further, if we do not ask, we have no right to resent not receiving.

Relating to Others

1. We agree that we may each have friends of either sex. However, neither of us shall select close personal friends from the special friends of the other.

2. We agree that we will regard private and personal matters between us as privileged communication and will not discuss them with others.

3. We agree to protect each other's good name and reputation with relatives, friends, and others in the community.

4. We agree not to embarrass each other in public by any distasteful behavior, including sarcasm or uninvited teasing, and that excuses such as being angry or being under the influence of alcohol do not remove the responsibility for such behavior.

Children

1. We each agree to take responsibility to ensure that no unplanned pregnancies result from our union, and to inform the other of contraceptive measures employed.

2. Inasmuch as we are now expecting our first child, we want to commit ourselves to 18 years of love, nurturance, care, and protection for that child.

3. However, we also agree to keep our relationship primary after the child is born and to resist the erosion of our relationship by the consuming demands of a child.

4. We agree to share equally any and all aspects of child rearing. Moreover, each parent will accept the responsibility for his or her relationship with each child.

5. We agree that a united front is better for children, but that we have a right to disagree about what is best for the child. However, we each agree not to prejudice a child toward the other. We further agree not to make a child a confidant.

Finances

1. We agree to regard our relationship as a financial partnership.

2. We agree to share equally all our income, property, and re-sources.

3. Any assets that either of us acquires in the future will be owned and used jointly.

4. If anything should happen to either one of us, the other pledges to use whatever he or she inherits for our child.

Privacy and Time Apart

1. We agree to allow each other privacy—time and space apart from the other—even though this may threaten the sense of control; that some time apart shall be private time, used at one's personal discretion, without requirement of detailed explanation.

2. We agree to the following specific arrangements:

    a. Before we have a child each partner may make separate plans for Monday and Tuesday. These are days set apart and we will not question each other about what we did, whom we saw, etc.

    b. After our child is born Mona will retain this schedule. Alex will have the same privileges on Wednesday and Thursday.

    c. Each of us will also take two weeks a year to go away alone and do as he or she wishes.

Resolving Disagreements

1. We agree to talk about our differences at the invitation of either party.

2. We accept some conflicts and differences of opinion as natural and to be used as occasions for growth.

3. We agree to try to resolve differences that cause either of us pain and anguish.

4. If either party initiates a discussion, the other party will be obligated to participate and try to resolve the disagreement.

5. On these occasions we will avoid judging and fault-finding and will sincerely strive to resolve our differences.

Consideration of Separation/Dissolution

1. We agree that since we are seriously involved we will not separate lightly. We will each make a serious effort to understand the proc-

ess whereby we grew apart and our own part in it. And we will allow time for healing.

2. We agree that threats of separation or leaving are ploys of intimidation and are to be avoided. This awareness is especially important because we want to maintain confidence and trust in the endurance of this relationship.

3. Should one partner decide upon separation and the other oppose it, we agree to participate fully in six months of counseling sessions with the professional person of our mutual choice. We agree that no unilateral decisions will be made until after the counseling period.

4. We agree that if we separate each party will foster the best possible relationship between our child and the other parent. We will not attempt to sway a child and we will not use a child to gain power over the other parent or to selfishly support our own bad feelings.

5. We agree that the custodial parent shall make visits by the other parent convenient and regular. The noncustodial parent agrees to stay involved with each child and to assume care of the children at least two days per week (or to arrange for responsible caretaking for those days). Each agrees to avoid any sabotage of the other parent's care and discipline. We agree to make every effort to stay in geographical proximity until the children are 15 years old, and if this is not possible, the noncustodial parent will have charge of the children for two months in the summer of each year.

6. We agree that figures settled upon for maintenance and/or child support should be reconsidered each year because of current inflation rates, cost-of-living increases, and changes in the financial status of each person. We agree that there should be no negligence whatsoever in these payments.

7. Each partner agrees to maintain a $100,000 life insurance policy on himself/herself for each child until the child reaches the age of 18, as assurance that the child's support will not be cut off by the death of one parent.

Contract 9: A Contract Between a Widower and Divorcee, with Provisions for Pay for Household and Child-Care Services

Tom, a 50-year-old plumber, owns a lucrative plumbing contracting business. Two years ago his wife died, leaving him with two children, now 10 and 14. Tom met Linda at a Parents Without

Partners meeting and they have been seeing each other regularly for the past year. They care for each other deeply, and have recently decided to live together. Neither of them wants to marry, but both want the companionship and "family" the other can provide.

Tom's children are having problems in school, needing more attention than he is able to give them while running his business full time. Linda is recently divorced and the mother of an 11-year-old girl. She finds herself unable to secure a satisfactory job after 15 years as a full-time housewife with no college education. She wants to return to school to study accounting, but cannot afford it; in fact, she is having an exceedingly difficult time managing financially.

Linda is willing to stay home and care for the house and both Tom's and her children, but she wants to be compensated for her work and to be assured that she will not later be penalized by the loss of Social Security and other benefits. Tom and Linda agree to a contract that will assure Linda of money and employment benefits in exchange for her full-time housework and child care.

Financial Arrangement

1. Linda will work in the home full time, supervising the children and taking care of all domestic chores (including cleaning, laundry, cooking, entertainment, and gardening) for a beginning salary of $250 per week.

2. Linda's salary will be subject to nondiscretionary readjustments tied to changes in the cost of living, and merit increases at Tom's discretion.

3. Linda will be entitled to two days off each week. She can spend these days either away from the home or in the home. If she wants to spend part of her days off learning bookkeeping and accounting, Tom promises to make his employees' time available to her for at least two hours a week.

4. Tom will make Social Security payments for Linda, as an employee. He will arrange a private pension plan for her, and will arrange for complete medical and hospital insurance for her and her daughter.

Property and Support

1. Each party will retain her or his separate property.

2. Tom will provide a house, its furnishings, and a car for their joint use, but he will retain title and ownership of these assets.

3. Tom will support the family and will have full responsibility for support of his own two children; Linda will have no financial support obligations with regard to Tom's children.

4. Tom will have full responsibility for supporting Linda's child during the time this agreement is in effect, but if it terminates this obligation will end.

Sexual Relations

Sexual relations will be by mutual consent only. Because Tom has had a vasectomy, no birth control measures will be necessary. Neither party wants additional children.

Vacations, Entertainment, and Education

1. Tom agrees to take Linda on a three-week vacation in Europe during their first summer together, and thereafter they will arrange at least one three-week vacation per year (not necessarily in Europe).

2. Linda agrees to entertain Tom's friends and/or relatives at dinner at least twice a month.

3. Tom will pay Linda's tuition costs for two classes per semester at a community college until she earns an accounting degree.

Termination

1. Either party can terminate this agreement by giving the other party a 90-day notice.

2. If Linda terminates the agreement, she will be entitled to severance pay at the rate of one month for every year the agreement has been in effect.

3. If Tom terminates the agreement, Linda will be entitled to severance pay at the rate of three months for every year together.

4. Tom will take out a bond to insure his ability to make severance payments.

5. Neither party will have any additional responsibility toward the other or the other's children after termination. Both will retain their own separate property.

Religion

Linda agrees to take the children to church at least twice a month.

Death

Each party agrees to assume full responsibility for the other's children in the event the other dies during the time this agreement is in effect. Tom agrees to make ample provision in his will for the support of Linda and the children.

Contract 10: A Separate Property Contract to Avoid the Potential Consequences of the <u>Marvin</u> Decision

Judith Rose and Joseph Gans are both full professors at an Ivy League university. They have been living together for six years in a house which they own as joint tenants. After reading about the California Supreme Court decision in *Marvin* v. *Marvin*, they decided to make explicit their intentions with respect to property. The following excerpts from their agreement, drafted by an attorney, contain provisions to protect each party against potential "Marvin" claims.

Independent Persons

1. Judith Rose and Joseph Gans are two independent persons.
2. Each of the parties has a secure job as a professor at a major university and has achieved a measure of material independence.
3. The parties have entered a relationship in consideration of mutual affection with no expectation of material or economic gain.

Intention to Define Property Rights

1. The parties intend to define and clarify their respective rights to the property of the other and to their jointly owned property.
2. The parties intend *to avoid* any interests which, except for the operation of this agreement, they might otherwise acquire in the property of the other as a consequence of their relationship.

Financial Disclosure

The parties to this agreement have fully and completely disclosed to each other the nature, extent, and probable value of all their separate properties, estates, and expectancies. A complete summary of this disclosure is attached as Exhibit A.

Intent that Property Remain Separate

1. The parties desire that all property presently owned by either of them of whatsoever nature and wheresoever located and all income derived therefrom and all increases in the value thereof, shall be and remain their respective separate property, except as otherwise specified below.

2. The following events shall under no circumstances be evidence of intent by either party or of an agreement between the parties to transmute their separate property interests into jointly owned property:

   a. The taking of title to property, whether real or personal, in joint tenancy or in any other joint or common form
   b. The designation of one party by the other as a beneficiary of his or her estate
   c. The commingling by one party, of his or her separate funds or property, with jointly owned funds or property, or with the separate funds or property of the other party
   d. The joint occupation of a separately owned residence

Definition of Jointly Owned Property of the Parties

1. The parties own the following property as joint tenants with the right of survivorship:

   a. Their residence at 608 State Street
   b. A Steinway piano located at the above address
   c. Paintings and art objects as specified in Exhibit B
   d. A 26-foot sailboat as specified in Exhibit C
   e. Two automobiles as specified in Exhibit D

2. Henceforth, except as described in #1 above, and as the parties may otherwise specify in writing, the *salaried* earnings of the parties from the university (but not their income from other sources) and the property acquired by the parties from their salaried earnings shall constitute their only jointly owned property.

Mutual Release of Marvin v. Marvin Rights

It is mutually agreed that each party waives, discharges, and releases any and all claims and rights, actual, inchoate, or contingent, in law and equity which he or she may acquire in the separate property of the other by reason of such relationship, including, but not limited to:

a. The right to a family allowance
b. The right to a probate homestead
c. The rights or claims of dower, courtesy, or any statutory substitutes therefor as provided by the statutes of the state in which the parties or either of them may die domiciled or in which they may own real property
d. The right of election to take against the will of the other
e. The right to declare a homestead in the separate property of the other
f. The right to act as administrator of the estate of the other

Modification or Waiver

This agreement shall continue in force until it is modified by a written agreement executed by both parties.

Execution and Acknowledgment

In witness whereof, the parties hereto have executed this agreement on the 6th day of July, 1979.

PART IV

Contracts and the Evolving Law

This section of the book examines the legal consequences of alternatives to traditional legal marriage. While its primary focus is on contractual alternatives it also reviews the legal consequences of living together without a contract.

Chapter 13 considers contracts between husbands and wives. It first analyzes the traditional legal treatment of contracts between married spouses, and then explores the recent developments in the case law. In the last decade a number of courts have begun to recognize the legitimate interests of husbands and wives who wish to arrange their relationships by contract.

The following two chapters consider the legal consequences of the major alternative to marriage: unwed cohabitation. Chapter 14 reviews the legal consequences of living together without a contract, while Chapter 15 analyzes the legal consequences of living together *with* a contract; it examines the effects of a contract on unwed cohabitation.

Chapter 14 begins with a review of the sociological data on the growing incidence of cohabitation between unmarried adults. It then investigates the legal consequences of cohabitation and the wide variety of state and federal regulations that negatively affect cohabiting couples both during an ongoing relationship and at the point of dissolution.

Chapter 15 then analyzes the extent to which a contract improves the legal situation of unwed cohabitants. It too begins with a review of the traditional law and its refusal to recognize the validity of contracts between unmarried men and women. The second part of the chapter explores recent developments in the law, spurred by the 1975 California Supreme Court decision in *Marvin v. Marvin*. The cases that follow *Marvin* have drastically improved the prospects for a man and woman who wish to order their relationship by contract—whether in writing or by oral agreement. The chapter ends with an exploration of the evolving case law and prospects for the future enforcement of intimate contracts like those proposed in this book.

CHAPTER 13

Contracts Between Husbands and Wives

Since no existing legislation authorizes the type of contract we have proposed within a legal marriage, the possibility of securing judicial enforcement of these contracts must be appraised in light of precedents established in the courts. This chapter undertakes that task.

The first half of the chapter focuses on the legal tradition: it reviews the traditional law, and examines the traditional standards for reviewing agreements between husbands and wives. While the courts have historically refused to enforce most contracts between husbands and wives, this traditional judicial attitude has clearly begun to change. Some dramatic shifts in judicial rulings in recent years suggest that these contracts are now increasingly likely to be recognized as valid and binding.

The second half of the chapter focuses on new developments in the law. It begins with a review of the five cases that have established the new doctrine of recognizing fairly negotiated contracts between spouses. We then examine the courts' new standards for reviewing these contracts and contrast the likely results under contract law standards versus family law standards of review. The chapter ends with a discussion of the advantages of contract law doctrines.

Although this chapter focuses on contracts between husbands and wives, it inevitably touches on some of the issues that are examined in Chapter 15 which deals with contracts between unwed cohabitants. In order to avoid duplication, we shall postpone discussion of the future prospects for both kinds of contracts until the end of Chapter 15.

The Traditional Law

A contract between a husband and a wife was regarded as an impossibility in common law because husband and wife were considered to be a single entity and the law did not recognize one-party contracts.[1] The Married Woman's Property Acts in the nineteenth century granted married women limited power to contract, and thereafter certain kinds of contractual agreements between husbands and wives became widely accepted.[2] However, two basic restrictions on all contracts between husbands and wives were maintained: first, no contract could alter the essential elements of the marital relationship, and second, no contract could be made in contemplation of divorce, other than at the time of marital separation.*

Contracts May Not Alter the Essential Elements of Marriage

A basic legal doctrine, repeated over and over in the annals of family law, is that "a bargain between married persons or persons contemplating marriage to change the essential incidents of marriage is illegal."[3] The two provisions in the traditional marriage contract which the courts consistently considered as "essential obligations" were the husband's duty to support his wife, and the wife's duty to serve her husband.

The courts have dealt with these issues primarily when spouses have sought either to eliminate one of these essential obligations (for example, by an agreement that the husband will not have to support the wife) or to ensure payment to one spouse for performing an essential obligation (usually by an agreement to pay the wife for her domestic services). In the first instance, the contract was voided because it violated public policy; in the second, the contract was

*These "separation agreements" are discussed further on page 342.

voided for lack of consideration—that is, the lack of a fair exchange. If, for example, a wife is already bound to perform domestic services by law, her husband gains nothing in exchange for a promise to pay her. In addition, a party cannot legally contract to perform that which she or he is already bound by law to do.[4]

Contracts that relieved the husband of his obligation to support his wife were deemed to violate public policy because they subjected society to the potential burden of supporting the wife. The courts' rationale for refusing to enforce these contracts is articulated in a 1908 Wisconsin decision:

> The law requires a husband to support, care for, and provide comforts for his wife in sickness, as well as in health . . . . The husband cannot shirk [this requirement], even by contract with his wife, because the public welfare requires that society be thus protected so far as possible from the burden of supporting those of its members who are not ordinarily expected to be wage earners, but may still be performing some of the most important duties pertaining to the social order. Husband and wife . . . cannot vary the personal duties and obligations to each other which result from the marriage contract itself.[5]

The courts have applied the same rationale to void contracts that tried merely to modify the husband's duty of support, regardless of the wife's ability to support herself or the parties' expectations. For example, in the 1974 Illinois case of *Eule* v. *Eule*,[6] a woman previously married six times and a man previously married nine times (three times to each other) decided to marry each other for the fourth time. Prior to their fourth marriage, they executed an agreement that stated their uncertainty about the success of their marriage. They fully disclosed their assets (the husband was worth $600,000, the wife $45,000) and both parties waived their respective rights to legal support in the event of separation or divorce during their first seven years of marriage, regardless of fault. Their agreement stipulated that the wife would receive $50,000 at the time of the husband's death. The couple separated 18 months later, and Mrs. Eule asked for temporary alimony. The court decided the "waiver clause" was invalid, because the husband had sought to avoid his legal duty of support.

Contracts that alter the wife's obligation to provide domestic services have similarly been invalidated in court. The issue has been raised in cases in which a husband agreed either to pay his wife for her domestic services or to reimburse her with a share of a farm or family business. For example, in the 1961 Iowa Supreme Court case of *Youngberg* v. *Holstrom*, the court held "It is well settled that a husband's agreement to pay for services within the scope of the marital relation is without consideration and contrary to public policy."[7] Similarly, in a 1968 North Carolina case, the court held that farm work and caring for the husband's sick relatives were duties for which the wife could not recover payment. "Under the law," the court declared, "a husband has the right to the services of his wife as a wife, and this includes his right to her society and her performance of household and domestic duties."[8]

The courts have traditionally defined the wife's duty very broadly, assuming that all her labor in any family enterprise—not only in the home, but also on a farm or in a family business—"belongs" to her husband. Thus, in a 1974 Wisconsin case the judge ruled that a business operated by both spouses as a partnership belonged only to the husband, because the wife's efforts constituted the "discharge of her wifely obligations" rather than the acts of a business partner.[9]

Even assuming the validity of the rule that prohibits payment for the wife's "normal" domestic services, there appears to be little rational or legal basis for invalidating a contract that provides a wife payment for services outside the scope of usual domestic obligations.[10] In fact, in examining such cases, one begins to suspect that in many instances the courts have used the rationale of "public policy" or "lack of consideration" to invalidate contracts that seemed to them questionable for entirely different reasons. For example, in many of these cases the husband has died and the wife seeks to recover on an alleged oral contract, claiming her husband promised to leave her money or property in his will. In other cases a vigorous disagreement has arisen between the two parties regarding the terms (or even the existence) of an alleged oral contract. Still others involve contracts not negotiated at "arm's length" that would, if enforced, result in an injustice. Thus it seems the courts have relied on the dubious rationale of upholding the essential obligations of marriage to invalidate contracts that they viewed as dubious or unjust.

But the issues raised in these cases are by no means unique to contracts between husbands and wives, and sound legal principles have been developed outside family law to handle them. The contract law standards used to examine alleged oral contracts, disputed oral contracts, and contracts that unjustly enrich one party could easily be applied to marriage contracts as well. The use of these relatively enlightened contract doctrines would certainly be preferable to reliance on the outmoded family law doctrine that "a bargain to change the essential incidents of marriage is illegal."

Although courts have been scrupulous in preventing spouses from contracting to alter the husband's duty to support and the wife's duty to provide domestic services, they have allowed wider latitude with regard to marital property. For example, in California, couples are allowed to make agreements reversing or modifying the characterization of either separate or community property.[11] They can also transfer or agree to transfer property, waive property rights in each other's estates, and provide for each other by will.[12]

Thus persons with property have gained considerable freedom to contract concerning some of the economic aspects of their relationships. The practice of allowing couples to contract about property but not about support, however, not only seems arbitrary but in fact may produce discriminatory results. For obvious reasons, the distinction operates to disadvantage couples who possess little or no property—that is, by and large, working- and middle-class couples.

The designation of sex-stereotyped "duties" as "essential incidents of marriage" is also questionable. Under recent developments in the law of equal protection, husbands alone can no longer be solely responsible for support during marriage any more than following divorce.* The same analysis should apply to service obligations. Both would surely be in violation of the proposed Equal Rights Amendment as well. Further, while it is traditionally argued that allowing husbands and wives to contract regarding their relationship promotes inflexibility, it is clear that forcing them to accept a relationship whose fundamental structure is dictated by the state is far more inflexible.

Contracts May Not Contemplate or Encourage Divorce

Just as legally married couples may wish to enter into enforceable contracts altering the traditional sex-stereotyped roles within marriage, they may wish to negotiate agreements to provide for support and property in the event of divorce. Such agreements have traditionally been unenforceable because: "A bargain to obtain a divorce or the effect of which is to facilitate a divorce is illegal."[13]

*Orr v. Orr, 440 U.S. 268 (1979) which is discussed in Chapter 2, page 44.

Thus if a husband and wife wanted to establish the amount of alimony or maintenance that one spouse would receive in the event of a dissolution, or if they wanted to agree beforehand that no alimony would be awarded, their agreement would invariably be held invalid. Similarly, an agreement to divide their property in a specific way, or an agreement according one spouse a specified amount of money in lieu of a property claim, would almost always be unenforceable in court.

An exception to this rule has allowed couples to contract *after* they have decided to separate or divorce. The rationale for this exception was that since the spouses had already agreed to separate, their contract could no longer be an incentive to divorce.[14] In addition, because the court could determine their financial arrangements upon separation, it was thought "that the parties should be permitted to enter into a fair agreement between themselves covering the same things upon which they could obtain relief in court."[15] Finally, courts assumed that only at the point of separation could the parties reasonably predict and contract for their future.

The general rule, however, has been that antenuptial agreements (contracts made before marriage) or postnuptial contracts (contracts made after the date of marriage) cannot include provisions for divorce.

Apparently, two concerns underlie this rule: provisions for divorce are thought (1) to encourage divorce and (2) to facilitate collusion in the manufacture of grounds for divorce.

Fear of encouraging divorce is illustrated by the 1968 North Carolina case of *Mathews* v. *Mathews* in which a husband promised to give everything he had to his wife (and their children) if he ever left her. The court held the agreement unenforceable because it encouraged the wife to "goad the husband into a separation":

> If such an agreement as the one alleged by respondent were enforceable, it would induce the wife to goad the husband into separating from her in order that the agreement could be put into effect and she could strip him of all of his property. Our society has been built around the home, and its perpetuation is essential to the welfare of the community. And the law looks with disfavor upon an agreement which will encourage or bring about a destruction of the home.[16]

Here again, one suspects that the court simply relied on a convenient excuse to invalidate a contract it deemed "unfair" for other reasons.

A similarly circuitous rationale is evident in a 1973 Iowa case, *In re Gudenkauf,*[17] in which a couple signed an antenuptial agreement that precluded either party from acquiring any rights in the property of the other by virtue of their marriage. Their agreement was intended in part to prevent the wife from receiving alimony in the event of a divorce. Thirteen years later the marriage dissolved and the wife, then 63, sought alimony. The court granted her request and held the antenuptial contract void as contrary to public policy because it facilitated and encouraged the husband to file for divorce.

There are three problems with the courts' voiding of these contracts "because they encourage divorce." First, if such a contract gives one party a financial inducement to seek a divorce, it must give the other party an equally strong incentive to preserve the marriage; thus it cannot serve *only* to encourage divorce. Second, by allowing advance agreement on issues of importance, the contract may promote marital harmony and may even facilitate marriages that otherwise would not occur. For instance, a very wealthy man might hesitate to marry unless he could be sure his assets would not be dissipated by a divorce.[18]

The third and major fallacy in the antidivorce rationale is the assumption that it is sound public policy to discourage planning for the contingency of divorce, irrespective of the parties' needs. Even though the state has a legitimate interest in fostering and protecting marriage and in trying to encourage spouses to live together, most states no longer discourage divorce when the relations between husband and wife have broken down and "the legitimate objects of matrimony have been utterly destroyed."[19] Liberalized divorce laws and the rising divorce rate reflect the increased acceptance of divorce for marriages that are not satisfactory. In this context it seems reasonable to expect the state to allow couples to make realistic plans for the possibility of divorce.

The second reason courts have annunciated for prohibiting contracts in contemplation of divorce is to prevent parties from fabricating grounds for divorce in order to dissolve a marriage when they would not be legally entitled to do so.[20] However, the widespread adoption of no-fault divorce laws, which abolish the requirement that one must show "fault" to obtain a divorce, has greatly diminished the relevance and likelihood of this kind of collusion. By 1980 only two states (Illinois and South Dakota) still retained fault as the *only* basis for divorce.* Other states have either abolished all grounds for divorce or added a no-fault option, thus allowing the parties the freedom to determine when to dissolve their marriage. Hence the fear of collusion to dissolve a marriage without legal grounds is clearly an outmoded reason for voiding these contracts. Parties to other kinds of relationships are allowed to anticipate and provide for dissolution;[21] the state should similarly encourage forethought and planning in the marital arena.

Traditional Standards of Review

In addition to the above limits on contracts between husbands and wives, the courts have typically subjected antenuptial contracts to standards more rigorous than those traditionally applied in contract law because they are alert to the special possibility of fraud or unconscionability in the negotiation of such contracts,[22] and the likelihood of hardships resulting from changed circumstances.

Fraud and Unconscionability

The courts have viewed husband–wife contracts with caution because of the fear that one spouse, typically the husband, will have greater financial experience and business acumen than the other, and will take unfair advantage of a partner "blinded by love." For example, if a contract is drafted by the husband's lawyer, and is not clearly explained to the wife, and if the wife has no lawyer of her own to advise her, the court is likely to put the burden on the husband to prove that his wife's consent was fairly obtained.

Of course all contracts are void if they have been obtained through fraud, duress, or undue influence in the original negotiation.[23] Nevertheless, because some courts have feared that contracts between intimates are especially vulnerable to such subversion, they have used the potential for abuse as a justification for refusing to uphold contracts between husbands and wives.

Other courts have been willing to review husband–wife contracts, but have imposed more stringent standards of review than those that are normally required for commercial contracts. As Professor Homer Clark explains, "many courts take the view that pro-

---

*In 1980 Pennsylvania was the most recent state to add irretrievable breakdown to its other grounds for divorce. 23 P.S. Sec. 201.

spective spouses are in a *confidential relationship* . . . [in which] a special trust or reliance is placed by one of the parties on the other."[24] The standards for reviewing contracts in confidential or fiducial relationships stand half way between the general contract law standards and traditional family law standards. Contract law standards typically require great deference to the private choices and decisions of the contractors. On the other hand, a substantive review of the contract is characteristic of areas dominated by public policy, such as family law. As Professor Marjorie Shultz notes, contracts in confidential relationships, such as the relationship between an attorney and a client, the executor of an estate and the beneficiary, and between a corporate officer and a corporation, are subject to a vigorous review that includes a substantive review for fairness which is atypical for contract law. For example, when a corporate officer sells property to the corporation, the substance of the contract (i.e., the fairness of the price) may be reviewed. Thus contracts between those in a confidential relationship require a middle tier standard of review in which courts consider substantive questions of fairness as well as the procedural questions of fraud and duress typically posed by contract law standards.

Thus, when examining contracts between husbands and wives, as in other confidential relationships, the courts have typically imposed "an affirmative duty upon each spouse to disclose his or her financial status" as a condition to enforcement.[25]* In addition, each spouse must fully understand the legal consequences of the agreement. As Professor Homer Clark explains, the courts have typically required that the husband

> . . . make a full disclosure of the extent of his property and of the amount the wife is to receive at the time the agreement is made. Furthermore, many courts create a presumption that the agreement is unfair, and the husband loses unless he can rebut the presumption. He may do this by proof that he made a full disclosure, that the wife had independent legal advice, and that she executed the agreement with

*However, as Professor Marjorie Shultz notes, the standards for disclosure are in the process of change in contract law. Expertise or unequal access to information is increasingly being seen as providing one party with an unfair advantage in contractual negotiations. While the old norm for disclosure in contract law allowed the omission of information as long as the information relayed was correct, recent decisions indicate increased sensitivity to the possibility of fraud through omission. Similarly, the courts are now recognizing that an unfair advantage may be obtained through knowledge, so that unequal access to information may establish a more stringent burden of disclosure.

full understanding of its implications. In some states proof of either full disclosure or independent advice is sufficient.[26]*

While the language of these requirements suggests that they seek to protect the wife, that is clearly a result of the woman's traditionally inferior position with respect to both assets and financial experience. It is the weaker party, of whatever sex, who is protected.

It would seem, then, that the courts have already developed the doctrinal tools necessary to handle problems of fraud or unconscionability that may arise in antenuptial or postnuptial agreements. Concern about these issues should therefore not serve to bar more widespread recognition of legitimate contracts between husbands and wives.

Hardship from Changed Circumstances

A second concern expressed by courts wary of contracts between husbands and wives has been that a contractual bargain may cause hardship for one or both parties if their circumstances change. The courts have traditionally cited this concern in voiding contracts between spouses that provide for financial arrangements in the future.[27] As the courts have reasoned, even the most scrupulously fair negotiations, carried out with full disclosure of the assets of both parties and with sound legal advice for both parties, can result in a contract that, although fair at the time of negotiation, may be unfair years later owing to intervening events.

Once again, there is a precedent in contract law for dealing with such difficulties. At common law, to be sure, the difficulty of performing one's contractual obligations did not discharge the duty of a promissor. Today, however, under the approach accepted in most American courts, impossibility of performance may well release a party from a contract.[28] Although the general rule is that difficulty or improbability of accomplishment without financial loss is not sufficient to release a party from a contract,[29] this is a rapidly

---

*Clark notes that "in most cases where the agreement makes inadequate provision for the wife, the husband is unable to rebut the presumption and the agreement is held invalid. In the rare case where there is full disclosure and understanding of the agreement on the wife's part, but where the consideration is still inadequate, *the wife's bad bargain is enforced against her.*" Homer Clark, *The Law of Domestic Relations* (St. Paul, Minn.: West Publishing Company, 1968), pp. 524–25 (emphasis added).

changing area of contract law and there is a growing tendency to apply more liberal standards to commercial contracts involving severe financial loss.[30] These newly articulated contract doctrines seem particularly appropriate for application to marriage contracts. For example, if the supervening events that make performance impracticable are willfully or negligently caused by one party, the burden will fall on him or her;* where neither is at fault, the burden may be apportioned.[31]

New Trends in the Law

In recent years, courts in Florida, Illinois, Oregon, Nevada, and California have adopted a much more realistic approach to contracts between husbands and wives. Although at present these courts' attitudes are representative of a small minority nationwide, their willingness to discard outmoded legal doctrines signals a general trend toward increased recognition of reasonable contracts between husbands and wives. Further, although these courts thus far have dealt overwhelmingly with cases involving support and property upon divorce, the new legal doctrines established by their decisions may easily be extended to agreements affecting ongoing marriages. The five cases that established the new law in this field are briefly reviewed below.

The first case, *Posner* v. *Posner*,[32] involved an antenuptial agreement between a divorced millionaire, Victor, and a 27-year-old saleswoman, Sari. Prior to their marriage the parties had been dating for five years during which time Victor paid Sari's rent, took her on business trips, and gave her expensive presents. When Victor was reluctant to marry again because he wanted to protect his fortune, Sari proposed an antenuptial agreement and Victor assented to the proposal. Their agreement provided for Sari to receive $600 a

---

*While some critics of the contractual model have asserted that such fault-based standards are in conflict with no-fault divorce, as Professor Carol Bruch has pointed out, it is important to distinguish between economic fault (such as the deliberate misappropriation of another's property) and the moral fault that formerly provided grounds for divorce. No-fault divorce laws allow spouses to obtain a divorce without fault-based grounds for the divorce. But all states with no-fault grounds have provisions to deal with economic fault by compensating a person whose spouse has deliberately dissipated or misappropriated funds or property belonging to the other. Personal conversation, October 13, 1980.

month in alimony if they divorced. Five years later they divorced and Sari sued for a larger alimony award.

As we noted above, the courts' traditional practice was to invalidate any agreement that set or waived alimony in contemplation of a future divorce. However, when they were faced with the Posner antenuptial contract in 1970, the Florida Supreme Court recognized that Florida's recent liberalization of divorce laws "require[d] a change in the rule respecting antenuptial agreements settling alimony and property rights of the parties upon divorce." It concluded that "such agreements should no longer be held to be void *ab initio* as 'contrary to public policy.' "[33] The court ruled that antenuptial agreements dealing with alimony and property upon divorce should be tested by the same standards as those dealing with the property rights of spouses in each other's estate upon death. Thus, the court ruled, if the antenuptial agreement was a valid and binding agreement between the parties under the conditions at the time it was made, it should be upheld like any other valid contract.

In the second case, *Volid* v. *Volid*,[34] an Illinois appellate court upheld an antenuptial agreement written by a 60-year-old grandfather entering his fourth marriage and a 40-year-old school teacher. The agreement provided for the wife to receive $50,000 as a lump-sum settlement if divorce occurred within three years of the marriage and $75,000 if divorce occurred thereafter. The marriage lasted slightly more than three years. Under the contract, the $75,000 due was to be paid at the rate of $600 per month for 125 successive months. In upholding this agreement, the court specifically rejected two traditional excuses for voiding similar contracts. First it noted that the husband did not attempt to shirk his duty of support. He had made a generous provision to ensure it. Second, the court asserted that rather than encouraging divorce, such contracts may promote marital stability:

> The most frequent argument made for holding agreements limiting alimony invalid is that such agreements encourage or incite divorce or separation. There is little empirical evidence to show that this assertion is well founded. It is true that a person may be reluctant to obtain a divorce if he knows that a great financial sacrifice may be entailed, but it does not follow from this that a person who finds his marriage otherwise satisfactory will terminate the marital relationship simply because it will not involve a financial sacrifice. *It may be equally cogently argued that a contract which defines the expectations and re-*

sponsibilities of the parties promotes rather than reduces marital stability.[35]

Further, the Volid court asserted that "public policy is not violated by permitting these persons prior to marriage to anticipate the possibility of divorce and to establish their rights by contract."[36]* However, it cautioned that the traditional safeguards of contract doctrine must obtain: "as long as the contract is entered with full knowledge and without fraud, duress or coercion [the contract should be upheld]."[37]

In the third case, the 1973 divorce of Mr. and Mrs. Buettner, the Nevada Supreme Court similarly applied normal contract standards to review (and uphold) an antenuptial agreement between two divorced persons:

[A]s with all contracts, courts of this state shall retain power to refuse to enforce a particular antenuptial contract if it is found that it is unconscionable, obtained through fraud, misrepresentation, material nondisclosure or duress.[38]

The agreement at issue in *Buettner* v. *Buettner* provided that in case of divorce the wife would be given the couple's house, all household goods and furniture, and $500 a month for five years (a sum of $30,000). After five months of marriage the husband filed for divorce and asserted that the prenuptial agreement was invalid. The trial court agreed with him and awarded the wife a dining room set, a couch, and a total of $2,000 payable over a one-year period.

The Nevada Supreme Court reversed this decision and upheld the parties' original agreement, concluding that antenuptial agreements which set forth alimony and property rights upon divorce were no longer void as contrary to public policy. However, the *Buettner* court reserved the right to invalidate antenuptial agreements in certain extreme circumstances:

We have now come to the conclusion that antenuptial agreements concerning alimony should be enforced unless enforcement deprives a

*Here the court also took notice of the growing incidence of divorce and the reasonableness of considering its consequences: "It would be anomalous to hold that the parties cannot plan and agree on a course of action in the event that the marriage is unsuccessful and ends in divorce. This is particularly true where the parties are older and where there is little danger that either party would be without support. The incidence of divorce in this country is increasing, and consequently more persons with families and established wealth are in a position to consider the possibility of a marriage later in life."

spouse of support that he or she cannot otherwise secure. A provision providing that no alimony shall be paid will be enforced unless the spouse has no other reasonable source of support.[39]

Also in 1973, the Oregon Supreme Court, in *Unander* v. *Unander*,[40] sided with this newly emerging judicial trend by declaring that a large number of citizens need "to be able to freely enter into antenuptial agreements in the knowledge that their bargain is as inviolate as any other."[41] This decision is especially significant because the Oregon court articulated the importance of according marital partners the same freedom of contract that other contracting parties enjoy.

The Oregon case involved a premarital agreement between two persons who had each been divorced. The husband, "a man of property," was making substantial alimony and child support payments to his former wife. The agreement at issue provided for the new wife to receive $500 a month alimony and a $25,000 life insurance policy in the event of divorce. In upholding this agreement, the court explicitly overruled its own decision in a 1970 case invalidating an antenuptial agreement in which the wife agreed to forgo all claims to alimony. The court now said its previous position that "such agreements encourage divorce" was of "extremely doubtful validity."[42]

The final and most far reaching case was decided by the California Supreme Court in 1976, *In re Marriage of Dawley*.[43] *Dawley* involved an unmarried schoolteacher who became pregnant unexpectedly. She and the father of the unborn child decided on a temporary marriage because the woman feared her job would be terminated if she gave birth as an unwed mother. The couple wrote an antenuptial agreement in which the father, an engineer, agreed to support the wife and her child from a previous relationship for a period of 14 months. This would enable her to take a leave of absence from her tenured teaching job and to give birth to and care for the child. The husband also agreed to support the child to age 21. The agreement further provided that earnings acquired during the marriage would be held separate. In addition, each spouse disclaimed all rights, including community property rights, to the property of the other spouse.

The couple lived together for eight years instead of 14 months. When the couple divorced the trial court found that during those eight years the parties had abided by their promises concerning separate property. However, the woman challenged the validity of their original agreement, claiming, among other things, that it "violated public policy by denying her support."

The California Supreme Court upheld the agreement, *candidly acknowledging that it was made in contemplation of divorce*. In doing so, the court explicitly rejected the past dictum, which it had affirmed as recently as 1973, that antenuptial agreements "*must* be made in contemplation that the marriage relation will continue until the parties are separated by death."[44] The court said the new test of the validity of these contracts was whether the language of the contract itself *objectively promoted* dissolution of the marriage. (It would seem, at least empirically, that this one did not, inasmuch as the couple remained together for eight years instead of the contemplated 14 months.)

In establishing this new standard, the California court indicated it would not try to reconstruct the parties' "subjective" thoughts and wishes because "under a test based upon the subjective contemplation of the parties, neither persons dealing with the parties, nor even the parties themselves, could rely on the terms of an antenuptial agreement."[45] The court further recognized: "Neither the reordering of property rights to fit the needs and desires of the couple, nor realistic planning that takes account of the possibility of dissolution, offends the public policy favoring and protecting marriage."[46]

Taken together, these five cases established three new principles for reviewing contracts between marital partners. First, instead of following tradition and holding illegal all antenuptial agreements that contemplate divorce, these courts all viewed such contracts as valid legal agreements, provided they meet the test of traditional contract standards. Thus, as the *Buettner* court stated, agreements between married persons, like all other contracts, will not be upheld if it is unconscionable, or obtained through fraud, duress, nondisclosure or misrepresentation. Second, instead of dichotomizing contracts pertaining to support and contracts dealing with property, these courts considered both subjects appropriate for contractual ordering and, in a clear departure from previous policies, upheld contracts that limit alimony as well as those that assign property rights.

Third, and most important, these courts extended to marital partners the same freedom to contract that has been traditionally accorded to other contracting parties. Thus these courts have said that marital partners entering into agreements should have the same assurance as other contractors that the courts will enforce the terms of their agreements.

Before we examine how these new standards will work in practice, it is important to note the areas in which the courts have *not* modified the traditional legal doctrine. No court has yet upheld a husband's attempt to contract away his obligation for support *during marriage*. (However, as we have already noted, neither will any court *enforce* a husband's obligation to support his wife during marriage.) Thus, the law in this respect has remained unchanged. Nor have the courts yet upheld contracts in which the husband agrees to pay the wife a salary for her domestic services, although this issue has not been tested before one of these more liberal courts in recent years. It is almost certain that these courts would uphold an agreement to pay the wife for her domestic services with a property award (instead of a salary), provided the contract was negotiated in accord with traditional contract standards.

Thus couples wishing to enter such agreements should be cognizant of the limits of the current law. But they can reasonably expect that the courts will be increasingly loath to disallow fairly negotiated contracts governing the spouses' financial rights and obligations.

In ruling on the five cases discussed above, the courts have implied that they already have appropriate standards for reviewing contracts between husbands and wives. What are these standards? In reexamining the standards of review the courts have applied thus far, it becomes apparent that they fall into two (somewhat contradictory) categories: those embodied in the law traditionally used to review contracts, and those embodied in the law traditionally applied to review family cases. Thus the *Volid* and *Buettner* courts talked about invalidating contracts that were unconscionable, or obtained through fraud, misrepresentation, material nondisclosure or duress—questions typically raised in contract law. However, the *Posner* court discussed questions of "fairness" and "changed circumstances," standards familiar to family court judges who evaluate separation and divorce agreements by current standards of adequacy.

Let us now examine the different consequences that may result from these different standards of review.

New Standards for Review: Contract Law or Family Law?

Personal contracts between spouses are raising some legal questions that are virtually without precedent in existing statutory and case law. Largely for that reason, the courts, in their attempts to adjudicate such questions, have been inconsistent in selecting standards for review of antenuptial agreements. The result is that even within a single state we may see courts relying on contract doctrine in some cases and on family law doctrine in others. In general, when the court invokes the standards of contract law, it upholds the contract. When family law standards are applied, however, the contract is likely to be modified in accord with the court's own standards of fairness. This section briefly examines these two legal traditions. It then urges and demonstrates the usefulness of contract doctrines in resolving difficult cases.

Contract Law

Traditional contract doctrine tends to treat contracts with great deference. As long as a contract has been fairly negotiated, it is assumed to express the true intentions of its makers, and the court is constrained to uphold its validity. Thus the courts have traditionally given effect to all forms of business contracts as long as they have been freely agreed to (that is, without misrepresentation, fraud, duress, etc.) by responsible adults. The standards of review under contract law are *procedural standards*. They focus on the negotiation process—the circumstances surrounding the initial agreement —and have been established to ensure that the parties are fully informed and acting voluntarily when they enter the contract. The judges do not examine the content of the contract, or attempt to evaluate its wisdom. Nor do they care whether the parties still want to adhere to the contract, or whether it will cost one of them a lot of money. Furthermore, even if judges themselves consider the agreement unfair or unwise, they are nevertheless generally bound to enforce the terms of a fairly negotiated contract.

The facts in *Potter* v. *Collin*[47] afford a case in point. In that case a wealthy 81-year-old man and a poor 47-year-old woman executed an "explicit" nine-page antenuptial agreement that provided $20,000 to the wife on the husband's death, but included a waiver by the wife of any interest in the husband's property. After the husband died, the wife challenged the contract's validity. In 1975 a Florida appellate court upheld the agreement even though it was "unreasonable and penurious," because the wife had entered into it with a sound mind. In fact, she had been told by her lawyer it was "bad business" to sign it.

Another 1975 Florida case, *Singer* v. *Singer*,[48] eventuated in a similar resort to contract law, but with some ambiguous undertones. In that case a couple made an antenuptial agreement providing $500 per month in alimony for the wife in the event of a divorce unless she were to obtain a divorce on the grounds of adultery, in which case she would receive $1200 monthly. After eight years the husband sued for divorce. The wife countersued, claiming that the husband had committed adultery, but this allegation was stricken prior to trial and never reinstated. Nevertheless, the court awarded the wife alimony of $1200 per month. The appellate court reduced her award to $500 monthly, stating that in the absence of changed circumstances, the trial court was bound by the alimony provisions of the agreement.

While this decision purportedly turned on contract law—that is, the agreement was supposedly treated like any other valid agreement—the appellate court's reference to "changed circumstances" echoed a different standard of review, a standard traditionally used in family law cases. As we shall see, this standard has allowed family court judges to examine agreements in light of the current situation of the parties, and to invoke a more subjective standard for reviewing contracts (i.e. one that permits their own definitions of fairness to intrude).*

Family Law

Family law has already developed a sizable body of doctrine to deal with separation agreements, divorce agreements, and other postnuptial agreements. This doctrine requires that judges evaluate the

---

*This is a subjective standard in that it is based on the judge's subjective assessment of fairness. It is also subjective in that the outcome is likely to vary from judge to judge. Judges, however, are likely to consider their judgments objective in that they permit a third party, who is not directly involved in the situation, to examine the case "objectively." They also point to the fact that they are guided by legislation and case law precedents, both of which limit personal bias. Nevertheless, a review for fairness inevitably allows a judge more discretion than the nonsubstantive procedural review characteristic of contract law.

"merits" of all such agreements to ensure that they are "fair," "equitable," and "just." In some states courts have applied the same standards of evaluation to the review of premarital and marital contracts. These family law standards permit the courts a great amount of discretion to inquire into the relative circumstances of the parties and to pass judgment on various contract provisions—with the result that judges have often freely modifed agreements or discounted them altogether in accord with their own notions of justice and fairness.

Thus, in contrast to the *procedural review* required by contract law, family law requires a *substantive review* of the content of an agreement. It allows the court to make judgments about the fairness of specific provisions—some of which it may decide to invalidate—while contract law typically requires that the provisions of the contract be treated with deference.

In reviewing the recent developments that followed the *Posner* decision, Professor Homer Clark, writing in 1979, asserted that the law seems to be developing in the direction of permitting spouses to contract about their financial obligations upon divorce "*provided* the agreement meets the requirements of fairness made for all such agreements [and provided] that the agreement makes adequate provision for each spouse in view of the needs and resources of each."[49] Clark goes on to note that the provisions must be adequate and fair both at the date of execution of the agreement and at the date of enforcement—a standard that would allow judges considerable latitude. The family law tests of adequacy and fairness clearly allow a judge to modify a contract that does not make what the court considers "an adequate provision" for a dependent wife (or husband).

For example, in the 1974 Illinois case of *Eule* v. *Eule*, although the court recognized the "trend in the law" to uphold these antenuptial agreements if they are fair and reasonable, the court nevertheless went on to invalidate the agreement in question because it provided that the wife waive all claims to alimony or support if the marriage was dissolved within seven years, and the court did not consider that fair and reasonable.[50]

A second example of the amount of judicial discretion that family law standards allow is provided by a 1976 Indiana case. In *Tomlinson* v. *Tomlinson* the court upheld an antenuptial agreement in which a wife waived any interest in her husband's property upon divorce, but emphasized that "such an agreement is not binding on the court."[51] It went on to state that "a valid agreement is but one factor to be considered among the several factors upon which the court customarily relies to make an equitable distribution of property."[52] In other words, the agreement may be valid, but the court is not required to enforce it.

No doubt an argument can be made in favor of these family law standards because they allow the court the latitude to achieve "just" results. Further, it can be asserted that the relatively rigid contract law standards may lead the courts to impose harsh results—for as long as a court must treat an agreement as binding it will not be able to forestall unforeseen hardships.

However, this position fails to recognize that the continually evolving doctrines of contract law are equally well suited to deal with the problems of unforeseen hardships. In examining these doctrines below I will argue that they are better equipped than family law doctrines to handle marital contracts—and do not allow for the uncertainty and subjectivity that are the major disadvantages inherent in a substantive review. A primary function of the contract is to provide the parties with the stability that ensues from settled rights and duties; the prospect of subjective judicial review can only undermine this stability.

Applying Contract Doctrine to Difficult Cases

Mutual mistake. One contract doctrine that is available to minimize the potential hardship of a marital agreement is the doctrine of mutual mistake.* If two parties have negotiated a contract that is based on erroneous assumptions or misunderstandings which go to the basis of the contract, the provisions of the contract may not reflect choices the parties would have made had they been fully knowledgeable. Contract doctrine is well equipped to prevent injustice in such a case, as it allows either the recision of the contract or its reformation as an appropriate remedy.[53]

Applying the doctrine of mutual mistake to marital contracts can be illustrated by a case that was decided under family law

---

*The rule has been stated in this manner: "Where a mistake of both parties at the time of contract was made as to a basic assumption on which the contract was made has a material effect on the agreed exchange of performances, the contract is voidable by the adversely affected party unless he bears the risk of mistake. . . ." American Law Institute, *Restatement (Second) of the Law of Contracts*, Tentative Draft No. 10, Chap. 12, Sec. 294 (1975).

rules. In *Garnett* v. *Garnett*,[54] the husband and the wife signed an agreement upon divorce when they were under the mutual misapprehension that the wife was seriously diabetic and would soon be incapable of self-support. The husband agreed to pay all of the mortgage payments on their home, which the wife would occupy and own. He also agreed to pay the maintenance, upkeep, and utilities for the home, to provide his wife with an automobile and to pay for its insurance, gasoline, and service. After the divorce both parties remarried. The husband then suffered a loss of income, while the wife recovered her health, continued working at her job, and earned a generous salary. The court used the family law standards of "changed circumstances" and "fairness" to eliminate all of the husband's contractual obligations except the mortgage payments on the wife's home (which the court considered part of the property division rather than support).

In this extreme case, where both parties were misinformed when they made the agreement, the same outcome would have been possible under the doctrine of mutual mistake. Here an agreement over essential conditions was reached in large part because both parties misunderstood the actual state of the wife's health. Had they known the truth at the time of the agreement, no doubt they would have written a different contract.

However, contract law would have led to different results if the original diagnosis of the wife's illness had proved to be correct. In that case, while family law standards of review might still permit a modification of the agreement because of changed circumstances (that is, the husband's reduced earning capacity), contract law standards would not, since the possibility of a change in his earning capacity would have been foreseeable at the time of contracting. From a public policy perspective, the latter result is clearly preferable because it upholds the enforceability of fairly negotiated contracts between spouses. As noted above, marital partners, like other contracting parties, must be able to rely on the terms of their agreements and know that their enforceability is assured. Without such assurance husbands and wives will not be able to plan for the future, as their plans and agreements will always be open to change and the subjective prejudices of the courts. Thus contract law is preferable because it is essential that marital agreements be treated like all other contractual obligations and that their enforceability be guaranteed.

Impossibility. The contract doctrine of impossibility may also be applicable in hardship cases. Under this doctrine, a party may be relieved of an obligation if an intervening event, which neither party could have foreseen at the time they entered into the contract, makes the performance of the obligation either impossible or impracticable.[55] Thus, the court may modify a contract provision that becomes unduly burdensome because the parties were unable to reasonably anticipate some event that affected their capacity to perform.

For example, if a husband has agreed to support his ex-wife with earnings from his medical practice and he subsequently loses his sight in a car accident, the court could use the doctrine of impossibility to modify his original agreement.* The same result could be reached in family law under the doctrines of changed circumstances and fairness. However, if the facts of this case are changed to resemble a more typical (and more predictable) situation, results of contract law and family law again diverge. For example, if the doctor simply remarries, has four children with his new wife, and wants to reduce his support of his former wife so that he can better support his new dependents, family law would probably justify a modification of the original agreement because of changed circumstances, while contract law would uphold the original agreement.

Unconscionable contracts. The preceding analysis deals with difficult questions that arise when parties make good-faith agreements with incomplete knowledge of the existing facts or without foreknowledge of contingencies that will make performance impracticable. Traditional contract doctrine is also well equipped to deal with another difficult situation—that in which one party attempts to take unfair advantage of the other.

In some such instances, the court may find an agreement unconscionable. As Professor Corbin noted, "there is sufficient flexibility in the concepts of fraud, duress, misrepresentation, and undue influence, not to mention differences in economic bargaining power, to enable the courts to avoid enforcement of a bargain that is shown to be unconscionable by reason of gross inadequacy of consideration accompanied by other relevant factors."[56] Where the terms of a marital contract seem unduly one-sided, courts may inquire into the surrounding circumstances at the time of the contract to ensure

---

*If, however, he had disability insurance and therefore continued to have a substantial income after the accident, his obligations might be reduced rather than eliminated.

that the bargain struck was the free choice of both parties. Since couples that are married or about to be married are in a confidential relationship, it is reasonable for the courts to require the highest standards normally applied to confidential relationships—full disclosure at the time of contracting. These standards can serve as an important safeguard against abuse. For example, the *Posner* court articulated the appropriate standards:

> Freedom to contract includes freedom to make a bad bargain. But freedom to contract is not always absolute. The public interest requires that antenuptial agreements be executed under conditions of candor and fairness.
>
> . . . The relationship between the parties to an antenuptial agreement is one of mutual trust and confidence. Since they do not deal at arm's length they must exercise a high degree of good faith and candor in all matters bearing upon the contract.

Similarly, under equitable principles, a party will be denied specific performance where such performance would constitute a grossly unfair demand.

This discussion is not intended to suggest that contract doctrines should give courts unfettered discretion to modify marital contracts whenever one party appears to have received a better bargain than another. Such a result would merely cast family law doctrine in a different guise, and that clearly would not lead to a just or fair administration of marital agreements. Instead it is hoped that in the vast majority of cases courts will give effect to contracts that are fairly negotiated and will do true justice to the parties' expectations. However, where a bargain is egregiously one-sided, the courts would have sufficient flexibility under contract rules to effect an equitable adjustment of the rights of the parties.

CHAPTER 14

Living Together Without a Contract: Social Patterns and Legal Consequences

This chapter examines the present-day legal consequences of unwed cohabitation—of living together without marriage and without a contract. The first section discusses the numerical incidence and social meaning of cohabitation in the United States. The second section considers the legal consequences of cohabitation during an ongoing relationship. The third reviews the legal consequences when a relationship is terminated by separation or death.

Social Patterns and Trends

In the winter of 1977, Jimmy Carter, who had just assumed office as the President of the United States, urged members of his staff to get married instead of "living in sin."[1] While the President's view of unmarried cohabitation may have inspired some marriages among his aides, it appears to have had little effect on the citizenry at large. The intervening years have seen a steady increase in the number of single people of opposite sex who are sharing homes. In the gray language of the U.S. Census, by 1978 there were 2.2 million unmarried persons "sharing a household with an unrelated adult of the opposite sex."[2] These 2.2 million individuals comprise 1.1 million households.

The rise in unmarried heterosexual cohabitation was most dramatic in the 1970s. Starting from 1960 base-line data, the number of unmarried couples rose from 439,000 in 1960, to 523,000 in 1970, to 957,000 in 1977, to 1,137,000 in 1978.[3] This reflects a dramatic 117 percent increase between 1970 and 1978. As Paul Glick and Graham Spanier observed, "rarely does social change occur with such rapidity: indeed, there have been few developments relating to marriage and family life which have been as dramatic as the rapid increase in unmarried cohabitation."[*]

It is likely that these figures substantially underreport the actual amount of unmarried cohabitation. One of the cohabitants may have an "official" residence elsewhere or may actually maintain his or her own apartment even though living with the partner most of the week. This is especially common when one of the partners has children: the other partner often maintains a separate apartment (which the adults may use when they want to be alone). In addition, if the female partner is involved in postdivorce litigation and faces the possibility of having her alimony or child support reduced, she is unlikely to report that an adult male is living in her household. If one considers these sources of underreporting along with the underreporting that is inevitable in shifting and short-lived relationships, the actual number of couples involved in a cohabitation relationship may be closer to 2 million—twice the number reported by the U.S. Census.

The number of two-person, same-sex households has also increased in recent years, but census data give no indication of what proportion of these are homosexual relationships.[†]

[*]Glick and Spanier were referring, more specifically, to the 19% increase in unwed cohabitation between 1977 and 1978. Paul C. Glick and Graham B. Spanier, "Married and Unmarried Cohabitation in the United States," *Journal of Marriage and the Family*, (1980):19–30.

[†]Since "many young adults live with someone of the same sex while attending college or while working before marriage," the census data on same-sex partnerships are limited to "those living in two-person households which are maintained by a person 25 years or older." In 1977 there were more than a half million of these households, involving about one million persons, divided about equally between men and women. Of course many of these couples were not involved in homosexual relationships, but there is no way to ascertain the parties' relationship from census data. Paul C. Glick and Arthur J. Norton, "Marrying, Divorcing, and Living Together in the U.S. Today," *Population Bulletin* 32, no. 5 (October 1977): 35.

There are three sociologically important features of the recent increase in heterosexual cohabitation. The first is its *increased prevalence among young adults*. According to Paul Glick, senior demographer at the U.S. Bureau of the Census, the most dramatic rise in heterosexual cohabitation has been among young people: the number of heterosexual couples between 18 and 25 increased more rapidly than *any* other census category of household from 1960 to 1970 and, as Glick notes, even then, the number was "probably incompletely reported."[4] By 1978, 42 percent of the cohabitors were under 25, and 59 percent were under 35.[5] As early as 1974 Macklin reported that 25 to 30 percent of the college students surveyed said they had "cohabitated" with someone of the opposite sex at some time during their college years. *

The second important feature of the recent period is the evidence of an increased number of cohabiting relationships *among people of all ages*. In 1978, 32 percent of the heterosexual cohabitors were between 25 and 44 years of age, 15 percent were between 45 and 64, and an additional 11 percent were over 65.[6] This indicates that the attractions of cohabitation as an alternative to marriage are increasing for people throughout the life cycle, from never-married singles to middle-aged divorcees, to retired pensioners. As Glick noted, by 1975 one out of five older men who shared living quarters with a nonrelative was living with a female partner.[7]

Third, and perhaps most important, is the *increased acceptability* of cohabitation among the "normal" population and the *"respectable" middle class*. In the past, cohabitation has been confined largely to the young, the poor, the bohemian, and the very rich: it has been an option chosen by generations of nonconformists and wealthy persons who wanted to (and could afford to) challenge society's mores, as well as by the very poor who had nothing to lose by nonconformity.[8] Similarly, in other cultures, even those in which consensual unions have long been the *predominant* form of house-

---

*Although the definition of cohabitation varies from study to study, it usually includes a relationship between two unwed persons of the opposite sex who share the same household for a relatively long time. Occasional or irregular overnight visits are not included. However, Macklin does include arrangements in which one or both persons maintain a separate residence (in a dorm or an apartment) in addition to their joint household. Eleanor D. Macklin, "Cohabitation in College: Going Very Steady," *Psychology Today*, November 1974, pp. 53–59. The percent ranges from 9 percent at a small liberal arts college in the Midwest to 36 percent of the student population at a major state university. Macklin also indicates that the likelihood of cohabitation increases with higher class standing, a less restrictive university housing policy, and a higher male–female student ratio.

hold (as in certain Caribbean societies), cohabitation has occurred primarily among the lower classes. What is different today is the evidence of cohabitation among more "respectable" segments of U.S. society: it is now perceived as an option for couples of all ages and class levels. As Herma Hill Kay and Carol Amyx observe:

> They live near you—in a house, apartment, or trailer, in urban centers, small towns, or on farms. They may both be professionals or wage earners; they may work separately or together in various enterprises of their own; one of them may act as a homemaker while the other works outside the home for pay. They share your neighborhood activities, your civic concerns, your national and international problems. Their life-style may be avant-garde or traditional. They may be a man and a woman, two men, or two women. In one respect, however, they differ from most couples: they are not married.[9]

Census data, though limited, provide some indication of the spread of cohabiting couples in the "normal" population. A quarter of the currently cohabiting couples have one or more children living with them, and that suggests a relatively stable family relationship. Second, in contrast to the common belief that cohabitation is confined to the protected liberal atmosphere of academia, only a quarter of young cohabiting couples have one or both partners enrolled in college.[10] The other three-quarters live in the mainstream of society. Finally, recent census data indicate that unmarried couples include persons of all ages and levels of education and income.*[11] This suggests that those who were previously most likely to cohabit, such as the young and the poor, are still cohabiting, but they have now been joined by a new population—the middle-aged, middle-class adults who now consider cohabitation a normal option.

In order to assess the sociological importance of cohabitation it is important to ask whether it is becoming institutionalized as an alternative to marriage, or whether it is a new phase in the courtship process in which couples set up households before (rather than af-

---

*This is not to say that the demographic characteristics of cohabiting couples show no differences from the married population. Cohabiting couples are more likely to live in large metropolitan areas, to have lower income levels and higher unemployment rates, generally, than married couples. Female cohabitants who have never been married are more likely to be employed than are married women of the same age. In addition, when compared to married couples, cohabiting couples in which neither partner had been previously married, had high levels of educational attainment, with both partners completing their college education. Glick and Spanier, "Married and Unmarried Cohabitation in the United States," *Journal of Marriage and the Family*, (1980): 19–30.

ter) they get married. There is some evidence to support each of these perspectives.

The view of cohabitation as a new step in the courtship process is supported in a limited way by some of the (admittedly nonrepresentative) research on college student cohabitants.* While these cohabitants apparently attach a wide range of meanings to their relationships, sociologist Eleanor Macklin found that at Cornell University about half of the cohabitants (43 percent) viewed living together as a prelude to marriage or as a way of "developing" a lasting relationship. However, the other half (46 percent) expressed a less permanent view of their commitment—a "let's see" attitude of planning to stay together only as long as the relationship remained mutually satisfying.[12]

This variation in attitudes suggests that, among the young, cohabitation is not yet "institutionalized" either as a form of engagement or as a distinct alternative to marriage. This lack of institutionalization makes it entirely possible for two people to begin living together with two different sets of expectations. For example, sociologist Pat Jackson found that males and females often have different aims in deciding to live with a person of the opposite sex.[13] Jackson (who also worked with a nonrandom university-based sample) found that while most men entering a relationship considered cohabitation as a preferable alternative to marriage, the majority of the women hoped it would develop into marriage. These women tended to view cohabitation as a calculated risk which, if all went well, would serve to persuade the men to formalize the relationship. Not surprisingly, the greatest outside pressure toward that end came from the couple's parents, and especially from the woman's parents.†

It is clear, however, that other cohabitants, college and noncollege couples alike, hold the view that their relationship is not a trial engagement but a practical alternative to marriage. For some it is a permanent replacement for traditional marriage; for others it is a

---

*Although college students comprise only a quarter of the young cohabitants, almost all the sociological research on cohabitation has focused on them because researchers can easily gain access to them.

†In contrast, among Swedish cohabitants, Trost found no difference between men and women in the percentage who entered the union with the intention of having it result in marriage. In addition, very few of these Swedish couples (less than 10% of both men and women) reported any pressure from their parents to get married. Jan Trost, *Unmarried Cohabitation*, (Vasteras, Sweden: International Library, 1979).

temporary alternative.* For example, the young career-oriented woman who wants to devote her primary energies to her work may intentionally avoid marriage because she does not want to be trapped by the traditional domestic responsibilities of a wife. As one explained:

> When we lived apart we ate every meal together. Now we don't eat together all the time. If I had been married I would have felt the pressure of filling the wife-and-cook role. I believe in marriage but I'm not ready for it yet. I want a career first.[14]

U.S. Census data show a signficant increase in the percentage of never-married women in the 20 to 24 age group (from 28 percent in 1960 to 43 percent in 1977).[15] This could reflect a developing pattern of delayed marriage (perhaps until after a period of cohabitation), or it could reflect an affirmative choice to remain single and/or cohabit instead of entering marriage. While it is too early to predict whether these women will eventually marry, it is clear that many young people are cautious about making lifelong commitments in today's uncertain and rapidly changing world. If cohabitation can successfully serve the seemingly incompatible goals of independence and emotional closeness, it will undoubtedly be an increasingly attractive alternative to traditional marriage.

Whatever the reasons for cohabitation among young people, it is evidently also the preferred option for some once-married middle-aged and older persons. Many divorced women and men are determined to avoid the pitfalls of another legal commitment, and many older widows and widowers are constrained by circumstance to hold on to survivors' benefits from their earlier marriage. These cohabitants are much more likely than the young to explicitly reject marriage and to choose living together as a reasonable and satisfying alternative.

In fact, a *majority* of cohabiting couples include at least one divorced partner. A 1975 survey showed that one-half of the men, and three-fifths of the women in cohabiting relationships had been

---

*Those for whom cohabitation is a temporary relationship seem to be more common, since 63% of all cohabiting households in 1977 had been together less than two years. Paul C. Glick and Arthur J. Norton, "Marrying, Divorcing, and Living Together in the U.S. Today," *Population Bulletin* 32 no. 5 (October 1977). This is in contrast, again, to Trost's Swedish sample, in which 68% of the couples cohabiting at the time they were first interviewed were either married or still cohabiting three and a half years later.

previously married.[16] These previously married cohabitants were evenly dispersed among the age categories (less than 35, 35–54, 55 and over), while in contrast, 85 percent of the never-married cohabitors were in the youngest age group.

From a sociological point of view, then, cohabitation is worth studying because it is challenging the traditional institutions of marriage and family: although cohabiting unions currently constitute only one percent of all households, and only 2.8 percent of all couples living together in the United States, it is likely their numbers will increase. Indeed, if the trends in other Western countries are any indication of what will happen here, cohabiting couples will soon become a significant social minority. In Sweden, for example, studies show the number of cohabiting couples increasing steadily during the past 20 years. Sociologist Jan Trost reports that unwed cohabiting couples accounted for only 1 percent of all Swedish unions in 1960; by 1970 they were about 7 percent of the total; and by 1974, 12 percent.[17]

Similarly, the cohabitation rate (the percentage of couples living together unmarried) has increased substantially in other countries in Western Europe. According to Trost, the rate was 7% in the Netherlands in 1979 and 8% in Finland in 1978. In Norway the rate grew from 3% to 5% between 1973 and 1977, and in Denmark the rate increased from 8% in 1974, to 10% in 1977, to 13% in 1979.[18] Clearly Sweden and Denmark have the highest known cohabitation rates in the Western world, with approximately one out of eight couples in the population living together without marriage.

Cohabitation is significant from a legal perspective as well, because it presents a challenge to many of the traditional boundaries of family law. In reading the following pages one may be surprised at the archaic state of the current law. Clearly, new laws and new legal remedies are needed to deal with this emerging family form.

The Legal Consequences of Living Together

Most couples do not think much about the legal implications of their actions when they begin living together. Nor are they typically aware of the legal consequences that can arise when their relationship ends. However, as we will see, most of the protections afforded by the state to persons who form legal unions are not extended to unwed cohabitors. Some of these protections involve privileges and benefits during marriage; others become evident only at the critical junctures of death and divorce. For example, Kay and Amyx summarize the legal rules and rewards incident to marriage in California:

> Legal marriage is created by a formal ceremony solemnizing the relationship. Its incidents include the spouses' right to live together in marital cohabitation; the power to confer legitimacy upon their children; equal ownership of the community property produced by either spouse during the marriage; the assumption of mutual obligations of marital and child support; the power to declare a marital homestead; the right to file joint income tax returns; and the right to legal redress against third parties who destroy or diminish either spouse's enjoyment of the consortium of the other.[19]

In addition, married couples have access to state-financed forums for resolving disputed claims upon divorce. Taken all together, these legal rules and forums provide otherwise unprepared married couples with an efficient system for dealing with the unexpected; they thereby minimize the resulting hardships. For example, if one spouse is killed in an airplane accident, the state has rules for allocating the decedent's property in the absence of an explicit will, and for guaranteeing a share of it to the surviving spouse. By contrast, if one member of a cohabiting relationship dies without a will, the surviving partner has no legal right to the property held in the other's name under the intestate succession laws of any of the fifty states, even if the property was acquired through their joint efforts.* As we shall see, the contrast thus exemplified applies to scores of other situations in life and in death.

In this section we will examine the legal consequences of living together during an ongoing relationship. In the next section we will consider the legal consequences of cohabitation at death or dissolution.

Cohabitation and Fornication as Criminal Acts

Fifteen American states and the District of Columbia have statutes that make cohabitation a crime.† These statutes vary in their defi-

---

*However, he or she may be able to claim ownership of some of the property by virtue of an oral contract entered into with the decedent, as discussed in Chapter 15.

†Alabama, Arizona, Florida, Georgia, Idaho, Illinois, Kansas, Michigan, Mississippi, North Carolina, Rhode Island, South Carolina, Utah, Virginia, and Wisconsin. Toni Ihara and Ralph Warner, *The Living Together Kit* (New York: Fawcett Crest, 1979).

nitions of cohabitation and in the penalties prescribed for violators. For example, in Virginia cohabiting must be "lewd and lascivious," but in Wisconsin all that is required is openly living with a person "he knows is not his spouse under circumstances that imply sexual intercourse."[20] Similarly, penalties may be as stiff as three years imprisonment in Massachusetts or as minor as a warning for first offenders in New Mexico.[21]

Most states also have statutes that prohibit fornication, which is defined as sexual relations between unmarried persons. Cohabitors may be subject to criminal penalties for fornication if it is "inferred" from the act of cohabiting. In addition, many states retain laws prohibiting sodomy, oral copulation, and adultery—even between consenting adults.[22]

While the laws prohibiting cohabitation, fornication, and certain other sexual acts remain on the books in many states, they are rarely enforced, for two reasons. First, they involve problems of proof: after all, most couples do not perform their "illegal" acts in public, and spying on couples is not generally considered a proper police function. In fact, some states have added the requirement that the illegal behavior be "open and notorious" precisely to prevent overzealous enforcement of these laws.[23] Second, because the "new morality" of the sixties and seventies has increased public acceptance of sexual acts between consenting adults, community norms no longer encourage vigorous enforcement of these laws.

Nevertheless, as long as these laws remain on the books they can be used selectively to harass people whom the police (and influential segments of the public) define as "undesirable," such as those in communal living situations. Similarly, these laws provide a potential vehicle for the harassment of cohabiting couples, for as long as an act remains illegal, it can bring criminal penalties in the community that chooses, for whatever reason, to exact those penalties.

Government-supported Benefit Programs

Unmarried cohabitants are not eligible for any of the Social Security benefits for old age, survivors, disability, or death that typically accrue to spouses.[24] For example, a divorced wife married ten years or longer can collect Social Security benefits from her husband's account; an unmarried woman who has lived with a man for the same length of time cannot. Similarly, a married couple over 65 is qualified to receive two Social Security checks each month—one for the husband and one for the wife; even if one spouse has never earned a salary or wages during the marriage, he or she is entitled to spousal benefits (typically one-half the wage earner's entitlement) after age 65. However, if a man of 65 is living with a 65-year-old woman who is not his wife, but nevertheless has been wholly dependent on him for twenty years, the couple can receive only one monthly check—none for the dependent cohabitor.

Until recently, some older couples were better off with respect to Social Security benefits if they lived together as cohabitants instead of getting married. If the woman was a widow collecting maximum widow's benefits and the man was collecting maximum benefits himself, marriage would reduce their aggregate benefits to only one and one-half times the man's stipend. The 1978 amendments to the Social Security legislation eliminated this "marriage tax" and allowed both to retain their benefits after marriage.

Unmarried couples are typically denied benefits provided for spouses in other areas of social welfare. For example, unrelated persons living together cannot receive veteran's and unemployment benefits available to related dependents. Similarly, worker's compensation benefits, available to dependents of a worker who is injured and dies on the job, have long been limited to the worker's legal relatives.[25] However, this may be beginning to change, especially in more liberal states like California. In 1979, in the case of *Department of Industrial Relations* v. *Workers' Compensation Appeals Board*, a California appellate court upheld an award of a death benefit to Jeremy Tessler, a woman who had been living out of wedlock with the decedent Gary Bradburn for 4 months prior to his work-related death.[26] The court held that Jeremy was a dependent, as required by statute, because she and Gary had pooled their assets, shared expenses, and planned to marry.

Of course, this California decision does not bind other states, but a recent U.S. Supreme Court decision on food stamps does. In *U.S. Department of Agriculture* v. *Mareno*, the court concluded that it was a violation of Equal Protection to restrict food stamp benefits to households in which members are related.[27] Cohabitants are in a similarly improved position with respect to receipt of welfare benefits and AFDC (Aid to Families with Dependent Children). The Supreme Court has held that a needy parent who is living with an unmarried partner cannot be denied welfare benefits.[28]

However, such aid may bring special burdens: it may be conditioned on the recipient's willingness to identify the father of an out-of-wedlock child to enable local authorities to bring suit for paternity and child support against him.

Taxation

One economic distinction between marriage and cohabitation is the different amount of taxes couples must pay under federal and state laws—although here the married couple does not always reap the greater reward. The major "tax benefits" of marriage accrue to the married couple in a traditional relationship, in which the husband works to support the family and the wife is a full-time homemaker. This couple has a considerable tax advantage over a cohabiting couple. However, if the married woman is employed outside the home, the couple is no longer likely to be treated with favor; in fact, there is a "marriage tax" on the two-wage-earner family. They will probably pay a higher tax than two single people with the same combined income.

For example, in 1977 a married couple with a single income of $10,000 paid about $500 less in federal taxes than two cohabitants with the same single income. At $20,000 of income the "marriage benefit" rose to over a thousand dollars, and at $30,000 of income it was close to two thousand dollars.[29]

Cohabitors, however, are likely to be better off than married couples if there are two wage earners in the partnership. In 1977, nonmarital cohabitors paid 477 fewer tax dollars if each person earned $10,000. The tax advantage of cohabitation was close to $2,000 if the parties each earned $20,000, and $4,330 if each earned $30,000.

There is another potential tax disadvantage of cohabitation when the couple relies on a single wage earner. The nonearning partner might be required to report the day-to-day living expenses he or she receives to the Internal Revenue Service as taxable income. While a husband is legally required to support his wife, a cohabitor has no such legal obligation. Attorney Gary Randall argues that any income or support tendered in a cohabiting relationship can be viewed as "payment for services rendered," and may therefore be taxable.[30]

Some single-income cohabiting couples have attempted to improve their tax position by having the employed person claim his or her partner as a legal dependent in order to gain an additional deduction. Although the Internal Revenue Service has generally taken the position that unmarried cohabitors cannot claim each other as dependents, the only formal restriction on this type of claim is that a dependency deduction cannot be used when the relationship between the taxpayer and the dependent violates a local law.[31] In states where cohabitation is not illegal, such as California, it may therefore be possible for the working partner to claim the nonworking partner as a dependent.

Private Insurance and Credit

Efforts to obtain insurance can present sizable problems for couples living together. For example, because insurance companies typically require that the policy owner have an "insurable interest" in the insured, and because they assume that only relatives have such an interest, it has been rare for an insurer to write a policy that allows one cohabitant to insure the life of the other.[32]

Other difficulties arise with auto and home insurance policies that routinely extend coverage to all "residents of the household." Many companies narrowly interpret this clause to include only members of the insured's family. Similarly, family medical and hospitalization coverage is generally limited to the insured's spouse and dependent children (and frequently excludes illegitimate children).[33]

The problems that unmarried couples have incurred in trying to obtain various types of insurance may, however, soon decrease. Both the growing numbers of cohabitants, and the passage of laws (in a few states) that prohibit discrimination on the basis of marital status, are making insurers more willing to do business with unmarried partners.[34] For example, in one unusual case from the 1979 Washington, D.C. Court of Appeals, it was held that unmarried couples are protected by the Equal Credit Opportunity Act, which bars discrimination on the basis of marital status (among other grounds).[35] The case involved an unmarried couple who applied for a mortgage to buy property on Capitol Hill. Their application was rejected because they were not married and neither one had sufficient individual income to establish credit worthiness. The court reasoned that, since their incomes would have been aggregated if they were married, the refusal to aggregate them was discrimination on the basis of marital status.

The Legal Position of Children in Unwed Unions

When a cohabiting couple has children and fails to legitimize them, a host of legal problems may follow, both for the child and for the child's natural parents. In this section we will consider the legal position of the illegitimate child. In the following section we will examine the legal position of the parents.

Historically, children of unwed mothers have been denied most of the legal rights accorded legitimate children. In common law the illegitimate child had neither the right to support from his natural father nor the right to recover from the father's estate if the father died without making him a beneficiary of his will.[36] Some laws went so far as to invalidate testamentary gifts to illegitimate children in excess of a certain percentage of the deceased father's estate.

But the law has changed considerably since then. As the social stigma associated with illegitimacy has decreased, so have its legal consequences. Although illegitimate children still do not enjoy all the rights of legitimate children, a series of recent Supreme Court decisions has rapidly moved the law in that direction.

In 1973, in *Gomez v. Perez*,[37] a mother went to court to compel her daughter's natural father to contribute to the child's financial support. A Texas court denied her claim, but the U.S. Supreme Court characterized the denial of child support as a violation of the Equal Protection Clause of the Constitution. It held that illegitimate children are entitled to support from their natural fathers in the same manner as legitimate children (provided, of course, that paternity has been proven).

In a second 1973 case, *New Jersey Welfare Rights Organization v. Cahill*,[38] the Court invalidated a regulation of the New Jersey "Assistance to Families of the Working Poor" program for the same cause. The contested regulation provided benefits only to families of two opposite-sex adults "ceremoniously married" to each other with one or more legitimate minor children of their own. Its effect was to deny benefits to illegitimate children, and the Court ruled that illegal.

The rights of illegitimate children after the death of a natural parent are somewhat less clear. In 1968, in *Levy v. Louisiana*,[39] the Supreme Court granted illegitimate children an equal right to recover damages for the loss of their natural father. However, three years later, in *Labine v. Vincent*[40] (another Louisiana case) the

Court upheld a Louisiana law that barred an illegitimate child from inheritance in the absence of a will. In *Labine* the natural father had acknowledged his paternity in writing, but died without leaving a will. The U.S. Supreme Court reasoned that since the father could have overridden the law simply by making a will, the child was not unfairly deprived of the right to inherit.

The Court's reluctance to erase all disabilities of illegitimate children is further reflected in the 1976 case of *Matthews* v. *Lucas*,[41] which involved dependency benefits under the Social Security Act. The Act provides benefits to surviving legitimate children of a deceased wage earner without requiring them to prove their dependency on the decedent. Illegitimate children, on the other hand, must establish proof of both paternity and dependency in order to receive benefits. The Supreme Court upheld the different requirements as reasonable (in view of the absence of close family ties and frequent uncertainties concerning paternity). However, the Court has since relaxed this position. In *Trimble* v. *Gordon*,[42] (which presented a factual situation virtually indistinguishable from *Labine*) the Court upheld the right of two illegitimate children in Illinois to inherit from a father who died without a will.

Thus, although the general trend in recent cases has been toward the expansion of rights for illegitimate children, some obstacles remain. The *Matthews* case, for example, shows that where administrative convenience or government funds are involved, discrimination against illegitimate children may still be allowed. In addition, in order to qualify for any of the benefits discussed above, paternity must first be proved.

Paternity suits may be both costly and painful,[43] but they can easily be avoided by having an unwed father acknowledge the child as his. It would be wise for all unmarried couples with children to prepare a formal acknowledgment of paternity as a protection for their children's rights in all possible contingencies.

This need not be an elaborate document. It should clearly affirm that *x* and *y* are the parents of a particular child. The statement should be signed by both parties and notarized. In some states such an acknowledgement, when coupled with the father's acceptance of the child into his home, serves to legitimize the child. In others, it entitles the child to support and other benefits from the natural father.

Although a paternity statement could be drafted by a non-lawyer it would still be wise for the mother and father to consult a lawyer to see what the law of their state requires with respect to witnesses, whether the document should be recorded, etc.

But even a paternity statement from the parent(s) may not always be sufficient to protect the rights of an illegitimate child. A New York statute, for example, requires a court decree of paternity to enable the child to inherit without a will, a provision which the U.S. Supreme Court upheld in 1978 as rationally related to the proper administration of decedents' estates in *Lalli* v. *Lalli*.[44] As a consequence, the plaintiffs in that case, Robert Lalli and his sister, were denied a distribution from their father's estate even though they presented affidavits and other documents that demonstrated that their father had acknowledged them as his children. *

Many states now have statutes that retroactively "legitimate" certain classes of illegitimacy. For example, in many states a child becomes legitimate if its parents marry; in others the father's "public acknowledgement" or his having "received the child into his home" operate to legitimate the child.[45] For example, in California,[46] a child is considered legitimate if his or her unmarried parents live together, or if the father acknowledges paternity by having the child visit or live with his family. Furthermore, one California court decided that a child was legitimate because the parents had lived together for two years and were cohabiting when the mother became pregnant, even though the couple separated before the child was born. In this case the court reasoned that the child had been received into the father's family *in utero*.[47]

Illegitimate children are now generally in a better legal position in the seven states which have adopted the Uniform Parentage Act.† That Act, designed to establish substantive legal equality for all children regardless of the marital status of their parents, provides, in part, that a man will be presumed to be the father of a child if he and the child's natural mother are, or have been, mar-

___

*Although the court recognized that compliance would impose a hardship on some illegitimate children, it upheld the statute nonetheless because it bore a rational relationship to the proper administration of estates, i.e., to minimize fraudulent assertions of paternity. *Lalli* v. *Lalli* 99 S. Ct. 518 (1978) at 526.

†The Uniform Parentage Act provides substantive legal equality for all children regardless of the marital status of their parents. As such, the Act embodies the ruling of a series of U.S. Supreme Court cases in the late 1960's and early 1970's mandating equal legal treatment for legitimate and illegitimate offspring in several areas except intestate succession from the child's father.

As of 1979, the following states had adopted the act: California, Colorado, Hawaii, Montana, North Dakota, Washington, and Wyoming.

ried to each other and the child is born during the marriage, or within 300 days after the marriage is terminated; or have attempted to marry prior to or after his or her birth, but the marriage is deemed invalid; or if he receives the child into his home and publicly acknowledges the child as his natural child.

The Legal Rights of Unwed Parents

Concurrent with the growing acknowledgement of rights for illegitimate children, we have experienced an expanding recognition of the rights of unwed parents, especially of fathers. Traditionally, the mother of an illegitimate child had an exclusive right to govern the child's life; the father had no claim whatsoever. But in the landmark case of *Stanley* v. *Illinois*,[48] the Supreme Court began to carve out a sphere of rights for the father.

Stanley involved an unmarried couple who had lived together intermittently for 18 years. During that time they had three children. When Joan Stanley died, the State of Illinois declared the children wards of the court, and placed them in the care of a court-appointed guardian. Peter Stanley brought suit to regain custody of the children, claiming he had been denied equal treatment under Illinois law. The state law provided that married parents and unwed mothers could not be deprived of their children without a hearing and proof of their neglect; however, a father need only be proved unwed to be deprived of his children. Mr. Stanley's fitness as a parent was considered irrelevant.

The U.S. Supreme Court agreed with the plaintiff and held that unwed fathers must be granted the same parental rights as married parents or unwed mothers. As a result of this decision, the father of an out-of-wedlock child today has a claim to his child. The mother may no longer have absolute power to prevent a child's exposure to the father—unless she can prove it would be detrimental to the child.[49]

We noted above that it would be wise for unwed fathers to acknowledge paternity in writing to protect the child's rights. This acknowledgement may also enhance the father's rights—to visitation, custody, recovery for wrongful death, etc. In addition, an acknowledgement of paternity can give force to a couple's written agreement for ongoing child support, as well as for custody in the event of death or dissolution. While their agreement would not be binding on the court under the present state of the law, most courts tend to follow the parents' wishes in custody awards.

Property

Suprisingly, most states make little distinction between married persons and cohabitants with respect to property rights in an on-going relationship. In the 42 common law states both husband and wife retain their own earnings and property as separate property (see Chapter 2). Thus in most cases married men and cohabiting men alike are entitled to keep their earnings and whatever property they acquire, and to spend, save, or sell it as they wish; nor do they have any claims to their partners' earnings. Similarly, the married woman who works in the paid labor force is in the same position as the cohabiting woman who earns a salary or who accumulates property: each is entitled to her own earnings and neither has any right to her partner's earnings.

Much the same holds true for the full-time homemaker in either relationship (unless she lives in one of the eight community property states). Whether married or not, she has no legal right to her part-ner's income or to the property he acquires in the course of their relationship. Although the married woman has the theoretical ad-vantage of being entitled to support, in practice both she and the cohabiting woman are "entitled" only to what their male partners choose to give them.

In the eight community property states, however, the married woman is in a far superior position. As a legal wife she owns half of the income and wealth her husband accrues and can spend it or otherwise dispose of it as she chooses—to buy food or clothing, to take a trip, to pay for an operation, to buy presents for others, or to pledge as credit for any of these expenses. In contrast, the cohabit-ing homemaker in a community property state typically has no le-gal claim to the earnings or property her partner accumulates in the course of their relationship.*

In summary, then, although the married woman has a signifi-cant legal advantage in the eight community property states, she has remarkably little advantage over the cohabiting woman during an ongoing relationship in the 42 common law property states.

*Recent changes in the law as a result of the 1975 California Supreme Court decision in *Marvin* v. *Marvin* are discussed in Chapter 15.

However, as we will discover in the next section, when either relationship is terminated by death or dissolution, major differences surface nationwide.

Legal Consequences at Death and Dissolution

Not surprisingly, most of the litigation dealing with the rights of individuals who have lived together occurs after their relationship has ended, and centers on property acquired in the course of the relationship. Problems concerning the division or award of property can arise in the context of both death and dissolution. In either event the traditional judicial and legislative response has been the same: unless a couple has an explicit written agreement to the contrary, the law tends to leave matters "as they are." Thus at the time a relationship is dissolved, whoever has legal title to property is allowed to keep it as his or her own. Typically, this has meant that the male retains the property because most relationships, marital and nonmarital alike, have been based on a sex-typed division of rights and duties in which the man is the wage earner, the woman the homemaker, and the wage earner "owns" the property acquired through his wages. While a homemaker may ask the courts for "equitable" relief, and indeed may be deemed morally entitled to it in the eyes of some courts, she has no "legal right" to "his" money or property.

After legal marriage, in contrast, the homemaking wife is entitled by law in most states to alimony and an "equitable" share of her husband's property upon divorce. As his widow she is usually assured a nonbarrable share of his estate. An unmarried woman, however, has no "right" to her partner's property after dissolution or his death.

Many unmarried homemakers have challenged this rule in the courts in attempts to obtain a share of the money or property acquired by a wage-earning male in the course of their relationship. Some have sought payment for homemaking services; others have asked for an interest in the property acquired through the couple's joint efforts. In both cases the traditional courts have been singularly unresponsive to the women's claims. A brief examination of these cases is instructive, although we will postpone our discussion of the most recent developments in the law to Chapter 15.

Claims for Payment for Services Rendered

The courts have employed two rationales in denying unmarried co-habitants payment for services they have provided. In one line of cases the validity of the claim has been denied because of the parties' illicit, or *meretricious*, relationship (a meretricious relationship is one in which the parties openly cohabit without marriage). In the second line of cases the services at issue are assumed to have been given as a "gift."

Meretricious relationships. To illustrate the first rationale, consider the following case. In *Willis* v. *Willis*[50] a woman sought to recover for the value of the services she performed for a man with whom she had lived. The woman alleged that, aside from performing "wifely" duties, she had maintained the man's rooming house and worked in his cabaret as a hostess and entertainer. The court nevertheless found these services "incidental" to her illicit sexual relationship with the man and decreed that she should not be compensated. The court reasoned as follows:

> [A] woman who knowingly and voluntarily lives in illicit relations with a man cannot recover . . . for services rendered him during such relationship. . . . [S]uch cohabitation being in violation of principles of morality and chastity, and so against public policy, the law will not imply a promise to pay for services rendered under such circumstances.[51]

It is important to note that the courts make a clear distinction between a "meretricious" relationship and one in which at least one party mistakenly, but in good faith, believes herself or himself married (legally termed a "putative" spouse). The law has traditionally protected putative spouses and allowed them to receive many of the benefits of a valid marriage. Meretricious spouses, as we have seen, have received no protections, and indeed one suspects that some courts have considered it appropriate to mete out special punishment to the woman who is party to a meretricious relationship.

Gratuitous services. The second rationale the courts have commonly used to deny compensation for services between cohabitors presumes that one person's services are freely given to the other as a "gift." For example, in the 1975 Oregon case of *York* v. *Place*,[52] the plaintiff sought recovery for the services she had provided for a man during the eight years they lived together before his death. The couple had jointly built a house and worked on his farm. The woman cooked, did the housework, and performed the "other chores a farm wife generally does." She also used her $1,500 savings to pay for materials for the house and for furniture and appliances. At the time of death the couple's only income came from the man's Social Security. The court, however, denied the plaintiff's claim for compensation because

> . . . in the normal course of human affairs persons living together in a close relationship perform services for each other without expectation of payment. Payment in the usual sense is not expected because the parties mutually care for each other's needs. Also because services are performed out of a feeling of affection or a sense of obligation, not for payment.[53]

In this case there was evidence that Place had promised York the farm after he died, and witnesses testified that he had told them the farm would go to her at his death. But even this testimony was insufficient to overcome the court's presumption that her services were (or should have been) performed without expectation of payment.

The *York* court's presumption derives from legal precedents established in the handling of claims of spouses or relatives. In those cases the courts have traditionally held that services are performed out of love or obligation, and not in expectation of property or payment. Nonmarital relationships are held to fit within this rule because they are "close relationships"[54] analogous to marriage. But inside or outside marriage, such a blanket rule with respect to services rendered seems open to question.

Claims for a Share in Property Accumulated

Although the financial stakes in *York* were relatively low, the same principle would apply irrespective of the amount of property at issue. If the estate had flourished while the couple lived together, the woman would have been without remedy—even though her services had enabled the man to acquire a great deal of property for their mutual benefit—because the rule, simply stated, has been that a person who willfully lives in a sinful relationship acquires no property rights. Sometimes (but not in the *York* case cited above) when a meretricious spouse has contributed *funds* toward a joint investment, she may be allowed to recover her investment. However, in the past these doctrines have been applied only to situations in which the woman made a *financial* investment. If she contributed only services (as a housewife and a mother), the courts have almost uniformly held that as a meretricious spouse she is not entitled to recover an interest in any resulting property.

Two California cases reflect the courts' historical intransigence concerning the value of household services. In 1943, in *Vallera* v. *Vallera*,[55] an unmarried couple lived together for two years. During that time, using earnings provided by the man and services provided by the woman, they accumulated property worth $60,000. Because California is a community property state, the woman claimed a half interest in the property when the relationship dissolved. The California Supreme Court rejected her claim because she had contributed only services—not funds.

The rule that prevents the homemaker from recovering for her services inevitably works against the woman—while the man is allowed to retain the entire fruits of their joint efforts. As Justice Curtis concluded in his dissenting *Vallera* opinion:

> Unless it can be argued that a woman's services as cook, housekeeper, and homemaker are valueless, it would seem logical that if, when she contributes money to the purchase of property, her interest will be protected, then when she contributes her services in the home, her interest in property accumulated should be protected. Just because the man, who in the instant case was equally guilty, earned the money to buy the property, should not bar the woman from any rights at all in the property, although her services made the acquisition possible. Such a rule gives all the advantages to be gained from such a relationship to the man with no burdens.
>
> . . . To permit the defendant to retain the entire fruits of their joint efforts is contrary to the dictates of simple justice.[56]

Vallera left in some doubt the question of whether a woman's nonwifely services might give rise to an interest in property acquired in the course of a cohabiting relationship. In 1962, in *Keene* v. *Keene*,[57] the California high court clarified that point with a majority "No"—thus reaffirming its refusal to compensate a woman for any services whatever when rendered in a nonmarital union.

Keene involved a couple who had cohabited for 18 years. When they began living together, in 1946, the man owned only a rundown ranch. Ten years later, he was able to sell this ranch, by then vastly improved, and all the flocks and herds on it for a substantial figure. The money from the sale was then invested in furniture and real estate businesses. Before the sale of the ranch, the woman in the case engaged in various farm chores such as raising turkeys and chickens, sowing and harvesting of crops, herding cattle, and clearing the land, in addition to performing wifely duties. After the ranch was sold she helped with the business operations.

The court rejected the woman's claim that her services in operating the ranch (and business) entitled her to an interest in the property. Only a monetary contribution, the court insisted, would entitle her to a property interest. Once again, however, one of the justices issued a vigorous dissent that attacked the double standard in this rule. Justice Peters argued that the majority opinion told a woman who had "sinned," by knowingly entering into a meretricious relationship, that she would not be permitted to share in the property she helped to accumulate. But the man involved would be allowed to retain the property, even though he had "sinned" to an equal degree.

This is not to imply, however, that only women have suffered from the court's intransigence concerning property rights in nonmarried cohabitation. Although the woman is much less likely to acquire title to property in such a relationship, a male who does not have title is equally disadvantaged. For example, in *Creasman* v. *Boyle*,[58] when Harvey Creasman and Caroline Paul began living together in 1939 each of them owned an old car and little else. Later that year, Caroline contracted to purchase in her name a parcel of real estate containing a one-bedroom house. She made a $90 down payment on the property with money they received from the sale of Harvey's car.

The next year Harvey went to work in a shipyard, where he was continuously employed until 1946. The payments for the property were made with the money Harvey earned while he and Caroline lived together. In addition, using his own labor and materials paid for with his wages, Harvey built two additional rooms onto the house. Meanwhile, Caroline performed housekeeping tasks and attended to their business affairs.

Caroline died after the couple had lived together for seven years, and in 1947 Harvey sought to recover his property interest: half of the real property (now worth $3,000) and $1,700 in a savings account held in Caroline's name but accumulated from the proceeds of savings bonds Harvey purchased in the course of his employment. The Washington State Supreme Court denied his claim, holding that property acquired by an unmarried couple who live together as husband and wife belongs to the party who has legal title. The court found that the couple had acquired the property with full knowledge of the implications of their meretricious relationship and therefore "presumed, as a matter of law, that the parties intended to dispose of it exactly as they did dispose of it."[59]

This reasoning indicates to what extent the courts have been willing to ignore the facts of a case and fall back on legal fictions. The courts in most states still follow the rule employed in *Creasman* and regard the jointly acquired property of meretricious partners as "belonging to the one in whose name the legal title to the property stands"[60]—even when the actions of the parties suggest that they intended to share everything.

The Exceptions: Explicit Contracts, Putative Spouses, Common-Law Marriage

Traditionally there have been three exceptions to the legal rule that treats the property accumulated by unwed cohabitants as the sole property of the person who holds the legal title. The first, now being recognized by a growing number of states, is the case in which unmarried cohabitants have formulated an explicit agreement, or contract, with respect to the disposition of their jointly acquired property. Because the legal status of contracts between unmarried cohabitants is discussed at length in Chapter 15, it will not be detailed here. However, it is important to emphasize that the written contract is undoubtedly the most effective way for unmarried cohabitants to protect their rights and interests in property they have jointly acquired.

The other two cases are not really "exceptions" to the legal doctrine outlined above. Rather, they are the result of a special set of legal interpretations developed to protect parties who *intend* to assume the status of legal marriage but who, through neglect or error, have failed to do so.

The first of these is the putative spouse doctrine, created to prevent injustice to persons who mistakenly, but in good faith, believe themselves legally married. Such a situation arises when a ceremonial marriage is found to have been void or voidable as, for example, when one party has secured a faulty divorce or has failed to obtain a divorce and lied about it to the new partner.

The party or parties who mistakenly believe themselves to be married are known as putative spouses, and the law has traditionally allowed such persons to receive many of the incidents of a valid marriage. For example, the Uniform Marriage and Divorce Act provides that any person who has cohabited with another in the good faith belief that they were married, may acquire the rights of a legal spouse to property, maintenance, and support. Most of the putative spouse cases involve women who have been deliberately misled by men, and the doctrine affords these women many of the rights of a legal wife.[61]

Kay and Amyx summarize the rights of a putative spouse in California:

> In California the only requisite for putative spouse status is a good faith belief that one is validly married.
>
> The courts have granted the putative spouse the right to an equitable division of the property that would have belonged to the community in a valid marriage. If no such property is available for distribution, the putative spouse may be awarded a lump sum representing the reasonable value of the household services rendered by the putative spouse in excess of the value of maintenance and support furnished by the other party. No case has awarded the putative spouse permanent alimony, and dictum in one case suggests that no such right exists. When the relationship is terminated by death, the surviving putative spouse has been awarded all the quasi-marital property as well as a spousal share of the decedent's separate property. The putative spouse has been accorded the right to bring suit for the wrongful death of the deceased partner, and to recover worker's compensation death benefits as a surviving widow as well as benefits due a surviving spouse under the public employees retirement fund. Since children born of void or voidable marriages are deemed legitimate in California, putative spouses have the same rights and obligations toward their children as do married persons.[62]

The status of putative spouse derives from a legal marriage analogy, for—unlike meretricious spouses, who deliberately elect not to marry—the persons whose rights are governed by this doctrine have chosen to be married. Though the marriage upon which a party has relied is shown to be invalid, the law seeks to equate that party as closely as possible with a legally married person.[63]

The final exception, the case of common-law marriage, is similarly derived from an analogy to legal marriage, and it too pertains to people who believe themselves to be married as well as to people who behave like married persons. While only 13 states currently recognize common-law marriage,* in these states the law gives the couple many of the rights of legal spouses. The doctrine that validates these unions typically requires that the parties *intend* to enter a marriage-like relationship, and hold themselves out to the community as husband and wife.[64]

Thus while both putative spouses and persons in common-law marriages appear to be exceptions to the legal doctrine that governs unmarried relationships, they might be called exceptions that prove the rule. It is precisely because these people intend to establish marital unions that they are accorded a legal status similar to that of persons legally married. However, as we have seen, cohabitants who have willfully lived in "sinful" relationships have historically acquired none of the rights or incidents of legal marriage.

*Alabama, Colorado, Georgia, Idaho, Iowa, Kansas, Montana, Ohio, Oklahoma, Pennsylvania, Rhode Island, South Carolina, Texas and the District of Columbia. From Homer H. Clark, Jr., *Cases and Problems on Domestic Relations*, third edition (St. Paul, Minn.: West, 1980).

CHAPTER 15

To <u>Marvin</u> and Beyond: Contracts Between Unwed Cohabitants

Chapter 14 discussed the courts' historical reluctance to assume that property rights arise from cohabitation, and suggested that couples who live together should enter a written contract to protect their respective rights to assets acquired during their relationship. Here we will examine how contracts between cohabitants have been and are likely to be treated in the courts.

The first section of this chapter reviews the traditional law and the lack of recognition accorded to contracts between unmarried cohabitants in the past. We then discuss new developments in the law, focusing primarily on the trend-setting opinion of the California Supreme Court in *Marvin* v. *Marvin* in 1976. The third section explores the profound effects of the *Marvin* decision in other states. The chapter concludes with an exploration of future prospects for the enforcement of intimate contracts.

The Traditional Law

In the past, most courts have been reluctant to enforce contracts between unmarried cohabitants. In her classic analysis of the property rights of de facto spouses, Professor Carol Bruch points to three impediments in the traditional law: first, a sexual relationship between the parties often rendered their contract illegal; second, doctrines applied to business transactions were used to invalidate their contracts; and third, the courts refused to recognize the value of the homemaker services as adequate consideration for the contract.[1] Let us briefly examine each of these obstacles.

The Illegality of Illicit Sexual Services

Courts have traditionally refused to uphold contracts between unmarried cohabitants because they did not want to give effect to agreements for "illicit sexual services." This reasoning stemmed from the dubious assumption that all contracts between unmarried cohabitants were in fact contracts for prostitution—the illegal agreement of one party (typically the man) to pay for the sexual services of the other party (typically the woman).

If contracts between unmarried cohabitants were based on an illegal benefit—or in the words of contract law, on "illegal consideration"—they were not entitled to enforcement in a court of law. All legal contracts must be based on something of value or "consideration." In business contracts the consideration has typically been money, property, goods, or services. The traditional courts have managed to ignore the fact that most contracts between unmarried cohabitants are based on similar kinds of consideration. Instead they have assumed that the only "services" exchanged are the illicit sexual services of one party in consideration for the property or support of the other, and therefore have held that this illegal sexual consideration invalidated the contract.

This position is illustrated by the early (1898) New York case of *Vincent* v. *Moriarty*,[2] which involved a couple who lived together for eleven years after agreeing to pool their property and earnings. During their cohabitation they purchased a house and furnishings in the man's name and saved money, which the man kept in his possession. They jointly accumulated $10,000, which they applied to the mortgage on the house. In addition to housekeeping duties, the woman continued her dressmaking business, took in boarders, and raised the couple's child. She reported that they had lived together for mutual love and affection, and she believed that the assets they had accumulated during their cohabitation were "theirs."

After they separated the man kept the home and property which he argued belonged to him alone. The woman sued to recover her share under the terms of their pooling agreement. Although the trial court upheld the contract and ordered an equitable division of the property, the appellate court reversed the trial court's decision. In a forceful defense of traditional morality, it held that because the consideration included immoral concubinage, the entire contract was unenforceable:

> It is difficult to imagine a more audacious challenge to a court of justice for the enforcement of an immoral contract than that which appears in this complaint. It will be observed that it contained no allegations disclosing such a condition as arises when a young girl, ignorant and unfamiliar with the wiles of men, is deceived and betrayed into an illicit union, where a court might sometimes be astute in seeking methods to avoid injustice. Here, the plaintiff alleges that she had contracted with the defendant to enter into a state of concubinage, asking a court of equity to sanction the contract and award her the price of her shame.[3]

One flaw in this traditional position is that it ignores the fact that there is an exchange of sexual services. Both the woman and the man provide sexual services for *each other*. A second glaring flaw is that it fails to recognize the nonsexual services that a woman typically provides. For example, in *Vincent* the woman not only cared for the children and the household and thereby contributed to the man's earning capacity, she also conducted a dressmaking business. Surely the court could have recognized the monetary value of her contribution had it wanted to. However, it clearly did not want to; rather, it was intent upon making her pay for violating society's mores—and it did this by preventing her from acquiring the property to which she was entitled.

The courts' punitive attitude toward women who have chosen to live in "sinful" relationships is further illustrated by the more recent (1958) case of *Wellmaker* v. *Roberts*.[4] This case involved an unmarried couple who contracted to build a house and live in it together. They agreed that the woman would finance the construction and the man would provide the labor. After the house was completed, the man breached the contract and began living in it with another woman. The court rejected the first woman's contract claim for return of her money because part of the consideration was a promise of illicit cohabitation.

In these traditional cases, the courts have flatly denied cohabitants their normal rights to contract about their property simply because they are living together. The courts have focused on the couple's sexual relationship and have used that as an excuse to invalidate what would otherwise have been a binding and enforceable agreement.

In a minority of states, including California, the courts adopted a slightly more liberal position and were willing to uphold property agreements between cohabitants that could be severed from "the illegal consideration". That is, if the contracting parties could, to the court's satisfaction, separate the sexual relationship from the property agreement, the property agreement would be upheld.

This severability principle was initially set out in the 1932 California case of *Trutalli* v. *Meraviglia*,[5] which involved a couple who had lived together for eleven years after agreeing to pool their earnings for their mutual benefit. The woman performed household services, while the man was employed outside the home. The man held title, in his name alone, to all the property they had acquired together.

The trial court found two separate agreements in this domestic arrangement: one was an agreement to live together without marriage and to openly assume the marital relationship; the second was an agreement to pool their joint labors. The woman was awarded a half-interest in the two parcels of real estate held in the man's name. The California Supreme Court upheld the trial court's award and concurred in viewing the property agreement as "separate and distinct" from the sexual agreement:

> While the trial court found that the parties agreed "upon the making and entering into" the agreement of cohabitation that they would invest their earnings in property to be held jointly by them, it did not find that this later agreement was a part of, or that it was in any manner connected with, their agreement to unlawfully cohabit together. The two agreements, although made at the same time, are separate and distinct contracts, and neither is made dependent upon the other.[6]

This reasoning has been followed fairly consistently in subsequent California cases. For example, in a 1954 case, *Bridges* v. *Bridges*,[7] an unmarried couple formed an agreement calling for the pooling of their joint assets, work, labor, and services. The man worked as a salesman and the woman took care of their six children from prior marriages, improved their property, and performed housekeeping duties. After the couple separated, the man claimed the pooling agreement was invalid because it was based on an illegal sexual relationship. However, the court rejected his argument and upheld the contract:

> Appellant contends that as a matter of law an agreement found to have existed between the parties was unenforceable for having been made in contemplation of and because of the promise of meretricious relationship. There is nothing in the record which furnishes a basis for this contention. Neither party testified that there was any agreement that the parties would pool their assets and share their accumulations in contemplation of meretricious relations nor do the findings of the court contain such matter by implication. Nowhere is it expressly testified to by anyone that there was anything in the agreement for the pooling of assets and the sharing of accumulations that contemplated meretricious relations as any part of the consideration or as an object of the agreement.[8]

Even in California, however, relief has been denied where the court believed that the pooling agreement could not be severed from the cohabitation. In the 1950 case of *Hill* v. *Estate of Westbrook*,[9] for instance, a man and woman lived together for sixteen years. During that time, in addition to performing "wifely" duties, the woman assisted the man in his store and waited on customers. She also worked in a shirt factory and used her earnings for his benefit. Although the trial court found, in her favor, that the man had promised to provide for her in his will (which he failed to do) and to reimburse her for her services in "living with him as man and wife during all of said time and bearing the said Charles Westbrook two children,"[10] the appellate court reversed this judgment and ruled that the woman could not recover the money because it could not distinguish which part of the award was for the promise to live together and bear children, for which the court ruled no recovery could be allowed.

This decision indicates that even the less tradition-bound courts have sanctioned a double standard that punished women who lived in "illicit" relationships while rewarding their male partners. For when courts refuse to enforce contracts between unmarried cohabitants, the typical result is that the woman is deprived of a share in the jointly accumulated property, while the man is allowed to keep much more than his share.

Application of Market Place Concepts

The second impediment to agreements between unwed cohabitants has been the courts' refusal to enforce contracts unless they meet standards required of commercial contracts. Two conditions in particular have provided a barrier: (1) the need for an express or explicit agreement and (2) the need for adequate consideration.

Typically the law has required that enforceable contracts formed in the market place reflect an express agreement between two parties. One party must have agreed, either in writing or orally, to do X in exchange for the other's doing Y. Perhaps one has pledged to deliver goods in exchange for the other's paying him a stated sum of money. While it seems reasonable to assume that most commercial dealings are based on these explicit agreements,* they are clearly not normative in intimate relations. Close friends, relatives, and lovers are much more likely to assume that they can count on each other. An explicit agreement to provide care, support, or affection seems unnecessary at best, and an affront to the relationship at worst. Indeed an unlimited all-encompassing commitment is the very essence of parental concern, friendship, and romantic love. Thus the commercial standard that assumes all contracts are explicit may bar legal recognition of the less formal understandings that are characteristic of intimate relationships.

In addition, in the less common situations in which intimates do make explicit contracts—such as a promise to support a daughter through college if she tutors her brother in math—their contracts are much less likely to be written down. Although most oral contracts have the same legal standing as written contracts, their existence is more difficult to prove. That burden of proof becomes especially severe if the courts rely on commercial or business standards to judge their existence and validity.

These commercial standards of proof are, in fact, increasingly inappropriate because recent developments in contract law reflect a new recognition of the need for noncommercial standards to deal with oral agreements between relatives.[11] For example, let us say that a niece cares for an aging aunt and uncle who promise to leave her their home in return for her services. After her aging relatives

---

*Even a business deal that closes with a handshake is typically based on a history of prior business, shared assumptions about normal business practice, and a substantial body of business law to provide the basis for an implied agreement.

die, the niece discovers that their original will, leaving the house to their nephew, has never been changed. Under traditional contract law, the niece's claim would have been dismissed. But, more recently, the courts have developed commonsense doctrines of equity to preclude such harsh results. As Professor Carol Bruch observes, over time the traditional commercial requirements for written promises have been gradually replaced by "quasi-contractual doctrines that would provide equitable results."[12]

Nevertheless, as Professor Bruch also notes, these developments in the common law of contracts have, in the past, typically been overlooked by courts faced with implied contracts between unmarried cohabitants. The courts have insisted instead on the unnecessarily rigid requirements of proof in formal commercial contracts.

Adequate Consideration and the Value of Personal Services

A final issue raised by commercial contract standards is the question of adequate "consideration." As noted above, all contracts require that both parties give up something in exchange for what they receive. In commercial contracts the consideration typically is a sum of money or a piece of property with a market value. But in contracts between intimates, the consideration provided by the female partner is often household services, which the courts have refused to recognize as adequate. One excuse, as discussed above, has been that the only services the female partner provides are sexual services, and that sex is illegal consideration. A second excuse, discussed in Chapter 14, is that the nonsexual services the woman provides are intended as "gifts," which do not require recompense, rather than one side of an exchange. A final position is that nonsexual services such as homemaking and child care have so little monetary value that they are not sufficient consideration for the man's agreement to support or to share property.

Thus the third major flaw in the traditional legal position is its failure to recognize the extent and value of the nonsexual services the female partner typically provides in a cohabiting relationship. And yet, while the courts have negated the value of the woman's contribution in the cases we have reviewed, it is clear that the woman and her partner do not view her contribution as worthless or as a gift: both typically assume the woman has earned a share of the parties' assets, such as the house or the business, in return for her efforts. Nevertheless, the traditional courts have ignored these expectations.

New Trends in the Law

In 1976 the state Supreme Courts in Oregon and California took a bold step forward and upheld the contractual rights of openly cohabiting couples. The courts in these states have begun a major transformation of the law with two important cases: *Latham* and *Marvin*.

The Latham Case in Oregon

In 1976 the Oregon Supreme Court discarded the two traditional approaches to contracts between unwed cohabitants—the conservative stance of rejecting all agreements between unmarried cohabitants, and the more liberal stance of recognizing only those agreements in which the sexual relationship was severable. It decided that even the severability principle was a dubious legal distinction which often stood in the way of just results.

In *Latham* v. *Latham*,[13] the Oregon court was faced with an agreement between unmarried parties who had agreed to live together as if they were husband and wife. In consideration for the woman's "living with [the man], caring for and keeping after him, and furnishing and providing him with all amenities of married life," the man had agreed to pay her one-half of the property accumulated during the agreement. The man, however, refused to give the woman any of the $100,000 worth of property that had been accumulated, contending that the agreement was void as against public policy because the consideration was future illicit cohabitation. The Oregon court upheld the agreement and awarded the woman half the property. In so doing it noted that past reluctance to enforce contracts between cohabitants had typically resulted in an unjust deprivation for the female:

> The application of the principle that such a contract will not be enforced has often resulted in the male keeping the assets accumulated in the relationship and the female being deprived of what she jointly accumulated. Although the parties have been jointly accumulating property for 19 years, that would be the result in this case if the principle were applied. While not condoning the parties' conduct, such a result seems to be unduly harsh.

For these reasons we hold that such an agreement is not void. We are not validating an agreement in which the only or primary consideration is sexual intercourse. The agreement here contemplated all the burdens and the amenities of married life.[14]

The Marvin Case in California

In discussing the *Marvin* case it is important to distinguish the 1976 California Supreme Court opinion,[15] which articulated new legal principles, from the 1979 trial court decision on remand,[16] which dealt with the facts of the case. For our purposes the California Supreme Court opinion is more significant. That decision not only created new legal precedents, it also established a new sociological approach to unwed cohabitation—signaling a new recognition (and acceptance) of changing social mores. As Professor Henry Foster and attorney Doris Jonas Freed observe, the Marvin decision was "avant-garde in the sense that the court took cognizance of the obvious fact that more and more couples, in California and elsewhere, were engaged in nonmarital cohabitation and that such a change of mores warranted a reconsideration of public policy regarding their rights."[17]

Marvin was initiated by Michelle Triola Marvin, a singer who lived with the actor Lee Marvin for close to seven years, from 1964 to 1970, without marriage. Michelle alleged that she and Lee had an oral contract. The contract entitled her to half of the property that Lee acquired while they were living together, and to support for the rest of her life. According to Michelle their contract had the following provisions:

1. They would live together and combine their efforts and earnings.
2. They would share equally any property accumulated as a result of their efforts.
3. They would represent themselves to the public as husband and wife.
4. Michelle would provide services as "companion, homemaker, housekeeper, and cook."
5. Michelle would give up her career as an entertainer to devote herself full time to providing services.
6. Lee would "provide for all the plaintiff's financial support and needs for the rest of her life."[18]

During the years they lived together, substantial real and personal property (including motion picture rights worth more than $1 million) was acquired in Lee Marvin's name. At the end of seven years, Lee asked Michelle to move out of the house. He promised to give her $850 a month for the next five years. After eighteen months he refused to provide further support. Michelle then sued him for breaching their agreement.

The trial court originally granted Lee's motion to dismiss the suit because Michelle had suffered no legally recognizable injury, but the California Supreme Court reversed that decision. It held that if Michelle's allegations could be proven, she would have a valid contractual claim and could recover half of the property. The case was then remanded (i.e., returned) to the trial court for a hearing of the evidence.

The California Supreme Court decision in *Marvin* established three important legal precedents, negating each of the three traditional legal barriers discussed in the first section of this chapter. First, as noted above, it adopted a revolutionary view of unwed cohabitation, setting new standards for appropriate public policy. In response to Lee Marvin's contention that the alleged contract violated public policy because it was so closely related to the "immoral" character of the couple's relationship, the court announced a new standard: "A contract between nonmarital partners is unenforceable only to the extent that it explicitly rests upon the immoral and illicit consideration of meretricious sexual services."[19] The *Marvin* court thus took the scarlet letter off the chest of unwed cohabitants,[20] assuring them the same rights as all other contracting parties. As the court stated:

> The mores of the society have indeed changed so radically in regard to cohabitation that we cannot impose a standard based on alleged moral considerations that have apparently been so widely abandoned by so many. . . . In summary, we base our opinion on the principle that adults who voluntarily live together and engage in sexual relations are nonetheless as competent as any other persons to contract respecting their earnings and property rights.[21]

The second important precedent established by the Marvin decision was the extension of equitable remedies to cohabiting couples. The *Marvin* court expressed a willingness to look beyond traditional doctrines of commercial law and to recognize the diversity of semicontractual and equitable remedies that could be used to provide "justice" for parties in intimate relationships. Although Michelle Marvin alleged that she and Lee Marvin had an express contract (i.e., an explicit agreement), the California Supreme Court clearly stated that it was appropriate to look beyond express contracts and to grant relief on other contractual and equitable theories as well: "In the absence of an express contract, the courts should inquire into the conduct of the parties to determine whether the conduct demonstrates an implied contract, agreement of partnership, or joint venture, or some other tacit understanding between the parties."[22]

The third important principle established by the *Marvin* decision was the recognition of the value of homemakers' services. The court held that household services could provide sufficient consideration for an agreement to share or divide property acquired during the relationship. The *Marvin* court noted that prior case law was inconsistent in its treatment of property accumulated through joint efforts. On one hand, if a partner made a financial contribution, the courts recognized that person's right to a portion of the accumulated property. On the other hand, however, the cases "held that a nonmarital partner who rendered services in the absence of express contract could assert no right to property acquired during the relationship."[23]

In rejecting this traditional position the *Marvin* court pointed to the unfairness that typically resulted when the homemaker's services were disregarded. As it noted:

> Unless it can be argued that a woman's services as cook, housekeeper, and homemaker are valueless, it would seem logical that if, when she contributes money to the purchase of property, her interest will be protected, then when she contributes her services in the home, her interest in property accumulated should be protected.[24]

Thus the *Marvin* court affirmed the value of the homemaker's contribution and, in so doing, provided an equitable as well as a contractual basis for homemakers to assert their rights to property acquired during unwed cohabitation.

After Marvin: New Standards and New Cases

How have the courts dealt with alleged contracts between unmarried partners since *Marvin*? What standards will they use in the future?

In April 1979 the National Law Journal reported that the principles articulated in *Marvin* were supported in seventeen states, while only four states rejected them.* What standards have the courts used to make these decisions?

Some indication of the new standards is offered by sequential questions posed by Judge Arthur Marshall of the Los Angeles Superior Court when he examined the evidence in the *Marvin* case on remand in 1979.[25] First, he asked, is there proof of an express contract between the parties, either in writing or as attested to by the partners? If not, is there proof of an implied contract? If not, is there an equitable doctrine that is appropriate to do justice to the "reasonable expectations" of the parties?

Let us briefly examine each of these standards and see how they have been applied by other states.

Finding an Express Contract

As noted earlier in this chapter, an express contract is *an explicit* agreement between two parties. It can be oral or in writing. In either case, it is a conscious and voluntary understanding between the parties representing their mutual consent to certain terms and conditions.

We all make express contracts in the course of our everyday lives —agreeing to pay a neighbor's son or daughter for watering our lawn or babysitting, promising to share the cost of a wedding present with a relative, or agreeing to reimburse a car pool driver for the cost of gasoline. Although people in long-term relationships— friends, neighbors, and relatives—rarely put their agreements in writing, they are valid contracts nevertheless.

The main disadvantage of an oral agreement is that neither party can point to a piece of paper that clearly specifies its terms. Typically, however, both parties abide by the agreement. In addition

---

*The seventeen states that support *Marvin* are California, Connecticut, Illinois, Kentucky, Massachusetts, Michigan, Minnesota, New Hampshire, New Jersey, New York, Oklahoma, Oregon, Texas, Utah, Washington, Wisconsin, and Wyoming. *National Law Journal*, 1, no. 31 (April 16, 1979):14. This tally is somewhat suspect because some of the decisions cited predated *Marvin* and involve other issues. In addition, the Illinois Supreme Court rejected *Marvin* in the 1979 *Hewitt* cases discussed below.

The four states reported to reject *Marvin* are Arizona, Arkansas, Florida, and Georgia. However, a Florida trial court has recently given recovery under an express oral contract.

they usually tell their family and friends about their plans and expectations, and this provides support for their agreement from the larger social community.

If, however, the parties have a disagreement about the terms of their oral contract, the one who seeks to enforce the agreement (in court) faces a more diffficult burden of proof than a party to a written contract. He or she will first have to prove the existence of the contract. Then he or she will have to substantiate his or her claims about the terms of the contract—without the aid of a written document. This can be done by pointing to the circumstances surrounding the agreement, to statements or promises made in the presence of family or friends, and to evidence of the parties' compliance with the terms of the contract in the past.

The difficulty of proving an oral contract is illustrated by the *Marvin* case. In the trial court's rehearing of the case Michelle claimed that she and Lee had an express contract to share property: she claimed that Lee told her "that what I have is yours and what you have is mine."[26] But Lee denied that he had made that statement and denied that he had ever agreed to share his property with her. On the contrary, he asserted that he had told Michelle that he did not want any financial responsibilities in connection with the relationship. Furthermore, his attorneys contended that the statement "What I have is yours," if made by Lee, was not made with contractual intent and was too vague to enforce as a contract.[27] Finally, they argued that the conduct of the Marvins during their relationship did not demonstrate any sharing which would provide evidence for the existence of an agreement to share their property. Lee and Michelle each maintained separate bank accounts, Michelle deposited all of her earnings in her separate account, and Lee purchased property in his name alone.[28] On the basis of these conflicting claims and in the absence of evidence of financial pooling, Judge Marshall concluded that there was no express agreement to share property.

In contrast, express oral agreements were found and upheld in two 1980 cases, one in New York and one in Oregon. The New York case, *Morone* v. *Morone*,[29] involved an agreement to share property, while the Oregon case, *McHenry* v. *Smith*,[30] involved a contract for support.

In *Morone* a couple lived together for twenty-three years, produced two children, and presented themselves to the community as married. Frances Morone alleged that she and Frank entered into a partnership agreement in 1952 in which they orally agreed that she would furnish domestic services, that Frank was to have full charge of business transactions, and that the net profits from the partnership were to be divided equally. She also alleged that Frank "commanded that she not obtain employment" and that he agreed to support, maintain, and provide for her in accordance with his earning capacity and that he would "take care of her and do right by her."[31]

The New York Court of Appeals overturned a lower court's dismissal of Frances Morone's complaint, and held that an express contract between unmarried persons living together is enforceable provided it does not rest upon illicit sexual behavior as consideration.

The express contract in the Oregon case was a support-tradeoff agreement, similar to those discussed in the Appendix to this book.* In *McHenry* v. *Smith* the Oregon Court of Appeals affirmed an award of $16,000 damages to a woman who sued the man with whom she had cohabitated for four years. The man broke his promise to "work and support her" after she had worked and supported him while he was writing a book and unemployed.[32] The oral agreement was for them to pool resources and establish a home and live together. She was also to render services as companion, cook, homemaker, gardener, and housekeeper. After the man completed his book, he reestablished his career and refused to support her in accordance with their agreement.

In addition to questions of proof, express agreements must be based on adequate consideration: "the consideration must be something of value and cannot be illegal."[33] As noted above, at issue here is the couple's sexual relationship and the extent to which the courts are willing to disregard it when they examine contracts for property or support between unwed cohabitants. The states that have ruled on this question to date can be divided into three groups. The first group, which adopts the *traditional* position, holds that if any part of the consideration for the agreement consists of sexual relations, the entire agreement is invalid. The second group, typified by the *Marvin* decision, subscribes to the *severability* doctrine. It is willing to uphold contracts between cohabitants as long as they are not explicitly based on meretricious consideration. The third group, typified by the 1976 *Latham* decision in Oregon, totally rejects the sex-

*See page 429.

as-illegal consideration doctrine and is willing to *uphold contracts* that include *a sexual relationship* and the consideration of "providing a partner with all the amenities of married life." Let us briefly examine the post-*Marvin* cases in each group.

The traditional position, discussed in the first section of this chapter, was to declare the contract void if it was "tainted" by an illegal sexual relationship between two parties. Recent decisions in Georgia, Tennessee, and New York have applied this rule to invalidate property agreements between unwed cohabitants.

In 1977, in *Rehak* v. *Mathis*,[34] a woman who lived with a man for eighteen years in a jointly purchased home was denied any interest in the house, any compensation for her services, and any right to support, because the Georgia Supreme Court found that their contract was based on immoral consideration, precluding any basis for recovery.

The applicant, Hazel Rehak, alleged that she and Archie Mathis jointly purchased a home. For the first two years she made all the payments. After that each of them paid one-half of the monthly installments. They lived in the house together for eighteen years, during which time Hazel Rehak cooked, cleaned, and generally cared for Mathis's "comforts, needs, and pleasures." She further alleged that on numerous occasions Mathis told her that the house belonged to them jointly, and that he would support and take care of her and her financial needs for the rest of her life.

In denying her claims to a share of the property, the Georgia Supreme Court declared: "It is well settled that neither a court of law nor a court of equity will lend its aid to either party to a contract founded upon an illegal or immoral consideration."[35]

In a forceful dissent Justice Hill argued:

> Where a man hires a maid to clean house for him, his obligation to pay wages is enforceable in court even though he seduces her. . . . I do not find evidence that the female in this case agreed to make house payments in consideration of the man's promise to seduce her or to cohabit with her illegally.[36]

In 1979 and 1980 courts in New York and Tennessee similarly rejected the claims of female cohabitants upon finding their contractual relationships void and against public policy.[37] In *McCall* v. *Frampton* for example, McCall was living with Frampton while legally married to another man.[38] The New York court held her agreement with Frampton void since their relationship was one of adultery.*

Rejecting the anachronistic morality of the traditional doctrine, a second group of states have adopted a middle level standard of upholding contracts that do not explicitly rest on illicit consideration. For example, in *Kozlowski* v. *Kozlowski*[39], a 1978 New Jersey court followed the severance theory articulated in *Marvin*. It awarded a woman cohabitant of fifteen years $55,000 on an express contract that her partner would support her for the rest of her life.

The Kozlowskis began their cohabitation when Thaddeus promised that he would divorce his wife and marry Irma. He persuaded her to leave her husband and move in with him—promising that they would get married as soon as they each got divorced. After she obtained a divorce they had a serious disagreement because it became clear that he did not really intend to get divorced or to marry her, but rather planned—and preferred—to continue cohabiting without marriage. They separated briefly, but he pleaded with her to return, promising that he would take care of her and provide for her for the rest of their lives. He insisted that he needed her and that they would both be happy if she would only come back and resume her functions in the household.

Believing his promises, she moved back into the house they had previously shared, and again "performed services of value to defendant, including housekeeping, cooking, food shopping, serving as his escort and companion and entertaining his business associates and customers as he desired." She also provided him with emotional support and raised their children.

After fifteen years of cohabitation it became obvious that Thaddeus had another romantic interest, no longer loved Irma, and wanted to be rid of her. She was crushed and hurt and "left in a huff." Without Irma's knowledge Thaddeus had instituted a suit for divorce from his legal wife. After the divorce was granted he married the other woman, who was thirty years younger than Irma.

The New Jersey court held that the "apparent illicit relationship engaged in by the parties" did not in itself bar relief, and found that the parties had entered a severable express contract when they resumed their relationship after the separation.

---

*After this book went to press, the decision was reversed on appeal.

The third approach, exemplified by the *Latham* court in Oregon, rejects the sex-as-illegal-consideration doctrine and thus the need to sever the sexual relationship from the financial contract. *Latham* held that the parties' sexual relationship was not illegal (because Oregon had repealed its former "lewd or lascivious cohabitation" statute) and that adequate consideration was provided by the woman's promise to live with the man, care for him, and furnish him with all the amenities of married life. Along similar lines a 1973 Michigan court totally rejected the illegal consideration doctrine (both parties were guilty of adultery) and found an express oral agreement to pool assets and share property.[40]

A final issue, which these cases have resolved, is the clear recognition of homemaker services as adequate consideration for an agreement to share property or provide support. Attorneys Foster and Freed note that there is less danger that an express agreement will be challenged if it is a partnership agreement (or a joint enterprise which contemplates the joint financial efforts of both partners) than if one party contributes wages and the other contributes services in the home. Nevertheless, they conclude that the value of the homemaker's contribution has now been clearly established by *Latham* and *Marvin*.[41]

Finding an Implied Contract

An implied-in-fact contract is an agreement that is *inferred from the behavior* of the parties even though they may not have formulated an explicit agreement.

If, for example, there is clear evidence of the parties' mutual intent to share property, and if each of them has actually shared his or her property with the other during the relationship, then the court can legitimately infer a contract from the facts of their relationship. The major difference between an express and an implied-in-fact agreement is that an express agreement "is evidenced by words while an implied agreement is evidenced by conduct."[42]

In *Marvin* the California Supreme Court directed the courts to "inquire into the conduct of the parties to determine whether that conduct demonstrates an implied contract or implied agreement of partnership or joint venture or some other tacit understanding between the parties."[43]

Several courts have followed the *Marvin* directive and have examined the intentions and behavior of unwed cohabitants who have not made an explicit agreement. For example, in 1978 the Oregon Supreme Court found an implied contract in the intent and behavior of an unwed couple in *Beal* v. *Beal*.[44]

Beal involved a couple who bought a house together (a month after they got divorced in 1972). Both contributed to the down payment on the house, and the deed listed them as husband and wife. Raymond Beal made most of the monthly payments on the house while all of Barbara Beal's income was used for family expenses. After they lived together in the house for two years Barbara moved out and Raymond remarried. Raymond made all of the subsequent house payments by himself.

The Oregon Supreme Court focused its review on the intentions of the parties. In a clear explanation of their procedure and the rationale for upholding implied contracts the court stated:

> We believe a division of property accumulated during a period of cohabitation must be begun by inquiring into the intent of the parties, and if an intent can be found, it should control that property distribution. While this is obviously true when the parties have executed a written agreement, it is just as true if there is no written agreement. The difference is often only the sophistication of the parties. Thus, absent an express agreement courts should closely examine the facts in evidence to determine what the parties implicitly agreed upon.[45]

This analysis led to the conclusion that the parties "intended to pool their resources for their common benefit during the time they lived together."[46] This was evident from the fact that Barbara contributed her entire income to maintain the household, from their living arrangements, and the fact that neither made any effort to keep separate accounts or to total their respective contributions for reimbursement purposes. The Oregon Supreme Court therefore decided that each party owned one-half of the house. To adjust the equities after Barbara moved out, the case was sent back to the trial court to consider how much she owed Raymond for the house payments he had made, and how much he owed her for rent (for the time that he lived in the house with his new wife).

Although Barbara Beal contributed wages to the family treasury, implied contracts involving homemaker services have also been upheld. For example, in *Carlson* v. *Olson*[47] the Minnesota Supreme Court found an implied contract between Laura Carlson, a housewife who did not work outside the home, and Oral Olson. Carlson and Olson lived together for twenty-one years without being married, although they held themselves out as a married couple to neighbors, family, and friends. Together they raised a son and acquired a modest home and some personal property.

When Laura decided that she no longer wanted to live with Oral she went to court to obtain half of the property they had accumulated. Even though the house deed listed them as "husband and wife" and as joint tenants, Oral claimed that the house was his alone because he had supplied all of the money (approximately $30,000) for its acquisition and improvement from his own salary. (The only exception was $1,000 supplied by Laura's mother for a remodeling project.) He also claimed that he was the sole owner of the furniture, automobile, boat, trailer, and other items of property they had accumulated. Finally, he countersued Laura for past due rent, which he claimed she owed him for living in his house for seventeen years.

The trial court, however, supported Laura's claims. It found evidence that the parties had intended to share their accumulations, and accordingly divided their property equally. It held that the funds and improvements Oral made on the property were irrevocable gifts to Laura "in consideration for the wifely and motherly services she performed during the period of their cohabitation."[48] The Minnesota Supreme Court upheld the trial court's decision, quoting *Marvin* on the value of homemakers' services and the rights of unwed cohabitants to have their reasonable expectations upheld. It concluded that the Minnesota courts should also

> . . . enforce express contracts between nonmarital partners . . . In the absence of an express contract the court should inquire into the conduct of the parties to determine whether that conduct demonstrates an implied contract . . . or some other tacit understanding between the partners.[49]

A similar analysis led the court to find an implied agreement in the 1978 Connecticut case of *Dosek* v. *Dosek*.[50] *Dosek* involved a couple who lived together for seven years. During that time the woman adopted the man's name and gave birth to his child. The court found that the couple had agreed (1) to combine their incomes for the purpose of living together as a family unit and (2) in the event of separation, to divide their assets equally.

An implied contract with very different terms was found by a New York judge in *McCullon* v. *McCullon* in 1978.[51] In *McCullon* the woman, Susan, agreed to forgo employment and to provide domestic services in return for the man's promise to provide future support and a home. The McCullon relationship continued for over twenty-eight years, during which time three children were born and raised.

At the beginning of the relationship Susan McCullon stopped working as a nurse's aide to devote her full time to housekeeping for Leonard. She took his surname and wore a wedding ring. Although Susan did not obtain a divorce from her previous husband until five years after she began to live with Leonard, the parties were always known as husband and wife and were introduced to friends and relatives as such. They had joint bank accounts, filed joint income tax returns, and took joint title to their home as tenants by the entirety.

In a somewhat strained decision the New York judge found both a common-law marriage (from the couple's sojourns in Pennsylvania) and an implied contract based on (1) twenty-eight years of cohabitation during which Susan tended house and Leonard paid the bills and (2) Leonard's statement that he would always care for her. On the basis of the McCullons' implied contract for future support, the judge ordered Leonard to pay alimony, child support, and counsel fees.

It would be wrong, however, to imply that all courts have followed *Marvin* in recognizing implied contracts. In 1980 the highest New York court explicitly rejected the possibility of recovery on an implied contract, and thereby implicitly overruled the *McCullon* decision just discussed. In this case, *Morone* v. *Morone*,[52] recovery was still permitted as the court found and upheld an express contract to share property.

An even more tradition-bound decision was made by the Supreme Court of Illinois in 1979. It overturned a lower court's finding of an express oral contract after seventeen years of cohabitation in which the woman supported the man through dental school, raised their three children, assisted him in his practice, and believed his promise of shared property and lifelong support. This case, *Hewitt* v. *Hewitt*,[53] is especially distressing because the Illinois court denied Mrs. Hewitt any relief, declaring that the public policy of supporting the institution of marriage was of substantially greater importance than the rights of the immediate partners.

Victoria and Robert Hewitt began living together in June 1960 when both were students at Grinell College in Iowa, and she became pregnant. Robert told her "that they were husband and wife and would live as such, no formal ceremony being necessary," and that he would "share his life, his future, his earnings and his property" with her.[54] The parties immediately announced to their respective parents that they were married and thereafter held themselves out as husband and wife. In reliance on Robert's promises, Victoria devoted her efforts to his professional education and to helping him establish his dental practice of pedodontia, obtaining financial assistance from her parents for this purpose. She assisted him in his career with her own special skills and, although she was given payroll checks for these services, she placed them in a common fund. Robert, who had no funds at the time their relationship began, earned over $80,000 a year at the time of the suit as a result of their joint efforts. In addition he had accumulated large amounts of property, some owned jointly and others owned separately by him alone. During their seventeen-year union Victoria raised three children and provided Robert with every assistance a wife and mother could give, including entertaining designed to enhance his social and professional reputation.

The original trial court dismissed Victoria's complaint, but the intermediate court reversed their decision and found an express oral contract. It stated that because the parties had outwardly lived a conventional married life, Victoria's conduct had not "so affronted public policy that she should be denied any and all relief." The Illinois Supreme Court, however, reversed this decision and explicitly rejected the *Marvin* policy of providing redress for unwed cohabitants because, it believed, to give recognition to these relationships would seriously undermine the institution of marriage.

While this discussion illustrates the growing trend toward recognition of implied-in-fact-contracts, cases like *Hewitt* and *Morone* suggest the pitfalls of assuming that all states will uphold the *Marvin* doctrines. Nevertheless, traditional states like Illinois and New York do appear to be in the minority. And with each passing year additional states are affirming the legitimacy of inferring a property agreement from the parties' behavior during the relationship.

Fair Dealing and Equitable Remedies

The most controversial aspect of the *Marvin* opinion was the court's directive for situations in which neither an express nor an implied-in-fact agreement was evident. In those situations, the *Marvin* court stated, the courts may employ equitable doctrines such as constructive trust, quasi-contract, or other equitable remedies, to achieve a fair division of property between the parties. In a now famous concluding footnote the California Supreme Court suggested that trial courts might employ "whatever equitable remedy may be proper under the circumstances."[55] Before discussing the cases it is necessary to explain briefly these equitable doctrines.

As we noted above, the courts may infer a contract from the intent and behavior of the parties. These implied-in-fact contracts are significantly different from implied-in-law contracts, which are contracts that the law imposes to ensure that the parties are dealt with fairly. Implied-in-law contracts are not concerned with the parties' intentions—instead they reflect the law's concept of appropriate behavior and fair dealing. Although implied-in-law contracts are typically referred to as quasi-contracts, they are not really contracts at all—in the sense of being freely contracted agreements. Rather they are contracts that the law imposes to achieve equitable results.

As Professor Carol Bruch explains, the prototype for the concept of an implied-in-law contract is *Chase* v. *Corcoran*, in which a boat that had been found adrift was repaired by the men who found it.[56] The boat's owner sought to recover the boat but refused to pay the finder for the repairs. He claimed that since he had not contracted for the repairs he was not bound to pay for them. While it is clear that the owner had no intention of contracting for the services rendered, the Supreme Court of Massachusetts held that he nevertheless had to pay for them because it would be unfair for him to enrich himself at the finder's expense.

Thus an implied-in-law contract is imposed to avoid unjust results without regard to the parties' intentions. "Known as unjust enrichment or quasi-contract this doctrine focuses on the unseemly enhancement of one party's wealth at the improper expense of another."[57]

One example of the application of these equitable principles is found in the New Jersey court's opinion in *Kozlowski*, discussed above. The judge reasoned that it would be unfair to allow Thaddeus Kozlowski to enjoy the benefits of Irma's labor without providing her with some equitable compensation. He observed that Irma had devoted fifteen years to living with Thaddeus; providing him with the necessary household services and emotional support to permit him to successfully pursue his business career; performing housekeeping, cleaning, and shopping services; running the household; and raising their children. In return Thaddeus had literally forced her out of the household without any ongoing support or the wherewithal for her survival.

The judge ruled that the

> . . . unjust enrichment of one party at the expense of the other will not be tolerated. . . . [I]t would be inequitable to allow the recipient to enjoy the benefit (of her services) without compensation. . . . [Q]uasi-contractual remedies should be available where the circumstances justify compensation for valuable household services in the absence of an express agreement. A quasi-contract is . . . based upon the equitable principle that whatsoever it is certain that a man ought to do, that the law supposes him to have promised to do.[58]

To prevent unjust enrichment of one partner at the other's expense, a partner who provides services may recover in *quantum meruit*—"the reasonable value of household services rendered, less the reasonable value of support accorded."[59] Aside from the somewhat difficult and bothersome task of demonstrating the value of services rendered, *quantum meruit* depends on a cohabitant's showing that the value of services rendered exceeds the value of support received. That may prove difficult if a cohabitant has enjoyed a lavish life-style during the cohabitation as, for example, Michelle Marvin had. However, even more modest levels of support may be considered adequate to offset the value of services rendered if judges underestimate and miscalculate the value of household services (as discussed in Chapter 3 of this book).

It is ironic that the judge in *Kozlowski*, who seemed to understand the extent of Irma's contribution, concluded that the services that Irma rendered were offset by the value of the compensation she had received in weekly support, clothing, trips, vacations, medical benefits, and jewelry. He therefore based his order for Thaddeus to continue to support her on their implied contract rather than on her claim for *quantum meruit*.

On the other hand, two other states have supported rather substantial *quantum meruit* claims. A 1978 Massachusetts court upheld a jury verdict awarding a woman $1,350,000 against the decedent's estate on the basis of *quantum meruit* where the plaintiff alleged an oral agreement by the decedent to leave his entire estate to her if she stayed with him and performed social, domestic, and business services for him.[60] And, in a 1978 New Hampshire case, a woman who had cohabited with and maintained a business relationship with a man for over five years before his death was recognized to have "a cause of action in *quantum meruit* for the fair value of the intimate, confidential and dedicated personal and business services which she gave the decedent for years."[61]

Quantum meruit has been criticized for imposing the incidents of legal marriage on unmarried cohabitants.[62] Foster and Freed contend that "much of the confused and 'far out' discussion of *Marvin* and its implications (such as the erroneous claims that it forces men to support their lovers or that it imposes marriage on cohabitants) derives from this aspect of the opinion."[63] Nevertheless, in the absence of an express or implied contract, *quantum meruit* may provide an important basis for compensating an unwed cohabitant for years of unpaid services.

Another type of remedy suggested by the *Marvin* court involved resulting or constructive trusts.

A resulting trust, like an implied-in-fact contract, is a trust that is inferred from the behavior of the parties. If, for example, the circumstantial evidence suggests that the parties intended one of them to hold property in his or her name in trust for the other, a resulting or implied-in-fact trust is established.[64] A constructive trust, in contrast, ignores the parties' intentions. Like an implied-in-law contract it is imposed by the courts to do justice and to prevent the unjust enrichment of one party at the other's expense.

The courts have imposed a resulting or a constructive trust upon cohabitants in a few post-*Marvin* cases, forcing the partner who used household funds to acquire property in his or her name alone to account to, and share the proceeds with, the untitled partner.

For example, in a 1977 Wisconsin case, *Doyle* v. *Giddley*,[65] Sherry Doyle asked the court to prevent Richard Giddley from selling the property they had accumulated during the four years they cohabited. Sherry contended that she "contributed a substantial sum of money to the household which was used to buy furnishings and a home" (that were owned in Richard Giddley's name alone).[66] Sherry alleged that she had contributed the income she received from her work at Oscar Meyer and from monthly child support to joint household expenses and to joint purchases of property. Over four years this amounted to a substantial sum of money. Richard, however, purchased their house and furnishings in his name and claimed that they therefore belonged to him alone. Sherry in contrast contended that Richard held the property in trust for her.

In granting Sherry's request, the Wisconsin court held that it had the jurisdiction to prevent the unjust enrichment of one person (i.e.

Richard) at the expense of the other (Sherry), and that if it refused to take action it would promote injustice by letting the stronger party keep the contributions of the weaker party. A 1978 Utah court used similar quasi-contract principles to effect an equitable distribution of property between an unwed couple in *Edgar* v. *Wagner*.[67]

In *Doyle*, as in most cases of resulting or constructive trusts, the woman contributed money as well as services. In an influential article Professor Bruch noted that increased recognition of the homemaker's worth will expand the reach of resulting trust theory. Courts will more readily recognize that contributions of labor are also contributions to a spouse's earning capacity, and thus to the money and property accumulated during the relationship.[68]

Before completing this section on recent cases, two qualifications are in order. First, although we have discussed express agreements, implied agreements, quasi-contract, and equitable remedies as conceptually distinct, in actual practice these claims and their remedies are usually intertwined. Second, this discussion has, if anything, underestimated the range of possible bases for claims and the range of innovative solutions available for relief. For example, after rehearing *Marvin* on remand, Judge Marshall awarded Michelle $104,000 as rehabilitative alimony, citing the Supreme Court's famous footnote 25, which encourages courts to fashion other equitable remedies as circumstances require. Clearly *Marvin* opened the door—we have just begun to see what lies beyond.

Beyond Marvin: Prospects for the Future

One of the most significant features of the *Marvin* decision is its effort to fashion flexible remedies to support the parties' reasonable expectations. This means that trial courts are left with an enormous amount of discretion. On one hand, *Marvin* is to be applauded for recognizing the diversity among unwed cohabitants and for giving trial courts an opportunity to tailor their remedies to the particular circumstances and understandings of the parties. On the other hand, the lack of specific guidelines in *Marvin* leads to some uncertainty as to how it should—or will—be applied.* As Justice Clark noted in his dissent from the majority *Marvin* opinion, it is not clear

* As Professor Herma Hill Kay observed, "*Marvin* enjoys the singular honor of being one of the most misunderstood decisions of modern times." H. H. Kay and Carol Amyx "*Marvin* v. *Marvin*: Preserving the Options," *California Law Review* 65, no. 5, (September 1977): 37.

what circumstances are necessary for each type of recovery, what the limits to recovery should be, and which remedies are cumulative and which are exclusive.[69]

Nevertheless, despite the uncertainty, it is possible to outline *Marvin*'s impact on the following types of contracts between unwed cohabitants: agreements about rights and obligations during the relationship; agreements specifying how property will be held during the relationship and how property will be divided upon divorce or death; and contracts that specify support obligations and obligations to children. Each of these is examined below.

But before discussing these general areas, let us digress briefly to look at *Marvin*'s impact in one community studied by two Stanford law students. In 1980 Jan Hansen and Patricia Schneider interviewed a small sample of ten family law attorneys in the San Francisco Bay Area.[70] Together these attorneys represented fourteen claimants and defendants in *Marvin*-type cases.

Hansen and Schneider found that the single most important factor influencing the attorneys' decisions to take a *Marvin* case was the amount of money involved, as the uncertain state of the law made it an expensive investment for them.[71] While there was a lack of uniformity in the attorneys' predictions about the outcome of specific hypothetical cases, there was considerable consensus among the attorneys as to what factors were important in determining the results of a *Marvin* case. The attorneys ranked the parties' understanding regarding their relationship as the most important factor. This was followed by the parties' economic arrangements, children born during the cohabitation, and holding out to the public as husband and wife. The parties' economic arrangements, including the manner of holding property and the relative contribution of each, would, of course, also be relevant to a determination of the parties' intentions and understandings about the relationship.

Holding out as husband and wife and the presence of children were considered important by some attorneys because they implied an agreement to live together in a marriage-like relationship, and by other attorneys because these factors would be likely to evoke a judge's sympathy.

Although not included in the list Hansen and Schneider used, "reliance" and the duration of the relationship were also mentioned as important. However, their influence on the decision was less clear-cut. For example, a young woman was more likely to evoke sympathy if she gave up some of her best years, especially if she was justifiably naive in her reliance. On the other hand, her need was likely to be less than that of an older woman who evoked less sympathy (she was more likely to have entered the cohabitation with "her eyes wide open") but was nevertheless more disadvantaged by the end of the cohabitation.[72]

Of less importance, the attorneys ranked the age of the parties, the reason for termination, the division of household chores, and the parties' relative incomes (although this last-mentioned factor appears to have been the basis for Judge Marshall's award of $104,000 in rehabilitative alimony to Michelle Marvin).

This example suggests that attorneys are not yet certain whether the standards of contract law or family law will be used to adjudicate *Marvin* claims. As discussed in Chapter 13, if contract law is used, then the intent (and behavior) of the parties is paramount. If, however, family law is used, then current circumstances (such as income) and need become more salient.

Let us now consider the more general question of *Marvin's* impact on unwed cohabitants. In this discussion we shall also refer to married partners because *Marvin* extended the contractual rights of parties in both types of relationships. In fact, *Marvin* has meant that both married and unmarried partners now have a far better chance of having their agreements upheld in a court of law.

Rights and Obligations During the Relationship

As noted in Chapter 13, the courts have traditionally refused to honor husband–wife contracts that alter the "essential elements" of the marital relationship—that is, contracts to pay for household services or to relieve a spouse of the obligation to support.[73] To the extent that these rules are explicitly based on sex role stereotypes, such as barring the husband's waiver of support or the wife's pay for domestic services, they are certain to fall on constitutional grounds. In addition, it is extremely doubtful whether such rules could be justified on public policy grounds even if they were sex-neutral.

To date, however, the courts have not faced the type of contract suggested in this book. To examine their prospects it may be useful to distinguish between provisions about financial matters and those that regulate the interpersonal relationship.

Both married and cohabiting couples can be relatively confident about the validity of a contract that regulates the financial aspects of their relationship. The courts have long upheld various forms of property contracts between spouses within marriage, and the cases following *Marvin* suggest the willingness of many state courts similarly to uphold those between unwed cohabitants. Thus agreements to hold property jointly or separately, to pool earnings and assets, to create trusts, or to exchange services for an agreement to share property should increasingly be upheld.

Different contingencies arise with respect to contracts that regulate a couple's interpersonal relationship. While agreements to divide housework, postpone education, or abide by a time management plan are more likely to be upheld if they include provisions for liquidated damages, the courts have traditionally been reluctant to become involved in disputes within an ongoing relationship. Family law has traditionally assumed that a breach of contract that is serious enough to result in litigation is also likely to result in termination of the relationship, and it is therefore unnecessary and inappropriate for the courts to be involved in disputes in an ongoing relationship. However, many couples would prefer a means of resolving disputes within a relationship—without having to contemplate dissolution. Couples who want to be assured of settling disputes that arise during their relationship may wish to borrow the concept of arbitration used in labor law or to provide for marriage counseling in their contracts, as do some of the contracts in Chapter 12.[74]

At least one American court, the Conciliation Court of Los Angeles, has already instituted a system to foster this type of arrangement.[75] That court, with the assistance of trained marital counselors, helps married and divorced couples negotiate a written contract, called a conciliation agreement, that closely resembles the type of contract we advocate. This contract is then given a judicial stamp of approval and thereafter becomes technically enforceable through contempt citations from the court. Although the court has only rarely exercised this enforcement power, preferring instead to rely on the psychological and emotional force of the agreement to support its provisions, judicial sanctions are available when necessary.

In general, enforcement of a contract within an ongoing relationship is more likely if contractors adopt one of the techniques suggested above and make specific provision for counseling, arbitration, or specific liquidated damages.

Property Ownership upon Dissolution

Express contracts governing the ownership and distribution of property between both married spouses and unwed cohabitants are generally likely to be upheld. The principal recent development in this sphere is the court's increased willingness to recognize implied contracts and equitable remedies for distributing property as well. As Professor Carol Bruch noted, by 1980 most courts had limited or dispensed with public policy defenses to property claims between unwed cohabitants and had recognized "the legal sufficiency of domestic services as a form of consideration and as a measure of unjust enrichment."[76] The remedies available to cohabitants now tend to approximate those previously made available only to married persons.[77]

Support

Although the traditional courts made a clear distinction between agreements about property and agreements about support, recent cases (such as *Dawley* for married couples and *Marvin* for unmarried) have suggested increased awareness of the arbitrary nature of this distinction. They have also indicated a growing acceptance of contracts about support. Thus an agreement to trade A's support at time 1 for B's support at time 2, or an agreement to exchange household services at time 1 for support at time 2, should face a good chance of being upheld.

As we note above, claims based on an express contract, especially a written contract (which minimizes the issue of proof) between both married and unmarried partners, are likely to be upheld. Recent decisions of the State Supreme Courts of Alaska, California, and New Jersey have explicitly recognized the enforceability of agreements for support between cohabitants, and Professor Bruch has predicted that courts which now recognize property agreements between nonmarital partners will extend similar recognition to support contracts.[78] In addition, equitable remedies should increasingly be utilized to prevent unjust enrichment and to protect the reasonable expectations of the parties.

Provisions for Children

The Courts are most likely to resist enforcement of contractual provisions about children, especially if the court considers them detrimental to the child. This resistance does not conflict with the position advocated in this book. While it is hoped that the courts will generally respect the written intentions of the parties, arrangements that are clearly harmful to children obviously do not merit court approval.

Contract provisions regarding child custody are usually honored by courts if judicial review indicates they accord with the child's best interests.[79] Owing to the vagaries of judicial discretion, however, parents can never be sure that the arrangement they have negotiated will be upheld as long as there exists a possibility that a judge will consider some other arrangement preferable for the child. If a contract specifies which spouse is to have custody of the children in the event of separation, the other spouse can challenge the agreement and obtain custody if he or she can convince the court that the child's best interests will thus be served.

If the parent who has agreed to take custody later refuses to do so, it is not likely that specific performance would be available. It would also be unwise, because an unwilling parent is not likely to be an effective custodian. However, the monetary damages to the injured parent could be computed. Thus some effect could be given to the parents' provisions through an assessment of the monetary consequences of the shift in custody. For example, money damages can be awarded to the injured party if a custody provision is breached. If moving or household arrangements must be made for a child, their cost can be calculated, and the spouse who has reneged on the custody obligation can be required to reimburse the other spouse for the actual costs of rearing the child. Unfortunately, no comparable remedies are available to the spouse who was assured custody under an agreement but is subsequently deprived of this right. The resulting psychological stress and thwarted expectations would be more difficult, but not impossible, to compute in dollar terms.

The right to receive support from his or her parents legally belongs to every child, and parents cannot ordinarily contract away this right.[80] However, they might specify by agreement which parent will bear the burden of support, and such provisions may give rise to legal difficulties. Let us say, for example, that A and B agree to have a child with the understanding that A will assume full financial responsibility for the child. If upon dissolution of that marriage A in fact accepts this responsibility, the court is not likely to interfere. However, if later on A decides that the financial burden is too great and goes to court to obtain some relief from B, it is likely that the court will require B to contribute to the child's support. B thereupon has a cause of action against A for breach of the agreement and can sue A to recover whatever amount B was required by the court to pay. If a couple wants to be as certain as possible that one partner is relieved of any financial obligation for a child, they probably should include a contract provision specifying that if that partner is required by a court to pay support, he or she will be entitled to reimbursement from the other partner. It is not certain, however, whether a court would uphold this type of agreement or reject it as unconscionable.

In one recent California case however, a man fathered a child at the mother's request relying on her promise that she would not hold him financially responsible. In *Fournier* v. *Lopez*,[81] Esther's doctor had told her that she would have to have an operation within a year or two that would totally destroy her ability to bear children. She was childless and asked Arnold to father her child. Arnold, who was already supporting two children, told her he could not afford the financial responsibility. Esther then promised she would raise the child herself and assume the entire financial responsibility alone. The California Court of Appeal upheld the contract and ruled that as long as the mother was financially able to support the child, she must bear the burden by herself.

Although this is clearly an unusual case, it provides a fitting end to this chapter, for it suggests the far-reaching effects that the new doctrines are likely to have. It is also an appropriate case to close this book for it illustrates how far the courts have come in their efforts to give effect to the intentions and expectations of the parties —as expressed in their contractual agreements.

APPENDIX

An Empirical Study
of Intimate Contracts

This appendix examines a sample of contracts that couples have written as alternatives to traditional legal marriage.* The research reported here was originally designed to gather empirical data to "test" some assertions I made about contracts in a 1974 *California Law Review* article. In that article I argued that legal marriage impedes egalitarian relationships because it imposes sex-based rights and responsibilities on husbands and wives. I suggested that couples seeking more egalitarian relationships might benefit by writing their own marriage contracts. This research was undertaken to examine the extent to which contracts might indeed further that goal and provide a viable structure for intimate relationships. It had three major aims:

1. To determine and describe the types of intimate contracts couples would write

*This report was written with Carol M. Dixon, Joyce Adair Bird, Neil McGinn, and Dena Robertson and was originally published in *Alternative Lifestyles*, 1, no. 3 (1978):303–78. Copyright 1978 Lenore J. Weitzman. All of the authors worked on the California Divorce Law Research Project at the Center for the Study of Law and Society, University of California at Berkeley, and wish to thank the Center and the National Institute of Mental Health (grant no. MH 27617) for their support. We would also like to thank Carol Bruch, William J. Goode, Susan Feller, and Joseph Barberi for their suggestions on an earlier draft of this paper.

2. To analyze the extent to which these contracts support more egalitarian family patterns
3. To compare the relationships established by contract with those established by traditional family laws

Because of the length of this appendix, a word about its organization may be helpful. The first section discusses the research methodology, the second describes the three types of contracts studied. The content of the contracts is then discussed in ten topically arranged subsections: aims and expectations, duration, property ownership and management, support and work arrangements, domicile and household tasks, interpersonal relations, children, wills and inheritance, changes in the contract, breach of contract penalties, and dissolution.

The summary and conclusion draws together the research data to address the two basic questions that motivated the research:

1. To what extent do contracts support more egalitarian family relationships?
2. To what extent do contractual relationships differ from traditional legal marriage?

To briefly anticipate our findings, we found that, first, the contracts encompassed a wide range of relationships: while a large number sought to establish an alternative structure for a "marriage-like" relationship, others were written for a trial union, and still others were written by legally married couples who wanted to modify the spousal obligations imposed by family laws. This diversity in relationships established by contract stands in marked contrast to the single family form that the law imposes on all who enter legal marriage.

Second, the relationships established by contract were more egalitarian than those established by traditional legal marriage. All of the contractors in some measure rejected the legally imposed model of marriage. Most repudiated the sex-based division of family rights and responsibilities, with its resulting *hierarchical* (and patriarchal) family structure, and tried instead to establish relationships that were more like partnerships in their apportionment of rights, responsibilities, and benefits.

It would be inaccurate, however, to characterize all of the contracts as strictly egalitarian. Considerable variation occurred within the sample of contracts we studied, and some of the couples (primarily those already married) contracted for fairly traditional family roles. For example, the married couples who planned to have children tended to assign child care responsibilities to the female partner. Nevertheless, even these "traditional" contracts departed from the marriage contract imposed by the law. For example, those that provided for a division of labor by sex also contained provisions to ensure compensation for the partner who assumed homemaking and child care responsibilities. Furthermore, they treated income and property acquired by either partner during the relationship as "community property," and thereby sought to guarantee both partners an equal share in the results of the partnership.

This is believed to be the first empirical study of intimate contracts to be published, although the topic has received considerable attention from the mass media[1] and other researchers have reported work-in-progress at professional meetings.[2]

Methodology

In the past almost all antenuptial contracts were written by wealthy individuals or by previously married persons who had property they wanted to control.[3] The limited reports of current contracts, however, suggest that today they are quite likely to be aimed at avoiding the restrictions of legal marriage and structuring a more egalitarian (and individually tailored) relationship.[4]

Because little is known about the demographic and social characteristics of couples who write the new type of intimate contract (we failed to locate a single study that estimated their distribution in the population), we were hard pressed to locate a representative sample. Our original plan—to obtain a sample of these contracts from attorneys—was thwarted when an informal poll of likely attorneys revealed that none had negotiated more than a few personal contracts (as of 1977), and that a great many contracts were being written entirely without legal advice. Consequently, we abandoned hope of drawing a random or representative sample and decided to focus instead on *an admittedly nonrepresentative group.*

The contracts we surveyed were obtained from students in an upper-division sociology course on sex roles and the law at the University of California in 1977. After completing readings in employment and family law, these students were given the choice of writing an employment discrimination brief or writing an intimate contract.[5] To satisfy the contract option, a contract had to be "real"—that is, it must have been discussed and signed by both of the contracting parties, and it had to relate to a genuine relationship. (About three quarters of the writers were themselves a party to the contract.*) The contract option elicited a total of 59 valid contracts.

We were surprised to find that many had been notarized, which we interpreted as an indication of the seriousness of the parties. Nevertheless, we wish to acknowledge frankly the limitations of this research. Because the sample was drawn solely from a relatively well-educated, young, middle-class population of college students, our findings cannot be readily generalized to the larger population. The prime contribution of this study therefore rests in its descriptive and suggestive value. The contracts we studied reflect a wide variety of expectations and concerns and therefore provide a rich source of data for exploratory research.

As expected with any small sample, some of the differences among subgroups did not meet the test of statistical significance. We have reported differences that proved significant at the 95 percent level of confidence. However, because significance tests are based on the assumption of a random selection of cases, even "significant" findings from a nonrandom sample must be considered tentative.

In addition, our data indicate some strong correlations between the purpose of the contract (e.g., those within marriage versus those written as an alternative to legal marriage) and its content. These findings should provide a basis for comparison for future studies of other class and age groups.

The Three Types of Relationships

The contracts we examined covered three types of relationships. The first involved already married couples who wrote "contracts within marriage." They comprised 22 percent of the sample and are referred to below as *the married group*.[6]

The second type of relationship was a prelude to marriage, or a "trial" union, for those who planned to marry but wanted to live to-

*Approximately 73 percent of the students wrote contracts to which they were a party, while 20 percent wrote contracts for others. The writer's involvement was not clear or classifiable in the remaining 7 percent of the contracts.

gether first. Couples in this category represented 24 percent of the sample. A careful examination of their contracts persuaded us that they could not be considered conventionally "engaged" couples. Only a few had participated in the traditional rituals of engagement—the formal announcement, the engagement party, the symbolic ring—and all planned to live together during their trial union. We decided to refer to them as the *premarried group.*

Members of the third and largest group, the *cohabitors*, chose a contract as an *alternative to legal marriage.* Most of these couples explicitly rejected legal marriage and sought to establish a radically different structure for their relationship. The cohabitors constituted 47 percent of the total sample.[7]

If one considers the broad range of intimate relationships that can be established by contract, the contract writers in this sample represent a limited segment of the potential population: none were engaged in group relationships, none had great wealth or property, and none were seriously in debt. Also missing were second or third-marriage contracts with their unique emphasis on the children and/or spouses of former unions. Our original sample included one same-sex "platonic" contract for the duration of a trip to Europe and three homosexual contracts, but they were excluded from the subsequent analysis because their subgroups were too small to analyze separately and they could not be appropriately combined with any of the other groups.

Aims and Expectations

Most of the contracts (87 percent of the total sample) began with an explicit statement of the couple's aims, goals, and expectations for the relationship. The statistics cited in this section are based on this subsample (57 couples).[8] In light of the new priority given to personal growth and fulfillment in marriage, it is not surprising that the most commonly expressed aims of these contracts were love and emotional support (62 percent), career goals (54 percent), personal growth (50 percent), and education (48 percent), with 85 percent listing more than one of these aspirations. Only one-fifth of the contracts mentioned bearing or rearing children as a goal of the relationship.

Each of the three groups placed a different emphasis on the aims and expectations that they included in their contracts.

Aims and Expectations of Married Couples

Contracts within the married group reflected a strong concern with career development; in fact, almost all the married couples mentioned careers (83 percent). Education, emotional support, and childrearing goals followed, each discussed by over half (59 percent) of the marrieds. Slightly fewer mentioned personal growth as an explicit aim of the relationship.

Married couples' contracts projected two contrasting approaches to careers. The first sought to guarantee both partners an equal opportunity to pursue a career; the second focused on the husband's career. As the following contract provision suggests,* those who adopted the first approach viewed equality of opportunity as a basic aim of the relationship:

> Lillian and Joseph believe that their individuality should be able to develop within as well as outside their marriage, and that both should be able to pursue their desired educational and career goals. In order that they are assured the opportunity to achieve these goals, they wish to have a legally enforceable understanding regarding the future. . . .

The second approach assumed that the man's career concerns would be primary and the wife would be his "helpmate," providing companionship, affection, and support to further his advancement. The following contract excerpt illustrates this perspective:

> Cheryl enters into the contract with the expectation of a lifetime relationship with Larry as a loyal friend, loving husband, and supportive father to their future children. As a wife, she takes the responsibility of household care and cleaning, cooking, and care of the children while Larry is at work. . . . Larry expects to be provided with warm companionship, *affection, and rational guidance* in problems that he may encounter in life, . . . he also expects that Cheryl will provide *moral support*, instill confidence, and make a diligent effort to keep *her body physically healthy and attractive*. [Italics added]

In its expectation that the wife will attend to her husband's psychological well-being and guarantee her personal appearance, the bargain articulated in this contract extends well beyond the traditional domestic service–economic support exchange.

---

*In this and all subsequent quotations extracted from the contracts, the names have been changed to preserve the writers' anonymity. If a contract is cited more than once, a new pair of fictional names has been chosen for each citation.

But even in some male-oriented contracts it is evident that both partners realize the wife is giving up a potential career to perform other duties and on both counts deserves to be compensated. This is, of course, very different from the expectation in a traditional legal marriage in which the wife's career potential is ignored and it is assumed that her only role is that of full-time housewife and mother. In the new contracts the wife's contribution and sacrifice of an alternative career is clearly acknowledged. For example:

> Diane agrees to give up her potential career since it will not fit in with the lifestyle necessary to Rick's [military] career. . . . Rick realizes that Diane will have to give up her career for his sake and that her help will be essential to his advancement. . . . He is willing to compensate for her efforts by providing a good future for them. . . . Rick will provide her with security, a good standard of living, and the opportunity to travel.

Although the nature of the compensation the wife will receive is not made explicit here, we shall see that these vague promises of a bright future have often been translated into a number of specific obligations in other sections of these contracts.

Aims and Expectations of Premarried Couples

The aims and expectations of the premarriage couples were less clear cut. Love and emotional support, and career goals (54 percent each) led their lists, but almost as many mentioned personal growth and educational aims (46 percent each). Few premarried contracts mentioned childrearing goals, whereas more than half of the married couples said these goals were central.

The major goal of these contracts was the growth of a relationship that would culminate in marriage. The contractual period was seen as a trial time for the parties to grow, individually and as a couple:

> The aim and purpose of the relationship is to allow Cathy and Arnold to be together while finishing off their school years. The future expectation is that it will work out well enough to allow them to spend their entire life [sic] together.

A characteristic feature of the premarrieds' aims was their lack of specificity:

> . . . that we remain in love with each other, live together as a family, care for and aid each other, make decisions that are mutually beneficent, and live together as long as we both are happy.

Aims and Expectations of Cohabiting Couples

The cohabitors emphasized love and emotional support (64 percent) and personal growth (56 percent), giving less importance to educational and career goals (36 percent). Childrearing goals were almost never mentioned (4 percent).

The *affective* nature of the cohabitors' expectations contrasts sharply with the *career* orientation of the marrieds. Cohabitors wrote of love, respect, compassion, support, trust, caring, and friendship. For example:

> The aims and expectations for our relationship are (a) to establish and maintain a relationship based on *mutual love, trust, respect,* and *friendship*; (b) to allow each partner to maintain their *individuality* and *grow along with* each other rather than through each other; (c) to support each other both financially and *emotionally* [italics added].

And whereas the married couples focused on the *future*, the cohabitors emphasized emotional satisfaction in the *present*. They often referred to their goals in psychological terms (striving for "personal growth" and "personal space" as well as "mutual support" and "intimate sharing"). A prominent theme in these contracts is commitment to love and emotional support, rather than to specified time, place, or status goals. The cohabitors hoped to keep their relationships "open" and "flexible"; in fact, one couple went so far as to rule out any specific mutual aims or expectations:

> Sonia . . . and Marv . . ., both students, would like to contract for a relationship that is quite *unstructured*, and at this time is not headed toward any *specific aim or goal*. . . . Personal goals are of the utmost importance and predominate over any mutual goals. This allows for and facilitates a separation if personal goals conflict. [italics added]

Although there is considerable overlap in the aims of all three types of relationships, they emphasize different goals. The contrasts among the groups are most marked with respect to career and childrearing goals, as indicated in the accompanying graph.

Duration

The vast majority of the contracts (81 percent, or 48 contracts) discussed the duration of the relationship. Of these, half were open-ended, describing a relationship of indefinite duration, while the

Aims and Expectations for the Relationship†

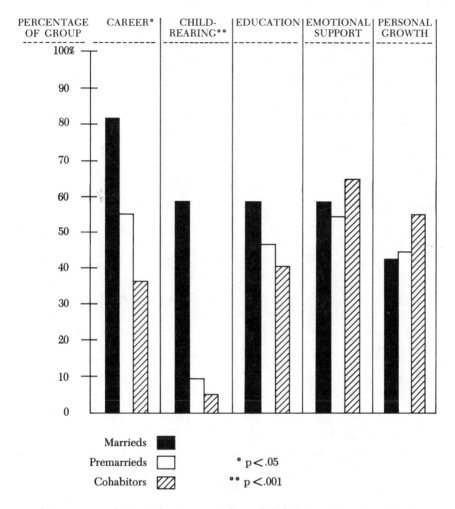

†Percentage of Marrieds, Premarrieds, and Cohabitors Who Mentioned
Each Area in Statements of Aims and Expectations for the Relationship

other half limited the contract to a specified number of years or the
attainment of a specific goal (such as graduation from law school).
The average duration, when specified, was three years.

The married couples were the least likely to specify the duration
of their contracts, but the marrieds who did discuss it affirmed their
commitment to a lifelong relationship. The premarrieds were similarly inclined to contract for an open-ended relationship, while the
cohabitors were slightly more likely to opt for a fixed term. How-

ever, not all couples who wrote fixed-term contracts planned to terminate the relationship at the end of the contract period. Rather, many of them saw the contract termination date as an appropriate time to rethink and renegotiate the terms of the contract with the expectation of renewal. For example:

> Since both parties expect to be students for the next few years, a specific time period seems to be too arbitrary. Therefore, this contract will be renegotiated each time the educational status of either party is changed (i.e., degree completion even if that degree is not the final step in the educational process), since a change in status may bring changes in income, property, debts, etc.

Property

Almost all the contracting couples discussed property arrangements, indicating a widespread belief that these arrangements should be settled at the beginning of a relationship. Provisions covered not only physical property (such as real estate) and personal possessions (such as TV sets and stereos), but also anticipated income. More than a third of the couples appended a list of their present assets or pledged to do so by a specific date.

Property Ownership

Nearly all contracts recognized two kinds of property: precontract property (owned by each partner before entering the relationship), and postcontract property (acquired during the contract period).

Precontract property. Almost two-thirds of the contracts allowed each person to retain his or her precontract assets as separate property. The remaining one-third converted these assets into what we shall refer to as community property. (Here we refer simply to joint and equal ownership as distinct from the legal system of community property which entails more complex arrangements and far-reaching consequences.)

A significant difference emerged between cohabitors and the two other groups with respect to the ownership of precontract property. Roughly one-half of the married and premarriage couples (55 percent) chose to relinquish their individual ownership and to contribute their precontract property to the newly formed partnership. In contrast, only 15 percent of the cohabitors decided to treat precontract assets as community property. The rest chose to retain their rights to the property they owned when they entered the relationship.

The cohabitors' decisions to maintain their separate ownership of precontract property is consistent with their general emphasis on maintaining individuality within the relationship. It also explains our finding that cohabitors were significantly more likely than the other groups to list their present assets (57 percent, compared to 25 percent for marrieds and premarrieds), for it makes sense to keep written records when items are separately owned.

Postcontract property. Most couples in the sample (88 percent) chose to regard property acquired during the contract period as community property. Although group percentages differed here (100 percent of the marrieds and premarrieds designated all such assets as community property, in contrast to 76 percent of the cohabitors), *the high overall percentage of couples who opted for community property reflects an overwhelming preference for the "partnership" model of a relationship.* As a typical contract stated, "We believe our life together to be a partnership; therefore all property will be mutually owned."

The dramatic preference for sharing principles and community property ownership of all the assets acquired during the relationship is certainly one of the most important findings of our inquiry. And it holds across the three types of intimate contracts. This finding underscores the inappropriateness of the separate property system of the 42 common law states that still treat the earnings and assets of each spouse as his or her separate property. While these states deny the all-important partnership aspect of marriage, our data, by contrast, highlight its continued strength and importance. In fact, even in fixed-term relationships, where couples anticipated the probability of separation, 84 percent elected to share ownership of everything acquired during their union.

Management and Control of Property

The term *property management* typically relates to day-to-day decisions about the disposition of income or assets. *Control* refers to the ultimate authority to buy, sell, pledge, or otherwise encumber property. Most of the couples who discussed management and control of property (60 percent of the sample) treated them as a unitary dimension. Of these, 88 percent chose an egalitarian arrangement and planned either to share equally or to alternate both management and control. Typically this meant joint control of property and mutually agreed-upon decisions about expenses.

The preference for joint and equal control is very significant when compared to the provisions of the traditional marriage contract. The full-time housewife in most states has no legal access to the income and assets her husband acquires during their marriage. In contrast, the majority of these tailor-made contracts have given both partners an equal right to utilize, on a daily basis, the income and assets that accrue to the community.

A minority of the couples (25 percent) felt both partners should have some discretionary money of their own and therefore reserved a monthly sum for each partner's personal expenses. "Mad money," sports equipment, clothing, cosmetics, books, tuition, and gifts were specifically mentioned as discretionary expenses. This is but one illustration of the flexibility of the contract model, and the ease with which contracts can be tailored to fit the unique needs and wishes of the parties.

Debts

Only slightly more than half of the contracts (56 percent) mentioned debts. Among those that did, a surprising 71 percent of the married and premarried couples decided to make their existing or precontract debts a community obligation, thus pledging joint responsibility for the debts and obligations their partners had incurred in the past. They thereby extended their commitment to sharing beyond traditional community property principles—and far beyond the separate property assumption of the common law property states. Although many of these contract writers are young, it is likely that some of them had substantial educational loans that became community obligations.

As expected, the cohabitors were significantly less likely to assume their partner's existing (precontract) debts. Indeed, not one cohabiting couple made precontract debts a community obligation. The cohabitors were similarly more likely to make postcontract debts a separate obligation (42 percent as opposed to 22 percent of the married and premarriage couples). Thus the cohabitors were more likely to keep separate both their economic resources and their economic obligations.

Support and Work Arrangements

The vast majority of the contracts set forth an arrangement whereby the burden of family support was to be assumed equally by both parties. Arrangements, in rank order, fell into the following four patterns:

1. *Alternating support*, in which each partner takes a turn at supporting the couple, typically while the dependent partner is in school (32 percent)
2. *Combined responsibility for support*, in which support obligations are shared equally or proportionately (32 percent)
3. *Individual responsibility for self-support*, in which each partner is responsble for his or her own support (21 percent)
4. A *single breadwinner*, in which one partner is solely responsible for the support of both partners (12 percent)

Under an *alternating support* arrangement, one partner agrees to support the other temporarily, usually through a period of education or job training. When this period expires, the roles are reversed. Those who favored this tradeoff scheme were obviously prepared to make joint plans for many years ahead. For example:

> Barry agrees to support Jill through her final year of college and during any time she should wish to return to graduate or professional school. Upon completion of her B.A. degree, Jill agrees to support Barry through four years of dental school . . . [but] if their partnership should dissolve after the completion of dental school, Barry will continue to support Jill at the rate of one-half of his annual income for four years.

Most couples who agreed to *combined responsbility for support* assumed both partners would be full-time wage earners. While most of these contracts talked of "equal contributions," the writers were clearly aware that equality could be operationally defined in various ways, from equal monetary contributions to equal contributions of effort. Thus, they anticipated and planned for disparities between the partners' occupational aspirations, career advancement, and income. Their practical solutions to these potential "problems" indicate a keen sensitivity to the traditional relationship between income and power, and a strong commitment to finding ways to ensure that both partners would be equal within the relationship. For example, as one couple stipulated: "There may be times when a contribution that is equal on its face will in fact place a greater or less burden on one of us. Adjustments shall be made for this kind of situation."

Several contractors specified how they would handle large differences in the partners' earning power. Most rejected the notion that the partner who earns the higher income is entitled to more privileges. Instead, all earnings would be treated as the product of joint efforts:

> Candice and Terry consider themselves equal partners in the relationship and will treat all income, property and other assets as products of our joint efforts, regardless of who earns the income at any time.

Another method for handling income differences required each partner to contribute the same proportion of his or her income (80 percent, for example) to a joint account, and retain the remainder for personal expenses. Several couples explicitly rejected this scheme because it gave superior financial power to the person with the greater income. They agreed instead to have each partner retain a specific (and equal) amount of money for personal expenses while contributing the remainder to the joint account.

Others simply provided for adjustments in each person's contribution to the household expenses when one person began to earn more:

> [If] one person suddenly begins to earn a proportionately larger salary than the other, then his/her responsibility for household expenses shall be increased accordingly, based on the concept that each of us wishes to contribute equally, according to our ability.

A majority of contracts (57 percent) also included specific provisions in case of one partner's job layoff, illness, disability, or maternity leave. They typically agreed to continue treating the nonearning partner as "a partner who is still making an equal contribution to the collective enterprise, which must, of course, be defined more broadly than a mere economic partnership." All these clauses reflect a highly sophisticated concept of "equal contribution" and indicate that the contractors' commitment to share their burdens goes well beyond a simple division of household expenses.

The two other arrangements—*individual responsibility* for self-support and the *single breadwinner* pattern—are straightforward and need no explication here.

As expected, support and work arrangements varied with the types of relationships. The most common support arrangement among married couples provided for alternating support (64 percent), followed by the shared support arrangement (27 percent). Only one married couple placed sole responsibility for family support on one partner, and none chose to make each individual responsible for his or her own support, reflecting once again their view of their relationship as a partnership or joint endeavor.

The premarrieds and cohabitors were similarly unlikely to rely on a single breadwinner. The premarrieds were divided about evenly among the three remaining schemes. The cohabitors were more likely to choose shared support (38 percent) than individual support (29 percent) or alternating support (25 percent).

A clear and persistent pattern emerges when we compare married couples and cohabitors. The marrieds were consistently more likely to provide for a sharing and pooling of assets—that is, they were more *community-oriented*. The cohabitors, in contrast, were more concerned about preserving their *individuality* and more likely to provide for separate property, separate debts, and separate support. In addition, even when they agreed to joint control over income and property, as a group the cohabitors were more likely to set aside a portion of their incomes to be spent at the earner's discretion (33 percent, vs. 16 percent of the marrieds and premarrieds).

Even so, all three groups planned relationships that more closely approximated a partnership (in contrast to the hierarchical model of a relationship imposed by traditional legal marriage) in that *a full 88 percent of the couples adopted schemes whereby both partners would contribute to family support.* Hence they clearly did not expect the male partner to assume the sole breadwinning role—nor did they expect the female to be a full-time homemaker. Even those couples who saw the male as the chief provider commonly anticipated intermittent employment for the woman:

> Tom will be the primary supporter of the family. However, Nancy will work in addition, between her graduation and credential program; and before the children; and after the children are in junior high school.

Domicile and Household Arrangements

Household arrangements were discussed in virtually all of the contracts (98 percent). The concerns most often specified had to do with the choice and location of domicile, and the division of responsibility for household tasks.

Domicile

Most couples (90 percent) planned a joint domicile. Although traditional family law gives the husband the right to choose the family domicile, the majority of these contracts (60 percent) gave both partners the right to make this decision, either together or alternately. For example:

> Dick and Sharon will live where their schooling takes them. When Sharon is in school, she will chose the location. When Dick is in school, he will choose. However, if there is no employment available for the other party (e.g., no hospitals for Sharon's residency while Dick is in school), a new location must be sought.

Only 18 percent of the contracts allowed one person to choose the family domicile: the male in 14 percent of the cases, the female in 4 percent. The remaining couples left the choice to the partner (sex unspecified) with the more important school and/or job-related needs. This category, while phrased in terms of career priorities, often had the effect of tacitly giving the right of decision to the male because his career was often given priority. For example:

> Steven and Judy both wish to reside in San Rafael. Should Steven's law practice be relocated, Judy agrees to transfer her career to the new location. Steven's career will be of major concern to the partnership since it will be the main source of support for the family.

If we combine the males who had job-related power with those given unconditional power, the proportion of "male" choices increases from 14 percent to 30 percent. Thus, *a significant minority of couples still subscribed to the traditional legal notion that the choice of domicile rests with the male.* As expected, this occurred significantly more often among the married and the premarried couples than among the cohabitors: half of the married group and a third of the pre-marrieds said choice of domicile would be the male's, compared to only one-tenth of the cohabitors. Although we have noted the persistence of the traditional minority, it is equally significant to point out that *a clear majority rejected* the traditional model and chose to give both parties the right to make this important decision.

Household Tasks

The majority of the contracts reflected an egalitarian approach to household tasks: in only one contract was the female given overall responsibility for all such tasks. Most couples planned either to "share equally" (26 percent) or to "take turns" (26 percent). For example:

> There will be no sexual division of labor. Housework will be split in half so that each partner will be assigned half of the work one week and half of the work the other week, alternating specific tasks.

Another fifth of the contracts (21 percent) allocated tasks "proportionately," in line with other responsibilities or temperamental preferences. The remainder left the overall division of labor vague or unassigned but specified responsibility for certain "trouble areas" in a sex-neutral fashion.

Even if we cynically assume that the women would do most of the housework in the 21 percent of the households where tasks are allotted "proportionately," that situation would be established by less than one-fourth of the contracts. Thus the majority of our contractors departed from the traditional legal norm. This is evident in two ways: first, they rejected the assumption that domestic tasks are solely the woman's responsibility, and second, they rejected the assumption that housework is not "real work" deserving of compensation, as we shall see.

It is clear that the contract writers considered household tasks "real work." For example, some contractors calculated the time each partner would work outside the home and allocated household work hours on a par with paid employment so that both partners would work an equal number of hours:

> The important item here is that both parties work approximately the same total number of hours per week. That is, hours at the job plus hours doing household responsibilities equal the partner's hours. At no time will the amount of wages made by a party take precedence over number of hours in this agreement.

A few couples specified that the partner performing more household services would receive a sum of money or a half share of all earned income, or some sort of tradeoff in leisure time or other privileges. But the major form of recognition of the value of household duties is evident from the penalties prescribed for their neglect. Almost half of the contracts assigned penalties for nonperformance of household chores, some in the form of a direct monetary fine, others in the form of payments by the "guilty" party to the partner who did the work (or to the person they hired to do it). For example:

> In the event that one party fails to perform his/her household tasks within two days of appointed time, . . . the second party may perform the task and demand to be reimbursed for his/her time at the rate of $15.00 per hour.

Among those contracts that made specific task assignments, chores were generally assigned in a sex-neutral fashion. For example, cooking was most often "shared equally" (30 percent) or done by "taking turns" (27 percent). The female partner was assigned sole responsbility for cooking in 22 percent of the contracts, the male in 14 percent. (When one person was assigned all the cooking, the other person was often assigned all the cleanup; thus meal preparation was more often "shared" than might be apparent from the cooking arrangements alone.)

Similarly, other routine household jobs such as laundering, mopping floors, watering plants, and cleaning the oven were most often shared or alternated. The only sex-based division of labor appeared in the responsibility for car maintenance (85 percent assigned it solely to the male) and shopping (42 percent assigned it solely to the female).*

Interpersonal Relations

Personal relations between the two partners were discussed in 57 contracts. A majority of these contracts discussed surnames (86 percent), and sexual relations (67 percent). Less than half discussed re-

---

*The overall sharing of household tasks along egalitarian lines brings into focus a *function* of intimate contracts: they provide *a rational context in which it is possible to "consciously" structure a relationship in accord with an egalitarian ideology.* For example, in a recent study of cohabiting and married college men and women, Stafford et al. found that while most couples divided household labor along traditional lines, *some* couples were able to break out of the traditional mold by the force of a conscious ideology. (Rebecca Stafford, Elaine Backman, and Pamela Dibona, "Division of Labor Among Cohabiting and Married Couples," *Journal of Marriage and the Family* 39, no. 1 (1977):43–57.) Our study suggests that the process of negotiating a contract in the early stages of a relationship may provide a normative framework for translating ideological beliefs into day-to-day practice.

ligion (41 percent), and ways of resolving disagreements (40 percent); therefore these topics are given less attention below.

The reader should note that the percentages reported in this section are based on the number of couples who discussed each topic, not on the total sample.

Surname

The contractors were almost evenly divided in their decisions about surnames. On the one hand, a significant minority of the couples (47 percent) decided that both persons would assume the male's surname. On the other hand, a sizable minority (41 percent) agreed that each person would retain his or her own name. In a few cases the woman planned to use a hyphenated surname, and in each of these the male retained his own name. No male planned to assume his partner's surname, not even as an adjunct to his own.

We were frankly surprised by the large number of couples who followed the traditional legal pattern and chose to adopt the male's name. *This is clearly one of the most conservative features encountered in these contracts.* Both instrumental and expressive reasons were given for the decision:

> Both parties will use Donald's surname to simplify credit terms and the use of a joint account.

> As far as the name she shall have, I insist that she carry mine. This is something we both feel is mandatory. It would make us feel more as one.

Those who opted to retain their surnames also offered both practical and ideological justifications:

> Each person will keep his or her own surname in the interest of their careers.

> Because we feel that a name is central to a person's identity, and because we believe it is important for a woman to retain her independent identity, Sandra will keep her own surname, as will Bill.

Surname decisions were closely related to marital status. The assumption of the male's surname was the preferred option in the more traditional relationships of marriage (73 percent) and premarriage (69 percent). However, it is important to note that even

within the most "traditional" contract group—the marrieds—
slightly more than one-fourth of the couples deviated from the traditional norm. In contrast, only a fourth of the cohabitors chose the
traditional option, while 75 percent of them elected to keep their
own names.

The "traditionalism" of the surname decision was significantly
related to childbearing plans. The majority of couples planning to
have children also planned to use the male's surname (72 percent).

Sexual Relations

Of the 38 couples who discussed sexual relations, *87 percent expected a sexually monogamous relationship.* Only one-tenth of the
couples explicitly allowed for sexual activity outside the contract relationship, usually with the expectation that the outside activity
would not be concealed from the partner:

> This relationship is not necessarily monogamous . . . the decision to
> have extra-relationship sex is recognized as an important, emotional,
> and volatile one; however, this choice is open, with the provision that
> the other party must be told before it happens and at least 30 minutes
> of discussion time allowed. As with money, this is done . . . for clarifi-
> cation and communication . . .

We were surprised to find that such a large majority of the contracts upheld the traditional norm of sexual monogamy. We were
also surprised to find the cohabitors, as a group, as likely to agree to
a sexually exclusive relationship as the marrieds. These findings
may reflect the youthful, middle-class composition of the sample as
well as the contractors' general idealism and commitment to their
intimate partner.*

The 24 couples who mentioned *sexual access* all stated that their
sexual relations would be solely by mutual consent. This finding notably contrasts with the law's traditional assumption that a husband has an unqualified right to sexual relations with his wife.

Religion

Only 41 percent of the contracts mentioned religion. Perhaps some
couples thought religion was not a proper subject for contractual

---

*We carefully examined the contracts of the few nonmonogamous couples in
our sample in an attempt to find distinguishing patterns, but found none.

negotiation; others undoubtedly felt it was not an important part of their lives. In fact, some of the couples who mentioned religion sought explicitly to *exclude* it from their relationship. For example, one couple provided an escape clause if either party "became religious":

> Both Matt and Sandy are agnostic and uncommitted to any religion. If one partner does find themselves [sic] involved and committed at some future time, then the other party has the option to cancel the contract.

In general, discussion of religion, when it appeared, was brief and nonspecific. For example, only half specified what religion would be practiced, or referred to frequency of church or synagogue attendance.

The single most important concern of couples who discussed religion was their children's religion and religious instruction. Three-fourths of their contracts dealt with this issue. Some designated the religion their children would follow, others outlined the religious training their children would receive, and still others agreed to allow their children to choose their own religion.

This finding suggests that a wish to ensure "good" childrearing provided the primary motivation for including religion in the contracts. Whatever the religiosity of these contracting parties, most of them saw religious guidance as an important part of a child's education. The association is underscored by the fact that nearly two-thirds of the couples who planned to have children discussed religion, compared to one-third of those who did not plan children.

Contrary to our expectations, the married couples were not more likely to discuss religion than the other two groups. The majority of couples in all groups (an overall 59 percent) omitted all mention of religion.

Resolving Disagreements

Approximately 40 percent of the contracting couples attempted to establish procedures for resolving their future differences. Half of them laid out specific ground rules for the tone and tenor of their disagreements. Some couples attempted to minimize the hostility of their arguments, others agreed not to argue when they were very angry, and still others prohibited the use of violence. Many of these provisions demonstrated the couples' awareness of effective communication techniques:

> Parties will not make disparaging comments directed at other party during arguments. Neither party will raise his/her voice above a reasonable level during an argument. Each party will allow the other to complete his/her statement before replying. Neither party will leave the premises before conclusion or resolution of an argument without consent of the partner.

Some of the provisions for resolving disagreements were highly personal and indicated the couple's awareness of the types of language, behavior, insults, and *ad hominem* remarks that had hurt each other in the past. For example:

> . . . no party may roam about refusing to speak to the other unless the other refuses to calm down, quiet their voice, and speak naturally. . . . Profanity is not acceptable . . . nor are slurs on inadequate sexual performance or lack of sexual attractiveness.

Many couples apparently believed that a "well-regulated" argument would be less likely to cause permanent damage to their relationship.

More than half of the couples agreed on procedures to deal with persistent disagreements. The three most frequently mentioned contingency plans were (1) setting aside time to discuss differences, (2) seeking professional counseling or other third-party assistance, and (3) abiding by the decision of an arbitrator. Each of these provisions was included in one-half of the contracts.

The finding that half of the couples who discussed disagreements were willing to involve third parties is somewhat surprising. It indicates a high level of confidence in professional counseling and mediation. In fact, only one couple expressly prohibited either partner from discussing the couple's differences, and explicitly rejected the involvement of third parties in their private affairs.

A third of the contracts provided for a graduated series of contingency measures, with each successive measure to be implemented only upon the failure of its predecessor. Generally, the first step involved some form of discussion between the parties. If that failed, the parties would seek professional help. Finally, if professional help did not eliminate the dispute, a neutral third-party arbitrator (generally *not* a court of law) would be called in to settle the matter once and for all. Some of the couples opting for this scheme also agreed that if none of the specified measures solved the disagreement, the relationship would terminate.

No group was significantly more likely than the others to include provisions for resolving disagreements. However, cohabiting couples were more apt to lay down ground rules for arguments and resolving disagreements themselves, while marrieds were much more likely to agree to seek professional help.

In establishing procedures and guidelines for dispute resolution, the people who have written their own contracts are entering an area where there has long been a legal void. The traditional legal contract nowhere requires comparable settlement efforts before dissolution (although optional conciliation courts are now available in some states).

Children

Plans to Have Children

Children were mentioned in 92 percent of the contracts. Half of the couples (51 percent) indicated they did not want children, 41 percent planned to have children, and the remainder were undecided. However, many of these decisions appear to be tentative, as two-fifths of the contracts provided for later review of the subject, with the later decision, in almost all cases, to be a joint decision.

As might be expected, there was a correlation between plans for children and marital status. Marrieds and pre-marrieds were more likely to plan to have children (56 percent and 78 percent, respectively) than were cohabitors (33 percent). The causal direction of this relationship is unclear. On one hand, it is possible that couples who choose the more traditional relationship of marriage are predisposed to want a traditional "family." On the other hand, couples may first decide they want children and therefore (because of societal pressures, convenience, health insurance, legal consequences, etc.) conclude they had best get married. The latter speculation is supported by Hassett's finding that the large majority of college students "believe that raising children is best done within the legal bonds of marriage."[9] Similarly, some of the cohabitors in our sample indicated that a future decision to have children would require a renegotiation of their contract because they viewed children as part and parcel of a legal marriage.

It should be noted, however, that the correlation between legal marriage and the expectation of children was far from perfect; not all children were planned within legal marriage. Indeed, a third of the cohabiting couples planned to have children. However, these cohabitors were the ones most likely to envision a long-term relationship "suitable" to raising children.

The fact that a good half of the couples in the sample chose not to have children may indicate another shift away from traditional patterns. Here we must be cautious, however, for nearly one-half of those who said they did not want children provided for second thoughts in a subsequent review. Moreover, since our society continues to view procreation as essential to marriage, and parenthood as necessary for personal fulfillment, especially for women,[10] couples who elect to remain childless will probably continue to face formidable pronatalist pressures. These forces are recognized in the comments one couple appended to their contract:

> Children—our greatest discussion arose here. I raised the issue of children in a serious way—we should not become parents just because everybody does it, or because we want to see if we can raise children. I feel that the decision to raise children involves a dedicated commitment. If we fail as parents, our children will be the ones to suffer, and being a parent is the one thing I want to succeed at most in life. . . .
>
> Children can bring joy, excitement, pride, love and much more into a relationship. They can bring the parents together very closely as they watch them grow. But when we have children, we must want them dearly and love them and dedicate ourselves to them, for the rest of our lives.

This unusually articulate statement may hold a clue to why, in spite of social pressures and the general bias in favor of childbearing in marriage, so many couples in our sample expressly agreed not to have children. Other couples expressed more instrumental concerns—fearing that children were simply incompatible with a two-career family.

Birth Control and Unplanned Pregnancies

Responsibility for birth control was discussed in 86 percent of the contracts. Over half of the agreements made the female either solely responsible (27 percent) or responsible until an effective male contraceptive is available (31 percent).* Responsibility was shared or alternated in another one-third of the cases. The male was assigned primary responsibility in only two cases.

Approximately two-thirds of the couples who discussed the issue of childbearing had contingency plans for unplanned pregnancies. While one-fourth of the couples rejected the possibility of an abortion, a slightly larger number, close to a third of the couples, considered abortion a likely option. A recurring theme in these contracts was the woman's right to make the final decision because she had "the right to control her own body."

Contingency plans varied somewhat with marital status. Not surprisingly, the cohabitors, who were less likely to want children, were more likely to formulate plans for unexpected pregnancy. However, 65 percent of the couples who planned children (eventually) also discussed contingency plans for an untimely or unplanned pregnancy. Plans for abortion were also related to marital status. Married couples were less likely than cohabitors to discuss abortion; and when they did discuss it they were more likely to reject it.

Child Care

The large majority of the couples who wanted children (81 percent) specified who would have the responsibility for child care. Of these, the sample was almost evenly divided between traditional and egalitarian child care arrangements.

Those couples who assigned the primary responsibility for child care to the woman typically expected the man to continue working while the woman would interrupt her career. A typical provision:

> During the first five years of their children's lives, Joyce will quit work and stay home with the children. The children will be two years apart in age; therefore, Joyce will be out of the labor force for seven years. She will then return to pursue her career.

Similar results were found in Huang and Leonard's 1976 study of married and cohabiting couples in college: most respondents felt

---

*The stipulation that "the female partner will assume responsibility for birth control until a more effective male contraceptive becomes available" was mentioned in a contract cited in the original Weitzman article (which was read by the contractors of the present sample) and reflects the impact of what can be seen in retrospect as a poorly chosen example.

that both partners should work until a child was born, at which time the overall preference was for the female to remain at home.[11]

In only one case was primary child care assigned to the male. It seems that the sex-role stereotype of women as caregivers is harder to relinquish than most other stereotypes. In fact, *the rearing of children is one of the two areas in our sample of contracts in which the egalitarian ethos failed to dominate.* *

This finding is somewhat attenuated, however, by the fact that contracts assigning child care to the woman often included expectations of "help" from the male partner (and others). For example:

> On weekends and evenings Dave will take a substantial load of child care responsibilities from Jane to give her leisure time. A babysitter will come in one night a week so that Jane and Dave can have time to themselves for some leisure activity.

In addition, in contrast to traditional arrangements, these contractors typically allocated substantial compensation for the childrearing partner. One such provision stated:

> If one party stays home with the children and temporarily stops working, the other partner will pay the first [partner] one-half of his/her income until the child is placed in a day care center.

It is also important to note that a sizable minority of the couples (42 percent) maintained egalitarian norms and planned to share or alternate responsibilities. For example:

> All child-care tasks will be shared equally. The parties will take turns staying home from work to care for children if necessary. Child care on weekends and discipline will also be shared equally. If one partner does not complete his/her tasks, he/she will pay the other the salary of a private nurse.

Financial Arrangements for Children

Among couples who planned children, their financial support was to be shared in about half the cases (most specified "equal" contributions, a minority specified proportional contributions). In the other half the children's financial support was assigned to the male. As expected, these financial assignments were directly linked to the child care arrangement. Half of the couples accepted the tradition-

---

*The choice of surname, discussed above, is the other: 47 percent of the contracting couples chose to adopt the male's surname.

al male obligation for child support and the traditional female obligation for child care. The other half of the couples planned to share both types of responsibility. Provisions for children in the event of divorce or dissolution (that is, for child support and custody) are discussed below in the section on dissolution.

Wills and Inheritances

One-half (51 percent) of the contracts contained some provisions for making wills, usually a simple statement of plans to draft mutual wills at a later date. For example:

> Both parties agree to make wills within ninety days of signing this contract so that in case of death their share of all community property and funds will go to the remaining party.

Traditionally, the husband has been the spouse most likely to write a will, for two reasons. First, most husbands expect to predecease their wives; and second, in most states husbands expect to predecease their wives; and second, in most states husbands are assumed to "own" the family property and therefore to have exclusive right to dispose of it. Thus the husband has customarily drafted a will largely to ensure economic support and "protection" for his widow. The same rationale lies behind state inheritance laws that guarantee a widow a fixed share of her husband's estate whether he leaves a will or not.

The contracting couples in our sample, however, apparently viewed wills as sex-neutral. Both partners planned to write wills, and two-thirds of the couples who mentioned wills chose to leave all property to the surviving partner. Very few wills included provisions for third parties, such as parents or siblings, but 42 percent planned to leave part of their estate to their children.

Couples who planned to have children were more than twice as likely to discuss wills as those who planned to remain childless (85 percent vs. 36 percent), and nearly two-thirds of these couples mentioned children in connection with wills. Of these, about 60 percent excluded their children as long as one spouse survived, while 40 percent granted the children a share outright. (In contrast, Sussman et al. found that 85 percent of testators left the entire estate to the surviving spouse, despite the existence of surviving children.[12])

Married couples were slightly more likely to mention wills than premarrieds and cohabitors (70 percent vs. 50 percent each), and were significantly more likely to follow the traditional assumptions and to provide for a widow (rather than for a widower). As expected, couples planning permanent relationships were more likely to discuss wills (61 percent) than were couples who wrote limited-duration contracts (36 percent).

Contract Review and Breach of Contract

Changing the Contract

The couples in this sample recognized the importance of contract flexibility. Nearly two-thirds discussed the likelihood of their relationships changing over time and accordingly adopted some provision for reviewing the contract at a later date.

Slightly more than half of those who provided for contract review (56 percent) either set a specific date for the review or provided for periodic reviews (ranging from every six months to every five years). In addition, nearly one-quarter of the couples allowed for ad hoc reviews at the request of either party. For example:

> If for any reason, one person is unhappy about a specific provision, he/she may demand a negotiation of that particular section, giving at least two week's notice.

No significant differences emerged among the marrieds, premarrieds, and cohabitors with respect to review provisions.

Damages for Breach of Contract

Slightly less than half (44 percent) of the contracts included provisions for the payment of damages when one party failed to keep his or her part of the bargain. Those that did, typically required the violator to pay liquidated damages—that is, a monetary fine calibrated to the amount of damage caused by the breach. In some cases, however, severe breaches would trigger the termination of the relationship.

The majority of the damages were set for two kinds of violations: a breach of an agreement to be sexually monogamous, and a breach of an agreement to perform specific household tasks. Together, and in roughly equal proportions, these two accounted for 60 percent of the first-mentioned offenses.* The specification of these two behaviors may indicate their particular importance in the minds of the contractors, or it may simply reflect the partners' perception of which provisions are most likely to be violated.

The most frequently prescribed penalties were monetary damages, specified in 57 percent of the contracts. Some couples established a schedule of fines (typically for specific tasks and interpersonal items, such as not cleaning up, or not calling to say one would be home late), while other contracts required the offending party to pay commensurate costs:

> If a breach of contract is made concerning household or child care responsibilities, the nonconforming partner must pay the amount necessary to hire a maid or a babysitter to cover his or her share of the responsibilities.

Along these lines, several couples established an hourly pay rate for the partner who chose to perform the neglected task instead of hiring outside help:

> In the event that one party fails to perform his/her household tasks within two days of appointed time, . . . the second party may perform the task and demand to be reimbursed for his/her time (from the nonperforming partner's cash fund) at the rate of $15.00 per hour.

Several couples devised unique penalties. For example, one couple who objected to financial penalties for nonfinancial matters, substituted appropriate verbal and psychological punishments instead. Another couple created an imaginative penalty for infidelity: the offending party was required to pay for three dates between the injured party and a person of the opposite sex.

While most of the couples preferred to determine their own penalties and to grade them according to their personal estimates of the seriousness of the offense, a few wanted penalties to be set by a court of law. This "solution" has several disadvantages. It is likely to be expensive and time-consuming to carry out, compared to preestablished penalties, and it may encourage unnecessary litigation. It also carries the risk of facing a court that does not share the par-

---

*This percentage slightly underrepresents the number of contracts that included damage provisions for violation of household task or fidelity agreements. A few other couples gave first mention to other types of offenses, such as property breach, wage breach, or noncare of children, and then gave second- or third-place mention to infractions in the areas of household duties or fidelity.

ties' values and may be unwilling to award damages for pain and suffering (in contrast to those for monetary losses). On the other hand, there are certain types of breach that are difficult to anticipate and final recourse to the courts (or an arbitrator whom both parties trust) may be helpful in dealing with breaches caused by unanticipated events.

Traditionally, the only penalty the law has imposed for a breach of the marriage contract (such as adultery or nonsupport) has been to grant the innocent party a divorce. In that case, the breaching party has typically been required to "pay" for his or her fault in the divorce settlement: adulterous wives have been denied alimony, and husbands at fault have been penalized by the loss of property or by high support orders.[13] The intimate contracts in this sample follow the legal pattern insofar as they provide for dissolution of the relationship when one partner violates an agreement to be sexually monogamous. In contrast, however, *not one* contract mentioned dissolution as a penalty for neglect of household duties. Financial penalties were prescribed for these violations.*

Couples who planned to have children were much more likely than those not planning children to specify damages for infidelity (75 percent vs. 13 percent), while couples who hoped to remain childless were much more concerned about the violation of household task agreements (88 percent vs. 25 percent). Similarly, couples who established community property regimes were more likely to specify damages for infidelity (54 percent vs. 0), while couples with separate property contracts more frequently specified damages for the nonperformance of household tasks (100 percent vs. 46 percent).

The pattern of these findings reflects a basic difference in the nature of the couples' commitments. Couples who planned to pool their property and rear children together envisioned a more complete merger of their lives and a mutual commitment to a long-term relationship. They were less concerned with the division of labor in the household than with the partner's commitment to the union. An act of infidelity was seen as a serious threat to the relationship because it would undermine their emotional and affective commitment to each other. In contrast, couples who kept their property separate and did not plan to have children together were more concerned with the day-to-day conditions of their lives than with a

---

*This may suggest that the couple anticipates a problem in securing compliance with these task assignments and may be establishing penalties—in advance— to create an additional pressure for compliance.

long-term total commitment. They therefore concentrated on minimizing daily inconveniences and penalized those who neglected household responsibilities.

Dissolution

Almost all of the contracts (90 percent, or 53 documents) included some discussion of dissolution. The remainder of this section is based on those contracts.

Conditions for Dissolution

Surprisingly, only one-third of the couples specified the conditions under which dissolution would occur. Slightly more than half (56 percent) provided for a "pure no-fault dissolution," allowing either party to terminate the relationship upon request (with adequate notice). The rest set a fixed date for termination or adopted some combination of the two approaches.

Some of those who allowed dissolution at one party's request nevertheless required some prior attempt at counseling or reconciliation. For example:

> Dissolution will not occur until parties have had at least three months of professional marriage counseling, either separately or jointly. Conciliation attempts must be made by both parties, prior to termination. Termination can take place three months after conciliation attempts have failed.

Termination Fees

Very few couples (only 12 percent) imposed a fee or penalty on the party who chose to terminate the contract. Thus the overwhelming majority rejected traditional legal notions of responsibility and fault, and were not interested in penalizing the person who initiated the dissolution.

Among the small minority of couples who did impose penalties, some elected to award less property to the partner responsible for the dissolution. Others imposed a termination fee as a way of adjusting inequitable consequences of the dissolution. For example, a man who terminated a marriage before his wife finished school could be required to pay such a fee if he had been allowed to finish his education before she returned to school. In most cases these tradeoff arrangements were treated as purely financial exchanges elsewhere in the contract. But in the few cases discussed above an additional termination fee was imposed.

Division of Community Property

On major advantage of a marriage contract (or a contract in lieu of marriage) is its potential utility in minimizing court battles over property and support at the point of dissolution. A large majority of the couples (79 percent) discussed division of the community property. Married couples in the sample were less likely than the others to discuss property division, but this may reflect their awareness of and satisfaction with California community property law. (California law provides for an equal division of the property acquired by a couple during their marriage. However, marital partners may opt for an unequal division by written agreement.) For unmarried cohabitors, in contrast, the legal situation is much less certain. Because most states have no provisions governing the division of their assets, *the only way in which cohabitants can ensure a desired division of jointly acquired property is by contract.*

Almost all the contracts that provided for the division of community property divided it equally (83 percent). Many couples handled this division in one short sentence:

> Upon separation, each party will take his or her separate property, and any jointly owned community property will be divided equally.

No differences were found among the proportions of married, premarried, and cohabiting couples who opted for an equal division. Recognizing, however, that they might disagree about what was community property and what separate, or about what constituted an equal division, several couples also arranged for arbitration to help in the evaluation and allotment.

A number of couples established procedures to ensure that a business or a professional practice would not be needlessly dissolved: typically, the operating or practicing partner would be permitted to retain the enterprise intact but must reimburse the other partner for one-half of its value. Some contracts further specified how this reimbursement was to be paid (in assets or cash). Monthly payments over a period of years were often explicitly ruled out because this arrangement would deprive the inactive partner of equal use of the capital. Thus the operating partner might be required to secure a loan to satisfy the reimbursement requirement.

Other couples anticipated the problem of allocating nondivisible assets (including, in one case, "fur persons"):

> In the case of dissolution, each person shall get a portion of the community property in the following manner. All community funds (money) shall be split evenly. All community (including fur persons) shall be chosen alternately (one person claiming an item, then the other claiming one, etc. . . . with who chooses first being decided by lot).

Less than a fifth of the total sample discussed the division of debts. Of those who did, only one couple assigned debts according to "fault." As expected, the couples who wanted to maintain separate property and separate debts during their relationship reaffirmed these principles in the event of dissolution.

Provisions for Partner Support After Dissolution

The issue of who shall support whom, and to what extent, is often a troublesome one in legal divorces. It is also frequently cited as an area in which marital contracts (or contracts in lieu of marriage) can do a great service in minimizing court battles upon dissolution. More than half of the contracts that discussed dissolution (57 percent) included provisions for support.

Couples contracting for relationships of indefinite duration were significantly more likely than fixed-term contractors to discuss support provisions (70 percent compared to 42 percent). Similarly, nearly all the would-be parents discussed postdissolution support (88 percent), whereas only about a third (36 percent) of the couples not planning children made support agreements. Thus, length and depth of commitment was positively correlated with concern for support.

Three-fifths (62 percent) of the couples discussed the traditional male obligation to support the female, and over half of these (58 percent) stated flatly that the male would have *no* support obligations upon dissolution. Typically, such a provision was coupled with a statement indicating that neither partner would sustain a support obligation.

When support responsibility was specified, it was frequently written as a sex-neutral obligation; either party having "need" or deserving "repayment" would be supported by the other. However, only 58 percent of the contracts explicitly relieved the man of an obligation to support, whereas 80 percent explicitly relieved the woman—an interesting sign of the persistence of tradition.

Although the percentage of couples who rejected any female responsibilities for support was equally high across groups, large differences emerged with regard to the male's support obligation. While three-fourths of the cohabitants and two-thirds of the premarrieds rejected the notion that the man should support the woman after dissolution, only 13 percent of the married couples relieved the man of all such obligations. Moreover, our first suspicion—that this finding was a spurious result of plans for children—was not confirmed. Married couples were more likely to opt for continuing male support of the female irrespective of their plans for children. Legally married couples were simply more traditional. Since they opted for more traditional roles during marriage, the women were more likely to be dependent on the men for postdivorce support. Furthermore, they tended to view postdivorce support as a form of compensation for the wife's services, career sacrifices, and aid in building the husband's career. For example:

> Matthew will pay Carol one-third of his annual salary for seven years (after dissolution), which is as long as they decided she should not have a full-time career outside the home, so that she could care for the children in a manner they agreed.

In accord with our early expectations, couples planning children were indeed more likely than not to continue the male's support obligations after dissolution. Of those who planned children, 64 percent expressly agreed to have the male partner support the female partner. On the other hand, well over three-fourths (81 percent) of couples not planning children relieved the male partner of any such obligation.

The amount of support.   The majority (70 percent) of the couples who created support obligations proved quite imaginative in developing formulas to determine the amount of support. In fact, these formulas reveal a lot about their various rationales for requiring support. Analysis disclosed four major justifications.

1. *Need and ability to pay.* The first basis for support is similar to the standard commonly applied by courts in no–fault divorce states; the comparative needs and finances of the parties. One contract read:

> Support payments made, if any, will be contingent upon the salaries made by each partner. If both partners earn $10,000 a year or more, no support payments will be made. But if only one partner earns more than $10,000 a year, payments will be made until the poorer partner's income rises to at least $10,000 a year or that partner remarries.

2. *Compensation for past services.* Some couples imposed a support obligation on one partner as a means of compensating the other for past childrearing or domestic services:

> Nick will pay Karen one-fourth of his annual income for as many years as the relationship has lasted. . . . It is agreed that this is not alimony, but a reimbursement for Karen's care of the children during this time. This payment will continue regardless of her remarriage.

3. *Compensation for forgone career opportunities.* Several couples imposed a postdissolution obligation on one party to compensate the other for having passed up career opportunities in order to further the relationship or the other partner's career:

> If no children are born, Ron agrees to pay Diane 30 percent of his income in compensation for the years of her career that she has lost. This applies until Diane remarries or until her income is within 10 percent of his.

4. *Reimbursement for past support.* Sometimes postdissolution support was intended to settle the balance on a tradeoff arrangement. If the party who provided support during the relationship did not receive the support he or she was promised during the union, he or she could be compensated after dissolution:

> If this relationship terminates on or before the three-year period, both parties agree that Kristin will compensate Rod for the support that he will have provided for her. For every month that Rod assumed responsibility for the support of Kristin, Kristin shall in turn give Rod $400.

Although judges may well consider similar factors in awarding spousal support or alimony, the last three of these standards have rarely been articulated as valid justifications for support awards. In fact, in 1975 one New York judge made headlines when he awarded an executive secretary (who had supported her husband through law school and a six-year marriage) five years of support so that she could continue in medical school.[14] His decision was reversed on appeal. Because the higher court's ruling remains the law in most states today, contracts that require reimbursement for past support (or services) provide the best, if not the only, means of assuring compensation after dissolution.

Duration of support. Although some couples specified the number of years a support obligation would continue, most linked its duration to the length of the relationship—typically, a year of support for every year the couple stayed together.

An equally common arrangement linked the duration of post-dissolution support to the completion of a tradeoff arrangement. For example:

> Lori will be responsible for Todd's educational expenses and support for four years. Todd will then be responsible for Lori's educational expenses and support for the following four years. If the partnership should dissolve at any time during these eight years, this contract stipulates that each shall have the following financial obligation to the other: (1) If dissolution occurs during the first four years, Lori will pay Todd's remaining tuition (which may be up to four full years in graduate school) and $350 a month in living expenses. The amount paid in living expenses will be tied to the cost-of-living index to allow for automatic increases. (2) If dissolution occurs during years 5 through 8, Todd will have the above obligation for Lori's tuition and living expenses.

Other couples adopted the more traditional pattern of tying the duration of support to the remarriage of the supported partner:

> Taylor agrees to support Naomi at the rate of three-eighths of his gross monthly income. This will continue if she returns to work, but will cease if she remarries.

Child custody. Custody provisions were closely linked to expectations about child care. Of those who wanted children and who specified custody plans, 40 percent stipulated that the female would have sole custody. Custody was split or given to the male in slightly more than one-tenth of the cases. The remaining half of the couples drafted less specific custody provisions, providing for custody to be awarded to the parent "most able to provide care," or "who is best qualified," or "who is closer to the children."

Child support.   Child support obligations were discussed by 78 percent of the couples who planned children. Slightly more than half (57 percent) agreed to share support responsibilities by making "equal" or proportional financial contributions. For example:

> Child care will be equally shared by both parents if their incomes do not differ by more than 10 percent. If their incomes differ by more than 10 percent, then the one with the greater income will pay a greater percentage of child support, the amount to be determined by the difference in the parents' incomes. . . . In any case, the parent who has custody of the children will receive $100 per month from the other parent for assuming the responsibility for child care.

It is interesting to note that the majority of these contracts recognized the value of the nonmonetary contribution of the custodial parent. For example:

> Upon dissolution, Steve agrees to provide Kay with full financial support for the children and child care expenses, and to compensate her for her own time in caring for them at the going rate for private nurses for the hours that they are not in school. This will continue until they are of legal age. He also agrees to use the income from various insurance and stocks to support their higher education.

While over one-half of the couples agreed to share child support obligations, a substantial minority (29 percent) chose the traditional pattern and imposed the obligation of supporting the children solely on the male partner. There was no comparable assignment of the total obligation for child support to the female partner.

The duration of child support obligation was rarely specified; when it was, it was set at age 18, or age 21, or "until college graduation." Only one couple pledged to support their children through graduate or professional school "if student loans are not available."

We expected the three groups to vary in the allocation of child support responsibilities. However, once we controlled for plans to have children there were no significant differences.

Summary and Conclusion

We began this research with three aims: to describe and compare different types of intimate contracts, to analyze the extent to which these contracts support egalitarian family forms, and to compare the relationships established by contract with those established by traditional family law. Having described and compared the intimate contracts, we now turn to the latter two questions.

To what extent do these contracts support more egalitarian family forms? Looking at the sample as a whole, it is evident that the cohabiting couples were the group most likely to establish egalitarian relationships, the married couples least likely, with the premarrieds somewhere in between. To highlight the contractual provisions that are most supportive of egalitarian family forms, it seems useful to compare the two extremes, the cohabitors and the married couples.

These two sets of contracts reflect two basic differences: an individualistic vs. a collective orientation, and contrasting styles of allocating decisions and responsibilities. Let us briefly examine each of these dimensions. First, the cohabitors were more likely to stress each person's *individuality*—both psychologically and financially —and to give each partner independence and power in roughly equal amounts. The women tended to retain their own surnames, and the partners were likely to keep their property and debts separate and to assign each partner separate responsibility for his or her own support. In contrast, the marrieds, who viewed themselves as a *community*, tended to treat both property and support as joint endeavors.

Earlier we contrasted these behaviors in terms of their individualistic vs. collective orientation. Here we wish to stress the power consequences of these differences. When a couple creates a joint enterprise or a community, they open the door to dominance by one partner. From the view that the two are "one" and their futures inextricably linked, it is relatively easy to progress to decisions that further the male's career—in the interest of the collectivity. It is also easy for the partners to fall into the traditional family roles of dominant husband and helpmate wife. In contrast, when partners retain individual responsibilities for their own support, property, and careers, both are forced to make independent decisions and maintain the measure of control that gives each one an independent power base.

These assertions about the relationship between property control and power may seem contradictory in light of our earlier contention that the overwhelming preference for community property among couples in this sample is a reflection of their egalitarian ideals. We argued that this preference fosters a "partnership" model for intimate relationships, a model seen as especially desirable from the perspective of the homemaking partner for its recognition of the value of that partner's contribution to the union. Thus, the community property system was viewed as a means of overcoming many of the property inequities suffered by married and unmarried women in the past.

However, let us now stress that the advantages of the *community property* system are most important in a single-income family— that is, in the traditional family, in which the husband earns most or all of the family income while the nonsalaried wife cares for household and children. In these circumstances, *separate property laws* give the husband the right to retain, as his alone, all the income and property he acquires during the marriage. However, the consequences of the separate property system are different for a family with *two incomes.* In a two-income family the separate property system allows both partners to maintain the ownership and control of their own income, and thus accords each an independent financial base.

Some would argue that the two-income family also benefits from the more equitable distribution of property that the community property system provides.* Pointing to current employment discrimination against women, the lower salaries women receive, and the continued subordination of women's careers to the needs of their husbands and families, they assert that community property is the only way to "equalize" the burden that women typically shoulder. Others, however, contend that even women who earn less than their male partners are better off keeping control of their own property because separate property facilitates their individuality and affords them a relatively secure financial base.

The couples in this sample seem to subscribe to the first view in their overwhelming choice of the community property option. Although few of them planned to rely on a single income (almost all expected both partners to work and share the burden of support), they seemed to believe the community property system offered the best way both to equalize their efforts and to share the results. As we have noted, they were alert to the potential power consequences of unequal incomes; indeed, many of them formulated special pro-

*As we noted in Chapter 3, law professor Susan Prager argues that most marriages, especially two-career marriages, are based on sharing principles. "Sharing Principles and the Future of Marital Property Law," *UCLA Law Review* 25, no. 1 (1977):1–22.

visions to ensure that greater earnings would not confer greater power within the relationship.

None of our married or premarried couples chose to hold their property separately. In contrast, 25 percent of the cohabitors chose to do so. One-fourth does not constitute a majority, to be sure; nevertheless, these stalwarts reflected the "independence concerns" that were typical of the cohabitors as a group and distinguished them in an important way from the married couples.

A second significant difference between the cohabitors and the marrieds can be seen in their modes of making decisions and allocating responsibilities. The cohabitors were much more likely to contribute equally to decisions and to share responsibilities equally. For example, only 11 percent of the cohabitors allowed the male to control domicile decisions, compared to 57 percent of the marrieds. Similarly, in the allocation of responsibilities, the married couples were more likely to assign household tasks to one person, to assign the male the responsibility for support, and to assign child care responsibilities to the female. The last difference is especially significant: fully 80 percent of the cohabitors agreed to share child care responsibilities, in contrast to 20 percent of the marrieds.

The differences between the married and cohabitant groups also dramatize *the variety of ways in which relationships established by intimate contracts can differ from those established by legal marriage.* Clearly, the contracts written by the cohabitors differ most sharply from the legal norm because these couples explicitly aimed at establishing a different form of relationship. The overwhelming majority of them rejected every provision of the traditional marriage contract. First, they viewed the household as jointly headed: only 25 percent of the women chose to adopt the male's surname and only 11 percent allowed him to choose the family domicile.

Second, they rejected the law's traditional assignment of support responsibilities. Not one cohabiting couple assigned sole responsibility for family support to the male; instead, all adopted some sort of agreement to share the burden either through an alternating or a joint support arrangement, or by agreeing that each would be self-supporting. Furthermore, they rejected the male's traditional obligation to support the family after dissolution.

Third, the cohabitors rejected the woman's traditional obligations in the home in favor of having both partners share domestic and child care responsibilities. The latter is an especially significant departure from traditional legal norms—only 20 percent of the co-habitors assumed the woman would be solely responsible for children, while 80 percent agreed to share child care and nurturance.

Apart from renouncing these time-honored expectations, the cohabitors departed from tradition in at least two other important respects: only a third of them planned to have children, and only half of them expected their relationship to last "indefinitely." All these nontraditional choices suggest that the type of relationship they envisioned was significantly different from the lifelong union assumed by family law. However, it would be inaccurate to portray these relationships as diametrically different in all respects. The overwhelming majority of the cohabiting couples wanted a monogamous sexual relationship, indeed, viewed it as essential to their emotional intimacy. Furthermore, they continued to emphasize the importance of love, tenderness, and various forms of mutual support.

A somewhat more subtle comparison between a contract relationship and the legal marriage prescription is provided by the married couples. As we have seen, the married couples, as a group, were the most committed to a traditional family, and many of them viewed the furtherance of the male's career as a primary concern of the partnership. Only a fourth of them stipulated that the wife would not use her husband's surname, and only half of them gave the woman an equal right to choose the location of the family domicile. Thus, they were largely supportive of the traditional assumption that the husband is head of the family.

However, the married couples did not subscribe to all the sex-based prescriptions of traditional legal marriage. They were more likely to structure their family as a partnership than as a hierarchy; and most of them expected both partners to be employed and to contribute to family support. The married couples who planned children were somewhat more likely to make the male primarily responsible for support, but even among this subgroup half of the couples agreed to share family support responsibility.

As we have seen, traditional assumptions regarding a sexual division of labor within marriage have served as justification for the husband's ownership and control of property. In a strong break from this tradition, every married couple in our sample agreed that property acquired during the contract period would be treated as community property. Half of the marrieds further agreed that property owned by either party before the marriage would be converted to community property. Of those marrieds who discussed the disposition of community property in the event of dissolution, all but one couple decided the property would be divided equally; the exceptional couple tied property division to child custody arrangements.

This aspiration to equality extended into the realm of domestic responsibilities as well, with three-fourths of the married couples agreeing to share household tasks. If this finding seems less than startling in view of the fact that most of our married couples also planned to share family support responsibilities, it should be remembered that in traditional arrangements most wives with full-time jobs continue to carry the full burden of household duties in addition to their paid employment.

Finally, with respect to the fourth provision of the traditional marriage contract, the majority of the married couples who planned children (60 percent) followed the traditional norm by assigning child care responsibilities to the wife; nevertheless, a very significant minority planned to share these duties. In addition, those who assigned child care to the wife defined her role in nontraditional ways: the husbands were often committed to some participation in caring for the children, and the wives were typically guaranteed some form of compensation for their responsibilities. Further, in the event of divorce, the man's support obligation generally was to include payment for the woman's caretaker services in addition to conventional child support payments—another indication of the value these couples accorded to the woman's labor. It is also noteworthy that only 56 percent of the married couples planned to have children in the first place, once again indicating their disposition to depart from traditional legal assumptions about the goals of marriage.

In summary, in contrast to traditional legal marriage, *both the married and the cohabiting contracts were likely to structure intimate relationships as partnerships* and to effect an equalization of rights and responsibilities. While it is unclear whether the contract process itself or the desires of the contractors had more to do with the egalitarian character of the documents, it is evident that the contract structure uniquely facilitates the formation and perpetuation of a partnership model of marriage.

Notes

Introduction (pp. xv–xxiii)

1. Sir Henry Sumner Maine, *Ancient Law* (London: Oxford University Press, 1931), p. 141.
2. Philip Selznick, *Law, Society, and Industrial Justice* (New York: Russell Sage Foundation, 1969), p. 53.
3. Maynard v. Hill, 125 U.S. 190, 211 (1888).
4. Griswold v. Connecticut, 381 U.S. 479 (1965).
5. Loving v. Virginia, 388 U.S. 1 (1967).
6. Henry Foster, "Marriage: A 'Basic Civil Right of Man,' " *Fordham Law Review* 37 (1968):51.
7. Loving v. Virginia, 388 U.S. 1, p. 12.
8. See, generally, Barbara Brown, Ann Freedman, Harriet Katz, and Alice M. Price, *Women's Rights and the Law: The Impact of the ERA on State Laws* (New York: Praeger Publishers, 1977).
9. Ibid. p. 87.
10. Ibid.

Introduction, Part I: The Legal Tradition: Terms of the Traditional Marriage Contract (pp. 1-3)

1. William Blackstone, *Commentaries on the Laws of England*, vol. 1 (1765):442.

2. United States v. Yazell, 382 U.S. 341, 359 (1966) (dissenting opinion).

3. Max Radin, "The Common Law of the Family," *National Law Library* 6 (1939):175.

4. It is interesting to note that the law today takes the opposite position with regard to custody preference, almost invariably granting custody to the wife. The events that led to the legal change in the custody presumption are beyond the scope of this book, but suggest an intriguing area for historical research.

5. Barbara Babcock, Ann E. Freedman, Eleanor Holmes Norton, and Susan Ross, *Sex Discrimination and the Law: Causes and Remedies* (Boston: Little, Brown & Co., 1975), p. 563.

    The wife could not bring charges against the husband for rape or assault and battery because she could not sue in her own name and because rape was defined as forcible intercourse by a man with "a woman not his wife." In addition, as Babcock, et al. noted (p. 562): "The husband could go to court to get control of her property, its profits and rents, and her wages. He could have her forcibly returned to him if she ran away." Citing Mansfield, *The Legal Rights, Liabilities and Duties of Women* (1845), p. 273.

6. Homer Clark, *The Law of Domestic Relations* (St. Paul, Minn.: West Publishing Co., 1968), p. 229.

7. Ibid., p. 226.

8. Leo Kanowitz, *Women and the Law: The Unfinished Revolution* (Albuquerque: University of New Mexico Press, 1969), p. 40 (footnotes omitted). By 1882 the Married Women's Property Acts had also become the law in England.

9. Ibid., p. 40.

10. The property disadvantages that married women continue to face are discussed in Chapters 2 and 3.

11. California was the first state in the United States to adopt a no-fault law that completely abolishes fault-based grounds for marital dissolution. California's no-fault divorce law allows dissolution of the marriage when "irreconcilable differences have caused the irremediable breakdown of the marriage" (*California Civil Code*, Section 4506

[West 1970]). By substituting this standard of marital breakdown for the old fault-linked grounds (such as adultery or mental cruelty) for divorce, the California law allows the individuals to decide for themselves when and why they want to dissolve their marriage.

Chapter 1: The Husband Is Head of the Family (pp. 5–22)

1. See Herma Hill Kay, "The Married Woman's Loss of Identity," in Kenneth Davidson, Ruth Ginsburg, and Herma Hill Kay, *Text, Cases and Materials on Sex-Based Discrimination* (St. Paul, Minn.: West Publishing Co., 1974), pp. 117–30. Also published separately as *Sex-Based Discrimination in Family Law* (St. Paul, Minn.: West Publishing Co., 1974), pp. 117–30 (hereinafter cited as *Discrimination in Family Law*).

2. As Inger Margrete Pedersen has observed, single women often have more legal advantages than married women. See "The Status of Women in Private Law," *Annals* 375 (1968):44–51.

3. Barbara A. Brown, Ann E. Freedman, Harriet N. Katz, and Alice M. Price, *Women's Rights and the Law: The Impact of the ERA on State Laws* (New York: Praeger Publishers, 1977), p. 104 (hereinafter cited as *Women's Rights and the Law*).

4. Ibid., p. 100.

5. Ibid.

6. Kay, *Discrimination in Family Law*, p. 119, citing 1972 data.

7. Leo Kanowitz, *Women and the Law: The Unfinished Revolution* (Albuquerque: University of New Mexico Press, 1969), p. 11 (hereinafter cited as *Women and the Law*).

8. Ibid., p. 11.

9. Stanton v. Stanton, 30 Utah 2d 315, 318–19, 517 P.2d 1010, 1012 (1974).

10. Stanton v. Stanton, 421 U.S. 7 (1975).

11. Barbara Brown, Thomas Emerson, Gail Falk, and Ann Freedman, "The Equal Rights Amendment: A Constitutional Basis for Equal Rights for Women," *Yale Law Journal* 80 (1971):940.

12. See, e.g., Bacon v. Boston Elevated Ry., 246 Mass. 30, p. 31, 152 N.E. 35, p. 36 (1926).

13. See, e.g., In re Kayaloff, 9 F. Supp. 176 (S.D.N.Y. 1934).

14. See, e.g., Michigan Statutes Annotated, Section 25.181 (1970). This was ammended by Public Acts 1975, No. 40.

15. "A Wife by Any Other Name," review of *Mrs. Man* by Una Stannard, *The Spokeswoman* 8, no. 5 (November 15, 1977):12.

16. Ibid.

17. This example is drawn from the "Memorandum on the Right of Married Women to Retain or Regain Their Birth Names," The Women's Rights Project of the American Civil Liberties Union Memorandum to Affiliates and Liaison People (September 1972) pp. 2, 3.

18. Forbush v. Wallace, 405 U.S. 970 (1972), *aff'd per curiam*, 341 F. Supp. 217 (M.D. Ala. 1971).

19. Kay, *Discrimination in Family Law*, p. 125.

20. Whitlow v. Hodges, 539 F.2d 582 (6th Cir.), *cert. denied*, 97 S. Ct. 654 (1976).

21. *Halsbury's Laws of England* states that any name change by a woman upon marriage today in England is at her choosing and not as a matter of law or legal tradition (vol. 19, 3d ed., 1957, section 1350, p. 829), and "[t]here is no statute law which regulates the right of any person . . . to change his surname. . . ." (vol. 22, 3d edition, 1970, p. 1211).

22. For example, in State *ex rel* Krupa v. Green, 114 Ohio App. 497, 501, 177 N.E. 2d 616, 619 (1961), the Ohio court states: "It is only *by custom*, in English speaking countries, that a woman, upon marriage, adopts the surname of her husband in place of the surname of her father. The State of Ohio follows this custom, but there exists no law compelling it."

   Most states, including California, have no statutes on a married woman's name. See Mary Jane Hamilton, "Female Surnames and California Law," *University of California at Davis Law Review* 6 (1973):405–21. As of 1975 Hawaii was the only state that had an explicit statute directing that "every married woman shall adopt her husband's name as a family name." However, this statute was held unconstitutional in 1975 (Cragun v. Hawaii, Hawaii 1st Dir. Ct. 1975).

23. Walter v. Jackson, 391 F. Supp. 1395 (E.D. Ark. 1975); Banks v. Banks, 42 Cal. Appl.3d 631,117 Cal.Rptr. 37 (1974); Custer v. Bonadies, 30 Conn. Supp. 385, 318 A.2d 639 (1974); Marshall v. State, 301 So. 2d 477 (Fla. App. 1974); In re Hauptley, 312 N.E. 2d 857 (Ind. 1974); Stuart v. Bd. of Supervisors of Elections, 226 Md. 440, 295 A.2d 233 (1972); In re Lawrence, 133 N.J.Super. 408, 337 A.2d 49 (1975), *rev'g*, 128 N.J. Super. 312, 319 A.2d 793 (1974); In re Halligan, 46 App. Div. 2d 170, 361 N.Y.S. 2d 458 (1974); State *ex rel*. Krupa v. Green, 114 Ohio App. 497, 177 N.E. 2d 616 (1961); Dunn

v. Palermo, 522 S.W.2d 679 (Tenn. 1975); Kruzel v. Podell, 67 Wis. 138, 226 N.W.2d 458 (1975).

24. "Names," *Corpus Juris Secondum* 65 (1966): sec. 11, subsec. 1; "Name," *American Jurisprudence*, 2d ed. 57 (1971): sec. 10.

25. Pennsylvania Attorney General, *Opinion*, no. 62 (1973); *Michigan Attorney General Biennial Report* (1973), p. 824; Secretary of Com. v. City Clerk of Lowell, 366 N.E. 2d 717 (1977).

26. In re Lawrence, 128 N.J.Super. 307, 327–28, 319 A.2d 790, 801 (1974, as quoted in Herma H. Kay, *1975 Supplement to Sex-Based Discrimination in Family Law* (St. Paul, Minn.: West Publishing Co., 1975), p. 70.

27. Ibid.

28. In re Lawrence, 133 N.J. Super. 408, 337 A.2d 49 (1975).

29. In re Mohlman, 26 N.C.App. 220, 216 S.E.2d 147 (1975).

30. Brown et al., *Women's Rights and the Law*, p. 104.

31. Ibid., p. 331, citing Oklahoma statutes re fault, Wisconsin statutes re alimony, and Arkansas, Kentucky, South Dakota, and Wisconsin statutes re minor children.

32. Ibid., citing New Jersey and Washington statutes.

33. In re Marriage of Banks, 1 Civ. 34453; Sup.Ct. 656–810, 42 Cal. App. 3d 631, 117 Cal. Rptr. 37 (1974).

34. In re Marriage of Banks, 42 Cal. App. 2d at 631, 117 Cal. Rptr. at 39.

35. Egner v. Egner, 133 N.J. Super, 403, 337 A.2d 46 (1975).

36. This is the language from a companion case decided the same day, In re Lawrence, 133 N.J. Super. 408, 337 A.2d 49 (1975).

37. Egner v. Egner, 133 N.J.Super. at 406–7, 337 A.2d at 48 (1975).

38. Although one does not need a court order to change one's name, in many situations having a court order as proof can be extremely helpful. Three useful sources of information are: "Booklet for Women Who Wish to Determine Their Own Names After Marriage" (available for $2.25 from the Center for a Woman's Own Name, 261 Kimberley, Barrington, Ill. 60610, 1974); Una Stannard, *Married Women v. Husband's Names: The Case for Wives Who Keep Their Own Names* (available for $2.25 from Germainbooks, San Francisco, Calif. 94114, 1973); and Priscilla MacDougall, "Married Women's Common Law Right to Their Own Surnames," *Women's Rights Law Reporter* 1, no. 3 (Fall/Winter 1972–73):2–14.

For a survey of other countries' approaches to female surnames, see Symposium, "The Status of Women," *American Journal of Comparative Law* 20 (1972):585.

39. The anxiety experienced by certain segments of our society when faced with the assertion that a married woman's surname should not be dictated by that of her husband, can be seen in Senator Ervin's dissent to the passage of the Equal Rights Amendment, which focused on this issue. See Senate Report No. 689, 92d Cong., 2d Sess. (1972):50–52.

40. Brown et al., *Women's Rights and the Law*, pp. 108–09.

41. Ibid.

42. Ibid, p. 111.

43. Homer Clark, *The Law of Domestic Relations* (St. Paul, Minn.: West Publishing Co., 1968), pp. 149–51 (hereinafter cited as *Domestic Relations*); Kanowitz, *Women and the Law*, pp. 46–52.

44. This was the wording of the Ohio Code Section 3103.02 (1972) repealed effective 9/23/74 by 135 v. H. 322, Section 2 *Ohio Revised Code* Ann. 1980.

45. Brown et al., *Women's Rights and the Law*, p. 111.

46. In re Paullin, 92 N.J.Eq. 419, 113 A. 240 (1921).

47. This was the rule in California until May 1, 1973. See also Samuel v. University of Pittsburgh, 375 F. Supp. 119 (W.D. Pa. 1974), holding that residency rules that presume the domicile of a married woman to be that of her husband are violative of equal protection. Under this ruling, married women who are state residents are entitled to lower tuition regardless of their husbands' residence.

48. This example comes from Barbara Allen Babcock, Ann E. Freedman, Eleanor Holmes Norton, and Susan C. Ross, *Sex Discrimination and the Law: Causes and Remedies* (Boston: Little, Brown & Co., 1975), p. 577.

49. Ibid.

50. Kay, *Discrimination in Family Law*, p. 127.

51. Brown et al., *Women's Rights and the Law*, p. 113.

52. The voting tabulation is current as of 1977 (from Brown et al., *Women's Rights and the Law*, p. 113). The source of the other data is the *Report of the Committee on Civil and Political Rights to the President's Commission on the Status of Women* (1963), p. 21, table 2, which, in turn, was prepared by the Women's Bureau, U.S. Department of Labor. The figures reflect the situation as of March 6, 1963. There appears to be no more recent state-by-state tabulation of the domicile laws for candidacy, probate, and jury service.

53. Kanowitz, *Women and the Law*, p. 52.

54. Colquitt Walker, "Sex Discrimination in Government Benefit Pro-

grams," *Hastings Law Journal* 23 (1971):281–82. But see the recent invalidation of unemployment compensation statutes that impose a special eligibility requirement on persons who terminate employment because of "marital, parental, filial, or domestic obligations." Kistler v. Industrial Comm., 556 P.2d 895 (1976).

55. Cavallo v. Cavallo, 79 Misc. 2d 195, 359 N.Y.S.2d 628 (S.Ct. 1974).

56. Santarsiero v. Santarsiero, 331 A.2d 868 (Pa. Super. 1974).

57. See, e.g., Younger v. Gianotti, 176 Tenn. 139, 138 S.W.2d 448 (1940); Estate of Wickes, 128 Cal. 270, 60 Pac. 867 (1900).

58. Carlson v. Carlson, 75 Ariz. 308, 256 P.2d 249 (1953).

59. Carlson v. Carlson 75 Ariz. at 310, 256 P.2d at 250 (emphasis added).

60. See generally, Robert Seidenberg, "Dear Mr. Success: Consider Your Wife," *The Wall Street Journal*, February 7, 1976, p. 12, col. 1.; and Myrna M. Weissman and Eugene S. Paykel, "Moving and Depression in Women," *Society* 9, no. 9 (July/August 1972): 27.

61. G. J. Berkwitt, "Corporate Wives: The Third Party," *Dunn's Review* (August 1972):61–62.

62. Alice Lake, "The Revolt of the Company Wife," *McCalls's* (October 1973), p. 26. Lake quotes one executive whose company transferred its offices from New York to Denver as saying, "Management thought I should run home, tell my wife, pick up the kids and go. But since my wife shares responsibility for the household, she is entitled to share in decision making."

63. Robert Seidenberg, "Moving On to What?" *Mental Hygiene* (Winter 1975):11 (emphasis added).

64. On the growing number of two-career families, see, generally, Rhona Rapoport and Robert Rapoport, *Dual Career Families* (Middlesex, Eng., and New York: Penguin Books, 1971); and Rhona Rapoport and Robert Rapoport, *Dual-Career Families Re-examined: New Integrations of Work and Family* (New York: Harper Colophon Books, 1977).

65. U.S. Department of Labor, Bureau of Labor Statistics, "Married Persons' Share of the Labor Force Declining, BLS Study Shows," *News*, USDL 77–191 (March 8, 1977). Computed from table 4.

66. Lynda L. Holmstrom, *The Two-Career Family* (Cambridge, Mass.: Schenkmann, 1972), pp. 30–32 (hereinafter cited as *Two-Career Family*).

67. Rhona Rapoport and Robert N. Rapoport, "The Dual Career Family," *Human Relations* 22 (1969):3–30.

68. Michael P. Fogarty, Rhona Rapoport, and Robert N. Rapoport, *Sex, Career and Family* (London: Allen & Unwin, 1971).

69. Ibid., p. 464. A contrary finding for a national sample of young American, white women college graduates and their spouses is reported by R. Paul Duncan and Carolyn Cummings Perrucci, who found that "the wife's employment . . . is not a deterrent to familial migration" (p. 260). In addition, "the relative 'fullness' of the wife's work role . . . as measured by her occupational prestige or her relative contribution to the total family income, and opportunities for employment in her field elsewhere . . . do not affect migration probability." "Dual Occupation Families and Migration," *American Sociological Review* 41 (April 1976):252.

70. Holmstrom, *Two-Career Family*, p. 38. See also pp. 000–000 in the Appendix for a description of the variety of domicile arrangements made by two career couples.

71. Beth Dunlop, "Mixed Marriages: Couple vs. Careers," *The Miami Herald*, February 10, 1977, p. 6–G, cols. 2–3.

72. See, for example, Judy Klemesrud, "Marriage in Academe Reflects the Changing Status of Women," *New York Times*, November 13, 1972, sec. C., p. 42, cols. 1–6. One couple who lived in Washington, D.C., and Los Angeles reported that one of the most difficult aspects of living apart was convincing friends they were not getting a divorce.

73. Naomi R. Gerstel, "The Feasibility of Commuter Marriage," in *The Family*, Peter J. Stein, Julia Richmond and Natalie Hannon, eds. (Reading, Mass.: Addison Wesley, 1977), pp. 357–66.

74. Ibid., p. 364.

75. Weintraub v. Weintraub, 356 N.Y.S.2d 450 (Fam.Ct. 1974).

76. Blair v. Blair, 199 Md. 9, 85 A.2d 442 (1952), as cited in Kay, *Discrimination in Family Law*, p. 127.

77. Clark, *The Law of Domestic Relations*, p. 261.

78. Ibid, p. 272.

79. Brown et al., *Women's Rights and the Law*, p. 119.

80. Ibid, p. 118.

81. Swartz v. United States Steel Corp., 293 Ala. 439, 304 So. 2d 881 (1974).

82. Brown, et al., *Women's Rights and the Law*, p. 118. In a footnote to a 1980 U.S. Supreme Court decision it was noted that 42 states and the District of Columbia now allow recovery by a wife or couple. American Export Lines, Inc. v. Alvez, ——— U.S. ———, 100 S. Ct. 1673, 1679 (1980) fn 11.

83. Ibid.

Chapter 2: The Husband's Responsibility for Support (pp. 23-59)

1. Homer Clark, *The Law of Domestic Relations* (St. Paul, Minn.: West Publishing Co., 1968), p. 181 (hereinafter cited as *Domestic Relations*).

2. Herma Hill Kay, "Sex-Based Discrimination in Family Law," in Kenneth Davidson, Ruth Ginsburg, and Herma Hill Kay, *Text, Cases and Materials on Sex-Based Discrimination* (St. Paul, Minn.: West Publishing Co., 1974), p. 139. Also published separately as *Sex-Based Discrimination in Family Law* (St. Paul, Minn.: West Publishing Co., 1974) (hereinafter cited as *Discrimination in Family Law*).

3. Ibid., p. 139; Clark, *Domestic Relations*, p. 186.

4. Commonwealth ex. rel Lebowitz, 227 Pa. Super. 593, 307 A.2d 442, p. 443 (1973), quoting 18 *Pennsylvania Law Encyclopedia* Husband and Wife, Sec. 2, p. 6 (1959) (emphasis added).

5. Friedrich v. Katz, 341 N.Y.S.2d 932, 934, 73 Misc. 2d 663, 664 (1973) (footnotes omitted).

6. State v. Barton, 315 So.2d 289 (La.Sup.Ct. 1975).

7. State v. Barton, 315 2d at 291.

8. Clark, *Domestic Relations*, pp. 187-88.

9. Thomason v. Thomason, 56 Ala.App. 206, 289 So.2d 627 (Ala.Civ. App. 1974).

10. Dill v. Dill, 262 Ga. G2. 231, 206 S.E.2d 6 (1974).

11. Clark, *Domestic Relations*, pp. 28, 227.

12. Isabella H. Grant, "Marital Contracts Before and During Marriage," *The California Family Law* (Berkeley, Calif.: Continuing Education of the Bar, 1962), p. 160. Chapter 14 provides a more complete discussion and analysis of the legality of contracts that attempt to alter the husband's traditional duty to support.

13. See, e.g., Kershner v. Kershner, 244 App.Div. 34, 278 N.Y.S. 501 (1935), affirmed, 269 N.&. 655, 200 N.E. 32 (1936), which held that a wife's waiver of support would not be enforced. In addition, her agreement to support her husband would not be enforced.

14. Clark, *Domestic Relations*, pp. 219-20 (footnotes omitted) (reprinted with permission).

15. Caleb Foote, Robert J. Levy, and Frank E. Sander, *Cases and*

Materials on Family Law, 2d ed. (Boston: Little Brown & Co., 1976), p. 752.

16. Leo Kanowitz, *Women and the Law: The Unfinished Revolution* (Albuquerque: University of New Mexico Press, 1979), p. 57.

17. See, generally, Colquitt Walker, "Sex Discrimination in Government Benefit Programs," *Hastings Law Journal* 23 (1971):281 –83.

18. John Kenneth Galbraith, "Economics and the Public Purpose," cited in Judith Areen, *Cases and Materials on Family Law* (Mineola, N.Y.: The Foundation Press, 1978), p. 75 (hereinafter cited as Areen, *Family Law*).

19. The following draws heavily from Ann Bingaman, "The Impact of the ERA on Marital Economics," *Impact ERA* (Millbrae, Calif.: Les Femmes Publishing, 1976), p. 116 (hereinafter cited as Bingaman, "Impact of the ERA").

20. Rasmussen. v. Oshkosh Savings and Loan Association, 35 Wis. 2d 605, 151 N.W.2d 730 (1966), as researched and summarized by Norma Briggs in *Real Women Real Lives: Marriage, Divorce, Widowhood* (Wisconsin Governor's Commission on the Status of Women, 1978), p. 19 (hereinafter cited as *Real Women Real Lives*).

21. Areen, *Family Law*, p. 197. The last three states to change were Idaho in 1974, Nevada in 1975, and Louisiana in 1979 (effective 1980).

22. Corpus Christi Parish Credit Union v. Martin, 358 S.2d 295, 1978. The summary in this text was prepared from interviews with attorneys Sylvia Roberts, general counsel, and Phyllis Segal, staff attorney for the NOW Legal Defense and Education Fund, January 1979, and from NOW–LDEF materials.

23. Cert. denied, 47 *Law Week* 3246, Oct. 10, 1978.

24. Public Law 93–495, Titles V and VII, 93d Cong., 2d Sess., amending 15 U.S.C., Sec. 1601 et seq.

25. Ralph E. Smith, "The Movement of Women into the Labor Force," in *The Subtle Revolution: Women at Work* (Washington, D.C.: The Urban Institute, 1979).

26. Margaret Gates, "Credit Discrimination against Women: Causes and Solutions," *Vanderbilt Law Review* 27 (1974):414–15. Gates cites a Sears Roebuck explanation for this policy: "[I]t is expensive for creditors to open two accounts per family and, as between the husband and wife, they prefer to deal with the man."

27. Barbara Ann Kulzer, "Law and the Housewife: Property, Divorce and Death," *University of Florida Law Review* 28(1975):11 (hereinafter cited as "Law and the Housewife").

28. *Real Women Real Lives*, p. 44, excerpting the case of Norris v. Norris, 16 Ill.App.3d 897, 307 N.E.2d 181 (1974) (reprinted with permission).

29. Kulzer, "Law and the Housewife," p. 16.

30. Ibid.

31. Ibid.

32. Bingaman, "Impact of the ERA," pp. 212–22.

33. *Real Women Real Lives*, p. 18, summarizing the case of Estate of Budney, 2 Wis.2d 389, 8b N.W.2d 421 (1957).

34. Kulzer, "Law and the Housewife," pp. 37–38.

35. In re Weger, 71 Wis.2d 484, 238 N.W.2d 522 (1975).

36. Ibid., quoted in *Real Women Real Lives*, p. 85.

37. McGuire v. McGuire, 157 Neb. 226, 59 N.W.2d 335 (1953).

38. Ibid., p. 238.

39. Blanche Crozier, "Marital Support," *Boston University Law Review* 15, no. 1 (January 1935): 33 (hereinafter cited as "Marital Support").

40. Joan M. Krauskopf and Rhonda C. Thomas, "Partnership Marriage: The Solution to an Ineffective and Inequitable Law of Support," *Ohio State Law Journal* 35, no. 1 (1974):564 (hereinafter cited as "Ineffective Law of Support").

41. Commonwealth v. George, 358 Pa. 118, 56A.2d. 228 (1948).

42. Ibid., at 231.

43. Ibid.

44. Crozier, "Marital Support," p. 33.

45. The U.S. President's Citizens' Advisory Council on the Status of Women, *The Equal Rights Amendment and Alimony and Child Support Laws*, 1972, p. 38.

46. Krauskopf and Thomas, "Ineffective Law of Support," pp. 566, 569.

47. Garlock v. Garlock, 279 N.Y. 337, 18 N.E. 2d 251 (1939).

48. Krauskopf and Thomas, "Ineffective Law of Support," p. 569.

49. Harry D. Krause, *Family Law* (St. Paul, Minn.: West Publishing Co., 1976) (hereinafter cited as Krause, *Family Law*).

50. Barbara Brown, Ann Freedman, Harriet Katz, and Alice M. Price, *Women's Rights and the Law: The Impact of the ERA on State Laws.* (New York: Praeger Publishers, 1977) p. 87.

51. Restatement of Restitution, sec. 113, as cited in Krause, *Family Law*, p. 138.

52. Krause, *Family Law*, p. 137, citing J. Madden, *Persons and Domestic Relations*, 1931, pp. 183–98.

53. Krauskopf and Thomas, "Ineffective Law of Support," pp. 572–73.

54. Ibid.

55. For a historical discussion of alimony, see Vernier and Hurlbut, "The Historical Background of Alimony Law and Its Present Statutory Structure," *Law and Contemporary Problems* 6 (1939):197.

56. Clark, *Domestic Relations*, p. 42.

57. All American states except Indiana, Texas, and Pennsylvania now have alimony or spousal support statutes.

58. Orr v. Orr, 440 U.S. 268 (1979).

59. Ibid.

60. Henry H. Foster and Doris Jonas Freed, "Orr v. Orr: The Decision that Takes Gender Out of Alimony," *Family Advocate* 1, no. 4 (Spring 1979):8.

61. Ibid.

62. Lenore J. Weitzman and Ruth B. Dixon, "The Alimony Myth: Does No-Fault Divorce Make a Difference?" *Family Law Quarterly* 14, no. 3 (Fall 1980) (hereinafter cited as "The Alimony Myth"). This does not include token awards of $1 a year, which allow the courts to retain jurisdiction over the award in the future. In California the term "spousal support" has replaced the word "alimony."

63. National Commission on the Observance of International Women's Year, "... *To Form a More Perfect Union* ..." *Justice for American Women* (Washington, D.C.: U.S. Government Printing Office, 1976).

64. Paul Harold Jacobson, *American Marriage and Divorce* (New York: Rinehart, 1959), p. 126.

65. Weitzman and Dixon, "The Alimony Myth," p. 155.

66. Ibid., table 2, p. 157. The following discussion of alimony in California is drawn from this paper.

67. Alimony is deductible by the husband and taxable as income to the wife, *Internal Revenue Code of 1954*, secs. 71, 215. Child support payments are not usually deductible by the husband sec. 71 (b).

68. Weitzman and Dixon "The Alimony Myth," table 3, p. 159.

69. Lenore J. Weitzman, *No-Fault Divorce in California*, unpublished manuscript, Center for the Study of Law and Society, University of California at Berkeley, 1979.

70. Barbara Everett Bryant, *American Women Today and Tomorrow*

(Washington, D.C.: U.S. Government Printing Office, 1975), p. 24.

71. Stuart Nagel and Lenore J. Weitzman, "Women as Litigants," *Hastings Law Journal* 23 (1971):189–91. See also Maxine Virtue, *Family Cases in Court* (Durham, N.C.: Duke University Press, 1956), p. 92.

72. I am indebted to my research assistant Neil McGinn for his critical reading of this section.

73. Robert Brannon, "The Male Sex Role: Our Culture's Blueprint of Manhood, and What It's Done for Us Lately," in *The Forty-five Percent Majority*, Deborah S. David and Robert Brannon, eds. (Reading, Mass.: Addison-Wesley Publishing Co., 1976), p. 22 (hereinafter cited as "The Male Sex Role").

74. Robert Gould, "Measuring Masculinity by the Size of a Paycheck," *Ms.*, June 1973, p. 20.

75. Lillian Rubin, *Worlds of Pain: Life in the Working Class Family* (New York: Basic Books, 1977), p. 171 (hereinafter cited as *Worlds of Pain*).

76. Mirra Komarovsky, *Blue Collar Marriage* (New York: Random House, 1964).

77. Joseph T. Howell, *Hard Living on Clay Street: Portraits of Blue Collar Families* (Garden City, N. Y.: Anchor Books, 1973), p. 100.

78. Rubin, *Worlds of Pain*, p. 174.

79. Myron Brenton, *The American Male* (New York: Coward-McCann & Geoghegan, 1977), ch. 7 (hereinafter cited as *The American Male*).

80. Brannon, "The Male Sex Role," p. 23.

81. Olof Palme, "The Emancipation of Man," *Journal of Social Issues* 28, no. 2 (1972):237–46 (hereinafter cited as "Emancipation of Man").

82. Myron Brenton, "The Paradox of the American Father," reprinted from *The American Male*.

83. Brenton, *The American Male*, p. 207, citing Princeton sociologist Marvin Bressler.

84. Jack Nichols, *Men's Liberation: A New Definition of Masculinity* (Middlesex, Eng.: Penguin Books, 1975), p. 135.

85. Palme, "Emancipation of Man."

86. Warren Farrell, *The Liberated Man: Beyond Masculinity; Freeing Men and Their Relationships with Women* (New York: Random House, 1975) p. xxvi.

87. Elliott Liebow, *Tally's Corner* (Boston: Little, Brown & Co., 1967), p. 86.

88. Kay, *Discrimination in Family Law*, pp. 140–41.

89. Women's "trained incapacity" to deal with money and mathematics begins at an early age and is reinforced throughout the social system. See, generally, Lenore J. Weitzman, *Sex Role Socialization* (Palo Alto, Calif.: Mayfield, 1979); and Sheila Tobias, *Math Anxiety* (New York: W. W. Norton, 1978).

90. The following analysis is drawn primarily from Susan Plover, "Trusts and the Mistrusted Widow," unpublished student paper, George Washington University Law School, May 24, 1971 (hereinafter cited as "Trusts and the Mistrusted Widow").

91. Ralph J. Goldberg, "Trusted Wife," *Trusts and Estates*, December 1968, pp. 1100–04. (Emphasis added.)

92. Plover, "Trusts and the Mistrusted Widow," p. 12.

93. Krauskopf and Thomas, "Ineffective Law of Support," p. 581.

94. Krause, *Family Law*, p. 116.

95. Ibid.; and Herma Hill Kay, "The ERA and Family Law: The Last Frontier for Change," keynote address to the National Conference on Women and the Law, Madison, Wis., 1977, p. 7.

96. Personal conversation with Professor Homer Clark, October 1980.

97. Morris Ploscowe, Henry H. Foster, Jr., and Doris Jonas Freed, *Family Law: Cases and Materials*, 2d ed. (Boston: Little, Brown & Co., 1972), pp. 146–47; and Krause, *Family Law*, p. 116.

98. Calloway v. Munzer, 57 Misc. 2d 163, 291 N.Y.S. 2d 589 (1968).

99. Marilyn Alexander, "The Way We Were," *San Francisco Sunday Examiner and Chronicle*, California Living Magazine, January 11, 1976, p. 6, cols. 2, 3.

100. Report of NOW Conference on Marriage and Divorce, *New York Times*, January 21, 1974, p. 32, cols. 7–8.

Chapter 3: The Wife's Domestic Responsibility (pp. 60–97)

1. Rucci v. Rucci, 23 Conn. Supp. 221, 224, 181 A.2d 125, 127 (Super. Ct. 1962).

2. Rucci v. Rucci, 23 Conn. Supp. at 224.

3. Barbara Brown, Thomas Emerson, Gail Falk and Ann Freedman,

"The Equal Rights Amendment: A Constitutional Basis for Equal Rights for Women," *Yale Law Journal* 80 (1971):940.

4. William L. Prosser, *Handbook of the Law of Torts*, 3d ed. (St. Paul, Minn.: West Publishing Co., 1964), p. 894.

5. McMillan v. Felsenthal, 482, S.W. 2d 9 (Texas 1972).

6. Bradesku v. Antion, et al., 21 Ohio App.2d 67 50 Ohio Op.2d 137 (1969), 255 N.E.2d 265, cited in Harry D. Krause, *Family Law: Cases and Materials* (St. Paul, Minn.: West Publishing Co., 1976) p. 178 (hereinafter cited as *Family Law*).

7. Golding v. Taylor, 23 N.C.App. 171, 208 S.E.2d 422 (1974); and Shrock v. Goddell, 528 P.2d 1048 (Or.1974) cited in Krause, *Family Law*.

8. "Wife Stolen, Man Gets $80,000," *San Francisco Chronicle*, October 24, 1979, p. 3, cols. 1–4.

9. Felsenthal v. McMillan, 493 S.W.2d 729 (Texas 1973).

10. Bradwell v. Illinios, 83 U.S. (16 Wall) 130, p. 141 (1893).

11. Muller v. Oregon, 208 U.S. 412 (1908). Much of the Brandeis brief was actually written by Josephine Goldmark.

12. Muller v. Oregon, 208 U.S. 412, pp. 421, 422 (1908).

13. Goesart v. Cleary, 335 U.S. 464 (1948); Contra, Sail'er Inn, Inc. v. Kirby, 5 Cal.3d 1, 485 P.2d 529, 95 Cal Rptr. 329 (1971). See Leo Kanowitz, *Sex Roles in Law and Society* (Albuquerque: University of New Mexico Press, 1973), pp. 364–81, for a discussion of the legality of protective state laws regarding hours and weight-lifting restrictions for women in light of Title VII of the 1964 Civil Rights Act, 42 U.S.C. Sec. 2000e. On pregnancy see, generally, the cases discussed in Chapter 4.

14. Hoyt v. Florida, 368 U.S. 57 (1961) at 62.

15. The Court's most recent standard, articulated in Craig v. Boren, 429 U.S. 190 (1976), is that the gender classification must serve "important governmental objectives and [be] substantially related to achievement of those objectives" to be upheld.

16. Kahn v. Shevin, 416 U.S. 351 (1974).

17. Geduldig v. Aiello, 417 U.S. 484 (1974).

18. Joan M. Krauskopf "Partnership Marriage: Legal Reforms Needed" in *Women into Wives: The Legal and Economic Impact of Marriage*, Jane R. Chapman and Margaret Gates, eds. (Beverly Hills, Calif.: Sage, 1977) (hereinafter cited as "Partnership Marriage").
Citing Tryon v. Casey, 416 S.W.2d 252 (K.C. Ct. App.) (1967).

19. Joan M. Krauskopf and Rhonda C. Thomas, "Partnership Marriage: The Solution to an Ineffective and Inequitable Law of Support", *Ohio State Law Journal* 35, no. 1 (1974):558–60, citing Wallis v. City of Westport, 82 Mo. App. 522 (1900) (hereinafter cited as "Ineffective Law of Support").

20. Blanche Crozier, "Marital Support," *Boston University Law Review* 15 (1935):28.

21. Gunnar Myrdal, *An American Dilemma*, Vol. II, (New York: Pantheon, 1944), p. 1073.

22. Krauskopf and Thomas, "Ineffective Law of Support," p. 563.

23. Sylvia Law and Nadine Taub, "Constitutional Considerations and the Married Woman's Obligation to Serve," unpublished manuscript, n.d. (ca. 1976) (hereinafter cited as "Obligation to Serve"). The authors are respectively professors at New York University Law School and Rutgers Law School.

24. John Kenneth Galbraith, "The Economics of the American Housewife," *Atlantic*, August 1973, pp. 78–83.

25. Krauskopf and Thomas, "Ineffective Law of Support," p. 579.

26. Krauskopf, "Partnership Marriage."

27. Susan Westerberg Prager, "Sharing Principles and the Future of Marital Property Law," *UCLA Law Review* 25, no. 1 (October 1977) (hereinafter cited as "Sharing Principles and Marital Property").

28. Skaar v. Department of Revenue, 61 Wis.2d 93, 211 N.W.2d 642 (1973).

29. This case is excerpted from Wisconsin Governor's Commission on the Status of Women, *Real Women Real Lives: Marriage, Divorce and Widowhood* (Madison, Wisc., 1978), pp. 20–21 (hereinafter cited as *Real Women Real Lives*) (reprinted with permission).

30. Stern v. Department of Revenue, 63 Wis. 2d 506, 217 N.W.2d 326 (1973).

31. Murdoch v. Murdoch, 1 W.W.R. 361 (Sup. Ct. Canada, 1974).

32. Case summary from Wisconsin Commission on the Status of Women, "Why We Need Marital Property Reform" (mimeographed), September 1976, p. 5.

33. State ex rel. George v. Mitchell, 230 S.W.2d 117 (Sp. Ct. App.) (1950).

34. DiFlorida v. DiFlorida, 333 A. 2d 66 (1975).

35. Citizen's Advisory Council on the Status of Women, *Recognition of Economic Contribution of Homemakers and Protection of Children in Divorce Law and Practice* (Washington, D.C.: U.S. Gov't Printing

Office, 1974), p. 6 (hereinafter cited as *Economic Contribution of Homemakers*).

36. Wirth v. Wirth, 38 App.Div. 2d 611, 326 N.Y.S.2d 308 (1971).

37. Henry Foster and Doris Jones Freed, "Marital Property Reform," *Family Law Quarterly* 8 (1974):174–75.

38. Homer Clark, *The Law of Domestic Relations* (St. Paul, Minn.: West Publishing Co., 1968), p. 227.

39. Ibid. See also the discussion of contracts between husbands and wives in Chapter 13 of this book.

40. Youngberg v. Holstrom, 252 Iowa 815, 108 N.W.2d 498 (1961).

41. Frame v. Frame, 120 Tex. 61, 36 S.W.2d 152 (1931).

42. Taylor v. Taylor, 26 N.C.App. 592, 216 S.E.2d 737 (1975).

43. See Alvarado v. Alvarado, 22 Ill.App.3d 1, 316 N.E.2d 561 (1974).

44. Brooks v. Brooks, 48 Cal.App. 347, 351; 119 P.2d 970, 973 (1941).

45. In re Estate of Sonnicksen, 23 Cal.App. 2d 475, 73 P.2d 643 (1st Dist. 1937).

46. See, generally, Carolyn Shaw Bell, "Social Security: Society's Last Discrimination," *Business and Society Review*, Autumn 1972, p. 45, and Deborah Pisetzner Klein, "Women in the Labor Force: The Middle Years," *Monthly Labor Review*, U.S. Department of Labor, November 1975, p. 13.

47. *Real Women Real Lives*, p. 22.

48. Herma Hill Kay, "The Married Woman's Loss of Identity," in Kenneth Davidson, Ruth Ginsburg, and Herma Hill Kay, *Text, Cases and Materials on Sex-Based Discrimination* (St. Paul, Minn.: West Publishing Co., 1974), p. 142. Also published separately as *Sex-Based Discrimination in Family Law* (St. Paul, Minn.: West Publishing Co., 1974), pp. 117–30 (hereinafter cited as *Discrimination in Family Law*).

49. Louise Kapp Howe, "Just a Housewife," *McCalls*, November 1975, p. 107 (hereinafter cited as "Just a Housewife").

50. Ann Oakley, *The Sociology of Housework* (New York: Pantheon, 1975), p. 25.

51. *Economic Contribution of Homemakers*, p. 6.

52. Law and Taub, "Obligation to Serve," p. 26.

54. Krauskopf, "Partnership Marriage," p. 102.

54. Kay, *Discrimination in Family Law*, p. 144.

55. Howe, "Just a Housewife," p. 154.

56. Krauskopf, "Partnership Marriage," p. 95, citing Johnston, "Sex and

Property: The Common Law Tradition, the Law School Curriculum and Developments Toward Equality," *New York University Law Review* 28 (1973):1066.

57. Wendy Edmond and Suzie Fleming, "If Women Were Paid for All They Do" in *All Work and No Pay: Women, Housework, and the Wages Due* (Bristol, England: The Power of Women Collective and the Falling Wall Press Ltd., 1975), p. 7 (hereinafter cited as "If Women Were Paid").

58. Lillian B. Rubin, *Women of a Certain Age: The Midlife Search for Self* (New York: Harper & Row, 1979). p. 147.

59. Edmond and Fleming, "If Women Were Paid," p. 11

60. Law and Taub, *Obligation to Serve*, p. 27.

61. Nona Glaser, "The Caste Position of Women: Housewifery," paper presented at the Annual Meeting of the American Sociological Association, New York, September 1, 1976, p. 2.

62. Carolyn Shaw Bell, "Alternatives for Social Change: The Future Status of Women," Working Paper #14, Dept. of Economics, Wellesley College, Wellesley, Mass., April 1975, p. 13.

63. Edmond and Fleming, "If Women Were Paid," p. 7.

64. Wendyce H. Brody, "Economic Value of a Housewife," Research and Statistics Note 9–1975, U.S. Dept. of HEW Pub. No. SSA–75–11701, p. 2.

65. "How Much is a Homemaker Worth?" *Washington Star*, September 11, 1976, p. B–5.

66. Scott, "The Value of Housework: For Love or Money," *Ms.*, July 1972, p. 59.

67. Law and Taub, *Obligation to Serve*, p. 4.

68. Evelyn Kaye "Housewife Power." *Parents*, August 1979, pp. 40–44. *Sacramento Bee*, Aug. 6, 1980. See also C. Bruch "Property Rights of De Facto Spouses including Thoughts on the Value of Homemakers' Services," *Family Law Quarterly*, X:101 (1976).

69. R. Posner, *Economic Analysis of Law* (Boston: Little, Brown & Co., 1972), pp. 79–80.

70. Law and Taub, *Obligation to Serve*, p. 4.

71. Posner, *Economic Analysis of Law*, p. 80.

72. Robert J. Levy, *Uniform Marriage and Divorce Legislation: A Preliminary Analysis*, a report prepared for the Special Committee on Divorce of the National Conference of Commissioners on Uniform State Laws (Chicago: National Conference of Commissioners on Uniform State Laws, 1968), p. 165.

73. Marriage and Family Commission of NOW, "Suggested Guidelines in Studying and Comments on the Uniform Marriage and Divorce Act" (mimeographed), April 11, 1971, p. 2 (hereinafter cited as NOW "Comments").

74. Jessie Bernard, *Women and the Public Interest: An Essay on Policy and Protest* (Chicago: Aldine, 1971), p. 115.

75. NOW "Comments," p. 72.

76. Thomas D. Schaefer, "Wife Works So Husband Can Go to Law School: Should She Be Taken in as a 'Partner' When 'Esq.' Is Followed by Divorce? or Can You Have a Community Property Interest in a Professional Education?" *Community Property Journal* 2, no. 2 (1975):85.

77. Ibid., pp. 85, 98.

78. Morgan v. Morgan, 81 Misc. 2d 616, 366 N.Y.S. 2d 977 (1975), as modified on appeal 383 N.Y.S. 2d 343 (1976).

79. Inman v. Inman cited in "Postgraduate Divorce: Is a Degree 'Property' to be Divided?" *New York Times*, August 31, 1979, p. A14, col. 4.

80. See, generally, In re Marriage of Foster, 42 Cal.Ap.3, 577 (1974); In re Marriage of Lopez, 38 Cal.Ap. 3, 93 (1974); In re Marriage of Barnett, 85 Cal.Ap.3, 413 (1978).

81. Fred Kennedy and Bruce Thomas, "Putting a Value on Education and Professional Goodwill," *Family Advocate* 2, no. 1 (Summer 1979):3.

82. Ibid.

83. In re Marriage of Brown, 15 Cal.Ap.3d 838 (1976); In re Marriage of Fithian, 10 Cal.Ap.3rd 592 (1974).

84. Douglas Anne Munson, "Putting a Value on Insurance Policies," *Family Advocate* 2, no. 1 (Summer 1979):10–13.

85. Ibid.

86. Prager, "Sharing Principles and Marital Property," pp. 7–9.

Chapter 4: The Responsibility for Children (pp. 98–134)

1. Skinner v. Oklahoma, 136 U.S. 535, 541 (1942).

2. Miller v. Miller, 132 Misc. 121, 122, 228 N.Y.S. 657 (1928).

3. Reynolds v. Reynolds, 85 Mass. (3 Allen) 605 (1862).

4. Reynolds v. Reynolds at 610.

5. Hooks v. State, Miss, 197 So.2d 238 at 240 (1967).

6. Coleman v. Coleman, 291 N.E.2d 530 at 534, 32 Ohio St.2d 155 (1972).

7. David Daube, *The Duty of Procreation* (Edinburgh: Edinburgh University Press, 1977).

8. Ibid., p. 31.

9. Henry Foster and Doris Jonas Freed, "Life with Father," *Family Law Quarterly* 11, (1978):321–22 (hereinafter cited as "Life with Father").

10. Robert H. Mnookin, "Child Custody Adjudication: Judicial Functions in the Face of Indeterminancy," *Law and Contemporary Problems* 39, no. 3 (1975):226, 233–34 (hereinafter cited as "Custody Adjudication").

11. William Blackstone, *Commentaries on the Law of England*, p. 493; cited in Foster and Freed, "Life with Father," p. 325.

12. King v. De Manneville, 102 Eng. Rep. 1055 (K.B. 1804).

13. Foster and Freed, "Life with Father," p. 341.

14. Francine D. Blau, "The Data on Women Workers, Past, Present, and Future," in A. H. Stromberg and S. Harkess, *Women Working: Theories and Facts in Perspective* (Palo Alto, Calif.: Mayfield, 1978), p. 38.

15. Mnookin, "Custody Adjudication," p. 235.

16. Ibid.

17. Washburn v. Washburn, 49 Cal. 2d 581, 122 P.2d 96 (1942).

18. Alan Roth, "The Tender Years Presumption in Child Custody Disputes," *Journal of Family Law* 15, no. 3 (1972).

19. Krieger v. Krieger, 59 Idaho 301, 81 P.2d 1083 (1938).

20. Green v. Green, 137 Fla. 359, 360, 188 So. 355, 356 (1939).

21. Wojnarowicz v. Wojnarowicz, 48 N.J. Super. 349, 353, 137 A.2d 618 (Ch. Div. 1958).

22. Kirstukas v. Kirstukas, 14 Md. App. 190, 286 A.2d 535, 538 (1972).

23. Cox v. Cox, 532 P.2d 994, 996 (Utah 1975) (emphasis added).

24. Commonwealth Ex. Rel. Lucas v. Kreischer, 450 Pa. 352, 299 A.2d 243 (1973) (emphasis added).

25. See, for example, John Bowlby, *Child Care and the Growth of Love* (1965), and others cited in James Levine, *Who Will Raise the Children: New Options for Fathers (and Mothers)* (Philadelphia, Penn.: J. B. Lippincott Co., 1976), p. 41.

26. See, for example, R. Levy and P. Ellsworth "Legislative Reform of Child Custody Adjudication," *Law and Society Review*, Nov. 1969, p. 4.

27. Robert J. Levy, *Uniform Marriage and Divorce Legislation: A Preliminary Analysis* (n.p., n.d.; ca. 1968), p. 224 (hereinafter cited as *The Uniform Act*).

28. The three states were Oklahoma, South Dakota, and Utah. Mnookin, "Custody Adjudication," p. 235.

29. According to Mnookin, as of 1975, 31 states had statutory provisions for the award of custody in the best interest of the child. "Custody Adjudication," p. 236.

30. See, generally, Andrew S. Watson, "The Children of Armageddon: Problems of Custody Following Divorce," *Syracuse Law Review* 21 (1969):56 (hereinafter cited as "Children of Armageddon").

31. National Conference of Commissioners on Uniform State Laws, 1971, *Uniform Marriage and Divorce Act* (Chicago, 1971), p. 46. See also Levy, *The Uniform Act*.

32. Lenore J. Weitzman and Ruth B. Dixon, "Child Custody Awards: Legal Standards and Empirical Patterns for Child Custody, Support and Visitation After Divorce," *University of California at Davis Law Review:* 12 (1979):473–521 (hereinafter cited as "Child Custody Awards"). This figure is based on responses of 95 percent of the judges hearing family law cases in the greater Los Angeles area.

33. Walter D. Johnson, "Divorce, Alimony, Support and Custody: A Survey of Judges' Attitudes in One State," *Family Law Reporter* 3 (1976):4003 (hereinafter cited as "Divorce, Alimony, and Custody").

34. Ruth Bader Ginsburg and Herma Hill Kay, *Sex-Based Discrimination: 1978 Supplement* (St. Paul, Minn.: West Publishing Co., 1978), p. 2; citing Arends v. Arends, 30 Utah 2d 328, 329, 517 P.2d 1019, 1020 (emphasis added) (hereinafter cited as *1978 Supplement*).

35. Ibid., citing Gordon v. Gordon, 557 P.2d 1271 (Okla. 1978).

36. Foster and Freed, "Life with Father," p. 332–33

37. In chronological order of the research, mothers were awarded custody of their children in 76 percent to 80 percent of the cases in Hennepin County, Minnesota between 1875 and 1939; in 81 percent–87 percent of the cases in Ohio between 1900 and 1949; in 85 percent of the cases in New Haven County between 1919 and 1932; in 83 percent–87 percent of the cases in Kansas between 1927 and 1939; in 68

percent of the cases in Maryland in 1929; in 86 percent of the cases in Cook County, Illinois, between 1945 and 1948; in 84 percent of the cases in Missouri from 1948 to 1955; in 74 percent of the cases in New Jersey in 1949; and in 82 percent of the cases in Tennessee in 1949. Paul H. Jacobson, *American Marriage and Divorce* (New York: Rinehart & Company, 1959), pp. 131–32.

38. William J. Goode, *Women in Divorce* (New York: The Free Press, 1965), p. 29.

39. Maine Department of Health and Welfare, *Social Casework Services in a Divorce Court* (1960).

40. William Lawrence [Note], "Divided Custody of Children After Their Parents' Divorce," *Journal of Family Law* 8 (1968):58. The lowest reported figure for mother custody was 74 percent in Tippecanoe County, Indiana. Harold T. Christenson and Hanna H. Meissner, "An Analysis of Divorce in Tippecanoe County, Indiana," *Sociology & Social Research* 40 (1956):248.

41. Weitzman and Dixon "Child Custody Awards," Table 2.

42. Bradwell v. Illinois, 83 U.S. (16 Wall) 130, 141 (1873).

43. Muller v. Oregon, 208 U.S. 412, 421 (1909).

44. Hoyt v. Florida, 368 U.S. 57, (1961).

45. General Elec. Co. v. Gilbert, 429 U.S. 125 (1976).

46. Barbara Babcock, Ann E. Freedman, Eleanor Holmes Norton, and Susan Ross, *Sex Discrimination and the Law* (Boston: Little, Brown & Co., 1975), p. 315.

47. As Evelyne Sullerot notes, throughout the history of patriarchal society "the reproductive function of women has appeared at the same time both as their justification in the world and the reason for their subordination. From this follow all the other features of woman's position. . . ." Evelyne Sullerot, *Women, Society and Change,* trans. by Margaret Scotford Archer (New York: McGraw-Hill, 1971), p. 20.

48. Brief for Appellees at 41, Geduldig v. Aiello, 94 S. Ct. 2485 (1974).

49. Scolmon v. Scolmon, 66 Wis. 2d 761, at 770, 226 N.W.2d 388, at 392.

50. See, for example, Stanley v. Illinois, 405 E.S. 645 (1972) in which the U.S. Supreme Court held that the presumption that an unwed father is an unfit parent is unconstitutional as a denial of both due process and equal protection.

51. Lila Tritico, "Child Custody: Preference to the Mother," *Louisiana Law Review* 34 (1974):884.

52. State ex rel. Watts v. Watts, 350 N.Y.S.2d 285 (N.Y. Fam. Ct. 1973).

53. Peter S. Title, "The Father's Right to Child Custody in Interparental Disputes," *Tulane Law Review* 49 (November 1974):201 (hereinafter cited as "Father's Right").

54. Ibid., p. 113.

55. *Family Law Reporter*, vol. 2 (1975), p. 1029.

56. Ibid.

57. Brim v. Brim, 532 P.2d 1403 (Okl. App. 1975).

58. Carper v. Rokus, 230 N.W.2d 468 (Neb. 1975).

59. Margaret Mead, "Anomalies in American Post Divorce Relationships," in P. Bohannon, ed., *Divorce and After* (Garden City, N.Y.: Doubleday, 1970), p. 110.

60. See, generally, Watson, "Children of Armageddon," p. 61.

61. See, generally, pamphlet published by Equal Rights for Fathers, P.O. Box 6367, Albany, Calif. 94706. (n.d., ca. 1974).

62. Levy, *The Uniform Act*, p. 225.

63. Weitzman and Dixon "Child Custody Awards," pp. 516–17 and table 9.

64. Joseph Goldstein, Anna Freud, Albert J. Solnit, *Beyond the Best Interest of the Child* (New York: Free Press, 1973), p. 7.

65. Estes v. Estes, 261 La. 20, 258 So. 2d 857 (1972).

66. Ibid.

67. See S.v.J., 367 N.Y.S.2d 862 at 863 (Sup. Ct. 1975).

68. Moezie v. Moezie, Superior Court of the District of Columbia, 1973, Family Division Docket #35 35–71.

69. Dockum v. Dockum, 522, P.2d 744 (Colo. App. 1974). See also Shaw v. Shaw, 402 S.W. 2d 222 (Ark. 1971); and Hammett v. Hammett, 239 So.2d 778 (Ala. Ct. Civ. App. 1979).

70. In re Guyer, 238 N.W.2d, 794 (Supreme Ct. Iowa 1976).

71. McCreery v. McCreery, 218 Va. 352, 237, S.E.2d 167 (1977), cited in Ginsburg and Kay, *1978 Supplement*, p. 113.

72. E. Mavis Hetherington, Martha Cox, and Roger Cox, "Beyond Father Absence: Conceptualization of Effects of Divorce," unpublished paper presented at meetings of the Society for Research in Child Development, Denver, Colorado, April, 1975, p. 7 (hereinafter cited as "Beyond Father Absence").

73. Margaret Mead, "Some Theoretical Considerations of the Problems

of Mother–Child Separation," *American Journal of Orthopsychiatry* (1974):24.

74. Hetherington et al., "Beyond Father Absence," p. 7. In a study of motherless families in Canada, Schlesinger and Todres found that while fathers also felt the social stigma of being a single parent they did not feel as isolated as the divorced mothers (because of their employment). Benjamin Schlesinger and Rubin Todres, "Motherless Families: An Increasing Societal Pattern," *Child Welfare* 8 (1976): 553–58.

75. Title, "Father's Right," p. 203, citing Benedek and Benedek, "New Child Custody Laws: Making Them Do What They Say," *American Journal of Orthopsychiatry*, 42 (1972):829.

76. National Commission on the Observance of International Women's Year, ". . . *To Form a More Perfect Union . . ." Justice for American Women* (Washington, D.C.: U.S. Government Printing Office, 1976), p. 105.

77. La Rosa v. La Rosa, 83 Misc. 2d 1059, 373 N.Y.S.2d 985 (Sup. Ct. 1975).

78. Homer Clark, *Law of Domestic Relations* (St. Paul., Minn.: West Publishing Co., 1968), p. 490.

79. Personal conversation, February 15, 1978. Chambers' research is discussed later in this chapter on pages 132–133.

80. Guidelines and schedule approved by the King County Superior Court Judges on April 28, 1977 and Johnson, "Divorce, Alimony and Custody," p. 4010.

81. Walzer, Stewart B. "The Economic Realities of Divorce," in John J. Kennelly, James P. Chapman, eds., *The Trial Lawyer's Guide* (Mundelein, Illinois: Callaghan & Co., 1968), p. 347.

82. Martha Griffiths, "Child Support Collection Among Welfare Families," *Congressional Record*, December 4, 1974, H 11291 (hereinafter cited as "Child Support").

83. Weitzman and Dixon, "Child Custody Awards," pp. 495–98.

84. Thomas Espenshade, *The Cost of Children in the United States*, University of California, Berkeley, Population Monograph Series, no. 14 (1973).

85. Weitzman and Dixon, "Child Custody Awards," p. 497.

86. Karen Seal, "A Decade of No-Fault Divorce," *Family Advocate* 1 (Spring 1979):10, 11–14.

87. "A New Estimate of Child-Rearing: $254,000 to 18," *Peninsula Times Tribune*, October 21, 1980, A–7, col. 1.

88. Philip Eden, "How Inflation Flaunts the Court's Order," *Family Advocate* 1 (Spring 1979):2–5.

89. Stuart Nagel and Lenore J. Weitzman, "Women as Litigants," *Hastings Law Review* 23 (1971):190.

90. Griffiths, "Child Support," H 11292.

91. Kenneth Eckhardt, "Deviance, Visibility and Legal Action: The Duty to Support," *Social Problems* 15 (1968):470–77.

92. Fred H. Steininger, "Study of Divorce and Support Orders in Lake County, Indiana, 1956–1957," submitted to Lake County Welfare Board. Cited in Henry Foster and Doris Freed, *Law and the Family —New York* (Rochester, N.Y.: Lawyers Cooperative Publishing Co., 1966), p. xv.

93. Barbara Everitt Bryant, *American Women Today and Tomorrow* (Washington, D.C.: National Commission on the Observance of International Women's Year, U.S. Government Printing Office 1977), p. 24. Although this figure remained consistent among other subgroups, only 30 percent of the black mothers were awarded child support.

94. U.S. Bureau of the Census, "Divorce, Child Custody, and Child Support," *Current Population Reports*, series P–23, no. 84 (June 1979), pp. 3–4.

95. Ibid.

96. More recently Jones, Gordon, and Sawhill confirmed the finding that payment performance deteriorated as time elapsed from the date of the divorce. They found that both the probability of receiving support and the amount of support declined as the number of years increased. Carol Adaire Jones, Nancy M. Gordon, and Isabel V. Sawhill, *Child Support Payments in the U.S.: Urban Institute Working Paper 992-03* (Washington, D.C.: The Urban Institute, 1976), p. 78 (hereinafter cited as *Child Support Payments*).

97. The reported percentage for full compliance varies from a low of 22 percent of all fathers (in a 1973 study of AFDC fathers cited in Jones, Gordon, and Sawhill, *Child Support Payments*, p. 29) to a high of 38 percent (in Eckhardt's data on fathers in the first year after the court order).

98. Foster, Freed, and Midonick more conservatively estimate that there are arrearages in at least 50 percent of the cases. Henry H. Foster, Jr., Doris Jonas Freed, and Millard L. Midonick, "Child Support: The Quick and the Dead," *Syracuse Law Review* 26 (1975):1157–94.

99. Diane Serafin Blank and Jerema Rone, "Enforcement of Inter-

spousal Support Obligations: A Proposal," *Women's Rights Law Reporter* 2, no. 4 (1975):13 (hereinafter cited as "Enforcement").

100. The reported percentage varies from a low of 21 percent of the mothers in the IWY study who reported they never received a single payment to the 47 percent reported by Steininger.

101. Marian P. Winston and Trude Forsher, *Nonsupport of Legitimate Children by Affluent Fathers as a Cause of Poverty and Welfare Dependence*, December 1971 (revised April 1974) (Santa Monica, Calif.: Rand, 1975) (hereinafter cited as *Nonsupport*).

102. Ibid., p. 16.

103. Griffiths, "Child Support," H 11292.

104. Cited in E. Uhr, "Child Support: The Evaded Obligation," *Focus* 4, no. 1 (Fall 1979):7–8.

105. Ibid.

106. Ibid.

107. "Child Support," *U.S. Congressional and Administrative News* 4 (1974):8147.

108. Winston and Forsher, *Nonsupport*, p. 16.

109. Table III–4 in Jones, Gordon, and Sawhill, *Child Support Payments*, pp. 29–30, citing a 1973 AFDC study, vol. II–A, p. 22, table 7.

110. Blank and Rone, "Enforcement," p. 14.

111. Ibid.

112. 42 U.S.C. §653 (Supp. 1978)

113. California Civil Code, §4701.

114. Ibid., §4370.C.

115. David L. Chambers, *Making Fathers Pay: The Enforcement of Child Support.* (Chicago: The University of Chicago Press, 1979) (hereinafter cited as *Making Fathers Pay*).

116. "The Solution to Non-Support: Jail the Parent," *Marriage and Divorce Today* 3, no. 19 (1977):2. (A report of David Chambers' research.)

117. Chambers, *Making Fathers Pay*, pp. 90–91. Smaller counties also had higher collection rates.

118. "Making Fathers Pay Child Support," *Marriage and Divorce Today* 5, no. 22 (1980):2–3.

119. Chambers, *Making Fathers Pay*, p. 118.

120. Ibid., pp. 118–119.

121. Ibid., p. 258.

Introduction, Part II: Legal Assumptions Versus Social Reality (pp. 135-138)

1. Ogburn, "The Changing Family," *The Family* 19 (1938):139.
2. Norman Ryder, "The Family in Developed Countries," *Scientific American* 231 (Sept. 1974):128.
3. William J. Goode, *World Revolution and Family Patterns* (New York: The Free Press, 1963).

Chapter 5: The Lifelong Commitment (pp. 139-152)

1. Quoted in Max Rheinstein, *Marriage Stability, Divorce and the Law* (Chicago: University of Chicago Press, 1972), p. 3 (hereinafter cited as *Marriage Stability, Divorce and the Law*).
2. Ibid., p. 20.
3. *Book of Common Prayer*, "Solemnization of Matrimony."
4. Rheinstein, *Marriage Stability, Divorce and the Law*, p. 24.
5. Ibid.
6. Ibid.
7. Herma Hill Kay, "A Family Court: The California Proposal," in Paul Bohannan, ed., *Divorce and After* (Garden City, N.Y.: Doubleday, 1970), p. 221.
8. Homer Clark, *The Law of Domestic Relations* (St. Paul, Minn.: West Publishing Co., 1968), pp. 242–43.
9. Rheinstein, *Marriage Stability, Divorce and the Law*, p. 41.
10. Elizabeth Cady Stanton, Susan B. Anthony, and Mathilda J. Gage, *History of Woman's Suffrage* (New York: Fowler & Wells, 1881), vol. I, p. 720.
11. But cf. Barbara Ann Kulzer, "Law and the Housewife: Property, Divorce and Death," *University of Florida Law Review* 28 (1975):35, for the exceptional case of New Jersey.
12. "Testimony before Joint Hearings of the Matrimonial Law Committees of the New York County Lawyers' Association and the Association of the Bar of the City of New York," January 14, 1972, p. 3.
13. Mathews v. de Castro, 429 U.S. 181, 182, 50 L. Ed. 2d 389, 97 S.Ct. 431 (1976).
14. These data are summarized from U.S. Bureau of the Census, "Di-

vorce, Child Custody and Child Support," *Current Population Reports*, series P–23, no. 84 (1979):7, table 1 (hereinafter cited as "Divorce, 1979").

15. "Divorces, Three Times Amount in 1959," *Marriage and Divorce Today* 5, no. 34, (April 7, 1980):2.

16. Kingsley Davis, "The American Family in Relation to Demographic Change," in *Commission on Population Growth and the American Future, Research Reports* 1, *Demographic and Social Aspects of Population Growth*, Charles F. Westoff and Robert Parke, Jr., eds. (Washington, D.C.: U.S. Government Printing Office, 1972), pp. 246–47.

17. Ibid., p. 247 (emphasis added).

18. U.S. Bureau of the Census, "Marriage, Divorce, Widowhood and Remarriage by Family Characteristics: June 1975," *Current Population Reports*, series P–20, no. 312 (August 1977):12.

19. Paul C. Glick and Arthur J. Norton, "Marrying, Divorcing, and Living Together in the U.S. Today," *Population Bulletin* 32, no. 5 (October 1977):37 (hereinafter cited as "Marrying, Divorcing and Living Together: 1977").

20. U.S. Bureau of the Census, "Number, Timing, and Duration of Marriage and Divorces in the United States: June 1975," *Current Population Reports*, series P–20, no. 297 (1976):6 (hereinafter cited as "Number, Timing and Duration of Marriages and Divorces: 1975").

21. Ibid.

22. Raymond Payne and Barbara B. Pittard, "Divorce in the Middle Years," *Sociological Symposium* 3 (1969):115.

23. Jurate Kazickas, "After 25 Years—Divorce: More and More Longtime Marriages End," *Sacramento Bee*, May 29, 1973, p. B4 (hereinafter cited as "After 25 Years").

24. James Bossard and Eleanor Boll, "Marital Unhappiness in the Life Cycle," *Marriage and Family Living* 17 (1955):10, 14.

25. Angus Campbell, Philip E. Converse, and Willard L. Rogers, *The Quality of American Life: Perceptions, Evaluations, and Satisfactions* (New York: Russell Sage, 1976), p. 325.

26. Paul C. Glick, "Children of Divorced Parents in Demographic Perspective," *Journal of Social Issues* 35, no. 4 (1979):180.

27. Ibid.

28. William J. Goode, *World Revolution in Family Patterns* (London: Free Press, 1963), p. 81.

29. Lenore J. Weitzman, "No Fault Divorce in California," unpublished

ms, Center for the Study of Law and Society, University of California at Berkeley, 1979.

30. See for example, *Marriage and Divorce Today* 5, no. 29 (March 3, 1980):2.

31. Prudence Brown and Roger Manela, "Changing Family Roles: Women and Divorce," *Journal of Divorce* 1, no. 4 (Summer 1978):315–328.

32. Quoted in *Marriage and Divorce Today* 3, no. 52 (August 14, 1978):2.

33. Jessie Bernard as quoted in Kazickas, "After 25 Years," p. B4.

34. Spence and Loner, "Divorce and the Life Course of Middle Aged Women," unpublished paper presented at meetings of the American Sociological Association, August 1971.

35. Anna Quindlen, "Self-Fulfillment: Independence vs. Intimacy," *New York Times*, November 28, 1977, p. 1.

36. Ibid., p. 36.

37. Hugh Carter and Paul C. Glick, *Marriage and Divorce: A Social and Economic Study*, rev. ed. (Cambridge, Mass.: Harvard University Press, 1976), p. 55 (hereinafter cited as *Marriage and Divorce*).

38. Bernard as quoted in Kazickas, "After 25 Years," p. B4.

39. Isabel V. Sawhill, Gerald E. Peabody, Carol A. Jones, and Steven B. Caldwell, "Income Transfers and Family Structure," *The Urban Institute Working Paper 979–03*, Washington, D.C., 1975. Results from income maintenance experiments suggest that the "independence effect" also results from the guarantee of income to women through welfare or income maintenance payments. Michael T. Hannan and Nancy Brandon Tuma, "Income and Marital Events: Evidence from an Income Maintenance Experiment," *American Journal of Sociology* 82 (May 1977):1186–1211.

40. Sandra L. Hofferth and Kristin A. Moore, "Women's Employment and Marriage," in *The Subtle Revolution: Women at Work*, Ralph E. Smith, ed. (Washington, D.C.: The Urban Institute, 1979), p. 108.

41. Anne Locksley, "On the Effects of Wives' Employment on Marital Adjustment and Companionship," *Journal of Marriage and the Family* 42, no. 2 (1980):337–346.

42. Jon Nordheimer, "The Family in Transition: A Challenge from Within," *New York Times*, November 27, 1977, p. 74.

43. Glick and Norton, "Marrying, Divorcing and Living Together: 1977," p. 20, table 9.

44. U.S. Census, "Divorce, 1979," p. 8, table 2.

45. Carter and Glick, *Marriage and Divorce*, p. 55.

46. Glick and Norton, "Marrying, Divorcing and Living Together: 1977," p. 8.

47. U.S. Census, "Number, Timing and Duration of Marriages and Divorces: 1975," p. 14.

48. See discussion of recent cases in Nevada, Illinois, Florida, and Oregon in Chapter 1.

49. Robert Schoen and Verne E. Nelson, "Marriage, Divorce, and Mortality: A Life Table Analysis," *Demography* 2, no. 2 (May 1974):267, 285.

Chapter 6: First Marriage, No Remarriage (pp. 153–167)

1. Homer Clark, *The Law of Domestic Relations* (St. Paul, Minn.: West Publishing, 1968), p. 27. Clark states that "The typical antenuptial agreement is made by older people who are about to be married, who have been previously married and who have considerable property whose disposition they may wish to control."

2. See, generally, Peter D. King and Howard L. Firestone, "Antenuptial Contract: A Useful Alternative," *University of San Fernando Valley Law Review* 4, no. 2 (1975):251.

3. Paul C. Glick and Arthur Norton, "Marrying, Divorcing and Living Together in the U.S. Today," *Population Bulletin* 32, no. 5 (1977):7 (hereinafter cited as "Marrying, Divorcing and Living Together: 1977").

4. Ibid.

5. William J. Goode, "Pressures to Remarry: Institutionalized Patterns Affecting the Divorced," in N. Bell and E. Vogel, eds., *A Modern Introduction to the Family* (London: Free Press, 1968), p. 331.

6. Glick and Norton, "Marrying, Divorcing and Living Together: 1977," p. 7.

7. U.S. Bureau of the Census, "Number, Timing and Duration of Marriages and Divorces in the United States: June 1975," *Current Population Reports*, series P–20, no. 297 (1976):3 (hereinafter cited as "Number, Timing and Duration of Marriages and Divorces: 1975").

8. Hugh Carter and Paul C. Glick, *Marriage and Divorce: A Social and Economic Study* (Cambridge, Mass.: Harvard University Press, 1976), p. 440 (hereinafter cited as *Marriage and Divorce*).

9. Bureau of the Census, "Number, Timing and Duration of Marriages and Divorces: 1975," p. 3. This ratio is based on persons between 50 and 75 years old in 1975.

10. U.S. Bureau of the Census, "Marriage, Divorce, Widowhood, and Remarriage by Family Characteristics: June 1975," *Current Population Reports*, series P–20, no. 312 (1977):8.

11. Bureau of the Census, "Number, Timing and Duration of Marriages and Divorces: 1975," p. 4.

12. Glick and Norton, "Marrying, Divorcing and Living Together: 1977," p. 8.

13. Frank F. Furstenberg, "Recycling the Family: Perspectives for a Neglected Family Form," *Marriage and Family Review* 2, no. 3 (1979):1, 12–22 (hereinafter cited as "Recycling the Family").

14. Ibid., pp. 6, 36. Between 1972 and 1975, for example, the remarriage rate for divorced men declined by 17 percent, and the patterns for women were similar. Carter and Norton believe the economic recession of the mid 1970s may explain some of this decline; however, they also point to the growing proportion of divorced men and women who are apparently opting not to remarry and suggest that this may herald a future overall decline in the remarriage rate.

15. U.S. Bureau of the Census, "Perspectives on American Husbands and Wives," *Current Population Reports*, series P–23, no. 77 (1978):7.

16. Bureau of the Census, "Number, Timing and Duration of Marriages and Divorces: 1975," p. 2.

17. Furstenberg, "Recycling the Family."

18. *Stepfamily Bulletin* 1 (Fall 1980):1.

19. The 13 percent figure was reported in *The Spokeswoman* (September 1980):12. The 20 percent figure was reported in the *Stepfamily Bulletin* 1 (Fall 1980):1.

20. Andrew Cherlin, "Remarriage as an Incomplete Institution," *American Journal of Sociology* 84, no. 3 (1978):634–50 (hereinafter cited as "Remarriage").

21. Ibid.

22. Jessie Bernard, *Remarriage: A Study of Marriage* (New York: Dryden Press, 1956).

23. Leslie Aldreidge Westoff, *The Second Time Around: Remarriage in America* (New York: Viking, 1977), pp. 4, 41 (hereinafter cited as *Second Time*).

24. Personal interview with Dr. Jacqueline Bourgonne, July 1980, Sheffield, England.

25. Cherlin, "Remarriage."

26. Liz Einstein, *The Stepfamily Web* (forthcoming, 1981).

27. Ann Goetting, "Former Spouse–Current Spouse Relationships," *Journal of Family Issues* 1, no. 1 (1980):58–80.

28. "Today's Major Clinical Issue: The Remarriage Family," *Marriage and Divorce Today* (December 1979):2.

29. Ibid., Westoff, *Second Time*, p. 42.

30. Cherlin, "Remarriage."

31. Paul Bohannan, "Divorce Chains, Households of Remarriage, and Multiple Divorces," in Paul Bohannan, ed., *Divorce and After* (New York: Doubleday, 1970), pp. 127–39.

32. Anne C. Schwartz, "Reflections on Divorce and Remarriage," *Social Casework* 49 (1968):213.

33. U.S. Department of Health, Education and Welfare, "Advance Report: Final Divorce Statistics, 1975," *Monthly Vital Statistics Report* 26, no. 2 (May, 1977):2.

34. This assertion is based on 1960 data. See Carter and Glick, *Marriage and Divorce*, pp. 21–24.

35. "Elderly Weddings," *San Francisco Chronicle*, November 16, 1976, p. 22, col. 1.

36. By 1985 the population of persons 65 and older may reach 26.7 million, or 11.4 percent of the total U.S. population. "Profiles of Elders in the United States," *Statistical Bulletin* (Metropolitan Life), vol. 56 (April 1975):8.

37. U.S. Department of Health, Education and Welfare, "Advance Report: Final Marriage Statistics, 1975," *Monthly Vital Statistics Report* 26, no. 2 (May, 1977) p. 5 (hereinafter cited as "Marriage: 1975").

38. "Likelihood of a Golden Wedding Anniversary," *Statistical Bulletin* (Metropolitan Life), vol. 57 (February 1976):4, 6 (hereinafter cited as "Golden Wedding Anniversary").

39. The percentage for bridegrooms is 63 percent. These statistics are computed from Department of HEW, "Marriage: 1975," p. 5, table 4.

40. The concerns of the elderly themselves must be distinguished from those of relatives. Infringement on the rights of the elderly by those who seek to impose a guardianship in order to prevent an older person's entry into marriage and thus ensure a prospective inheritance, is raised in Note, "The Disguised Oppression of Involuntary Guardianship: Have the Elderly Freedom to Spend?" *Yale Law Journal* 73 (1964):676.

41. Henry H. Foster, "Marriage and Divorce in the Twilight Zone," *Arizona Law Review* 17, no. 2 (1975):456.

42. Letter to the author, January 1974.

43. *San Francisco Chronicle*, February 26, 1974, p. 4, col. 1.

44. See, generally, William H. Masters and Virginia E. Johnson, *Human Sexual Response* (Boston: Little Brown & Co., 1966).

45. See, e.g., Bette Dewing Brabec, "Being Our Age and Learning to Like It," *Prime Time: For the Liberation of Women in the Prime of Life* 2, no. 1 (1974):5; and Susan Sontag, "The Double Standard of Aging," *Saturday Review of Society* 55, no. 39 (1972):29.

46. Robert Schoen and Verne E. Nelson, "Marriage, Divorce, and Mortality: A Life Table Analysis," *Demography* 2, no. 2 (1974):285.

47. "Golden Wedding Anniversary," p. 5.

48. Ibid., p. 4.

49. Paul C. Glick, "Some Recent Changes in American Families," *Current Population Reports*, series P–23, no. 52 (1976):3.

50. James A. Peterson, "Marriage and Love in the Middle Years," *Public Affairs Pamphlet*, no. 456 (1970):2–3.

51. Paul C. Glick and Robert Parke, Jr., "New Approaches in Studying the Life Cycle of the Family," *Demography* 2 (1965):187.

52. Jessie Bernard, *The Future of Marriage* (New York: World, 1972), p. 68.

53. Lawrence S. Kubie, "Psychoanalysis and Marriage," in Victor W. Eisenstein, ed., *Neurotic Interaction in Marriage* (New York: Basic Books, 1956), p. 12.

54. Ibid.

55. Jessie Bernard, "Infidelity: Some Moral and Social Issues," in R. Libby and R. Whitehurst, eds., *Renovating Marriage: Toward Sexual Life-styles* (Danville, Calif.: Consensus Publishers, 1973), pp. 75–76.

Chapter 7: Separate Roles for Husband and Wife (pp. 168–189)

1. William J. Goode, *World Revolution and Family Patterns* (New York: The Free Press, 1963), p. 59 (hereinafter cited as *World Revolution*).

2. "In 1890 most employed women were working on farms, in domestic or personal service, teaching, or in the clothing and textile industries. In 1963 [fewer] than one out of 10 employed women [were] in domestic service." Goode, *World Revolution*, p. 61. By 1974, only 3.9 percent of employed women were service workers in private households. Women's Bureau, U.S. Department of Labor, *1975 Handbook on*

Women Workers 297 (1975):84 (hereinafter cited as *Women Workers: 1975*).

3. William J. Goode, *The Family* (Englewood Cliffs, N.J.: Prentice-Hall, 1964), p. 75.

4. The following statistics, unless otherwise noted, are from Ralph E. Smith, "The Movement of Women into the Labor Force," in *The Subtle Revolution: Women at Work*, Ralph E. Smith, ed. (Washington, D.C.: The Urban Institute, 1979); pp. 1–15 (hereinafter cited as "Women into the Labor Force").

5. Ibid., pp. 4–5.

6. Ibid., p. 4.

7. Valerie K. Oppenheimer, *The Female Labor Force in the United States* (Berkeley, Calif.: University of California Institute of International Studies, 1970), p. 187.

8. Francine D. Blau, "Women in the United States Economy," in *Women: A Feminist Perspective*, Jo Freeman, ed. (Palo Alto, Calif.: Mayfield, 1975).

9. Women's Bureau, U.S. Department of Labor, *Women Workers Today* 1 (1976):1 (hereinafter cited as *Women Workers Today*).

10. Ibid., pp. 1–2.

11. Francine D. Blau, "The Data on Women Workers, Past, Present and Future," in *Women Working: Theories and Facts in Perspective*, Ann H. Stromberg and Shirley Harkess, eds. (Palo Alto, Calif.: Mayfield, 1978), pp. 37–38 (hereinafter cited as "Data on Women Workers").

12. Smith, "Women into the Labor Force," p. 14.

13. Ibid., p. 11, fig. 2; and Women's Bureau, *Women Workers: 1975*, p. 26, table 11.

14. Smith, "Women into the Labor Force," p. 14.

15. U.S. Bureau of the Census, "A Statistical Portrait of Women in the U.S.," *Current Population Reports*, Special Studies Series P–23, no. 58 (1976):26 (hereinafter cited as "Women in the U.S."). This figure is based on ever-married mothers.

16. Smith, "Women into the Labor Force," p. 11, fig. 2, and p. 14, table 1.

17. Women's Bureau, *Women Workers: 1975*, p. 31, table 7–5.

18. Women's Bureau, U.S. Department of Labor, *Why Women Work* (rev. July 1976).

19. Smith, "Women into the Labor Force," p. 12.

20. Ibid.

21. Stephen Rawlings, "Perspectives on American Husbands and Wives," *Current Population Reports*, U.S. Bureau of the Census, Special Studies Series P-23, no. 77 (1978) (hereinafter cited as "Perspectives").

22. Carolyn Shaw Bell, "Working Women's Contributions to Family Income," *Eastern Economic Journal* 1 (1974):198.

23. Ibid.

24. Rawlings, "Perspectives," p. 36, table 28A.

25. Personal interview with Cynthia Epstein, June, 1979.

26. Clair Vickery, "Women's Economic Contribution to the Family," in *The Subtle Revolution: Women at Work*, Ralph E. Smith, ed. (Washington, D.C.: The Urban Institute, 1979):159–200.

27. "Life Insurance Industry Adapts to Women's New Role," *Marriage and Divorce Today* 5, no. 9 (October 15, 1979):1.

28. Rawlings, "Perspectives," p. 36, table 28A.

29. Howard Hayghe, "Families and the Rise of Working Wives—An Overview," *Monthly Labor Review* 99, no. 5 (1976):17.

30. "The 59¢ Majority," News Release, National Organization for Women, Washington, D.C., August 26, 1980.

31. Bureau of the Census, "Women in the U.S.," p. 27.

32. Women's Bureau, U.S. Department of Labor, *Women Workers Today* (1976), p. 9.

33. Ibid.

34. Blau, "Data on Women Workers," pp. 48–49. See also Isabel Sawhill, "The Economics of Discrimination Against Women: Some New Findings," *Journal of Human Resources* 8 (1973):383–96, for a review of this research. On the persistent decline in women's occupational, economic, and educational achievements, compared to those of men, see Dean Knudsen, "The Declining Status of Women: Popular Myths and the Failure of Functionalist Thought," *Social Forces* 48 (1969):183.

35. R. Stephen Warner, David T. Wellman, and Lenore J. Weitzman, "The Hero, The Sambo, and the Operator: Three Characterizations of the Oppressed," *Urban Life and Culture* 2, no. 1 (1973):60–61.

36. Richard J. Meislin, "Poll Finds More Liberal Beliefs on Marriage and Sex Roles, Especially Among the Young," *New York Times*, November 27, 1977, p. 1.

37. Ibid.

38. Jessie Bernard, *Future of Marriage* (New York: World, 1972), pp. 3–53.

39. Ibid.

40. See, generally, Betty Friedan, *The Feminine Mystique* (New York: Norton, 1964); and A. Koedt, E. Levine, and A. Rapone, eds., *Radical Feminism* (New York: Quadrangle, 1973).

41. Smith, "Women into the Labor Force," p. 2.

42. Goode, *World Revolution*, p. 56.

43. Kristin A. Moore and Isabel V. Sawhill, "Implications of Women's Employment for Home and Family Life," in *Women Working: Theories and Facts in Perspective*, Ann H. Stromberg and Shirley Harkess, eds. (Palo Alto, Calif.: Mayfield, 1978), p. 207 (hereinafter cited as "Implications").

44. Stephen J. Bahr, "Effects on Power and Division of Labor in the Family," in *Working Mothers: An Evaluative Review of the Consequences for Wife, Husband and Child*, Louis W. Hoffman and F. Ivan Nye, eds. (San Francisco: Jossey-Bass, 1975), p. 185 (hereinafter cited as "Effects on Power").

45. Mary Jo Bane, *Here to Stay: American Families* (New York: Basic Books, 1976), p. 80 (hereinafter cited as *American Families*).

46. Constantina Safilios-Rothschild, "Dual Linkages Between the Occupational and Family System: A Macrosociological Analysis," *Signs* 1, no. 3, pt. 2 (Spring 1976):52 (hereinafter cited as "Dual Linkages").

47. Goode, *The Family*, pp. 74–75.

48. Bahr, "Effects on Power," p. 184.

49. Rothschild, "Dual Linkages," p. 53.

50. Ibid.

51. William J. Goode, "Why Men Resist," *Dissent* (Spring 1980).

52. Caroline Bird, *The Two Paycheck Marriage: How Women at Work are Changing Life in America* (New York: Rawson, Wade Publishers, 1979), pp. 61–62 (hereinafter cited as *The Two Paycheck Marriage*).

53. Moore and Sawhill, "Implications," p. 207.

54. Kathryn E. Walker and Margaret E. Woods, *Time Use: A Measure of Household Production of Family Goods and Services* (Washington, D.C.: American Home Economics Association, 1976).

55. Bane, *American Families*, p. 80.

56. Elise Boulding, "Familial Constraints on Women's Work Roles," in *Women and the Workplace*, M. Blaxall and B. Reagan, eds. (Chicago: University of Chicago Press, 1976), p. 112.

57. Myra H. Strober, "Women and Men in the World of Work: Present and Future," in *Women and Men: Changing Roles, Relationships*

and Perceptions, L. Cater and A.F. Scott, eds. (New York: Aspen Institute, 1976), p. 136.

58. Ibid.

59. John P. Robinson, "Housework Technology and Household Work," in *Women and Household Labor*, Sarah Fenstermaker Berk, ed., (Beverly Hills, Ca.: Sage Publications, 1980).

60. Julia A. Bricksen, William L. Yancey, and Eugene P. Ericksen, "The Division of Family Roles," *Journal of Marriage and the Family* 41, no. 2 (1979):301–314.

61. This is the central thesis in Elizabeth Bott, *Family and Social Network* (New York: Free Press, 1957). Bott focuses on the tightly knit network in working-class neighborhoods in London, but her analysis seems as accurate for the blue-collar families in the United States studied in Komarovsky, *Blue-Collar Marriage* (New York: Random House, 1964).

62. Arlene Skolnick, *The Intimate Environment: Exploring Marriage and the Family* (Boston: Little, Brown & Co., 1973), p. 311. See also Leonard, "The Fathering Instinct," *Ms.*, May 1974, p. 52.

63. M. Komarovsky, "Cultural Contradictions and Sex Roles: The Masculine Case," *American Journal of Sociology* 78 (January 1973):882.

64. Herma Hill Kay, "Making Marriage and Divorce Safe for Women," *California Law Review* 60, no. 6 (1972):1695–96 (footnotes omitted).

65. *Women Today* 3, no. 26 (1973):3.

66. "Trends—Paternity Leave," *Marriage and Divorce Today* 5, no. 25 (February 4, 1980):4.

67. See, for example, Robert A. Fein, "Research on Fathering: Social Policy and an Emergent Perspective," *The Journal of Social Issues* 34, no. 1 (Winter 1978):122–35, and Glenn R. Hawkes, "Who Will Rear Our Children?" *The Family Coordinator* 27, no. 2 (April 1978): 159–66.

68. Rochelle Wortis, "The Acceptance of the Concept of the Maternal Role by Behavioral Scientists: Its Effects on Women," *American Journal of Orthopsychiatry* 41 (1971):733.

69. The following section is paraphrased from Lenore J. Weitzman, Deborah Eifler, Elizabeth Hokada, and Catherine Ross, "Sex-Role Socialization in Picture Books for Preschool Children," *American Journal of Sociology* 77 (1972):1125. See also C. Amyx, "Sex Discrimination," *California Law Review* 62 (1974):312.

70. Talcott Parsons, "Family Structure and the Socialization of the Child," in *Family Socialization and Interaction Process*, T. Parsons and R. Bales, eds. (Glencoe, Ill.: Free Press, 1955), pp. 35, 80.

71. Philip E. Slater, "Parental Role Differentiation," in *The Family: Its Structure and Functions*, R. Coser, ed. (New York: St. Martin's Press, 1964), pp. 350–70.

72. Lois W. Hoffman, "Effects on Child," in *Working Mothers: An Evaluative Review of the Consequences for Wife, Husband and Child*, L. W. Hoffman and F. Ivan Nye, eds. (San Francisco: Jossey-Bass, 1975), p. 164 (hereinafter cited as *Working Mothers*).

73. "Working Mom's Study," *The Spokeswoman* 9, no. 11 (May 1979):7.

74. Lois Hoffman, "Effects on Child," in *Working Mothers*, p. 163.

75. Dolores Gold and David Andres, "Relations between Maternal Employment and Development of Nursery School Children," *Canadian Journal of Behavioral Sciences* 10, no. 2 (1978):116–29. Gold and Andres, "Comparisons of Adolescent Children with Employed and Nonemployed Mothers," *Merrill-Palmer Quarterly* 24, no. 4 (1978): 243–54.

76. Alice Rossi, "Equality Between the Sexes: An Immodest Proposal," in *The Woman in America*, Robert Lifton, ed. (Boston: Houghton Mifflin, 1964), p. 113.

77. Bart, "Mother Portnoy's Complaint," *Trans-Action* 8 (November–December 1970):113.

78. F. Ivan Nye, "Effects on Mother," in *Working Mothers*, p. 224.

79. Donald St. John-Parsons, "Continuous Dual-Career Families: A Case Study," *Psychology of Women Quarterly* 3, no. 1 (Fall 1978):30–42.

80. Rucci v. Rucci, 23 Conn. Super. 221, 224, 181 A.2d 125, 127 (1962).

81. See 65 Am. Jur. 2d, Rape § 27.

82. Pepper Schwartz, "Female Sexuality and Monogamy," in *Renovating Marriage: Toward New Sexual Life-Styles*, R. Libby and R. Whitehurst, eds. (Danville, Calif.: Consensus, 1973), p. 214.

83. William H. Masters and Virginia E. Johnson, *Human Sexual Response* (Boston: Little, Brown, 1966).

84. See, generally, Anne Koedt, "The Myth of Vaginal Orgasm," in *Radical Feminism*, A. Koedt, E. Levine, and A. Rapone, eds. (New York: Quadrangle, 1973), pp. 198–207.

85. Sandra Coyner, "Women's Liberation and Sexual Liberation," in *Sexuality Today and Tomorrow: Contemporary Issues in Human Sexuality*, S. Gordon and R. W. Libby, eds. (North Scituate, Mass.: Duxbury Press, 1976), pp. 59–71.

86. David R. Mace, "Sex in the Year 2000," in *Sexuality Today and Tomorrow: Contemporary Issues in Human Sexuality*, S. Gordon and R. W. Libby, eds. (North Scituate, Mass.: Duxbury Press, 1976), pp. 398, 400.

87. Ruth Dixon, "Measuring Equality," *Journal of Social Issues* 32, no. 3 (1976):23.

88. Bird, *The Two-Paycheck Marriage*, p. 73.

89. Ibid.

90. Ibid.

91. Philip and Lorna Surrel, "The Redbook Report on Sexual Relationships," *Redbook*, October 1980, p. 79.

Chapter 8: The White Middle-Class Bias (pp. 190–203)

1. Jacobus tenBroek, "California's Dual System of Family Law: Its Origin, Development, and Present Status," *Stanford Law Review* 16 (1964):257–317 (pt. 1); 900–81 (pt. 2); and 17 (1965):614–82 (pt. 3) (Hereinafter cited as "The Dual System").

2. Ibid., pt. 2, p. 978.

3. Ibid., pt. 1, pp. 257–58.

4. Jerome E. Carlin, Jan Howard, and Sheldon Messinger, *Civil Justice and the Poor: Issues for Sociological Research* (New York: Russell Sage Foundation, 1967), p. 9 (hereinafter cited as *Civil Justice and the Poor*).

5. Ibid., p. 9.

6. TenBroek, "The Dual System," pt. 3, p. 614.

7. Kenneth W. Eckhardt, "Deviance, Visibility and Legal Action: The Duty to Support," *Social Problems* 15 (1968):470–77.

8. Ibid.

9. Henry H. Foster and Doris Jonas Freed, "Unequal Protection: Poverty and Family Law," *Indiana Law Journal* 42 (1967):202 (emphasis added; hereinafter cited as "Unequal Protection").

10. TenBroek, "The Dual System," pt. 1, p. 258; pt. 2, pp. 900–81.

11. Monrad G. Paulsen, "Juvenile Courts, Family Courts, and the Poor Man," *California Law Review* 54 (1966):694 (hereinafter cited as "Courts and the Poor"); quoting in part from Martin Tolchin, "Experts Wonder if Family Court Is Doing Its Job," *New York Times*, January 18, 1964, p. 24, col. 3 (reprinted with permission).

12. Cited in Paulsen, "Courts and the Poor," p. 695.

13. Carlin, Howard, and Messinger, *Civil Justice and the Poor*, p. 13.

14. Ibid., p. 14.

15. E. Ehrlich, *Fundamental Principles of the Sociology of Law* (Cambridge, Mass.: Harvard University Press, 1936), p. 238.

16. Foster and Freed, "Unequal Protection," pp. 193–94. Unlike tenBroek, Foster and Freed do not believe that the law on the books is discriminatory—but they do agree with tenBroek's strong indictment of the law in practice. As they note: "[The law] in operation produces discrimination because historically the indigent cannot afford the luxury of formal justice."

17. Paulsen, "Courts and the Poor," p. 712.

18. See, generally, Henry H. Foster, "Common Law Divorce," *Minnesota Law Review* 45 (1961).

19. Testimony before the California Assembly Interim Commission on Judiciary (Los Angeles, January 8–9, 1964), *Transcript of Proceedings on Domestic Relations* 71, pp. 92–93.

20. See, generally, Gerhard O. W. Mueller, "Inquiry into the State of a Divorceless Society: Relations Law and Morals in England from 1660–1857," *University of Pittsburgh Law Review* 18 (1957):545–78.

21. Herbert O'Gorman, *Lawyers and Matrimonial Cases: A Study of Informal Pressures in Private Professional Practice* (New York: The Free Press, 1963), pp. 22–23. At the time O'Gorman conducted his study, adultery was the only ground for divorce in New York.

22. Boddie v. Connecticut, 401 U.S. 371 (1971).

23. Jerome Carlin and Jan Howard, "Legal Representation and Class Justice," *U.C.L.A. Law Review* 12 (1965):382–83 (hereinafter cited as "Legal Representation").

24. The relatively few private attorneys available to the poor tend to be the least well trained and the least likely to conform even to the minimal standards of the bar. These lawyers are invariably at the lower end of the profession in academic achievement, and because of the insecurity of their practice they are most likely to succumb to temptations to exploit clients. Jerome Carlin, *Lawyers' Ethics* (New York: Russell Sage Foundation, 1966), pp. 22–30, 71–73.

25. Carlin, Howard, and Messinger, *Civil Justice and the Poor*, p. 47.

26. Ibid., p. 49.

27. According to Kay and Philips, the Legal Aid societies have typically either refused to process divorces when one party has deserted the family or agreed to do so only under conditions not imposed by private lawyers on their paying clients. Herma Hill Kay and Irving Philips, "Poverty and the Law of Child Custody," *California Law Review* 54, no. 2 (1966):726 (hereinafter cited as "Poverty and the Law of Child Custody").

28. Carlin and Howard, "Legal Representation," p. 415.

29. Interview with staff attorney, Mobilization for Youth Legal Services, New York City, January 1977.

30. Paulsen, "Courts and the Poor," p. 699.

31. Ibid. (emphasis added).

32. TenBroek, "The Dual System," pt. 3, p. 649.

33. Kay and Philips, "Poverty and the Law of Child Custody," p. 410 (reprinted with permission).

34. Foster and Freed, "Unequal Protection."

35. Kay and Philips, "Poverty and the Law of Child Custody," p. 734, citing Bernice Boehm, "The Community and the Social Agency Define Neglect," *Child Welfare* 43 (1964):459.

36. Justice Wise Polier, *A View from the Bench: The Juvenile Court* (New York: National Council on Crime and Delinquency, 1964) p. 26, cited in Paulsen, "Courts and the Poor," p. 710.

37. Relf v. Weinberger, 372 F. Suppl, 1196, 1199 (D.D.C. 1974) (emphasis added).

38. This is a summary of Robert Winch, et al., *Familial Organizations* (New York: The Free Press, 1977).

39. Andrew Billingsley, *Black Families in White America* (Englewood Cliffs, N.J.: Prentice Hall, 1968), p. 33.

40. Joyce Aschenbrenner, *Lifelines: Black Families in Chicago* (New York: Holt, Rinehart and Winston, 1975), p. 6 (hereinafter cited as *Lifelines*).

41. Ibid., p. 3.

42. Carol B. Stack, *All Our Kin: Strategies for Survival in a Black Community* (New York: Harper Colophon Books, 1974), p. 121 (hereinafter cited as *All Our Kin*).

43. Ibid., p. 122.

44. Ibid., p. 126.

45. See, for example, Robert Staples, "Toward a Sociology of the Black Family: A Theoretical and Methodological Assessment," *Journal of Marriage and the Family* 33, no. 1 (1971):130 (hereinafter cited as "Towards a Sociology of the Black Family"); and Ulf Hannerz, *Soulside: Inquiries into Ghetto Culture and Community* (New York: Columbia University Press, 1969).

46. Stack, *All Our Kin*, p. 112 (quoted with permission of the author).

47. Charlotte Robinson, "Black Marriages—Victims of the Affluent Rat Race," *San Francisco Chronicle*, April 25, 1976, p. 24, col. 1. Robinson refers to the divorce rate for all black families, not just for lower-class families. However, the rate is highest among lower-class families.

48. Lee Rainwater, "The Crucible of Identity: The Negro Lower-Class Family," *Daedalus* 95 (Winter 1965):255.

49. Ibid., p. 255.

50. Stack, *All Our Kin*, p. 125.

51. Aschenbrenner, *Lifelines*, p. 4.

52. Stack, *All Our Kin*, p. 125.

53. Robert Staples, "Towards a Sociology of the Black Family," p. 131.

54. Elliot Liebow, *Talley's Corner* (Boston: Little, Brown & Co., 1967), p. 78.

55. Francine D. Blau, "Women in the Labor Force: An Overview," in *Women: A Feminist Perspective*, Jo Freeman, ed. (Palo Alto, Calif.: Mayfield, 1975), p. 211.

56. Ibid., p. 215.

57. U.S. Bureau of the Census, "A Statistical Portrait of Women in the U.S.," *Current Population Reports*, Special Studies Series P-23, no. 58 (1976):60.

58. Stack, *All Our Kin*, p. 90.

59. Aschenbrenner, *Lifelines*, p. 70.

60. Kay and Philips, "Poverty and the Law of Child Custody," p. 726.

61. Stack, *All Our Kin*, pp. 48–49.

62. Moore v. East Cleveland, 97 U.S. 1932 (1977).

63. Ibid., at 1940.

Chapter 9: One Man, One Woman — No Exceptions (pp. 204–223)

1. Caleb Foote, Robert J. Levy, Frank E. A. Sander, *Cases and Materials on Family Law*, 2d ed. (Boston: Little, Brown & Co., 1976) (hereinafter cited as *Family Law: 1976*).

2. Cleveland v. United States, 329 U.S. 14 (1946).

3. Foote, Levy, and Sander, *Family Law: 1976*, p. 593.

4. Reynolds v. United States 98 U.S. 145 (1878).

5. Ibid., p. 145.

6. Caleb Foote, Robert J. Levy, and Frank E. A. Sander, *Cases and Materials on Family Law* (Boston: Little, Brown & Co., 1966), p. 220.

7. Testimony of the California State Department of Social Welfare before the California Assembly Interim Commission on Judiciary, (Los Angeles, January 8–9, 1964) *Transcript of Proceedings on Domestic Relations* 71, pp. 92–93.

8. Homer H. Clark, *Law of Domestic Relations* (St. Paul, Minn.: West Publishing Co., 1968), pp. 67–70, on presumptive validity of second marriages.

9. In Re Atherly 44 Cal. App. 3d 758, 119 Cal. Rptr. 41 (1975).

10. Observations in the court of Judge Robert Kroninger, Superior Court of Alameda County, California, In Re Marriage of Scherr, Case No. 445394.

11. See, generally, Bennett Berger, Bruce Hackett, Sherri Cavan, Gilbert Zickler, Mervyn Millar, Marilyn Noble, Susan Theiman, Richard Farrell, and Benjamin Rosenbluth, "Child-Rearing Practices of the Communal Family," in *Family in Transition: Rethinking Marriage, Sexuality, Child-Rearing and Family Organization*, A. Skolnick and J. Skolnick, eds., (Boston: Little, Brown & Co., 1971), pp. 509–23; Bennett Berger, Bruce Hackett, and Mervyn Millar, "The Communal Family," *The Family Coordinator* 21 (1972):419–27; Sara Davidson, "The Hippie Alternative: Getting Back to the Communal Garden," in *Family in Transition*, A. Skolnick and J. Skolnick, eds. (Boston: Little, Brown & Co., 1971), pp. 523–42.

12. Comment, "All in the 'Family': Legal Problems of Communes," *Harvard Civil Rights–Civil Liberties Law Review* 7 (1972):410–11.

13. This is the general impression one receives from the articles in note 11 above and from Benjamin Zablocki, *The Joyful Community* (New York: Penguin, 1971).

14. Jessie Bernard, *The Future of Marriage* (New York: World Publishing, 1972), pp. 205–06. See also James W. Ramey, "Emerging Patterns of Innovative Behavior in Marriage," in *Sourcebook in Marriage and the Family*, M. B. Sussman, ed. (Palo Alto, Calif.: Houghton Mifflin, 1974), p. 56.

15. Carmen Massey and Ralph Warner, *Sex, Living Together and the Law: A Legal Guide for Unmarried Couples (and Groups)* (Berkeley, Calif.: Nolo Press, 1974), p. 178 (hereinafter cited as *Sex, Living Together and Law*).

16. Lee Goldstein, *Communes, Law and Commonsense: A Legal Manual for Communities* (Boston: New Community Projects, 1974), p. 7 (hereinafter cited as *Communes, Law and Commonsense*).

17. Massey and Warner, *Sex, Living Together and Law*, p. 175.

18. 7 U.S. C.A. § 2012(e), as amended.

19. Moreno v. United States Department of Agriculture, 345 F. Supp. 310 (D.D.C. 1972).

20. Goldstein, *Communes, Law and Commonsense*, p. 34.

21. Ibid., p. 41 (reprinted with permission).

22. See, generally, Note, "Excluding the Commune from Suburbia: The Use of Zoning for Social Control," *Hastings Law Journal* 23 (1972):1459; Note, "Burning the House to Roast the Pig: Unrelated Individuals and Single Family Zoning's Blood Relation Criterion," *Cornell Law Review* 58 (1972):138.

23. Palo Alto Tenants Union v. Morgan, 321 F. Supp. 908 (N.D. Cal. 1970).

24. Village of Belle Terre v. Boraas, 94 S. Ct. 1536 (1974).

25. Palo Alto Tenants Union v. Morgan, 321 F. Supp. 908 (N.D. Cal. 1970).

26. Ibid.

27. Belle Terre v. Boraas, 416 U.S. at 9, 94 S.Ct. at 1541.

28. Riverside v. Reagan, 270 III App. 355 (1933).

29. From Moore v. East Cleveland, 97 U.S. 1932 (1977), 52 L.Ed.2d 531.

30. Rademan v. City and County of Denver, 526 P.2d 1235 (Colo. 1974).

31. Association for Educational Development v. Hayward, 533 S.W. 579 (Mo. 1976).

32. Town of Durham v. White Enterprises, Inc., 318 A.2d 706 at 709 (1975).

33. City of White Plains v. Ferraioli, 34 N.Y.2d 300, 357 N.Y.S.2d 449, 313 N.E.2d 756 (1974).

34. Berger v. State, 71 N.J. 206, 364 A.2d 993 (1976).

35. Arlie Hochschild, "Communal Life-Styles for the Old" in *Intimacy, Family and Society*, A. Skolnick and J. Skolnick, eds. (Boston: Little, Brown & Co., 1974), p. 565.

36. Marino v. Mayor and Council of Norwood, 77 N.J. Super. 587, 187 A.2d 217 (1963).

37. Ibid., p. 221.

38. Michael Alan Barcott, "Village of Belle Terre v. Boraas: A 'Sanctuary for People,' " *University of San Francisco Law Review* 9, no. 2 (1974):409.

39. Morris Ploscowe, Henry H. Foster, and Doris Jonas Freed, *Family Law: Cases and Materials* (Boston: Little, Brown and Co., 1972), p. 377 (hereinafter cited as *Family Law*).

40. See Daniel E. Murray, "Ancient Laws of Adultery," *Journal of Family Law* 1 (1961):89.

41. Ploscowe, Foster, and Freed, *Family Law*, p. 378.

42. See Commonwealth v. Call, 38 Mass. (21 Pick.) 509 (1839).

43. Ploscowe, Foster, and Freed, *Family Law*, p. 378 list Arkansas, Louisiana, Nevada, New Mexico, and Tennessee as states not having criminal statutes against adultery.

44. Ibid. p. 379.

45. Ibid.

46. Robert N. Whitehurst, "The Monogamous Ideal and Sexual Realities," in *Renovating Marriage: Toward New Sexual Life-Styles*, R. Libby and R. Whitehurst, eds. (Danville, Calif.: Consensus, 1973), p. 42.

47. Alfred C. Kinsey and Paul Gebhard, *Sexual Behavior in the Human Female* (Philadelphia: W. B. Saunders, 1958), p. 437.

48. Morton Hunt, *The Affair* (New York: New American Library, 1969), p. 11 (quoting Dr. Gebhard, successor to Dr. Kinsey as Director of the Institute for Sex Research at Indiana University, as to a 1968 estimate).

49. Morton Hunt, *Sexual Behavior in the 1970's* (New York: Dell, 1974), p. 253 (emphasis added; hereinafter cited as *Sexual Behavior*).

50. John F. Cuber and Peggy B. Harroff, *Sex and the Significant Americans: A Study of Sexual Behavior Among the Affluent* (Baltimore, Md.: Penguin, 1966), p. 62.

51. Ibid., p. 159.

52. Ibid., p. 62.

53. See, generally, Gilbert D. Bartell, *Group Sex: An Eyewitness Report on the American Way of Swinging* (New York: P. H. Wyden, 1971); James R. Smith and Lynn R. Smith, *Beyond Monogamy: Recent Studies of Sexual Alternatives in Marriage* (Baltimore, Md.: Johns Hopkins University Press, 1974) (hereinafter cited as *Beyond Monogamy*); and Roger W. Libby and Robert N. Whitehurst, *Renovating Marriage: Toward New Sexual Life-Styles* (Danville, Calif.: Consensus, 1973) (hereinafter cited as *Renovating Marriage*).

54. Hunt, *Sexual Behavior*, p. 22.

55. See, for example, Simone de Beauvoir's candid discussion in "The Question of Fidelity," *Harper's Magazine*, November 1964, p. 64.

56. Brian G. Gilmartin, "Sexual Deviance and Social Networks: A Study of Social, Family, and Marital Interaction Patterns Among Co-Marital Sex Participants," in Smith and Smith, *Beyond Monogamy*; see also Roger W. Libby, "Extramarital and Co-Marital Sex: A Review of the Literature," in Libby and Whitehurst, *Renovating Marriage*.

57. Robert Seidenberg, *Marriage Between Equals* (Garden City, N.Y.: Anchor Press, 1973), p. 122.

58. Pepper Schwartz, "Female Sexuality and Monogamy," in Libby and Whitehurst, *Renovating Marriage*, pp. 211, 215.

59. Ibid., pp. 223–24.

60. For a review of the religious background for modern social and legal biases against homosexuals, see R. A. Basile, "Lesbian Mothers I," *Women's Rights Law Reporter* 2, no. 2 (1974):5–7; Marilyn Riley, "The Lesbian Mother," *San Diego Law Review* 12 (1975):800–808 (hereinafter cited as "Lesbian Mother").

61. Cf. J. Bouvier, *The Institutes of American Law* 102 (1851) from Harry D. Krause, *Family Law: Cases and Materials* (St. Paul, Minn.: West Publishing Co., 1976), p. 9.

62. Sections 201 and 207 as cited in Kenneth M. Davidson, Ruth B. Ginsburg, and Herma H. Kay, *Sex-Based Discrimination: Text, Cases and Materials* (St. Paul, Minn.: West Publishing Co., 1974), p. 199.

63. Baker v. Nelson, 291 Minn. 310, 312, 191 N.W.2d 185, 186 (1971); appeal dismissed, 409 U.S. 810 (1972).

64. Baker v. Nelson, 291 Minn. 310, at 311, 191 N.W.2d at 185–86 (footnote omitted).

65. Jones v. Hallahan, 501 S.W.2d 588 (Ky.Ct.A-p.1973). The U.S. Supreme Court has never ruled on this issue. However, in 1976 it did uphold Virginia's criminal prohibition of homosexual acts, in Doe v. Commonwealth's Atty. for City of Richmond, 44 U.S.L.W. 3545 (1976). This suggests that the Supreme Court is not inclined to include homosexual acts among those protected by privacy, much less to validate homosexual marriages.

66. Del Martin and Phyllis Lyon, *Lesbian/Woman* (San Francisco: Glide, 1972), p. 103.

67. "The Legality of Homosexual Marriage," *Yale Law Journal* 82 (1973):580 (hereinafter cited as "Legality of Homosexual Marriage").

68. E. Carrington Boggan, Marilyn G. Haft, Charles Lister, and John P. Rupp, *An American Civil Liberties Union Handbook: The Rights of Gay People* (New York: Avon Books, 1975), pp. 104, 106 (hereinafter cited as *The Rights of Gay People*).

69. Anonymous v. Anonymous, 325 N.Y.S.2d 499, 67 Misc. 2d 982 (1971).

70. Ann.Code Md, Art. 62, Sec. 1.

71. Florida Legislative Investigation Commission, "Homosexuality and Citizenship in Florida," Florida Legislature, 1964, cited in Riley, "Lesbian Mother," p. 851.

72. Baker v. Nelson, 291 Minn. 310, at 312, 191 N.W.2d 185 (1971).

73. Boggan et. al, *The Rights of Gay People*, p. 107; see also "Legality of Homosexual Marriage."

74. *Congressional Record*, vol. 118, sec. 4389 (daily ed., March 21, 1972). From "Legality of Homosexual Marriage," p. 584.

75. Singer v. Hara, 11 Wash.App. 247, 522 P.2d 1187 (1974).

76. J. D. MacFarlane, "The Validity of Homosexual Marriage under ERA," *Equal Rights Monitor* 2, no. 5 (1976):2.

77. Nan D. Hunter and Nancy D. Polikoff, "Custody Rights of Lesbian Mothers: Legal Theory and Litigation Strategy," *Buffalo Law Review* 25, no. 3 (1976):691 (hereinafter cited as "Custody Rights of Lesbian Mothers").

78. Bennett v. Clemens, 230 Ga. 317, 196 S.E.2d 842 (1973).

79. Hunter and Polikoff, "Custody Rights of Lesbian Mothers," p. 732. At the Eighth National Conference on Women and the Law, attorneys representing lesbian mothers were advised to have the mother stipulate to her homosexuality if they could not prevent it from being brought to the court's attention. By so stipulating, they advised they could at least avoid a parade of witnesses attesting to it.

80. O'Harra v. O'Harra, No. 73–384 E (Ore. Cir. Ct., 13th Jud. Dist., June 18, 1974), aff'd, 530 P.2d 877 (Ore. App. 1975).

81. O'Harra v. O'Harra, 530 P.2d at 877.

82. Hunter and Polikoff, "Custody Rights of Lesbian Mothers," p. 706.

83. Nadler v. Superior Court, 255 Cal. App.2d 523, 63 Cal. Rptr. 352 (1967).

84. Ibid., p. 354.

85. Del Martin and Phyllis Lyon, "Lesbian Mothers," *Ms.*, October 1973, p. 79.

86. Riley, "Lesbian Mother," p. 831.

87. Mitchell v. Mitchell, No. 240665 (Cal. Super. Ct., Santa Clara County, June 8, 1972).

88. Shuster v. Shuster, No. D–36868 (Wash. Super. Ct., King County, Dec. 22, 1972).

89. Isaacson v. Isaacson, No. D–36867 (Wash. Super. Ct., King County, Dec. 22, 1972).

90. "Custody and Homosexual Parents," *Women's Rights Law Reporter* 2 (1974):20.

91. Schuster v. Schuster, No. 36876 (Wash. Super. Ct., King County, Sept. 3, 1974), reported in *Family L. Rptr.* 1 (1974):2004.

92. People v. Brown, 49 Mich. App. 358, 212 N.W.2d 55 (1973).

93. Ibid., p. 59.

94. Commonwealth v. Bradley, 171 Pa. Super. 587, at 593, 91 A.2d 379 (1952) at 382.

95. In re J. S., and C., 129 N.J. Super. 486 at 497, 324 A.2d 90 (Ch. 1974).

96. In re Jane B., 85 Misc. 2d 515, 380 N.Y.S.2d 848 (Sup. Ct. 1976).

97. In re Jane B., at 525, 380 N.Y.S.2d at 858.

98. See, for example, Nigel Nicholson, *Portrait of a Marriage* (New York: Bantam, 1973), which describes an upper-class English marriage during which both partners had homosexual affairs but were deeply committed to each other and to their marriage.

Chapter 10: The Case for Intimate Contracts (pp. 227–254)

1. K. McWalter, "Marriage as Contract: Towards a Functional Redefinition of the Marital Status," *Columbia Journal of Law and Social Problems* 9 (1973):636–37 (hereinafter cited as "Marriage as Contract").

2. As quoted in Susan Edmiston, "How to Write Your Own Marriage Contract," *Ms.* 1, no. 1 (Spring 1972):66, 68.

3. See, for example, Resolution 10 adopted at the National Conference of the National Organization for Women (NOW), May 1974, which provides in part:

   Whereas, woman's position in a society rises no higher than woman's position in the marriage relationship, and Whereas, marriages are based on unwritten contracts, many of which fail to insure equality of the marriage patterns, and
   Whereas, many of the inequalities we are combatting in employment, education, etc., are based on the inequalities existent in the marriage relationship,
   Therefore, be it resolved
   That NOW set as one of its highest priorities in 1974–75 equality in the marriage relationship . . . (NOW, October 1974 at 8).

4. Marriage Contract of Harriet Mary Cody and Harvey Joseph Sadis, in "To Love, Honor and . . . Share: a Marriage Contract for the Seventies," *Ms.* 1, no. 1 (1973):62–64, 102, 103. I was surprised to find this statement repeated in a large number of the marriage contracts I examined as potential samples for Chapter 12.

5. Laura Rausmussen, "Interspousal Contracts: The Potential for Val-

idation in Massachusetts," *Suffolk University Law Review* 9 (1974): 185.

6. Ibid.

7. J. Gibson Wells, "A Critical Look at Personal Marriage Contracts," *The Family Coordinator* 25 (1976):36–37 (hereinafter cited as "A Critical Look at Personal Marriage Contracts").

8. See, generally, H. Blumer, *Symbolic Intractionism; Perspective and Method* (Englewood Cliffs, N.J.: Prentice Hall, 1969).

9. Wells, "A Critical Look at Personal Marriage Contracts," p. 36.

10. Karl Fleischmann, "Marriage by Contract: Defining the Terms of the Relationship," *Family Law Quarterly* 8, no. 1 (1974):29 (hereinafter cited as "Marriage by Contract").

11. Ibid., p. 36.

12. Ibid., p. 35.

13. See, generally, Meyer Elkin, "Conciliation Courts—The Reintegration of Disintegrating Families," *The Family Coordinator* 22, no. 1 (1973):63 (hereinafter cited as "Conciliation Courts").

14. Dorothy Linder Maddi, "The Effect of Conciliation Court Proceedings on Petitions for Dissolution of Marriage," *Journal of Family Law* 13, no. 3 (1974):557–58.

15. Elkin, "Conciliation Courts," p. 66.

16. James Crenshaw, "A Blueprint for Marriage: Psychology and the Law Join Forces," *American Bar Association Journal* 48 (1962):126.

17. *Preface to the Sixth Annual Report of the Conciliation Court of Los Angeles County*, January 1970, 11 North Hill Street, Los Angeles, CA 90012.

18. Ibid.

19. Ibid.

20. Fleischmann, "Marriage by Contract," p. 27.

21. Clifford Sager, Helen S. Kaplan, Ralph H. Grundlach, Malvina Kremer, Rosa Lenz, and Jack R. Royce, "The Marriage Contract," *Family Process* 10, no. 3 (1971):312.

22. Ibid.

23. See also Clifford Sager, *Marriage Contracts and Couple Therapy* (New York: Brunner/Mazel, 1976); and Clifford Sager and Bernice Hunt, *Intimate Patterns, Hidden Patterns in Love Relationships* (New York: McGraw Hill, 1979).

24. A. L. Scoresby, F. J. Apolonio, and G. Hatch, "Action Plans: An Approach to Behavior Change in Marriage Education," *The Family Coordinator* 23 (1974):343–37.

25. Ruth Ihne, "Marital Contracts," unpublished paper prepared for Yale Legislative Services, Yale Law School, July 1976, p. 5 (hereinafter cited as "Marital Contracts").

26. Ibid., pp. 5–6.

27. K. McWalter, "Marriage as Contract" p. 636.

28. Max Rheinstein, "The Transformation of Marriage and the Law," *Northwestern University Law Review* 68 (1973):463, as cited in Margaret Sokolov, "Marriage Contracts for Support and Services: Constitutionality Begins at Home," *New York University Law Review* 49, (December 1974):1186 (hereinafter cited as "Contracts for Support and Services").

29. Sokolov, "Contracts for Support and Services."

30. Ibid., p. 1187.

31. Ibid., pp. 1241–42.

32. Wells, "A Critical Look at Personal Marriage Contracts," pp. 35–36.

33. Ibid., p. 36.

34. Ibid.

35. Posovsky v. Wolfe, *Lackawanna Jurist* 50 (1949):246, 249 (emphasis added).

36. See, generally, Ian R. Macneil, "The Many Futures of Contracts," *Southern California Law Review* 45, no. 43 (1965):44; and Sokolov, "Contracts for Support and Services," pp. 1187–90.

37. See, generally, McDowell, "Contracts in the Family," *Boston University Law Review* 45, no. 43 (1965):44; and Sokolov "Contracts for Support and Services," pp. 1187–90.

38. Uniform Commercial Code, Section 1–102 (3), 1–203, 2–302 (1).

39. Sokolov, "Contracts for Support and Services," p. 1188.

40. Ihne, "Marital Contracts," p. 17.

41. Ibid., citing Belcher v. Belcher, 271 So. 2d 7, 12 (1972).

42. Charles Gamble, "The Antenuptial Contract," *University of Miami Law Review* 26 (1972):719 (hereinafter cited as "The Antinuptial Contract").

43. Stilley v. Folger, 14 Ohio 610, 614 (1846), cited in Gamble, "The Antenuptial Contract," pp. 719–20. This portion of the Stilley opinion was quoted with approval more recently in Osborn v. Osborn, 10 Ohio Misc. 171, 226 N.E. 2d 814 (1966) (counseling judges to be both chivalrous and circumspect), and in Rocher v. Rocher, 13 Ohio Misc. 199, 232 N.E. 2d 445 (1967).

44. Ihne, "Marital Contracts," p. 19.

45. Ibid., quoting Barbara Babcock, Ann Freedman, Eleanor Norton, and Susan Ross, *Sex-Based Discrimination and the Law* (Boston: Little, Brown & Co., 1975), p. 632, n.75.

46. Ihne, "Marital Contracts," p. 22.

47. Homer Clark, *Law of Domestic Relations* (St. Paul, Minn.: West Publishing Co., 1968), pp. 28–29.

48. Ihne, "Marital Contracts," p. 24.

49. For a more complete discussion of the traditional conditions under which performance will be excused, see J. D. Calamari and J. M. Perillo, *Contracts* (St. Paul, Minn.: West Publishing Co., 1970), Chapters 10 and 11.

50. U.C.C. Section 2–617. The *Restatement of the Law of Contracts* (St. Paul, Minn.: American Law Institute, 1932), p. 843, indicates that impossibility is an excuse for nonperformance. Impossibility is defined in section 454: ". . . impossibility means not only strict impossibility because of extreme and unmeasurable difficulty, expense, injury, and loss involved." The Uniform Commercial Code recognizes commercial impracticability as an excuse for nonperformance. Corbin, *Contracts* (St. Paul, Minn.: West Publishing Co., 1950), pp. 642, 1325, and 1333 also deals with the issue of impracticability as an excuse for nonperformance.

51. See Wells, "A Critical Look at Personal Marriage Contracts."

52. Norman Sheresky and Marya Mannes, "A Radical Guide to Wedlock," *Saturday Review of Society* 55 (1972):33–38.

53. United Steelworkers v. American Mfg. Co., 363 U.S. 564 (1960). Discussing the enforceability of arbitration clauses, the Court stated: "The processing of even frivolous claims may have therapeutic values of which those who are not a part of the plant environment may be quite unaware." Cited in Sokolov, "Contracts for Support and Services," p. 1242.

54. Sokolov, "Contracts for Support and Services," p. 1240 (emphasis added).

55. See, for example, Michael Wheeler, *No-Fault Divorce* (Boston: Beacon Press, 1974).

56. Sokolov ("Contracts for Support and Services," p. 1245) argues that the family courts and conciliation services that already exist, such as the conciliation bureaus of New York's family court, would provide suitable environments for dealing with married couples' contracts. See McLaughlin, "Court-Connected Marriage Counseling and Divorce—the New York Experience," *Journal of Family Law* 11 (1971):517.

57. See, generally, Alexander Lindey, "Arbitration in Matrimonial Matters," *Arbitration Journal* 1 (1937):345.

58. Most family law cases are resolved by private agreement; only 10 percent of them are contested in court. Henry Foster and Doris Freed, *Law and the Family* (Rochester, N.Y.: Lawyers Cooperative Publishing Co., 1966), p. viii.

Chapter 11: Topics and Provisions for Intimate Contracts (pp. 255–290)

1. Karl Fleishmann, "Marriage by Contract: Defining the Terms of the Relationship," *Family Law Quarterly* 8, no. 1 (1974):30–31.

2. Ibid., p. 31.

3. Ibid.

4. For an illuminating discussion of the many perspectives on this issue see Marilyn Fabe and Norma J. Wikler, *Up Against the Clock* (New York: Random House, 1979).

Chapter 13: Contracts Between Husbands and Wives (pp. 337–359)

1. The United States v. Yazell, 382 U.S. 341, 361 (1966) (Black, J. Dissenting).

2. The third clause of the Statute of Frauds, found in most states, provides that promises made in consideration of marriage (other than mutual promises to marry) must be in writing and signed by the party to be charged. Homer Clark, *The Law of Domestic Relations* (St. Paul, Minn.: West Publishing Co., 1968), pp. 27–28 (hereinafter cited as Clark, *Domestic Relations*).

3. American Law Institute, *Restatement of the Law of Contracts*, Sec. 487 (1932) (hereinafter cited as *Restatement of Contracts*).

4. *American Jurisprudence*, 2nd ed. vol. 41, "Husband and Wife," Secs. 320, 322 (1968) (hereinafter cited as *Am. Jur. 2d*). See also Note, "Interspousal Contracts: The Potential for Validation in Massachusetts," *Suffolk Law Review* 9, no. 1 (1974):197.

5. Ryan v. Dockery, 134 Wis. 431, 434, 114 N.W. 820, 821 (1908).

6. Eule v. Eule, 24 Ill. App. 3d 83, 320 N.E. 2d 506 (1974).

7. Youngberg v. Holstrom, 252 Iowa 815, 823, 108 N.W. 2d 498, 502 (1961). See also *Am. Jur. 2d* 41, "Husband and Wife," Sec. 320 (1968); Clark, *Domestic Relations*, p. 227.

8. Mathews v. Mathews, 2 N.C. App. 143, 162 S.E. 2d 697, 698 (1968).

9. Stern v. Wisconsin Dept. of Revenue, 217 N.W. 2d 326 (Wis. 1974).

10. Note, "An Analysis of the Enforceability of Marital Contracts," *North Carolina Law Review* 47 (1969):827.

11. Grant, "Marital Contracts Before and During Marriage," *California Family Law* (1961):156–159 (Berkeley, Calif.: Continuing Education of the Bar).

12. Ibid. p. 159. One spouse can agree to assume the obligation to support the other's children; they can both agree that, after marriage, the earnings of either one or both shall be the separate property of the one who earns them.

13. *Restatement of Contracts*, Sec. 586 (1932).

14. Clark, *Domestic Relations*, p. 521.

15. Graham v. Graham, 33 F. Supp. 936, 940 (E.D. Mich. 1940). See also California Civil Code Sec. 4802.

16. Matthews v. Matthews, 2 N.C. App. 143, 162 S.E. 2d 197, 99 (1968).

17. In re Gudenkauf, 204 N.W. 2d 586 (Iowa 1973).

18. See for example, Posner v. Posner, 233 So. 2d 381 (Fla. 1970) discussed on pages 347–348.

19. Hill v. Hill, 23 Cal. 2d 82, 141 p. 2d 417, 422 (1943; citations omitted).

20. Clark, *Domestic Relations*, pp. 526–28.

21. See California Corporations Code Secs. 15029–43.

22. Clark, *Domestic Relations*, pp. 28–29.

23. See, e.g., California Commercial Code Sec. 2–302.

24. Homer H. Clark "Antenuptial Contracts," *University of Colorado Law Review:* 50 (Jan. 1979):144 (hereinafter cited as "Antenuptial Contracts").

25. Ibid.

26. Clark, *Domestic Relations*, pp. 524–25.

27. Ibid., pp. 28–29.

28. *Restatement of Contracts*, Sec. 457.

29. *Am. Jur. 2d* 17, "Contracts," Sec. 402.

30. Ibid.

31. Arthur L. Corbin, *Corbin on Contracts* (St. Paul, Minn.: West Publishing Co., 1952), sec. 1354 (one vol. ed.).

32. Posner v. Posner, 233 So. 2d 381 (Fla. 1970), rev'd on other grounds on rehearing, 257 So. 2d 530 (Fla. 1972).

33. Posner v. Posner, 233 So. 2d at 385. It is to be noted that two years later the Posner contract was held to be void on rehearing as the wife did not have full knowledge of her husband's wealth at the time they contracted. Posner v. Posner, 257 So. 2d 530 (Fla. 1972).

34. Volid v. Volid, 6 Ill. App. 3d 836, 286 N.E. 2d 42 (1972).

35. Volid v. Volid, 6 Ill. App. at 391, 286 N.E. 2d at 46 (1972) (emphasis added).

36. Volid v. Volid, 6 Ill. App. at 392, 286 N.E. 2d at 47.

37. Volid v. Volid, 6 Ill. App. at 392.

38. Buettner v. Buettner, 89 Nev. 39, 505 P. 2d 600 (1973).

39. Buettner v. Buettner, 89 Nev. at 45, 505 P. 2d at 604.

40. Unander v. Unander, 506 P. 2d 719 (Ore. Sup. Ct. 1973).

41. Unander v. Unander, 506 P. 2d at 721.

42. Unander v. Unander, 506 P. 2d at 720.

43. In re Dawley, 17 Cal. 3d 342, 551 P. 2d 323, 131 Cal. Rptr. 3 (1976).

44. In re Higgason, 10 Cal. 3d 476, 485 516 P. 2d 289, 295, 110 Ca. Rptr. 897, 903 (1973).

45. In re Dawley, 17 Cal. 3d 342, 351, 551 P. 2d 323, 329, 131 Ca. Rptr. 3, 9 (1976).

46. In re Dawley, 17 Cal. 3d at 366, 551 P. 2d at 333, 131 Cal. Rptr. at 13.

47. Potter v. Collin, 321 So. 2d 131 (Fla. App. 1975).

48. Singer v. Singer, 318 So. 2d 439 (Fla. App. 1975).

49. Clark, "Antenuptial Contracts," pp. 150–51.

50. Eule v. Eule, 24 Ill. App. 3d 83, 320 N.E. 2d 506 (1974).

51. Tomlinson v. Tomlinson, 352 N.E. 2d 785, 791 (Ind. App. 1976).

52. Ibid.

53. Miller v. Stanich, 202 Wis. 539, 230 N.W. 47 (1930).

54. Garnett v. Garnett, 526 P. 2d 549 (Ore. 1974).

55. See American Law Institute, *Restatement (Second) of the Law of Contracts*, Tentative Draft No. 9, chap. 11, sec. 281, 1974.

56. Arthur L. Corbin, *Corbin on Contracts* (St. Paul, Minn.: West Publishing Co., 1963), vol. 1, chap. 5, sec. 128, p. 551.

Chapter 14: Living Together Without a Contract: Social Patterns and Legal Consequences (pp. 360–384)

1. In an informal talk with staff members of the U.S. Department of Housing and Urban Development on February 10, 1977, Jimmy Carter was quoted as saying: "We want to protect that integrity of the family. We need a stable life to make us better servants of the people. So, those of you who are living in sin, I hope you'll get married." *San Francisco Chronicle*, February 11, 1977, p. 1, col. 6.

2. U.S. Bureau of the Census, "Marital Status and Living Arrangements: March 1978," *Current Population Reports*, series P–20, no. 338, (May 1979):3 and table D (hereinafter cited as "Living Arrangements: March 1978").

3. Paul C. Glick and Arthur J. Norton, "Marrying, Divorcing, and Living Together in the U.S. Today," *Population Bulletin* 32, no. 5 (October 1977):32 (hereinafter cited as "Marrying, Divorcing, and Living Together").

4. Paul C. Glick, "A Demographer Looks at American Families," *Journal of Marriage and the Family* 37, (1975):11–12.

5. U.S. Census, "Living Arrangements: March 1978" p. 4, table D.

6. Ibid.

7. Paul C. Glick, "Living Arrangements of Children and Young Adults," paper presented at the annual meeting of the Population Association of America, Seattle, April 1975.

8. "Living Together," *Newsweek*, August 1, 1977, p. 46, col. 1 (hereinafter cited as "Living Together").

9. Herma Hill Kay and Carol Amyx, "*Marvin v. Marvin:* Preserving the Options," *California Law Review* 65, no. 5 (September 1977):937 (hereinafter cited as "Marvin and Options") (reprinted with permission).

10. Glick and Norton, "Marrying, Divorcing and Living Together," p. 34.

11. Ibid., pp. 34–35.

12. Eleanor D. Macklin, "Heterosexual Cohabitation Among Unmarried College Students," *The Family Coordinator* 21 (1972):467.

13. Pat Jackson, "Discussions of Unmarried Heterosexual Cohabitation Among Middle Class Youths: The Old and the New," unpublished

paper for Sociology 292, University of California at Davis, 1976, pp. 13–15.

14. "Living Together," p. 47.

15. Glick and Norton, "Marrying, Divorcing and Living Together," p. 6.

16. Paul Glick and Graham Spanier, "Married and Unmarried Cohabitation in the United States," *Journal of Marriage and the Family* 10 (1980):19–30.

17. Jan Trost, *Unmarried Cohabitation* (Vasteras, Sweden: International Library, 1979).

18. Ibid.

19. Kay and Amyx, "Marvin and Options," pp. 939–40.

20. VA Code Section 18, 2–345; Wisconsin State Ann. Section 944.20. See also Toni Ihara and Ralph Warner, *The Living Together Kit* (New York: Fawcett Crest, 1979), p. 15 (hereinafter cited as *Living Together*).

21. Mass. Gen. Laws Ann. Ch. 272, Section 16 (West 1970); NM Stat. Ann. Section 30–10–2 (1978). As recently as 1974 Morgan King could boldly state that "Cohabitation is a crime in 27 states . . ." Morgan D. King, *Cohabitation Handbook* (Berkeley: Ten Speed Press, 1975), p. 120.

22. Ihara and Warner, *Living Together*, p. 15.

23. See Carmen Massey and Ralph Warner, *Sex, Living Together and the Law*, (Berkeley: Nolo Press, 1974) pp. 21–30, 62–63 (hereinafter cited as *Living Together and the Law*).

24. Ihara and Warner, *Living Together*, p. 119.

25. Nora Lavori, *Living Together, Married or Single: Your Legal Rights*, (New York: Harper and Row, 1976), p. 207, (hereinafter cited as *Living Together, Married or Single*).

26. Department of Industrial Workers v. Workers Compensation Appeals Board 94 Cal. App. 3d 72 (1979).

27. U.S. Department of Agriculture v. Mareno 413 U.S. 528, 93S.Ct.2821 (1973).

28. King v. Smith, 392 U.S. 309 (1968).

29. These statistics are computed from the 1978 tax tables.

30. Gary C. Randall, "Living Together Can Be Very Taxing—Especially If You're Unmarried and the IRS Is Watching You," *Family Advocate* 1, no. 3 (Winter 1979):4.

31. Lavori, *Living Together, Married or Single*, p. 155.

32. Barbara Hirsch, *Living Together: A Guide to the Law for Unmarried Couples* (Boston: Houghton Mifflin Co., 1976), p. 61.

33. Ibid., p. 71.

34. Ihara and Warner, *Living Together*, p. 111.

35. Markham v. Colonial Mortgage Service Company, 605 F. 2d 566 (1979).

36. Caleb Foote, Robert J. Levy, and Frank Sander, *Family Law*, 2d ed. (Boston: Little, Brown & Co., 1976) (hereinafter cited as *Family Law*).

37. Gomez v. Perez, 409 U.S. 535 (1973).

38. New Jersey Welfare Rights Organization v. Cahill, 411 U.S. 619 (1973).

39. Levy v. Louisiana, 391 U.S. 68 (1968).

40. Labine v. Vincent, 401 U.S. 532 (1971). But cf. Weber v. Aetna Casualty and Surety Company, 406 U.S. 164 (1972).

41. Matthews v. Lucas, 427 U.S. 495 (1976).

42. Trimble v. Gordon, 97 S. Ct. 1459 (1977).

43. See Harry D. Krause, *Family Law: Cases and Materials* (St. Paul, Minn.: West Publishing Co., 1976), pp. 447–49.

44. Lalli v. Lalli, 99 S. Ct. 518 (1978).

45. Foote, Levy, and Sander, *Family Law*, p. 644.

46. California Civil Code, Section 230.

47. Lavell v. Adoption Institute, 185 Cal. App. 2d 557, 8 Cal. Rptr, 367 (1960). Professor Henry Foster as quoted in Leslie Bennetts, "Unwed Parents: The Arrangement Seems Legitimate to Them," *New York Times*, March 24, 1978, p. A15, col. 3 (hereinafter cited as "Unwed Parents").

48. Stanley v. Illinois, 405 U.S. 645 (1972).

49. Foster, as quoted in Bennetts, "Unwed Parents."

50. Willis v. Willis, 49 P.2d 670 (Wyo. 1935).

51. Ibid., at 680.

52. York v. Place, 544 P.2d 572 (Ore. 1975).

53. Ibid., at 574.

54. Ibid.

55. Vallera v. Vallera, 21 Cal. 2d 681, 134 P.2d 761 (1943).

56. Ibid., at 686–87.

57. Keene v. Keene, 67 Ca. 2d 657, 371 P.2d 329 (1962).

58. Creasman v. Boyle, 196 P. 2d 835 (Wash. 1948).

59. Ibid., at 841.

60. Ibid., at 839.

61. See, generally, Herma Hill Kay, *Sex-Based Discrimination in Family Law* (St. Paul, Minn.: West Publishing Co., 1974).

62. Kay and Amyx, "Marvin and Options," pp. 940–41 (citations omitted).

63. Ibid., p. 941.

64. Massey and Warner, *Living Together and the Law*.

Chapter 15: To <u>Marvin</u> and Beyond: Contracts Between Unwed Cohabitants (pp. 385–415)

1. Carol S. Bruch, "Property Rights of De Facto Spouses Including Thoughts on the Value of Homemakers' Services," *Family Law Quarterly* 10 (1976):106–107 (hereinafter cited as "De Facto Spouses"). The following discussion is drawn from Professor Bruch's analysis

2. Vincent v. Moriarty, 31 App. Div. 484, 52 N.Y.S. 519 (1898).

3. Vincent v. Moriarty, 31 App. Div. at 486–87.

4. Wellmaker v. Roberts, 213 Ga. 740, 101 S.E. 2d 712 (1958).

5. Trutalli v. Meraviglia, 215 Cal. 698, 12 P. 2d 430 (1932).

6. Trutalli v. Meraviglia, 215 Cal. at 700, 12 P. 2d at 431.

7. Bridges v. Bridges, 125 Cal. App. 2d 359, 370 P. 2d 69 (1954).

8. Bridges v. Bridges, 125 Cal. App. 2d at 362–3, 270 P. 2d at 71.

9. Hill v. Estate of Westbrook, 95 Ca. App. 2d 599, 213 P. 2d 727 (1950).

10. Hill v. Estate of Westbrook, 95 Ca. App. 2d at 602.

11. Bruch, "De Facto Spouses," pp. 109–110.

12. Ibid., p. 110.

13. Latham v. Latham, 274 Ore. 421, 547, P. 2d 144 (1976).

14. Latham v. Latham, 274 Ore. at 426–27, 547 P. 2d 144 at 147 (emphasis added).

15. Marvin v. Marvin, 18 Cal. 3d 660, 557 P. 2d 106, 134 Cal. Rptr. 815.

16. Marvin v. Marvin, A Memorandum Opinion issued by Judge Arthur K. Marshall of the Los Angeles Superior Court, April 17, 1979, 5. Fam. L. Rep. 3077 (1979).

17. Henry H. Foster and Doris J. Freed, "Marvin v. Marvin: New Wine in Old Bottles," *The Family Law Reporter* 5, no. 26 (May 8, 1979), Monograph No. 1, pp. 4001–4012, (hereinafter cited as "New Wine").

18. Marvin v. Marvin, 18 Cal. 3d at 666.

19. Marvin v. Marvin, 18 Cal. 3d at 669, (emphasis in original).

20. Personal conversation with Professor Carol S. Bruch, September 25, 1980.

21. Marvin v. Marvin, 18 Cal. 3d at 831.

22. Marvin v. Marvin, 18 Cal. 3d at 669.

23. Marvin v. Marvin, 18 Cal. 3d at 828.

24. Marvin v. Marvin, 18 Cal. 3d at 828, quoting from Justice Curtis' opinion in Vallera v. Vallera, 21 Cal. 2d 681, 134 P. 2d 761 (1943).

25. Memorandum Opinion, Superior Court of Los Angeles County, Case No. C23303, April 18, 1979, *Family Law Reporter* 5, no. 24, pp. 3077–3085.

26. Trial transcript, Los Angeles Superior Court Case *C23303, Vol. 33, p. 6024, lines 4–7.

27. Closing Brief for Defendant Lee Marvin, Case No. C23303, Superior Court of Los Angeles County, April 1979, pp. 12–13 (hereinafter cited as Closing Brief for Lee Marvin).

28. Ibid., p. 15.

29. Morone v. Morone, 50 N.Y. 2d 481 (June 6, 1980).

30. McHenry v. Smith, Ore. Ct. App., 4/14/80, released 5/5/80, *Family Law Reporter* 6, p. 2553.

31. Morone v. Morone, 50 N.Y. 2d 481.

32. McHenry v. Smith, Ore. Ct. App., April 14, 1980.

33. Foster and Freed, "New Wine," p. 4003.

34. Rehak v. Mathis, 238, S.E. 2d 81 (Ga. 1977).

35. Rehak v. Mathis, 238 S.E. 2d 82.

36. Ibid., at 83.

37. Roach v. Buttons, Feb. 29, 1980, Tenn. Ch. Ct., *Family Law Reporter* 6, p. 2355 and McCall v. Frampton, N.Y. Sup. Ct., Nassau Co., April 18, 1979, *Family Law Reporter* 5, p. 3015.

38. Ibid.

39. Kozlowski v. Kozlowski, 164 N.J. Super. 162, 395 A. 2d 913 (July 12, 1978).

40. Tyranski v. Piggins, 44 Mich. App. 570, 205 N. W. 2d 595 (1973).

41. Foster and Freed, "New Wine," note 29, p. 4010.

42. Closing Brief for Lee Marvin, p. 22 (emphasis added).

43. Marvin v. Marvin, 134 Cal. Rptr., 815, 831.

44. Beal v. Beal, 577 P. 2d 507.

45. Beal v. Beal, 577 P. 2d 510.

46. Ibid.

47. Carlson v. Olson, 256 N. W. 2d 249.

48. Carlson v. Olson, 256 N.W. 2d 251.

49. Carlson v. Olson, 256 N. W. 2d 255.

50. Dosek v. Dosek, *Family Law Reporter* 4, no. 51 (October 1978): 2828–29.

51. McCullon v. McCullon, 96 Misc 2d 962 (10/31/78).

52. Morone v. Morone, 50 N.Y. 2d 481.

53. Hewitt v. Hewitt, Sup. Ct. of Illinois, 1979, 77 Ill. 2d 49, 31 Ill. Dec. 827, 394 N.E. 2d 1204.

54. Ibid.

55. Marvin v. Marvin, 18 Cal. 3d at 684, N. 25.

56. Bruch, "De Facto Spouses," p. 124. Citing Chase v. Corcoran, 106 Mass. 286 (1871).

57. Ibid.

58. Kozlowski v. Kozlowski, 395 A. 2d 913 (1978) at 917–918.

59. Foster and Freed, "New Wine," p. 4007.

60. Green v. Richmond, 337 N.E. 2d 691 (Mass. 1975) cited in Foster and Freed, "New Wine" n. 90.

61. Hamiston v. Bushnell, N.H. Sup. Ct. 11/15/78.

62. Foster and Freed, "New Wine," p. 4007.

63. Ibid.

64. Bruch, "De Facto Spouses," p. 122.

65. Doyle v. Giddley, Wis. Cty., Ct., Dane City, 6/16/77, Case #74–435, *Family Law Reporter* 3 (Oct. 4, 1977):2730.

66. Ibid., p. 2.

67. Edgar v. Wagner, S72 P. 2d 405, Utah 1978 cited in Foster and Freed "New Wine," n. 80.

68. Bruch, "De Facto Spouses," p. 123.

69. Marvin v. Marvin, 18 Cal. 3d at 684.

70. Jan Hanson and Patricia Schneider, "*Marvin* v. *Marvin*: Am Empirical Analysis of the Implementation of a Higher Court Ruling," Di-

rected Research for Professor Michael Wald, Stanford Law School, August 1980 (hereinafter cited as "Empirical Analysis of Marvin").

71. Ibid., p. 53. The findings that follow are summarized from pages 48 to 53.

72. Ibid.

73. See especially pp. 338–341.

74. See for example, the section on enforcement of Contract 7 involving counselling and arbitration clauses.

75. James Crenshaw, "A Blueprint for Marriage: Psychology and the Law Join Forces," 48 *American Bar Association Journal*: 126 (1962).

76. Carol S. Bruch, "Non-marital Cohabitation in the Common Law Countries: Patterns of Judicial and Legislative Response," *American Journal of Comparative Law* 29 (1981):107–108, n. 26–27.

77. Ibid.

78. Ibid., p. 117.

79. Clark, *Domestic Relations*, p. 549. Another conception of the child's interest would try to preclude dissolution when children are involved. This view would limit the option of contracts to childless couples in order to safeguard against marital breakdown in families with children: "(A)s long as breakdown does demonstrable social damage—as it surely must, particularly where children are involved—any system that would invite separation of the spouses must be regarded as highly dubious in terms of social policy. *The obvious solution is to limit the term-of-years option* (term contracts) *to childless couples only, with the option to expire upon pregnancy.*" McWalter, "Marriage as Contract: Towards a Functional Redefinition of the Marital Status," *Columbia Journal of Law and Social Problems* 9 (1974):638 (emphasis added).

80. Clark, *Domestic Relations*, p. 549.

81. *Fournier* v. *Lopez*, Ca. Ct. App. 1st Dist. 12/27/78, reported in *Family Law Reporter* 5 (Jan. 1979):2204–05.

Appendix: An Empirical Study of Intimate Contracts (pp. 417–458)

1. See, for example, Susan Edmiston, "How To Write Your Own Marriage Contract," *Ms.* 1, no. 1 (1972):66; Alex Kates Shulman, "Living by Contract," *Life*, April 28, 1972, p. 43 (hereinafter cited as "Living by Contract"); and "To Love, Honor and Share," *Ms.* 1, no. 12

(1973):63, 64, 102–3 (hereinafter cited as "To Love, Honor and Share").

2. See, for example, Marvin B. Sussman, "Marriage Contracts: Social and Legal Consequences," paper presented at the 1975 International Workshop on Changing Sex Roles in Family and Society, 1975; and Lucy Jen Huang and Wilbert M. Leonard II, "The Marriage Contract and Gender Roles," paper presented at the 71st annual meeting of the American Sociological Association, New York, 1976 (hereinafter cited as "The Marriage Contract and Gender Roles").

3. Homer Clark, *The Law of Domestic Relations* (St. Paul, Minn.: West, 1968), p. 27.

4. *Ms.*, "To Love, Honor and Share"; and Shulman, "Living by Contract."

5. The students had read Weitzman's article on "Legal Regulation of Marriage" and had participated in a class discussion of contracts within and in lieu of marriage. The article contained a list of suggested topics for inclusion in the contracts.

6. Thirteen contracts were identified as marriage contracts. Ten of these were written by couples already married. The remaining three were prepared by couples who were soon to marry (within months). We refer to all these couples as members of the "married group."

7. The exact nature of the relationship was discernible in 55 of the 59 contracts; the four contracts that did not fit into one of these groups are excluded from the analysis whenever the type of relationship is being taken into account.

8. Contracts that mentioned relationship aims and expectations only tangentially were excluded from this section. All of the 52 contracts considered in this analysis included explicit statements regarding the aims and expectations of the relationship as a preface to further provisions.

9. James Hasset, "A New Look at Living Together," *Psychology Today*, December 1977, p. 83. See also Donald W. Bower and Victor A. Christopherson, "University Student Cohabitation: A Regional Comparison of Selected Attitudes and Behavior," *Journal of Marriage and the Family* 39, no. 3 (1977):447–52.

10. See, generally, Judith Blake, "Coercive Pronatalism and the American Population Policy," in *Pronatalism: The Myth of Mom and Apple Pie*, Ellen Peck and Judith Senderowitz, eds. (New York: Thomas J. Cromwell, 1964).

11. Huang and Leonard, "The Marriage Contract and Gender Roles," p. 6.

12. Marvin B. Sussman, Judith N. Cates, and D. T. Smith, *The Family and Inheritance* (New York: Russell Sage, 1970), p. 89.

13. Lenore J. Weitzman and Ruth M. Dixon, "The Alimony Myth: Does No-Fault Divorce Make a Difference?" *Family Law Quarterly* 14, no. 3 (Fall 1980):141–85.

14. Morgan v. Morgan, 52 A.D.2d 804, 383 N.Y.S.2d 343 (1976).

Index

A list of court cases by subject follows the Index on page 535.

A *topical list of the court cases discussed in this volume follows in the
succeeding three columns.*